MASTERPLOTS II

POETRY SERIES

MASTERPLOTS II

POETRY
SERIES

1

A-Conn

Edited by

FRANK N. MAGILL

SALEM PRESS

Pasadena, California   Englewood Cliffs, New Jersey

Copyright © 1992, by SALEM PRESS, INC.
All rights in this book are reserved. No part of this work
may be used or reproduced in any manner whatsoever or
transmitted in any form or by any means, electronic or
mechanical, including photocopy, recording, or any information storage and retrieval system, without written
permission from the copyright owner except in the case
of brief quotations embodied in critical articles and re-
views. For information address the publisher, Salem
Press, Inc., P.O. Box 50062, Pasadena, California 91105.

∞ The paper used in these volumes conforms to the
American National Standard for Permanence of Paper
for Printed Library Materials. Z39.48-1984.

Library of Congress Cataloging-in-Publication Data
Masterplots II: Poetry series/edited by Frank N. Magill
  p. cm.
  Includes bibliographical references and index.
     1. Poetry—Themes, motives. I. Magill, Frank
  Northen, 1907-   .
PN1110.5.M37   1992   91-44341
809.1—dc20   CIP
ISBN 0-89356-584-9 (set)
ISBN 0-89356-585-7 (volume 1)

PUBLISHER'S NOTE

Masterplots II, Poetry is the eighth set in the Masterplots II series, which complements the original twelve-volume *Masterplots*, Revised Edition (1976). The *Masterplots II* series began in 1986 with the four-volume American Fiction set, which was followed by sets on Short Stories (1986, six volumes), British and Commonwealth Fiction (1987, four volumes), World Fiction (1988, four volumes), Nonfiction (1989, four volumes), Drama (1990, four volumes), and Juvenile and Young Adult Fiction (1991, four volumes).

The scope of *Masterplots II, Poetry* is broad, both historically and internationally. Its six volumes examine 760 individual works of poetry—ranging from seventh century Chinese verse to twentieth century poetry from around the world—that have not previously appeared in the Masterplots series. The majority are English-language poems, but a significant representation of poems in translation is also included, with many of them being works by winners of the Nobel Prize in Literature. In all, works by 275 poets, writing in more than ten languages, are featured.

The poetry of Elizabethan England is represented by fourteen of William Shakespeare's best-known sonnets, as well as poems by Edmund Spenser, Sir Philip Sidney, and Christopher Marlowe. Seventeenth century poems found here include John Milton's "Lycidas," Robert Herrick's "Delight in Disorder," and Andrew Marvell's "To His Coy Mistress." Eighteenth century poets whose works are featured include Alexander Pope and Samuel Johnson. The Romantic poets are well represented, from John Keats (ten poems, including "Ode to a Nightingale") to William Wordsworth (eleven poems, including "Ode: Intimations of Immortality"), William Blake, Percy Bysshe Shelley, Samuel Taylor Coleridge, and George Gordon, Lord Byron. By the nineteenth century, poets in many countries, writing in many different languages, were influencing one another more than ever before; American poet Edgar Allan Poe (represented by six of his best-known poems, including "The Raven"), for example, exerted a strong influence on the French poets of his century, who in turn influenced succeeding generations of writers in English and other languages. Because of this, the works of such poets as Charles Baudelaire and Stéphane Mallarmé, represented here (along with many other European poets), have a double importance. Pivotal American poetic works of the nineteenth century are also covered; among them are nine poems by Walt Whitman and ten by Emily Dickinson.

Coverage of twentieth century poetry extends from the beginning of the century to the 1980's, with important works of Symbolist, Surrealist, modernist, Beat, and confessional poetry all being treated. Among them can be found T. S. Eliot's "The Love Song of J. Alfred Prufrock," W. H. Auden's "Musée des Beaux Arts," William Butler Yeats's "The Second Coming," Hart Crane's *The Bridge*, Allen Ginsberg's "Howl," and Sylvia Plath's "Daddy." Twelve winners of the Nobel Prize in Literature are also covered, among them Boris Pasternak (Russian), Nelly Sachs (German), Pablo Neruda (Chilean), Eugenio Montale (Italian), Odysseus Elýtis (Greek), Czesław Miłosz (Polish), and Wole Soyinka (Nigerian). In addition to poets whose

v

place in the literary canon has long been established are poets whose work has gained recognition in the latter part of the twentieth century, such as Carolyn Forché, Garrett Hongo, and Sharon Olds. A range of ethnic voices is included, from African American (among them Michael S. Harper, Langston Hughes, and Nikki Giovanni) to Native American (Leslie Marmon Silko and N. Scott Momaday) to Asian American (David Mura and Cathy Song) to Hispanic (Victor Hernandez Cruz and Alberto Rios).

Masterplots II, Poetry is arranged alphabetically by title; poems in translation are presented with the title that is best known to English-speaking readers. Each essay is divided into four sections. The ready-reference top matter gives the author's full name and birth and death dates, then lists the type of poem (such as lyric, narrative, or elegy). The year the poem was first published, either in a book or a periodical, is given. In the case of English-language poems that first appeared in a periodical, the first collection in which the poem was published is also listed. For poetry in translation, the title under which the poem first appeared is given after the date of first publication; that information is followed by the title and date of an accessible English-language collection in which the poem can be found. The text of the essay is divided into three sections. "The Poem" presents an overview of the work—the events, situations, or objects the poem describes. "Forms and Devices" looks closely at the poetic devices the poet uses, such as imagery, metaphor, and meter. "Themes and Meanings" examines the underlying concerns being expressed in the work.

At the end of volume 6 are reference features to aid the reader further. The Bibliography, divided into two sections, lists sources for further study: the first section covers general critical and theoretical studies; the second section, arranged by poet, lists secondary sources about the major poets covered. As is standard in the *Masterplots II* series, there is a Title Index and an Author Index. The Title Index also includes first lines of poems that appear in the set as numbered poems (such as Shakespeare's sonnets). In addition, a Type of Poem Index groups poems by sub-genre—such as lyric, narrative, epic, elegy, and ode—allowing easily accessible comparisons of works within a single genre.

We wish to acknowledge the contributions of the many fine academicians and other writers who contributed articles to *Masterplots II, Poetry*. A list of their names and affiliations appears in the front matter to volume 1.

CONTRIBUTING REVIEWERS

Howard C. Adams
Frostburg State University

Michael Adams
Fairleigh Dickinson University

Amy Adelstein
Independent Scholar

Patricia Alkema
Independent Scholar

David J. Amante
University of North Carolina—Charlotte

Christopher Ames
Agnes Scott College

Terry L. Andrews
Independent Scholar

Anu Aneja
Ohio Wesleyan University

Andrew J. Angyal
Elon College

Raymond M. Archer
Indiana University at Kokomo

Stanley Archer
Texas A&M University

Frank Ardolino
University of Hawaii at Manoa

Dorothy B. Aspinwall
University of Hawaii at Manoa

Bryan Aubrey
Maharishi International University

William Baer
University of Evansville

Jim Baird
University of North Texas

JoAnn Balingit
University of Delaware

Thomas Banks
Ohio Northern University

Stephen M. Baraban
Independent Scholar

Judith Barban
Winthrop College

Terry Barr
Presbyterian College

David Barratt
Chester College, England

Melissa E. Barth
Appalachian State University

Sharon Bassett
California State University, Los Angeles

Robert Bateman
Concord College

Stephen Benz
Barry University

Gordon N. Bergquist
Creighton University

Dorothy M. Betz
Georgetown University

David Biespiel
University of Maryland

John Biguenet
Loyola University, New Orleans

Cynthia A. Bily
Siena Heights College

Nicholas Birns
New York University

Richard Bizot
University of North Florida

Neil Blackadder
Princeton University

Robert G. Blake
Elon College

Gerard Bowers
Willamette University

Kevin Boyle
University of Iowa

Colin Brayton
University of California, Berkeley

Hans-Peter Breuer
University of Delaware

William D. Brewer
Appalachian State University

Patricia Pollock Brodsky
University of Missouri-Kansas City

David Bromige
Sonoma State University

C. L. Brooke
Cleveland State University

Keith H. Brower
Dickinson College

Mary Barnes Bruce
Monmouth College

Carl Brucker
Arkansas Tech University

Maria Budisavljević-Oparnica
Arizona State University

Paul Budra
*Simon Fraser University, Vancouver, B.C.,
   Canada*

Edmund J. Campion
University of Tennessee

Thomas J. Cassidy
University of Wisconsin — Marshfield

John Steven Childs
Polytechnic University

Balance Chow
Rollins College

Paul Christensen
Texas A&M University

C. L. Chua
California State University, Fresno

John R. Clark
University of South Florida

Norris B. Clark
University of Akron

Richard Collins
Louisiana State University

Laura Cowan
University of Maine

Beverly Coyle
Vassar College

George Craddock
Concord College

Stephen H. Crane
University of South Florida

Barry Crawford
University of California, Riverside

Peter Crawford
Independent Scholar

Vance Crummett
University of Wisconsin — Milwaukee

Thomas M. Curley
Bridgewater State College

Koos Daley
Adams State College

Richard Damashek
Illinois Benedictine College

Robert Darling
Keuka College

Jonathan Daunt
University of California, Davis

Dean Davies
Mesa State College

William V. Davis
Baylor University

Dennis R. Dean
University of Wisconsin — Parkside

Cameron K. Deaver
Independent Scholar

Bill Delaney
Independent Scholar

Scott D. Denham
Davidson College

Matts Djos
Mesa State College

Barbara Drake
Linfield College

John Drury
University of Cincinnati

Doris Earnshaw
University of California, Davis

Bruce L. Edwards
Bowling Green State University

Clifford Edwards
Fort Hays State University

Robert P. Ellis
Worcester State College

CONTRIBUTING REVIEWERS

Edmund L. Epstein
City University of New York, Queens College

David Lawrence Erben
University of South Florida

Thomas L. Erskine
Salisbury State University

Angela M. Estes
*California Polytechnic State University, San
Luis Obispo*

Sandra K. Fischer
State University of New York—Albany

Ray Fleming
Pennsylvania State University

Terri Frongia
University of California, Riverside

Janice Moore Fuller
Catawba College

Samuel B. Garren
North Carolina A&T State University

Jill B. Gidmark
University of Minnesota

Erlis Glass
Rosemont College

Laurie Glover
Claremont Graduate School

Nancy Goldfarb
University of Michigan

Lois Gordon
Fairleigh Dickinson University

Sidney Gottlieb
Sacred Heart University

James Green
Arizona State University

Glenn Grever
Illinois State University

William Grim
Ohio University

Jeffrey D. Groves
Harvey Mudd College

James Hale
Central Washington University

Tina Hanlon
Concord College

Nelson Hathcock
St. Xavier College

John C. Hawley
Santa Clara University

David M. Heaton
Ohio University

Hartmut Heep
University of Illinois at Urbana-Champaign

Terry Heller
Coe College

John Hildebidle
Massachusetts Institute of Technology

William Hoagland
Northwest College

Alan Holder
Hunter College

Hilary Holladay
University of North Carolina—Chapel Hill

Whitney Hoth
Fort Hays State University

Ed Ingebretsen
Georgetown University

Charles Isenberg
Reed College

Barry Jacobs
Montclair State College

Helen Jaskoski
California State University, Fullerton

Michael Jeffrys
Independent Scholar

Geri Johnson
Loyola University, New Orleans

Ralph Robert Joly
Asbury College

Kirkland Jones
Texas Southern University

Marlene Kadar
York University

Robert Kaplan
University of Arizona

Cynthia Lee Katona
Ohlone College

MASTERPLOTS II

Heidi Kelchner
University of South Florida

Sherrill Keller
Central Washington University

Steven G. Kellman
University of Texas—San Antonio

Frank L. Kersnowski
Trinity University

Gunilla Theander Kester
University of North Carolina—Chapel Hill

Judith Kitchen
State University of New York, College at Brockport

Judith Kleck
Central Washington University

Kathleen L. Komar
University of California, Los Angeles

Paula Kopacz
Eastern Kentucky University

Robin Kornman
Princeton University

Paul R. La Chance
Frostburg State University

Christine de Lailhacar
State University of New York Maritime College

R. T. Lambdin
University of South Florida

Joshua Landy
Princeton University

Kathleen Margaret Lant
California Polytechnic State University, San Luis Obispo

Peter Lapp
Queen's University, Kingston, Ontario, Canada

Carlota Larrea
Pennsylvania State University

Eugene Larson
Los Angeles Pierce College

Terry Lass
Columbia College

Anne LeCroy
East Tennessee State University

L. L. Lee
Western Washington University

Bruce H. Leland
Western Illinois University

Jordan Leondopoulos
St. John's University

Leon Lewis
Appalachian State University

Thomas Lisk
University of South Carolina—Sumter

James Livingston
Northern Michigan University

Russell Lord
Plymouth State College

Janet McCann
Texas A&M University

Clarence McClanahan
Diablo Valley College

James McCorkle
Hobart and William Smith Colleges

Howard McCrea
Independent Scholar

Gardner McFall
The Cooper Union for the Advancement of Science and Art, New York

Ronald E. McFarland
University of Idaho

Richard D. McGhee
Kansas State University

Kevin McNeilly
Queen's University, Kingston, Ontario
University of Western Ontario, Canada

Lois A. Marchino
University of Texas—El Paso

Laura Martin
Emory University

Thomas Matchie
North Dakota State University

Clark Mayo
California State University, San Bernardino

CONTRIBUTING REVIEWERS

Aparajita Mazumder
University of Illinois at Urbana-Champaign

Laurence W. Mazzeno
Mesa State College

Kenneth W. Meadwell
University of Winnipeg, Manitoba, Canada

Muriel Mellown
North Carolina Central University

Michael J. Meyer
Concordia University Wisconsin

Vasa D. Mihailovich
University of North Carolina—Chapel Hill

Maureen W. Mills
Central Michigan University

Robert A. Morace
Daemen College

Bernard E. Morris
Modesto Junior College

Dean de la Motte
Guilford College

Russell Elliott Murphy
University of Arkansas at Little Rock

Thomas Mussio
University of Michigan

John M. Muste
Ohio State University

Susan Nagel
Independent Scholar

Elizabeth Nelson
St. Peter's College

Cynthia Nichols
North Dakota State University

Emma Coburn Norris
Troy State University

George O'Brien
Georgetown University

Peter D. Olson
Hillsdale College

James Panabaker
Queen's University, Kingston, Ontario, Canada

Pamela Pavliscak
University of North Carolina—Chapel Hill

Thomas Amherst Perry
East Texas State University

Francis Poole
University of Delaware

Joseph Powell
Central Washington University

Jonathan L. Price
California State University, Sacramento

Charles Pullen
Queen's University, Kingston, Ontario, Canada

Dean Rader
State University of New York at Binghamton

Philip Raisor
Old Dominion University

Jerrald Ranta
University of Wyoming

Rosemary M. Canfield Reisman
Troy State University

Donald Revell
University of Denver

Jeanette A. Ritzenthaler
New Hampshire College

Len Roberts
Independent Scholar

Claire Robinson
Maharishi International University

Jill Rollins
University of New Brunswick, Quebec, Canada

Carl Rollyson
*Bernard M. Baruch College
City University of New York*

Heather Rosario-Sievert
*Hostos Community College
City University of New York*

Joseph Rosenblum
University of North Carolina—Greensboro

Robert L. Ross
University of Texas—Austin

Stan Sanvel Rubin
State University of New York, College at Brockport

Christine F. Sally
University of South Florida

Phyllis J. Scherle
Indiana University at Indianapolis

Marilyn Schultz
California State University, Fullerton

Jeffrey Schwartz
Greenwich Academy

D. Dean Shackelford
Concord College

Anne Shifrer
Utah State University

Anne W. Sienkewicz
Independent Scholar

Thomas J. Sienkewicz
Monmouth College

Karla Sigel
Eastern Kentucky University

Carl Singleton
Fort Hays State University

Genevieve Slomski
Independent Scholar

Marjorie Smelstor
University of Wisconsin—Eau Claire

Katherine Snipes
Eastern Washington University

Jean M. Snook
Memorial University of Newfoundland

Steven P. Sondrup
Brigham Young University

George Soule
Carleton College

Virginia Starrett
California State University, Fullerton

Thomas J. Steele
Regis University

Karen F. Stein
University of Rhode Island

Ingo Roland Stoehr
University of Texas—Austin

Stefan Stoenescu
Cornell University

Elisabeth Strenger
Brandeis University

Michael Stuprich
Ithaca College

Ernest Suarez
Catholic University of America

Alvin Sullivan
Southern Illinois University—Edwardsville

James Sullivan
California State University, Los Angeles

David Sundstrand
Citrus College

Charlene E. Suscavage
University of Southern Maine

Catherine Swanson
Independent Scholar

Marie Gerenday Tamas
Rutgers University

Betty Taylor Thompson
Texas Southern University

Jonathan L. Thorndike
Rocky Mountain College

John H. Timmerman
Calvin College

Christine D. Tomei
Allegheny College

Lewis Turco
State University of New York, College at Oswego

Von E. Underwood
Cameron University

Julia A. Urla
University of Michigan

Sue Walker
University of South Alabama

Ron Welburn
Western Connecticut State University

Julia Whitsitt
Texas Tech University

Barbara Wiedemann
Auburn University at Montgomery

CONTRIBUTING REVIEWERS

John Wilson
Independent Scholar

Anna M. Wittmann
Medicine Hat College, Alberta, Canada

Cynthia Wong
Western Illinois University

Qingyun Wu
California State University, Los Angeles

Howard Young
Pomona College

Harry Zohn
Brandeis University

LIST OF TITLES IN VOLUME 1

MASTERPLOTS II

POETRY SERIES

"A"

Author: Louis Zukofsky (1904-1978)
Type of poem: Poetic sequence
First published: " 'A' — Second Movement," 1932; "From 'A,' " 1933; *"A"-12*, 1959; *"A" 13-21*, 1969; *"A"-24*, 1972; " 'A'-22, Part 1," 1973; " 'A'-22, Part 2," 1974; "From 'A'-23," 1975; *"A" 22 & 23*, 1975; *"A"* (complete poem), 1978

The Poem

"A" is one of the longest poems in the English language, numbering more than eight hundred pages. It was written over a forty-six-year period (1928-1974) and is divided into twenty-four sections (referred to as movements) that differ widely in length, from the single page of "A"-16 to the 242 pages of "A"-24. *"A"* is generally considered to be the greatest poetic achievement of the twentieth century Objectivist school of poetry, which was led by Louis Zukofsky and included George Oppen, Lorine Niedecker, Charles Reznikoff, and Carl Rakosi.

The title *"A"* is significant in that it is not only the first word of the poem but also an indefinite pronoun and as such is a response to Zukofsky's earlier poem, "Poem beginning 'the' " (1926). The twenty-four movements of *"A"* suggest the twenty-four hours of the day—that is, the solar day representing the totality of human civilization. The *a* of *"A"* is also the first step in the poet's attempt to comment upon this process literally from *a* to *z* (the *z* of Zukofsky, that is).

"A"-1 begins with a description of a performance of Johann Sebastian Bach's *St. Matthew's Passion* at Carnegie Hall in New York City on April 5, 1928. The dichotomy between intellect and emotions is examined and is continued in "A"-2, in which the narrator Zukofsky engages in a debate with the eponymous character Kay. The death of one Ricky (in reality, the suicide of Ricky, the brother of Whittaker Chambers, who was one of Zukofsky's fellow students at Columbia University) is mentioned in "A"-3. "A"-4 is concerned with origins, and specific references are made to the poetry of Yehoash (the pen name of the Yiddish poet Solomon Bloomgarden). The dichotomy between intellect and emotions that was first seen in "A"-1 and "A"-2 is rehashed in "A"-5. "A"-6 constitutes a reexamination of "A" 1-5, which the reader now discovers to have been only a preamble to the central aesthetic question posed by the poet: "*Can*/ The design/ Of the fugue/ Be transferred/ To poetry?" (page 38).

"A"-7 and "A"-8 concern themselves with the worsening conditions of the Great Depression and constitute Zukofsky's effort to examine the roles of the individual and society within the contexts of three intellectual constructs that strive for universal validity and will only be fully revealed in "A"-12: Marxist economics, Einsteinian physics, and Pythagorean music theory. The interweaving of these and other ideas is a poetic approximation of the interplay of musical lines in the fugue. "A"-8 functions, then (as do "A"-12 and "A"-24), as a summation and amalgamation of all that has transpired so far in the poem.

"A"-9 provides lyrical relief from the literary pyrotechnics of the preceding movement and is the poet's paean to memory, the recollection of love as well as musical themes. In "A"-9, music is equated with action, action being remembrance, a necessary prerequisite, in Zukofsky's mind, for the existence of love. By the time of "A"-10, the Great Depression is over, and the Nazi occupation of Paris and the regime of Marshall Pétain are being examined.

"A"-11 and "A"-12 both examine the tightly knit and loving relationships among the members of Zukofsky's immediate family, including the poet, his composer wife Celia, and their violinist son Paul. The 135 pages of "A"-12 are longer than the previous eleven sections of the poem combined. In "A"-12, the specific nature of the relationships or harmony among the members of the Zukofsky family is examined in universalizing contexts symbolized by the many references to the works of those who strove for the totality or "universal harmony" of artistic creation, such as Pythagoras, J. S. Bach, Arnold Schönberg, William Shakespeare, James Joyce, and Johann Wolfgang von Goethe.

"A"-13 and "A"-14 are movements that signal Zukofsky's retreat into a very personal and hermeneutic poetic world. "A"-13 is an attenuated description of a walking tour of New York City taken by the poet and his son. In "A"-14, which mostly consists of three-line stanzas with two or three words per stanza, Zukofsky limits his syntax so severely that the words become direct images rather than metaphors of the objects and ideas they are trying to describe. "A"-15, "A"-16, and "A"-17 are concerned with Zukofsky's musings on history and his appropriation of the literary montage techniques utilized by William Carlos Williams in *Paterson* (1946-1958). "A"-15 contains an English approximation of the Hebrew of the Book of Job and describes the tragic events of the early 1960's: the assassination of President Kennedy, the Bay of Pigs fiasco, and the deepening American involvement in the Vietnam War. "A"-17 includes a chronology of the writing of *"A"* and the rest of Zukofsky's canon, as well as an extended tribute to the poetry of Williams.

"A"-18 and "A"-19 provide an interesting contrast. The former movement concerns itself with the theme of societal decline. Zukofsky makes additional references to the Vietnam War as well as to Edward Gibbon's *The History of the Decline and Fall of the Roman Empire* (1776-1788) and works by Henry Brooks Adams, including *Degradation of Democratic Dogma* (1919) and *The Education of Henry Adams* (1907). "A"-19, however, is concerned with renewal—specifically, Paul Zukofsky's very promising career as a concert violinist, which is given impetus by his participation in the Paganini Violin Competition, held in Italy. Paul Zukofsky's career as one of the foremost performers of avant-garde music forms the topic of "A"-20.

"A"-21 is Zukofsky's idiosyncratic English translation of Plautus' Latin play *Rudens*. The play within the poem is indicative of Zukofsky's efforts at translation (particularly the poetry of Catullus) and is somewhat analogous to the literary influence of Shakespeare, a lifelong infatuation for Zukofsky. *Rudens* is a recognition comedy, set outdoors for the most part, which contains a storm scene; as such, it is reminiscent of Shakespeare's play *The Tempest* (1611). "A"-21 is connected to the rest of the poem not thematically but as a testimony to the literary work in which Zukofsky was engaged and as a symbol of the past as present and the permanence of art as opposed to the vagaries of history.

"*A*"-22 and "*A*"-23 are perhaps the most densely textured, difficult to comprehend, and personal sections of the poem. They constitute Zukofsky's attempt to resolve the many themes of the poem, to seek the unity and totality of human existence. "*A*"-22 and "*A*"-23 point toward the resolution of Zukofsky's aesthetic dilemma in "*A*"-24 and also make oblique references to his final poetic work, *80 Flowers* (1978). Zukofsky's poem, therefore, progresses from poem as music (music in both the literal and the Pythagorean sense) to a resolution of the "music" of humanity with that of nature.

"*A*"-24 is a summa of Zukofsky's entire poetic career. Here the "music" of Zukofsky's poetry leaves the abstract Pythagorean realm and becomes literal music. The implied counterpoint of the earlier sections of the poem becomes actual musical counterpoint. "*A*"-24 also reveals how inextricably linked were Zukofsky's work and family life; this section is and is not a work of Zukofsky's. As a birthday present, Celia Zukofsky gave her husband a work entitled "L. Z. Masque," which became "*A*"-24. This work consists of four different texts by Louis Zukofsky that are set to selections from George Frideric Handel's *Pièces pour le clavecin*. The result is a five-part "score" in which music (Handel's pieces), thought (Zukofsky's book of essays entitled *Prepositions*), drama (Zukofsky's play, *Arise, Arise*), story (the poet's short story "It was"), and poetry (excerpts from earlier sections of "*A*") are simultaneously presented. The gift of "L. Z. Masque" delighted the poet, who realized that it contained the solution to the resolution of his lifetime's work.

Forms and Devices

"*A*"-24 exhibits a dazzling display of poetic forms and devices, many of which are derived from musical procedures. Leitmotifs—that is, short recurring phrases—occur throughout the poem. "*A*"-8, "*A*"-12, and "*A*"-24 are long movements in which poetic approximations of the musical fugue are attempted. One of Zukofsky's common "fugue" themes is the use of Bach's name as an acrostic. Bach's name was used by the composer himself and many others as the theme of musical fugues (in German musical notation, B-A-C-H equals the notes B flat-A-C-B natural). Zukofsky uses Bach's name in "*A*"-12, "*A*"-23, and several other movements of the poem as an acrostic representing the words *B*lest-*A*rdent-*C*elia-*H*appy. This acrostic is later transformed into a representation of *B*aruch Spinoza (Hebrew *baruch*, blessed)-*A*ristotle-*C*elia-*H*ohenheim (the last name of the medieval scientist Paracelsus).

The sonnet is a favorite poetic form of Zukofsky's. "*A*"-7 is very close to being a crown of sonnets, in which seven sonnets are linked; the last line of each of the first six sonnets becomes the first line of the next sonnet, and the last line of the seventh sonnet repeats the first line of the first sonnet. "*A*"-9 is a double canzone, two sets of five sonnets, in which the last word of each line of the first set is used as the last word of each corresponding line of the second set. "*A*"-9 also employs the standard musical canzona rhythm of long, short, short.

Unusual forms and devices abound in "A." "A"-10 approximates a medieval troped Mass, in which words and music were added to the text and music of the original Gregorian chants of the Mass. Zukofsky calls "A"-13 a partita (a baroque musical suite, a collection of instrumental dance pieces in varying moods and tempi), and he divides this movement into five subsections that in meter and spirit are roughly analogous to the allemande, courante, sarabande, gigue, and chaconne of the baroque dance suite. "A"-19 consists of two-word lines. This section is concerned with Paul Zukofsky's appearance in the Paganini Violin Competition in Italy; therefore, the two-word lines are meant to represent the up and down motions of bowing the violin. "A"-20 makes references to Paul Zukofsky's interest in modern music, particularly dodecaphonic (or twelve-tone) music. This movement consists of four twelve-line stanzas with introduction and epilogue and is meant to approximate the variations on the tone row of a dodecaphonic musical composition.

"A"-22 and "A"-23 are similarly structured, each consisting of one thousand lines in which twenty five-line stanzas (with five words per line) precede and follow a main body of eight hundred lines. Both movements begin with the word "an," continuing the precedent of the "An" songs found in "A"-14 and displaying once again the wealth of meaning Zukofsky found in simple words.

Themes and Meanings

It is not surprising that the themes and meanings of a work as long and complicated as "A" cannot be distilled into a neat package. The meaning of "A" is really the meaning of life itself, whether or not there is a unity or unifying force by means of which the entire universe may be understood or into which it may be subsumed. The thematic structure of "A" is therefore correspondingly dense. A cursory (and very incomplete) list of the thematic material of "A" includes the music and life of J. S. Bach, birds, flowers, horses, labor, love, eyes (both the subjective "I" and the objective seeing "eye"), Zukofsky's family, Spinoza, Aristotle, Paracelsus, Pythagoras, Karl Marx, leaves, light, and Shakespeare.

The creation of the twenty-four movements of "A" was designed by Zukofsky to occupy a lifetime of work and to be a commentary on the lifetime that was being occupied by the process of creating the poem. Zukofsky's fascination with the linguistic possibilities of small and seemingly insignificant words such as pronouns is an attempt to extrapolate the universal from the microcosmic or the individual, and is influenced by the *Cantos* of Ezra Pound (1917-1970) and James Joyce's *Ulysses* (1922). The Pythagorean and Boethian concept of the harmony of the spheres (the tripartite categorization of actual musical harmony, the "harmony" among individual human beings, and the cosmic "harmony" linking everything in the universe) is omnipresent in "A." By utilizing an extremely dense structure of themes or leitmotifs, Zukofsky presents analogues of universal harmony in his examinations of himself (as poet attempting to find an individual poetic voice) and of his relationships with his wife and son.

Also present throughout the poem is the tension arising from the dichotomy between historical determinism and the contingent nature of art. The indefinite articles "a" and "an," therefore, seem to represent the unlimited possibilities of art, as opposed to the definite article "the," which symbolizes the eschatology of historical forces represented by Marxist thinking and Judeo-Christian theology, both of which Zukofsky ultimately rejected.

History and art become somewhat reconciled for Zukofsky in "A" in that both are acts of remembrance. The historian "remembers" events that have already transpired while the artist seeks the remembrance of the eternal verities implicit in the autonomous work of art. Memory, the human capacity for the self-understanding of recurring (or even contingent) patterns of existence, found its analogue not only in the casual repetitions of the poetic refrain but also in the more organic type of repetition found in musical forms. The evolutionary "musicalization" of "A," from the report of a musical performance in "A"-1 to the actual notated musical score of "A"-24, is a process whereby Zukofsky equates music with the human (and humane) capacity for remembrance.

At the end of "A," Zukofsky has found no ultimate resolution or single key to the understanding of the interconnectivity of the individual with his fellow humans, of mankind with nature, or of the present with the past and future. Unlike the similarly grandiose *Cantos* of Pound, however, which deal with similar ideas and end on a note of defeat, Zukofsky's "A" is triumphant, life-affirming, and open-ended, implying poetic and human possibilities left to be examined. Zukofsky's conclusion is that there is neither a hermeneutic key to understanding existence nor a grand Hegelian synthesis of the disparate elements of the cosmos. There remains, however, the universal "fugue" in which each voice sounds its music simultaneously. Understanding the individual life, the nature of art, the history of mankind, or the cosmos will always be, in Zukofskian terms, a close and objective examination of the particularities of existence as they appear before the poet's eye.

William Grim

ADONAIS

Author: Percy Bysshe Shelley (1792-1822)
Type of poem: Elegy
First published: 1821

The Poem

Adonais is a long poem, running 495 lines in fifty-five Spenserian stanzas. As the poet states in his subtitle, it is "An Elegy on the Death of John Keats." The younger Keats, an acquaintance and fellow Romantic poet whom Percy Bysshe Shelley had invited to visit with him in Italy, had been seeking warmer climes to relieve the tuberculosis which eventually took his life, at the age of twenty-six, on February 23, 1821.

The poem's title requires the reader to pause and reflect momentarily on Shelley's highly conscious design. In keeping with the conventions of the pastoral elegy, Adonais is the fictive name which Shelley assigns John Keats. Readers familiar with Greek mythology will certainly hear an echo of Adonis in the name; he was the decidedly handsome youth whom the goddess Venus loved and who also died a tragic and early death, being killed by a wild boar. One familiar with Judaic traditions might also hear Adonai in Shelley's choice of name. Adonai in Hebrew means God or Lord, and is a substitute for the ineffable name which even the name Jehovah only betokens.

If it seems presumptuous for Shelley to hint at a godlike quality to the young man whose death he is mourning, it is easier to see an intended symmetry: As a poet, Keats shares a spiritual identity both with a mortal beloved of the gods and with the godhead itself, and he is the inheritor of both the classical and biblical traditions that compose Western culture — an heir, that is, of the ages.

The poem opens boldly with a single, undeniable fact and the poet's response to it: "I weep for Adonais — he is dead!" Stanzas 2 through 35 will present a parade of mourners who, with the poet, have come to grieve. The poet pitifully urges the fallen Adonais' mother, Urania, to awaken to lead the mourners at his bier; in her, Shelley combines both the Venus of the Adonis myth (Venus Urania is one of the goddess' titles) and Urania, the muse of astronomy. That latter may seem an odd choice unless one knows that Adonais' ultimate destiny is an eternity represented by the stars.

For the moment, however, there is only despair, and readers are urged to "weep for Adonais — he is dead!" Stanza 9 brings as leaders of the solemn procession the dead shepherd/poet's "flocks" — his dreams and inspirations. Continuing through stanza 13, there is a cataloging of the personifications of all those thoughts and feelings, attitudes and skills, which made his genius, as they view the corpse in shocked disbelief. Awakened by the grieving poet as well as by the figure Misery, Urania appears in stanza 22, and the poet repeats his lament: "He will awake no more, oh, never more!" In the wild distraction of her grief she urges her son to arise, to awake; her pleas are in vain.

Stanzas 30 through 34 bring a select group of human mourners. The "Pilgrim of Eternity," to anyone familiar with Byron's first great work, *Childe Harold's Pilgrimage* (1812-1818), is George Gordon, Lord Byron. The next is the Irish poet Thomas Moore, whose themes also comment on the sorrows and losses wrought by time's passage. Finally, stanzas 31 through 34 present a Shelleyan self-portrait: "one frail Form" who has "fled astray," "his branded and ensanguined brow," a brow "like Cain's or Christ's."

This image is not simply of himself but of the poetic soul in general as a gentle, high-strung creature who, as an outcast, survives the darts of his callous fellow mortals with dignity and a quiet grace. The image spurs a substantial shift in the poet's attitude toward Adonais' death.

To this point, the poet has lamented his and others' helplessness to make sense of that death. In stanza 37, however, the poet reflects on a fit punishment for the "nameless worm" and "noteless blot" who is the anonymous and highly critical reviewer of Keats's *Endymion* (1818), who, in Shelley's eyes, drove John Keats/ Adonais to an early grave. The worst punishment that Shelley can contrive is that such a scoundrel should live: "Live thou, whose infamy is not thy fame!/ Live!" Faced with the contradiction that he would wish a long life upon the miscreant who took his hero's life, in stanza 38 the poet bursts open the gates of consolation that are required of the pastoral elegy: "Nor let us weep that our delight is fled/ Far from these carrion kites."

Adonais "is not dead . . ./ He hath awakened from the dream of life." Shelley turns his grief from Adonais to "we" who must live on and "decay/ Like corpses in a charnel," and after a series of stanzas (39-49) in which he celebrates the richer and fuller life that Adonais must now be experiencing, the poet becomes mindful that he is in Rome, itself a city rife with visible records of loss and decay. Moreover, he is in the Protestant cemetery there, where Shelley's three-year-old son is buried as well; and yet, as if mocking all despair, a "light of laughing flowers along the grass is spread." Nature does not abhor death and decay, he sees; it is humans, who fear and hate in the midst of life, who do.

"What Adonais is, why fear we to become?" he asks in stanza 51. The reversal of attitude is completed, and in stanza 52 Shelley makes the most profound profession of faith in the everlasting and transcendent to be found in all English poetry. It is life's worldly cares — that obscuring and distracting "dome of many-coloured glass" — not Death that is the enemy and the source of human despair. "Follow where all is fled," he urges, and he goads his own heart into having the courage to face not extinction but "that Light whose smile kindles the Universe." The poem concludes by imagining Adonais to be a part of "the white radiance of Eternity." As the poem ends, "like a star," the soul of the dead poet "Beacons from the abode where the Eternal are."

Forms and Devices

Adonais is a pastoral elegy, a highly stylized composition adhering to rules, or conventions, that hark back at least two thousand years to such Greek poets as Theocritus, Moschus, and Bion. Shelley had in fact translated into English Bion's *Lament for Adonis* and Moschus' *Lament for Bion*; he would have been familiar with the form, even had he never studied those classical sources, through the seventeenth century English masterpiece, John Milton's "Lycidas."

In general, the pastoral deals with an idyllic imaginative landscape where it is always May and the pastures and hills are always green. Despite renowned uses of pastoral conventions in poems from the late sixteenth century such as Edmund Spenser's *The Shepheardes Calendar* (1579) and Sir Walter Raleigh's "The Nymph's Reply to the Shepherd," by Shelley's own time the pastoral mode had fallen into disuse among serious English poets. Some of this development was attributable to changing social conditions; pasture lands had been fenced off, and the Industrial Revolution was making England a less bucolic nation. The eighteenth century critic Samuel Johnson had also poked fun at the pastoral's sanitized view of the lives of shepherds, pointing out that they generally smelled quite bad; in 1798, William Wordsworth had pointedly subtitled *Michael* (published in 1800), his realistic narrative of an elderly shepherd struggling to make ends meet, "a pastoral," as if to sound the death knell, in English poetry, of this long-standing literary tradition.

Indeed, it may seem strange that Shelley should choose to lament Keats's death in such an artificial and constrained format as the pastoral requires. If his feelings of grief were genuine, one might ask, why not have expressed them in plain, or at least far less contrived terms. The pastoral allows the poet to exercise, nevertheless, the option of poeticizing the event. From that perspective, Shelley, who was quite capable of using a wide range of poetic styles and expression, was first of all doing his fellow poet a high honor by eulogizing him in a structure unique to poetic discourse.

Also, Keats's own poetry often harked back to pastoral themes if not actual modes. "Ode on a Grecian Urn" is only one outstanding example, and all of Keats's poetry is rich in an appreciation of life's simple pleasures and beauties — and of the pain that their loss can cause.

Shelley adheres to all the traditional formal pastoral constraints — and more — in producing his elegy. In keeping with the tradition, he does not identify the characters by their actual names, but by their shepherd names or by characteristics typical of natural rather than social environs. Since the tradition is Greek, he harks back to classical myth and imagery. Keats's poetic efforts, as noted previously, are his flocks. The procession of mourners is appropriately arrayed in flowers and other vestiges of spring; even in the depths of his grief, the poet never fails to remind the reader that it is in fact the springtime of the year.

Themes and Meanings

In his preface to *Adonais*, Shelley called Keats one of the writers "of the highest genius who have adorned our age." Shelley saw in the tragedy of Keats's untimely death a comment on the mindless cruelty that the world inflicts upon the sensitive soul. Shelley imagined that Keats's illness and death were the direct result of an anonymous and vituperative review of Keats's ambitious poem *Endymion*. That review, which is now known to have been written by an individual named John Wilson Croker, had been published in the influential *Quarterly Review* for April, 1818. Shelley was not alone in his opinion that the negative reaction had broken the young Keats's heart; Byron was of the same opinion.

Shelley's poem is therefore a sincere act of public mourning and reaffirmation in the face of an apparently needless and certainly tragic death; yet it is also a literary broadside of the first order. Its pointed and feeling attack on the pettiness of the quarterly reviewers in the face of the poetry which Shelley and his fellow Romantics were producing (and in the process, altering the nature of English poetry for generations to come) itself follows a long tradition harking back at least as far as John Dryden's *Mac Flecknoe* (1682) and Alexander Pope's *The Dunciad* (1728-1743). With typical Romantic *élan*, nevertheless, Shelley turns both the pastoral elegy and the literary satire into a stirring commentary on the larger purpose of death in an unfeeling and violent physical universe.

Shelley's decision to utilize the pastoral mode is particularly telling. In its earliest formulations, it was an Edenic vision, a harking back to greener, happier, sunnier times. It is likely that no one has ever imagined that the pastoral described, or was intended to describe, a true human condition. Only the most coldhearted, however, can fail to hear in its eternal springtime optimism the dearest longings of the human heart for peace, ease, and contentment.

In this regard, even the elegaic pastoral is compelled to render the experience positive by poem's end, for while no poet can deny the undeniable reality of bodily death, the pastoral's very idealizations require one to imagine a transcendent reality as the true locus of all human hopes and aspirations. In its spirited exultation that light shall triumph over darkness, that the true shall endure the violence done them through hatred and spite, and that all of nature conspires yearly to reward humankind with renewals and resurrections that can take the breath away, *Adonais* reaffirms life in the very act of lamenting an individual's death.

Russell Elliott Murphy

ADVICE TO A PROPHET

Author: Richard Wilbur (1921-   )
Type of poem: Lyric
First published: 1961, in *Advice to a Prophet and Other Poems*

The Poem

"Advice to a Prophet" is composed of nine quatrains with an *abba* rhyme scheme. The formal structure of the poem is appropriate to its serious content. Richard Wilbur begins the poem by addressing a hypothetical prophet who needs to appear in reality to persuade the human race to eliminate the weapons of twentieth century warfare, which can annihilate life on earth. The poet imagines that the prophet, when he states this danger, will be "mad-eyed" from being ignored. Consequently, the prophet needs the poet's advice on how to tell the truth in effective language.

The poet imagines that the prophet will not speak of humanity's "fall," like the prophets of the Old Testament, but will beg people in "God's name" to have self-pity. The poet begins to offer advice in stanza 2, telling the prophet not to speak of the "force and range" of weapons, because people cannot imagine numbers so large or the destructive power to which they refer. Similarly, the poet explains in stanza 3, the prophet's talk about the death of the human race will have no effect, because humanity is incapable of imagining an unpeopled world.

Instead, the poet recommends in stanza 4, the prophet should speak of the changes the use of weapons would cause in the natural world. These are comprehensible because they are familiar. Humanity has witnessed changes brought about by natural processes, such as a cloud dispersing or a vine killed by frost. Also, the poet states in stanza 5, people have watched deer flee into a forest and birds fly away, disturbed by human presence. A pine tree growing at a cliff's edge, its roots half-exposed, about to fall, is also a familiar sight. The poet returns to the effects of war on nature in stanza 6, providing an example from history. The ancient city of Xanthus was burned so severely in war that the debris of the Xanthus river caught on fire, stunning the trout.

After focusing attention on changes in the natural world, the poet recommends, in stanza 7, that the prophet ask what humanity would be without nature. The poet explains that nature is a "live tongue," giving images, such as "the dolphin's arc, the dove's return," that people use to express their own thoughts and feelings. The poet gives more examples in stanza 8: the rose, representing love, and the shell of a locust, expressing the idea of the soul leaving a body at death. Images from nature also enable people to represent ideal selves—perhaps graceful like the dolphin or faithful like the dove. In the concluding stanza, the poet asks if human language would be possible without the images of nature. He tells the prophet to ask if human hearts would "fail" if people had only the "worldless rose." Without the oak tree, could there be ideas like "lofty" and "long standing"?

Forms and Devices

In "Advice to a Prophet," Wilbur uses a variety of verbal devices, most of which exemplify ways in which human language and nature depend on each other for meaning. He uses personification to show how human characteristics are projected onto things in the natural world. The leaves are "untroubled," the stone has a "face," and the locust is "singing." Nature, itself, is a "live tongue." In this construction, "tongue" is also a metaphor for nature. The poet uses "glass," or a mirror, as another metaphor to represent nature. Wilbur also draws a metaphor from the language of weaponry, in "rocket the mind," where "rocket" means to go beyond the mind's capacity to imagine, as well as to destroy the mind.

In this context, other words take on double meanings. The phrase "death of the race" refers to the human race but also suggests the arms race. If people do not end the arms race, the human race itself may end. "The locust of the soul unshelled" implies the shells of weaponry as well as the literal shell of a locust. Some double meanings in the poem are expressed in puns. When the poet refers to ways nature "alters," he evokes the "altars" of religious worship, indicating that nature should be treated with reverence. Similarly, he puns on "arc" in "the dolphin's arc, the dove's return," making an allusion to Noah's "ark" and the story of the first destruction of the world by flood.

Wilbur makes other allusions to the Bible. When he writes that the prophet will not speak of humanity's "fall," he refers to the fall of Adam and Eve in the garden of Eden. He also evokes Old Testament prophecies of coming plagues of locusts. The historical allusion to the destruction of Xanthus by fire reminds the reader of the biblical prophecy that the second destruction of the world will be by fire. It is likely that the poet intends the reference to Xanthus to evoke modern parallels—the destruction of Nagasaki and Hiroshima by the fires of atomic explosion. These events made it clear that the destruction of the world by fire is possible. In this context, the phrase "the dreamt cloud" brings to mind the mushroom cloud accompanying the explosion of atomic and nuclear weapons.

When Wilbur writes that nature may become a "glass obscured" by the use of such weapons, he alludes to the biblical idea that in this world people see as through a glass, darkly. By using variations of the word "dream" as a metaphor representing human perception, the poet implies a need for clear vision. Wilbur's prophet, himself a figure of biblical tradition, hopes to clarify human sight.

Themes and Meanings

By giving advice to the prophet, Wilbur thereby becomes the prophet, obliquely assuming one of the poet's traditional roles. Just as the prophet is "mad-eyed from stating the obvious" without being listened to, the poet in the modern world is for the most part unread, his role as prophet forgotten. It is ironic that the poet is speaking to himself. By addressing the prophet as "you," however, he calls on the reader to become the prophet and to pass on the word of the poet's vision. Wilbur's view of life on Earth is summarized in the titles of two of his other poems: "A World Without Objects Is a Sensible Emptiness" and "Love Calls Us to the Things of This World."

The first of those titles finds expression in the poet's idea of a "worldless rose." There can be no world without objects. If there were, it would be a sensible emptiness: nothing there to see, touch, smell, taste, or hear, and no one there to do these things. There can be no "worldless" human beings. The poet believes this is obvious, perhaps so obvious that it has been forgotten. How else can he explain why human beings allow weapons to exist that are capable of destroying the world?

The other title mentioned above, "Love Calls Us to the Things of This World," expresses the attitude Wilbur believes people should have toward all things of nature, including themselves. Love is the opposite of war. The things of this world are exemplified throughout "Advice to a Prophet"—the lark and the dove, the horse and the deer, the dolphin and the trout, the rose and the vine, the jack-pine and the oak tree and its locust. By viewing these things as "words" spoken to us by the "living tongue" of nature, Wilbur draws on the transcendental tradition of Ralph Waldo Emerson, Walt Whitman, and Henry David Thoreau.

For these writers every natural fact is a symbol of a spiritual fact. The "living tongue" of nature speaks the language of God; spirit is incarnate in nature. Humanity can have heaven on Earth and save its collective soul if it answers the poet-prophet's "call" and "believes" in nature—which is "God's name." If this were so, people would not allow weapons to exist. The world might become one modeled on Wilbur's poem "The Baroque Wall-Fountain in the Villa Sciarra," in which he envisions Saint Francis of Assisi's desire for the "dreamt land/ Toward which all hungers leap, all pleasures pass." The imagined land is Eden, and Wilbur believes humanity can return to it—if people do not destroy it first.

James Green

ADVICE TO KING LEAR

Author: Turner Cassity (1929-   )
Type of poem: Lyric
First published: 1986, in *Hurricane Lamp*

The Poem

"Advice to King Lear" is a short lyric poem of thirteen lines that are divided into two stanzas. The first stanza has six lines, and the second stanza has seven; the same end rhyme is employed for all thirteen lines. Turner Cassity has made his reputation by writing structured verse. "Advice to King Lear" was included in his 1986 collection *Hurricane Lamp*. Like many poems in this collection, "Advice to King Lear" is a compressed creation in which Cassity wryly combines the profound past with the seemingly ordinary present. The poem combines the Shakespearean tragedy *King Lear* (c. 1605-1606) and the bizarre Texas setting in which it is being staged.

Cassity reprints as an epigraph a description from *San Antonio: A Pictorial Guide*, which states that the Arneson River Theatre is unique because its stage stands on one side of the San Antonio River, but its grass seats are located on the other side. The final comment of the guide notes that "Occasional passing boats enhance audience enjoyment." This particular setting fits well with Cassity's use of the ironic. As the title states, the narrator of the poem will be advising King Lear. The first word of the poem is "Unlikely," which—as becomes evident as the poem progresses—is a definite understatement; the unlikely and the unusual are common in Cassity's poems. (Other poems in *Hurricane Lamp* that illustrate this theme include "News for Loch Ness," "A Dialogue with the Bride of Godzilla," and "Scheherazade in South Dakota.") After the "Unlikely," Cassity contrasts the locale where the play is being staged and the artificial weather that must be created in order to produce *King Lear* correctly. The San Antonio area is a "semi-desert," and on the night of the play, the night is "azure." To create the illusion that there is a storm on stage, the crew must resort to the use of a wind machine. Through it all, "Advice to King Lear" juxtaposes King Lear's tragedy against the almost silly notion of staging the play in a place where the locale, not Shakespeare's instructions, dictates the ending.

With King Lear's situation becoming increasingly desperate, the freak coincidence happens, and "Pleasure craft now part the placid water." The stage weather has become "glummer" with each succeeding act, but the poet interjects that no matter where *King Lear* is staged, a "mummer's still a mummer." A mummer is an actor, and therefore the opening has been created for something "unlikely" to happen in this particular production of *King Lear*. Circumstances allow King Lear to alter his fate, if he wishes, and take the advice finally given to him as the "pleasure craft" passes: "Get on the boat, Old Man, and go to summer."

Forms and Devices

Cassity structures his poetry in a traditional manner. His subjects may vary greatly, but he adds power to his point of view by compressing his observations into poems that usually employ metered lines and dense syntax. Cassity is a disciplined poet who has been compared with such poets as Yvor Winters and Alexander Pope. Cassity's technique and socially conscious themes link him with Winters' formalist school of poetry, and he is like the eighteenth century poet Pope in his reliance on wit and the frequent use of satire. In "Advice to King Lear," he makes use of his varied poetic strengths without seeming overcontrived.

Since the rhyme scheme is the same throughout the poem, Cassity adds variation by means of alliteration. The first four lines of the poem end with words that end in *ure*. Each of these words— "azure," "seizure," "pressure," and "foreclosure"—has a strong *s* sound, which unites the words. The last two lines of the first stanza and the first two of the second stanza have final words that end with *ter*. Each of these words— "matter," "stutter," "glitter," and "water"—draws its power from the pronounced *t* sound. Four of the last five lines of the poem finish with words that end in *mer*. The one line that does not stop with a word ending in *mer* ends with the word "dumber." Since the *b* is silent in "dumber," the sound effect for all five lines is the same. The sound that is made by the words ending these lines— "glummer," "mummer," "dumber," "drummer," and "summer"—is the lazy *um*, which could be described as a trance-inducing sound. Each of the sound choices that Cassity has used heightens the total emotional impact of "Advice to King Lear."

Cassity does not write easy poems, but there is a payoff if they are closely read. He is never obscure for obscurity's sake; the reader of "Advice to King Lear" should be somewhat familiar with Shakespeare's *King Lear*. The correct emotional response to the poem will come out of an intellectual understanding and appreciation of Western literary tradition. It is also necessary to appreciate Cassity's sense of playfulness in combining literary tradition and rather absurd contemporary circumstances. The charm of "Advice to King Lear" comes from the poet's dextrous wit. In the end, the winning quality of the poem is its ability to seem sophisticated without taking itself too seriously.

Themes and Meanings

The Arneson River Theatre is almost too good a creation to be true for a poet like Cassity. He recognized the possibility of exploiting its unique setting in order to expand the choices for a more spontaneous solution to the tragedy of *King Lear*. In the first stanza, the reader is introduced to the connection between the desertlike setting of the theater and the gloomy weather conditions that must be artificially generated. The poem opens up at this point to be more than merely contrast; it is also about what it takes to stage the play and keep the financial backers from worrying about "foreclosure." By the end of the first stanza, the reader has been introduced to the difficulty of staging a tragedy that is occurring on the heath, both logistically and financially.

Cassity, by writing about the staging of a Shakespeare play, also suggests the playwright's habit of occasionally having the characters step outside their roles to make offhand remarks about being in a play. Cassity does this himself in "Advice to King Lear." By the middle of the second stanza—after the "Pleasure craft" have already appeared—the poet inserts the line "Outdoors or in, a mummer's still a mummer," which refers to the fact that actors are merely playing roles; if the situation presents itself, actors can step out of their written characters and expand plot solutions. The narrator of the poem speaks to Lear and presents the mounting evidence for him to act on his own, for him to reject his gloomy end. The narrator mentions that his "fool can only grow forever dumber" and that his heirs will "march one to their different drummer." Since this is the case, the passing of a pleasure craft is a wonderful opportunity for Lear to follow the narrator's advice: "Get on the boat . . . and go to summer." The boat becomes a marvelous theatrical prop. Whereas the wind machines were used to impose a prescribed set of circumstances, the local boat serves to make *King Lear*—the dusty old tragedy—new and alive in the present. The situation is liberating not only for the players, but also for the viewing audience. In witnessing the staging of *King Lear* at this particular theater in San Antonio, the audience must rely on illusion for the play to seem comprehensible, but the river between the stage and the seats has allowed the unusual to happen. "Advice to King Lear" is a fine example of Cassity's poetic gifts: Structure and content work together to make the poem wholly balanced in terms of tone, which allows Cassity's wit to shine through.

Michael Jeffrys

AENEAS AT WASHINGTON

Author: Allen Tate (1899-1979)
Type of poem: Dramatic monologue
First published: 1933; collected in *The Mediterranean and Other Poems*, 1936

The Poem

"Aeneas at Washington" is a thirty-nine-line poem in blank verse. It utilizes an occasional Alexandrine or six-beat line, very likely in oblique tribute to the hexameter line of the Latin poetic source, Vergil's *Aeneid* (c. 29-19 B.C.) for Allen Tate's hero/speaker, Aeneas.

The poem opens with Aeneas in medias res, recounting an episode from Vergil's epic. In this particular episode, Vergil borrows from a narrative technique used in one of his Homeric sources, the *Odyssey* (c. 800 B.C.). In that far more ancient epic, Homer, rather than directly relating to the audience Odysseus' adventures on his return voyage, has Odysseus himself tell his hosts, the Phaiakians, the story of his travels. In the same way, Vergil, who is writing for a Roman audience to celebrate Imperial Roman values, has his hero, Aeneas, tell Queen Dido of Carthage the story of the night Troy finally fell to the Greek forces which had been besieging the city for nine years. So, too, Tate begins with Aeneas virtually in midsentence as he is describing the horribly bloody moment in which Neoptolemus, the son of the dead hero Achilles, mercilessly slaughters the Trojan king, Priam, and his queen, Hecuba, along with their children, as they huddle near the altar to Athena.

As the title informs the reader, however, while this Aeneas may be the man of whose exploits Vergil sang, those ancient times and places are far behind him now; he is instead in Washington, D.C., the capital of a modern, industrial state whose institutions are in many ways modeled on those of imperial Rome. If Tate brings Aeneas into the modern world, he nevertheless does not update him. That is to say, this Aeneas is the same hero found in the *Aeneid*, embodying and espousing the same value structure: "I bore me well," he says, "[a] true gentlemen, valorous in arms/ Disinterested and honourable." Details are missing, but this speaker is indeed the mythic hero whose devotion to family and duty is his foremost attribute, along with his acquiescence to the demands of destiny and the will of the gods.

If there is something vital missing from Tate's hero, it is an upbeat attitude. For one thing, the poem is entirely in the past tense. Aeneas is looking back, true, but even the contemporary world is cast in terms that are past, as if some irrevocable closure has gripped the Republic. While the Aeneas who first encounters Dido in Vergil's epic is bone-weary from his travails, in Tate's hands Aeneas has become a world-weary, perhaps even cynical or skeptical figure. He is not the forward-looking hero who will bring his refugee followers to a new home in Italy; now he says that their "hunger" ultimately was fit for "breeding calculation/ And fixed triumphs" out of the "vigor of prophecy," as if the results were not worth the centuries-long promise and the effort.

In lines that seem to echo popular patriotic songs such as "America the Beautiful," one hears how Aeneas views those results in this later New World, America, itself the supposed flower of the same ancient Greco-Roman culture that bred Vergil and his epic hero. The "glowing fields of Troy" become "hemp ripening/ And tawny gold, the thickening Blue Grass," reminders of Tate's native Kentucky, positive enough images surely; nevertheless, "the towers that men/ Contrive," rather than the towers of Ilium, are, one must imagine, the skyscrapers of commerce and smokestacks of industry, cluttering the skies.

Aeneas closes by relating how he stood once "far from home at nightfall/ By the Potomac" and, seeing the Capitol's "great Dome" lit up at night and reflected in those waters, could no longer recognize "The city my blood had built"; instead, he thought of that older city, Troy, and "what we had built her for."

Forms and Devices

In "Aeneas at Washington," Tate weaves a web of literary and historical allusion so tightly that the poem cannot profitably be explored without bringing to it a measure of the literary and cultural erudition the poet does. It is as if Aeneas traverses the intervening centuries in the course of the poem, beginning in ancient Carthage but simultaneously setting sail from Troy for America as well as for Italy. The British spelling of "honourable" and the Elizabethan "victualing," for example, give the reader a sense that he or she might be in an intervening heroic era—Shakespearean England—which coincides with the time during which the New World was first being explored and settled.

A devoted student and practitioner of modern poetry, Tate knew that in adept hands, as T. S. Eliot had vividly demonstrated in poems such as *The Waste Land* (1922), the literary device of allusion could give a semblance of order and meaning to contemporary events and crises which otherwise might seem chaotic, random, and pointless. For example, in the poem, Tate applies a single extended historical and literary allusion to comment on a complex sociocultural and political process, very much as if the allusive element were a musical counterpoint to the unfolding surface theme.

To appreciate the allusion, readers must realize that Vergil's Aeneas is not a Greek or Trojan but a Roman hero. One also needs to know that Vergil wrote not to celebrate Homeric Greece but imperial Rome, specifically in the person of the emperor Caesar Augustus. Furthermore, one needs to know that America's founding fathers modeled many of the republic's concepts and institutions, including the very notion of representative democracy, on Roman precedents, particularly the Roman Senate. Finally, one must keep in mind that the Capitol building in Washington, D.C., is modeled after an ancient Roman temple to Jupiter situated on the Capitoline hill and that it was Jupiter who saw to it, in Vergil's epic, that Aeneas abandon his private life and get down to the business of fulfilling a destiny that would be a public, not a private, boon and accomplishment.

Through this tangled series of connections the poet is commenting with a compounded irony on an America founded on the principle of individual liberty yet now serving the cause of collectivity and realpolitik. In this way, Tate is able to utilize as innocuous a device as the historical/literary allusion to comment on the crisis of individuality and self-fulfillment in the banal anonymity of the modern industrial state.

Themes and Meanings

If "Aeneas at Washington" has a single theme, it is the corruption of an ideal. This ideal is, in Tate's view, so pervasive and ancient that he cannot attempt to describe its corruption except in sweeping cultural and mythic terms.

During the 1930's, the Great Depression was both undermining America's faith in the free enterprise system and threatening the tenuous balance between urban and rural segments of society. Even without this economic crisis, the increasing industrialization and urbanization of American culture, along with the United States having become entangled in Old World affairs as a result of World War I, was increasingly provoking debate about the national purpose. Some were insisting that the republican virtues upon which America had been founded—respect for the individual, for the common man, for self-sufficiency and self-reliance—were in danger of succumbing to the hollow necessities of internationalism.

A leading force in this call for a restoration of those republican virtues was a group of Southern thinkers and writers who called themselves the Agrarians. The Agrarian movement included such important literary figures as John Crowe Ransom, Robert Penn Warren, John Gould Fletcher, and Kentucky-born, Tennessee-educated Allen Tate. Despite its harking back to the classical past, "Aeneas at Washington" is a product of the Agrarian movement. It sees in the present-day corruption of traditional values and ideals a national dilemma that transcends contemporary issues.

At the heart of the problem, Tate is saying, is the concept of the city and what it represents. In this regard, the provincial beauty of Troy is the civilized ideal against which the crass materialism and imperial vainglory of ancient Rome and its present-day counterpart, Washington, D.C., pale in comparison—yet the irony is that Rome was the result of the mythic attempt to rebuild Troy. Finally, then, the poem suggests that human history has become a devolutionary process amid which the ideals of a golden age, with its pastoral myth, remain only to taunt humankind into regret at how low it has fallen despite high aims.

Russell Elliott Murphy

AFFLICTION (IV)

Author: George Herbert (1593-1633)
Type of poem: Lyric
First published: 1633, in *The Temple*

The Poem

George Herbert includes five poems entitled "Affliction" in the first half of his collection of lyrics. Perhaps this is one way of emphasizing how difficult and yet important it is to understand the experience of affliction fully. These poems form a loosely linked sequence, and together they dramatize a variety of responses to suffering and propose several ways of connecting human with divine grief. "Affliction" (I) is perhaps the most well-known and successful of these poems, particularly because it seems to be deeply autobiographical, dramatizing what many critics interpret to be the pains and frustrations that inescapably plagued Herbert in both his secular and his devotional life. In some ways, though, "Affliction" (IV) is equally powerful: It narrates a life of pain and disappointment from the inside, focusing not on the steps of a persona's career in the "world of strife," as in "Affliction" (I), but on a nearly hallucinatory vision of one's self being fragmented, tortured, and then miraculously reformed.

The five six-line stanzas are addressed to God, but at the beginning of the poem, the speaker is so guilt-ridden and disoriented that he approaches God fearfully. "Broken in pieces," he imagines God as a tormentor hunting him, and he seeks not help but oblivion. Twice he speaks of himself as a "wonder," underscoring the fact that the "normal" perception of one's place in the world—indeed, in the cosmos— has given way to a "tortured" sense of being stretched between heaven and earth.

The poem shifts rapidly from one image of distress to another. As in so many other poems by Herbert, one of the great afflictions of life is a heightened consciousness, and in stanza 2, the speaker is figuratively attacked by his thoughts, imagined as knives that wound body and soul alike. The self in extreme pain can only interpret experience in terms of that pain: Even the potentially promising image of a vessel watering flowers is part of a nightmarish vision of continual assault.

For the rest of the poem, the speaker's distress is presented in terms of a violent rebellion that disrupts life on all levels: personal, political, and cosmic. Order, obedience, and control seem to have vanished, and everything seems dangerously unstable. Chaos is self-destructive, leading to the death of the rioting "attendants" and "elements" as well as the speaker, and it is also murderous, threatening even God, who is closely bound up in the life of the persona. The only hope is that God will intervene and scatter "All the rebellions of the night."

It is only in the last stanza that the speaker can envision some "relief." Through God's powerful action, the rebellious forces of grief can be brought back to work to praise God and help rebuild the persona's damaged self. The poem ends with a description of order restored and the self reintegrated, on the way to "reach heaven, and much more, thee." This is, however, only a plea, and although the end of the poem is much more calm and assured than the beginning, the imagined security of the conclusion is not yet an accomplished fact.

Forms and Devices

Herbert is a master at using poetic form to underscore his themes. At the beginning of "Affliction" (IV), the shape and sound of the lines embody the fragmentation and nervousness of the speaker. Iambic meter is Herbert's basic unit here, but he varies it to add emphasis of different kinds. For example, he opens with a trochaic substitution—that is, the first word is accented on the first syllable rather than the second, as it would be in an iambic pattern. This not only dramatically accentuates the key word "Broken" but also disrupts the rhythm of the entire first line so that it is halting and jerky rather than smoothly flowing. A similar substitution in line 4 places an accentual stress on "Once," and thereby heightens the rhetorical contrast between what he was previously—a "poor creature," but presumably less miserable—and what he is "now"—a "wonder." Other subtle touches make the first stanza even more irregular and unstable. Lines 1 and 4 each contain nine syllables instead of eight, the norm for the other stanzas, and since the last syllable in each is unaccented, they form a so-called "feminine" rhyme, a technique often used to weaken the closure usually conveyed by rhyme. Finally, by repeating the word "wonder," Herbert adds a kind of eerie echo effect that underscores the speaker's obsessive concentration on his pain.

By the last stanza, though, the form of the poem helps underscore the dramatic improvement in the speaker's state of mind. The repeated words are not "wonder" and "wound," as they are earlier, but "day by day," conveying a new sense of patience and trust in time as allied with progress, not decay. Metrical substitutions accent words that are encouraging rather than frightening: "Labor," for example, which situates the speaker in a world of "praise" rather than pain. Finally, the rhymes are strong and subtly reinforce the transformation of "grief" into "relief" and the restored intimacy of "me" and "thee."

The state of mind of the speaker of "Affliction"(IV) is expressed not only by his speech patterns but also by the imagery that he uses. Through most of the poem, he seems to be ransacking his vocabulary to seize upon as many figures of pain and chaos as he can find: He is broken, hunted, forgotten, and tortured. Much of the energy of the poem comes from the rapid shifts among images and metaphors as he tries to give coherent representation to a self he feels is under attack, but ironically, what he brings to life in most of the poem is a picture of unruly "attendants" and "elements" that threaten to destroy the world. The crucial turn in "Affliction" (IV) comes when he shifts suddenly to a deeply felt plea to God and a description of God's role in this "strife." The comparison of God to a "sun" is commonplace but powerful, and the vision of the "light" dispersing "All the rebellions of the night" is infinitely refreshing to the troubled speaker. For all the implied militancy of this simile, Herbert is careful to end on a gentle note. The sun—and he presumably has

Christ in mind as well, the "son" of God—tames and rebuilds rather than destroys. This is crucial because the rebellious powers are not so much inveterate and external enemies, but rather parts of the persona's self—"My thoughts," "my attendants." He is consoled and redeemed by transforming affliction from a rebellious power into part of a process ending in praise of God.

Themes and Meanings

"Affliction" (IV) is a meditation on the experience of human suffering and its role in one's devotional life. Like many of the Psalms, to which Herbert alludes repeatedly throughout *The Temple,* this poem suggests that one of the key tasks in life is not to eradicate suffering—an impossibility—but to understand how it can deepen, not dissolve, one's faith, and how it can be balanced by the deep joys of that faith. Herbert is one of the great poetic analysts of physical and spiritual pain, and "Affliction" (IV) acutely voices the thoughts of a person leading a life based on the premise "I suffer, therefore I am." At its darkest moments, this poem shows that suffering leads to more suffering, but in its much more optimistic conclusion, it suggests that suffering is the preparation for a return to intimacy with God. Herbert's other poems titled "Affliction" focus more directly on the way in which human suffering is linked to the far greater sacrificial suffering of Christ. This is implicit rather than explicit in "Affliction" (IV), where Herbert emphasizes not Christ's agony but his ability to turn all "grief" to "relief." Because of Christ's power, manifested every day like the sun, human suffering is endurable and meaningful. The poem does not—and perhaps cannot—dramatize exactly how this works, but its presentation of the miracle of recovery is stirring: The opening plea to stay hidden from the Lord gives way to the concluding plea to grow ever closer to "heaven" and "thee."

What is at stake in "Affliction" (IV) is not only the self but, the speaker would have the reader believe, the entire world. The first two stanzas are a meditation on personal suffering, but the next two stanzas suddenly introduce terms that turn the internal struggle into a microcosmic focal point of all the chaos and disorder of the world at large. Many of the writers of the early seventeenth century were painfully aware of the turbulence of their times and brooded over what seemed to be increasing social, religious, political, and even cosmic instability. John Donne's comments on how "new philosophy" calls everything into doubt are well-known, but Herbert's poems also tend to picture a world in which (to use Donne's words) all coherence is threatened. To use an even more compelling example, "Affliction" (IV) is as close as Herbert comes to William Shakespeare's grim vision of life in *King Lear* (c. 1605-1606). Like Lear, Herbert's speaker is bound upon a wheel of fire, stretched "Betwixt this world and that of grace," and his mental distress is a mirror of an external world of strife, plots, rebellions, and the threat of nothingness. "Nothing" is a key word in *King Lear;* it is also a word Herbert places at almost the exact center of this poem.

If the world of "Affliction" (IV) temporarily pivots on nothingness, however, it does not end there. The miracle that does not happen in *King Lear* does happen—or is at least powerfully imagined—in Herbert's poem. The true "wonder" is not, as the speaker first thinks, the way affliction tortures but, as he finally learns, how it elevates.

Sidney Gottlieb

AFTER APPLE-PICKING

Author: Robert Frost (1874-1963)
Type of poem: Meditation
First published: 1914, in *North of Boston*

The Poem

Robert Frost preferred to write within the traditional forms and patterns of English poetry, scorning free verse, comparing its lack of form and metrical regularity to playing tennis without a net. "After Apple-Picking" is not free verse, but it is among Frost's least formal works. It contains forty-two lines, varying in length from two to eleven syllables, with a rhyme scheme that is also highly irregular; many of the rhyme lines are widely separated. There are no stanza breaks. Frost intends to evoke a mood of hesitation and drowsiness, as if the speaker were about to drop off to sleep and is no longer fully in control of his thoughts.

The poem is written in the first person; the speaker is someone who has worked long and hard but is now on the verge of being overwhelmed by fatigue and the depth of the experience. The details of his activity are recalled in contemplating the dream he expects to have. The poem is filled with images drawn from the speaker's experience with the pastoral world; the events he remembers all took place on a farm, specifically in an apple orchard. He has climbed a ladder to pick apples; even when he has finished, he can almost feel the rungs of the ladder beneath his feet. The smell of the apples is pervasive, and he can still hear the sound of the wagons carrying loads of apples into the barn.

All the sensory images are pleasant, but they have become distorted, as if the pleasant dream could become a nightmare. The speaker finds that the large harvest for which he had wished has become excessive: He has "had too much/ Of apple-picking." He recalls the details of the work with pleasure, but he is half afraid of the sleep he feels coming on. On the edge of sleep, he remembers not only the ripe apples successfully picked but also those that fell and were considered damaged and had to be sent to the cider mill. He knows that his sleep will be troubled by the failures more than by the successes. He is not sure about the nature of the sleep he is about to drop into—whether it will be ordinary sleep, more like a hibernation, or more like death.

Forms and Devices

The irregularities of line length and rhyme scheme, so unusual in a Frost poem, are noteworthy; they provide an almost staggering effect to "After Apple-Picking," as if the speaker were literally reeling with fatigue. More important, the meters are highly irregular, especially in the frequent short lines: "As of no worth," for example, where two unaccented syllables precede two stressed syllables, or "Were he not gone," in which every syllable receives almost equal emphasis.

Reinforcing this impression of fatigue is the sense of disorientation which affects his senses: Images of smell, sight, movement, hearing and touch are all used. The speaker's vision is compared to looking at the world through a thin sheet of ice which would distort and cloud what was seen. He has been off the ladder for a while, but he still can feel its rungs under his feet as well as its swaying. The apples he will see in his dreams are distorted, magnified to show every mark. He still hears the sound of the wagons.

As is often the case in Frost's poems, the language is poetic without being stilted. It is not really the language of common speech—no colloquial language is used— but with the carefully planned metrics, the language conveys the sense of someone speaking aloud. The richness of the imagery, reinforcing the drowsiness of the speaker's mood, also contributes to this effect.

The entire poem is a kind of extended metaphor, in which the activity of harvesting apples represents other kinds of activity, but Frost avoids metaphorical imagery, choosing instead precise images and rhythmic patterns which tend to fall, reinforcing the dominant theme of the fatigue of the narrator: "For all/ That struck the earth,/ No matter if not bruised or spiked with stubble,/ Went surely to the cider-apple heap/ As of no worth." The language also supports the sense that the experience being described has become excessive: "There were ten thousand thousand fruit to touch,/ Cherish in hand, lift down, and not let fall."

Themes and Meanings

Much of Frost's poetry, like "After Apple-Picking," describes ordinary events taking place in a rural setting, often on the kind of farm where he lived for many years. Many poems also use such settings to pose broad questions concerning the meaning of human life and the relations between man and the natural world. Few of these poems are as clearly allegorical as this one.

The lessons of "After Apple-Picking" could be applied to almost any line of endeavor which the participant loves and enjoys but finds exhausting, partly because of the loving effort required. For Frost himself, the poem most likely is intended to describe his feelings about poetry, after writing it over a period of years.

There is an anomaly in this, for "After Apple-Picking" was written when Frost was thirty-nine, still a relatively young man, while the poem seems to represent an old man's feelings. The explanation may be that the poem was composed in 1913, immediately after *A Boy's Will* (1913), his first book, had been published. The book had come out after many years of struggle and had received little favorable notice. "After Apple-Picking" may have been a response to that disappointment, an expression of his uncertainty about his future as a poet.

In any case, the speaker had wished for a full and productive life in poetry, and he feels that he has had that. Never having desired any other kind of life, he has given all of his devotion to poetry and is able to believe that he has succeeded; the harvest has been a full one, perhaps even fuller than he had hoped for or expected. He has written a large number of poems and can feel confident that they are good.

Now, however, he is forced to realize that the experience has drained him. He cannot forget any aspect of it, nor does he regret having lived as he has, but he has no desire to continue. Furthermore, his mind focuses on the failures, symbolized by the fallen apples: the poems he started and could not find a way to finish, the ideas which would never find clear expression in his poems, perhaps even the poems which he finished but was dissatisfied with and had to discard. What should have been an entirely satisfying experience turns out to have left him dissatisfied, less proud of what he achieved than concerned about his failures.

Having come to the end of an experience, he is also troubled by uncertainty about what lies ahead. He uses the image of the hibernating woodchuck to symbolize this question. Perhaps the sleep he goes to will be only an ordinary "human sleep," from which the speaker will arise, presumably refreshed and ready to go on with his life. Perhaps, however, it will be a sleep like the animal's hibernation, an oblivion extending over a long period of time and ending in a world entirely different from the one the sleeper left. The questions also raise an issue that Frost was often concerned with—that of what, if anything, may lie beyond death. In a poem entitled "The Onset," he uses the cycle of seasons to suggest that death is only temporary, like winter, but in "After Apple-Picking" he provides no such assurances. The early hopeful image of the ladder pointing "Toward heaven" is not confirmed by the conclusion of the poem.

It is typical of Frost's approach to the larger questions of life that he does not provide or even suggest an answer to the questions he raises, preferring to leave the reader to find the way to his or her own answers. The poem finally leaves the impression that the sensory enjoyment of the endeavor provides its true justification, but that the larger issues it implies are beyond human understanding.

John M. Muste

AFTER SOMEONE'S DEATH

Author: Tomas Tranströmer (1931-   )
Type of poem: Lyric
First published: 1966, as "Efter en döda," in *Klanger och spår;* collected in
   Selected Poems, 1981

The Poem

"After Someone's Death" is a poem of three stanzas of four lines each. As in many of Tomas Tranströmer's poems, this one begins with the appearance of a story, but by the end, the series of disconnected images do not seem to add up to a coherent narrative. It is the speaker's visual (rather than organic) ordering of things that holds the poem's various images together. The title suggests the discontinuity between life and death; it is the time after someone's death that the poem considers. The speaker is not identified as the one who specifically experiences the death of another person, and this general detachment may allow the speaker to talk of a more universal condition. It is not uncommon for people to experience the death of another person. The reference to "us" in the first stanza may therefore refer to all people.

In the following two stanzas, the speaker addresses more directly a "you" in the poem. The other person is depicted in familiar situations such as shuffling on skis on a winter's day and feeling his or her "heart throbbing." In these depictions, the speaker seems to be consoling the other person by reminding him or her of activities in which the living and breathing human body can still engage.

The speaker assumes some responsibility for the emotional well-being of the person who has possibly experienced someone's death. Tranströmer establishes the mood of this situation in the first stanza when he makes note of the "shock" that follows death. The "cold drops" here suggest the numbness induced by shock. The repetition of "cold" and the way it "consumes" the living warmth in the second stanza reinforce this idea.

The third stanza highlights the difference between being dead and feeling dead. When someone literally dies, the one who remains often feels deadened by this fact. The latter, suffering from the cold truth of death, must be reminded of the blood that still pulses in his or her own self. Nevertheless, the speaker is sympathetic toward this apparent lack of emotional feeling and understands that the other person is gripped by a sense of unreality. It is at this time that "the shadow feels more real than the body" or, in other words, when the gloominess is the actuality.

The last two lines shift away from the interpersonal concerns. The image of a samurai and his armor made of "black dragon-scales" ends the poem, and it seems peculiar to the more cosmic and humanist concerns of the earlier lines. As well as being disconnected from the rest of the poem, this last image may even be considered shocking. In this respect, the lines contribute to the mood or effect of the poem, rather than provide a satisfying closure to the never-ending pain that the death of another person causes.

Forms and Devices

At one time Tranströmer was a practicing psychologist, and his work enables him to employ many strategies to speak about the unspeakable. How else do humans come to understand what death means unless they first realize what psychological and emotional effects visit them after someone else dies?

The poem does not appear to be logically developed because the grief caused by death forces one to reconsider the outside world. After death, the world is transformed; it is irrational, since everything seems inexplicable. If the poem develops in discontinuous fashion, it is the poet's attempt to correspond the reality of the experience to the unreality of death. The speaker of the poem acts as a kind of mediator between the fact of death and the emotional impact of the one who remains after the dead. The world is seen through the eyes of the other who is suffering, and the pain is interpreted through the components of the physical world. If objects are transposed in this presentation, this may be caused by the way in which personal affliction has filtered the images.

The poem begins with the effect of the "shock"; it takes the form of "a long pallid glimmering comet's tail." Already, the poem establishes the sense of lifelessness in the cosmic metaphor. Unfortunately, this lack of vitality is all-encompassing ("It contains us") and alters even inconsequential things such as television sets. The movement from the personal (grief) to the universal (comets) and then to the quotidian (televisions and aerials) suggests the rapidness with which the shock of death affects all aspects of existence. The reference to the passive act of watching blurred television pictures speaks of a psychological condition as well. One does not have heart for much else, and rather than be left with one's own pain, it is easier to displace it by letting external images flicker across one's consciousness.

In the second stanza, the cosmic and technological realms transpose into a natural one; it is as though the speaker requests that the one suffering get up and go outdoors to refresh the body and the mind. The speaker gently paints this picture: "You can still shuffle along on skis in the winter sun" indicates that once, perhaps as a past joyous activity, "you" used to be uplifted by skiing in the woods.

In the second half of the stanza, however, the speaker returns to the sympathetic tone and considers how the innocent act of skiing itself could have drastic consequences. The comparison of the remaining tree leaves to "old telephone directories" suggests that one might think again of dead things or of things that have since passed away.

By the third stanza, the speaker acknowledges the endlessness of pain itself and, again, gently reminds the other that it is "still beautiful" to be alive. Like the groves with bare trees, though, one feels the vast emptiness: Even the "samurai looks insignificant beside his armor." What was once plenitude and substance becomes devoid of meaningful substance.

Themes and Meanings

"After Someone's Death" is a poem that depicts the emotional shock that people experience as a psychological condition after someone has died. Against the lurid pain itself, the poem offers a message of consolation without denying the inevitable fact of mortality.

After a death, everything feels unreal and unnatural. The poem encapsulates this mood by presenting images and situations that do not bear obvious, or organic, relation to one another. A way to interpret this strategy of discontinuous images is to consider the manner in which the mind's eye perceives the world when one is going through an emotional upheaval. The constant shifts in perception signify disturbances in the normal or usual order of experience.

Despite the overwhelming sensation of grief, the poem emphasizes everyday or familiar situations, both to show how these are transformed by the fact of death and to urge one to return to these things since they constitute life. Beyond that, the poem suggests that the natural course of life always ends with death and that all things are changed by this fact. Not surprisingly, then, the images share a common trait: The comet's tail, the television pictures, the skiing, "last year's leaves" on the trees, and the throbbing heart are all things that move or are in motion. If the shock renders one incapacitated, the poem focuses on movement or mobility to depict the inevitability of things changing.

While the poem's tone is gentle, even consoling, the message resists being glib or appearing naïve. The poet Tranströmer, who understands the archipelago of his native Stockholm, perceives the complexities of the human mind as well. Death, the poem reveals, invades emotional life in much the same way modern technology has embedded itself in daily life—both disorder the images of experience. In television, for example, news reports, commercials, and entertainment programs appear in irrelevant order, but one is not unduly troubled by these jumps. If the poem seems fragmented and random in the way images appear, Tranströmer is expressing the conditions of modern experience in some of its disjointed facets.

The poem does not pretend to offer unprecedented wisdom about death; neither does it attempt to discredit the pain that death can cause to those still living. It does attempt, however, to suggest that death is a part of all life, no matter how unreal one feels after it has occurred to someone else. It is usually after someone else's death that one is reminded of his or her own impending death.

On this note, the poem ends enigmatically with the image of the samurai beside his armor. This image suggests that, in the end, all humans are but warriors beside the apparel they don to face (or to fight or confront) the world. Finally, one rests alongside the things that contained one in life, as one also departs from that which was once himself or herself.

Cynthia Wong

AFTER THE SURPRISING CONVERSIONS

Author: Robert Lowell (1917-1977)
Type of poem: Epistle/letter in verse
First published: 1946, in *Lord Weary's Castle*

The Poem

"After the Surprising Conversions" is a forty-six-line poem on a historical event in colonial New England, a common subject for Robert Lowell. The title indicates that the poem takes places after the conversions and destructive religious enthusiasm that swept southern New England in the wake of the sermons of Jonathan Edwards. Edwards is explaining and, in a sense, justifying the origins and development of the event to an unknown correspondent.

The speaker of the poem is Edwards himself; the poem is based upon his letter of 1736, "A Faithful Narrative of the Surprising Work of God in the Conversion of Many Hundred Souls in Northhampton and the Neighboring Towns and Villages." The tone of Lowell's re-creation of the letter is very different from the fervor that occasioned it. Edwards comments matter-of-factly on the suicides and on how "it began to be more sensible"—it can now be sorted out and understood more fully.

The origins of the religious awakening began with one man, who "came of melancholy parents." There were, however, signs of hope in his life. He would watch the wind touch a tree and think of God's beneficent creation. He was predisposed to "loving," but "he durst/ Not entertain much hope of his estate/ In heaven." Edwards preached one Sunday on Kings, a historical book of the Bible that is an unlikely source for such momentous events. Immediately after, the melancholy gentleman, Josiah Hawley, who was in fact the uncle of Edwards, "showed concernment for his soul." This concern immediately leads him to preach the difficulty of salvation to others, and he "dreamed/ That he was called to trumpet Judgment Day/ to Concord." In May, he "cut his throat." Edwards seems to ascribe the cause of this suicide to the nature and family background of Hawley; it is a means by which Edwards justifies his own role in the episode.

After this event, others suddenly began to fear for their spiritual state, cutting their throats after urging others to do the same. A madness and despair about God's grace seized them; the only answer was suicide. Edwards ascribes these terrible events to Satan and, curiously, to God: "God/ Abandoned us to Satan." The religious gains that had been achieved earlier by Edwards are now undone in the religious madness that follows. It is interesting that Edwards seems to deny or attenuate his own responsibility for the suicides and passes the responsibility to God. The God who empties the land and allows Satan to take over is not Jesus, but Jehovah, the God of wrath.

The last lines of the poem deal with teeming and fecund nature. The fullness of the unpicked apple trees and the spawn of the bass are a rebuke to those who have lost themselves in abstract and abstruse religious speculation. Nature is life-giving, and the way of Edwards' God leads only to self-destruction.

Forms and Devices

The poem is written in a loose iambic pentameter that does not call attention to itself, although the pattern is regular and the syllables are exact. There are a few significant changes in the iambic pattern; the spondees of line 42 (" 'Cut your own throat. Cut your own throat. Now! Now!' ") consciously violate the established meter, reflecting the violence of the awakening. The variation of the meter at the beginning of line 40, "Jumped at broad noon, as though some peddler groaned," also supports the changed view of those who once took their salvation for granted.

The poem consists of run-on couplets that hide their formal nature. Since the couplets consistently run on, the reader is hardly aware that they are couplets until he or she closely examines the poem. So there is an underlying recurrence that gives order to the seemingly casual conversational style of the letter and the violent events that it describes. The interaction between a fixed form and terrible and irrational events provides a tension that is not resolved until the end of the poem, when nature returns as a presence.

There are some interesting opposing images in the poem. The melancholy man broods on "terror," but earlier "loving shook him like a snake." Love gives way to death, and the landscape that was a sign of God's goodness seems to disappear until the end of the poem. The demand to "Cut your own throat" is described in a strange but appropriate simile "as though some peddler groaned/ At it in its familiar twang." Death has, in Lowell's strange reformulation of Edwards, become a commodity to be sold to those gullible or guilty enough to buy. Even the time period of the events, "Hard on our Lord's Ascension," contrasts with the later lines, "The breath of God had carried out a planned/ And sensible withdrawal from this land." The beneficent Jesus who has completed his mission of redemption and ascends to heaven is transformed later in the poem into a wrathful Jehovah.

The last image pattern is very different from what has gone before. Images of nature return to stand against the cutting of throats. The visual and aural images of the cracking apple trees filled with "unpicked apples" and the "small-mouth bass" breaking water, "gorged with spawn," are a counterpoint to the selling of death and the despair that leads to suicide.

Edwards' actual words make up about one-third of the poem. Lowell borrows phrases and occasionally whole sentences and surrounds them with his own language, so the poem filters the spirit of Jonathan Edwards through the mind and art of Robert Lowell. The extensive use of such historical elements in a poem is very unusual. Lowell manages to preserve the integrity of these elements, but they have been turned into an artistic creation, a unified poem; this is not merely a historical curiosity.

Themes and Meanings

Robert Lowell was a member of the famous Lowell family, prominent in Boston society. In this poem, he seems to feel that he must explore the Puritan past of New England to discover guilt and transgressions that will help him and his readers come to better terms with the heritage of the past. Lowell does not falsify that earlier and very different world. He does, however, focus on the irrationality and terror of early America rather than the repression that so many others have noted. Moreover, he has recovered the voice of that early world, and the Puritans condemn themselves in their own words.

At the time when the poem was written, Lowell was a devout Catholic convert with a history of manic-depressive illness. *Lord Weary's Castle* is a testament to that newfound faith. It is clear that Lowell believed that his madness did not come from his religion, as it does in "After the Surprising Conversions": For him, religious conversion was a way to overcome madness.

The Puritan God in the poem seems to be a destroyer, not a preserver: "The breath of God had carried out a planned/ And sensible withdrawal from this land." If he is not leveling the land, he is abandoning it to Satan to do with as he will. It is the fear that they cannot appease this God that leads Josiah Hawley and those who follow him to take refuge in suicide. The Catholic deity is very different for Lowell; for example, in the sixth section of "The Quaker Graveyard in Nantucket," he speaks of "Our Lady of Walsingham," whose shrine holds out hope to man and the world. The virgin is an intercessor for man and is very different from a wrathful Jehovah.

The overt meaning of the poem in the story of the conversions and suicides is supported by the imagery. The passages on nature at the end of the poem are especially significant. This section, one of Lowell's additions to Edwards' letter, speaks in a tone that is very different from that of the preceding sections. The descriptions and images suggest the continuation of nature: "Sir, the bough/ Cracks with the unpicked apples, and at dawn/ The small-mouth bass breaks water, gorged with spawn." Man ignores the goodness of nature, since the apples are "unpicked," and the sexual suggestion of the bass's "spawn" is a principle of life, not the self-willed death and life denial of religious terror. Lowell clearly believed that his new religion, Catholicism, was life-giving, and he continually associates it with natural images. The Puritans do not pick the fruit, but let it rot; the Garden of Eden has been abandoned.

James Sullivan

THE AFTERNOON OF A FAUN

Author: Stéphane Mallarmé (1842-1898)
Type of poem: Lyric
First published: 1876, as *L'Après-midi d'un faune*; collected in *An Anthology of French Poetry from Nerval to Valéry in English Translation with French Originals*, 1958

The Poem

The Afternoon of a Faun is Stéphane Mallarmé's most well-known poem. In slightly more than a hundred lines, it presents the dreamlike erotic reveries of a faun—a mythical creature of classical legend that, like the satyr, has a combination of animal features (such as horns and goatlike feet) and human features.

The poem opens with the faun becoming excited by two nymphs; he is disoriented, however, having just awakened. Finding himself alone, he realizes that the nymphs must have existed only in his dream. "Let me reflect," he muses. He addresses himself as "Faun," as if he were another being, and recalls the two nymphs: One is chaste, blue-eyed, and full of illusions; the other, more experienced, is "all sighs" and is like a warm breeze on his fleece. Suddenly changing direction, the faun describes himself as a musician playing his flute (satyrs and fauns were often imagined, like the god Pan, to be in the woods playing reed pipes). His playing is the "serene artificial breath/ of inspiration, which regains the sky" like evaporating rainwater.

The faun next addresses nature directly, asking the marshes to narrate how he was "cutting the hollow reeds" when he saw a flight of "swans, no! Naiads" (water nymphs). It is now midday, and the faun reflects on the fate of the one "who seeks the *la*"—both a musical tone and the French feminine article ("the"). After thinking of a kiss and lips that "purr," he weaves dreaming together with his playing of the pipes, thinking of entertaining nymphs with his solo and his "credulous song." He then decides to suck the juice out of grapes and be drunk until evening.

In the second half of the poem, his encounter with the two nymphs is described in more detail. To his own surprise, he comes upon them as they are sleeping by the water, entwined in each other's arms. He seizes them both, "not untangling them," and runs with them to a spot in the sun, ready for sexual delights. He must separate them, however (separate the "disheveled tangle/ of kisses" that the gods have put together), to pursue his pleasure, and he admits that parting them was his "crime." Moreover, it destroys the faun's lustful hopes, because they are then able to get away. It does not matter, he concludes philosophically, since there will be other nymphs in the future. He describes his passion as ripe, bursting pomegranates; his blood burns for those who will receive it. Suddenly he imagines embracing Venus, the queen of love herself, but just as quickly realizes that there would surely be punishment for such an outrageous act. The faun concludes by deciding to return to sleep, but he pauses to bid an enigmatic farewell to the two nymphs: "Sweet pair, farewell. I shall see the shades you became."

Forms and Devices

It was probably Paul Valéry, a poetic disciple of Mallarmé, who coined the term Symbolism, and *The Afternoon of a Faun* is a Symbolist poem. The Symbolist poets used words for their magical suggestiveness; *The Afternoon of a Faun* calls to mind Charles Baudelaire's "forest of symbols" because of its dense, complex style. It exemplifies Mallarmé's aesthetic that "to name is to destroy; to suggest is to create." The poem is indirect; it presents a cluster of images and ideas that the reader must help assimilate into a coherent work of art. Words and phrases are put together in ways that defy syntactic logic. Rational thought can flounder when it encounters a Mallarmé poem, and in reading Mallarmé one must keep one's sense of humor and spirit of adventure close at hand.

Beneath the poem's title appears the word "Eclogue"; an eclogue is a pastoral or bucolic poem that is traditionally in the form of a dialogue. Mallarmé indicates who will be speaking first: "The Faun." As the poem progresses, however, the reader realizes that this is a dialogue of one. The faun is debating with and reminiscing to himself alone, with alternating sections of the poem appearing in regular type and in italic type (in quotation marks) to indicate that different aspects of the faun are speaking. He is alternately relating his story and commenting on it—and on his present condition—as he does so. The sections in which he is specifically remembering his dream encounter with the nymphs are in italics.

There are recurring image patterns of heat and water, which are played against each other. The events (or perhaps the nonevents) transpire during a hot day, representative of the sexual heat being expressed; both the nymphs and the music that the faun creates on his pipe are linked to water. Overall, the tone of the poem is dreamy, erotic, and playful. Its images are sensual and strong— *"the splendid bath of their hair disappears/ In the shimmer and shuddering"* —although it is sometimes difficult to find the connections between them and therefore to make sense of them. The disjointedness does seem to convey the confusion of the faun himself, who is unsure if he was awake or asleep and who may be intoxicated during at least part of his interior monologue. His perpetually unsatisfied libido rules his reality and his fantasies; he sometimes sounds like a dreamy, lovesick adolescent. Before the Freudian concept of the libido, or sexual drive, had been established, and before the idea of stream-of-conscious narrative had been popularized, Mallarmé prefigured both in his faun's monologue.

Themes and Meanings

The primary effect of *The Afternoon of a Faun* is a dreamy eroticism combined with a sense of whimsy; the musical and sensual pleasure of Mallarmé's use of words is the hallmark of the poem. C. F. MacIntyre declared in *French Symbolist Poetry* (1958) that Claude Debussy's orchestral tone poem based on the poem is "one of the best guides into the mysterious realm of Mallarmé" and that Debussy "understood the intention better than the critics do." Although it may indeed be a mistake to try to read too much into the poem, *The Afternoon of a Faun* does make some intriguing comments on love, loss, and the creation of art.

The poem's pastoral, Arcadian setting—its woods, water, and flowers—and mythological allusions enhance its portrayal of erotic desire. The faun is a satyr or Pan figure, a whimsically oversexed creature, who fantasizes about sexual exploits with nymphs, yet the poem may also remind one of the more powerful Zeus, who assumed various forms in order to seduce women. As the faun relives his fantasy or dream, he finds himself in the world of the fabulous and in the role of storyteller. He recounts in detail the erotic sequence of arousal, passion, attempted conquest, and, finally, failure to consummate his lust. Words that form the language of love fill the poem—along with the verb "to love" (*aimer*) are such words as "chaste," "adore," "Venus," "kiss," and "nude."

Yet although the setting, with its soft colors and rich ("green gold") verdure, is ideal for a love scene, the poem emphasizes the challenges of love and the fact that the sexual act is not completed. The two nymphs that the faun is excited about have disappeared, and he is not even sure that they ever existed. The faun begins by announcing that he wants to "perpetuate" them, but the only thing that can be perpetuated is a dream or fantasy. Moreover, central to the memory is the "crime"—the loss of the nymphs at the very moment of copulation. One may note that the act the faun was attempting to perpetrate was also a crime; he was about to have sexual intercourse with the two nymphs after abducting them from the water's edge where they had been peacefully sleeping, intimately entwined in each other's arms. "Love" seems a less appropriate word than "lust" to apply to the poem.

One theme that underlies the poem concerns the act of artistic creation. Art, to Mallarmé, was created only with considerable sacrifice. He was always fascinated by the power of art (and of words, in particular), and the Symbolist poets in general sought to combine words in new ways that would produce mysterious effects similar to the magical effects and emotions that music can produce.

Mallarmé's faun is both a storyteller (in a sense, a poet) and a musician. The encounter with the nymphs may not have been real, but the story of it takes on its own reality; moreover, the music the faun plays is a crucial part of the poem. The only water or wind that is moving, the faun says early in the poem, is "poured" or exhaled from his twin pipes. Then he relates (after first asking the marsh itself to tell the story) that he was cutting reeds for his pipe when he saw "*an animal whiteness,/ reposing*"—a whiteness that became swans, then nymphs, flying up. Soon the faun decides to forget his frustrations ("But enough!" he cries) by playing his pipes, his "confidant." He will play a long solo to entertain whatever "beauties" may be about.

Then, in an allusion, Mallarmé unites the nymphs and the music: "Try then, instrument of flights, oh evil/ Syrinx, to flower again by the lakes where you wait!" Syrinx was a nymph who was turned into reeds after running from Pan; she was then turned into the very pipes upon which Pan played. Through this allusion the faun's frustration, the creative power of art, and the dream that is the poem become one.

Clarence McClanahan

THE AGE

Author: Osip Mandelstam (1891-1938)
Type of poem: Lyric
First published: 1922, as "Vek"; in *Tristia*, second edition 1923; collected in
Modern Russian Poetry, 1967

The Poem

"The Age" consists of four stanzas of eight-syllable lines, which are rhymed *ababcdcd* throughout. The title refers to the age in which Osip Mandelstam lived and which he addresses in the poem. It is one of several poems with a related theme—the poet's running dialogue (indeed, an argument) with his own age.

In the very first line, the poet addresses his age directly and immediately equates it with a beast ("My age, my beast"). This equation sets the tone for the entire poem. He expresses his puzzlement about his age by wondering who can fathom its true nature and who will be able to glue together the two centuries, the preceding and the present one, both of which the poet has witnessed. He sees that the present world is being built of blood; it is gushing from the throat of earthly things, so that only a parasite is trembling in expectation of good things on the threshold of new days.

In stanza 2, the poet maintains that every creature must carry its backbone and that every wave plays with this invisible spine. He calls the present age an infant and equates it with the tender cartilage of a baby. Because of the age's infancy, the cranium of life has once again been sacrificed like a lamb. To what cause the sacrifice is to be made, the poet does not state explicitly, although at the beginning of the third stanza he speaks of captivity. If one is to liberate himself from this captivity, one must "tie the knotty elbows/ Of days together with a flute," clearly hinting at a power that can accomplish the liberation. The poet again refers to the nature of the age as one of anguish: A viper in the grass becomes its measure.

In the last stanza, the poet seems to rejoice in a possible liberation, when the buds would swell again and the green shoots would spurt, but he quickly reminds himself that the backbone of the age is broken. He ruefully calls his age beautiful but pitiful, cruel and weak, looking at the past with a senseless smile—as a beast, once supple, looks at the tracks of its own paws. The poem ends on a resigned note, seemingly without a solution to the dilemma postulated at the beginning and explored in the middle of the poem.

Forms and Devices

"The Age" is built predominantly of metaphors. There is an intricate system of metaphors designed to hold together the structure (organism) of the entire poem. The principal metaphor is a beast standing for the age in which the poet lives. Other, smaller metaphors reinforce the main one. Several refer to the physical nature of the beast: pupils, the vertebrae, blood, backbone, the cranium, paws. Just as the beast is a live being, so is the age.

Other metaphors are also taken from the living world. Blood, the essence of life, is referred to as a substance that builds, a substance which can cement "the vertebrae of two centuries." It can also signify a loss of life, however, indicating that it can rip asunder, as well as cement ("gushing through the throat of things upon the earth"). A creature that must carry its own backbone is another example. A parasite referred to in the first stanza is also a live being depending for its existence on another living being. The tender age is compared to baby's cartilage, which is sacrificed like a lamb—another young being. Days have "knotty elbows," which must be tied if one is to find a solution. Finally, when the solution gleams as a possibility (although a fleeting one), the rebirth is metaphorized by buds and green sprouts.

The poet refers to the age as a living being, calling it at one point "the age of the infant earth." It rocks the wave of human anguish. Other references to the age/beast also reveal the connection with a living being. The age is addressed almost as a human being: "My beautiful, pitiful age." It can look backward; it can smile. It can also be cruel and weak.

Built into this system of metaphors is Mandelstam's depiction of the phenomena of life and death. The repeated references to a broken backbone allude to the possibility of, or nearness to, death. When the poet asks at the very beginning who will look into the age's pupils, he refers to an age-long method of checking whether life has turned to death. The mention of the sacrifice of a lamb is another age-old expression connected with death. The poem, in fact, is filled with metaphors that refer now to life, now to death. The separation of the one state from the other is tenuous; indeed, the beast is mortally wounded, and the end is only a matter of time. Finally, two additional metaphors should be mentioned. One is the wave, which stands for water or the sea and which can be interpreted as a metaphor for life. The other is a flute, which clearly refers to art and, more specifically, to lyric poetry.

Themes and Meanings

The overriding theme in "The Age" is Mandelstam's argument with the age in which he lived. The poem therefore makes it difficult to agree completely with those critics who have characterized him as aloof and unconcerned with happenings around him. On the contrary, he was very much concerned with the life outside of his admittedly secluded poetic world, as attested by direct references in this and many other poems.

"The Age" was written in 1922, only a few years after the beginning of the October Revolution in Russia and, more important, only two years after the "new age" in the Soviet Union had begun to take shape. Mandelstam was directly affected by the revolution, but only as a bystander—even as such, he was on one or two occasions close to losing his life. The external manifestations of change, danger, and loss were not so much on his mind as were the more important potential losses—those of human dignity and artistic freedom. For this reason, his characterization of his age as a beast refers primarily to the possible destruction of both of those values, which were always more precious to him than anything else.

In this light, the mood of the poem is essentially pessimistic. This is underscored primarily by the use of the beast metaphor, which usually carries dangerous and destructive connotations. The fact that the beast is young and dying, and is therefore a victim itself, does not diminish its destructive role. When coupled with the damage it has wrought, it is not surprising that the poet considers his age in mostly negative terms.

Mandelstam's hopelessness is relieved only for a moment when, in the third stanza, he allows for a possibility of a solution. He sees this possibility in the healing and rejuvenating power of art, as symbolized by a flute. He says clearly that, in order to lead life out of captivity and start anew, "one must tie the knotty elbows/ Of days together with a flute." Tying the knotty elbows of days simply means joining the old and the new, rather than rejecting the old or destroying it.

Throughout his life, Mandelstam believed in the high mission of art, and particularly of poetry. Amid the horrors of destruction and the rejection of everything that was different from the accepted dogma, he still hoped for a moment that art could save mankind. The hope is fleeting. The beast that was once "beautiful" and "supple" — a reference to the unfulfilled promises of the revolution — can now only look at the tracks of its own paws; "the cranium of life has been sacrificed" once again.

Vasa D. Mihailovich

AJANTA

Author: Muriel Rukeyser (1913-1980)
Type of poem: Meditation
First published: 1944, in *Beast in View*

The Poem

"Ajanta" is a long poem written in five subtitled parts: "The Journey," "The Cave," "Les Tendresses Bestiales," "Black Blood," and "The Broken World." The poem, written in free verse, is given form by the progression of the journey it describes, in which the poet goes into herself in search of a sense of the unity of life. It is an exploration of her spirit, mind, and body.

"Ajanta" is named for the great painted caves in India, famous for their magnificent religious frescoes painted by Buddhist monks. Muriel Rukeyser uses this setting in her poem to suggest the sacredness of her own interior places, her Ajanta, both psychic and physical. The figures of gods, men, and animals in the poem are accurate descriptions of the caves' artwork.

Part 1 provides an emotional setting for the poem; it also describes Rukeyser's life in the midst of war and annihilation (the poem was written during World War II). The poet, in her "full youth," wants "my fullness and not a field of war" and sets out on a journey "to the midnight cave." Profoundly disturbed to be living in a world that "considered annihilation," a world with "the dead boiling up in the ground," the poet resolves to travel alone to find "This cave where the myth enters the heart again." The "myth" is, in a sense, herself.

Actually, the cave is a metaphor for the place within, where she can evaluate experience and be at peace with herself. Although the frustrations and upheaval of war are almost overwhelming ("All the way to the cave, the teeming forms of death . . ."), she makes the "expiation journey" alone. It is her solitary quest to make amends, perhaps, for what she feels is her inability to prevent the dying happening or her inability to rechannel her frustration over the war. On the way, she performs a private ritual: "I blessed my heart . . ./ For it had never been unable to suffer." The blessing is both a talisman for safekeeping and confession of her own frustration with life. To free herself from this debilitating state, the poet seeks to know herself and find possibilities of renewal.

In part 1, the star under which she travels is called "Wormwood." The wormwood plant, which contains a bitter oil used to make absinthe (a nineteenth century drink so strong it was purported to cause forgetfulness and hallucinations), has been associated by name with any unpleasant or mortifiying experience. The war's profound effect on the poet's psyche is emphasized by the name Wormwood, but her belief in the vitalizing natural rhythms of the body is also alluded to: Wormwood was used in plant lore as an aphrodisiac.

Part 2, "The Cave," begins with a description of the cave, a description both literal and metaphorical. The "interlaced gods, animals, and men," religious representations painted on the walls, suggest the interconnectedness or vital union of things in a peaceful world. Because union is what the poet seeks in herself, these figures provide for her evidence that serenity is possible in a chaotic world: "The figures hold their peace/ In a web of movement."

The artwork at the Ajanta caves has been described as overwhelming; in the poem, the descriptive onslaught of things—earth, crystal, water, "pillars and prisms," riders, horses, and "Red Cow . . . running through the world"—overwhelms the reader. The cave is a place of intense feeling and emotion.

In the cave, where "the world comes forward in flaming sequences," the poet-traveler possesses her world at its most fulfilling:

> There is no frustration
> Every gesture is taken, everything yields connection . . .
> Water to sound, fire to form, life flickers
> Uncounted into the supple arms of love.

The unity she attempts to describe is conveyed in sexual images, but transcends the sexual; it cannot be confined to "the spaces of the body," which are "suddenly limitless." The idea of union, however, is best conveyed in the imagery of the body and its physical rhythms. The last ten lines of "The Cave" are an energetic and sensuous evocation of the life force consecrating itself: physical action transformed into timeless, boundless energy "in the web of time."

Part 3, "Les Tendresses Bestiales" (brutish caresses), describes a return to frustration (part of life's rhythm). Rukeyser examines her reaction to the frustration of lost love, one who has died, presumably in the war. The sequence is written from the perspective of a mariner on the water, peering at the sky to chart the way. She sees the constellations reconfigure to form a "body shining."

The images come into port next: the dark streets, the faceless whore, the whispering "checkered men," "The dice and the alcohol and the destruction," and finally the "Broken bottle of loss" are images of squandering and despair. Unchecked, these impulses can lead to self-destruction—"the glass/ turned bloody into the face."

She compares dealing with her emotions to trying to keep a ship's wheel steady in a storm: Losing control of the wheel as "the wave turns," she sees "the world bearing my grave,/ And your eyes open in earth." The loss of her love is still very vivid. In deep mourning, the poet envisions the world as a hostile place and finds herself sinking into it. Her search for "the midnight cave"—her place of healing—becomes more urgent than ever.

"Black Blood," part 4, is a brief and mysterious interlude in the poem. Her attempt to return to the cave pauses at a deserted harbor, a sinister place where a "woman laced into a harp/ screams and screams" (the poet unable to sing her song?) and "The Floating Man" (the moon?) "rides on the ragged sunset." Still grieving for her love and the world's destruction, the poet realizes that her "armored ghost of rage" is "powerless" and so implores: "touch my blood again." This request shaken out of sorrow is a turning point in her journey back to harmony. The advice coming from her innermost voice to "Try to live as if there were a God" is cautious and ironic, but nevertheless more hopeful than her previous state of mind.

The final part of the poem, "The Broken World," is a return to the cave; it ends the poem with two realizations. First, the poet reaches her Ajanta, "The real world where everything is complete." She has cast off her debilitating grief and now stands shadowless "on summer earth." Shadows, "the forms of incompleteness," stand for illusion, the mere outline one so often perceives of something without seeing what the thing really is. In the cave, though, shadows do not exist: "Here everything is itself."

The "Animals arrive,/ Interlaced, and gods/ Interlaced, and men/ Flame-woven." All things are connected, both peacefully and fruitfully. In Ajanta, at last, the poet can say "I stand and am complete." Her transformation into a unified being has come out of her great loss and her sense of the world's loss. Out of the cave (her search, herself), she has been reborn.

The second realization is that although the world is and always will be a broken world, people must live in it, for there is no way to be whole unless one's world "Enters the heart again" — even with its shadows and its "old noise of tears." The poet's rebirth has allowed her to welcome back the broken world and accept the struggles of living in it.

Forms and Devices

Rukeyser's energetic experiments in poetry were considered by many critics of the 1940's and 1950's to be loose in form and disorganized. During that time, traditional prosodic forms were more acceptable to many poets and critics, but Rukeyser was more interested in a poetry in which the material could generate its own form. She did not believe in grafting predetermined structures, such as metered patterns, onto her experiences for the sake of technical unity.

She seeks to convey the wholeness of experience. Thus, in "Ajanta," as many critics did not recognize, the sexual images not only serve as thematic unifiers but also help to weave the structural fabric of the poem. In "Ajanta," and many of the poems in *Beast in View,* sex becomes an organizing force as Rukeyser attempts to reproduce in language and sound and rhythm the rhythms of the body. She later praised Walt Whitman's poetry, in which "physical rhythms are the base of every clear line. . . . He remembered his body as other poets of his time remembered English verse." Such rhythms in "Ajanta" are especially apparent in the last ten lines of part 2, "The Cave," and in the "Animals arrive" sequence in part 5, "The Broken World." At the poem's climax, the rhythm suggests one trying to catch her breath, then slowly relaxing as the feverish pace calms toward the last line of the poem.

"Ajanta" conveys the force of sexual impulse — the need and desire for union, which is what the poet seeks in herself and with the world. The sexual impulse becomes a metaphor for unity at all levels of existence. Built into the poem are journeys toward a number of unions: the poet seeking the cave to enter it, the heart seeking its myth, the bereft lover seeking whatever will relieve her sorrow, the re-born traveler taking the world into her heart again.

The image of the cave, the poem's central extended metaphor, also unifies the poem. Besides its thematic importance, the cave image frames the poem. The first lines of parts 1 and 5 echo each other: "Came in my full youth to the midnight cave" and "Came to Ajanta cave." The repetition shows that the journey has come full circle, a closing device that indicates the poet has completed the journey.

The journey motif is crucial to the poem's unity. Each section finds the traveler in another phase of self-examination; that is, in another place, more or less close to her desired goal. The nautical terms used to describe certain legs of the journey (the deserted harbor, "night sailing the river," "the foghorn's word") also help unify the poem and indicate the elemental nature of the voyage.

Themes and Meanings

By choosing to make her journey by water, Rukeyser consciously uses the time-honored symbolism of water and sea voyaging. Water is the source of life, what we are born out of; it flows beneath the surface of things; it is the element of fertility, and it is always moving and changing. It is a favorite symbol, also, to indicate female life force and women's physical transformations. This poem is about transfor-mation and nurturing new life, or rebirth.

"Ajanta" opens *Beast in View*, Rukeyser's fourth book of poems. The "beast" she hunts on her spiritual voyage is not always in view — in "Ajanta" it remains hidden from her until her final reconciliation in the cave to which it has led her. The beast is her innermost self, what makes her who she is, what is vital to her being. The thematic energy of "Ajanta" is devoted to capturing the beast — herself in her own myth of herself — so that she can be a whole person again. Because the poem is about transformation, and adapting to changes in life and the world, the beast in "Ajanta" often appears in disguises. All these masks are part of the poet's person-ality and her changes. She seeks to unify them and accept them all: "the whore with the dying red hair,/ the child myself who is my murderer . . ." and later "the panther with its throat along my arm" and "the silver derelict wearing fur and claws."

The search for self-identity in "Ajanta," however, is not an end in itself. Begin-ning with descriptions of war atrocities, the poem reminds readers that to know oneself is vital also for the sake of the world in which one lives. The poet seeks the strong armor of self-knowledge, rather than the armor of rage, in order to know better how to aid the struggles of those who have been betrayed or who are suffering loss. The "world of the shadowed and alone" is a place in which the conscientious must fight for those in need and confront "the struggles of the moon." In "Letter to the Front" (also from *Beast in View*), Rukeyser praises the healing power that wo-men can offer the world, especially in time of war. She envisioned female sensi-bilities transforming traditional man, or the traditional masculine ideal. This vision laid a path for later women poets, such as Adrienne Rich, who continue to explore similar themes.

The cave is a symbol for female sensibility, mystery, and strength. It is a dark interior, a place of hiding or hibernation, a place of meditation, a vault from which one emerges reborn, as did Jesus. It is also a source of life: Its watery, quiet space nurtures, like a womb. Its interior can be mysterious yet comforting, black, and frightening, or cool and beckoning. "Ajanta," says Kenneth Rexroth (1905-1982), is "an exploration . . . of her own interior—in every sense." That is, as a poet and a woman, Rukeyser is interested in her mind and in her body's flesh and form and how they shape her quest for fulfillment. The beauty, complexity, and energy of "Ajanta" has made it one of her most famous and powerful poems.

JoAnn Balingit

ALL BREAD

Author: Margaret Atwood (1939-   )
Type of poem: Lyric/meditation
First published: 1978, in *Two-Headed Poems*

The Poem

"All Bread" is a short poem in free verse, comprising four stanzas of uneven length. The poem's central premise is the interdependence of humans and the earth and the cyclical rhythms of that relationship. A parallel interdependence between males and females is also implicit in this premise. Bread is the archetypal product of the earth, both the "staff of life" and an element of sacrifice and sacrament. The mundane yet important ritual of making and consuming bread shapes the poem and provides its central metaphor.

The poem's four stanzas trace the stages in the bread-making process, moving from field to kitchen to consumption, from drudgery to communion. Stanza 1 describes the growing grain which comprises all the elements of earth, vegetable and animal, living and dead. Humans plant and harvest the grain; they assemble the wood and water necessary to mill and cook it; the cook shapes it into loaves. Stanza 2 describes the baking process, evoking the moist heat and the aroma that gives bread-making its appeal. Stanza 3 defines bread's taste on the individual's tongue; and stanza 4 invokes perhaps the most meaningful part of the bread-making process: sharing bread.

The poem is written in the first person. Its tone is personal and intimate, as if a kitchen-table conversation were taking place while bread is being shared in a daily family or neighborly ritual. Stanza 4, though, takes on the cadence of a priest intoning the rites of Eucharist: "Together/ we eat this earth" is the benediction that closes the poem.

Forms and Devices

As is typical in Margaret Atwood's poetry and much of her prose, "All Bread" is permeated with the imagery of elemental, primordial life with which Atwood believes humankind is intimately bound. The poem's language is bare. Its words are largely monosyllabic, sparse and direct, very Anglo-Saxon, sometimes gross— the speech and imagery of peasants and laborers bound, often unwillingly, to the earth: "All bread is made of wood,/ cow dung, packed brown moss,/ the bodies of dead animals." These materials are obtained by "nine strokes/ of the axe." The making and consumption of bread is the shaping metaphor for Atwood's unoriginal vision of the life cycle as binding life and death irrevocably. At the poem's conclusion, Atwood's usually pessimistic outlook is leavened by an uncharacteristic optimism. Homely, rustic rituals, performed in field and kitchen, affirm humans' community with other humans and with the earth. Says critic Kathleen Vogt: "The bread of communion is the bread baked in the kitchen; it is a part of the processes of nature, which include death and life. These processes are a kind of sacrament in 'All Bread.' "

The intricate interweaving of death and life, destruction and creation, is suggested in the poem's juxtaposed images of ancient sacrificial rituals (especially of humans to pagan gods) and of the fecund warmth of pregnancy and birth evident in the description of the bread's rising and baking:

> nine strokes
> of the axe, skin from a tree,
>
> . . . .
>
> the row
> of white famine bellies
> swollen and taut in the oven,
> lungfuls of warm breath stopped
> in the heat from an old sun.

Sacramental ceremony is also suggested by "a silver dish" in which the loaves are offered to the oven.

Salt is the dominant image in stanza 3: "Good bread has the salt taste/ of your hands after nine/ strokes of the axe, the salt/ taste of your mouth. . . ." The ambivalence expressed through the rest of the poem's imagery is sustained here. Indispensable bread is indeed the salt of the earth but conversely requires the saltiness of blood, sweat, and tears expended in the labor of sustaining life. Despite this imagery of sacrifice, a tone of fulfillment is also discernible in stanza 3.

This tone carries the reader into stanza 4, where diction and mood become more quietly exalted. For the first time, more complex and connotative words occur, recalling the solemn, splendid liturgy of the Eucharist (or Communion) ritual. "Lift," "ashes," "devour," "consecrate," "broken," and "shared" all evoke Christ's devotions to his followers at the Last Supper: "Now as they were eating, Jesus took bread, and blessed, and broke it, and gave it to the disciples and said, 'Take, eat; this is my body' " (Matthew 26:26). The poem's final lines — ". . . Together/ we eat this earth"—bring it full circle, back to the earth where the residues of death and the elements of life are equally contained, and where the making and eating of humble bread is a reminder to humankind of its place in the cycle.

Themes and Meanings

"All Bread" expresses the core of Atwood's vision: humankind's love-hate relationship with the natural world, as well as with the dichotomies of its own nature. This vision is delineated through a voice that is ironic in tone, suitable for exploring the conflicts and ambiguities of humankind's struggles to survive both physically and psychically.

In an earlier poem, "Progressive Insanities of a Pioneer" (*The Animals in That Country*, 1968), Atwood defines the power struggle between humans and nature as "the tension/ between subject and object." Part of this tension lies in humans' recognition of nature as mainly predatory, and of human existence as a struggle both to survive and also to subvert these same predatory tendencies in the human character. The very real struggles of early Canadian settlers from Europe, many of whom were unsuited to the harsh Canadian climate and landscape, have provided Atwood with the perfect metaphor for exploring the nature-humankind relationship. In her own study, *Survival: A Thematic Guide to Canadian Literature* (1972), Atwood concludes the chapter "Nature the Monster" by observing, "Nature is a monster, perhaps, only if you come to it with unreal expectations or fight its conditions rather than accepting them or learning to live with them."

The speaker of "All Bread" begins by expressing outright distaste for natural processes: "All bread is made of . . .// the bodies of dead animals, the teeth/ and backbones, what is left/ after the ravens." Soon comes acknowledgment of how human labor on the earth can be consecrated by nature: "good water which is the first/ gift, four hours." Finally, there is a quiet acceptance of the relationship between humankind and nature: "to know what you devour/ is to consecrate it,/ almost." Critic Jean Mallinson observes, " 'All Bread' . . . records a kind of reconciliation with the muck of the world, the ooze and dung and dirt of it, which is part of the poet's dispraise of life in other poems."

Secondary in "All Bread" is a parallel aspect of conflict that also informs Atwood's vision: the power struggle between the sexes. As with the struggle between humanity and nature, the perspective of the poem evolves from forceful and ironic to calm and accepting. In the course of the poem, the speaker (whose tone and point of view are almost certainly female) makes reference to shared physical work and to the exclusively female pain of childbirth. Female imagery abounds in stanza 2, where the inextricable interweaving of death and life is strongest in the metaphors used to describe the bread baking. "Live burial under a moist cloth,/ . . . the row/ of white famine bellies," while somewhat glibly and gratuitously evoking the ovens of concentration camps, above all suggests the joyful pain of childbirth labor: "swollen and taut in the oven,/ lungfuls of warm breath stopped." References in stanza 3, where the tone becomes more intimate with the use of the second-person "you," are to shared sexual love— " . . . the salt taste/ of your hands after nine/ strokes of the axe, the salt/ taste of your mouth." Finally, in stanza 4, Atwood refers to the shared ceremony that celebrates life's sacraments such as marriage.

"All Bread" may be viewed as a personal epiphany, or revelation, in which the speaker contemplates, at first with ironic distaste but finally with benign acceptance, the paradoxical truth of existence: that death and life are inextricably entwined, and that human relationships, especially between the sexes, are founded on the same interdependence. In this poem, the sanctity of life, despite its elements of grossness and drudgery, is celebrated.

Jill Rollins

ALL MY PRETTY ONES

Author: Anne Sexton (1928-1974)
Type of poem: Lyric
First published: 1962, in *All My Pretty Ones*

The Poem

"All My Pretty Ones" is the title poem of Anne Sexton's intensely confessional second book of poetry, *All My Pretty Ones* (1962), and it reflects that volume's absorption with loss and death. This poem consists of five ten-line stanzas and resembles the form of most of the companion poems in the volume. The poem's title comes from William Shakespeare's *Macbeth* (1606), when Macduff mourns the loss of his wife and children. In March of 1959, Anne Sexton's mother died, followed in June of the same year by Sexton's father. "All My Pretty Ones" is a monologue addressed to Sexton's dead father as she sorts through her parents' possessions.

In the first stanza, Sexton looks over her father's meager "leftovers": a key, some stock certificates, clothing, a car, his will, and a box of photographs. She is recording a moment that many children must endure: the closing of a parent's affairs, the moment when the living children must literally discard artifacts not only of their parents' lives but also of their own. She sees her task as one of helping her father to free himself from the tangles of his now past life. The stanza concludes with her decision to throw away the items that she has found.

In the second stanza, Sexton continues to gaze on the photographs in the box, wondering at the images she sees, unable to identify many of the now long-dead people with any degree of certainty. She looks at a picture of a small boy in a christening gown—is it her father? She wonders if another picture is her great-grandfather. She concludes that her father's own death renders her search for names irrelevant; now she can never know, because the person who could have told her the importance of each face in the pictures has died. She ends the stanza by locking them—entombing them—in the album and throwing it away.

Stanza 3 continues the sifting and sorting process with a scrapbook that her father had begun the year Sexton was born. It contains memorabilia of historical events such as Prohibition and the crash of the *Hindenburg*. It also enables Sexton to recall some of her father's own history, such as his financial good fortune as a result of the war. Sexton swings the focus of the poem back to her father in the stanza's concluding three lines when she remembers her father's intention to marry a second time— only months after her mother's death—and her own distraught response. Her father died three days later.

This reflection forms the bridge to stanza 4, in which Sexton looks at pictures of her parents, photographs that reflect family history as well as family wealth. It is clear from these images that Sexton led a privileged life, yet she concludes this section with a reference to her father's alcoholism. The final stanza continues this reflection: Sexton finds her mother's diary, which elliptically records three years of her father's drinking. This, like the family pictures in stanza 4, Sexton decides to keep; they are artifacts that she hopes, in the poem's final three lines, will enable her to come to terms with her own mixed feelings about her father.

Forms and Devices

By using a fairly open line in "All My Pretty Ones," Sexton achieves a conversational tone in this interior monologue. The rhyme scheme is *ababcdcdee*, which gives a strict form to the poem, but a form whose meter and structure does not intrude on what could be termed the rhythm of everyday speech. By making individual lines within a stanza fairly long, Sexton adds to the somber tone of this encounter with her dead father, his dead past, and the end of her childhood. This form also makes the lines and stanzas heavy: Sentences continue for several lines, weighing the poem down and adding to the feeling of sadness that Sexton achieves in her description of what may be her first articulation of being an adult orphan. Controlled form plays an important part in Sexton's early poetry; the more difficult the emotional event, the tighter the form. In "All My Pretty Ones," she uses the structure to give an external control to a powerful moment.

Of equal importance is the strong visual sense that Sexton imparts to the poem. Much of what she describes relates to seeing: images of her dead parents, artifacts that symbolize aspects of her father's personality and life, pictures that freeze moments in her ancestors' lives and in her immediate family's past. Sexton offers a balanced description of these artifacts, allowing the reader to decide their importance to the woman who is sorting through the remnants of her parents' lives. It is the choice of things rather than what Sexton says about those things that makes the commentary poignant and powerful. Sexton frequently reports rather than analyzes, as in the case of her mother's diary in the poem's final stanza. Much like this older woman's account of her husband's alcoholism, "telling all she does not say," Sexton's poem shows rather than explains. In this regard, the photographs she sifts through in stanzas 2 through 4 do the same thing for the poet: They offer images, but they fail to explain why they were important ones to the man who kept them for all those years.

The power of "All My Pretty Ones" rests partly in its twofold focus. The poet reflects on her father's life and tries to make sense of it, as the reader does listening to her "conversation" with her now-dead parent. Also, in sorting out her father's world, Sexton is also sorting out her feelings for this man, someone who obviously was difficult for her to love unconditionally. The actions of the daughter move from discarding images and things in the first two stanzas to keeping images and artifacts "to love or look at later." The final stanza concludes this transformation, and the last couplet resolves the tension that Sexton has been building. She offers her dead father forgiveness. This final line repeats an image of enfolding that she used to conclude the previous stanza when she refolded the pictures of her father; in the last line of the poem, Sexton herself bends down over the material scraps that her father has left behind and forgives him.

Themes and Meanings

"All My Pretty Ones" is a poem about loss, about love, and about an adult daughter's relationship to her parents, in particular to her father. It also reflects the tone and focus of the book for which it is the title piece; in *All My Pretty Ones*, Sexton attempts to deal with her preoccupation with death, pain, and bereavement. An intensely personal poet, Sexton is generally described as a confessional poet, an artist whose own life provides much if not all of the material for her poetry. In the case of *All My Pretty Ones*, it is Sexton's emotions relating to her family and to God that are the foundation for the poems. Poems such as "All My Pretty Ones" are painful for the reader because of their intensely personal revelations and because the subject matter touches on fears, griefs, and disappointments that many readers will share.

The title of the book and the poem is taken from Shakespeare's *Macbeth*, in which Macduff expresses shock and grief over the murder of his entire family and makes the point relevant to Sexton's book that he cannot stop remembering the things "That were most precious to me." This is precisely what Sexton does in this poem and in the other pieces in the book. Not only does the book's epigram from *Macbeth* set the stage, but also her choice of an additional quotation from Franz Kafka establishes the book's purpose: In the passage, Kafka says that "a book should serve as the ax for the frozen sea within us." "All My Pretty Ones" is certainly an example of the catalytic function of memory and objects, not only books, for it is the poet's sifting through the artifacts of her parents' lives that breaks down her resistance and enables her to express her true feelings for her father. The act of closing her father's house gives her the opportunity to bring closure to her relationship with him: At the poem's conclusion, she has moved toward forgiveness and acceptance.

Melissa E. Barth

L'ALLEGRO

Author: John Milton (1608-1674)
Type of poem: Pastoral
First published: 1645, in *Poems of Mr. John Milton*

The Poem

This 152-line poem is non-stanzaic and is written in tetrameter couplets except for the first ten lines, which are alternating trimeters and pentameters. It is a companion piece to the slightly longer "Il Penseroso," with which a detailed comparison must necessarily be made.

"L'Allegro" means "the cheerful man," and the poem describes, in pastoral terms and in his own voice, the idyllic day of such a man in the countryside. It begins with the sun rising and takes the man through the pleasures of the day until the countryfolk's bedtime. After that, the man goes to the city and enjoys his evening in more sophisticated literary company.

The poem actually begins, however, with an invocation against "loathed Melancholy," personified as a horrific creature and seen as a state bordering on madness. In place of this monster, the cheerful poet welcomes Euphrosyne, or Mirth, who, mythologically, was the daughter of Venus and Bacchus, or perhaps of Zephyrus (the west wind) and Aurora (the dawn). As neither loving nor drinking figures significantly in the poem, it must be inferred that John Milton prefers the latter, less well-known genealogy. He invites Mirth, together with "the Mountain Nymph, sweet Liberty," to take him as one of her followers, to live "in unreproved pleasures free."

The remainder of the poem is more a pastoral fantasy of what such a day spent in Mirth's company would be like than an actual description of a particular day, as one might expect to find in a Romantic pastoral such as John Keats's *Sleep and Poetry* (1817) or *I Stood Tiptoe* (1817). As in classical pastoral, the countryside is idealized, and any unpleasantness, such as bad weather or painful labor, is removed. In fact, the poet becomes a spectator rather than a participant (such as a shepherd) in the pastoral activity. He imagines the lark rising at dawn, the hunt, and the cock crowing. As the sun rises, he observes typical country work, people, and animals, especially (as befits a pastoral) sheep and shepherds.

The landscape is an impossible one, in that meadows, castles, mountains, wide rivers, and woods all jostle one another for place. Similarly, the day dissolves from a working day to a rustic holiday, focusing on the merrymaking at suppertime. The folk tell one another legends and country tales as the ale circulates. With sunset, they go to bed.

Not so the cheerful man, who imagines himself now in "towred Cities" of a distinctly medieval flavor, with "throngs of Knights and Barons bold." A tournament is being held, then a wedding feast. Then the man goes to the theater to see the comedies of Ben Jonson or the young William Shakespeare. Finally, in his bliss, the poet calls for soft music and poetry that would rouse even the god Orpheus. If Mirth can give him all this, the poet vows to live always with her.

Forms and Devices

The verse form of "L'Allegro" is delightfully lyrical. The rhythm is light and joyful, and it is the single most important factor in creating the idyllic tone of the poem. Although the meter is tetrameter, the length of line is frequently seven syllables rather than eight. Regularly placed stressed syllables dominate; in the shortened lines, along with the rhyming effect of the couplet, they provide a strong musical beat. The stressed syllables have relatively few of the longer, "dark" vowel sounds. Consonants are also soft, as in "Lap me in soft Lydian Aires/ Married to immortal verse." The *l*, *m*, and *s* sounds echo exactly the sense. The sound and the rhythm are mellifluous and flow easily in long, relaxed sentences that have none of the grammatical complexity of John Milton's later style. The vocabulary, too, is simple, avoiding pedantic or latinate words.

The only verse that suggests any harshness is the opening section. This section also demonstrates that the poet is a man of learning; even if he does not care to show it in his diction, it shows in his easy use of classical myth. The verse form here is somewhat irregular. It alternates between trimeter and pentameter, with a complicated rhyming scheme (*abbacddeec*); it is basically iambic but is sometimes broken up, as in "And the night-Raven sings." This contrast, rhythmic as well as tonal, with the rest of the poem is striking and provides a dramatic opening.

Milton's use of mythological names is accomplished, and it goes well beyond the usual pastoral naming of shepherds with Latin or Greek names. Euphrosyne's genealogies are given, and clearly Milton understands the meaning of the Greek as "she who rejoices the heart." The most significant classical allusion, though, is to Orpheus, since this forms an extended concluding image and is picked up in "Il Penseroso." In "L'Allegro," the tragedy of the myth is played down, and the beauty and enchantment of music are stressed. Orpheus lies "on a bed/ Of heapt Elysian flowers" and, with such music as the poet delights in, would have "quite set free/ His half regain'd Eurydice." The Orphic myth can still contain celebration. The poet's delight in literature also suggests his learning, and the heady mixture of pastoral and literature suggests the work of Keats a century and a half later.

The landscape descriptions, diction, and images need to be read in contrast to "Il Penseroso." Here in "L'Allegro," the diction conveys light and radiance. The lark is mentioned, rather than the nightingale of the other poem. Although both birds are symbolic of the poetic imagination, one is a bird of day, the other a bird of night. In "L'Allegro," fields fill the landscape (rather than woods); there are people instead of solitude, so the poet walks "not unseen." (In "Il Penseroso," he says, "I walk unseen.") The literature mentioned in the poems also contrasts; here, there is comedy and medieval romance, whereas there one finds epic and tragedy. The music in "L'Allegro" is country songs; in "Il Penseroso," solemn organ tones.

Themes and Meanings

A number of interpretations have been suggested for the poem—or rather, for the pair of poems. One suggestion is that the young Milton, possibly still at the University of Cambridge, or possibly recently having been graduated, was using the form of a typical student dialectic exercise to conduct an argument, such as deciding "whether day or night is the more excellent" or comparing the merits of learning and ignorance. It could also be seen as marking the poet's return from Cambridge to his father's retirement home in the Buckinghamshire countryside, expressing both his joy at country life (together with its accessibility to London) and his thoughts on his still undecided future. The poem's pastoral landscape is rustic and English; it cannot be taken for a classical setting. If Milton's thoughts, as is most likely, were turning toward the vocation of literature, then the pastoral form would be the most appropriate genre for him to begin exploring, as the pastoral was seen classically as the one for "apprentice" poets. Certainly, Milton persisted in and mastered the genre in his youth.

The poems could also be seen, as could Keats's *Sleep and Poetry*, as the youthful explorations of the aspiring poet, encapsulating the intellectual excitement in imaginative fantasies and daydreams. If this is taken as the basis for an interpretation, it is possible to go further and see the two poems as Milton's setting out a poetic program for himself. The poem becomes, thus, not so much about day and night, comedy and tragedy, as about the inspiration to be found by the young poet in idyllic nature and the pastoral imagination founded on this and on Romance literature—inspiration that needs feeding. This is one possibility for him as a youthful, idealistic poet. The other possibility is explored in "Il Penseroso," which is perhaps the one he ultimately seems to prefer. Certainly, "L'Allegro" lacks the impressive coda to be found at the end of "Il Penseroso." The closure of the former is light-hearted, almost whimsical, and hypothetical.

Another possibility is to read the pair of poems as explorations of possible life-styles. The life-style of "L'Allegro" puts away melancholy as a disease, an infection to be avoided at all costs. Joy is to be found in a simple and active life, close to beauty and the rhythms of everyday life, yet keeping in touch with literature and the arts. Many a young graduate must have experienced the appeal of such a life. By contrast, "Il Penseroso" embraces studiousness and "high seriousness." Milton's life followed the latter path, but it can never be known whether he made that choice at the time he was writing these poems. The poem's thematic structures are open enough to allow various interpretations, and that openness is a part of their continued attraction.

David Barratt

ALTARWISE BY OWL-LIGHT

Author: Dylan Thomas (1914-1953)
Type of poem: Poetic sequence
First published: 1935, 1936; collected as "Poems for a Poem," in
Twenty-five Poems, 1936

The Poem

"Altarwise by Owl-Light" is a sequence of ten sonnets. The title is taken from the opening of the first sonnet, which describes the birth of Christ as producing an era of owl-like wisdom through the light of His altar. The last sonnet returns to vary the image of "altarwise" as a celebration of the effects Christianity has had on the history of the world: It has followed "the tale's sailor from a Christian voyage/ Atlaswise."

In the first sonnet, Dylan Thomas says that Jesus descended from Adam into the grave of life, the house of the flesh, which he made wise as the owl in the twilight of history. He is a gentle man who is the sun (Son) moving between the Tropic of Capricorn (the goat/life) in the Southern Hemisphere, on December 22, and the Tropic of Cancer (the crab/death) in the Northern Hemisphere, on June 22. He does battle with Abaddon as Satan/death by hanging on the cross by a nail. He is also the cock who announces a new day, hanging on his cross on one leg like a weather-vane rooster.

The second sonnet continues to present the complexities of the Christian Nativity, when death was made into a metaphor of spiritual rebirth. The child at a mother's breast is Christ whose mother is self-sacrificing, like the pelican who feeds her young with her own blood; Christ is the pelican itself, shedding his blood for others. As the sun/Son, Christ is a child of the Milky Way, and he moves through circles of the heavens, as up a ladder (Jacob's ladder, made from the crossed bones of death) from the cave of mortality.

Sonnet 3 shows the birth of the sacrificial lamb, the one who pays the debt of death incurred by the old bellwether, the old Adam. The new lamb butts down death when Christ is sacrificed on Golgotha, the place of skulls. At the crucifixion, Christ speaks out like Rip Van Winkle, who wakes from a long sleep to become a new person. The next sonnet voices eight questions asked by the young child (Christ?), ranging from how the Word can be measured to whether God is a man or a woman. The energy of "genesis" charges a spark of light to show love projected through history, shot across the great flood of time itself.

The Annunciation of Christ's coming occurs when the angel Gabriel comes like a sheriff with two guns in sonnet 5. He plays a trick on death, and he plays cards with time. He pulls three cards from his sleeve: God, the "king of spots," king over death; Jesus, the jack (of all trades), and Mary, with the great heart. Gabriel is drunk on his message of salvation, and he tells a strange story of his travels: from Adam out of Eden, across the ocean as Ahab-Noah-Jonah, to the place of the frozen angel (Satan in Dante's hell of ice), where death as a "black medusa" dwells and the sirens lure sailors into the Sargasso Sea.

The sixth sonnet is a cartoon of what God did in creating the universe, as described in Genesis, the book of life. It all began with the "word," as do all poems. The word is also Christ, the Word, who as the great rooster-cock of love pecks out the eye of the medusa—death. Still, the sirens sing to seduce the Adam of the flesh into their Sargasso Sea of sin. The genesis of sonnet 6 yields to the gospel of sonnet 7, where the Lord's Prayer is stamped "on a grain of rice," because rice must be planted in water to grow, like birth in the womb and rebirth in baptism. The leaves of the Bible grow from the tree of Calvary until spiritual wind turns death into life, words into poetry.

Sonnet 8 contemplates the crucifixion and passion of the suffering Christ, as viewed by his mother, Mary, and by himself. Jesus is the wound of Mary's womb, who is herself bent by the wound of the world. The rainbow of God's promise to Noah is repeated as the colors of the Trinity arching over the breasts of Mother Nature and Mary. In the last four lines, Jesus speaks as the thief of time and the physician who heals death. The next sonnet (9) is a contrast to sonnet 8. Whereas Christian burial is a way to eternal life, Egyptian burial is a futile effort to preserve the flesh in mummies and arks of parchment. The only resurrection for Egyptian mummies is the work of scholars who break into their tombs to study their dusty remains.

The final sonnet, sonnet 10, shows that the wise altar of sonnet 1 is the cross of the crucifixion ("the rude, red tree"). Here the Christian voyager has crossed the atlas to become wise enough not to be wrecked in the "dummy bay" of a false harbor. He is guided by Peter into a safe harbor, to which he holds the key ("quay"). Peter asks questions about the "tall fish" and the "rhubarb man," symbolic images of Jesus, who has restored the garden of Eden for all.

Forms and Devices

The sonnets of "Altarwise by Owl-Light" are lyrics of fourteen lines, divided into two logical parts: a sestet of six lines, followed by an octave of eight (a reversal of the conventional Italian sonnet). The rhyme scheme is *abcbac, dedefgfg*, but the rhymes are rarely exact; instead, they are slant rhymes or sight rhymes, as in the opening sonnet: "house" rhymes with "news," "furies" with "fairies," and "Adam" with "scream."

The sonnets are held together by the repetition of certain images, such as "altar," "cock," "bones," "cradle," and voyaging by water. Some of these images, such as Capricorn and Cancer, are drawn from astrology; others, such as mandrakes and pelicans, are from folklore. The sequence is dense; it rings with puns and obscure allusions. There are puns such as "genesis" and "gender" for biblical and sexual beginnings; sun for Son; and "rude, red" for "rood, read." Besides using frequent biblical allusions, the sequence employs numerous other literary allusions, such as Rip Van Winkle, and Herman Melville's Ishmael and the whale from *Moby Dick*

(1851). Biblical anecdotes are mixed with contemporary events to create surrealistic effects. Sonnet 4 describes the Nativity of Christ with imagery of modern photography; sonnet 5 describes the Annunciation as an episode from a Western film made in Hollywood.

Determined by a biblical chronology that passes from Genesis to Revelation, the sequence is a series of figurative snapshots which interpret Christian images as creative (sexual and literary) symbols.

Themes and Meanings

In "Altarwise by Owl-Light," Thomas weaves together several themes to produce a richly layered meaning of personal and universal experience. Most prominent of its themes are the surrealistic events of Christian history, the trials of human sexuality, and the joyful labors of poetic creativity. In the end, all are one and the same, identified by the mysterious force of language itself.

Christian history is portrayed as very individual, as the speaker of the sonnets may sometimes be the poet, sometimes Christ, and sometimes the mother of Christ. Crucial episodes of history are taken as moments of illumination for all time, past, present, and future: the Nativity of Christ is a significant repetition of the genesis of the world, of the creation of Adam, and it is significantly repeated in the birth of every person; the Crucifixion of Christ repeats the Fall of Adam, and every person's pain/death is a reenactment of the Fall and the Crucifixion; the Resurrection confirms the promise of new birth and new life for all, a return to Eden (the "flying garden") of the Old Adam through the New Adam of Christ.

Wherever there is creation, there is also some pain and, sometimes, there is comedy. The sequence follows the ironies and paradoxes of sexuality as blessing and curse: from the "hangnail cracked from Adam," to "the gender's strip," "marrow ladle," and "manwax," masculine crosses feminine sexuality with its "shapeless country," "milky mushrooms," and "house of bread." The theme of poetic creation crosses all with its elaboration of the major pun on the "Word" as the Beginning of All; hence, there is a "walking word," a "book of water," "medusa's scripture," "my fork tongue," and "a rocking alphabet." To create babies and poems is to create the world anew, to renew paradise and triumph over death; to joy in re-creation is to be wise, converting the atlas of the world into an altar of renewal.

Richard D. McGhee

AMAZING GRACE IN THE BACK COUNTRY

Author: Robert Penn Warren (1905-1989)
Type of poem: Narrative
First published: 1977; collected in *Now and Then: Poems 1976-1978*, 1978

The Poem

In "Amazing Grace in the Back Country," the aging Robert Penn Warren looks back with nostalgia and wry amusement at a revivalist camp meeting he attended in rural Kentucky when he was twelve years old. Although he was quite convinced at that age that he was indeed sinful, he "hardened his heart" and refused the "amazing grace" offered by the revivalists. The tone is ironic throughout, and the poem implies that human behavior is not noticeably different after repentance. Nevertheless, this poem is not contemptuous of the yearning for redemption and hope.

The first stanza presents an unflattering analogy between the meager trappings of the traveling evangelists and the half-bankrupt carnivals that pitched their tents in the same spot. The fat lady, the geek, the moth-eaten lion, the boa constrictor that eats calves, and the aging whores demonstrate the quality of entertainment available in the backcountry. Those who lingered with the whores were likely to acquire syphilis as an added price for their fun.

The boy sits with the others listening as "an ex-railroad engineer/ Turned revivalist shouted the Threat and the Promise." An old woman in worn-out black silk kneels beside the boy and determines to save him. "She wept and she prayed, and I knew I was damned,/ Who was guilty of all short of murder,/ At least in my heart." He remembers how he once walked down the street after dark "Uttering, 'Lust—lust—lust,'/ Like an invocation, out loud."

The boy gazes in mounting alarm at the rising hysteria around him. At last, he bolts from the tent, runs into the forest, and vomits while leaning against a tree. He crouches there "knowing damnation" until the ecstatic congregation, now singing triumphantly of "amazing grace," straggles back to the village. Each singer "Found bed and lay down,/ And tomorrow would rise and do all the old things to do,/ Until that morning they would not rise, not ever."

Meanwhile, the boy lies in the forest with his hand in the spring where he rinsed his mouth after being sick and wonders what grace he will ever find. The poem ends with the thoughtful reminder "But that was long years ago. I was twelve years old then." Warren was in his seventies when he wrote the poem.

Forms and Devices

The poem uses the natural cadence of speech, avoiding rhyme and consistent meter. Both lines and stanzas vary in length. The last line stands alone, suggesting the pause, pregnant with unspoken memories of the person who looks backward at scenes a lifetime away, yet still vivid in detail. The tone is carefully modulated to fit the emotional content.

Sometimes the diction is jocular, colloquial, and disrespectful, like that used by one who remembers the language of the time and place: "one/ Boa constrictor for two bits seen/ Fed a young calf; plus a brace/ Of whores to whom menopause now/ Was barely a memory." (One can imagine the country storyteller sharing a laugh with the farmers in the general store.) Yet even here, the colloquial diction quickly fades to the more circumspect wording of the older, wiser man who remembers the tragic possibilities of coarse fun with whores: "A new and guaranteed brand of syphilis handy — yes."

The tent-meeting scene again zooms in with the immediacy of only yesterday when the boy was confused about how sinful he really was. The reader must smile at the boy's discovery of "lust" as a newly minted word, somehow equivalent to some secret sin not yet clearly understood. It is appropriate for a poet to appreciate the evocative power of words. After all, in a theological sense, the boy was not wrong in realizing that the intent of the heart is morally significant.

The poem makes an unobtrusive but thematically suggestive use of symbols. It begins with attention to the setting by the woods "where oaks of the old forest-time/ Yet swaggered and hulked over upstarts." The "old forest-time" is a reminder that these villagers have not yet completely dominated the surrounding wild country, just as they have not successfully indoctrinated the boy.

In stanza 7 through stanza 9, the protagonist is observing the worshipers and listening to them from the viewpoint of the woods. "I stared/ Through interstices of black brush to the muted gold glow/ Of God's canvas." The boy stays in the woods until all the voices are silent, and the lights are out in the tent, and the stars "Had changed place in the sky, I yet lay/ By the spring with one hand in the cold black water/ That showed one star in reflection, alone." The wheeling stars, with their connotations of time and fate, support the implication that the single star reflected in the water may symbolize the protagonist's fate. Moreover, the boy keeps his hand in the spring where the star appears, suggesting that the spring is a natural symbol of an alternate source of inspiration for the person who has refused "amazing grace." The twelve-year-old persona is not necessarily sure of that choice or what it portends for the welfare of his soul. The older Warren who tells the story has the wisdom of hindsight, but he does not make a moral judgment in the matter.

Themes and Meanings

Contemporary writers who, like Warren, were born at the beginning of the twentieth century have lived through the most rapid and spectacular social changes of any comparable period of history. This is particularly true for the South, which lingered in the rural, agrarian mode longer than other areas of the United States. Presumably at least, the backcountry does not even exist anymore. There is no place quite so isolated in its social choices, so insulated from information about the outside world, and so limited in its resources for entertainment or inspiration.

Although this poem provides a humorous commentary on the limitations of life in the backcountry, particularly the emotional poverty that at times led to what some would call religious hysteria, Warren approaches this time with a gentle and tolerant mood. Warren was and remained an unbeliever of strict fundamentalist religion. Yet he recognized that it answered a need that all people have, especially those who cannot distract themselves with the toys of a modern industrial society.

No matter what the excesses of revivalist camp meetings, these emotional encounters renewed a dream of salvation in lives that were often grim and repetitive. They assuaged what the poet calls "The late-season pain gnawing deep at the human bone."

Traveling preachers in the backcountry were often totally untrained for their calling. It was literally a calling—that is, they responded to a personal call from God, leaving behind whatever mode of life or occupation they had devised to make a living. They probably read the Bible, at least superficially, but they excelled mostly in fire-and-brimstone oratory. With the threat of damnation, these preachers sought to coerce sinners into accepting the "amazing grace" of a forgiving God.

This poem suggests that the young Warren was more frightened than inspired by the Christian message. Whether this rejection stemmed from rebellion, from a renewed devotion to sin as the boy dimly perceived it, or from an unconscious covenant with another source of inspiration remains somewhat ambiguous. Considering the subdued implication of the star and the spring, one may assume that Warren felt closer to God in the woods than he ever did in the revivalists' tent.

Some of Warren's other meditative poems written late in his life indicate that the moral and theological questions of religion continued to be live issues. Perhaps he was not immune to "The late-season pain gnawing deep at the human bone." Such poems as "A Way to Love God" and "Trying to Tell You Something" suggest that the fear is gone but that the mystery of fate remains. The imagery of these poems comes more from nature than from organized religion to provide insight into meaning and human fate.

There are no answers in the sense of doctrine or easy promises for future bliss. There is only the tremendous reality of experience and the overwhelming drive in the poet to give that experience adequate expression. Yet there is a certain hope, not exactly of salvation, but of some new remarkable insight that comes only, perhaps, at the point of death.

Katherine Snipes

THE AMBASSADOR DIARIES OF
JEAN DE BOSSCHÈRE AND EDGAR POE

Author: Norman Dubie (1945-   )
Type of poem: Lyric
First published: 1977; collected in *The City of the Olesha Fruit,* 1979

The Poem

"The Ambassador Diaries of Jean de Bosschère and Edgar Poe" has three sections, the first and third containing twelve stanzas each, the second containing five. Each stanza consists of six free-verse lines. Although Norman Dubie's title refers to Edgar Allan Poe and poet Jean de Bosschère, the poem is about Conrad Aiken (1889-1973). From childhood on, Aiken loved Poe's work, and he admired the poetry of Bosschère. Like these poets, Aiken was an orphan. The word "ambassador" comes from one of the passages in Aiken's poem "Time in the Rock," parts of which Dubie used as epigraphs in this poem, and Aiken referred to his *Preludes for Memmon* (1931) as a "spiritual diary."

In section 1, Dubie addresses Aiken and then narrates an anecdote based on Aiken's poem "And in the Hanging Gardens," whose characters—a king, a princess, and a knave—were derived from Aiken and his parents. Dubie combines the king and the knave in a single figure and provides a historical name, King Henry VIII. The young king has thrown his drinking cup from a window of his castle and goes out in the rain, cursing it and his mother, to find it. When he does, he lies down at the edge of a meadow to sleep, but servants are coming to return him to his mother, who waits with dry linens. Dubie says that the king's quest reflects a desire to be down in the muddy fields, dreaming of a castle in the air. Referring to Aiken's fear of inheriting his father's insanity, Dubie asks if his king is sane. When Aiken was eleven, his father shot Aiken's mother and then committed suicide. Dubie pictures the boy going from his dollhouse in the garden to his parents' bedroom and discovering the bodies. It begins to rain, and the walls of the dollhouse become "walls of terror, everywhere."

In section 2, Dubie quotes from Aiken's "Goya"—"Why wake the ones who sleep, if awake they/ Can only weep." Positive change will not occur in the world unless disturbing truths about human nature and the human condition are brought to consciousness. One such truth is the finality of death. Referring to Aiken's "Cliff Meeting," Dubie would like to think such a meeting of lovers will come after death for the woman who has died, but the most he will say is that it will be an "absence" of everything that is "not pretty."

In section 3, Dubie pictures Aiken writing poetry to heal the wound caused by his parents' deaths. Although Aiken won a Pulitzer Prize and Sigmund Freud considered his novel *Great Circle* (1933) a masterpiece, Dubie tells Aiken: "They no longer read your poems." Suggesting a reason, Dubie says Aiken disgusted the sheriff with details about his parents' deaths—"You told the truth." After asking Aiken if he hated women, Dubie states that the "government of children is left to women," with "the Fathers leaving us" from the beginning. These lines relate to Aiken's poem "Landscape West of Eden," in which Eve wants to stay in Eden and Adam wants to explore beyond it. Dubie suggests that some children become "orphan-poets" because of this conflict; he wrote his first poem when he was age eleven. Referring to another of his poems, "Elegies for the Ochre Deer on the Walls at Lascaux," which includes three suicides, Dubie says he once compared "the heads of two/ Bald priests" to the "buttocks/ Of lovers fleeing into the trees." This image, combined with those of rain in the poem (collected in a reference to the biblical flood), suggests a new beginning. Love and poetry offer the possibility of a new Eden.

Forms and Devices

In addition to his use of literary and historical allusions, Dubie employs parallels in diction and syntax, including images of color and clothing, to establish relationships among characters and incidents in the poem. In section 1, he refers to a "dark courtesan" with "white braids" and to the "dark room that morning" where Aiken's parents died. In section 2, he tells of the "lady in white" who "fell down this morning" and to the child who ran to her aid, as Aiken ran to his mother's. The lady addresses the child as Peter, saying she had never felt so "carefree." Aiken believed that his mother, although dead, spoke to him. Dubie renders this in a passage derived, as was the name "Peter," from Aiken's poem "The Coming Forth of Osiris Jones": "There was a voice speaking" of a handkerchief, of a flower.

Dubie establishes another link with a color image when he refers to Aiken's "red-eyed dolls" and to children who are kept "scrubbed and red/ And crying" by their mothers. This also connects with King Henry's mother, waiting with dry linens, and with Aiken's mother, who "had washed" his legs. Dubie creates another parallel with the color yellow. King Henry has "yellow sleeves," and the Nazis burned *Great Circle* because they considered it a "yellow-book, decadent," which is ironic, because it was Henry VIII and the Nazis who were decadent. They parallel the "princes and priests" who wanted to "pickle Goya's feet" as well as the priests of literature who have banished Aiken's work from the canon of accepted texts. The reference to priests also connects with the bald-headed priests who contrast with the lovers of the poem's final stanza.

Also, in contrast to the king's "yellow sleeves," Goya "wore out the elbows of his sleeves." The king "sweeps" his slipper through the grass, whereas Poe, "wearing a shawl," coughs while "sweeping snow." Dubie contrasts the opulence of kings with the poverty of poets and artists. In another reference to clothing, Aiken's father "paused, while dressing," to murder Aiken's mother. Henry VIII lives on in infamy because he had two of his wives beheaded. Dubie writes that the king left "both the children and the women." Aiken, himself, was divorced from his first two wives and left his children with their mother. In another comparison, the king has "wild-pig in his beard" and Goya "drew a pig on a wall." In his fictionalized autobiography, *Ushant* (1952), Aiken tells of his mother drawing a pig to entertain her children, and in *Great Circle* he relates his nightmare about a crucified pig.

The study of these and other parallels in "The Ambassador Diaries of Jean de Bosschère and Edgar Poe" and the reading of works alluded to by Dubie in the poem do much to provide further insights into the works of both writers.

Themes and Meanings

Dubie's primary intention in "The Ambassador Diaries of Jean de Bosschère and Edgar Poe" is to draw attention to the work of Aiken. The epigraphs prefacing sections 1 and 3 of the poem give the reader a taste of Aiken's poetry—twelve lines of it—taken from one of Aiken's major works, "Time in the Rock." The numerous allusions to works by Aiken constitute an act of literary criticism: Dubie is saying that these works are important and should not be forgotten. Dubie's poem also expresses ideas that are central to Aiken's prose and poetry.

The focus on Aiken's life reflects Dubie's belief that the writer should engage in a sort of self-psychoanalysis to become aware of the forces that have determined or influenced his or her attitudes, beliefs, and actions. This consciousness provides the writer with the wisdom to avoid destructive patterns of behavior. Dubie shows Aiken beginning this process in the line of verse he writes following his parents' deaths— "Why did they whip poor Will?" Aiken was mentally and physically abused by his father, who would not have committed murder and suicide, Aiken believed, if he had developed such a consciousness. Aiken's father was one of those "who sleep," unaware of subconscious motivations. By mentioning the Nazis, Dubie reminds the reader of what can happen when an entire nation is "asleep."

Aiken believed that poetry not only allowed the poet to increase his or her individual consciousness but also served to advance the consciousness of the human race. By embodying the process of achieving self-knowledge and presenting the discoveries of the poet, it leaves a record for others to learn from and build on. As Aiken wrote in one of the passages from "Time in the Rock" that Dubie uses as an epigraph, the writer's job is "To be the ambassador/ Of all you are to all that is not you!" This sentiment raises the issue of literary tradition.

In "The Ambassador Diaries of Jean de Bosschère and Edgar Poe," Dubie writes that Aiken has been made a "childless" ambassador, meaning that his work has been relegated to the provinces of literary history, away from the mainstream of tradition, where it will not foster successors. By writing his poem about Aiken, however, Dubie means to correct this situation. Dubie becomes an inheritor of Aiken's work. As his allusions to Aiken's works demonstrate, Dubie has assimilated Aiken's consciousness, just as Aiken assimilated the consciousness of Poe and as future poets will assimilate the consciousness of Dubie. Many other writers also are the spiritual ancestors of these poets; in this way, the consciousness of the human race is increased.

James Green

AMERICA: A PROPHECY

Author: William Blake (1757-1827)
Type of poem: Narrative
First published: 1793

The Poem

America: A Prophecy is a narrative poem consisting of two parts, a thirty-seven-line section titled "Preludium" and a longer, 226-line section entitled "A Prophecy." It is written in long, unrhymed lines that seem to have been inspired in their shape both by the epic meter of Homer and by the iambic pentameter of John Milton, but that conform to neither.

The poem takes the American Revolution as its inspiration, but, even though George Washington and other founding fathers appear in it, the poem is by no means an attempt to write a history of the event. Rather, this poem is an attempt to create an extended metaphor glorifying the spirit of the revolution.

In *America,* William Blake is developing a cosmology of deities, some of whom had appeared in his earlier poems and many of whom were to appear in later ones, such as the poem "The Four Zoas." When the poem begins, Orc, a deity associated with fire and rebellion, based very much on the myth of Prometheus, has been chained by Urthona, who is a blacksmith and associated with the earth. He is being fed by the virgin daughter of Urthona, a sympathetic spirit also associated with the earth. Inspired by her presence, Orc breaks free of his chains to embrace her; she, in turn, is inspired to speak for the first time, and, at the end of this prelude, tells him of the struggle under way on "my American plains."

The main section of the poem, "A Prophecy," concerns the struggle between the Angel of Albion (England) and a number of characters and deities associated with the American colonies. George Washington early makes an impassioned speech to warn Americans that the Angel of Albion is on his way to imprison them, but after that, he and the other founding fathers named in the poem (including Thomas Jefferson, Benjamin Franklin, and Thomas Paine) have little to do. Most of the battle is between Orc and the Angel of Albion.

Orc arrives in a fiery burst to intervene between the Angel of Albion and the American colonists. The Angel of Albion recognizes him and demands to know what he is doing. Orc declares that he is defending the principle that "everything that lives is holy" against the idea that lives can be ranked according to their importance, which he sees the Angel of Albion as trying to enforce.

Beginning in line 76, the Angel of Albion tries to rally his "Thirteen Angels," representing the spirits of the original thirteen colonies. Led by Boston's Angel, who refuses to pay any more obedience to Albion, the Thirteen Angels throw down their scepters and stand united with Washington and other founding fathers. In line 142, the human governors of the thirteen colonies meet and, unable to break the mental chains binding them to England, surrender to Washington rather than join him.

The Angel of Albion sends plagues to defeat the colonies of America, but Orc intervenes and sends the plagues back onto the English. The plagues defeat the Angel of Albion, and Blake shows what he thinks of the official English poetry of his day by having a "cowl" of flesh and scales grow over the Bard of Albion (a stand-in for any of several British poet laureates of Blake's lifetime), who has hidden in a cave.

Then Urizen, at this point the most powerful of Blake's deities, appears. Urizen is described as old, pale, and bearded, and in this poem is associated with clouds and ice. He puts a stop to the revolt against Albion by trapping Orc in a white cloud for twelve years—possibly referring to the period between the end of the American Revolution and the execution of the king of France in 1793. The poem ends with a prophecy of the time when the five gates, meaning the five senses, will be burned away and mankind will be able to perceive infinity directly, the ultimate outcome Blake sees to the French and American revolutions.

Forms and Devices

Although Blake displays a rich feel for the rhythms and sounds of language in *America,* as he does in all of his work, in this poem he does not try to conform his poetic lines to any rigid structure. Typically, though, each line will have seven or eight hard stresses. Many lines have an iambic rhythm (every second syllable stressed), but usually it is interrupted by at least one other type of poetic foot (for example, two—or three—hard stresses in a row) at some point in the line. The effect is that every line seems to reflect the conflict of forces at work in the poem in general.

The larger accomplishment of this poem is that it weaves elements from mythology, from Milton's *Paradise Lost* (1667, 1674), and, of course, from the history of the American Revolution, into an original cosmology of Blake's own making. If the chained figure of Orc introduced at the beginning of the poem is derivative of Prometheus, the god in Greek mythology who defied the other gods by bringing fire to man and was therefore chained to a mountain by Zeus, he also owes much to Milton's Satan, condemned to the fires of hell for leading angels in revolt. Thus, when Orc tells the Angel of Albion, "I am Orc, wreathed round the accursed tree" (line 59), he is identifying himself with the serpent in the Garden of Eden, and more generally identifying himself with Lucifer when he refers to the "fiery Joy, that Urizen perverted to ten commands," meaning the Ten Commandments (line 61). Further, Orc identifies the rebellious spirit of the American colonies with his own rebellious spirit.

The poem, however, does not at any point become a meticulous allegory of the American Revolution. Although Orc's imprisonment may be read as a poetic rendering of the end of the war of independence, the events of the poem, such as the turning back of the plague meant for America onto the cities of Bristol and London, do not generally correspond to specific historical events. This is not a poem about the people and events of the revolution (and in fact, the Americans who are named and alluded to throughout the poem have little to do besides watch the main conflict) but about the spirit of the revolution. As such, its aim is to put this revolution into a context of revolt not only against political tyranny—the type of revolt Washington calls for in his brief but powerful speech—but generally against any tyranny that represses the potential for life.

This is why the poem is a "prophecy." It sees the American Revolution as part of a larger spiritual cleansing that will ultimately create a new world.

Themes and Meanings

America is a poem less about the importance of overthrowing political tyranny (though that is one of its concerns) than it is about the importance of overthrowing the ways of thinking and perceiving that Blake associates with political as well as spiritual tyranny.

In many ways, Orc's speech to the Angel of Albion in lines 59-75 is at the center of the meaning of the poem. In this section, Orc prophesies that he shall stamp the "stony law" of the commandments "to dust, and scatter religion abroad" (line 63), because they have served to shelter humanity from the "fiery joy" of living. This type of fire is only threatening to those (such as the Angel of Albion, and Urizen) who hide from it. Orc foresees a time when "Fires enwrap the globe, yet man is not consumed" (line 73), but in fact is transformed by the fire into a being who gleams like precious metals.

True to the spirit of Romantic poets such as Percy Bysshe Shelley and Lord Byron, with whom Blake is often associated, Blake uses fire as a basic metaphor for creativity. To someone who is afraid of it, it appears destructive. To someone who is not afraid of it, it is constructive. Religion has to be overthrown, according to Orc, because it prevents people from experiencing their own fires directly.

In fact, it is clear that for Orc this creative fire is the basic essence of life. Thus, when this fire is released through the destruction of religion, deserts will blossom. Those seeking "virginity," a term Blake does not use literally but understands as an innocent enjoyment of life's pleasures, "May find it in a harlot" (line 69). Orc's basic principle is that "every thing that lives is holy, life delights in life" (line 71). There are no isolated holy temples; everything that lives is a holy temple.

In view of such a high principle, the destruction that Orc unleashes may seem at first glance to be contradictory, but a closer examination shows that it is not Orc but the Angel of Albion who is responsible for this destruction. Orc does not create the plagues that rack London and Bristol; he merely deflects them from attacking the colonies. The Angel of Albion and his charges pay the price for trying to destroy the creative spirit of others.

The poem is called *America* because it is the revolt of the American colonies, its creative spirit, that receives Orc's attention. The revolution that the poem foresees at its end, when Orc frees himself again, is a much larger revolution, however: one that will free the human spirit throughout the world.

Thomas J. Cassidy

AMONG SCHOOL CHILDREN

Author: William Butler Yeats (1865-1939)
Type of poem: Meditation
First published: 1927; collected in *The Tower,* 1928

The Poem

William Butler Yeats's "Among School Children" is written in eight eight-line stanzas that follow a precise rhyme scheme. Along with the straightforward title, stanza 1 establishes the immediate context of the action in deliberately prosaic language. The speaker is visiting a schoolroom, and "a kind old nun," his guide for the day or perhaps the classroom teacher, is answering his matter-of-fact questions in a rapid, matter-of-fact way.

The tone and mood of the poem take a sharp turn in the couplet ending the first stanza, however; the speaker suddenly sees himself through the children's eyes as they "In momentary wonder stare upon/ A sixty-year-old smiling public man." The speaker is almost certainly Yeats himself; as a member of the Irish Senate, Yeats, just turned sixty, did in fact visit schools as a part of his official duties.

Seeing himself through the children's eyes inspires a reverie. He thinks of a child, a girl, whom he knew in his own childhood or youth. The facts are not quite clear, for the reader is told of a "childish day" but also of "youthful sympathy." Nevertheless, the young female is generally identified as Maud Gonne, with whom the poet first became acquainted and fell in love when she was in her late teens and he was in his twenties.

The reverie ends, but his eyes light upon one of the children, who looks amazingly like Maud when she was that age: "She stands before me as a living child." Seeing her as she looked then reminds him of what she looks like now, after the passage of nearly forty years. "Her present image" is of someone whom life has wasted and exhausted; she is "Hollow of cheek" as if she "drank the wind" and ate "a mess of shadows for [her] meat."

Thoughts of her then and now lead to thoughts of himself then and now. The years have not been kind in his case either, and, back in the present in the schoolroom, he decides that it is best to keep up a brave front and "smile on all that smile."

Yet he cannot shake the thought that human life appears to be a process of diminishment and gradual dispossession, if not outright defeat. He imagines what a mother—perhaps his own—would think, just having given birth, could she see that infant after he has lived through "sixty or more winters." Would she, he wonders, think the result worth the pain of her labor and of all her coming anxieties over her helpless infant's welfare?

In the final three stanzas, the personal note that has pervaded the poem is dropped as the speaker explores in rapid order the breadth and scope of all human thought and endeavor—from Plato to Aristotle and Pythagoras, from nuns to mothers to youthful lovers—seeking some solace for the tragic unraveling of dreams and hopes that human life seems to be. In a sudden burst of anger, the speaker excoriates all those images that people set before their mind's eyes to goad themselves and others into succeeding only at failing, and he tries instead to see human life as it is truly lived.

The vision that emerges is one in which neither devotion to others (motherhood) nor devotion to God (the nun) nor devotion to fulfilling selfhood (Maud Gonne) can alone be enough, for "Labour is blossoming or dancing." It is an ongoing process, not any final product. Therefore, one cannot isolate the individual from the passing moment by trying to imagine that at any one instant there is some greater or lesser being there; like the chestnut tree, a human life is all one piece, so one should be wary of trying to "know the dancer from the dance."

Forms and Devices

Yeats's is a poetry rich in complex webs of both personal and public symbols and allusions, and "Among School Children" is no exception. An example of this complexity can be found by examining the source of something as apparently superficial as the rhyme scheme. Ottava rima was introduced into English prosody by the early nineteenth century poet George Gordon, Lord Byron, who used it to great comic effect in poems such as his satiric masterpiece, *Don Juan* (1819-1824).

The Yeats poem is hardly satiric and is comic only by the broadest definition of the term, as one uses it when speaking of Dante's *The Divine Comedy* (c. 1320). Like · Dante, whose great poem begins with the otherwise unremarkable discovery that he has lost his way, Yeats uses a rather commonplace incident—a public official's visit to a classroom while touring a school—to explore the larger meaning and purpose of human life in general.

Because of the complexity of Yeats's technique, making such connections is not as farfetched as one might suspect. A symbol, like the allusion to outside texts and sources of information, can point in any number of directions, but it will always make a connection. The poet must connect private and public symbols and allusions in a careful order and to some greater thematic purpose.

Yeats's use of the myth of Leda and the swan offers a fine example. In the ancient Greek myth, Zeus came as a swan to rape the mortal Leda; from that union came Helen of Troy. Yeats's "Ledaean body," however, is something more than a knowledge of the myth alone can betoken. In his poem "Leda and the Swan," he sees in the myth a comment on the dangerous consequences of mixing divine elements with something as fragile as human nature. Furthermore, in other poems, Yeats identifies Maud Gonne with Helen of Troy as representatives of that beauty which is destructive.

That Leda also brings to mind childbearing and childrearing in a poem that focuses on children, childhood, labor, and birth suggests still further possibilities of meaning and illustrates that the apparent opacity of the poem is actually the result of combining a wide literary heritage with a compelling richness and interconnectedness of thought, feeling, and experience.

Themes and Meanings

The central themes of "Among School Children" are best exemplified in the central action: A sixty-year-old official is visiting with elementary school children. The age-old poetic themes of innocence versus experience, naïveté versus wisdom, and youth versus age permeate every stanza of the poem.

Yeats, who in his youthful work frequently dealt with incidents of passing and loss, virtually became obsessed with those themes as he became older and faced his own mortality in more real, less abstract terms. By this point in his career, Yeats was examining the consequences and effects of time's passage not only on the human body but also on the human spirit—both for the individual and for the race as a whole—invariably basing his meditations on personal experience.

In Yeats's hands, these timeless themes take on a profound significance, because while he views human life as tragic, his vision is not nihilistic. He never does actually enunciate what purpose human life may serve, but he does believe that there is a purpose. "Among School Children" illustrates how the individual might frustrate that purpose by imagining either that he is the master of his own destiny or that there is no such thing as destiny.

Maud Gonne serves as a prime example of this frustration of purpose. The poet, who is condemned to remember the brightness and promise of her youth, must live with the meaningless fruits of her actions now that the heartbreak and frustrations of her commitment to revolutionary Irish political causes have taken their toll both on herself and others. By cutting her fulfillment short, she has cut all the rest of humankind short.

Nor will Yeats exclude himself and others from the same condemnation. All fail in their choices and actions to face squarely the one insurmountable reality: Flesh ages, spirits flag, and human dreams wither. He thus accuses himself of having given up or given in ("I . . . had pretty plumage once" but now am "a comfortable kind of old scarecrow") and accuses nuns and mothers, as much as the Helens and Mauds of the world, of betraying the innocent, childlike spirit that fosters dreams and compels human choices.

People unwittingly create false images of what it is to be human, thereby creating false hopes and expectations. Yeats suggests that since there is no choice but to move forward, one should imagine the fullness of each moment as having an inextricable harmony with all others. Life is like a dance that does exist independent of a dancer but has no shape or form without the dancers.

Russell Elliott Murphy

AND DEATH SHALL HAVE NO DOMINION

Author: Dylan Thomas (1914-1953)
Type of poem: Lyric
First published: 1933; collected in *Twenty-five Poems*, 1936

The Poem

"And Death Shall Have No Dominion" is a poem in three nine-line stanzas of sprung rhythm. Each of the stanzas begins and ends with the title line, which echoes Romans 6:9 from the King James translation of the Christian New Testament: "Death hath no more dominion." The title and the refrain give the theme of the poem — resurrection — and introduce its characteristic rhythm and solemn tone.

The poem is built on repetition, and not merely of the title. Once the meaning of the first line is grasped, the entire poem is understood. Each of the intervening lines and images is simply another way of saying that the life force is immortal — that people's bodies may die but their spirits live on in the world.

The speaker of the poem is a grand and disembodied voice. There is no particular representative intended; there is no character whose words these are taken to be. The poem is an oratory; it is truth spoken out of the air.

The first stanza deals with the dead, who shall be made whole again at the end of time. The unity and wholeness of the universe is hinted at by an arresting rearrangement of elements that Dylan Thomas creates in the third line: "the man in the wind and the west moon." Man in the moon, man in the wind, west wind, west moon — it does not matter how the parts are arranged because all is one.

When dead men reach the final reckoning, therefore, even though their bodies are gone, "they shall have stars at elbow and foot." The paradox of having elbows and feet and yet no body reiterates the poem's theme of resurrection.

More important than the body is the spirit or the life force. "Though lovers be lost," the poet says, "love shall not." It is not people but people's spiritual force that shall endure.

There is much religious-sounding language in the first stanza, particularly many echoes of the language of the King James Bible: "naked they shall be one," "stars at elbow and foot," and "they shall rise again." There is no Christianity here, however. God is never mentioned, there is no talk of souls or of salvation, and the moment at which all shall or shall not happen is not specified as any sort of Judgment Day. Whatever happens to people happens because that is the nature of things, not because a supreme being has ordained it.

In the second stanza, Thomas treats the pain of life and death. Even if the pain should be bad enough for people's faith to "snap in two," they will still not suffer a final death. It is nature, not faith, that determines one's ultimate fate.

The last stanza connects one's life force to that of other natural beings — the birds and flowers. When people die, their life force may enter a daisy or the sun, but it will not simply end. Death shall have no dominion.

Forms and Devices

As is often the case with Thomas' poetry, much of the power of this poem comes from the sound of it. It should be read aloud to be fully appreciated. "And Death Shall Have No Dominion" is one of his poems that Thomas himself chose to record. When one listens to the poem, one is immediately struck by its rhythm. Gerard Manley Hopkins coined the term "sprung rhythm" to describe his own poetry in which the rhythm is based not on metrical feet, but simply on the number of stressed syllables in a line. The term is apt here. Two different readers reciting this poem are likely to stress different syllables within any given line, yet both readers will create the same effect of wavelike rhythm — strong, regular, and insistent.

Thomas creates this powerful rhythm by the careful selection of words and the crafting of lines. Nearly all of the words in the poem are monosyllabic and contain explosive consonants that create a sharp separation between words.

One line from the first stanza demonstrates this: "When their bones are picked clean and the clean bones gone." The combinations of consonants make it nearly impossible to elide words in this line. In "picked clean," the two hard *k* sounds demand to be sounded separately; in "clean bones gone," each of the three words begins with an explosive consonant, and the repetition of the *n* creates the effect of stress and echo. The line must be read slowly, distinctly, and rhythmically.

Most of the lines in the poem are punctuated at the end, and much of this punctuation is in the form of periods and semicolons. Again, this forces the reader to pause at regular intervals, enhancing the rhythm.

Repetition also aids rhythm in this poem. The most obvious example of this is the title line, which occurs six times in the poem, creating a rhythm of larger units that recede and echo back.

Repetition operates on a smaller scale as well. In the first stanza, three lines are structured to echo one another: "Though they go mad they shall be sane,/ Though they sink through the sea they shall rise again;/ Though lovers be lost love shall not." In the first two lines, repetition of the word "they" helps to create the wavelike effect, as do the words "lovers" and "love" in the third line.

Thomas has not created rhythm for its own sake, although his body of work clearly demonstrates that he was much taken by the beauty inherent in spoken language. This poem's rhythm, reminiscent of a Christian prayer or sermon, reinforces the solemnity and importance of its theme.

Thomas chooses to echo religious oratory, not to deliver a Christian message, but to offer his idea of resurrection in a ritual style that Christians will understand.

Themes and Meanings

The central issue in this poem is the nature of resurrection and, therefore, the essential nature of the life force being resurrected. By using echoes of the Christian Bible throughout the poem, Thomas demands that his views be seen in contrast to the Christian tradition in which he was reared.

Thomas has often been referred to as a pantheist. The word "pantheism" comes from the Greek *pan*, meaning all, and *theos*, meaning God. In other words, God and the universe are one, or God and nature are one. Although it is unlikely that Thomas ever used the term to describe himself, pantheism does seem to capture much of his system of belief. This idea is demonstrated in this poem as well as others, including "A Refusal to Mourn the Death, by Fire, of a Child in London" and "The Force That Through the Green Fuse Drives the Flower."

When Saint Paul said in his letter to the Romans that "death hath no more dominion," he meant that those who had chosen salvation would not suffer eternal damnation and spiritual death. Instead, they would be resurrected on the Day of Judgment and given new spiritual bodies.

Thomas makes it clear from the beginning that he sees things differently. When he states (and restates) that "death shall have no dominion," he carefully and deliberately leaves out the word "more." For Thomas, it is not a matter of death ceasing to have power—death has never been the end of life.

When people die, the poem says, their spirits live on. The issue of bodies is moot. When people die their spirits may next inhabit a flower ("Heads of the characters hammer through daisies") or something else, but their spirits will continue to live.

Faith, Thomas says in stanza 2, has nothing to do with it. Some may lose their faith ("Faith in their hands shall snap in two") as a result of the suffering inherent in life. Perhaps like Thomas they might turn away from the traditional faith of their childhood toward something else. Whatever they decide about God and the universe, their life force will not die because it is not the nature of this force to die.

Thomas does not use biblical echoes in "The Force That Through the Green Fuse Drives the Flower," even though its theme is similar to "And Death Shall Have No Dominion." If the essential message of the former poem is that human life and death are simply part of the natural cycle, then "And Death Shall Have No Dominion" takes this message one step further.

The use of biblical language forces the reader to juxtapose the two systems of belief. "And Death Shall Have No Dominion" is not only an oratory celebrating a pantheistic view—it is also an overt rejection of Christian beliefs.

Cynthia A. Bily

ANDREA DEL SARTO

Author: Robert Browning (1812-1889)
Type of poem: Dramatic monologue
First published: 1855, in *Men and Women*

The Poem

"Andrea del Sarto" is a meandering poem of 267 lines in blank verse, broken unevenly into three stanzas of 243, 23, and 1 line(s). The title identifies the subject of the poem, Andrea del Sarto, a distinguished artist of the Florentine School of painting. The poem is written in the first person, the speaker being Andrea, not Robert Browning. Andrea, conversing with his silent wife, Lucrezia, reflects on his life and art, thereby dramatically revealing his moral and aesthetic failure.

The poem begins with Andrea's placative request to Lucrezia to sit with him and not "quarrel any more." The failure of the marriage quickly becomes evident as Andrea acknowledges that her physical presence affords no guarantee of intimacy or rapport. His wife's consent to sit is rewarded with a promise that he will accede to her wishes, permitting Lucrezia's friends to dictate the circumference and price of his art. His most persuasive ploy for the pleasure of her company—even for a few evening hours—is his pledge to "shut the money" from his work in her hand.

As Andrea muses over the state of his life and his art, detailing his experiences and implying his dreams, he becomes an unconscious study in the complexity of failure: an artist possessing an uncommon aptitude for perfection in execution, but lacking the personal character traits to achieve success. Andrea views in all that he has touched—his life, his marriage, and his paintings—a "common greyness." He gropes desultorily for the cause of this diminution of his promise.

He first speculates that his failure is attributable to determinism; an authoritative, controlling god predestines individual accomplishments. Such rationale, however, is too simplistic for the sensitive, intelligent artist. He reflects on his potential. Self-confident, he affirms his innate genius: Unlike others, he does not have to struggle for perfection in line and color; for him, process is facile. Michelangelo has even identified him as a serious Renaissance contender—that is, he would be if he were as motivated and dedicated as the masters are.

Momentarily elated at his recollection and seeking to demonstrate this ability to his wife, Andrea almost presumes to correct a flawed line of a copy of a master painting; belatedly, however, withdrawing his brush from the surface of the painting, he surmises that technique is not the critical factor determining greatness. More significant is the soul of the artist. Ruminating further, Andrea ponders over Lucrezia's influence on his work: If she "had a mind," if she were spiritual rather than carnal, he might have triumphed. Perceptively, he concludes, however, that incentive is not an external, but an internal phenomenon.

Nostalgically, Andrea reflects on his year of prominence, basking in the favor of King Francis I and his royal court. Those golden years had ended abruptly at his decision to return to Italy and Lucrezia (at her request) and his embezzlement of money intrusted to him by the king for art purchases. Now, alienated from that glory, cuckolded—and aware of it—he prostitutes his art to delight Lucrezia and even to pay the debts of her lover.

The dispassionate Andrea seems resigned to the diminished state of his life and art as the second stanza begins. Experiencing guilt over his neglect of his aged, impoverished parents and his betrayal of the king, he purports consolation at "having" Lucrezia. His sense of frustration, however, continues; in one last effort at consolation, he speculates on the afterlife. He will compete successfully with Raphael, Leonardo da Vinci, and Michelangelo in the New Jerusalem. His obsession with Lucrezia and his resignation, however, surface once more: Even in heaven—at his choice—his wife will take precedence, negating any change in his performance.

The extent of Andrea's decadence is further emphasized in the concluding, one-line stanza: The effete husband, with seeming nonchalance, releases his wife to her lover at his casual whistle.

Forms and Devices

The dramatic monologue has become synonymous with Robert Browning's genius, and in "Andrea del Sarto" the poet probes the nature of one human failure. Form follows content, the language being informal as is natural in conversation. In harmony with the dwindling quality of Andrea's life, the tone is subdued, reflecting the passive resignation that feeds Andrea's impotence. In meter, also, the rhythm yields to the emotional tenor of the speaker's reverie, moving from the placid acceptance of the present through a lively reflection on his Fontainebleau years to the wistful contemplation of eternity. His low-pulsed "quietly, quietly the evening through" is interrupted by brief spurts of broken rhythm and faster-paced patterns: "Dream? strive to do, and agonize to do,/ And fail in doing."

The diction is sometimes oblique and indirect, conveying the ambiguity of Andrea's perception of truth. Browning also employs a rhetorical technique of questions and answers to advance the reader through time and provide details of the speaker's past. The questions are not directly responded to, but answers emerge through roundabout discourse: Andrea's "you turn your face, but does it bring your heart" arouses doubt concerning Lucrezia's affection for her husband, but his subsequent bribe—an offer to prostitute his art for her greed—turns the skepticism into a certainty that she is indifferent not only to Andrea but also to art in general.

Browning relies heavily on irony in "Andrea del Sarto." Overall there is a pervasive cosmic irony that Andrea, rarely gifted, lacks the ardor and capability to animate his paintings. Fate, too, seems to deny any personal or professional fulfillment; whatever the extent of his desire or the magnitude of his sacrifice, he falls short. Ironically, too, Andrea's introspection and his matter-of-fact observations about Lucrezia convey truths to the reader that he cannot even surmise. Incongruously, his words are often denied by the reality of his reverie: An assertion of "peace" initiates a return to the inner turmoil attendant to failure.

"A common greyness silvers everything," muses Andrea, thereby opening the monologue to the juxtaposition of two color images, "grey" and "golden," to symbolize mediocrity and transcendence, respectively. The concept of "grey" is expanded metaphorically in "toned down," "autumn in everything," "a twilight piece," and "a settled dusk now," becoming synonymous with Andrea himself. In marked contrast is "golden." Andrea's halcyon days in France were "golden." There he basked in the "golden looks" and wore "golden chains." Lucrezia, too, is included among these transcendent moments, Andrea making reference to her "hair's gold."

Themes and Meanings

"Andrea del Sarto" is a poem about success and failure in life and art, as expressed through the unconscious self-analysis of a sensitive, intelligent artist.

Andrea's mediocrity stresses the truth of a common Browning motif: "A man's reach should exceed his grasp." Unfortunately, such a premise negates success for Andrea (known in history as the "faultless painter"), for he possesses an ability for technique that others "agonize" to reach. Significantly, this excellence comes facilely: "I can do with my pencil what I know,/ What I see, . . ./ Do easily, too . . . perfectly." Yet, as Andrea theorizes, "In this world, who can do a thing will not;/ And who would do it, cannot, I perceive." Therefore, since Andrea is one who "can," he is ineffective.

His plaintive observation that others whose works lack precision "reach many a time a heaven" denied him reveals frustration; however, his very expertise, according to Browning's credo, signifies baseness and superficiality. Andrea's cognizance of his own ennui as, amoebalike, he is indifferent to criticism or praise, is indicative of a paralysis precluding an essential motivation, which would empower transcendence. Andrea should be "reaching that heaven might so replenish him/ Above and through his art."

Inextricably intertwined with the preceding theme is another, focusing on the balance between mind (art) and heart (love). For Andrea, love takes preeminence, and he evaluates all experience by the light in Lucrezia's eyes. In his art, Andrea's efforts are not determined by his own imagination, they are subjugated to the whims of his wife, as he commercializes his art to buy her a "ruff" or pay her lover's gambling debts. Even in France, his ultimate concern was not for self-realization or for meeting the king's expectations, it was for meriting Lucrezia's approval. At Lucrezia's request, he returned to Italy, forfeiting his promising career in France. Even Michelangelo's generous words of recognition serve only to impress his wife rather than arouse joy in his soul. His obsession has corrupted his values and destroyed his reputation. For love he became an embezzler and failed his parents.

Sacrificed, too, for love is Andrea's dignity. Servile, Andrea begs to hold his wife's hand; humiliated, he condones his wife's infidelity. His "moon" has become "everybody's." The epitomy of shamed manhood, he exercises an annoying forbearance as he releases his wife temporarily to the arms of her lover. The extent of

Andrea's demoralization is infinitely destructive, as shown by his final sacrifice: He forgoes his final opportunity for excellence. Even in eternity, he will "choose" Lucrezia and, therefore, deny his soul again. Andrea's unhealthy skewing of his life toward love has upset an essential balance between art and life, resulting in the betrayal of self and extinguishing the light of his soul.

Phyllis J. Scherle

ANGEL

Author: James Merrill (1926-   )
Type of poem: Lyric
First published: 1962, in *Water Street*

The Poem

This short, unrhymed exercise in free verse has the intimacy of a bit of private conversation about it. The poet, seated at his desk at a moment of creative frustration, his poem "thus far clotted, unconnected," notices a tiny angel hovering above his desk. Whether this is a figment of his imagination or a real spiritual intrusion is never made clear, and there are aspects of the description that possess intimations of the natural and the artistic worlds about them. The "whirring" sound leads directly to an association with the hummingbird, and its robes remind one of the colorful plumage of the tiny bird—robes which are described in terms of art, since Jan van Eyck is a fifteenth century Flemish painter whose work was bright and highly colored. There is, however, another association which may come to mind, getting its strength from the pointing finger; it may remind some readers of those small hanging mobiles, usually made of thin metal, painted gold, in which a figure, often an angel, cut out in profile and with arms outstretched, swings around in a circle, responding to air currents.

The tiny figure is pointing out the window with one hand. It is winter, and seemingly a particularly cold day, as evidenced by the smoke from the houses showing sharply in the crystal air and the haste with which people hurry by. The window seems to be in a house by the sea, since the speaker can see the sun's cold rays bouncing on the waves. With the other hand, the angel is pointing at the piano inside the room, upon which lies a copy of Erik Satie's Sarabande No. 1, a work that the speaker has never been able to learn to play well.

The angel's mouth is open, and the speaker imagines that he is poised either to speak or sing. The angel does not do either, but the writer thinks that if the angel were speaking, he would be chiding the writer for wasting his time trying to write when the obvious artistic successes of God and Satie are at hand to be admired. Defensively, the speaker thinks that is was wise of the angel not to have said anything of the kind, since there are arguments that could be made to suggest that neither God nor Satie created perfect works of art. In his chagrin, he also wonders at the presumption of the angel in admiring Satie. What is an angel doing admiring the works of an ordinary man? The angel has said nothing, but the speaker imagines his attitude toward the poem he is trying to write and is determined to show that he is not affected by the angel's presence. He gets back to the work of attempting to clean up the poem and give it some kind of artistic form. The angel, seemingly unimpressed by this show of busyness, unsmilingly shakes its head, making it clear that it does not approve even of the poem as it is printed.

Forms and Devices

Lurking behind this slender, witty lyric is a form that is usually developed into something rather more substantial, but which James Merrill has managed to keep small in this work. It is, in a sense, a "dramatic monologue" in the tradition of Robert Browning, but also reminiscent of the short, problem poems of John Donne. It starts *in medias res*, clearly in the middle of a situation which has developed to a point at which the poem begins. This gives the poem a kind of dramatic immediacy, a feeling of having inadvertently broken into a conversation which has been going on for some time. The reader is not sure of what has gone before, but the poem itself provides sufficient clues to the fact that somehow the speaker, who is a writer, has reached some kind of impediment, and his work is not going well. The angel provides him with the excuse for giving up, with the seemingly unassailable argument that the writer is striving beyond himself, presumptuous in assuming that he can make art; indeed, the argument is made more convincing by the admission by the writer that however much he desires to play the Satie composition, he cannot master it. The formidable counters of creative success used to discourage him are a sophisticated mix of the divine, the natural, and the artistic. God creates all, including the world, even in winter an object of awe. He also creates the angel, who is splendidly dressed in colors that connect him to the angels in the world of art, in the paintings of van Eyck. The angel sets the beauty and power of the spiritual, the natural, and the world of human artistic creation in the works of van Eyck and Satie, against the seeming failure of the speaker's text, thus far turgid and aimless compared with the angel's examples, "whole/ Radiant and willed."

As is the way of the "dramatic monologue," the problem is seemingly impossible of solution, but in the very act of contemplating its difficulties the character in trouble not only faces the difficulties, but learns to understand and confront them, and ultimately to move back into action. In this poem the writer asks himself why he should bother, given the example of past greatness, both spiritual and human. How can he hope to compete? Asking the question helps him to see that creative art is not all done, that both God and Satie have limitations in their respective creations. The poem is a process of understanding, of movement from modest despair through serious confrontation with the problem of choosing between being a cowed consumer of others' creative gifts and deciding to try once more, even in the face of the seeming disdain of the spiritual world. In the end, the writer gets his confidence back and is determined to try again, partly to annoy, if genially, the angel, who clearly thinks the writer incapable of reaching his goal, and partly to reestablish his place as a creator.

Much of the success of this poem depends upon its "smartness," its sophistication, which is not an uncommon element in Merrill's work. He is a writer whose work commonly shows up in the first instance in the pages of *The New Yorker* magazine, which has a reputation for appealing to educated, intelligent, worldly-wise readers. Merrill has wider and deeper ambitions than simply pleasing the intelligentsia, but this poem has a strong aura of cleverness, albeit tenderly expressed. It could be read without recognizing its "dramatic monologue" form, but it is much more effective, intellectually and aesthetically, when that is seen. Certainly the choice of Satie and van Eyck suggest a kind of fastidious aestheticism. Ludwig van Beethoven and Rembrandt van Rijn would have been too obvious, and one suspects too important, too powerful, to conform to Merrill's idea of himself as a second-line artist such as van Eyck and Satie: tasteful, circumscribed and not inclined to grand gestures. Merrill expects you to know what Satie sounds like: art upon art.

Themes and Meanings

"Angel" is a poem about the artistic process and the relation of the artist to the world of art, on the one hand, and the wonders of God's creation, on the other. Lighthearted and wry, it imagines the moment when the work of art is not going well, that moment when the artist is most likely to lose heart and give up, particularly if the overwhelming beauty and power of nature, even in its severest winter garb, is brought to the artist's attention. The temptation to quit is even more powerful when an example of the admired, finished, discrete art form (in this case, the charming Satie Sarabande No. 1) is thrust upon him, particularly since he cannot even play it. Not only is he being mocked as a producer of art, but also as an interpreter thereof.

The angel is an appropriate commentator on the writer's ability to make art, given the theological belief that one of the functions of angels is to sing the praises of God, the greatest Creator and, as such, the first and greatest artist. How can the poet sit there, fussing with his literary chaos, when he is surrounded by the power of God's example of making form out of confusion, and when the angel has pointed out to him the success of Satie, one of God's creatures who has proved his Godlike talents by producing the composition which the artist obviously much admired? If the poet cannot make art, he should give up trying and be content to adore those who can.

Merrill seems to be accepting the not uncommon idea that there is something divine about the artistic act. The angel seems to be denying the writer in the poem this gift, at least for the moment. The poem might be read, if not too exclusively or dogmatically, as a metaphor for the split personality of the artist, part human, part spiritual; the angel might stand for the artistic part of his own personality, discouraged by the failure to get the lines of poetry right, urging the writer to give up the attempt as presumptuous in the face of God's obvious creative force, on the one hand, and Satie's creative success on the human level, on the other. It is perhaps helpful to remember that this poem was originally called "Another Angel," which seems to suggest that this is not the first time the author has had this experience of artistic failure.

The poet, however, has the last laugh. The poem may be about not being able to write a poem, and how the artist's failure is deepened by lost confidence and by confrontation with creations, artistic, human, and spiritual that suggest his efforts are not only futile, as in his attempt at piano playing, but inconsistent with his real role as a consumer of art rather than a producer. He rejects that argument, however, despite the continuing disdain of the angel. What is more to the point is the "fact" of the poem on the page. In the very act of rejecting the angel's hints and getting back to work on his inchoate lines, confused and aimless as they are, he creates the poem "Angel" which is, cheekily, about the very experience of being assailed by the suggestion of his unworthiness as an artist. He proves the contrary in making the aesthetic object, the poem, in the very act of fighting for the right to do so.

Charles Pullen

THE ANGELS

Author: Rainer Maria Rilke (1875-1926)
Type of poem: Lyric
First published: 1906, as "Die Engel," in *Das Buch der Bilder,* second edition;
  collected in *Translations from the Poetry of Rainer Maria Rilke*, 1962

The Poem
  "The Angels" is a three-stanza poem of thirteen lines. In the original German
version, the rhyme scheme, *abab, cdcd, efeef,* nearly resembles that of an irregular
sonnet. The English translation does not seek to reproduce that rhyme scheme (with
the exception of the "seam" and "dream" rhyme at the end of lines 2 and 4), but it
does accurately reproduce Rainer Maria Rilke's use of alliteration in the second line
of each stanza, a use of alliteration that underlines poetically strategic images of the
nature and function of angels as Rilke conceives them to be. The poem is a reflection
on the nature of angels. One might well expect an emphasis on visual representation
and detail in a collection of poems whose German title translates into English as the
book of images or the book of pictures. In the poem "The Angels," the emphasis is
not on a visual image but rather on a mode of feeling and perceiving: Rilke's meditation here is on that which has not been seen.
  Rilke's lyricism has resonance with European Romantic poetry—that of John
Keats, Friedrich Hölderlin, William Wordsworth, and Novalis in particular. Unlike
in the typical Romantic lyric poem, however, where the poet speaking in the first
person focuses upon nature to present or resolve a problem, in Rilke's poem the
Romantic "I" of the poet gives way to the disembodied third-person speaker whose
observations on angels are filtered through his own modern and wounded sensitivity.
The details the speaking voice of the poet provides are unsettling because they suggest that angels with their "weary mouths" and their "yearning (as toward sin)"
participate in the same cosmic melodrama as mankind, even if their existence is on
a higher plane of reality.
  In the poem, the angels do no heroic deeds. They are silent statues or decorations
"in God's gardens," monuments without monumentality. There is little suggestion
of power, authority, or joy on the part of these creatures who are traditionally depicted as superior to man and next to God in the hierarchy of being. Indeed, these
twentieth century angels are lacking in the grandeur usually encountered in literature and the visual arts when angels are represented. Rilke's presentation will not
allow any traditional exaltation of their unique individual status, since he tells us
that they "Almost . . . are all alike."
  Rather than denying the existence of God, angels, or spiritual reality, Rilke rein-
terprets these concepts for his own age and that devastating reinterpretation reveals
the spiritual desolation of the individual in the modern age, in which the sensitive
human being seeks to make relevant received structures of value and belief. The
angels and, by implication, man, have been created by divinity as carefully wrought

works of art, but that creation appears to be surrounded in mystery. There is in Rilke's poem no hint of transcendence, of a special fate or bliss for God's creations.

Forms and Devices

There is an extraordinary tension in Rilke's poetry arising from the nature of the charged imagery that he employs. In his representation of the angels, he alternates between what appear to be realistic details and metaphysical details. The first line of the poem attributes physically, "mouths," to angels, and their souls are declared to be "without seam." The utilization of the words "mouths" and "seam" with their respective suggestions of the human and a physical division or demarcation contrasts with the word "soul," which, by definition is nonmaterial. These angelic beings reveal themselves to be the poet's attempt at interpretation of a dimly perceived spiritual concept rather than direct physical description. In this poem, *Sehnsucht* or "yearning" implies a passionate and unquiet desire on the part of the angels, and the defective nature of this desire is confirmed by the fact that it is directed toward "sin." This desire arises in the dreams of the angels as if to intimate that perfect beings (even God the Creator seems strangely cold and distant from his creations, the angels) do not exist in any sphere. In spite of the notion of otherness that angelic beings ordinarily suggest, these flawed creatures constitute a link with another creation, the flawed, spiritual/physical human species.

In representing and informing his own concept of angels, Rilke appears to be speaking about them, but in reality his discourse points to the complexity of his own interior life; he is actually revealing more about the quality of spiritual energies and anxieties that animate the poem. The poem provides few specific details about the angels' appearance. One might venture to say that these are not physical, but symbolic details.

The silent angels, compared to "intervals" in God's "might and melody," raise more questions than they answer. How are they like intervals? Intervals are the spaces that mark off one thing from another or that differentiate one segment from another of the same entity. The interval, as such, has no substance and can only be conceptualized and recognized in view of its relation to what it differentiates. The "bright souls" and "wings" point to a sphere associated with divinity, with God, yet the angels' "weary mouths" and "yearning" point back to the finite, physical world. One sees that structurally the angels differentiate the realms of the divine and the human. If they are intervals, gaps that mark off while they indicate God's power and harmony ("might and melody"), then in the poem they ultimately have no substance, and one might say that within this poetic frame of reference their position between God and man in no way enables them to function as intermediaries. In this poetic universe, God does not speak to or with his creations.

Themes and Meanings

In the twentieth century, such diverse poets as Wallace Stevens in America, Diego Valeri in Italy, and Dannie Abse in England, to name only a few, have utilized the figure of the angel in their poetry as a way of drawing together into one symbol their concerns about the nature and quality of the spiritual dimension of human life. In Rilke's "The Angels," this concern with the spiritual should not be seen as the conventionally religious concern of the orthodox believer, as Rilke had rejected, largely in reaction to his mother's superficial and narrow Catholicism, Christianity and its belief system. Precisely because Rilke's poetry is so committed to the sensuous aspects of nature, precisely because in much of his major poetry Rilke reveals the painter's eye for the contours and depths of physical reality, one comes to understand the spiritual as not opposed to or beyond the real, but as the usually unperceived extension of the real. "The Angels" seeks to explore, even illuminate, the basic texture of the spiritual dimension of human existence as the poet's vision of the angels tells of what the impoverished, post-Romantic imagination can still see even after the historical loss of traditional religious belief. These Rilkean angels are not the angels of Judeo-Christian tradition, but instead, complex symbols of the difficult relationships of the human to the divine when divinity itself is conceived of by the poet as an essentially aesthetic and moral ideal of power and harmony ("might and melody").

It is to this ideal of divinity that the poet implicitly compares himself in "The Angels." God is presented as an artist, a sculptor who through his own dispensations and actions gives life and meaning (though that meaning is difficult to discern, since it is hidden in the mystery of "the pages/ in the dark book of first beginning") to his creations. The poet as creator brings into existence his own poem; like God's control over His angels to the point of reducing them to mute and static figures in his garden, the poet's control of the figures of his poem seems all but absolute. It is for the poet to decide whether the poem will come into being — that is to say, whether he will exercise his power to create and impose unity and harmony on his creation. This notion of the absolute quality of the power of God and of the poet is called into question by the poem itself. Just as the angels, in spite of their "bright souls," manifest their inclination for "sin," thus revealing their defective or flawed nature, so does the poem reveal its technically flawed nature through the highly irregular structure of the last stanza, a five-line stanza that destroys any hope of structural symmetry or harmony. The five lines disrupt the symmetry of the previous two four-line stanzas; by the choice of five rather than six lines the technical or formal perfection of the fourteen line sonnet is forbidden.

Ray Fleming

ANGLE OF GEESE

Author: N. Scott Momaday (1934-   )
Type of poem: Elegy
First published: 1968; collected in *Angle of Geese and Other Poems*, 1974

The Poem

"Angle of Geese" is an elegy in six four-line stanzas. The poem presents an initial obscurity to the reader, for the subject and occasion are not immediately clear. The author evidently recognized the reader's potential difficulty; according to Matthias Schubnell, N. Scott Momaday wrote to his friend and mentor, Yvor Winters, that he proposed adding an epigraph to the poem: "For a friend on the death of his child."

In fact, the poem alludes to two separate incidents in the author's life. The first three stanzas express a plural "we": The occasion is the death of a child, and the speaker defines an intimate sympathy with the grieving parents in voicing the impossibility of finding words that "we" may find adequate to this moment. Words are not adequate; they are only superficial decoration for such a profound and inexplicable event as the death of a firstborn child. Custom and manners provide both a means and a barrier to the expression of feelings. The speaker feels almost able to comprehend the parents' grief; he attempts to sound the depth of their loss but is hard put to achieve any reconciliation to it.

The last three stanzas move to an earlier event in Momaday's life, the recollection of a hunt for wild geese. On that occasion, as the poet wrote about it elsewhere, he witnessed the calm but alert wariness of geese resting on water, then the rushing chaos as, at the first gunshot, they ascended from the water, and then the sudden, astonishing beauty of their flying formation. One goose had been hit, and the young man held it as it died. It is this event that is recollected in the elegy for his friend's child. The ancestral goose recalls the clan emblems that related the tribal peoples of America to their history and to the natural world; the great size of the goose also indicates that it is both real physical animal and spiritual ancestor from the early days of creation. The wedge formation of geese in the sky represents visually the intersection of time and eternity that is death. The speaker remembers that the goose fell awkwardly out of the sky, disrupting the perfect symmetry of the flying wedge of vibrantly alive animals. The animal died calmly, perturbed by neither expectation nor emotion; it was a full participant in its own being even in the act of dying. Its gaze lay fixed on the distant flock with neither longing nor regret until its end.

Forms and Devices

"Angle of Geese" is written in syllabic meter: The first and third lines of each stanza are each of five syllables, the second and fourth of seven syllables; there is no fixed pattern of accent (in contrast to metrical verse, in which a pattern of feet composed of stressed and unstressed syllables prevails). Syllabic verse is a favorite form of the author, and it is one that subdues the verse of a poem to a more proselike uncertainty of rhythm.

Further deemphasizing the verse form is the subtlety of the rhyme. The first and third lines of each stanza rhyme, but the second and fourth do not, reversing the more common pattern of the four-line stanza in English verse. The third stanza does suggest an off-rhyme in the second and fourth lines ending with "loss" and "repose," respectively, which is echoed in turn by the ending of the fourth line of the next stanza with "goose." The use of such near rhyme is characteristic of the poetry of Emily Dickinson, whom Momaday greatly admires, and who also wrote very movingly on the subject of the fundamental enigma of death. These suggestions of closing rhyme, however, remain tenuous and extremely subtle. The lack of rhyme to end each stanza correlates with the acknowledged inability of the speaker to come to any definitive statement of the meaning of so profound an event as death. The rhyme scheme supports the lack of closure, the ambiguity, that the speaker feels.

Other sound qualities in the poem are also extremely subtle. An example is the judicious use of alliteration. The device is notable in the first three stanzas. Stanza 2 contains six words that alliterate on the letter *m*, including "more" at the end of the second line, which is repeated immediately at the beginning of the third; the sound echoes again in the following stanza in "almost" and "mind," bridging the transition from the plural "we" to singular "I" as the speaker gropes for the "mere margin" of rest or acceptance of the event. One could speculate on the effect of this nasal consonant as a humming or murmuring sound appropriate to the muted emotions and desire to comfort that is expressed in the poem. The second half of the poem does not show sustained repetition of consonant alliteration, but subtle paired words: "so" and "symmetry" in the fifth stanza; in the sixth, "hope" and "hurt" in the first line, followed by "held" in the second; and "dark" and "distant" in the last line.

"Angle of Geese" is an example of the plain style identified in the work of Renaissance poets such as Ben Jonson and continuing through the tradition of English poetry down to twentieth century exemplars such as Louise Bogan and Thom Gunn. The style is characterized by controlled emotion—which may nevertheless be extremely intense—by precision of diction, and by little or no rhetorical ornamentation. Momaday even announces plain style as most appropriate to his subject in the first lines of the poem, which question the propriety or adequacy of language to "adorn" an event so profound as death. In keeping with this philosophy, the poet uses precise but measured language: Indeed, the term "measure" appears, as the speaker acknowledges the impossibility of determining the extent of such a loss. There is one brief exclamation, but that refers to the precisely ordered formation, the "symmetry," of the flying wedge of geese. The poem's only outright metaphor is the brief simile comparing the angle of the geese in flight as they disappear into the sky with the meeting of time and eternity that is death.

Themes and Meanings

In developing its themes relating to death, grief, and loss, "Angle of Geese" departs in significant ways from some traditional aspects of the elegy. In general, elegiac poems express the movement of a speaker through a process of grieving that comprises several phases. A typical formal elegy, including such famous examples as John Milton's "Lycidas" or Ben Jonson's "On My First Son," contains certain elements: an exposition of the loss, explaining who has died, and an expression of deep feeling—sorrow often mixed with outrage at the injustice and inexplicability of the particular loss. The elegist then typically introduces some philosophical statement regarding death: a universal principle that rationalizes death or endows it with some positive quality. Finally, the elegist will apply the universal principle to his or her individual situation and come to some reconciliation or at least resignation by placing the individual loss in a context of larger meaning. Sometimes hope or resolve for the future is expressed. Not all elegies contain all these steps, but at least some of them are characteristic of elegiac poetry.

Momaday, rather than moving discursively through the elegiac form, depends on the juxtaposition of the two events—the death of the child, and the remembered goose hunt—to imply by association the relationship of the individual death to the universal fact of death. The child's death remains beyond rational thought and language, an enigma and profoundly disturbing thought for which any attempt at explanation would be an impertinence. The death of the goose, on the other hand, is accepted as part of life (the hunt which killed the goose is suppressed in the poem, and the goose seems to fall spontaneously from the sky before the awed gaze of uninvolved watchers); the animal struggles neither for life nor against death, but remains a detached yet fully conscious participant in the cycle of nature.

Yet the poet makes no explicit connection between the natural cycle of life and death, as recognized in the memory of the animal's death, and the specific loss of the child. The two events are juxtaposed, and any connection between them must be left for the reader to infer. Such an inference might be made following the characterization of the goose as the "ancestral" goose. The term suggests the continuity between the human and natural world that Momaday finds is characteristic of Native American philosophies, in which man is part of nature, indivisible from its processes and kin to all its creatures. Such a philosophy finds usable wisdom in nature, transcending the enigma of death and the discontinuity between time and eternity. The suggestion of this continuity as relevant to the occasion of the child's death remains a suggestion, however; the meaning of death remains elusive, undecidable, and open. Hence, "Angle of Geese" lacks the closure of explicit reconciliation to the death being mourned and the addition of a promise or resolution for the future. Death, particular or abstract, remains a profound enigma, though sorrow may be tempered with friendship and sympathy.

Helen Jaskoski

ANIMULA

Author: T. S. Eliot (1888-1965)
Type of poem: Lyric
First published: 1929; collected in *Collected Poems, 1909-1962*, 1963

The Poem

"Animula" is written in irregularly rhyming iambic pentameter, with only one stanza break that separates the last six lines of the piece from the rest—almost as a brief litany. The title may have been suggested by a prayer of Hadrian to his soul, but T. S. Eliot began with his own adaptation of a line in Dante's *Purgatario* XVI, "There comes from his hand, like a wayfarer . . . the simple soul." Dante's "anima" is compared to a seeker of God who is deflected by daily trifles and follies.

Almost like the questing hero described by mythology scholar Joseph Campbell, the anima—or, here, the animula—moves in a world of wonders, now faring forward boldly, now retreating to some safe haven. It enjoys the Christmas tree, the natural world, and stags on a tray—it cannot tell fact from fantasy. The early venturesome innocence of the animula becomes daily more confused by the world of adult control, by perplexity between what "is" and what "seems." Awake and in pain caused by a conflict between desire and control, it seeks escape in dreams, in hiding behind books in a secret spot.

It grows; becoming selfish and misshapen as it learns, it is torn between desire, "the importunity of the blood," and the propriety of "may and may not." It is caught by its shadows and an awareness of death, and its end is in fragments of papers, dust, silence, and last rites.

In the major part of the poem, Eliot has a recollection that is somewhat similar to the one in William Wordsworth's "Ode: Intimations of Immortality" (in which "shades of the prison house surround the growing boy"). Eliot's vision, however, is much more terse and intense in its few words.

The second stanza, a pastiche of images, reflects on certain souls—the unknown Guiterriez and Boudin—symbols of those who "represent different types of cancer, the successful men in technology, the unknown killed in war" (Eliot, quoted in Ethel M. Stephenson's *T. S. Eliot and the Lay Reader*, 1974). No one has identified—probably Eliot intended it thus—the one who made a great fortune or the one who went his own way. Floret may be a symbol of Adonis or Actaeon, slain fertility gods. The two yew trees symbolize both death and resurrection.

The final line, a variation on the Hail Mary, "pray for us sinners now and at the hour of our death," may be seen as a statement of resurrection. "Death is life and life is death" pontificates Sweeney in *Sweeney Agonistes* (1932). The life in death in life imagery appears in many of Eliot's works: *The Waste Land* (1922), "The Hollow Men," and two other Ariel poems, "Journey of the Magi" and "A Song for Simeon."

Forms and Devices

Eliot presents the reader with images of physical things — table legs, toys, playing cards — mingled with feelings — chill, warmth, pleasure, and fear. All figure in the complex world of the small, growing soul.

The opening quoted line is echoed in line 24: "Issues from the hand of time the simple soul." Although God has sent the animula forth, time has perplexed and offended it. Where it was first bold, eager, rejoicing in wind or sunlight, it is now irresolute, selfish, and unable to move forward on its quest or backward to the innocence of fairies and fancy.

Eliot makes effective use of internal, oblique rhymes that are based on the concept of the poem's opening phrase. In the first seven lines, one finds "moving," "rising," and "advancing." These words are balanced, in the long stanza's last five lines, by "fearing," "denying," "leaving," and "living." The result is a sound pattern that suggests the continuity of life. Punctuation also creates emphasis on the movement of the soul. The first period, after "what the servants say," makes the break between childhood and the change of pace, the "heavy burden" which drives the soul to take refuge in second-hand learning. The soul, changed, hesitant amid shadow and specters, lives again only in the silence after "last rites."

The sudden change of tone in the last six lines is startling. One could well ask whether these lines have any connection with the preceding part of the poem. No single interpretation is possible, but the relationship between "living . . . after the viaticum" and "pray for us . . . at the hour of our birth" can be seen as implying continuity.

Eliot's poetry often includes such puzzling, apparently irrelevant references to unidentifiable persons and events; "A Cooking Egg," "Gerontion," and "Sweeney Agonistes," for example, have such inserts. One assumes good reason, yet one cannot find an entirely acceptable explanation. For those who enjoy Eliot, this is one of the persistent delights the poet offers.

Themes and Meanings

It is difficult to pin down exactly what "Animula" is about. It may concern the life quest of a soul, with no impressive ending or glorious triumph. It may be a reminder that life implies death and death, life. Grover Smith declared it to be "Eliot's most pessimistic poem," but it may be a promise of help for the helpless human condition.

The world of this "Animula" is not one of rare excitement, adventure, and challenge. It is the world in which most people live, with moments of joy (a Christmas tree, pleasure in the wind) and much pain and frustration — fear mingled with desire. Eliot may, indeed, be suggesting that peace only comes after death and that the strongest prayers are made "at the hour of our birth." Yet the promise of rebirth (if this is indeed his message) is a promise of something else, of another voyage through life that may be very unlike the one completed.

Taken in company with the other Ariel poems — "Journey of the Magi," "A Song for Simeon," and "Marina" — "Animula" fits into a pattern. The first two reflect on the meaning of Christ's birth, and both end on a note of death in this birth. "Marina" is a triumphant affirmation of life rising out of death. "Animula" may be seen as the bridge from the biblical events to the assurance of a life fully realized in "Marina."

Anna Le Croy

ANNABEL LEE

Author: Edgar Allan Poe (1809-1849)
Type of poem: Narrative
First published: 1849; collected in *The Works of the Late Edgar Allan Poe*, 1850

The Poem

"Annabel Lee" is in some ways a simple ballad—that is, a narrative poem intended to be recited or sung. The first four lines of the six-line first stanza are written in the traditional ballad stanza form. The rhyme scheme is *abab*, the first and third lines have four metrical feet, and the second and fourth lines have three feet. The language, too, is conventional for a ballad. The poem begins: "It was many and many a year ago,/ In a kingdom by the sea." This is the language of fairy tales, of beautiful princesses and their admirers, of great deeds and tragic consequences.

The poem is written in the first person, spoken by a man who was once the lover of "the beautiful Annabel Lee." The story, as it unfolds through six stanzas of six to eight lines each, is a simple one.

When the speaker and Annabel Lee were young ("I was a child and she was a child"), they loved each other passionately "in a kingdom by the sea." There is some evidence that the couple were actually married; at one point the speaker refers to Annabel Lee as his "bride." So great was their love that even the angels, who were "not half so happy in heaven," were envious of it. In their jealousy, the angels sent a chilling wind and killed Annabel Lee.

There are hints that it was not only the angels who disapproved of this courtship. The narrator reveals resentment of Annabel Lee's "highborn kinsmen" who take her away after death. He also takes pains to point out that those who were "older" and "far wiser" than the young couple did not understand the strength of their love. The clear implication is that the speaker was not the social equal of Annabel Lee and that the families did not bless their union.

It seems that the speaker's primary reason for telling his story is not to reminisce and enjoy again for a moment the pleasures of that great love. Instead, his purpose is to accuse those who tried to separate him from his Annabel Lee and to tell them defiantly that their machinations did not work. Although her death occurred "many and many a year ago," their love has not ended. The narrator is still devoted to her, still dreams of her, still feels that their souls are united. He has remained true to her; in fact, he has literally never left her side. He says in the poem's last lines that he spends every night lying next to her in her sepulchre by the sea.

The entire story is told in the words of Annabel Lee's lover, with no omniscient narrator to offer guidance. The reader must decide, then, how to interpret that story. Edgar Allan Poe may have intended this as a romantic tale of young lovers who could not be parted even in death. Perhaps, however, "Annabel Lee" is the demented reflection of a madman.

Forms and Devices

If "Annabel Lee" has become one of Poe's most popular poems, its popularity is probably attributable to its haunting rhythm, its lulling repetition. Like many of Poe's poems—and this is no slight to them—the sound is more significant than the thematic content. The story takes place "in a kingdom by the sea," and Poe takes great pains to capture the sound of the sea in his poem. A wavelike cadence is suggested by the rhymes on the three-foot lines; all the shorter lines in the poem end with the same *e* sound.

The echoing of "sea," "Lee," and "me" throughout the poem is hypnotic. Like the sound of waves in the background, the reader gradually stops being aware of the repetitive sound but is stirred by it on a subconscious level. Internal rhyme also contributes to this wavelike rhythm. In phrases such as "can never dissever" and "chilling and killing," the stressed syllables seem to receive a bit of additional stress because of the rhyme, and the effect is of regular, lulling pulses.

The poet uses the power of his rhythm to particular effect in stanza 5, where he breaks out of the established pattern of alternating three- and four-foot lines. In this stanza, he adds an extra three-foot line: "Of those who were older than we—/ Of many far wiser than we—." The unexpected change in rhythm jars the reader out of a lulled, dreamlike state for a moment, so that the irony of these two lines is not missed.

The hypnotic rhythm operates on another level through the repetition of entire words and phrases. Variations of "in a kingdom by the sea" occur five times in this forty-one-line poem, and the name "Annabel Lee" occurs seven times. Key words appear a surprising number of times in such a short poem; for example, "love" occurs six times in the first two stanzas.

Within individual lines, the repetition is even more striking. Lines such as "But we loved with a love that was more than love" are almost numbing; the reader is not expected to pause over such a line and analyze its logical sense, but simply to experience the accumulation of "love" after "love" and derive meaning (perhaps "sensation" would be more accurate) that way.

The dreamlike feeling of this poem is further enhanced by the poet's use of consonants that do not jar or explode, but rather glide smoothly. The poem is full of *m*, *n*, *l*, and *s* sounds, with very few harsh consonants. The only stressed word beginning with *t*, for example (excluding words beginning with *th*), is the dramatic "tomb" in the last line. The sound of the poem, then, is quiet, rhythmic, hypnotic. It is this haunting sound, not the story itself, that causes most readers to remember "Annabel Lee."

Themes and Meanings

The central question to be faced in interpreting "Annabel Lee" is what the reader is to think of the speaker's enduring love for Annabel Lee. Is he the model of a devoted lover, or is he mentally unbalanced? Based only on the words on the page, it is possible to make a good case for either view, but within the context of Poe's entire body of work, it would seem likely that the reader is dealing with the chilling story of a madman.

As already noted, the poem begins in the traditional form of a ballad. The speaker is calm, his language is straightforward, and his poetic form is tightly controlled. As the first stanza moves into its fifth line, however, the control begins to slip.

Instead of adhering to his ballad stanza form, the poet tacks on two more lines. The content of those lines is surprising, especially on a second reading of the poem. One might expect the speaker to announce his love for the maiden early in the poem as he sets the scene and introduces characters; instead, this speaker tells the reader—rather insistently—that "this maiden she lived with no other thought/ Than to love and be loved by me."

The exaggeration of "no other thought" could be taken merely as conventional rhetoric if the speaker were talking about his own feelings, but to declare that another person adored oneself so fiercely sounds wishful, even desperately so. The paranoia in the second through fifth stanzas is clear. The speaker feels that angels, demons, and kinsmen are all deliberately attempting to keep him from his love. The angels kill her out of malice, and "all men" know it. When Annabel Lee's "highborn kinsmen" come to entomb her dead body—a natural thing to do—all he can see is that they are taking her "away from me."

All this could perhaps be attributed to normal grief at the death of a loved one, were the death a recent one, the wounds fresh. Annabel Lee, however, died "many and many a year ago." One might wonder whether the speaker should be getting over the loss. Again, this instability on the part of the speaker is noticeable only on a second reading. Nothing he says in the first five stanzas is wrong enough to prepare the reader for the gruesome revelation in the sixth: that he in fact spends his nights lying beside Annabel Lee's dead body. Years after her death, she is still his "darling," his "life."

Cynthia A. Bily

ANYONE LIVED IN A PRETTY HOW TOWN

Author: E. E. Cummings (1894-1962)
Type of poem: Narrative
First published: 1940, in *50 Poems*

The Poem

The poem "anyone lived in a pretty how town" is basically a narrative with a strong lyric component—that is to say, it is a ballad. Written in nine variably rhyming quatrain stanzas, it does not show a normative or "running" verse foot, such as the iamb; therefore, the poem is written in podic prosody, a system of accentual verse that is sometimes called "folk meters." It is the prosody in which most nursery rhymes and folk ballads are written, which accounts for its strongly rhythmical quality. Specifically, the lines have four stresses, or are "tetrapodic."

E. E. Cummings was in many ways a sentimental poet, although he hid this sentimentality with all sorts of typographical, grammatic, syntactic, and rhetorical tricks and, sometimes, with a slangy and "wise-guy" level of diction, though that is not the case with this poem. Complicating his essential sentimentality was his rather sarcastic outlook on life: Cummings did not care for what he called "mostpeople," who, it seemed to him, were against culture and art and were too wrapped up in the quotidian—Cummings' "mostpeople" were what H. L. Mencken called the "boob-oisie." Very often this split-mindedness of Cummings led to what might almost be called a schizoid poetry, and no poem more so than "anyone lived in a pretty how town," which tells the story of a person named "anyone" and his lover, "noone" (that is to say "no one"). Anyone lived in a town where "women and men . . ./ cared for" him "not at all." They "sowed" their seeds of negativism in their dull lives. Some of their children guessed that there was someone in town, the woman named "noone," who loved him, yet even the children forgot this as they grew older. Nevertheless, "noone" loved "anyone" so much that his "any was all to her."

As life went along, the townsfolk lived their ordinary lives, "someones married their everyones," the children grew up, and "anyone" and "noone" grew older; "one day anyone died i guess/ (and noone stooped to kiss his face)." Nobody else paid much attention. Eventually "noone" died as well, and "busy folk buried them side by side." Still, life went on; people continued doing what they do in all seasons, beneath the rising and setting sun, moon, and stars, in all weathers.

That is the basic story, but it can also be read in a diametrically opposite way. Take, for example, line 4 of the third stanza, which can be read either as "noone loved him," or as "no one loved him." Stanza 7 might mean "one day anyone died," or "one day anyone died" (anyone at all); and either "noone stooped to kiss his face" or "no one" did. In what way are these two people, anyone and noone, to be distinguished from mostpeople? Are they to be distinguished at all? Are they, perhaps, representative of "someones" and "everyones"? There is a deliberate ambiguity about the story Cummings is telling.

Forms and Devices

From the very first line, the poem's ambiguity is seen to be a purposeful component of the poem, for Cummings uses the technique of hypallage: rearrangement of syntax — word order — in a sentence. "[A]nyone lived in a pretty how town" can be put back into a more normal form easily: "Anyone lived in how pretty a town," or "How anyone lived in a pretty town." He chose neither of these forms because he intended the poem to be ambiguous, and he chose a syntactic form that would imply both constructions, and perhaps others as well — for example, "How pretty a town anyone lived in." The second line continues and reinforces the double sense of the first; it could just as easily be read, "(with so many bells floating up, down)."

Like many ballads, this one has a refrain; in fact, it has more than one. There is a listing of the seasons which appears as line 3 of the first and second stanzas and line 2 of the last stanza. This is an "incremental" refrain, because it is slightly changed each time it appears — the order of the seasons is switched. A second refrain is "sun moon stars rain," which appears as line 4 of stanza 2, the first line of stanza 6, and the last line of the poem. The second time this refrain appears it is incremental, but the third time it reverts to its original order. A third demi-refrain is "Women and men (both little and small)," which appears incrementally one time as the first line of the last stanza, "Women and men (both dong and ding)," a reference to the sounds of the floating bells. A fourth is line 3 of stanza 2, "they sowed their isn't they reaped their same," which reappears in the penultimate line as "reaped their sowing and went their came."

This last refrain illustrates another rhetorical device that Cummings uses throughout the poem, antithesis in parallel constructions: "he sang his didn't he danced his did"; "and down they forgot as up they grew"; "she laughed his joy she cried his grief." These parallel repetitive schemas are mirrored in other lines that do not repeat but give almost the effect of refrains, as in the first line of the fourth stanza, "when by now and tree by leaf," and the first line of the penultimate stanza, "all by all and deep by deep," which continues into the next line, "and more by more." The rest of this stanza is similarly constructed.

All these sonic devices give the poem an extremely lyrical quality even though the rhyme scheme is not exact and at times, the lines do not rhyme. For example, although the poem begins with a rhyming couplet, the next two lines do not chime at all. The next stanza also begins with couplet rhyme, but the following two lines consonate (they off-rhyme). Consonance is often a feature of the anonymous folk ballad; here, it appears in a literary ballad.

The third stanza does the same thing, but the fourth goes back to the pattern of the first — though if one looks closely, one will see that the last line ends with the word "her," which light-rhymes with line 3 of stanza 1, "winter." An examination of the poem will disclose many other effects on the sonic level, including assonance ("how town"), alliteration, ("spring," "summer," "sang"), consonantal echo, as in the *m* sounds of stanza 2; both the cross-rhyme of "stir" and "her" and the internal consonance of "bird" and "stir" of stanza 4.

Themes and Meanings

The two major themes of "anyone lived in a pretty how town" are to be found in the first line or, rather, in the implications of the first line. One implication is, "how can anyone live in a pretty town" where nothing much goes on, where people are completely caught up in their everyday lives—where, though everyone is involved with everyone else, mostpeople do not really know or, in fact, care what their neighbors are really like? It is a rhetorical question because, in fact, most people do live in such a town—they are anyone and no one, of no particular significance except to one another on an individual basis. Anyone does mean something to noone, and that is the basic paradox of existence. Human beings—who, after all, are mostpeople—both care and do not care; both love and do not love; are important to one another and are not important at all.

These twin themes comprise thesis and antithesis; they make up a paradox. One theme appears to cancel out the other, but in fact does not: Both themes continue to exist and remain true. Thus, "anyone lived in a pretty how town" encompasses within its brief lyric tale two truths, not one, and these truths exist in tension with each other, each pulling and pushing against the other but remaining in a state of impossible equilibrium, which is the human condition. Humankind simultaneously treats itself with indifference and compassion, with cruelty and kindness, with trust and suspicion, and with many other antitheses one might list, all of which will, paradoxically, be true. E. E. Cummings, in this poem, managed to invent a poetic vehicle which exemplifies and illustrates these opposites, telling a story about mostpeople and individuals that is simultaneously a joyous and a sorrowful song.

Lewis Turco

APOLLO AND MARSYAS

Author: Zbigniew Herbert (1924-   )
Type of poem: Meditation
First published: 1961, as "Apollo: Marsjasz," in *Studium przedmiotu*; collected in
   Selected Poems, 1968

The Poem

"Apollo and Marsyas" is a meditation or reflection on the meaning of an ancient Greek myth. According to the legendary story, Marsyas, a satyr—part man, part animal—challenges the god Apollo to a musical contest. For a mortal to challenge a deity is always dangerous. Not only will the god or goddess almost invariably win but, in victory, the deity often takes vengeance on the opponent as well. Apollo does win the competition, and he punishes Marsyas by hanging him from a tree and stripping off his skin.

Risking a contest with Apollo was foolhardy for Marsyas: As a satyr, he ranked far below the gods. Satyrs, imagined as having a human body and the tail, ears, and sometimes legs of an animal, were associated with revelry, lechery, and the god of wine and excess, Dionysus. At the opposite extreme would be Apollo, god of the sun, poetry, music, medicine, and prophecy. Because of Apollo's link with reason, order, balance, and harmony, he would be a natural foe of Marsyas.

Zbigniew Herbert's poem describes the aftermath rather than the contest. In the first stanza, the contest has been decided. In the second stanza, Herbert describes the howling sound that Marsyas, tied to a tree, makes after losing his skin. Herbert interprets the howling as Marsyas' real music. In this poem, the contest has not ended but has only begun.

In the third stanza, Apollo is disgusted by the sound, which he hears while cleaning his musical instrument. Always self-controlled, Apollo has not been carried away emotionally by his victory but takes time to prepare his instrument for its next use. Removed from the painful aspects of life, Apollo's response is an involuntary "shudder."

The following stanza shows that Apollo's reaction is not the proper one. Apollo wrongly thinks that the howl of Marsyas is "monotonous," consisting only of one note, the vowel "Aaa." By challenging Apollo's judgment, Herbert is being not only audacious but also ironic. In the contest, Apollo's music represents "absolute ear," perfect pitch, but this is overruled by the poet: What seems to be true turns out to be otherwise. In the sixth stanza, the howl expresses the different parts of Marsyas' body. Herbert describes them as elements of nature: "mountains," "ravines," "forests," and "hillocks." The bones have become "wintry wind." Joining this "chorus" is Marsyas' "backbone," suspended in mid-air, deepening the sound and adding "rust."

In the ninth stanza, Apollo leaves, walking along the path of a formal garden. Perhaps sarcastically, he imagines that the sounds emitted by Marsyas may some day become a "new kind/ of art," perhaps "concrete." Apollo's smug departure is interrupted suddenly when a dead nightingale lands "at his feet." Startled, Apollo looks again at his defeated rival. To Apollo's surprise, the "hair" of the tree from which Marsyas is hanging has been transformed and is now "white/ completely."

Forms and Devices

Herbert's poem is based on allusion, an abbreviated reference to a historical or literary person, place, or event. The title and first two stanzas of the poem allude to the famous musical contest and to the loser's punishment. The poet assumes that the myth is sufficiently familiar so that the reader can supply the missing details. Herbert also assumes that the reader will know the qualities with which Apollo is associated. Apollo's link with reason, order, and harmony explains his "shudder" of disgust at the howl. Herbert also merely suggests Marsyas' identity as a satyr. Other than the detail of Marsyas' "tall ears" in the second stanza, Herbert treats Marsyas as a person.

"Apollo and Marsyas" does not have the formal appearance of a traditional poem. As in the original Polish, the stanzas of the poem vary considerably in length and the number of words in each line varies from one to several. In addition, only the first word of the poem, the two proper names, and the letter *A* are capitalized. Adding to the untraditional look of the poem is the almost complete absence of punctuation. The form and style of the poem announce that Herbert's treatment of the legend will be modern.

Until the sixth stanza, Herbert is sparing in his use of poetic devices. For example, few metaphors are used early in the poem. In the fifth stanza, however, Herbert departs from this straightforward style. Highly original metaphors describe the inner body of Marsyas as natural terrain. "Aliment," the alimentary system of organs for digesting food, such as the intestines, is transformed into "ravines," narrow valleys worn by running water. Lungs are compared to "rustling forests," as they are shaped like an inverted tree and the intake of air can make a "rustling" sound.

In the next stanza, the "backbone" of the satyr, the main support of Marsyas' body, is added to the sound. Metaphorically, the backbone represents Marsyas' strength of will. Despite his horrendous punishment, Marsyas remains true to his convictions: He has lost the contest but he has kept his principles.

In the tenth stanza, the nightingale falls at Apollo's feet. Because of the beauty of its song, the nightingale symbolizes romantic love, lyrical poetry, and intense emotion. The bird's death, therefore, is ominous. The blame is the god's for punishing Marsyas, as Apollo's victory has dealt a mortal blow to passion and lyrical poetry.

In the last stanza, the poem ends on a disturbing note. Shaken by the bird's fall, Apollo looks again at Marsyas. The tree's growth has turned white and, like the bird, it is dead. Although Marsyas lives and howls, two natural beings have perished as if in sympathy with the satyr's pain. The poem concludes with this ghastly image, and Apollo must be unsettled in his triumph.

Themes and Meanings

In "Apollo and Marsyas," Herbert departs far from the Greek myth. The poet restates the nature of the competition as one of "absolute ear" (Apollo) versus "immense range" (Marsyas). This parenthetical comment lets the reader know that Herbert sees the rivalry in terms of contrasting views of poetry. Apollo's strength, "absolute ear," indicates that his goals are purity, distance from life, and flawless form. To achieve formal perfection, a poet must restrict the subject matter. In contrast, Marsyas seeks "immense range," scope being more important in his music than purity, as he tries to encompass the wide variety of life. Herbert's sympathy with Marsyas' approach is revealed by the absence of formal symmetry in his poem.

Beginning with the fourth stanza, "Apollo and Marsyas" focuses on Marsyas' pain. The superficial interpretation of the howl is that the sound consists only of one vowel, *a*. As the letter *a* is the first letter of the alphabet, Herbert suggests, great pain may be the basis of human experience. The connection of the letter *a* with Marsyas' backbone supports the idea that pain is fundamental to language and poetry. The reference to "rust" implies the passage of time and links this cry to history. Poetry is one way that humans vent their pain throughout time.

An ambiguity present in the treatment of the vowel is its conflicting association with pleasure. Although Marsyas is in great pain, his sound expresses his body's "inexhaustible wealth." The description of his body includes pleasurable aspects, for example, the "sweet hillocks of muscle." As a satyr, Marsyas is identified with bodily pleasure, especially drinking and sex, in contrast to Apollo, a god distanced from ordinary human pleasures.

Instead of lamenting his skinned body, Marsyas is defiant. Perhaps influenced by Apollo's disgust, Marsyas celebrates the joys of the body at a moment when his suffers enormously. Preparing to depart, Apollo indeed may wonder who is the victor.

The god may also hesitate because of the effect of Marsyas' howl on nature. Herbert describes the deaths of the bird and the tree as brought about by fear. The nightingale lies "petrified" and the tree's "hair" has turned white. According to the Greeks, Apollo was capable of inflicting such terror that even the gods feared him. In punishing Marsyas, Apollo has created dreadful consequences: The bird of poetry and romance has died and a tree has ceased to grow.

Herbert's unusual use of the word "hair" to describe the growing part of the tree links human and natural life. By maiming the satyr, Apollo strikes a blow at the heart of nature itself. Marsyas' association with sensuality and the pleasures of the body indicates that punishing that side of life is not only wrong but also a crime. Sensual life is impure and is associated with animals, but the description of Marsyas' insides shows that the human body is an integral part of the earth. The god of reason and harmony recoils in disgust at the cry of a creature who indulges in pleasure, but Herbert sides with Marsyas, affirming a poetry which is all-inclusive. Herbert argues that the poet should accept and articulate all aspects of human existence, both great joy and rending pain. If the type of poetry represented by Marsyas

loses—poetry filled with the impure essences of sensual life—then the consequences will be serious. To Herbert, poetry cannot be separated from the earth.

Samuel B. Garren

ARCHAIC TORSO OF APOLLO

Author: Rainer Maria Rilke (1875-1926)
Type of poem: Sonnet
First published: 1908, as "Archaïscher Torso Apollos," in *Der neuen Gedichte anderer Teil*; collected in *New Poems (1908): The Other Part*, 1987

The Poem

"Archaic Torso of Apollo" is a sonnet divided into four stanzas, the first two stanzas containing four lines each, the last two containing three each. In the original German, the first two stanzas follow an *abba, cddc* rhyme scheme, while the last two stanzas together follow an *eef, gfg* scheme. In the German version, each line averages ten syllables in length. As is characteristic of the work of Rainer Maria Rilke throughout the two volumes of *New Poems*, the title unambiguously states the poem's subject matter, much as the title of a painted still life might refer the viewer directly to an object depicted therein.

In "Archaic Torso of Apollo," the poet depicts an ancient fragment of a statue of Apollo, the Greek god of the sun, of music, and of poetry. As one finds so often with the classical statuary now confined to museums, only the torso remains—the statue's legs, arms, and head have long been missing, leaving the poet to conjecture how the whole statue once must have looked. In the first line of the poem, the poet begins to describe the torso before him by calling attention to what is now missing. Once the statue had a head from which Apollo's eyes gazed forth brightly, "fabled eyes" about whose power the poet can now only wonder.

Yet the gaze that once must have been present in the statue's eyes, Rilke suggests, still seems to shine from the surface of the torso. This now-absent gaze, in fact, will haunt the entire poem. Its light, "turned down low," shines forth from the torso's breast and turns the curve of the upper thigh into a "smile." Although the statue is only a battered fragment, the now-absent light from the statue's eyes invests the remaining torso with a startling potency. Paradoxically, the very loss of those features which gave the statue of the god a recognizably human form has turned it into something more than human and truly mysterious. Battered by time, the torso has shed its human qualities and come to seem almost godlike, as though it were indeed an expression of natural force. This sense of the torso as something extra-human leads the poet in the third stanza to make what on the surface seems a contradictory comparison between the smooth stone of the statue and a "wild beast's fur."

The poet's perception undergoes its most radical transformation in the final stanza. There the vitality inside the statue seems to burst forth from its battered edges "like a star," and the gaze that the poet had directed toward the statue now seems to return to him from the torso itself. The final line enacts an even more dramatic shift, as the poem moves from description to declaration. The concluding statement, "You must change your life," is as forceful and uncompromising in the original German as it is in the English translation.

Forms and Devices

"Archaic Torso of Apollo" opens the second of the two volumes *New Poems (1907)* and *New Poems (1908): The Other Part*; a sonnet on the same theme, "Früher Apollo" ("Early Apollo"), opens the first. At this stage of his long and complex poetic career, Rilke was concentrating on writing short, intense poems that tended to focus almost exclusively on some particular object. While sometimes the poet focuses on an animal, a place, or, as in this case, an object of art, his aim is always to apprehend the object on its own terms, as something that stands apart fundamentally from his own nature. Often the subjects of the poems seem almost banal (a ball, a sundial, a panther in the zoo, and an apple orchard are some other examples), yet inevitably the poet moves from what might seem an unpromising beginning into increasingly resonant and mysterious depths.

"Archaic Torso of Apollo" contains three instances of metaphor, but much of the real force of the poem comes from Rilke's employment of the rhetorical device known as metonymy. Whereas in metaphor the poet's thought jumps from one level of meaning to another, in metonymy the poet focuses his attention on a small part of an object as a means of communicating his sense of the object as a whole. In this poem the poet's attention moves from the torso's breast to its thigh and genitals to the "shoulder's invisible plunge," yet there is little attempt to forge these perceptions into a rationally coherent unity. The effect resembles that of a cubist painting, in which the painter forces the viewer's perception to shift from one disparate glimpse to the next.

One might even argue that Rilke's use of metonymy is of more than merely technical interest, since fragmentation and the complex interplay between the part and the whole are among the principle themes of the poem. Just as the torso is fragmented, the poet is driven to describe it in a language of fragmented perceptions.

Significantly, too, Rilke begins the poem in the first-person plural ("We") and shifts to the second-person "you" in the course of the poem. By employing "We" in the opening line, Rilke creates a sense of identification between his sensibility and the reader's: Both are regarding the statue together. With both poet and reader standing in common awe of the torso, the shift to "you" in the course of the poem creates the sense that the command imparted at its close comes not from poet to reader but from torso to both. This pronoun shift creates the illusion of directing the reader's attention away from Rilke's response and toward the torso itself, so that the final declaration seems almost completely impersonal.

Themes and Meanings

Apollo was the god of the sun, of music, and of poetry; consequently, he came to be associated with principles of order, rationality, and harmony. Certainly Rilke would have expected his readers to be familiar with these associations, yet, while nothing in the poem explicitly denies them, it is interesting to note that his presentation of the god comes wholly in terms of the torso's immediate visual impact. Other than the "fabled eyes" mentioned in the second line, the poet apparently brings no preconceptions of Apollo to the torso. The message "imparted" by the torso seems to spring solely from the poet's sensuous apprehension of it, and the degree to which Rilke's presentation of Apollo coincides with the attributes traditionally assigned to the god is worth some consideration.

Rilke dedicated *New Poems (1908): The Other Part* "To my great friend August Rodin." In the years preceding the publication of the book, Rilke had served as a secretary at the sculptor's studio in Paris. Before meeting Rodin, Rilke had been chiefly a lyrical poet, writing poems focused primarily on his own inner moods. Unlike a poet, however, a sculptor cannot make his art solely from subjective feelings but must pay close attention to the materials with which he works. Being exposed to Rodin caused Rilke to consider a kind of poetry that dealt with the substantial qualities of things in much the way sculpture does. It follows, then, that in some of these poems Rilke would choose an actual sculpture for a subject.

Sculptors, carpenters, or others whose work involves actively making something recognize the importance of respecting and understanding their materials. For Rilke to explore this principle as a poet, however, especially to the profound degree he explores it in the two volumes of the *New Poems*, was a highly original conception. By making the simple yet fundamental shift of his attention outward to things, Rilke began to realize that the world outside human beings is every bit as interesting and meaningful as the world inside them.

For the sculptor or the carpenter, such attention might be a simple everyday habit, but for the poet of "Archaic Torso of Apollo," such attention leads to the startling and mysterious conclusion that, in looking closely at things, the things one looks at somehow seem able to look back. This realization leads to what might be taken as the torso's own concluding command, open-ended yet definite, for the reader alone to decipher.

Vance Crummett

ARCHER IN THE MARROW
The Applewood Cycles, 1967-1987

Author: Peter Viereck (1916-   )
Type of poem: Epic/lyric
First published: 1987

The Poem

Archer in the Marrow, subtitled *The Applewood Cycles, 1967-1987*, is an epic lyric poem composed of eighteen cycles, a preface, an epilogue, and notes. The preface identifies the speakers, establishes the poem's motifs, and presents an initial "Showdown on Land's End" to establish the conflict or war of contraries that is played out in dramatic fashion throughout the book. The epilogue provides both resolution and direction, a blank canvas that serves as prologue to a new spiral, and there is a lengthy "Appendix: Form in Poetry" that discusses the biology of verse and likens the rhythm of iambic pentameter to the throbbing of the human heart. Strict form in poetry, according to Peter Viereck, is the holy essence of human nature. The section of notes and the "Glossary of Names, Foreign Phrases, Classical, Biblical, and Historical References" were added at the publisher's request.

Peter Viereck's book-length poem serves as a rite of passage into a harmonious world of spheres that includes a rebirth of rhyme. Poetry is likened to human physiology, and this analogy links the matter of the appendix to the cycles of the poem.

The three main speakers of the poem (identified in lowercase letters) are the father, the son, and "you" — the human of today who imagines the voices of the father and the son; the son is both Jesus and Dionysus (the annually hacked mythical vine god is presented as the son's lost half). In addition, there is Eve, who is Mary Magdalene in the first cycle of the poem and Aphrodite in the last. A system of delineation helps determine who is speaking throughout. When the Father speaks, the text is set at the left margin; his voice is additionally indicated by the use of Roman numerals. The son's words are indented and represented by arabic numbers. The words of "you" are set in italics and quotation marks.

The text circles around the choice of whether to make a cross or a liberating arrow from the wood of the tree of knowledge in the Garden of Eden. If man should become more than a thing, determined by things, he must be "self-surpassing" (Viereck's term). According to medieval legend, the wood of the apple tree was used to make the cross upon which Jesus was crucified. The "archer" in the bone marrow symbolizes Viereck's idea that man should use applewood to make a liberating arrow rather than a cross.

The second section of the preface is entitled "Motifs," and Viereck begins it by stating that "Eden's forbidden appletree of knowledge lit man's eyes with consciousness" (page 15). This awakening causes a conflict between man, who wants to be "more than a thing, to expand from dot into circle" and his Father-god, who wants to keep the human toy blank-eyed and robotized. Thus a duel takes place at Land's

End—the beach on which a mutant "rogue" gene, the lungfish, man's forebear, first breathed air—and sets into play the motif of self-surpassing.

The discovery of lungs enables man to invade another realm—the sky—with the weapon known as human song or lyric poetry. The acquisition of this "formcraft" (Viereck's term) is an additional motif. It involves the biology of poetry that is discussed at length in the book's appendix. The blood of the poet is "Rh positive," Viereck says, and in *Archer in the Marrow*, the *Rh* is the twofold *Rh* of rhyme and rhythm. These two factors form the poet's rhapsody—the *rhaps* plus the *ody*—the "ode-stitching" of Viereck's crisscross pattern of verse. The swords of the book's dueling voices, then, are rhythms, not creeds, and the fight is for a living, body-rooted poetic form, instead of dead formalism or contemporary free verse.

The setting, or backdrop motif, of Viereck's drama—though he warns that *Archer in the Marrow* is a poem, not a tract or a play—has a ceiling meat hook and two big canvases set up by father and son. The artwork, like poetry's unparaphrasable uniqueness, is organic and nonverbal. Its pulse can be felt, and Rembrandt van Rijn's *Slaughtered Ox* and Jan and Hubert van Eyck's *Adoration of the Lamb* (one panel of the *Ghent Altarpiece*) set up a series of opposites: Hellenic and Hebraic, Dionysus and Jesus, Aphrodite and Eve, dust and loam, goatfoot and lamb. Only by means of free choice can man effect the reconciliation of these opposites. He must free himself from "the script writer in the sky" and by means of formcraft poach "creativity from its Creator" (page 16).

The final section of the preface begins the "Showdown on Land's End." The wine god, Dionysus, watches, and as modern man, or "you," is about to lose the duel, he is cast into timeless Part Zero.

Part Zero, a frozen realm outside time and space, begins the circling or "cycles." It is composed of Cycle One, "Up"; Cycle Two, "Hacked"; and Cycle Three, "Round"; in which "you" encounters the deaths of Jesus, the nailed son, and Dionysus. Cycle Three humorously juxtaposes Los Angeles and ancient Tarsus as east-west landmarks sway and are reversed in a "smog mirage" (page 40).

Two transitions follow. In the first, the father addresses an offstage "you" and claims that "it's not been easy being God." In the second, Dionysus comments that he is a "word-juggler, shape-juggler, world-juggling god, and quack" (page 54). He explains: "I'm Dionysus (or a wino pretending to be);/ Pan's one of my selves; on the Nile, Osiris another" (page 54). Part Zero dissolves, and man's various cycles follow. "Waltz," a section in a waltzlike 1-2-3 rhythm, measures the imprisoning birth-spawn-death—"dumped, dunked, done"—cycle of man. It contains an amusing counterpoint of dialogue between "you" and the son that makes reference to modern technology and poetry: "The devil was never the snake in the tree," the son says. "He's the snake in computers named 'Apple'" (page 64). Alluding to Emily Dickinson, "you" answers: "*A narrow fellow programmed me/ With gene tapes, Xerox at the bone*" (page 64).

In Cycle Five, the "Bread" cycle, a series of sestets, "you" asks the son as Dionysus to "Help us know deeper meanings," but the time for self-surpassing has not come; man's knowledge of applewood is incomplete. This cycle is set against a backdrop of "gas lights, high hats, and such incongruous pairs as Queen Victoria chatting with Freud and Andrew Carnegie with Marx" (page 71). The time is the late nineteenth century, which gives way to the late twentieth century backdrop in the "Epilogue to the Bread Cycle."

Cycle Six, "Rogue," is cast in the Devonian period of the Paleozoic Era. "You" becomes the lungfish and addresses future selves of 1987. Cycles Seven through Nine — "Salt," "Bells," and "Stain" continue "you's" quest toward self-surpassing as alternate dialogues with father and son and varying poetic forms punctuate the plight of the human toy's attempt to be more than a toy.

Part Two contains a prologue and four additional cycles: Cycle Ten, "Pish"; Eleven, "Eyes"; Twelve, "Book"; and Cycle Thirteen, "Auschwitz." In this latter cycle, "you" and the son argue about Nietzsche, the son's adopted brother, who predicted the slaughter of Jews. Part Three also begins with a prologue to cycles fourteen through eighteen: "Mek," "Core," an epilogue to "Core," "Choose," "Toward," and "Threads." *Mek* is the Hittite word for "power," and in this cycle, modern technology has surpassed Christianity as a significant and meaningful force. The result divides the outdated self and post-modern mechanics; the speaker is a male laboratory boss. In Parts Two and Three, Viereck explains that the father keeps his toys' apple-knowledge blinkered "by luring them to soar beyond that human frailty which is their true strength" (page 16).

"Part Zero Replayed" ends the poem. Opposites are united. The conflicts between the son and his pagan double, Dionysus, between Eve and Aphrodite, and between goatfoot and the lamb are resolved. The son tells "you" at the end of "Part Zero Replayed" that "God only fears one arrow: God's image, made human by Eve./ Now, archer in the marrow, stretch your own birth-cord's bow" (page 196). Wildness is freed. "You" concludes by saying: "Pierced hands . . . bending cross into crossbow./ Look: goatfoot Jesus on the village green" (page 211).

Forms and Devices

Archer in the Marrow embodies Peter Viereck's contention that poetry is inseparable from biology. Functional form is alive and liberating; mechanical or decorative formalism is dead.

The appendix of the book, subtitled "Form in Poetry: Would Jacob Wrestle with a Flabby Angel?" provides an assessment of Viereck's theory of poetic "formcraft." He asks if modern poetry is alive and has a structure, and points out that a metronome cannot feel; it is a mechanical tic. The rhythms of a lyric, however, are "the onomatopoeia of the flesh" (page 215). Life and poetry are organic recurrent vibrations. Viereck asserts that the formal poet marshals words "the way the body organizes its nervous system" (page 216). Enjambments are "synapses," and the thump-THUMP of the heart is the iambic pentameter of rhyme. Such anatomical functions as the "inhale and exhale of breath, systole and diastole of heart, pound and pause of pulse, in and out of coition, ebb and flow of tide" are all iambics (pages 219-220).

Trochees, according to Viereck, are iambics in reverse; dactyls and anapests are iambics with stutter. The Greek word for foot is iamb, the name of the scansion unit. Anatomy, then, is one of the arts, and biology forms a synthesis with poetry. Viereck maintains that rhyme should be extended into new areas of metrical and biological sensation. Poetry should be a rhythm message as well as a word message. While a word message is partly conscious and corresponds to the indicative or imperative in grammar, a rhythm message is partially unaware and is conditional or subjunctive. Poetry needs to concentrate on the nonverbal language of rhythm, which is the noncorporeal origin of form. "Strict form, in the broadest sense of 'form,'" Viereck claims, "may be both creator and product of the entire immortal macrocosm (as well as the microcosmic mortal poem)" (page 223).

Viereck's new form, "crisscross," rhymes the first two syllables of each line with the last syllables of other lines or of the same line. Its intent is to counter a "sloppy neglect of opening syllables and the pompous exaggeration of closing ones" (page 224).

Crisscross rhymes form the prosodic basis of *Archer in the Marrow*, and as poetry is freed from the deadwood, dead-end, formless wildness that is free verse, so is man led to self-surpassing, to a strict wildness in verse that Viereck sees as emancipating and earth-rooted. In the May/June, 1988, issue of *Poets & Writers*, he explains:

> This is why, in our post-modern era, we are witnessing a return, not to the dead mechanical "formalism," which free verse justifiably junked, but to a living, biological, content-expressing form. For if a definition of artistic creativity be demanded . . . then let us define it as expressive form: form for the sake of expressing an imperfection known as humanity.

Form, then, is neither artificial nor outdated. It is holy, a part of human nature. Although many poetic forms are used throughout the book, it is crisscross that liberates. When "you" asks at the end of the poem, "What makes two rival god-lies true for us?" the answer is crisscross—the poem's formcraft and the final appearance of "goatfoot Jesus on the village green" (page 211).

Themes and Meanings

The central theme of Peter Viereck's *Archer in the Marrow* is a crisscross. The first stroke of the crisscross is the biological nature of poetry as heartbeat and pulse, poetic formcraft, and strict wildness. It is the archer in the marrow of human bone who is liberated into making an emancipating arrow of applewood (the symbol of human self-surpassing). The battle fought by and among the father, the son, and the "you" of the poem is the other stroke of the crisscross, which is espoused by Viereck in the book's appendix: the split between form and ethics that resulted when the distinguished literary jury at the Library of Congress awarded Ezra Pound, in 1949, America's highest literary honor—the Bollingen Prize—for his, according to

Viereck, Fascist and racist *The Pisan Cantos* (1948).

Although Poundians claim that *The Pisan Cantos* are meaningless and that their symbolism is obscure, Viereck agrees with Charles Tomlinson's claim in *Poetry and Metamorphosis* (1983) that the main message of *The Pisan Cantos* was "to mourn the fall of Troy, "the Troy of the Axis powers," and to compare to the unheeded warnings of Cassandra his own Radio Rome warnings against "Jewish" Roosevelt's "Jew-Nited States" (*Archer in the Marrow*, page 235).

According to Viereck, in an article entitled "Pound at 100: Weighing the Art and the Evil," published on December 19, 1985, in *The New York Times Book Review*:

> One should never judge art by its politics. But Nazism was not a matter of politics or economics. It was a matter of ethics and of a metaphysics of evil — contagious evil. . . . Unlike politics, evil does fall within the purview of esthetic criticism, for it parches empathy and hence parches the artist's creative imagination.

The "Auschwitz" cycle of the book quotes Frau Cosima Wagner's diary note of 1881 about a theater fire that killed four hundred Jews: *"Richard Wagner makes a drastic joke to the effect that all Jews should be burned at a performance of* Nathan the Wise." The parallels between the Pound controversy and the *Archer in the Marrow* issue of "self-surpassing" are striking.

Pound had been an ardent follower of Benito Mussolini since 1920, and Viereck remembers one broadcast in particular in which Pound approved the massacre of the Eastern European Jews and warned the American Jews that their turn was coming (*The New York Times Book Review*, December 19, 1985). Viereck, a soldier in Italy in 1943, heard the broadcasts and believes that Pound lost, in those radio appeals, his human empathy and creativity. Pound's opinions were evil, but his sinister message became focused on literary politics rather than on the malevolent advocacy of slaughter. This resulted in the revival of propaganda poetry, which works neither as poetry nor as propaganda.

When Viereck publicly disagreed with the Bollingen Prize judges and with those who viewed Pound as a persecuted martyr rather than a Fascist who advocated death and torture, he was told by one critic "not to criticize the Pound-Eliot-Tate establishment, or he would no longer be publishable." Decades after the Bollingen controversy, Viereck continued to affirm that "energy should be mustered on the side of fallible yet self-surpassing humanity — not on the side of inhuman abstractions, bloodily inflicted on human beings for their own good" (page 237). Art should be saved from meddling politicians. Peter Viereck, then, is an archer in the marrow who liberates poetry from formless wildness by means of the invention of crisscross, a biology of rhyme, and who frees art from politics by fashioning an applewood arrow instead of a cross.

Sue Walker

ARIEL

Author: Sylvia Plath (1932-1963)
Type of poem: Lyric
First published: 1965, in *Ariel*

The Poem

On first reading, much of Sylvia Plath's poetry seems chaotic, and there is a sense of demoniacal negativity. Some critics have wondered whether her later poetry did not represent a surrender of reason to the turbulence of the emotions and a distraught, hypersensitive mentality. "Ariel," however, shows clearly the sense of control, order, and choice that characterizes her most mature lyrics. It describes in fragmentary, passionate, and almost hallucinogenic vividness an event in Sylvia Plath's life that occurred when she lost control of her horse, Ariel, and, losing the stirrups, clung to its neck while it ran for two miles at full gallop across an English pastoral landscape.

"Stasis in darkness," the first line, describes the moment when she is mounted on the horse but has not yet emerged from the stables into daylight beneath "substanceless blue" skies. A "tor" is a craggy hill, and together with the berry bushes and furrows of a ploughed field, it depicts the English landscape through which she rides at breakneck speed. The exultation of oneness with the raw power and dynamism of the horse hurtling forward produces the words "God's lioness." Is the lioness the rider, the horse, or—as the next line suggests—both, united in a "Pivot of heels and knees"? Actually, "god's lioness" is a literal translation of the Hebrew word "Ariel" which in Isaiah 29:1-3 and 5-7 is an admiring epithet for Jerusalem, a city both favored and cursed by God.

The third three-line stanza compares the ploughed furrows of the fields through which they ride with the sloping curve of the horse's neck, which the rider must try to grasp or she will fall. Details of the land blur at this speed, leading to quick images that are allusive and suggestive. Each rises for a moment in her vision and experience and disappears as the horse continues on. They pass bushes full of berries; the bushes seem to grab at the flanks of her horse or at her attention with their "hooks." In the next stanza, they are sensed as "black sweet blood mouthfuls."

She is no longer aware of the horse as a separate being but as a pure force that "Hauls me through air." She has become Lady Godiva, a heroine riding naked but for her long hair. Then, characteristic of Plath's style, in the midst of this frenzy of description comes a coldly intellectual observation as she considers her own body from a strange distance: "Dead hands, dead stringencies."

The separation of subject and object that is usual to acts of observation has disappeared by this point in her ride, and she becomes one even with the landscape: "And now I/ Foam to wheat, a glitter of seas." As the pace of the poem and the galloping of the horse pick up speed, wheat fields appear in her field of vision like waves of sea welling up into view. The cry of a child is heard, then the vision becomes a final pure experience of self uniting with sensation as she feels that she and the horse are a single arrow shot into the eye of the sun, dissolving there, as dew dissolves in the morning light.

Forms and Devices

The structure of "Ariel" is strict: ten three-line stanzas and a final single line for closure. The connections between the stanzas are strange, however, and they make it difficult to tell where one image or subject breaks off and another begins. For example, "God's lioness," which begins the second stanza, seems to refer by apposition to the "pour of tor and distances," the end of the first stanza. In the same way, there is frequently a sort of enjambment or connection between the last line of one stanza and the first of the next.

Ordinary similes and metaphors occur, but they are indicated by the slightest signs. "The furrow" is likened to the "brown arc/ Of the neck I cannot catch" by the words "sister to." The berries are compared to mouthfuls of blood by mere juxtaposition. "God's lioness" is both a metaphor and a complex allusion; the single word "Godiva" is yet another simile. The poem is rich with the resonances and figures of speech of traditional lyric. The poetic innovation here is in the supreme brevity with which these poetic figures are invoked. The meter is so brief that a complex image must be communicated in a few telegraphic words.

There is a general sense of rejection, dissolution, and emptiness in "Ariel": "substanceless blue," "Nigger-eye/ Berries," "hooks," "Flakes from my heels," "Dead hands," the verb "Melts." The sun is seen not as a sign of hope and power but as a red eye and a "cauldron."

The rhythm of "Ariel" has been called sexual, because its pace gradually quickens and crescendos to an orgasmic finish. Yet beneath this constant rise of energies is a sense of immense control—Plath's mastery of the changing energies of selfhood in lyric experience. The poet mentions herself again and again, tracking step-by-step the stages of her disappearance into pure sensation. The first-person pronoun establishes a rhythm for this progress in the second half of the poem: "I unpeel," "And now I/ Foam," "And I/ Am the arrow." One could almost say that the first six stanzas are the cause and the last four the effect. In the first six stanzas, she is propelled through a landscape; in the last four, the attention is drawn to the literal "I" of the poem.

"Dead hands, dead stringencies" creates a sudden pause in the headlong movement, and the reader must stop to think what this intellectual expression could mean. Then the beat is taken up again in a new key with the words "And now I/ Foam." In the end one can see that, despite the apparently overwrought intensity of the poem, a balance has been carefully crafted between feeling and observation, creating what Helen Vendler called "the coordination of intelligence and feeling."

Themes and Meanings

"Ariel" in many ways encapsulates the essence of the lyric form—a sense of nowness, of immediate experience which, because it is unconnected with any domestic narrative, captures the sublimity possible in pure sensation. At the same time, it contains the negativity that is an integral part of Sylvia Plath's vision. This sense of darkness, of fatality, was considered by her early critics to be inseparable from the theme of suicide that was explored in her novel *The Bell Jar* (1963) and that attracted her in life as well. Perhaps a more objective way of putting it would be to say that Plath attempted to see the world in a more honest and direct way; stripping sensation of its conventional meanings, she produced a new, dark vision of transcendence. This she expressed in a personal language with its own systems of classical allusions and correspondences. As she said in her 1956 journal: "[I]t is suddenly either all or nothing; either you break the surface shell into the whistling void or you don't. . . . The horror is the sudden folding up and away of the phenomenal world, leaving nothing. Just rags. Human rooks which say: Fraud."

In "Ariel" one can see this folding up of the phenomenal world and the abandoning in stages of conventional meaning; through tribulation, there is a movement to a new transcendence. This idea is expressed in the Hebrew meaning of the name she gave to her horse, "Ariel." This is the word used for Jerusalem when the prophet Isaiah predicts its tribulation—the period when the holy city will be invaded and the temple destroyed. After the time of its terrible trials, it will be purified and will achieve "deliverance in the apocalypse," as Caroline King Barnard has noted.

In the same way, the poet persona clinging to the fleeing horse gradually journeys through tribulation to a triumphant dissolving of the self. She lets fall the clothes of her conventional self-identity: "I unpeel—/ Dead hands, dead stringencies." This strikes a note of feminine rebellion, for that is the most familiar meaning of the Godiva story—the story of a woman who rides naked through a town as an act of protest. Judith Kroll has also pointed out a second meaning for Lady Godiva, which is her identification with the White Goddess, a female lunar deity discussed by Robert Graves in his exploration of Celtic goddesses.

Freed from external views of the feminine, the persona becomes the androgynous elfin essence of freedom, the Shakespearean Ariel from *The Tempest* (1611). That Ariel undergoes trials and then finds freedom, serving the magician Prospero for a period in order to gain final untrammeled liberation. At the same time, this liberation is a death to the old self, which dissolves like dew or disappears, flying like an arrow into the target, the red eye of the sun.

Robin Kornman

THE ARREST OF OSCAR WILDE
AT THE CADOGAN HOTEL

Author: John Betjeman (1906-1984)
Type of poem: Ballad
First published: 1937, in *Continual Dew: A Little Book of Bourgeois Verse*

The Poem

"The Arrest of Oscar Wilde at the Cadogan Hotel" is a mock ballad of nine quatrains. As the title indicates, the narrative recounts the arrest of the Irish writer and aesthete Oscar Wilde on April 6, 1895, on various charges of indecency. Wilde was convicted and jailed for two years.

John Betjeman had developed an early interest in Wilde, his life-style, and his theories of art. At Marlborough school, as a teenager, Betjeman had read of the Wildean theme that there can be no morality in art. Wilde, as spokesman for the aesthetic school (he was the so-called apostle of beauty), voiced views compatible with those of Betjeman, who flaunted his own dilettantism and anti-athletics position while at the University of Oxford.

The circumstances of Wilde's arrest were, for the most part, as Betjeman depicts them in the poem. Betjeman's account echoes particulars from the news accounts of the event. The first two stanzas describe Wilde as he awaits the pending arrest, although he has been forewarned by friends, who had urged him to flee the country. Here at the Cadogan, a place of highest respectability in Sloane Street, Wilde faces the ignominy of arrest, sipping Rhine wine and gazing through lace curtains at the "London skies."

The next four stanzas, reproducing Wilde's dialogue, reveal his immediate needs and concerns and, more important, his mental state. He requests additional wine from his close friend Robert Ross, pleads with Robbie for some understanding of the situation, and acknowledges Robbie's gift of the latest issue of *The Yellow Book*, the periodical of the aesthetic movement.

Furthermore, he voices his displeasure with what he perceives to be cretinlike service by the hotel personnel. He laments that neither of two lambskin coats is here, and orders that his leather suitcase be brought around later. In the seventh stanza, a thumping at the door, accompanied by a murmuring of voices, causes Wilde to complain of such din. Two plainclothes policemen enter. In the next quatrain, one of the policemen asks Wilde to accompany them quietly as they leave the Cadogan for the police station. The poem closes as Wilde rises, puts down *The Yellow Book*, staggers to the staircase, and is helped to the horse-drawn cab outside. He is described as being "terrible-eyed."

Forms and Devices

Typical of the ballad form, much of the action is developed through dialogue. Four stanzas plus one additional line (in parentheses) re-create Wilde's conversation.

One stanza reproduces the policeman's statement of arrest—rendered in a dialect clearly less cultured than Wilde's. The speech of each—in content and manner—is antithetical to that of the other. Wilde exudes social status; the policeman acknowledges and bends to that status as he asks Wilde "tew leave with us quoietly/ For this *is* the Cadogan Hotel."

The effect is reminiscent of Robert Browning's dialectics. Wilde's dialogue reveals a "soul in action" that is at least suggestive of those in Browning's dramatic monologues. Betjeman's poem also calls to mind the sixteenth century broadside ballads. Betjeman demonstrates here, as in so many of his poems, his fascination with particulars—details that capture the essence of a person or the atmosphere of a place. Betjeman's poem, in one sense, is a "period" piece—with its fastidious cataloging of turn-of-the-century details: hock and seltzer, Nottingham lace, *The Yellow Book*, the astrakhan coat, the morocco portmanteau, and a hansom.

Most of these period phrases are voiced by Wilde, however, so the effect may be more to characterize Wilde and his mind-set than to create a period piece. The same holds for the Wildean epigram in the fourth stanza: "Approval of what is approved of/ Is as false as a well-kept vow." Then, too, the subtitle of the collection in which this poem first appeared is "A Little Book of Bourgeois Verse." Its typography was highly stylized, and it had an ornate cover with imitation gilt-clasps.

Two striking details—especially in their stark contrast—are those describing Wilde's eyes. In the opening stanza, Wilde gazes "Through the Nottingham lace of the curtains/ Or was it his bees-winged eyes?" "Bees-winged" refers to the gauzy film that forms on old wine. It is as if his vision is hindered by his consumption of hock and seltzer, or perhaps his awareness is blurred by (or filtered through) aesthetics-tempered lenses. In the closing stanza, as Wilde staggers to the hansom cab, assisted by others, he is described as "terrible-eyed." Is he beginning to see through the haze of his temporal mind-set? Perhaps the description is an implicit answer to the question Wilde addressed to his friend Robert Ross in the third stanza: "Is this the end or beginning?/ How can I understand?"

Betjeman, who was interested in the typography of both the landscape and printing, employs a striking typographical design to heighten the dramatic and abrupt arrival of the police. Wilde's response to the pounding at the door is set in parentheses: "('Oh why must they make such a din?')." The intrusion of the police is boldly stated: "And Two Plain Clothes POLICEMEN came in." In its excess the technique is farcical.

Themes and Meanings

With its mixture of melodrama, farce, and tragedy, the poem projects an ambiguity that implies a moral neutrality. On the one hand, the piece is pure artistic self-indulgence—the work of a clever craftsman parading that cleverness. On the other hand, the poem evokes a sense of poignancy with its carefully crafted realistic detail and vivid depiction of what in all likelihood happened when Wilde was arrested.

That same kind of ambiguity prevails in terms of Betjeman's own attitudes about the aesthetic movement of which Wilde was so central a part. Betjeman wrote the poem while he was at Oxford, where he deliberately and openly cultivated a public profile laden with aestheticism. The poem, however, seems to run counter to that image. Much of his portrait of Wilde in the ballad is ironically negative—basically comic with hints of the absurd. In addition, the portrayals of both Wilde and the policeman border on the stereotypical.

The duality in Betjeman's recounting of Wilde's arrest is reflective of the emotional state of the central figure in the ballad. Warned of the pending arrest, Wilde seems Hamlet-like, torn between flight and standing his ground—fortified both by aesthetic precepts and, maybe, a vision of himself making one more, perhaps final, grand gesture befitting the "apostle of beauty."

The poem in its dialectical playoff between Wilde and the policeman matches two forces: the voice of individuality, even eccentricity, against the voice of civil authority—communal conformity. In another sense, it is the clash of art and the law, the artist and society. Betjeman's use of the palms image in the closing stanza makes a nod toward this point. As Wilde leaves the Cadogan Hotel, he brushes "past the palms on the staircase." The palms are emblematic of the world Wilde is leaving— the artist is being extracted from his aesthetic domain—assisted, indeed, marshalled from it on the arm of societal order.

For all of its farcical, absurd surface, the poem's undercurrent carries within it something hauntingly autobiographical. Betjeman was born into a wealthy family headed by a strong-willed father who wanted his son, an only child, to follow in his footsteps. Betjeman, who heard the call of the muse early in his life, struggled long and determinedly to practice his vocation against the paternally voiced pressures of the commercial world. Among Betjeman's best poems are those defending individuality against the crushing power of conformity.

Glenn Grever

THE ART OF POETRY

Author: Charles Tomlinson (1927-   )
Type of poem: Meditation
First published: 1955, in *The Necklace*

The Poem

Formally, this short poem is free verse, divided into five uneven stanzas. On the surface it seems obscure, a mixture of statements and images without much connection. There is no identifiable speaker, even though there is a mention of "we." The poem begins, not with any statement of subject, but with an assertion that "the mind" "feels bruised."

This sentence mixing abstraction and image, "mind" and "bruised," is followed by an image of light making white holes through black "foliage," succeeded in turn by a line that is both abstraction and image: "Or mist hides everything that is not itself." If the poem seems obscure, however, it nevertheless has a precise meaning. All the assertions and images are Charles Tomlinson's way of talking about poetry, by demonstration rather than mere precept. Even the apparently vague "we" becomes, clearly, "we poets."

The alternation of abstraction and image in these first two lines echoes the structure of the rest of the poem, for the second and third stanzas are a series of statements (one should especially note the statement almost in the center that "Proportions/ Matter"), whereas the last two stanzas are almost purely visual imagery. Still, these images require the reader's mind, as well as the poet's mind, to work. In those last stanzas, "green twilight" has "violet borders," a seemingly meaningless image until one thinks of the actualities of colors as evening comes down. The last four lines, describing butterflies, emphasize their "yellow" and then the colors— "scarlet" and "bronze"—of the flowers they are on. The poem is concerned with the effect of a process as well as with presenting static images.

The title of the poem, "The Art of Poetry," announces its subject matter and, by implication, offers an illustration of that subject matter. That title fits the poem into a long tradition of poems that take poetry itself as their subject, beginning with the *Ars poetica* (c.17 B.C.; *The Art of Poetry*) of the Roman poet Horace and continuing through innumerable treatments by later poets, often using the same title. Tomlinson's poem, despite its brevity, is a development of, as well as a reaction to, Horace and all the followers of Horace.

Horace wrote a long, discursive poem on poetic techniques and subjects; basically, he argues that a poem should be a unity, allowing variety in order to avoid simple uniformity. Horace was much concerned with the practical effect of the poem, holding that a poem should either teach or delight. Indeed, he suggested that it should do both ("he who mixes the useful with the sweet gets every vote"); the poem's pleasing qualities exist, essentially, so that the reader will accept the teaching. At the same moment, he attempted to illustrate his own precepts on how to write a poem. Tomlinson, in a much shorter space and using a different technique, is doing the same.

Forms and Devices

Tomlinson has called himself a phenomenologist; what this means to his poetry is that the concrete actuality of the world is primary. Moreover, he was trained as a painter; one would therefore expect visual images in Tomlinson's poetry, and they are there. He was also greatly influenced by certain modernist American poets such as William Carlos Williams and Wallace Stevens.

Those poets were, in their own right, influenced by the Imagist movement of the first part of the twentieth century, a movement that insisted upon the primacy of the image, especially the visual image. Neither Williams nor Stevens ever held that the image existed only for itself, however; it suggests, always, an intellectual element. As with the late poems of Wallace Stevens, Tomlinson's poems are not static images: His images suggest motion: "the light makes white holes," and "butterflies/ [are] Nervously transferring themselves." Motion is the very sign of the modern world, the world with which the poet must deal.

Tomlinson's lines, as well as whole stanzas, are discursive, not merely imagistic. Even in the discursive statements, however, there is either an image or an implied image. If "the mind feels bruised," the mind itself is somehow material, capable of being hurt. The following two lines, very imagistic, are designed to show what "bruises" the mind—the things of this world that are excessive or unclear. The second and third stanzas of the poem are nearly pure statement, but the following two stanzas of visual imagery respond to those two just as the last two lines of the first stanza respond to its first line. They illustrate the abstraction, giving it body.

The fact that the poem is in free verse is also an illustration of its abstractions; metrical poetry asserts uniformity, but not necessarily unity. Tomlinson's free verse suggests variety, but variety in a whole, emphasizing connections. The poem makes some use of run-on lines, even between the stanzas, as well as employing sentence parallelism, so that the ideas are connected by sound as well as by logic.

The poem's change from a mixture of statement and image through statements to images seems to reject any attempt at unity, but that change actually demonstrates unity. The images of twilight and of yellow butterflies moving from flower to flower are an illustration of how to see the world in order to find the proper proportions.

Moreover, in a traditional poem, the authority of an "I," the poet directly speaking about the craft on which he is an expert, clarifies and reinforces the teaching by identifying the source of the morality. The speaker of Tomlinson's poem, however, is simply an "authorial" voice; the voice speaks of "the mind" and then uses the impersonal "one" and finally "we," but even the "we" is a generalization for poets. Still, and paradoxically, that "authorial" voice, with its almost abstract tone, offers a kind of authority for the poem's implications simply because it is abstract and distant, not limited to some fallible individual.

Themes and Meanings

Every statement and every image in this poem functions directly with all the others. Together they are, despite the appearance to the contrary, a unity as well as a variety, a demonstration of the poem's "teaching" about what a poem should be. The poem is a demonstration that making poetry is a complex, difficult task.

It is not odd that poets should write about poetry itself. Of necessity, they must be concerned with the particulars of their craft. Yet poetry is not only a craft; it is also a way of knowing the world, so the poet is caught up in the questions of how one knows. Tomlinson has said that a poem "is a rite of passage through a terrain which, when we look back over it, has been flashed up into consciousness in a way we should scarcely have foreseen." That is, the poet gains an insight by writing a poem; the reader gains insight by reading the poem. The poem is not static, simply an object to be observed or contemplated with aesthetic delight. It does have an effect upon its audience; Tomlinson here agrees with Horace.

Yet the poem also orders the world around it. Tomlinson connects himself with the Romantic aesthetic, "with roots in Wordsworth and Ruskin," although his Romanticism is much modified by his modernism. The Romantics were concerned with the shaping power of the imagination. The image by itself is nothing "if it is merely that"; that attitude is at the very center of this poem. The poem is not only about what poetry should be, about its function in the world, but is also a poem about the process of creating poetry.

The "mind" that is "bruised" is the creative mind, acted upon by the external world, but also shaping the world. This "mind," in facing the actualities of the world, faces the problems of how to treat those actualities. The question, "how shall one say so," opening the second stanza, is really a question on what the creative process is—how, that is, the poet writes a poem that is true. The answer is given in the two-word sentence that connects the second and third stanzas: "Proportions/ Matter." The mind of the poet must find the balances in the world, but finding those balances is not easy— "It is difficult to get them right." The last two stanzas, then, seemingly pure images, are not only about nature; they also show what the creative mind can and must do with the realities.

L.L. Lee

THE ART OF POETRY

Author: Paul Verlaine (1844-1896)
Type of poem: Lyric
First published: 1882, as "Art poétique"; in *Jadis et naguère*, 1884;
   collected in *Selected Poems*, 1948

The Poem

"The Art of Poetry" is divided into nine quatrains with a rhyme scheme of *abba* (the French *rime embrassée*), though the C. F. MacIntyre translation of the poem has a rhyme scheme of *abab*. Each verse has nine syllables. The title suggests an addition to the venerable tradition begun by the *Ars poetica* (c. 17 B.C.), in which the Latin poet Horace established rules for the writing of poetry. He inspired countless others, notably the English poets of the Renaissance and the seventeenth century Frenchman Nicolas Boileau, to write their own treatises. Paul Verlaine's title is intended both seriously (the poem is, in fact, a guide to poetic composition) and ironically (the poem incites aspiring poets to break the rules).

The poet addresses the reader not as a distant critic does his audience, but as a mentor would address his pupil: In line 5, the reader is addressed as *tu*—the familiar form of "you" in French. In the poem's first stanza, the speaker stresses the importance of music, which is best achieved through uneven rhythm. Verlaine has chosen his own unusual meter well, for the nine-syllable line is uneven or odd (in French, it is "impair," meaning any number not divisible by two), and this gives Verlaine's poetry a light, elusive quality.

In the poem's second stanza, the reader is exhorted to choose his or her words freely, unafraid of mistakes; nothing is better than that "tipsy song/ where the Undefined and Exact combine." "Tipsy" implies the visionary euphoria of unrestrained poetry.

The third stanza extends this vision into a description of the truly poetic, represented by a series of objects, all of which underscore what the fourth stanza calls the shades of colors—never the primary, well-defined colors themselves. Like the music of the poem's beginning, these images suggest a twilight world of free-floating poetry, unfettered by rules: a veiled eye, a bright day "quivering with light," a "confusion of stars."

Stanza 5 marks a return to prescription, with a warning against epigram, harsh wit and laughter, and "all that garlic of vulgar dishes." This gastronomical metaphor reflects the fact that the most refined *haute cuisine* uses bold spices sparingly, if at all. The analogy is clear: Heavy-handed moralizing or content destroys the poetic subtlety of form, that vague, "soluble" quality mentioned in the poem's third line.

Thus far, Verlaine has used all of the senses but the sense of touch, to which he turns with violence in the sixth stanza: "Take Eloquence and wring his neck!" Even rhyme should be kept under watchful eye. Perpetrator of innumerable wrongs, rhyme is the invention of a crazy person or a "deaf child," a worthless bauble.

The poem ends (in stanzas 8 and 9) with an exhortation that returns to the first line: The poet should create music first, and the verse should wing like an amorous soul in flight, or run carefree in the morning wind, smelling of wild herbs. The final verse of the poem is abruptly ironic: "and all the rest is literature." "Literature" is intended pejoratively, to mean stiflingly traditional or academically acceptable poetry, in sharp contrast to the unshackled verse championed by Verlaine.

Forms and Devices

Verlaine's poetry was part of a larger movement in French poetry that occurred in the mid to late nineteenth century. Simply stated, poets increasingly favored oblique, suggestive poetry over the direct expression of events or emotions through clear metaphorical imagery. Musicality became as important as any message the poet might wish to impart, and this emphasis on form became known as "art for art's sake." Thus in "The Art of Poetry," Verlaine concentrates on the poem as an object in itself, not a vessel of meaning imposed from without.

The poem's metaphors continually remind the reader that a poem should be experienced on its own terms. Verlaine suggests such experience with the five senses: hearing ("music," "rhythm," "song," "flute and horn," "laughter"); sight ("the veiled and lovely eye," "Color," "shade"); taste ("garlic of vulgar dishes"); smell ("smelling of wild mint, smelling of thyme"); and touch ("Take Eloquence and wring his neck," "hold Rhyme in check").

Verlaine's poem, however, is not a random series of images. He has his own messages to communicate, and perhaps the most important is his insistence that poetry be suggestive. To avoid being the slave or victim of something else ("Epigram's an assassin! Keep/ away from him, fierce Wit, and vicious/ laughter"), the poem must never state directly, but should instead inhabit an elusive and allusive twilight region; it must have the fleeting beauty of music, or a "veiled and lovely eye." Poetry must never be too clear or well-defined. Verlaine describes his ideal verse variously as "vague in the air and soluble," "quivering," "confusion," "nuance," "dream," "a quick-wing'd thing and light," "a soul in flight," "Happy-go-lucky," running "disheveled . . . where the dawn winds lure."

Although the poet bemoans the "wrongs of Rhyme," his own "The Art of Poetry" is extremely regular in structure. While somewhat rare, the nine-syllable line has a long history in France, and the quatrain is the most common stanza form in French poetry. It is important, then, to note that Verlaine does not condemn rhyme outright, but qualifies that it sounds "hollow and false when filed." Verlaine simply condemns a regularity that, at its worst, approaches the mechanical.

The choice of nine stanzas further underscores the poet's ambivalence toward poetic structure. On the one hand, it reinforces the unevenness of his own verses recommended in the poem's second line: "a rhythm uneven is best." On the other hand, a certain typically French symmetry is sustained by the nine stanzas of nine-syllable verses.

The poem's final words do not resolve its paradoxical treatment of poetic form, but instead seal it permanently in irony: "and all the rest is literature." "Literature" here means the great tradition of French poetry, and Verlaine no doubt had in mind the predictable cadences of the twelve-syllable Alexandrine that dominated this literature from the seventeenth century to his day.

Themes and Meanings

Verlaine contends that poetry should be musically suggestive, "vague and soluble," not something the reader can separate neatly into formal or thematic topics. As its title suggests, however, the poem remains a manifesto, and has practical advice for the apprentice poet. Yet this is advice that Verlaine himself does not always follow, and both his ambivalence and the poem's imagery reveal him to be a transitional figure in the history of nineteenth century French poetics.

The young Verlaine was associated with the Parnassiens (c. the 1860's), a group of poets who celebrated art for art's sake but who also insisted upon an impassive or objective precision they often compared to sculpture or painting. Clearly, in "The Art of Poetry," Verlaine has abandoned such rigor for the fluidity of the Symbolists (c. the 1880's), of whom he is considered both an influence and an early member. For him there is "nothing more dear than the tipsy song/ where the Undefined and Exact combine." The poem's first line—"De la musique avant toute chose" ("You must have music first of all")—can be translated "music above all," for music displaces the sculptural metaphor so dear to the Parnassiens, to whom Verlaine perhaps alludes in calling rhyme a "trinket for a dime,/ sounding hollow and false when filed." The poet repudiates *la lime* ("the file"), a favorite image of the Parnassiens.

Two poetic tendencies are criticized in "The Art of Poetry": form that is too regular, even monotonous; and a preponderance of content, or moral messages, at the expense of poetic qualities. Although form is given priority over meaning, by form Verlaine means a vague, uneven poetry that suggests "Never the color, always the Shade,/ always the nuance." Traditional form and content are both rejected, for together they create the classical French clarity in which verse is considered the mere garment of an idea that already exists. The clear preference in "The Art of Poetry" for music, shades, nuance, dream, flight, wind, and odor—as opposed to color, epigram, wit, eloquence, rhyme, and literature—indicates why the older Verlaine inspired a generation of French Symbolists to attempt an intangible, ineffable poetry of suggestion. With his consistent use of rhyme, line length, and stanza, however, the poet stops far short of poetic nihilism.

Finally, "The Art of Poetry" teaches a lesson—in spite of itself—that transcends French literary history. It both reveals the difficulty of simultaneously prescribing and following rules for poetic composition. For Verlaine, the task is particularly vexing, for his practical recommendations are all negative. Yet in his very failure to make specific suggestions, the poet has brilliantly made his point, that "Only by shade is the trothal made/ between flute and horn, of dream with dream!"

With fleeting images of liberation expressed in traditional poetic structure, Verlaine creates his own "tipsy song/ where the Undefined and Exact combine."

Dean de la Motte

AS THE DEAD PREY UPON US

Author: Charles Olson (1910-1970)
Type of poem: Elegy
First published: 1957; collected in *The Distances*, 1960

The Poem

As with other poems Charles Olson wrote in the 1950's, "As the Dead Prey Upon Us" is composed in open form using a variety of stanza patterns, from long strophelike paragraphs to short, lumpy passages dense with imagery. Olson's "Projective Verse" essay, published in 1950, sets forth his strategies for writing poetry, which include the use of the typewriter as an instrument for designing how a poem is to be read as well as for picturing the precise patterns in which a poet's ideas form and fuse together into lyric language. Thus, a "projective" poem should be read as an arrangement of language in which the mental processes of conceiving and composing poetry are reenacted. "Closed form," Olson argued in his essay, smoothed away the precise details of thinking in poetry and manufactured a generalizing, abstract mode in which all the details of imaginative articulation are lumped together and given an overriding and uniform rhythm of speech.

"As the Dead Prey Upon Us" begins with the perception that the ghosts who haunt humans represent those parts of people that have not had the chance to live fully. The ghost may signify a repressed or constrained part of someone's personality or an unresolved conflict nagging at the back of the mind. Hence, when the speaker complains that his mother's death continues to haunt him, he begins by observing that the dead are unacknowledged facts of self. One is free of them only when one has confronted each of them and given them their freedom, that is, allowed them to enter consciousness and to find their relation within the rest of one's awareness. These repressed events or memories are "the sleeping ones," and the speaker bids them to awake and thus to "disentangle from the nets of being!"

The poem is divided into two sprawling sequences of unnumbered stanzas, although only the second section bears a Roman numeral, II. Usually, Olson will mark off the segments of discourse in a poem according to a simple pattern. Part 1 of a long lyric sequence sets up the conditions in which a thinking process will ensue, in which a variety of isolated elements taken from different sources in experience, including dreams, are carefully sifted and their internal relations worked out. Once this operation is complete, a second section or part begins with a richer, more figurative proposition that sets out to interpret what the first part has "assembled." The second discourse thus synthesizes, imagines, and philosophically investigates the "formal" construct, a process in which the new form is woven into the context of other knowledge possessed by the poet. An Olson poem is thus the carefully staged reenactment of how the mind works to understand itself when seized by creative activity, such as dreaming.

In this instance, the speaker is aroused by the irritating insistence of a dream he has had of his dead mother. Olson's mother had died five years before, on Christmas day, 1950. Other poems on her death (such as "In Cold Hell, in Thicket") attest both the closeness of his relationship to her and his need to understand her loss. The speaker has awakened and now recounts his dream to himself (and to the reader) in an effort to decipher its twisted plot.

The progression of stanzas introduces the reader to the other features of the dream: a visit to a tire store, where he may have observed the mechanic working under his car while replacing the tires; a vision of his mother surrounded by other dead souls in the living room of his house, where a film projector is showing a film against one of the walls; and in another room, an American Indian woman walks a blue deer around in circles, a deer that speaks in an African-American dialect or like an old woman as it looks for socks or shoes to wear, "now that it was acquiring/ human possibilities." This latter image of the evolving deer generates the discussion on the "nets of being," the laws that govern human identity and set it apart from other orders of nature, animals, and angels. To be human, the speaker notes, is to be limited to the "five hindrances," the five senses of the body from which awareness derives.

Human awareness is a niche in reality that dreaming expands and contradicts. The speaker must try to resolve the differences between what he has dreamed from his unconscious and what he understands as waking awareness, the world perceived by sense and logic. To Olson, the continuum of real human thought should begin with sense and reason and extend into myth and visionary insight. The speaker's dilemma is that he is of two minds that do not connect except here, in this poem, where the reader finds him puzzling out the meaning of a dream in his waking state. The situation is ironic, the perfect representation of the problem of divided nature Olson wishes to resolve.

The self-analysis of the speaker moves quickly through a cascading procession of different stanza shapes; the deeply indented ones are in counterpoint to the stanzas arranged along the left margin. Each time the thought darts inward, the speaker is seized by a new fact taken from memory, or that has flashed from the psychic depths. The passions of the speaker rise as he grapples with his theme of inner division, the spirit-haunted psyche that plagues his dreams and troubles his waking life.

In part 2, the dream state is likened to an underworld of souls lying at the bottom of the mind; hell is interior, a psychological cave within the mind's recesses where spiritual events occur out of the range of conscious attention. This dimension of the dream mind transforms the world of sense into a magic realm of distorted, quick-changing, mysterious properties, most of them made from what was once daily, routine experience, as when the automobile comes alive and mounts the speaker in his dream and then becomes a white chair. The speaker talks freely with the spirits who mill around in his house, a scene reminiscent of Odysseus' descent into the underworld in the *Odyssey* (c. 800 B.C.). The blue deer is an animal soul "becoming" human. Yet, the poem ends as things return to their original identities as mother, son, and a blue deer that "need not trouble either of us."

Forms and Devices

Perhaps the most intriguing device in the poem is the use of the dream itself, both as a second reality and as a level of figurative language whose meanings are not merely fantasy but a dimension of hidden meanings, repressed by some function of consciousness. The poem operates as a vehicle in which this second language of the dream is interpreted into lyric speech. The poem draws language from one side of the intellect into the other, as if from an exotic corner of mental space into that of conscious life. The poem reproduces how lyric language is made: Items from the peripheral, shadowy voices of the unconscious are drawn into an argument in which their significance is revealed and incorporated into the rational structure of the poem.

The elegiac form of the poem uses a string of narrative fragments as the links to be joined, in which the mother's appearance in the dream will be understood. All elegies work by remembering the deceased, but Olson's poem considers the remembering process a therapeutic necessity of the griever. As is often the case with Olson's speakers, his persona here has an investigative attitude toward his situation; he remembers events as if they were clues to a mystery, the solution to which will relieve him of a psychological burden. Things that make no sense at first begin to unfold another world within, as cars turn into beasts, animals talk as they approach human stature, and magical transformations occur at any moment. In essence, everything in the poem has a "soul" and is alive and sentient, capable of expressing its true nature in the dream state.

Themes and Meanings

Although "As the Dead Prey Upon Us" is, on the surface, an elegy in which a son mourns the memory of his deceased mother, it is essentially a poem about the mythological imagination that comes awake in dreams and springs forth in fits of inspiration. The poet who recalls his dream is involved in the act of composing language derived from the mythological depths of his unconscious. Olson spent much of his life defending myth as primal vision, but modern culture has rejected the function of myth and looks now to empirical analysis as the means for grasping the truth of events. Olson's speaker longs to decode the narrative of his dream but gropes blindly among its shimmering clues. His struggle to understand his dream is a portrait of the artist attempting to express his imagination: both face the unconscious with perplexed ignorance of its language.

The difference between what one sees with the "five hindrances" and what one dreams is that in waking, things are separate, scattered, inert, but in dreams, one thing becomes another, each connected by invisible threads that together make up the "nets of being" that is the central image of the poem. The speaker demands that this "sleep" state of mind, the dreaming function, awake and become an active part of his intelligence. His demand is to himself, and by addressing the "souls" directly he attempts to close the gap between the two faculties of his awareness. Happiness is that state in which the dream has entered consciousness and enjoys complete understanding. Hell is the limbo of unlived ideas, the ghosts that long to become part of the living self.

Olson's deep interest in Mayan hieroglyphs—the stylized characters and symbols that adorn their stone pillars, or stelae, and ziggurat-like temples—may also figure in this poem. His interest in Mayan language and art arose from his conviction that their art combined both sides of human intelligence, the mythological and the factual. The great bas-reliefs found at Chichén Itzá, Uxmal, and Palenque depict a human figure surrounded by natural objects, including plants, animals, numbers, and astronomical computations. Such was the richness of the intellectual life of a people who had not divided their mental functions into fantasy and reality, as Western culture had done. The totality of mind included both figurative, imaginative products and sensory experiences, the one nurturing the meaning of the other.

"As the Dead Prey Upon Us" attempts to restore a way of thinking in which the dream communicates to reason, uttering an insightful message about the self through its mythic figures and its magic landscape. That is what the detective persona in the poem attempts to penetrate, as if he were an archaeologist at the site of his own intellect, with its buried treasures and its mystical inscriptions. Olson describes the fullness of Mayan intellectual life in his essay "Human Universe," in which he talks eloquently about the dual role of mind in expressing mythological or dreamlike narratives as well as mathematical and scientific facts about nature. Both are valid acts of thought—each approaches the world from its own perspective—but in the end together they define a "heaven" of continuous vitality underlying nature.

Paul Christensen

THE ASH

Author: William Heyen (1940-　)
Type of poem: Lyric
First published: 1977; collected in *The Ash*, 1978

The Poem

"The Ash" is a lyric poem in eleven stanzas of four lines each. It is written in controlled free verse, with two to four stresses per line. The title refers to a tree—the mountain ash—which becomes a central symbol in the poem (and in the sequence with which it was published). As well as designating flowering nature, however, the name of the tree inevitably carries with it connotations of decay and death.

The poem opens with direct quotation—the complaining voice of the poet's sick friend, whom he is visiting in the hospital. The poem is composed of two interwoven voices, but it is not an actual dialogue. The friend's voice is present tense, immediate. Until the final stanza, the poet's response is past tense, reflective. He is narrating this encounter as if after the fact. The reader never learns what, if anything, he said in response to the ill man's bitterness. Instead, in traditional lyric fashion, the reader overhears the poet's thoughts. In the second stanza, the poet relates simply how a nurse gave the ill friend "lithium and thorazine"—medication used to fight depression. The third stanza gives a vivid picture of the friend in the hospital bed. One again, the reader hears the friend's voice, which runs into the fourth stanza, denouncing the doctors, hospital, and staff.

Repelled, the poet closes his eyes and thinks of "my mountain ash," the tree of the title, which is now (in May) "in white bloom." The poet's reverie of "home" becomes the center of the poem, running through the next four stanzas. The thought of the tree awakens his senses; in a series of intensely physical images, he remembers its "perfume-menstrual smell," and pictures (and seems to hear) the bees "maddened" for its blossoms. This leads him to thoughts of natural decay.

In stanza 9, the poet awakens from his reverie. His attention returns to his immediate surroundings—the hospital room. For the third time, the reader hears directly the voice of the friend, who is now recognizably seriously ill, in spirit as well as body. The poet refers to his friend's remarks as "hate-vapors"; they are a litany of things the friend "hates": books, seasons, children, the dead.

In stanza 11, for the first time, the poet also speaks in present tense (although not aloud—again one "overhears" him). He describes his friend being moved from ward to ward, seemingly without cure, ever closer, it seems, to death. The poem ends neither with the voice of the friend nor with the poet's past-tense narration. Instead of escaping from the scene before him, the poet asks a question: "Where will this end?" What "this" implies is ambiguous: Does he mean the friend's illness, the friend's bitterness, or his own responsibility to confront both of these? The poet's last, tentative statement is one that again removes him from the hospital and returns him in imagination to the outside world, to nature, to the tree.

Forms and Devices

"The Ash" depends for its effect on sharp, sensuous imagery that allows the reader to see the contrasting pictures of the sick friend — "eyes glazed,/ but fists clenched" — and the mountain ash, "in white bloom." There are many images that appeal vividly to the other senses as well: smell, sound, touch, and taste. The sound of the bees is reproduced through the device of onomatopoeia: "humming their hymns of blue flame" actually sounds like bees swarming. This is not an especially "musical" poem in the traditional sense of identifiable rhythmic patterns, but there is a strong controlling voice — the poet's — which occupies the center of the poem with a single grammatical unit running through seven complete stanzas. This long sentence is richly alive with the sounds of the natural world, the "music" of Nature's bloom and decay.

Juxtaposition is the main structuring technique. The probably dying man contrasts with the tree's springtime blooming. The poet's complex voice is opposed to his friend's flat declarations of antipathy, expressed in a diction and syntax as simple as a child's. The poet's intense reverie is set against the ill man's half-conscious state; the shrunken perspective of the hospital room, its "sick-room odors" and "twisted smiles," is balanced by the larger world outside.

The poem works to create the remembered ash as its central symbol, one that somehow combines life and death, flowering and decay, and thereby offers solace to the poet confronted by his friend's illness and negativity. The repeated final image of the circle echoes the description of the ash as "my oval" and seems to symbolize some larger connection to all things in nature, perhaps the hope of another life beyond the body's decay — one that will never end.

Themes and Meanings

"The Ash" is a poem of spiritual affirmation in the face of death. Its underlying theme is the search for transcendence. It presents two points of view on death. The sick friend exemplifies Dylan Thomas' famous injunction to "Rage, rage against the dying of the light." The poet, however, finds balm for the physical and spiritual decay of man not in any specific religious beliefs, but in a vision of the teeming life of nature, which itself is filled with decay and dying. The poem suggests that if, in nature, beauty and decay are inextricable ("blossoms of white filth"), then, for man, despair need not be the only perspective on death. Unlike the friend, the poet refuses to allow the fact of mortality to turn him against life. Against the friend's "hate-vapors," the poet embraces "my own oval of flowering ash." The pain of consciousness, the consciousness of death, is answered by the body's capacity for natural experience. There is at least a hint of possible transcendence in the poet's vision of a larger beauty: "the rainbow glaze of mucous,/ the milky beauty of pond-scum." Such images suggest that physical decay may not be absolute. By imaginatively opening his senses, by immersing himself in the natural rhythms — rather than mentally holding out against them — the poet embraces an identity larger than individual consciousness and seems to discover a body beyond the "sick-room odors." His is, however, a vision that does not deny death. Finally, the image of the circle suggests unity, wholeness, connecting him to his friend's dying—from which, at first, he turned away. Both of them are "circling," but the friend's circle is "lower," closer to the earth. The poet is "outside" this final circling—but, crucially, only "for now." Somehow, he is able, at the end of the poem, to accept even his friend's impoverished spirit, to merge the friend's death with an intimation of his own. The tree becomes the comforting symbol of a realm that includes both of them, containing life and death in a larger whole, the way the friend's bitter resistance is contained within the poet's larger affirmation.

The theme of transcendence intimated in "The Ash" is more fully developed in the sequence of six poems that William Heyen subsequently published under that title. The second poem is "The Ash: Its End," which takes place in June, when the tree has lost its blossoms and is perceived as "almost pure spirit at its end." The next poem, "The Eternal Ash," is set in August, when the tree's "berry clusters/ already tinged orange" are "bending its body/ almost to breaking." Yet the ash is seen as somehow eternal, "its changes mine, delusion," a matter of limited human perception. The fourth poem, "The Flowering Mountain Ash Berry," is a single four-line sentence that takes the cycle further, into the phase of regeneration, by describing the tree's "sperm floating in the air," impregnating earth, the earth itself becoming "one luminous oval seed." The fifth poem, "The Zenith Ash," is a September prayer. The poet explicitly addresses a divine power to which the tree's luminous presence has somehow given access. The tone is urgent: "If I, in human error, lose her,/ even You, my Lord, will curse me." Acknowledging "the slanting cancerous rays/ of autumn sunlight" as divine, the poet sees the ash as a token of divinity, "my ash of praise." The sixth and final poem completes the circle. "The Friend" takes place in winter. We hear again the dying man's bitterness as the poet heard it: "I hate the chairs, the words,/ the winds, the bastards." This time, however, the poet, returning home from a visit to the hospital, has an experience of transcendence: "I stepped/ from my car onto the shocked bone/ of my body, and walked// into the snow-sheathed tree." At the end, he is able to say goodbye to his "dead friend" and even "to love the dead."

Stan Sanvel Rubin

ASHES

Author: Philip Levine (1928-   )
Type of poem: Lyric
First published: 1979, in *Ashes: Poems New and Old*

The Poem

"Ashes" is a free-verse, single-stanza poem that is forty-one lines long. The title points to what a life comes to upon death, and it immediately establishes a mood of fatalism. Ashes are the result of fire, and fire in this poem is a metaphor for life's toil and labor. The poem is written in the first person, and the poet addresses the reader as early as the fourteenth line, telling the reader that "You can howl your name," but the wind will turn it to dust. The direct address links the poet to his reader.

"Ashes" begins at dusk with the poet musing, the classic pose for lyric poetry. Philip Levine sees smoke rising from a field of cotton, from which the workers have already returned several hours earlier. The image of the smoke is the point of departure in the poem—and will become the point of closure as well—as is the bus that passes by the poet and carries the blue-collar laborers home.

While the poet watches the bus pass, he wonders about the workers' fate, the fate of the poor who make their living in the only back-breaking jobs they can get. He wonders about the children who die every day, about the women who curse the very hours of their lives, and about the men who "bow/ to earn our scraps." By saying "our," Levine links himself to the men, suggesting that he, too, in writing the poem, is a laborer, a recorder of their experience, and thus, vicariously at least, experiences their suffering. Yet he only wonders about these people, and in that pose he exposes the differences between the poet and those who inspire him. The answer he provides about their life, which provides the poem's title, is cryptic only in the sense that it is metaphoric: "with fire there is smoke, and after, ashes." That, Levine suggests, is the fate of all people.

Next the poem imagines the darkness coming down for the night, but it is a night representative of all nights. The people go to sleep tired, and when they sleep they dream "of sleep/ without end." That state is fleeting, however, as morning comes in the next line like a blood stain on the sky; the workers are up dressing in clothes that are still warm, though damp, from the day before.

Meanwhile, as the workers head back to the fields, the poet is sleeping. This is a more dramatic difference between them, causing Levine to ask of the reader, "Do you want the earth to be heaven?" The answer given is a call to pray for "all you'll/ never be." Here the poem returns to the imagery of its beginning. In a list of options of what one may never be—"a drop of sea water" or a "small hurtling flame"—is the poem's final image of a "fine flake of dust that moves/ at evening like smoke at great height/ above the earth and sees it all." The image of smoke here represents the vision of the poet as well as the inspiration for poetic vision.

Forms and Devices

Levine has always been attracted to images of fire and smoke, and this poem typifies that interest. His concern, ultimately, is a consideration of living and dying, with which poetry finally must deal. In this sense, the poem's imagery is imbued with an elegiac tone as well as a defiant one.

Levine connects these tones by linking violent and tranquil images—that is to say, he finds an image's internal sense of paradox. For example, fields of cotton are often thought of as a quiet, almost pastoral image. Cotton-picking is hard, back-breaking work, but here the work is made harder because the fields are burning, an image that signifies the life of the laborer. Second, the earth is often thought of as Mother Earth, but it is anything but motherly in this poem. The poet is affected by this contrast. He questions why the earth would let children die and women curse and why it will eat lives the way people "eat/ an apple, meat, skin, core, seeds." He questions why people must tear a living "from the silent earth." The traditional image of the earth as benign and generous has been transformed into an image of affliction and distress.

In addition, Levine finds a paradox in the light. Traditionally, first light is a romantic image, going back to the Greek poet Homer's epithet of "rosy-fingered dawn." Dawn is a beginning, a new start. Yet in "Ashes," the first light "bloodies the sky," and beneath it the cotton-pickers are "bruised by the first hours" of that new sun. These paradoxes have a dramatic effect as they build throughout the poem. Building that kind of energy is a characteristic of Levine's poetry. He gives his images an urgency they might not otherwise have by endowing them with an emotional life: The bus creaks like a tired body; the earth is silent while the people suffer; answers hurt as much as questions; the sun bleeds the way people bleed.

Another device that is effective in this poem is the poet's direct address to the reader. By implication, Levine is suggesting that his readers are like the laborers and like him. All suffer and see suffering. One can "howl" one's name, call attention to oneself in a great burst of sound, but the wind will "blow it into dust." He tells readers that a person could "pledge" a "single life," but the earth "will eat it all."

By addressing readers, he pulls them deeper into his experience. One feels what the poet feels. This is the device for the poem's final movement, the prayer. The poet advises: "go down on your knees/ as though a king stood before you,/ and pray to become all you'll/ never be." One often thinks of hard work as the proper path to take to improve one's lot. Typically, however, Levine suggests that prayer will do as well, because—as the cotton-pickers demonstrate—hard work only begets more hard work.

Themes and Meanings

Readers familiar with Levine's work, his poetry of social protest, will recognize in this poem one of his familiar themes: the endurance and courage of men and women. It is their tenacity that lets them wake from the "dream of sleep/ without end" and return to the fields. It is their tenacity that brings them to his attention and makes him write about their lives.

One of the primary concerns in this poem is that the worker's fate is a life of what could be called "tired bodies" — one is caught in an endless cycle, like riding a bus to and from work, where everyone's face is "wide-eyed with hunger." In this sense, this lyric is not concentrated on an interior vision or revelation, as many lyric poems since the Romantic era have been. Instead, it is a public outcry, a loud "No!" shouted at the sky and at the earth. It presents the poet as someone who may best be described as a seer-activist. Levine is angry. He is angry at the earth in particular, because it burns lives into ashes, and even these ashes are blown away in the wind. He does not express sorrow, however; in another poem, "Red Dust," he writes that he does not "believe in sorrow;/ it is not American." What is American, "Ashes" implies, is work, and the work is never done.

The work of the poet is to see the "meat, skin, core, [and] seeds" of other lives and other suffering. By not feeling sorrowful about the cotton-pickers' lives — though feeling pain for them, empathizing with their general hardship — Levine allows room in his emotional response for something positive. Ironically, he finds in the ashes, at the poem's end, hope. Levine's habit has always been to celebrate the possible. The prayer motif at the end of the poem suggests that prayer cannot hurt. In the least, if the prayer is fulfilled and one does become a "fine flake of dust that moves/ at evening like smoke at great height/ above the earth and sees it all," one will be able to unite with the workers' suffering by also becoming a part of the visionary sky. A more knowing and sensitive aura will perhaps permeate the earth.

Thus, finally, "Ashes" is a poem about burial, but a burial in the sky. The prayer for empathy and vision that concludes the poem circles back to its beginning, to the "last winds of afternoon" that blow the smoke of hardship across the lives of those working on a hostile earth.

David Biespiel

ASTROPHIL AND STELLA

Author: Sir Philip Sidney (1554-1586)
Type of poem: Poetic sequence
First published: 1591

The Poem

Sir Philip Sidney composed *Astrophil and Stella* (Astrophil is sometimes spelled "Astrophel") between 1581 and 1583, most likely in the summer of 1582. A sequence of 108 sonnets and eleven songs, it is an important work in the history of English poetry for several reasons.

As the initial sonnet sequence of any scope in English, it domesticated a form in England that had been perfected in Italy by Francesco Petrarca—best known as Petrarch—in the fourteenth century, and that was later imitated in France and elsewhere in Europe. Earlier English poets had written sonnets but without making any attempt to weave them into a unified work of substantial proportions. The sonnet sequence does not, strictly speaking, tell a story but presents a series of reflections on, or lyrical celebrations of, a single subject. The preferred Renaissance subject was love, especially the love of a man for a woman who, for one reason or another, does not respond to his entreaties.

Second, *Astrophil and Stella*, first published five years after Sidney's death from a war injury in the Netherlands, touched off a vogue of late Elizabethan sonnet writing that climaxed in William Shakespeare's great cycle and thereafter persisted as an important poetic form down into the twentieth century. Sidney's sequence is thus one of the most influential works of poetry in the annals of English literature.

Finally, the work remains one of the best examples of its type. It plumbs the psychology of the lover, Astrophil ("star-lover"), as he contemplates the beautiful Stella ("star"), who marries another man and gives little encouragement to Astrophil because of her need to guard her reputation. Some of the individual sonnets, particularly Sonnet 31, "With how sad steps, O Moon, thou climb'st the skies," have become anthology favorites of readers unfamiliar with the sequence as a whole.

Astrophil and Stella bears tantalizingly autobiographical references to its author, whose first name is included in "Astrophil," as it is spelled by most modern editors and presumably intended by Sidney, and to Penelope Devereux, daughter of the earl and countess of Essex. There is a family connection, for after her husband's death Lady Essex married Sidney's uncle, the earl of Leicester. There is no independent historical confirmation of a love affair between Sidney and Penelope Devereux, but it is difficult to read the sequence carefully without concluding that some sort of affair took place.

Stella is, in a number of respects, the conventional heroine of medieval and Renaissance love poetry, but she boasts, in addition to her blonde hair, fair skin, and rosy cheeks, unconventional black eyes, as did Penelope. In several of the poems, Sidney makes pointed allusions to her "rich" husband—and Penelope married Lord

Rich. In one poem, Astrophil's father is referred to as having subdued Ulster, an obvious parallel to an activity of Sidney's own father, a colonial governor of Ireland. Despite these and other autobiographical details, however, the author often establishes a considerable aesthetic distance between himself and Astrophil, who must be regarded primarily as a character rather than as a mere disguise for Sir Philip Sidney.

The sonnet sequence is not a novel and cannot be thought of as demonstrating a plot; rather, Sidney presents a series of emotional crises, internal—and occasionally external—conflicts, and solitary musings on the course of a love affair that is destined to remain unconsummated. In the first sonnet Astrophil, already smitten by Stella's charms, decides to "show" his love in verse with the hope of winning her favor, but he cannot find the appropriate words until his muse, disgusted with the lover's unavailing efforts to imitate other poets, counsels him in the final line of the poem to "look in thy heart and write."

Soon it occurs to Astrophil that he should be pursuing virtue and not mere earthly beauty, but he continues to concentrate, sometimes defiantly, on the latter, while at other times he justifies his course with logic-chopping mental gymnastics. He vows to revert to virtue, but the mere sight of Stella undermines his resolve. Another problem is Stella's coldness; her heart is a "citadel" against him, presumably because a rival already "enjoys" her. (Although Sidney may have known Penelope Devereux before her marriage, it appears unlikely that there was then any opportunity for intimacy between them.) Astrophil oscillates between regarding Stella as the epitome of virtue and wondering whether her scorn of his suit should be interpreted as mere ungratefulness to a passionately devoted lover.

Stella provokes his poems in a variety of ways. He excels in a tournament (Sonnet 41) because she is looking on, but, in a later one, fails out of preoccupation with her (53). Once he thinks that he has caught her looking lovingly at him (66), and finally he reports that she has given him the "monarchy" of her heart (69)—but conditionally, for he must love her platonically. Because his love has such a relentlessly physical component, however, this concession turns out to be only another form of torture.

Finally Astrophil manages to kiss Stella while she is sleeping (Second Song). This kiss, which turns out to be Astrophil's closest approach to success, he transmutes in his imagination to Stella kissing him—a development that sustains a half-dozen sonnets. There are two sonnets (numbers 83 and 84) celebrating a journey to Stella's house, but then comes a "change of looks" (86), which may be a premonition of Song 8, wherein Stella confesses her love for him but demands that he end his suit for the sake of her honor.

In Sonnet 93 he confesses to having "harmed" Stella in some way, and the seven sonnets following are all lugubrious in tone. In number 101 this mood gives way to concern over a sickness that has sent Stella to bed. She recovers, and the lover makes one more try, serenading her under her window. This poem, the last of the eleven songs, is a dialogue between the lovers that was set to music by Thomas Morley (*The*

First Book of Airs, 1600) and has become the most popular of Sidney's songs; in it, Stella finally dismisses Astrophil unequivocally. After this song, "Who is it that this dark night/ Underneath my window plaineth?" Astrophil composes several abject laments, but his quest has not been entirely in vain for he finds a kind of "joy" in the expression of his "woes."

Forms and Devices

As practiced by the Italians, the sonnet characteristically comprised an eight-line unit, the octave, rhyming *abba, abba*, and a six-line sestet, employing various patterns of *c* and *d*, or *c*, *d*, and *e* rhymes. Usually the beginning of the sestet marked a turning point in the content. For example, the octave might be primarily descriptive, the sestet reflective; or the octave might pose a problem, the sestet move to resolve it. The meter was normally iambic pentameter throughout.

From the first sonnet in Sidney's sequence, he shows a respect for convention and a willingness to depart from it. He begins with a hexameter sonnet, that is, one with an extra poetic foot in each line. Its octave rhymes *abababab*, the cross-rhyming pattern which Henry Howard, earl of Surrey, had introduced earlier in the century. The first half-dozen sonnets exemplify five different rhyme schemes and include a second poem in hexameter. Sidney tends to retain the Italian structure, as the initial words in the sestets of the first few poems— "but," "now," "for"— suggest. Although he is fond of a rhyming couplet at the end, he seldom employs a full stop at the end of the twelfth line, as Shakespeare would soon be doing, and thus does not often turn the couplet into a distinct structural feature of epigrammatic force.

In addition to the variety of his sonnet forms, Sidney achieves a flexibility beyond that of earlier sonnet makers such as Surrey and Sir Thomas Wyatt. He gives the impression of running easily in his sonnet harness and will make his turn at various points, sometimes delaying it, as in Sonnet 1, until the last line, where Astrophil's muse finally dispels his bafflement by urging him to look into his heart, or in Sonnet 71, where, after Astrophil struggles for thirteen lines to love Stella chastely and reasonably, "But ah, Desire still cries, 'give me some food.' " Within the constraints of his meter, Sidney effectively varies caesura, rhythm, and pace to convey a sense of a nimble mind at work and a spirited heart being put through its paces.

The larger structure of *Astrophil and Stella* includes shorter sequences, such as the sonnets on the kiss and the two about the journey to Stella's house already mentioned. There are enough awkward spots, however, to suggest that perhaps the poet did not have the opportunity to finish the sequence completely. Five of the songs, all interpolated between Sonnets 86 and 87, do not consort well together, and one of them, probably written earlier than the other poems, is tonally and thematically unrelated to the others. Nevertheless, as long as the reader does not expect the coherence of a novel, the effect of the whole has the consistency proper to a series of dramatic moments in the life of an intense but frustrated lover.

Sidney's characterization of Astrophil is surely one of his major poetic feats. Both Dante and Petrarch, in their different ways, had presented the character of the lover-from-afar, the complaining lover as a figure predates the sonnet sequence, but previous continental and English imitators of Petrarch had usually produced rather uninteresting complainers. Thomas Wyatt, the first English sonnet maker, did not produce a sequence, but the complaints of the lover in his thirty-two sonnets are, with few exceptions, in the same doleful mood.

Astrophil, of course, has his share of doleful moments also, but Sidney manages to achieve a comic perspective on his lover even while respecting his tribulations. Writing early in the heyday of Elizabethan comedy, Sidney shared in his contemporaries' enthusiasm for the drama and staged a series of dramatic effects in *Astrophil and Stella*. Astrophil is essentially a comic creation, which does not mean that he is trying to be funny, though he often is, or that he makes his way to a happy marriage at the end in the manner of Shakespearean comedy, but Sidney contrives to make his very seriousness amusing in ways varying from high to broad comedy.

It is a tribute to the deftness of Sidney's depiction of Astrophil that some readers can identify with the lover, that is, take him as seriously as he usually takes himself, while others, though remaining generally sympathetic, can smile when he finds his "mouth too tender" for the "hard bit" of virtue, and perhaps laugh outright when he applauds his own poetic achievement: "My lips are sweet, inspired with Stella's kiss." In their absorption with their beloved, with the ups and downs of love, and with themselves, lovers are frequently inconsistent and always potentially comical. Astrophil adds to the usual lover's quirks a grim determination to celebrate his love in verse along with a general inability to determine how his poems can best be produced. Thus he is found in the first sonnet slavishly imitating other poets and in Sonnet 74 swearing "by blackest brook of hell, I am no pick-purse of another's wit."

Sidney appears to have based Astrophil on himself, but in no very long stretch of time after the Penelope Devereux episode he was able to stand back and capture not just the frustration but the humor of the thwarted lover. If Astrophil had merely "been" Sidney, he would have been far less interesting than he is.

Themes and Meanings

Wit is both a quality and a theme of *Astrophil and Stella*. In the 108 sonnets he uses forms of the word forty-two times. (By comparison, Shakespeare uses the words "wit" and "wits" only nine times in 154 sonnets.) The Old English word *witan* meant "to know," and wit had for centuries referred to mental capacities, especially intelligence. Among Renaissance literary men, wit signified one's facility at literary invention, which is the aspiration of Sidney's lover first and last.

Sidney wrote the first important critical treatise in English, *An Apologie for Poetrie* (1595); it was also published as *Defence of Poesie* (1595) and is still known by both titles. It is an eclectic document drawing upon the thought of ancient authorities such as Plato, Aristotle, and Horace and blending in the theories of earlier Renaissance figures such as Julius Caesar Scaliger. Astrophil shares his creator's inclination to harmonize, if possible, the poetical and rhetorical pronouncements of many authorities. Neoclassicists of Sidney's time had metamorphosed Aristotle's mimetic theory into a recommendation to imitate other writers, so Astrophil is to be found, in his first sonnet, "turning others' leaves." While Astrophil is trying to be witty by imitating his predecessors, Sidney is being witty through wordplay: Other poets' "feet" merely get in Astrophil's way.

Sidney's lover has a particular fondness for Horace's famous dictum that poetry should "teach and delight" and his insistence on what came to be called "decorum," the choosing of stylistically apt expression. Astrophil has high hopes that through his verse Stella "might take some pleasure of my pain," and that through this pleasure she might come to "know." He has a difficult time finding the "fit words" that will achieve another Renaissance poetic aim, that of motivating Stella to go beyond just knowing, for "Knowledge might pity win, and pity grace obtain." It is this "moving" effect of poetry, by the way, which looms largest in *An Apologie for Poetrie*.

There is one thing that Astrophil has forgotten in his initial enthusiasm. Poetry is supposed to move men to virtue, and his love for the married Stella is not precisely virtuous, a fact which makes his muse's exhortation to look in his heart all the more dangerous. Thus, the task of wit becomes that of reconciling the claims of love and virtue.

Sonnet 34 is a dialogue with Wit. Astrophil writes "to ease/ A burdened heart." When Wit asks how such reminders of his distress can ease him, he replies that "Oft cruel fights well pictured forth do please." Yet is he not ashamed to "publish" his troubles (it should be noted that the verb does not mean "print"; Sidney published none of his works in that sense)? Astrophil responds that his poetry may win him fame, but Wit counters that wise men will regard it only as famous foolishness. Wise men do not have to listen to what they regard as foolishness, Astrophil points out, only to hear Wit taunt him: "What idler thing than speak and not be heard?" Astrophil must struggle on doubtfully: "with wit my wit is marred."

This poem illustrates a fact about the poet's (or would-be poet's) audience. Many love poems do not address the lady, and for some of them she would make the least appropriate audience. Poets have always written for people who can appreciate poetry rather than mere flattery. The ideal audience is the witty one which, so to speak, looks over Astrophil's shoulder while he is composing. This audience understands better than Stella what to make of the assertion nominally made to her in Sonnet 35, "Wit learns in thee perfection to express," or his insistence in number 64 that she is both his "wit" and his "virtue."

The comic masterpiece of the sequence is Sonnet 74, "I never drank of Aganippe well." Here Astrophil denies all contact with the muses, all claim to the "poets' fury" that a diplomatically propitiated muse might inspire. He is merely a "poor layman" who has not the slightest motivation for stealing from "another's wit." Yet he now claims poetic success. How can that be? After teasing his audience right down to the last line, he explains: "My lips are sweet, inspired with Stella's kiss," an explanation surely no part of any reputable theory of poetic invention. This sonnet, in which Astrophil steps quite out of character, represents one of Sidney's witty changes on the stolen kiss. In Sonnet 81, still dwelling on the famous kiss, Astrophil reveals that Stella wants "higher seated praise" and thus proposes that if she objects to his current variety of kiss-inspired wit, she must "stop" his mouth with more kisses. She will not comply, and in the next sonnet he is "full of desire, empty of wit."

Eventually Astrophil asks Stella to "dismiss" his wit "till it have wrought what thy own will attends" (Sonnet 107). Astrophil remains in this suspended emotional state. (Sidney himself soon married the daughter of Sir Francis Walsingham, Queen Elizabeth's principal secretary.) In *Astrophil and Stella*, the intersection of love and poetry constitutes wit. Love provides the subject matter, but Sidney makes his poetry out of Astrophil's helter-skelter attempts at finding "fit words." The idea was not entirely original. The greatest English poet before Sidney, Geoffrey Chaucer, had delighted in painting his own picture as ineffectual poet. Whereas Chaucer's persona suffers from lack of experience at love, however, Sidney's is almost too emotionally involved in his affair to remain coherent. Fortunately, his creator remains in control, manipulating poetic conventions, modifying them as the need arises, and wittily exploring the domain of wit.

Robert P. Ellis

AT MELVILLE'S TOMB

Author: Hart Crane (1899-1932)
Type of poem: Lyric
First published: 1926, in *White Buildings*

The Poem

"At Melville's Tomb" is written in four four-line stanzas that follow an irregular rhyme scheme. The reader is placed at the gravesite of the noted nineteenth century American novelist, Herman Melville, whose tales of the sea—most notably *Moby Dick* (1851)—are generally regarded as commentaries on humans coping with one another and nature in a vast, often inimical, and ultimately destructive universe. The speaker, while he may be inspired by Melville, shares with the reader his own personal feelings and observations as he stands "at Melville's tomb."

There is not the expected use of the first person. Rather, one is told what Melville, identified only by the third-person pronoun "he," must have felt and observed when he had stood apparently at the same spot where he is now buried— "wide from this ledge"—and, considering the flotsam and jetsam washing up onto the Atlantic shore, had reflected on the relationship not only between man and the sea but also between man and eternity.

The images are difficult, but not impenetrable. The reader is told that amid the wreckage, and hence the apparent waste, that the sea washes up exist records of human passings, "The dice of drowned men's bones bequeath[ing]/ An embassy"— that is, imparting some message from the past. What are ostensibly tokens of destruction and loss can in fact be constructive elements if one can read them effectively.

Melville, too, is a messenger from the past, known now only in his works; the poem, except for the final stanza, is written in the past tense. Any record is only a remnant of some greater and more actual whole, after all, so the "numbers" (not simply the dice, but those messages and meaning the past might hold) are "obscured." In the middle two stanzas, one is thrust from the safety of the shore into a confused and nightmarish world wherein the sea becomes a whirlpool, the whirlpool a seashell, and the seashell "one vast coil," until in a turmoil of language and image one's vision is swept downward into an incredible sinkhole of misguided or mistaken information— "A scattered chapter, livid hieroglyphs,/ . . . portent"— and in desperation one raises "Frosted eyes" to see on "lifted altars . . . silent answers [creep] across the stars."

This movement from tumult to silence, from a barrage of sensations to a single, quiescent image, may be welcome, but it is less than rewarding. Unlike the certain, but obscured messages that the sea offers, whatever is revealed by the stars comes without the benefit of words or images and therefore perhaps comes without meaning.

Instead, in the fourth and final stanza, which has the poem's only present-tense verb, "contrive," the reader is told that all human knowing is in a sense a contrivance. Human instruments are limited in their ability to discern the actual meaning that the sea or the universe holds. This is true not only of those instruments that nature provided, but also of the instruments that humans make. Thus, "Compass, quadrant and sextant [can] contrive/ No farther tides," simply because they are man-made measures only of what one needs to know in practical terms, not of what is there to be known.

When it comes to that vision found "High in the azure steeps," from which one would hope for more timeless messages, one is left, if not confused, at least asleep—"Monody shall not wake the mariner." The sea to which Melville, for one, had looked for an answer to the ageless human dilemmas of sorrow and death can offer only the "fabulous shadow," or distant reflection, of that higher and more enduring truth that the stars hold.

Forms and Devices

An examination of something as simple as Hart Crane's rhyme scheme gives insight into the complex technical virtuosities for which he is both renowned and criticized. The four-line stanzas combine blank verse and rhymed couplets virtually at will, with no attempt at creating a pattern, let alone repeating it from one stanza to the next.

This creation of anticipations that are then either discarded or confounded is in keeping both with Crane's poetry and with the period in which he wrote. The ultimate modernist poet, Crane worked with words the way a painter works with pigments, combining them into larger and larger blends of imagery and detail until even the most trivial subject-verb combinations—"he saw . . . he watched"—become entangled in complexities: "The dice of drowned men's bones he saw bequeath/ An embassy. Their numbers as he watched,/ Beat on the dusty shore and were obscured."

In a famous exchange of letters, Harriet Monroe, then editor of *Poetry* magazine, challenged Crane to clarify the apparent obscurity of this particular imagery. He was easily able to do so precisely because every word and its associations had been chosen and then constructed with great care toward both lexical and figurative meaning.

By using ambiguous syntactical elements as well, such as verbs that could be nouns—"portent wound," for example—Crane is able to make each image cluster serve double and often triple duty. Similarly, "this ledge" can be an actual point on an actual shoreline above the actual sea, or it could be a figurative description of a human plane of reference, making the sea the figurative emblem of eternity.

Meaning in a Crane poem often floats freely between all literal and figurative potentialities. What is difficult in his poetry can become easier to unravel and reconstruct once one understands that Crane never obscures merely for the sake of obscuring. Rather, if and when Crane does obscure normal meaning and syntax, it is done in order to arrive at a wider and therefore richer range of associations and connections.

Finally, Crane's poetry is steeped in both the English and American literary traditions. Besides the overt allusions to Melville's body of work, one might be reminded of Pip, who in *Moby Dick* survives a drowning only at the expense of his sanity; of the whirlpool in Edgar Allan Poe's *The Narrative of Arthur Gordon Pym* (1838); or of Samuel Taylor Coleridge's beleaguered Ancient Mariner—yet another nightmarish vision of the sea as a metaphor both for the destructiveness of nature and for the human spiritual condition. Such literary associations add to the richness and scope of Crane's own intentions.

Themes and Meanings

If there is a single theme to a poetic experience as rich and complex as the one "At Melville's Tomb" provides, it is that there are limits to human knowledge, yet that does not mean that there are limits to human vision. The poet warns one not to expect the typical from his poetry while nevertheless allowing one to imagine that there is some overriding and predictable formal order to the poem. To some degree, that is the message of the poem as well.

The more deeply one looks into things, the more obscure and confused one's vision becomes; however, the instant one casts one's eyes into the most expansive of vistas, one recognizes some overriding structure to time and space and eternity—even if one finds it impossible to say or to measure what that structure may be.

By avoiding the present tense, Crane pushes the reader into an epistemological quagmire. What one knows and how one knows it are revealed to be worthless pieces of information in comparison with the ultimate mystery: the momentary existence of the universe itself. In the process of resurrecting Melville and his vision, for example, the poet nevertheless keeps his reader mindful of the pastness of the present that Melville occupied, just as the "he" of the poem is examining information whose living, or useful, significance lies in the past.

The danger is in thinking that Crane is saying that one must therefore "know" nothing. By poem's end, Crane allows one to imagine only some future epiphany that may not even wake one. What is clearly absent is a knowable present, and that, for the living, feeling mind, is the biggest problem. If we can realize, however, as the poem suggests, that all one's so-called knowledge is in fact berthed in one's very unknowing—that it is, in very real terms, one's confusions and uncertainties that cause one to raise eyes and lift altars—then one can understand why the stars, even in their silence, offer something "fabulous." Their very silence tells a far more profound tale than the worldly detritus on the shores of human knowledge can ever repeat.

Russell Elliott Murphy

AT THE BALL GAME

Author: William Carlos Williams (1883-1963)
Type of poem: Lyric
First published: 1923, in *Spring and All*

The Poem

"At the Ball Game" is a short poem in free verse, its thirty-six lines divided into eighteen stanzas of two lines apiece. The title suggests events occurring at a traditional American pastime, a baseball game; its function, however, is darker, as what actually happens at the ball game shows a side of the American character that most people would prefer to keep hidden.

The poem is written in a third-person dramatic style, with the narrator commenting on the mood of the crowd as it watches the game and observes individuals in its midst. One never enters directly into the mind of anyone in the crowd, but one sees from this more objective perspective how quickly normal spectators can be transformed into a snarling pack.

"At the Ball Game" begins with a scene that most Americans will recognize: a crowd at a game existing for one purpose only—to delight in the beauty of "the exciting detail/ of the chase/ and the escape" (lines 5-7). The crowd, described with the personal third-person plural "they" and "them," may be witnessing a runner racing to first base; it may be witnessing an "error/ flash of genius" (lines 7-8) that either helps the runner reach base safely or sees him put out in the nick of time. It is of no real consequence to the crowd or poet whether the runner is "out" or "safe" ultimately; they simply want to see athletic prowess—the skill and grace of players enjoying and excelling in their sport.

The crowd, which was "moved uniformly" in the first two lines of the poem, is still described as being "beautiful . . . in detail" in lines 11 and 12. Immediately afterward, still within the same sentence, William Carlos Williams darkens the scene. The "beautiful" crowd is now "to be warned against/ saluted, and defied." The crowd is a potent force that can do more than appreciate the beauty of the game. What might it do in a lull in the action, or between innings, for example? What reverence or allegiance might it demand of those in its midst? Thus the crowd goes from being the protagonist of the piece to being the force of opposition.

In line 16, Williams changes his use of personal pronouns to the neuter "it": "It is alive, venomous/ it smiles grimly." "Its" force, moreover, is directed against those who traditionally stand out in the crowd: "The flashy female" and "the Jew" (lines 19 and 21). They are discussed, verbally abused with gossip or open jibes; they "get it straight," and what they get from the crowd is reminiscent of "the Inquisition" and of a "Revolution" (lines 23 and 24) in which those who are different are swept away, put out of sight.

The poem ends by reminding the reader of the potential beauty still residing in the crowd, living "day by day in them/ idly" (lines 27 and 28). While the "power of their faces" (line 30) harbors great beauty, it also contains and is most willing to emit horrible abuse in the form of the stares they have given earlier to those they do not like. This is Williams' final irony. In the summer solstice, at a normal gathering of fans at a ball game, people laugh and cheer "permanently, seriously" (line 35) at the same time that they ridicule and mentally attack others near them who simply want to enjoy the game and the summer day.

Forms and Devices

Since the poem is in free verse, it avoids many obvious devices. The two most obvious literary devices used in "At the Ball Game" are the images of the crowd and game — suggested by the way Williams phrases what are rather ordinary, colorless words — and the extended metaphor of the crowd itself representing any group of people that can shift its temper suddenly and drastically.

Though one must read to the end of the poem to determine exactly the sport being played (baseball being the dominant American sport played during the summer solstice), one can from the beginning imagine the scene of an enthusiastic crowd at a sporting event, sitting in a large stadium, thanks to Williams' suggestive diction. Although Williams never names the sport, his brief mentioning of the "chase," "escape," "error," and "flash of genius" helps one imagine various scenarios: a base runner caught in a run-down; a runner from third base trying to beat the throw from the outfield home; an error made as the outfielder bobbles the ball, or as the shortstop allows a ground ball to pass between his legs; or the "genius" of the runner eluding the tag from the catcher. These are a few of the possibilities regarding baseball that a few well-chosen words might cause one to imagine.

Just as one imagines these scenes and the crowd's exclamations of joy and delight, so might one imagine the ugly stares or verbal swipes of the crowd toward the overdressed young woman and the dark-skinned Jew who pass by, perhaps on their way to the restroom or concession stand, simply by the repetition of the otherwise vague phrase "they get it." By contrast, though, Williams' precise language enables the reader to see and hear the crowd turn into an unruly and crude mob through the use of the words "Inquisition" and "Revolution" — words that conjure more violent and threatening images of people being caught up in a mass frenzy.

The crowd as metaphor works equally as well to engender feelings of uneasiness within the reader — to keep the reader off-guard as to how he or she should feel about the crowd. Since most people have attended sporting contests, one knows how crowds can quickly go from being delighted to being ugly. Ideally, everyone is at the event for the same reason: to appreciate the skill of the athletes. Yet people not only turn on them if they err, they also turn on one another if they root for opposite teams, or if in their anxiety or boredom they need an outlet, a scapegoat. The beautiful crowd of people who seen harmless, innocuous, and only interested in apprehending beauty at one moment turn into a poisonous "It" capable of any sort of abuse in the next.

When one thinks of what sorts of mobs a few groups of people have changed into—lynch mobs, the Ku Klux Klan, or Nazis—one cannot miss the potential of Williams' metaphorical implications.

Themes and Meanings

"At the Ball Game" is a perfect example of Williams' desire to create a new kind of poetry. In keeping with other writers of the modernist period (roughly from the 1890's to the 1940's), Williams equates style with meaning: The way he structures the poem is integral to what he wants to say through the poem.

For example, just as the crowd changes with no warning from delighting in beauty to jeering at its own members, so the poem, with its lack of punctuation and refusal to end a thought at the end of a line, keeps the reader from reaching a full stop until the very last line. The reader thereby witnesses the abrupt transformations as they occur; he or she sees the crowd go from a "uniform beauty" to a deadly and terrifying "Inquisition" in a matter of seconds.

In this way, "At the Ball Game" strongly resembles Williams' well-known poem "The Red Wheelbarrow." The theme and style of "At the Ball Game" are dependent on the crowd, and what seems so simple at first becomes complicated by the end. For example, in reading the lines "So in detail they, the crowd,/ are beautiful/ for this/ to be warned against" (lines 11-14), one sees the continuation from line to line of a thought that instead of simply completing itself, transforms itself into something unexpected, challenging, and quite the opposite of where the thought started. The crowd's momentary beauty lulls one into perceiving what is only partially true; the reader is "warned" that the beauty of the crowd may be one's undoing—then, before one fully digests the warning, one discovers how transitory that beauty really is.

This transformation of seemingly continuous thoughts should then cause the reader to ask the central question: How can such an appreciation of skill and beauty coexist with such an abusive intolerance? Given America's internal conflicts and contradictions, however, Williams might ask, Why be so startled? It is perfectly normal, like a day at the ball game. The crowd, then, is simply like the whole of the American people. It is also like a poem: It may seem easy to read, but it may be quite difficult and even dangerous to comprehend.

Terry Barr

AUBADE

Author: William Empson (1906-1984)
Type of poem: Lyric
First published: 1940, in *The Gathering Storm*

The Poem

An aubade is a poem of love, usually sung by lovers at dawn after a night together. There is no fixed form for an aubade, and William Empson has chosen to use four sets of alternating five- and three-line stanzas, followed by two five-line stanzas with which the poem concludes.

Empson spent the 1930's as a university lecturer in Japan and China, and the poem seems to be set in the Far East. At some time in the middle of the night an earthquake is felt; the lovers are shaken awake by the first tremor, which is followed by a stronger quake. They decide to get up and part. There is some suggestion that the male lover would like harm to come to some others through the quake, and there is the first appearance of the ambiguous line, "The heart of standing is you cannot fly."

The woman dresses, and the male lover, the writer or voice of the poem, who sees himself as apprehensively insecure (a "guarded tourist"), suggests that she might want to leave through the garden, obviously to avoid being seen. This amuses the woman, who is clearly more secure; she will take a taxi, and he will go back to bed. Before she leaves they discuss as well as they can, since they seem to have a bit of a language problem, how she will deal with her husband. It is now obvious that the relationship is adulterous and that they are of different races. She makes it clear that she is not worried about the earthquake and the deaths it might have caused, but that her husband, who might also have been disturbed and might be calling for her, might discover that she is missing. The lover goes back to sleep, hoping that while he sleeps all their problems will be solved.

Guilty but defensive, he imagines that he is being chided for his selfishness in carrying on an illicit love affair when politics in Europe are so dangerous (it is the 1930's, the time of the spread of Fascism). He goes on rhetorically to reject the political, personal, and natural troubles of both East and West, seeing in the Japanese intrusions into Manchuria only another version of the same things that are happening in Europe. He does not care; what matters is his love affair.

The rejection of imagined advice and criticism is brought to a personal level as he imagines the criticism naturally arising from an affair between lovers of different races. He admits that, as in the case of the earthquake, the wisest thing would be to get out of the affair before the matter gets out of hand, but the poem ends with a repetition of the "heart of standing" line, which by now clearly suggests that he will remain and continue the relationship. What begins, then, as a description of incidents occurring as a result of a middle-of-the-night earthquake and the parting of two lovers to avoid possible discovery, develops, in the last four stanzas of the poem, into a monologue in which the male lover—guilty, apprehensive, and defensive—rationalizes their conduct set against the wider problems of the world; he refuses either to abandon his love or to allow its importance to him to be debased.

Forms and Devices

The aubade has a long history in European poetry; it can be found in France, and particularly in Provence, by the end of the twelfth century, and has always had a touch of impropriety about it in its suggestion of secret assignation and regret as the lovers must part as the light of day comes on. Sometimes there is a husband to be deceived; sometimes it is simply a matter of sexual congress outside wedlock. It can use a wide tonal range and often ranges from celebration, through chagrin, to torment. Empson chooses to mix the form with two other interests which often appear in his poetry. The second half of the poem is strongly indebted to his admiration for the problem poems of John Donne, in which the enthusiasm of the male lover is rhetorically attacked by an outside voice and provides the lover with the opportunity to "argufy" in poetry, as Empson put it. This poem makes use of the disastrous nature of natural calamities, such as earthquake and flood, to diminish the importance of the love affair, but also makes use of the serious political and military adventures of the 1930's (which were to lead eventually to World War II in 1939)—not without some pertinence, since this is an affair between a Caucasian and an Oriental.

Another element in the poem, for which Empson is also strongly indebted to John Donne and the Metaphysical poets in general, is the ambiguity of the language. Empson's main reputation is as a critic, and in his most famous book, appropriately named *Seven Types of Ambiguity* (1930), he explores the way in which literary artists use words and phrases which have, quite deliberately, more than one meaning, and may sometimes have several. There is, as a result, an uneasy sense that things are being said in the poem which are not quite clear and often may be taken in more than one way. The poem is a peculiar combination of straightforward narrative and confusing repetitions which seem to mean not quite the same thing as they reappear throughout the poem. "It seemed the best thing to be up and go" and "The heart of standing is you cannot fly" are used in this manner, but they are also used in the aesthetic structure of the poem as alternating endings for the five- and three-line stanzas as a kind of choral repetition and a show of technical prowess.

Part of the problem of uncertainty about what is being said in the poem can be solved when it is recognized that the first three sets of double stanzas are in the past tense, a "telling" of the incident, perhaps to the person addressed rhetorically at the beginning of the seventh stanza. That narration, however, is mixed with comments on the incident made by the speaker, often unclear in meaning, and with snatches of conversation between the lovers which are sometimes hard to understand since they are conversing in a kind of shorthand not uncommon for people who know each other well. There is, as a result, a vivacity and immediacy, but also a sense of the reader being an outsider, not entirely sure of what is happening. For example, two sentences, although not consecutive, make sense if thought about for a moment. "Some solid ground for lying could she show?. . . None of these deaths were her point at all." If somewhat perversely confusing, they probably are part of the conversation about her reason for leaving. The seriousness of the earthquake and the possible deaths that might have occurred are not the reason she feels she must go; the reason is simply that her husband might have been calling for her. If he finds that she is not at home, what can she say to keep him from uncovering her infidelity? Perhaps she can lie and say that she was out looking about. The lover lamely suggests "saying Half an Hour to pay this call." Clearly this would seem suspicious in the middle of the night, and he immediately concedes that "it seemed the best thing to be up and go."

The second half of the poem is in the present tense as the lover defends himself against the good advice that he has no intention of taking. It is somewhat more straightforward but occasionally lapses into a kind of conversational shorthand, which is so common in John Donne's poems of romantic enthusiasm confronted by common sense; like Donne's lover, this man has a quick, sophisticated way with language and a tendency to say things ambiguously.

Themes and Meanings

It has been said of Empson's poetry that it provides the reader with the sensation of feeling sure that the poem is good, both aesthetically and intellectually, without the reader quite knowing what it means. This is not so severely the case with "Aubade," which could be described as being only occasionally, only seemingly, meaningless. At the most obvious level, it is what it says it is: an aubade, a love song on the necessity of the loved one to steal home, not because the night is over, but because everyone's sleep has been disturbed by an earthquake which may also have disturbed the unsuspecting husband who may notice the absence of his wife. Lovers in aubades usually complain about the intrusion of the light; in this case, a much more unusual and more destructive aspect of nature has intruded on the bliss of the lovers.

As is always the case, the lovers are reluctant to part; they are made aware of the facts of life, however, and are sufficiently cautious not to flaunt them. If they are to continue their affair, they must be careful—and that is one of the meanings of the "heart of standing" line. They must not do anything too romantic, which seems to be the meaning of the first use of the line and, perhaps, the second one, where the necessity of providing a solid lie is recognized. The third time the line appears, it may suggest something of a variation on that idea: that they can do no more than keep still until they know the consequences of their conduct. When it appears in the criticism of their conduct, it may be a repudiation of more serious worldwide matters, which proves how deeply they love—real lovers are proven to be so by their refusal to be distracted by the troubles of the outside world. Its last use is a rejection of the idea that their racial differences make it necessary for them to part and for the lover to leave and end the affair. Empson indulges in a very subtle manipulation of the idea of rising that any Metaphysical poet would immediately understand. The statement in itself has an obvious meaning: It would be the wisest thing for the two lovers to part. Yet that must be seen in the light of the other statement about the "heart of standing" precluding flight. It, too, is at first sight, simple. Obviously, one who stands cannot fly, but it can also mean that the heart (the lover) of standing (integrity) would not desert the loved one. Getting up to go, therefore, is not possible in the long run, though it may be necessary once in a while to protect the lovers from detection. "Standing" is character in action.

In the last stanza, however, it assumes the complicated, tricky reasoning of the Metaphysicals. One might get "up" to go, but there is another kind of "rising" which contradicts that retreat: the "rising" of erotic desire, where "up" is related to the heart, not the mind, and confirms the determination not to fly, but to remain with the loved one whatever the consequences. "Standing" now has a sexual implication.

This is not necessarily the only reading of the poem; it is a reading that attempts to make sense of the ambiguities in a way that is consistent with the more obviously factual elements in the work. It is possible to read this poem as a simple aubade and rationalization of an affair without worrying too fastidiously about what some of the more gnomic lines mean. The poem will work as poetry with a reasonable amount of "sense" even if the lines of ambiguity are taken as found, as bits of anarchic musing, tonally supporting the situation of ardor, uncertainty, and insecurity.

Charles Pullen

AUDUBON: A VISION

Author: Robert Penn Warren (1905-1989)
Type of poem: Poetic sequence
First published: 1969; collected in *Selected Poems 1923-1975*, 1976

The Poem

Robert Penn Warren once said that he had started *Audubon: A Vision*, about the American naturalist and painter of native birds John James Audubon, in 1946-1947, when he was reading Audubon's and other subhistories of early nineteenth century America. He was dissatisfied with it then and threw away what he had written. Twenty years later he suddenly remembered one line of his poem and immediately knew what he must do with it. The line he remembered is the only remnant of the original poem: "Was not the lost dauphin," which begins the first poem in this seven-part meditation on the mystery of identity.

This odd disclaimer derives from a legend which arose after Audubon's death that he was the lost Dauphin of France, son of Louis XVI and Marie Antoinette. He was, in fact, the son of a sea captain and his mistress. The obvious contrast between the fantasized origin and his humble beginnings provides the first irony in the question of his identity.

That the poem is called a vision suggests that the insight it provides is only partly derived from the known facts of Audubon's life. The first stanza ends with the assertion that he (Audubon) was only himself "and his passion—what/ Is man but his passion?" This suggests that the poem will inquire into the nature of Audubon's obsession with wild nature, which was the wellspring of his art.

The rest of this first poem imagines the painter's rapt attention to color, form, and the effects of light: how the great white heron looks black against a blood-red sunset, how the overflowing juice of blueberries that drool from a bear's yawn highlights the surprising whiteness of its teeth, and how the bee's wings glint like mica in the sunlight.

The second poem, entitled "The Dream He Never Knew the End Of," is a narrative about Audubon asking for shelter in an isolated forest cabin and then being rescued, at the last moment, from the old woman, his host, and her rascally sons who intended to murder him in his sleep. The three would-be killers are hanged in the morning—frontier justice as speedy and merciless as the crone's impulse to murder for the gold watch he had shown her the night before. Although this story may have some factual basis, it is told for its archetypal mythic nature—the recurring nightmare of a person drawn to the wilderness, recognizing that brute nature, especially unfettered human nature, can be dangerous.

Yet even here, when the persona's paralyzing terror evaporates, he sees something beautiful and dignified in the old woman. Though her sons snivel and beg, she remains calm and defiant, indifferent to fate. The persona, with spontaneous empathy, realizes that the gold watch was an emblem of a civilized, ordered world which had been denied her. With this understanding, he felt compassion, even love, rather than revulsion for his assailant.

The poems continue exploring Audubon's emotional bond to the timeless world of the wilderness, sometimes in philosophical terms, sometimes lyrical, sometimes simply factual. Unlike the old woman in the forest, Audubon had clear alternatives available. He had a wife and apparently loved her—but usually from a distance, communing with "dear Lucy" by letter and playing his flute alone in the forest after sunset. He could have been a successful trader on the frontier; he could have slept in a bed at home—but did not. Neither comfort nor money could lure him. He declined Daniel Webster's kindness when, Audubon himself wrote, he "would give me a fat place was I willing to/ have one; but I love indepenn and piece more/ than humbug and money [sic]."

Yet he did eventually succumb in some measure to fame and honor, even traveling to Europe, where he entertained his hosts by whistling bird calls of his distant forest. He wrote that he continually dreamt of birds. He even came back and lived at home with his wife, but clearly the wellsprings of his art were failing — "the mouthpiece/ Of his flute was dry, and his brushes."

Audubon died in bed, and the poet suggests that with him faded the timeless wilderness world of America: "For everything there is a season." Yet the last poem of the sequence, in which the poet speaks as his own persona, remembering his own fascination with nature from childhood, suggests that the dream of the timeless world never dies. It continues to inspire the artist, whether painter or poet, and offers a secret well of joy for those who both know and love the world. Warren's special affinity for Audubon's passion is understandable, since he himself aspired to be a painter of wildlife when he was a child.

Forms and Devices

The diction and the metaphors in this free-verse poem maintain a certain tension that prevents it from lapsing into either the purely sentimental or the purely Gothic treatment of nature. Although sometimes lyrical, as befits Audubon's passion for the wilderness, metaphors are sometimes startling, even unpleasant. The color of the dawn against which the great heron rises is "redder than meat." Later in the same stanza, it is the "color of God's blood spilt." The heron rises slowly as though "pulled by a string." The first of these curious metaphors may suggest a conventional attitude toward nature as savage, "red in tooth and claw." The second seems to introduce a religious element, perhaps redemption (or at least the need for it), while the third gives a peculiarly mechanical impression, as though all were part of some kind of elaborate stage setting.

Audubon, however, with the sensitivity of the painter, both marvels at the stage setting and mentally "corrects' the reality of the creatures he observes. Although the bird looks black against the red sky, Audubon names the genus and species and knows exactly the heron's true color. The undertone of potential savagery is caught again in the brilliance of a yawning bear's teeth, even though this particular bear is only eating berries and about to hibernate peacefully for the winter.

In the nightmare sequence, the images and metaphors suggest not the relatively innocent potential for violence in nature but a truly ominous quality, the degeneration possible in humans who know neither the natural curbs of instinct nor the social deterrence of law. Even the smoke rising, or rather sinking, from the chimney is described in disgusting terms: It "ravels,/ White, thin, down the shakes, like sputum." The words describing the old woman who opens the door are suspiciously like a child's version of a wicked witch: She is "strong-beaked, the haired mole/ Near the nose." One side of her face is in deep shadow, the other glows in the firelight. Later the woman spits on a knife as she sharpens it on a stone, and the reader remembers the slimey smoke like sputum.

The action becomes more surreal as it blends with remembered childhood nightmares. Although the uneasy visitor lying by the fire keeps his rifle loaded and cocked beside him, he becomes immobilized by a strange lassitude, as though helpless to defend himself. His rescue when three strong men burst in the door seems equally unreal, since no clue is given as to who they are or why they came.

Nevertheless, the later part of that section is surprisingly rational, relentlessly realistic in some details, as though to clear away all illusions. "The affair was not tidy," and later, "The affair was not quick: both sons long jerking and farting." The old woman, however, is "without motion, frozen/ In a rage of will, an ecstasy of iron, as though/ This was the dream that, lifelong, she had dreamed toward." In this usage, "dream" is almost synonymous with "fate," which casts another light upon the ambiguity of experience and choice.

After this dark night of the soul, the diction and metaphors are lighter, more informed with joy. The persona becomes more human and more comfortable with his life decisions. The section filled with quotes from Audubon's diaries or letters provides intimate glimpses of a varied personality. Sometimes he affirms the attitudes of the romantic naturalist, with his devotion to the noble savage view of the Native American: "He saw the Indian, and felt the splendor of God." Audubon wrote that he saw "the Man Naked from his/ hand and yet free from acquired Sorrow." In other words, the wilderness had the innocence of the world before the Fall of Man.

Other vignettes show Audubon as being as vulnerable to wounded pride as anyone, as when a pretty girl passed him by without so much as a nod, not remembering "how beautiful/ I had rendered her face once by Painting it/ at her Request with Pastelles [sic]."

The poem makes effective use of symbols. The most important of these is the gold watch that fascinates the old woman of the forest. It is the quintessential emblem of the man-made ordered world that humankind has superimposed upon nature, which knows only the ordering of the seasons and the pulses of instinct. The action of the heron, which seemed mechanical in its motion across the sky—but was not—is countered close to the end of the poem by a symbolic image of the truly mechanical contrivance. "The Northwest Orient plane, New York to Seattle, has passed, winking westward." This is one of the triumphs of the modern clock-oriented time—to keep the world on schedule; there is no more wandering around at will in a trackless wilderness.

Themes and Meanings

Audubon: A Vision develops three related themes that Warren used over and over in his fiction and poetry: the quest for identity, the loss of innocence, and reconciliation to the changes brought by time. The last two might be expressed in religious terms as the Fall and the Redemption. Warren was well acquainted with and skillful in the use of traditional Christian imagery, but he was more likely to consider these issues as psychological conditions or rites of passage than as religious doctrine. The psychological journey unfolds from an inner necessity.

Each of these themes has a double, or perhaps even a triple, layer of meaning in the poem. Each applies personally to Audubon, the naturalist and painter, and his quest for identity and validation for his life's work. Each applies as well to America as a whole, which was living through radical changes at the same time, losing its wild, free heritage of wilderness. Was the white man bringing "civilization" or simply corrupting an order more finely tuned to the needs of living things than anything men have invented since?

One cannot turn back the clock, however, or regain the original paradise (if, indeed, it ever existed—either in childhood or in the primeval forest). Warren does insist that the vision does not die, admitting that "For everything there is a season./ But there is a dream/ Of a season past all seasons." Some might call this sentimental, but Warren probably considered it an archetypal idea necessary to maintain one's moral equilibrium in a fallen world. It may also be the primary source of art: Audubon would probably not have painted pictures, nor would Warren have written poetry, without that dream.

This suggests the hidden third layer of meaning that may be assumed, given some knowledge of Warren's life. As suggested above, Warren himself aspired to being a painter of wildlife. He took lessons for a while as a child but learned that he was not especially talented in that field. Perhaps all stories are, in some measure, autobiographical. At least, the subject or plot of the tale introduces some compulsion upon the teller, because it rings true to his own experience. When the title calls this poem a vision, therefore, that may refer to Audubon's vision of the wilderness, to America's vision of itself, or to Warren's vision of Audubon living the life Warren coveted as a boy. He hints as much in the last section, called "Tell Me a Story," which begins:

> Long ago, in Kentucky, I, a boy, stood
> By a dirt road, in first dark, and heard
> The great geese hoot northward.

Moreover, there is at least one curious detail of the poem that seems to serve no significant function in the story except, perhaps, as a secret talisman of the author.

That infamous cabin in the forest had one other visitor for the night, who warns the protagonist in sign language of their hosts' evil intent and alerts the three men who burst in upon the group. This second, somewhat superfluous character, is an Indian who has a badly injured eye. The old woman laughs at the Indian, calling him a "durn fool" for accidentally putting out his own eye.

Oddly enough, a serious eye injury had a curious relevance to Warren's decision to become a poet rather than, say, an admiral of the Pacific Fleet—his dream at age sixteen. His father had been getting him an appointment at Annapolis, when a stone tossed carelessly in the air by a child struck Warren in the eye as he lay in the grass. Warren lost that eye, which prevented him from going into the Navy. He went to Vanderbilt University instead, where John Crowe Ransom and others discovered his ability to write and turned his attention to poetry. His career as a writer seemed, therefore, to have resulted from a fluke of fate. That accident was perhaps his own dark night of the soul, from which he emerged as a better man, or at least a different man, even as Audubon ironically learned a new compassion and understanding from the old woman of the forest.

The poet may speak for himself as well as for Audubon when he says, "His life, at the end, seemed—even the anguish—simple,/ Simple, at least, in that it had to be,/ Simply what it was." Perhaps this impression of one's fate as somehow predestined, even when it is partly instinctive, partly accidental, and partly consciously chosen, is simply another illusion of perspective:

> To wake in some dawn and see,
> As though down a rifle barrel, lined up
> Like sights, the self that was, the self that is, and there,
> Far off but in range, completing that alignment, your fate.

Katherine Snipes

AUGURIES OF INNOCENCE

Author: William Blake (1757-1827)
Type of poem: Poetic sequence
First published: 1863, in *Life of William Blake*, by Alexander Gilchrist

The Poem

Except for the first four lines, "Auguries of Innocence" (written in 1803 but unpublished until 1863) consists of a long series of couplets, each of which contains a proverb. Although William Blake may have intended to reorganize the couplets, the poem as he left it in manuscript has no clear order. For this reason, some editors of the poem have rearranged "Auguries of Innocence" by grouping the couplets according to theme.

"Auguries" means omens or divinations, and "Innocence," according to the subtitle of Blake's *Songs of Innocence and of Experience* (1794), is one of the two contrary states of the human soul. In Blake's poetry, innocence is related to existence in Paradise (what Blake calls Beulah) and is associated with the joy and spontaneity of childhood. Thus the title of "Auguries of Innocence" suggests that the poem will present omens from an innocent perspective, in which "the Infants Faith," not the cynic's mockery, is valid.

"Auguries of Innocence" begins with four alternately rhymed lines questioning the absolute nature of space and time. According to these opening lines, one can "see a World in a Grain of Sand," and Eternity can be contained "in an hour." This quatrain asserts that something infinitesimal can expand into immensity, an idea that prepares the reader for the rest of the poem, in which small proverbs are used to comment on such immensities as heaven, hell, and "endless Night."

At least some of these proverbs can be grouped roughly according to subject, but the poem as a whole is difficult to paraphrase. Most of the couplets in the first fifty lines of "Auguries of Innocence" mention animals, relating them to moral error, humans, heaven, hell, and the last judgment. As in the first four lines of the poem, there is a frequent movement from microcosm to macrocosm, from a caged robin to the rage of heaven, from a starving dog to "the ruin of the State." Several proverbs claim that animal abusers will be punished—for example, a man who angers an ox will never be loved by a woman.

Moreover, "Auguries of Innocence" attacks some favorite targets of Blake: those who are corrupted by power or money, and doubters. The poet declares that the armed soldier strikes the sun with palsy, the laborer is worth more than the miser, and the "Infants faith" is far greater than the mocker's doubt. "If the Sun and Moon should Doubt," one proverb claims, "Theyd immediately Go out." The last four lines of the poem contrast "those poor Souls who dwell in night" and perceive God as light to "those who Dwell in Realms of day" and know God in "Human Form." Like many of the preceding couplets, these last lines serve to challenge the beliefs of the literal minded.

Forms and Devices

The essential formlessness of "Auguries of Innocence" recalls Blake's "Proverbs of Hell" (a section of *The Marriage of Heaven and Hell*, 1790) — in both, Blake lists a series of provocative aphorisms that, collectively, represent a vision of reality. Thus "Auguries of Innocence" begins with the act of seeing "a World in a Grain of Sand" and ends with the assertion that God displays his human form to those who can correctly perceive Him. Even though the proverbs are haphazardly listed, they share a common vision. Moreover, each reading of the poem can be seen as a collaboration between Blake and the reader: Blake supplies the couplets, but it is up to the reader to see the connection between them, to learn to read them in a visionary way.

The model for a series of proverbs is, of course, the Bible, and in "Auguries of Innocence" Blake's proverbs often predict the future in true biblical fashion. For example, the poem contains prophecies of moral turpitude leading to disaster, such as "The Harlots cry from Street to Street/ Shall weave Old Englands winding Sheet." It is the nature of proverbs to be cryptic and suggestive, and several of the couplets are, like the poem itself, riddles in need of explication. Other aphorisms, however, are visionary, and some simply call for kindness to all living things — in "Auguries of Innocence," Blake strings contrasting proverbs together in a bewildering succession, perhaps suggesting the spontaneity and freedom from rules that characterize his vision of innocence. An advantage of these proverbs is that any one of them can be removed from the context of the rest of the poem and examined as a separate unit. Even readers who dislike the poem as a whole may find some proverb that interests them. Moreover, the use of the proverb gives the poem a biblical quality — these proverb-couplets seem appropriate as vehicles for the work's moral and visionary judgments. Clearly, an aphorism such as "Kill not the Moth nor Butterfly/ For the Last Judgment draweth nigh" is strengthened by its biblical echo.

Many of Blake's proverbs emphasize points by asserting startling cause-and-effect relationships. Thus the wounding of a skylark is said to stop cherubim from singing, and a gamecock prepared for combat frightens the rising sun. These hyperbolic declarations are clearly forceful — the message of many of the proverbs, that cruelty has consequences that reach far beyond the initial act, is powerfully made. Some readers will dismiss such wildly incongruous aphorisms as palpably absurd. How, some might ask, can the cry of a hunted hare tear a fiber from a brain? The poem has an aphorism for a reader who would make such an objection: "The Questioner who sits so sly/ Shall never know how to Reply." One should also remember that these are auguries of *innocence*. From the perspective of experience, it may seem ludicrous to suggest that someone who would hurt a wren will never be loved, but from an innocent point of view, harming a small bird must necessarily meet with universal disgust. These aphorisms have more in common with an "Infants faith" than with the logic of experience.

Themes and Meanings

In his prophetic works, Blake describes four types of vision: fourfold vision, the

highest visionary state; threefold vision, identified with Beulah (Paradise) and innocence; twofold vision, which is the realm of experience; and the single vision of
Newtonian physics and abstract reasoning. "Auguries of Innocence" deals primarily
with threefold vision, the mental state closest to the true enlightenment of fourfold
vision, and one should not, therefore, expect the poem to reflect either the realism of
experience or the formal consistency of abstract logic. For example, the couplet that
asserts that "Each outcry of the hunted Hare/ A fibre from the Brain does tear" does
not seem accurate in terms of experience or logic, but, from a more visionary perspective, such a statement can have much validity. It describes the consequences of
the physical act of rabbit hunting on the visionary ability of the hunter, who through
his cruelty falls from innocence to the less imaginative state of experience. Many of
the poem's couplets are, in fact, warnings about loss of vision as a result of acts of
cruelty, and the poem as a whole attests the fragility of innocence. Since innocence
is prized in the poem as the gateway to fourfold vision, the doubter who would mock
an infant's faith is seen as particularly criminal: "He who shall teach the Child to
Doubt/ The rotting Grave shall neer get out." The doubter's total lack of imagination
will ultimately trap him in the "rotting Grave" of the physical universe.

Thus the couplets of the poem, through a series of paradoxes and riddles, seek to
challenge and expand the reader's vision of reality. Those who are cruel, or who
become obsessed with rank, wealth, or power, can never see beyond the twofold
vision of experience to the threefold vision of innocence or the fourfold vision of
eternity. Moreover, those who put their faith in the visible universe are doomed from
the start: "He who Doubts from what he sees/ Will neer Believe do what you
Please."

The poem's last six lines describe two ways of seeing: *with* the eyes and *through*
the eyes. Seeing with the eyes leads the percipient to a mistaken faith in the visible
universe, but by seeing through the eyes, with imaginative vision rather than physical
sight, the percipient can break through the physical world and escape its "Night." To
those who dwell in this night of visible perception, "God appears & God is Light,"
but to the visionaries "who Dwell in Realms of day," God "does a Human Form
Display." As in the opening quatrain of the poem, the infinite is represented by the
particular: God can be visualized in human form just as the world can be seen in a
grain of sand or heaven in a wildflower. In essence, "Auguries of Innocence" reveals
the illusory nature of the physical universe in order to develop the reader's ability to
see the infinite in everything. This perceptual cleansing, Blake suggests, will ultimately lead to fourfold vision.

William D. Brewer

AUGUST MOON

Author: Robert Penn Warren (1905-1989)
Type of poem: Lyric
First published: 1979; collected in *Being Here: Poetry 1977-1980*, 1980

The Poem

"August Moon" is a poem of forty-seven lines dispersed among thirteen stanzas varying in length: The shortest stanza has only one line; the longest has eight. It is written entirely in free verse and is, therefore, typical of most of Robert Penn Warren's poetry in that imagery and metaphor are always the dominant vehicle of expression.

The title, though ostensibly a simple one, is highly suggestive both as a metaphor and as an image in itself. Literally, it is readily discoverable that the moon is bright and half-full, shining on a clear August night when literal heat and the clearness of the sky are at their zeniths. Metaphorically, such a moon represents the emotional intensity the poet feels for his beloved. As an image, it is indicative of the intellectual passion the poet experiences, not in the heat of the moment, but in the heat of his life.

The poem is written in the first person, both singular and plural. The use of "we" is not as a plural voice; rather, "we" is undoubtedly intended as a way to personalize the experience and to involve the poem's readers. Warren uses the second-person "you" in three instances. He does so not to suggest that he is addressing a second person, even the lover or the reader, but to talk to some component of his self.

The first stanza of the poem contains two metaphorical images: The August moon of the title is "Gold like a half-slice of orange/ Fished from a stiff Old-Fashioned." Similarly, it is "like a real brass button" on "an expensive seagoing blue blazer." The shining moon is the focus of all that it is near simply because of its overwhelming powers.

The third stanza is one of three in the poem to be emphasized by being set apart in a singular line. This line indicates the topic of the poem in the form of a question that the poet will answer as he proceeds: "What kind of world is this we walk in?" The preceding stanza had aroused the question through showing the poet's recognition of the stars surrounding the August moon, themselves contained in an "Eczema of glory."

In the next stanza, Warren gives the first part of this answer, though indirectly; it is the kind of world where people must die. He writes that "It makes no sense except/ . . . the body's old business" and lists three occurrences that typify death: "Your father's cancer, or/ Mother's stroke, or/ The cat's fifth pregnancy."

The plural "we" is used in the following two stanzas as the poet continues to answer the question of the poem. The reader is instructed that "we" walk in a world where communication is possible, although it is a "darkling susurration" that must be deciphered. It is also a world where time, though never directly mentioned, is counted by children at birthday parties.

In the eighth stanza, Warren tells the reader exactly the answer to this earlier question: "the point" is that one lives in a world in which the "counting of years" goes on for adults as well as for children, although in different ways. Toward the end of the poem, the poet compares life to a "pale path between treetops." Finally, he instructs the reader that the world is one in which travelers on life's journey should communicate by holding hands and not talking at all.

Forms and Devices

As is typical of Warren's poetry, imagery and metaphor dominate; the poem is devoid of standard poetic devices such as rhyme or alliteration. He conveys his message through a series of images, many of which are embedded in metaphors. The August moon itself is used to establish a mood of contemplation and a setting of quiet emotional intensity. The moon is set in the universe among the stars in the same way that the poet as an individual, his lover as another separate individual, and readers as yet another entity of individuals are set in the world to walk their respective paths through pale moonlight among darkened treetops. It is hopeless, the poet realizes, for these stars to attempt communication; so it is with all humans who "walk down the woods-lane." The stars attempt no communication, and neither should the individuals who are the "we" of the poem; the difference is that the individuals of this "we" can hold hands.

Initially, the moon is compared to the gold "half-slice of orange" in a drink and to a brass button on a blue blazer. It is a part of the physical universe, the most prominent, visible feature in the heavens (the "Eczema of glory"); yet it is entirely personalized in something so common, even mundane, as a button. The moon provides the setting both for the universe and for the people on earth who walk under it; the moon itself is set in the universe in time "By the tick of the watch." Children most successfully escape this concern with time. Adults cannot do so, for they are thrust into its reality "At random, like/ A half-wit pulling both triggers/ Of a ten-gauge with no target, then/ Wondering what made the noise."

Two other images are mysteriously embedded in questions in separate short stanzas near the end of the poem. The first of these is "Do you hear the great owl in distance?" Animals perhaps know the significance of the August moon and would attempt their own forms of communication. If the poet and his cotraveler(s) can hear the owl, they, too, can achieve a similar understanding. Then the poet asks, "Do you remember a childhood prayer— / A hand on your head?" This particular childhood prayer would be one prayed by another—by the adult who has, in the Protestant style of Warren's own youth, placed hands of anointment or ordination upon a child's head. Again, the impetus for such action is the communication of something important about the order and nature of a universal truth.

The last two metaphors are simple, even simplistic: "The track of white gravel leads forward into darkness." Life is, for those who would walk a gravel road, unpaved, yet white. It leads into darkness, the totality of which the travelers are spared only because of the light shed from the August moon. The darkness is and will remain all-encompassing, so the travelers are told to hold hands, walk on, and "speak not a word." Nothing that could be said is of importance, for only the moon will control the journey.

Themes and Meanings

Warren's purpose in "August Moon" is to explain some of the significant concerns of a traveler through life. These include one's station in and relation to the universe; one's place in the world in which one lives; the function and effects of time; and the proper perspective one should have as one proceeds into the inexplicable, cosmic darkness of the woods. Answers to all these questions relate to the August moon.

The walker through life is initially alone. One will remain that way if one steps out of line with nature by expressing oneself. (Ironically, this is exactly the function of the poet.) Individuals are like stars in that both possess (and are possessed by) a physical existence. In the face of the August moon, however, individuals can walk on in silence in order to maintain at least a semblance of companionship. One does so under the auspices of omnipotent time; here, the importance of time is simply that it makes one old.

At one point in the poem, Warren asks the question "who/ Wants to live anyway/ Except to be of use to/ Somebody loved?" The question is followed by a single-line stanza that questions the premise of that question: "At least, that's what they say." For the poet to suggest that others ("they") say this shows that he may not fully accept the idea himself. One can best be of service to someone one loves through companionship down the gravel road. A simple act such as holding hands in the pale moonlight under the treetops is what counts — not the counting of years. Older persons, perhaps, have little reason to count years, which already exist as an accomplishment. Rather, they count the importance of a single companion.

The world of words, as the poet shows, will not permit the deciphering of the night of one's life as it "Hardens into its infinite being." In this regard, finally, the poem is about how an older person prepares for an approaching death. Under the August moon, birthdays will no longer be counted because the counters will be gone, willfully having walked through life and on into the silence of the universe at some point on the white gravel path. The moon will become "lost in tree-darkness"; only stars will be visible. The poet will take his place in a universe of stars after walking through the life of this world governed by the moon. In making this passage, hand-holding and silence are the best for which he can hope.

Carl Singleton

THE AURORAS OF AUTUMN

Author: Wallace Stevens (1879-1955)
Type of poem: Meditation
First published: 1948; collected in *The Auroras of Autumn*, 1950

The Poem

"The Auroras of Autumn" contains 240 lines, divided into ten sections with twenty-four lines each. The title refers to the northern lights in autumn. The speaker first sees them as a serpent winding upwards, hungry to find a form for itself. The scene changes in the next section to a deserted, white beach cabin. Its whiteness is a memory, like clouds in winter. Autumn is a time for change, warning of winter. A man "turns blankly" as the sky makes change seem larger. The speaker feels utterly alone.

Section 3 begins, like section 2, with a farewell. Memory is focused on "mother's face," filling a room at evening. The aurora's lights are reflected from the windows, and the wind knocks at the door, "like a rifle-butt." The "farewell" continues, now focusing on the father, who is agreeable to everything. He enjoys change. He hears things that are not there, and he sees drama everywhere.

Section 5 examines the father's talent for imagining: He could fetch "pageants out of air"; and he made poems, though they were works "of barbarous tongue." These poems were the work of a man like Chatillon, an obscure sixteenth century writer who also said "yes" to everything. In the real world, the speaker objects, there is "no play" apart from mere existence.

In the next section, the poet, like his father, imagines nature's lights as a "theatre floating through the clouds": They become birds, volcanic smoke, floating in the sky's corridor. The "denouement" of this theatrical spectacle, however, cannot be completed because it has no inherent solution. The poet is defiant: Natural phenomena do not mean anything, or they mean whatever human beings allow them to mean. He boldly opens his door, but he is frightened. He is a puny "scholar" who sees by "one candle," when nature flashes out to overwhelm him, threatening "everything he is."

Section 7 reacts to this fear. The poet identifies the auroras with imagination, which leaps into the north, where it reigns supreme over all reality, displaying its energies in a proud burst of beauty. This imagination gets its energies from devouring reality: It is "the white creator of black," absorbing the planets to turn matter into energy. The speaker asserts that the aurora does not control its own destiny. It is an inscription on the blank of the heavens ("stele"), written there by the force that can both make and unmake it.

There is, the poet says in section 8, an innocence of time. Its existence is visible, as in "these lights" of the auroras in autumn. The poet reclines beneath them, "like children" secure "in the quiet of sleep," while mother sings. The next section continues this mood: The poet and his brothers lived each day as an adventure in the "outlandish." Each slept easily, fed on the honey of experience. In that innocent time, "fate" brought "freedom." Now, grown up and recalling innocence, the poet reconsiders the auroras: They are his mother soothing him for his fate. The autumn winds are sharp with the imminence of disaster. The auroras, however, are a shelter for imagination, cloaking darkness with a "flash" of innocence, so that the poet accepts death, which "may come tomorrow."

The concluding section is a tailpiece. The serpentlike auroras of autumn have been transformed into an imagination of "innocent earth." The auroras had been described in Section 7 as a regal figure crowned by a "diamond cabala." The conclusion asks a rabbi to explicate that text of gnostic wisdom. The poet imagines himself in "all lives" so he can know the world is noisy and hag-ridden, not a quiet Eden. The auroras join the winds of autumn to announce destruction; they are the "blaze of summer straw" seen "in winter's nick."

Forms and Devices

"The Auroras of Autumn" follows the rhythm of the meditation, from landscape observation, to focused detail from the natural scene, to personal associations from memory, to interpretation, and finally to a form of imaginative transcendence, signaled in the concluding section as "fulfilling his meditations."

This rhythm is made through eight (mainly) unrhymed tercets (three-line stanzas) in each of the poem's ten sections. While there is no standard rhyme scheme to the tercets, occasionally rhymes will occur to emphasize images and themes, as in the transition from the sixth to the seventh tercets of section 2: "fall" yields to "wall." More often, the sections contain "identical" rhymes (repetitions of the same word), as in "white" (section 2), "innocence" (section 8), and "world" (section 10). A form of rhyming occurs between sections, as certain words are repeated to form motifs of the theme throughout the poem as a whole: These include "wind," "changes," and "innocence."

The poem creates uncertainty and tentativeness with its interrogative mode of questioning the significance of what the senses report. It also makes difficult a certain identification of referents for pronouns (both demonstrative and personal). The title itself, however, hovers over all to suggest that the auroras of autumn will often serve as referents.

Images of light and wind, derived from the situation described by the title, dominate the figurative devices of "The Auroras of Autumn." While these images allude, sometimes subtly and sometimes obviously, to other poems by other poets (such as Percy Bysshe Shelley's *Mont Blanc* and "Ode to the West Wind," as well as to William Wordsworth's "Ode: Intimations of Immortality"), light as a figure for imagination and wind as a figure for communication do not need larger contexts to function clearly in Wallace Stevens' poem. The light of the auroras is transformed, though, to create a complication of its meaning: It is a "bodiless form" in section 1, "frigid brilliances" of color at the conclusion of section 2, "Boreal night" in section 3, an "ever-brightening origin" in section 4, an "Arctic effulgence flaring" in section 6, and a "blaze of summer straw" at the end of section 10. Similarly, the wind of autumn goes through several transformations: from the "cold wind" that "chills the beach" in section 2, to "windy grandeurs" knocking "like a rifle-butt against the door" of section 3, "the naked wind" that ends section 4, "a wind as sharp as salt" in section 9, and finally the "haggling wind" of section 10.

Themes and Meanings

While the light and wind imagery in "The Auroras of Autumn" may allude to poetry by Wordsworth, Shelley, and others (such as Walt Whitman), the more interesting indebtedness of the poem is to some of Stevens' own earlier poems. In particular, the refrain "Farewell to an idea" opening sections 2, 3, and 4 alludes to the poems Stevens published under the title *Ideas of Order* (1935), which included "Farewell to Florida" and "The Idea of Order at Key West." "Farewell to an idea," then, evokes an attitude of transformation in the poet's own life, poetic style and theme, or philosophical orientation. This marks Stevens' poem as a "hail and farewell" experience, in which he meets an object (or person) in passing on his way elsewhere. "The Auroras of Autumn" is a greeting to the spectacle of the northern lights at a time of transition (autumn) for the poet, who is looking for death (winter) in the flash of illumination provided by the auroras as his (innocent) imagination.

This theme of farewell allows the poem to be a vehicle for some private experiences from Stevens' life, such as those associated with his mother (her necklace and her hands in section 3, her singing in section 8) and his father (his eyes in section 4, his poems in section 5). Perhaps he refers to his brothers in section 5, as well as in section 9, where he may also refer to his wife as one whose "coming became a freedom" for himself and her. These personal, family "ideas" are sources of warmth but also obstacles to imaginative freedom; to them he must also bid farewell. Everything dissolves and disappears, everything is transformed, as both the light of the auroras and the wind of autumn signal.

The meaning of the poem is that everything changes, including the poet and his imagination. The power of change may be innocent or malicious, grimly benevolent, both just and unjust. The auroras of autumn are nothing in themselves without the innocent imagination; they are the inscriptions on a heavenly tablet, and they are the occasion for insight—not the insight itself. They do, however, as imagination's own power, illuminate ever so briefly the nature of a reality usually concealed by darkness, and what they reveal is a "harridan" world haggled "by wind and weather." This revelation, however frightening, is welcomed in the "nick" of time because it comes before winter and death overtake the poet or overwhelm "unhappy people" who think they exist in "a happy world."

Richard D. McGhee

AUSPICE OF JEWELS

Author: Laura Riding (1901-   )
Type of poem: Meditation
First published: 1938, in *Collected Poems*

The Poem

"Auspice of Jewels" is a poem in free verse that is divided into eight sections of irregular length. Although the title alludes to jewelry, the poem actually concerns the source of power, of luminescence, for women. In fact, the language of the poem is charged by the metaphor of light.

There are two groups of personae in the poem: "us" and "them," women and men. Laura Riding contrasts the two. Men believe they give significance to women by giving them objects of value. Actually, the significance of women is repressed or obscured by the gifts. In abandoning gifts, women become active rather than passive: "We have passed from plaintive visibility/ Into total rareness."

The poem begins with the assertion that men have weakened women through subterfuge: "They have connived at those jewelled fascinations." With constant shifting from "they" to "us," the poem leads the reader to realize that the speaker of the poem assumes an adversarial role as she comes to realize the extent to which she, as representative of women, has been repressed, compromised by the attention of men. This attitude is similar to that of Virginia Woolf, who classified a type of woman as "the angel in the house" in her essay "A Room of One's Own." Both writers contend that men, probably consciously, have belittled women by treating them as decorative objects rather than as human beings who, in their own right, possess intelligence and genius.

One can understand why Robert Graves so admired Laura Riding, his companion from 1926 to 1940. Throughout most of his writing, Robert Graves asserted the superiority of women to men and devoted much of his writing to correcting what he regarded as patriarchal corruptions of the literature of the matriarchy. Riding appears in the poem as a writer and a person who would elicit such a response.

The first three sections of the poem present woman as compromised in a male-dominated society. Sections 4 and 5 begin with the words "Until now," signaling that a change has occurred. The luminescence of women in the present of the poem is no longer merely reflected; it comes from within the women. Section 7 begins: "For we are now otherwise luminous," indicating that the source of luminosity has moved from without to within. The poem ends with section 8, a parenthetical comment on the "Gemmed ladies" who are still attended by those whose light they reflect. Riding did not expect the dominance of male history and tradition to change because women had seen the light, but she did expect change to occur in women (and men) who chose to live according to what she regarded as honest attention to life and truth. She thought of such people as living on the "inside," not simply on the outside. Such insiders, she believed, had the power to cause change.

Forms and Devices

References to jewels, the women who wear them, and the men who give them create the central metaphor of the poem. The metaphor causes the reader to consider whether women, like jewels, have significance only because of their assigned value, or whether their innate significance is no less valuable than that of those men who regard them as decorative.

The metaphor shifts in the fourth section to the unreflected luminosity of women, leading the reader to see that jewels have distracted women from their own power and worth. By using light as a metaphor, Riding evokes resonances that go far back into history and myth. In the Bible, God says: "Let there be light." In Greek mythology, Prometheus was punished for giving fire (light) to human beings, and Artemis was the Greek goddess of the moon. Light has been generally associated in religion with power and creativity; for example, Apollo, the god of poetry, drives his chariot, the sun across the heavens.

In her light metaphor, Riding contests the idea that women have only reflected light (power). She uses words such as "brilliance," "obscure," "twinkling," "gloom," "luminous," and "snuffed lanterns" to give the poem light, and to make the reader aware of the metaphor. The poem ends with a dreamlike stanza that tells the reader one last time that the language is figurative, not literal.

The contrast between "them" and "us" increases the metaphoric force of the poem by showing the recipients of the jewels to be passive. Those who are not bejeweled have their own power. This difference illustrates that the poem is concerned with the possession of power, not with the giving of gifts.

Themes and Meanings

The title "Auspice of Jewels" prepares the reader for a prophecy, since auspice actually means prophecy. The prophecy is that significance is inner for those women who know that they are human beings of significance and genius. In her life and writing, Riding never questioned either her significance or her genius.

In contrasting inner and outer reality, "Auspice of Jewels" adheres to a basic concern of Modernism. As Virginia Woolf noted in her essay "Modern Fiction," the popular writers at the beginning of the twentieth century adhered to a view that limited reality to physical characteristics. Since those characteristics were often of dress and accoutrements, social and economic class were presented as the major determinants of identity. The jewels in this poem illustrate that view. The inner value of a person is the proper concern of the artist.

Such a tendency to look inward was prevalent in the generation that emerged after World War I, since so many artists of that time, Riding among them, had viewed the horrors of that war and come to reject the ideals that were used to justify it. In *Goodbye to All That* (1929), Robert Graves wrote of his rejection of the society and culture that he viewed as responsible for the war.

Though Riding was certainly aware of such views as those held by Woolf and Graves, her views are her own. They are part of the awareness of the inner world that had been brought about by the writings of Sigmund Freud. They are also a response to the political activity of women at the time, whose efforts had earned for women the right to vote.

Riding believed, as have many others, that her poems spoke with power of a truth that is greater than the historical moment. "Auspice of Jewels" is a poem that ends with a reference to medieval times, when there were knights and ladies. With this reference, Laura Riding clearly moves her concern with significance and value from the momentary to the universal.

Frank L. Kersnowski

AUTO WRECK

Author: Karl Shapiro (1913-   )
Type of poem: Lyric
First published: 1941, in *Five Young American Poets*; collected in *Person Place and Thing*, 1942

The Poem

"Auto Wreck" is an impressionistic poem of three stanzas and thirty-nine lines that takes a hard look at the spectacle of injury and accident in a crassly technological world. The title, in trademark Karl Shapiro style, focuses attention on the unadorned, literalist description of a common event or experience.

In the first stanza, which comprises the first fourteen lines, the reader is situated, as it were, in front of an ambulance that is speeding toward the scene of an automobile accident; the reader is kept informed by an omniscient voice, which scrupulously provides both sensual and metaphorical detail that brings the reader uncomfortably close to both the horrifying event and his or her own matter-of-fact response to its horror.

The ambulance's red light pulses "like an artery," confronting the reader early with an image of blood, anticipating the arrival at the accident scene and preparing the reader for the sight of "stretchers . . . laid out, the mangled lifted/ And stowed into the little hospital." As the ambulance and its "terrible cargo" move away, the reader is left to contemplate the waiting physicians who will attempt to restore seeping life to the victims.

In the second stanza, the point of view shifts and the narrative voice becomes an introspective "we," implicating the reader as one of the "deranged, walking among the cops/ Who sweep glass and are large and uncomposed." These police officers, who are depicted as anonymous civil servants dutifully performing the tasks assigned them, are identified hauntingly by the impersonal singular pronoun "one": "One is still making notes," "One with a bucket douches ponds of blood/ Into the street and gutter," "One hangs lanterns on the wrecks that cling . . . to iron poles." The corps of officials and the spectators are united in their cold and predictable routine, beyond grief, beyond sympathy for the injured.

The third and longest stanza moves away from the accident scene to reflect on what the accident means. The poet punishes the reader with a series of hospital metaphors that puncture the reader's smug and complacent attitude toward the victims of technological disaster, which is mirrored in the inevitable carnage that high-speed, piston-driven vehicles precipitate. Throats as tight as "tourniquets," feet "bound with splints," this poem's readers try to speak through "sickly smiles" like "convalescents" attempting to make the best of a bad situation.

The auto wreck that occurred offstage in the poem's landscape has given way to the mental "wreck" that pushes one further toward one's "richest horror": The question "Who shall die?" turns into "Who is innocent?" While one contemplates the answers to these rhetorical questions, the poem takes a sudden turn toward a climax, surveying the more "natural" deaths of war, suicide, and cancer—each of which has its own logic and order.

Death by machine, by negligence, "invites the occult mind,/ Cancels our physics with a sneer," and disorients human beings' sensibilities and capacity to respond with compassion. One is left with a "denouement" splattered "across the expedient and wicked stones" of pavement and traffic lanes—whose silence speaks volumes about the increasing difficulty of discerning humane and human values in a world made alien by the presence of "empty husks of locusts," the wheels, motors, and steel bodies of the quintessential twentieth century innovation: the automobile.

Forms and Devices

To say that "Auto Wreck" takes its place among other "gut response to the world" poems that are characteristic of Shapiro's early craft is to say that his poems feature such subject matter as social injustice, the planned obsolescence and decay of man-made machines, and the alienation of modern humans from a world that barely resembles the one that was handed to them by their parents. "Auto Wreck," like similar Shapiro poems of the 1940's ("Hospital," "Washington Cathedral," and "University"), features obsessive, naturalistic treatment of the commonplace. It is the poet's intention to exaggerate the ordinariness of the mundane—or that which has become mundane by virtue of its perpetual presence or repetition—in modern culture in order to "defamiliarize" it and to enable one to see it as if for the first time.

In so doing, he is performing the function of art that was described by Soviet literary theorist Viktor Shklovsky, who believed that such defamiliarization works through poignant, graphic description of the real, a technique that borders on the surreal but stays safely this side of it by virtue of its intense view of the literal. In "Auto Wreck," this literalness is coupled with a metaphoric complement that combines the factual with the imaged; for example, in lines 9 and 10, "Stretchers are laid out, the mangled lifted/ And stowed into the little hospital." At first, the reader is meant to see a vehicle in which medical supplies are stored; next, to visualize a hospital on wheels. Shapiro thus achieves a marriage of the sensual and the analogous that forces the reader simultaneously both to look and to reflect on what has been seen.

As a result, many of Shapiro's stanzas feel as if they are being spoken in the first-person plural to fellow bystanders who are nodding silently in agreement. Although few explicit moral judgments are expressed in Shapiro's poetry, they linger, as they do in "Auto Wreck," on the edge of consciousness: "Already old, the question Who shall die?/ Becomes unspoken Who is innocent?" Such questions are raised only peripherally, however, never centrally.

Shapiro is adamant in embracing the view shared by the Southern "Fugitive" school of poets he admired that poetry with a "message" is mere propaganda. Shapiro's impressionistic poetics exalts immediacy, concreteness, and individuality. The crowd, the mob, is held at arm's distance, for it inevitably obscures the one, the individual life and its worth that the poet is at pains to make the reader see.

Shapiro has therefore always preferred a "low" or "common" English as the language of poetic life—a bridge or a concession to readers and poets who have tired of complex or contrived patterns or rhyme schemes. "Auto Wreck" exemplifies a poetic stance that is clearly opposed to that of the postmodernist poets, whom Shapiro has caricatured as propounding "apologies for the personal, the narcissistic, and the solipsistic, as well as for the tribal, antifamilial, and antinational ethos, drawn from both primitive and esoteric lore."

Themes and Meanings

"Auto Wreck" reveals what its author considers to be the terrible secret of modern life: the creeping indifference toward technological determinism, the simple violence of machine against human being in which everyone participates by failing to be troubled or moved by such disasters as automobile wrecks. Humanity sees but does not see; what is inherently unnatural or antihuman—traveling at high speeds in mechanical monsters that threaten both drivers and pedestrians—becomes the commonplace, the expected, and the normal.

One witnesses horrors and quickly dismisses them as part of the world one inhabits, a world that no one can control or understand fully: "We speak through sickly smiles and warn/ With the stubborn saw of common sense." Were one to understand it, the poet surmises, one would be even more horrified; hence, the better alternative is to register the horrific as the "official version" of an otherwise unbroken line of human catastrophes. It is not evil that should surprise one, but good; not failure, but success; not ugliness, but beauty; not revenge, but mercy; not despair, but hope.

The world of "Auto Wreck" is thus a sinister realm of everydayness. The details of horror are intensified by the images the poet chooses to portray his readers' response to that horror. Their "throats are tourniquets," their feet, "bound with splint," the badge of initiation into the labyrinth of stunned adulthood.

Whatever one chooses as tools for understanding become tools of ignorance, invitations to the deferral of meaning, preludes to the renunciation of "sense." One trusts one's senses but betrays one's mind; the longing for redemption or release from the mundane is but cruel illusion—a mocking and macabre invitation to either intellectual suicide or mad self-deception.

The "large and composed" cops in line 15 indifferently make "notes under the light" or "douche" "ponds of blood/ Into the street and gutter." Thus the threatened end of human life is transmogrified into the simple custodial task of sweeping the life source into the bowels of the city.

This thematic underscoring of a recurrent trait in Shapiro's poetry catches even the casual reader by surprise: Diction, image, metaphor—these must all be calculated to evince the proposition that in the modern world everything is arbitrary. Although things might have been otherwise, they are, in fact, not—indeed, they cannot be in a world run by machines. "Auto Wreck" thus becomes Shapiro's proto-typical accusation against a world that is bereft of the transcendent values that give human life meaning and purpose.

Bruce L. Edwards

THE AUTOPSY

Author: Odysseus Elýtis (Odysseus Alepoudhélis, 1911-   )
Type of poem: Lyric
First published: 1960, as "E autopsia," in *Éxi ke miá típsis yia ton ouranó;* collected in *The Sovereign Sun,* 1974

The Poem

"The Autopsy" is a short free-verse poem consisting of ten lines, the majority of which are long and flowing as well as rich and evocative. The remainder—the fifth, seventh, and tenth lines—are economic, almost laconic, and comment on or serve as links to the lines that precede or follow them.

The poem is written in the third person; this not only amplifies the objective, detached perspective that the title implies but also contributes to the analytical tone of the poem. The nostalgic, evocative language which the poet uses to describe the "findings" of the autopsy, however, belies this objectivity, thus creating the tension of the poem; this tension is sustained until the final line, which signals completion and fulfillment.

The poet permits only certain parts of the body to be dissected. Specifically, those parts are related to the senses through which he perceives the sources in the physical world which awaken and aid him in expressing his inner, poetic world.

First, the heart, the seat of all emotions, is examined and found to be permeated with the "gold of the olive root." The olive traditionally symbolizes peace, immortality, and the Golden Age. For Odysseus Elýtis, however, it is emblematic of Greek culture, its fruit having sustained the Greeks, physically as well as economically, through the olive oil trade. It is the quintessential Greek commodity, the "golden" gift of the gods. In the second line, the entrails are seized by "a strange heat," the result, apparently, of the poet's quest for light—whether in the candle's flame or in the coming of dawn. The entrails represent the physical self but also signify intuition, and Elýtis typically intuits in light the presence of pure spirit.

In the third line, the tactile sense is recalled, as the veins beneath the skin are likened to the "blue line of the horizon." This image occurs frequently in Elýtis, who, from the onset of his career, has elevated the landscape—and particularly the sea, sun, and sky—of his native land. The "cries of birds" in the fourth line also represent an element of this landscape, the divine realm of nature filtered through the subjectivity of the senses, which the poet has attempted to distill and express through poetry. If, in these attempts, he has been led astray or fallen short of the mark, "Probably the intention sufficed for the evil."

If the poet has succumbed to this evil in any way, the reader is told in the sixth line, it was the result of his own ingenuousness, his openness toward and his desire to participate fully in life, as evidenced by the vision of the "whole forest moving still on the unblemished retina." The forest symbolizes, on the one hand, society, and on the other, the realm of the psyche. In the seventh line, the brain, the reliquary of memory, is left empty. Only an echo of the poet's former ideal—the clear, inviolate sky—remains.

The auditory sense is summoned once again in the eighth line, which recalls more sea imagery; the sounds of the wind and the waves are, as is so often the case in Elýtis' work, almost palpable. In the ninth line, the poet cites the power of erotic love as one of the sources which have inspired his poetic voice. The tenth and final line acts as a coda, commenting on all that has preceded. It suggests that the poet has succeeded in entering and confronting life with purpose and courage and that his virtue will be rewarded with the promised renewal: "We shall have early fruit this year."

Forms and Devices

The most impressive device employed in the poem is the analogy of the autopsy, which the poet develops through a series of extremely effective, related metaphors, all of which reinforce the image of a surgeon performing this act. The analogy of the autopsy reinforces, in turn, the image of ritual sacrifice—the poet as an Adonis figure whose life has been dedicated to the quest for truth and beauty—which is implied in the regeneration indicated in the final line of the poem.

The imagery in this poem is typical of Elýtis' work in two respects: First, it evinces his roots in his native Greek tradition, and second, it reflects his fundamentally surrealist orientation. The Greek heritage, for Elýtis, is not merely that of classical Greece. Rather, it encompasses a number of indigenous sources, including pagan mysticism, animism, and nature worship, as well as the Byzantine, Eastern Orthodox, folkloric, epic, and demotic traditions. The Greek tradition is most frequently expressed in Elýtis' poetry, however, through the imagery of the sea. This sea imagery so dominated his early collections that, early in his career, he became known as the "poet of the Aegean."

For Elýtis, the seascape is not only the quintessential icon of Greece but also the only one that can convey the holistic worldview which he embraces, which constantly seeks to reunite man's physical and spiritual natures. In his poetry, the essence of things resides in the divine natural realm, which he perceives as a point of contact, a link between man's physical self and his divine inner world, the fusion of which Elýtis seeks to attain through the poetic act.

Surrealism enabled Elýtis to succeed in this effort to a great degree, as the images in "The Autopsy" attest. In the poem, the spiritual is constantly juxtaposed with the physical, and man and nature undergo a metamorphosis which renders the one indistinguishable from the other. The olive root becomes the human heart, the core of being; the blue line of the vein is transmuted into the horizon, and all that the body retains are the melancholic cries of birds and a few grains of fine sand. These incongruous juxtapositions are standard in the work of French surrealist poets such as Paul Éluard, to whom Elýtis is frequently compared. In Elýtis' work, however, they are always grounded in his native Greek environment. Moreover, Elýtis rejects the "automatic," unordered flow of thoughts, which the French surrealists admired; his poetry consistently reflects a clear, preconceived aim, subject unity, and the carefully controlled ordering of images.

Themes and Meanings

"The Autopsy" reflects the mature Elýtis, the poet who has acknowledged and reconciled himself to the presence of the tragic, but who, despite this acceptance, mourns the loss of the clear blue sky of his youth in these "remorses." He is no longer innocent; the once azure vault is now cloudy and polluted by the forces of chaos and destruction, and only a "dead echo" of it remains. His aim in the poem is to determine whether he has combated those malign forces fully and courageously.

The poem examines the poet's performance not only as an artist but as a human being as well. He assesses all the sources which have inspired his artistic life and evaluates, in addition, the events of his personal life. He finds that he has participated fully and served valiantly—"His eyes open, proud." He has lived with dignity as well as passion.

The poem is also about nature, specifically as a vehicle for penetrating the inner, spiritual realm of human existence. In Elýtis' terms, that means the world evoked by the interplay of water and light, which dominates the Greek landscape—hence the prevalence of sea imagery in his work. Yet the prevalence of nature in the poem reflects, as well, the particular affinity of the Greek for the landscape which has nourished him for so many centuries. The lull of the Aegean, the dazzling light of the sun on the sparkling water cast blue in the sky's reflection, wild birds crying above the edge of the horizon, and the omnipresent olive trees all permeate the Greek's entire being to a degree to which he himself is not fully aware, and it is this specific meaning which motivates Elýtis.

Finally, while the subject of the poem is the body of the poet, on a second level of meaning it is the body of Greece as well; in Elýtis' poetry, the poet and the country often seem inseparable. With tenderness and pride, the poet examines the timeless features of his country which constitute its unique essence, its Greekness. Taken from this perspective, the poem acquires a mythical dimension, which culminates in the reference to the resurrected Adonis in the enigmatic final line. Hence, it is not only the worthiness of the poet that is in question but also that of Greece itself. The final line, then, serves as an affirmation in both cases. Just as the poet has faced the forces of chaos and tragedy and emerged renewed, so too has his native land been strengthened by the centuries-long struggle against foreign domination and oppression. "The Autopsy" testifies to the worthiness of these sacrifices and celebrates the triumph of the human spirit.

Maria Budisavljević-Oparnica

AUTUMN BEGINS IN MARTINS FERRY, OHIO

Author: James Wright (1927-1980)
Type of poem: Lyric
First published: 1963, in *The Branch Will Not Break*

The Poem

"Autumn Begins in Martins Ferry, Ohio" is a short poem in free verse, its one-dozen lines divided into three unequal stanzas, forming an argument with two premises and an inescapable conclusion. The title of the poem both identifies the poem's locale and suggests the cyclical, seasonal, almost ritual quality of the football game which is the poem's central focus. In the bleak industrial Midwest of James Wright's poetry, the stylized violence of the gridiron takes the place of the traditional harvest festival celebrated by more peaceful, agrarian folk.

Wright wrote "Autumn Begins in Martins Ferry, Ohio" in the first person, and it is typical of many poems that he wrote, not behind the mask of a fictional persona, but in his own passionate voice. Wright was an advocate for both the confessional style and the poetry of personality, which were in vogue in the 1960's. It is quite logical, therefore, to identify the speaker of this poem with Wright himself, especially since Wright was born in Martins Ferry, Ohio, and grew up in that working-class community watching his father and others being brutalized by grueling factory work.

The first stanza of "Autumn Begins in Martins Ferry, Ohio" takes place in the Shreve High football stadium, where the first game of the season teases Wright "out of thought," much as John Keats is put into a reverie by his famous Grecian urn. As he sits in the stadium and observes the men around him, he cannot help but think of their lives outside the event, and he presents the reader with a grim picture of men whose work is physically and emotionally draining as well as ultimately unsatisfying. It is these broken men, these "Polacks" and "Negroes," who sit in the stadium "Dreaming of heroes." The poem strongly suggests that these men are both reminiscing about their own former greatness and reveling in the present victories of their sons.

In stanza 2, Wright extends his imagination to encompass the women of the community who, equally affected by the squalor of their lives, are "Dying for love." In a very short stanza of only eighteen words, Wright is able to characterize the family life of the spectators and the players of the game. These thwarted, needy women are one of the reasons "All the proud fathers are ashamed to go home."

Stanza 3 is a direct result of what the reader now understands was the argument of the first two stanzas. Men such as these, with wives such as these, mired in a situation such as this, are responsible for the spectacle of football, where all the combined frustrations of the parents are acted out in the beautiful and terrifying bodies of their sons, who are doomed to repeat the cycle of flowering and death as surely as the seasons perennially repeat themselves.

Forms and Devices

In his first two books, *The Green Wall* (1957) and *Saint Judas* (1959), Wright was composing clearly under the influence of Robert Frost and Edwin Arlington Robinson. In *The Branch Will Not Break*, where "Autumn Begins in Martins Ferry, Ohio" first appeared, Wright was turning away from the traditional verse forms represented by these mentors and embracing the poetic doctrines of Robert Bly and such foreign poets as Pablo Neruda, César Vallejo, and Georg Trakl, all of whom Wright had been reading and translating. What he borrowed from these widely varied sources, as well as from a number of Chinese poets, was a more spontaneous and visionary approach to poetry and a firm commitment to William Carlos Williams' famous dictum, "No ideas but in things."

It is not surprising, then, that the two most important poetic strategies in "Autumn Begins in Martins Ferry, Ohio" are diction and imagery. The brevity of the poem is only possible because of the haiku-like precision of the language and details. While the poem is not without figurative language—for example, the moving simile, "Their women cluck like starved pullets"—it relies more heavily on the freshness of its simple, powerful, and precise diction. This spare language becomes nearly apocalyptic in the last stanza of the poem, where the sons "grow suicidally beautiful" and "gallop terribly against each other's bodies." The choice of a word such as "gallop," more usually attributed to horses than men, helps the reader to see these young athletes as the powerful, graceful animals that they are, and makes the reader even more sensible of the degrading forces against which they must ultimately struggle. Wright is also addicted to the plain words of traditional Romantic poetry, and the word "beautiful" and "terrible" appear in this poem as well as throughout his work, as a kind of touchstone for his thoughts.

There is a strong pattern of animal imagery in "Autumn Begins in Martins Ferry, Ohio" which emphasizes the dehumanizing influence of the mines and the steel mills in these people's lives—it is no accident that the women are seen as chickens and the young boys as horses. While Wright's images are always strongly visual, they also appeal to the reader's other senses, as in the "gray faces of Negroes in the blast furnace at Benwood." Here the reader can not only see the ashen workers but can also feel the heat of the smoldering furnace.

Wright's great skill is his ability to turn three short images into an indictment of a whole way of life. If the game of poetry is one of compression, of saying the most about a subject in the least number of words, then Wright shows himself a consummate player in "Autumn Begins in Martins Ferry, Ohio."

Themes and Meanings

Sitting at the fulcrum of Wright's poetic career, "Autumn Begins in Martins Ferry, Ohio" is in many ways a compendium of Wright's major themes and concerns. Many of his poems are an attempt, by a mature and contemplative adult, to come to terms with the perceived horror of his American Gothic upbringing in a small Midwestern steel town. The "Polacks," the "Negroes," and the "ruptured night watchman of Wheeling Steel" who appear in "Autumn Begins in Martins Ferry, Ohio," are typical of the characters that populate Wright's industrial wasteland. His poems are littered with drunks, hobos, and murderers; his concern with the suffering of the derelict, the dispossessed, and the victim is clear. Also clear are Wright's feelings of guilt for not staying to suffer with them, his essential alienation from these characters and the environment in which they continue to live. While the men of "Autumn Begins in Martins Ferry, Ohio" are "Dreaming of heroes" and the women are "Dying for love," the poet sits in the football stadium and says, "I think." It is his penchant for thinking, and then writing poetry about what he thinks, which both isolates Wright from his background and ties him to it. Wright is one of the most regional of American poets, and this has contributed to both the strength and the narrowness of his poetic vision.

Wright certainly is not the first writer to mine this particular thematic vein: investigation of the predicament of society's outcasts, the outlaws and the orphans, the lepers and the debtors. Charles Dickens did it with more anger; Walt Whitman did it with more gusto; D. H. Lawrence did it with more sensuality; Thomas Hardy did it with more irony—but certainly no modern author has done it with more authenticity and sincerity than James Wright.

Cynthia Lee Katona

AUTUMN DAY

Author: Rainer Maria Rilke (1875-1926)
Type of poem: Lyric
First published: 1906, as "Herbsttag," in *Das Buch der Bilder*, second
  edition; collected in *Translations from the Poetry of Rainer Maria Rilke*, 1938

The Poem

"Autumn Day" is a short poem of twelve lines broken into three stanzas of 3, 4, and 5 lines. The original poem is predominantly in iambic pentameter (with the frequent substitution of stressed syllables to begin lines) and rhymes *aba, cddc, effef*.

The title of the poem recalls a familiar literary motif—autumn as the season of moving toward the end of a natural cycle. Autumn often calls up the melancholy feeling of things drawing to their close and reminds one of death. In this poem, the poet brings the reader to consider autumn's various aspects and what they might symbolize for man on a broader level.

The first stanza emphasizes autumn's association with endings, and so with death, by pointing out that the warm and nurturing days of summer have been great and full, and that now the creator who controls the seasons must curtail summertime in order to move on to autumn. The shadow being cast on the sundials symbolizes this act of divine curtailment. The almost biblical rhetoric with which the poet addresses the "Lord" in the first phrase adds a serious and spiritual tone to the poet's meditation. This same biblical tone returns in the last stanza of the poem.

Rainer Maria Rilke, however, also suggests the fullness of autumn as the time of ripe maturity and abundant harvest in stanza 2. The imminence of winter and death from stanza 1 is thus tempered by the ripening fruit and the "southern days" which bring life to its final perfection and fulfillment. Autumn becomes a time of full harvest and almost superabundance. Both the melancholy and the positive sides of the autumn day are embodied in these two stanzas.

The urgency of time running out, exemplified by the shadowed sundials of the first stanza, returns in the last stanza's first two lines as the poet echoes a biblical cadence and uses the repetition common in biblical passages. These lines admonish man that it is now too late to undertake life's primary tasks of building one's house or finding one's mate. Autumn—and the passing time it symbolizes—sweeps relentlessly forward. Like the leaves blown by the autumn wind, man too is driven along by time toward his own end. If he has not already attended to the important aspects of life and of love, he will not have time to do so as the year, and his life, draw to their close.

This last stanza also introduces the process of reading and writing into this natural cycle. Almost as in preparation for death, man will read and write long letters to leave behind. Writing thus becomes a link to some more permanent state. This poem itself is such a document of poetic permanence that outlasts the seasonal changes.

The last phrase of the German text, "wenn die Blätter treiben"—translated as "when the leaves are blowing"—has a dual meaning; "Blätter" can also mean the pages of a letter or a text. The term "leaves" also carries this dual meaning in English, although it is less commonly used. The word "leaves" thus connects the natural cycle (blowing autumn leaves) to the act of writing (the pages of a text being ruffled by wind) and unifies the natural and the human realms.

Forms and Devices

Among many minor poetic touches, Rilke employs two main devices in this poem. The first is the use of nature and its temporal cycle as a metaphor for man as he approaches the end of his life. This use of a strong central image is common to many of the poems in Rilke's collection *Das Buch der Bilder* (the book of pictures) in which this poem appears. The second characteristic is the biblical tone of the poem which adds a spiritual seriousness to the poet's ruminations.

The references to nature and to the natural cycle begin with the poem's first line. Summer and its growth are at an end; the shadows lengthen as night and the end of the year draw closer; the autumn winds begin to blow. In stanza 2, the references to nature continue as the fruits reach final ripeness in the warm late-summer days and the grapes achieve their final sweet fullness. While all of these images are familiar tropes for the end of the natural cycle, they also serve as metaphors for the end of man's life as well. As a part of nature, man too is subject to the winding down of time, to the end of abundance and the approach of winter and death.

This implied comparison is made explicit in the final stanza of the poem in which the poet's focus shifts from nature to man himself. It is man now who must realize that no time remains to him. He can no longer build or be fruitful. If he is alone as the end of his life approaches, he will remain alone. As the leaves in his path are blown by the autumn winds let loose in the first stanza, man too is driven restlessly forward toward his own end. Thus nature serves as the model for man's own progression in life.

To provide an even more serious mood for his meditations, the poet couches his thoughts in a tone reminiscent of biblical language. Not only does he address the "Lord" in the opening phrase, but he also echoes biblical rhythms and repetitions in the last stanza. This return to a biblical tone helps to bring the poem to full circle and to unify its natural and human components as well as adding the weight of biblical tradition to the poet's aesthetic contemplation.

Finally, Rilke uses stress and rhyme to emphasize his points. The unusual number of stressed syllables that open his lines (Lord, lay, bid, who, who) interrupt the more familiar iambic rhythm to call attention to the urgency and gravity of the situation. In the final stanza, the stresses pile up to create urgency in the phrases "Who has no house now will not build him one. Who is alone now will be long alone." The poem itself is propelled forward toward its end just as both the leaves and man are compelled to go on by the movement of time. This driving force is nicely preserved in the translations of the poem.

A formal characteristic of Rilke's German poem not easily carried over to the English translations is its rhyme scheme. Particularly in stanzas 2 and 3, Rilke uses rhyme to reinforce his message. For example, he rhymes *Tage* (days) and *jage* (pursue, chase, hunt) at the ends of lines 2 and 3 in stanza 2. He thus links the idea of time (days) with the idea of pursuit to produce the concept of time running out for nature and for man. In the final stanza, Rilke rhymes the second, third and fifth lines to similar effect. *Bleiben* (to remain), *schreiben* (to write), and *treiben* (to drive or push) rhyme and create a structure in which writing forms the bridge between remaining or enduring and being pushed or propelled by time. In the rhyme itself, Rilke indicates that even though we are driven unavoidably by time, writing may provide some form of human duration. The written word, the letter or the poem, helps us to endure beyond our own autumn and winter.

Themes and Meanings

"Autumn Day" is a poem about time running out. Nature is approaching winter and must employ all of its force to produce the final fullness of fruit and vine before winter sets in. Similarly, man approaches the twilight of his own life. He feels compelled to produce all the perfection of which he is capable before his time runs out in death.

The theme is not a new one. Many poets (William Shakespeare, for one) have used the impending end of a cycle of nature to symbolize human life. Such thoughts often trigger a sense of urgency and of intensification in human activity. Shakespeare in Sonnet 73, for example, cajoles his lover to love more intensely because of the thought of imminent departure: "This thou perceiv'st, which makes thy love more strong,/ To love that well which thou must leave ere long." Rilke's poetic persona does not have the comfort of a beloved, however; he is alone with his reading and writing, but his writing itself may offer him some means of enduring. Being alone may provide a melancholy tinge to Rilke's considerations, but his poem also focuses on nature's and life's fullness and sweetness. As in Shakespeare's case, the thought of losing that moment of fulfillment and perfection makes it all the more poignant.

Rilke's poem also reveals a persona ready to face autumn and the end of a temporal cycle. This is somewhat surprising, since Rilke was a young man of twenty-six when he wrote the poem in Paris in September, 1902. Poetic resignation or maturity of thought, however, does not necessarily depend on age. In this case, the poet is using his observations of nature and its seasons to think about his own future end as well as to intensify his present moment.

Kathleen L. Komar

AUTUMN LEAVES

Author: Jacques Prévert (1900-1977)
Type of poem: Lyric
First published: 1947, as "Les Feuilles mortes"; in *Soleil de nuit*, 1980; collected in *Our Huckleberry Friend: The Life, Times, and Lyrics of Johnny Mercer*, 1982

The Poem

"Autumn Leaves" is a short poem in free verse. Its forty-six lines are divided into four stanzas. The first and third stanzas contain twelve lines each, and the second and fourth stanzas have the same eleven-line refrain. The only punctuation in the entire poem is a period placed at the end of the last line. This almost complete lack of punctuation permits diverse interpretations of many lines because it is not at all clear exactly how one should interpret them. In many cases, two or three different explanations are grammatically possible.

The poem is written in the first person. The unnamed speaker is a man who is addressing a woman whom he used to love. Although their love for each other has now ended, he still feels an emotional bond with her. He addresses her with the intimate *tu* (for "you"), not with the formal *vous*. It is clear that these are two decent people "whom life has separated."

In the first stanza, the speaker calls upon his former lover to "remember the happy days" that now exist only in their memories. When re-creating these days of happiness, Jacques Prévert utilizes the imperfect tense in French. This is entirely appropriate because the imperfect tense refers to habitual past actions or to past actions that lasted for an extended period of time. These were wonderful days for them because "they were then friends." Their love is described as platonic and pure.

The title, "Autumn Leaves," occurs twice in the first stanza and once in the third stanza. Prévert states that "Autumn leaves are gathered together in a shovel" for disposal; similarly "memories" and "regrets" are carried away by the "north wind" "into the night of forgetfulness." These images of "wind" and "night" are richly connotative, suggesting the powerful and almost unconscious human need to remember pleasant experiences from the past. The speaker ends the first stanza by recalling a love song that she used to sing to him.

The identical eleven-line refrain that follows the first and third stanzas is written in a deceptively simple but very evocative style. The speaker imagines that this love song "resembles" them, and he tells her twice within five lines: "You used to love me/ I used to love you." The loss of love occurs slowly, in an almost imperceptible manner that Prévert compares to the "sea," which "erases on the sand/ the steps of disunited lovers."

In the third stanza, Prévert suggests once again that "autumn leaves, memories, and regrets" are all "gathered together in a shovel" for disposal, but the lovers choose to preserve their memories. Although they no longer love each other, he is thankful because she enriched his life and was his "dearest friend." He regrets nothing because he will always hear in his mind the love song that she used to sing to him. The emotional power of their love still influences their lives although they both realize that they can no longer live together.

Forms and Devices

"Autumn Leaves" illustrates very effectively the refined art of Prévert, who wrote in an apparently straightforward style and yet expressed deep feelings with which all readers can identify. The use of verb tenses in this poem does not seem to be complicated. Prévert, in fact, uses those verb tenses (specifically, the present indicative, the imperfect, and the compound past) that are most frequently used in spoken French. He avoids an overtly literary style, which would have created a barrier between his poem and certain readers. Prévert strove to attract readers who were alienated from extremely esoteric poetry. His poems deal directly with such basic human emotions as love, loss of love, grief, and despair.

The apparent simplicity of style and vocabulary in this poem should not cause one to overlook the subtle art of Prévert. He skillfully contrasts the present with several different periods in the speaker's past. Prévert's use of verb tenses is very effective in "Autumn Leaves." In this forty-six-line poem, there is only one verb in the present conditional and one verb in the future tense, yet each is used extremely effectively. Prévert begins this poem with a wish: "Oh! I would like you to remember/ the happy days when we were friends." If she still remembers their love, this will bring him much satisfaction, but he realizes that he may no longer be part of her memories. Only one future tense is used in this poem, and even then Prévert links it not with the present but with the past. The speaker tells his former lover: "And the song that you used to sing/ always always I will hear it." In "Autumn Leaves," Prévert evokes past feelings by using verbs in the imperfect tense; this is entirely appropriate because lovers cannot link the gradual development and fading of their love to specific events. In French, the compound past tense is used to describe single past actions that may still have a slight effect on the present. Prévert uses only one compound past tense in this poem. The speaker tells his former lover twice in the first stanza: "You see that I have not forgotten." Through the very effective repetition of these words, which he evokes in the third stanza with the question "How do you believe that I could forget you," Prévert suggests subtly that he has not forgotten her because he cannot bring himself to forget her. The repetition of both entire sentences and similar expressions also serves to reinforce the fact that this speaker once experienced a pure happiness that he can no longer recapture.

In the first and third stanzas, Prévert included the elegant lines: "At that time life was more beautiful/ and the sun was hotter than it is today." A warm summer sun brings one much pleasure, but it pales in comparison to the ecstasy that love alone enables one to experience, even if it is only for fleeting moments. Jacques Prévert's extremely effective use of French verb tenses allows his readers to appreciate more thoroughly the simple but profound psychological insights in this poem, whose eloquence and musicality have been recognized by several famous French singers, including Yves Montand, who have performed and recorded "Autumn Leaves."

Themes and Meanings

"Autumn Leaves" is a poem about the power of memory. "Les Feuilles mortes" literally means "Dead Leaves," suggesting the paradoxical coexistence of the past and the present. Although one may delude oneself into believing that one has completely recovered from the loss of love, modern psychology has shown that it is never possible to suppress completely painful experiences from the past. One may not, however, fully appreciate the degree to which the past has formed one's perceptions of reality and one's personality. The "leaves" of the past are never completely "dead." Seeing a certain thing may somehow remind one of experiences in the distant past. This process is called involuntary memory because one has made no conscious effort to recall these events. When the speaker sees someone collecting "autumn leaves" with a shovel before the wind can blow them away, this commonplace occurrence reminds him that it is also possible to collect things that are infinitely more significant: "memories" and "regrets." Recapturing his memories is bittersweet for the speaker because he recalls simultaneously moments of happiness and his loss of love. He realizes that regret cannot diminish his present sadness; he prefers to think of the fleeting moments of joy that he and his beloved experienced together. Although they no longer live together, he still appreciates the importance of their love in his life. He expresses the essence of his love with these two exquisite lines: "But my silent and faithful love/ still smiles and thanks life."

In "Autumn Leaves," Jacques Prévert wrote in a deceptively simple style that hides the subtle and profound psychological power of this poem. The vocabulary used in "Autumn Leaves" can be understood even by intermediate students of French. Prévert clearly wanted his poetry to be accessible to as many readers as possible. A poem such as "Autumn Leaves" can be interpreted at several different levels, and each interpretation reveals the refined artistry and sensitivity of Jacques Prévert.

Edmund J. Campion

AUTUMN SONG

Author: Paul Verlaine (1844-1896)
Type of poem: Lyric
First published: 1866, as "Chanson d'automne," in *Poèmes saturniens*;
collected in *French Symbolist Poetry*, 1971

The Poem

"Autumn Song" is the most famous poem from the collection of verse known as *Poèmes saturniens* (Saturnian poems), published when Paul Verlaine was only twenty-two years old. Like most of the French Symbolist poets of his day, Verlaine was enormously focused on the art of poetry for its own sake and often presented the soul of the artist and the creation of art as the only topics worthy of consideration.

Verlaine was singled out among his colleagues for his insistence on the notion that the poem must be musical. His often quoted theory, "De la musique avant toute chose" ("Music first and foremost"), is amply demonstrated in "Autumn Song." For this reason, many of his alliterations, phrasings, rhymes, and the poem's rhythm are untranslatable, leaving much of the powerful impact of "Autumn Song" diluted when the poem is not read in the original French.

Verlaine's genius was appreciated by many around the globe, and his influence on the Hispanic "Generation of '98" is widely documented. "Autumn Song" is one of the most quoted and most imitated poems of the late nineteenth century. The ennui expressed by the poet is a posture that was to be characteristic of his work for years to come, and the title, "Autumn Song," immediately marks this poem as one whose time and place do not celebrate vitality. The "song" is a lament of the process of withering. Decay was of great interest to the Symbolist poet, and here, Paul Verlaine begins his career as a young man who sees the parallels between an exhausted universe and the soul's fatigue. For the artist, it is a time to comment on his own frustration with his inability to experience exaltation through art whose meaning or message has dulled.

"Autumn Song" is a short poem of only eighteen lines, yet it is a complete composition. Composed mainly of rhyming couplets, it has been constructed like a musical score, with crescendo and decrescendo communicating in the classical lyric tradition. The intense feelings of the narrator are expressed through a first-person voice in deliberately plodding rhythm quite pronounced in the original French, formed with short meters that demonstrate a somber and disturbed tonality.

The first stanza begins with an image of a violin sobbing out a monotonous and languorous song that pierces the poet's heart. The personification of this musical instrument is a metaphor for the poet: He is the vessel through which the sadness of humanity is expressed.

Another sound is heard in the second stanza as the orchestration becomes more complicated. The clock strikes. As the hours proceed, time ticks onward. In contrast, the poet's memory returns to the past. The intrusion of this regression creates a counterpoint. Two melodies, as in a fugue, lend dimension to this stanza, and their simultaneous activities give the poem its tension. As his mind "strays," the poet weeps. Therefore, both the sobs of the autumn song and the tears of the poet create a groundswell of emotion at the end of the second stanza.

The poem is resolved in the third stanza by the annihilation of these feelings as he is left parched like a "dead leaf," transported "now here, now there," blown about by "ill winds" that leave him a passive object tossed about by unfavorable circumstance. The monotony of the autumn song is transposed to randomness and inconstancy.

Forms and Devices

The content of "Autumn Song" works brilliantly with its musicality, although its forcefulness has been impacted by translation. For example, the first two lines of the first stanza have been translated as "With long sobs/ the violin throbs." Although rhyme and rhythm are evident, the intended onomatopoeic device of the long, nasal *o* sound in "Les sanglots longs/ Des violons," which accurately bring to life the sound of a violin, is obliterated.

The "languor" of the poet's soul is mirrored in the sluggish rhythm of the poem. Although the use of imagery like autumn to express decay and a sadly playing violin to reveal a disquiet heart are devices that, to the poet of Verlaine's generation, would have seemed to be hackneyed Romantic clichés (certainly they would have elicited a bored reaction), Verlaine's use of meter elevates the poem from the banal to a thing of consummate beauty. Verlaine is exhibiting his skill as a technician here in order to show that even an "autumn song" — a timeworn theme or topic for the artist — can be treated in a new way if the poet pays attention to his craft. In contrast to the effusive and melodramatic Romantic poetic presentation, Verlaine's short meter demonstrates, through its gasping cadence, that nostalgia is not always comforting.

Irony is another poetic device prevalent in "Autumn Song." The irony of naming the poem "Autumn Song" while attempting to rejuvenate a frequently used theme is Verlaine's artistically self-conscious method of calling attention to his own purpose. He uses paradox, as well; for example, the soul is bathed in tears (life-sustaining water) at the same time it is dry "as a dead leaf." The title of this early collection of work, *Poèmes saturniens*, was chosen by Verlaine to provide an ironic message of his intent. "Saturnian" is a word that is associated equally with abundance, feasting, and merriment as it is with the astrological sign of sadness and the description of a gloomy temperament. Although the reader might think, at first glance, that the collection is a celebration of plenty, most of the works contained within are about the paucity of the poet's soul as a result of an unnamed pain and unlocated depression. The reader experiences these sensations not solely through visual imagery and metaphor, but through the rhythm of the music, which has, in effect, made the reader become the narrator through its psychological impact.

Themes and Meanings

"Autumn Song" is a poem whose intent is to create a literary atmosphere. Verlaine chooses familiar concerns—melancholia, nostalgia, and so on—and attempts to show his contemporaries how these themes can be treated in a fresh way. This emphasis is present not only in this first collection of poetry but throughout his later works as he presents poetry not for the sake of social or moral commentary but as paradigms of technical accomplishment. The structure and the harmony, the forms and sounds are of consummate importance to Verlaine. The poem must embody the sensation that the poet wishes to express and not function as merely a picture of it.

The Symbolist poets were sometimes known as "decadents." The label of "dandyism" or "decadent" was applied to some for their life-styles, but it was mostly a term used to characterize the poetry of artists such as Verlaine, Arthur Rimbaud, and Stéphane Mallarmé for a particular vision and aesthetic accord. The point of view in most of the poetry penned by Verlaine and his group expresses the world as seen through the eyes of a somewhat jaded and bored individual. Bored with conventional representation, Verlaine makes a strong argument in "Autumn Song" supporting the artistic credo of his fellow Symbolists in their attempt to revitalize poetry. He is "wounded" by the monotonous sounds of irritating music just as his sensibilities are offended by much of the clumsy and awkward poetry that was being written at the time. The Symbolists despised the kind of poetry that had little regard for innovation and instead preached morality to a wide, middle-class audience. The Symbolist poets, with their unexpected associations and hermetic symbols, addressed a more intellectual and cultivated audience. Hence, the subtle allusions to Charles Baudelaire's *Les Fleurs du mal* (1857; *Flowers of Evil*, 1909) in "Autumn Song" that pay tribute to Charles Baudelaire (who called his own collection "Saturnian") would have been known to only a select few despite the poem's seeming simplicity of subject.

Although the poet has control over his creation, he has no control over the state of sadness that envelops him. His poetry, measured and chiseled, fastidiously fashioned, contrasts with his own haphazard wanderings "now here, now there," and the care with which he creates the poem is out of keeping with his own personal "harried and sped" feelings, over which he exercised no composure. "Look to the poem," Verlaine is telling his reader, "not to the poet. For you will surely be deceived." The passivity expressed by the Symbolist narrator is a veil that thinly and exquisitely hides the aggressive, enthusiastic, and arduous honing of such radical poetry.

Susan Nagel

THE AVENUE BEARING THE INITIAL OF CHRIST INTO THE NEW WORLD

Author: Galway Kinnell (1927-   )
Type of poem: Poetic sequence
First published: 1960, in *What a Kingdom It Was*

The Poem

"The Avenue Bearing the Initial of Christ into the New World," a long poem in free verse, is divided into fourteen sections of varying lengths. The title suggests the setting for the poem, Avenue C in New York City's Lower East Side.

Although a first-person narrator does appear in section 9, essentially, the poem's concern is larger than a single consciousness: Galway Kinnell is more interested in revealing the complexities of urban life in twentieth century America than he is in telling secrets about his own personal life.

Instead of starting with ideas about a place or introducing central characters to the reader, Kinnell begins the poem with sounds: "pcheek pcheek pcheek pcheek pcheek." These are the sounds of recently hatched birds demanding their due; their mothers then "thieve the air/ To appease them." The first section continues to provide a variety of sounds not necessarily specific to the area of Avenue C: A tug on the East River "Blasts the bass-note of its passage"; a broom "Swishes over the sidewalk"; a pushcart moves "clack/ clack/ clack/ On a broken wheelrim"; and a man leaves a doorway, and the sounds he makes walking enter the poem and bring the notion of time with them: "tic toc tic toc tic." The section concludes without any pontificating by the poet; he is there, and he watches and records. Time passes, "the babybirds pipe down," and the poem's overture concludes.

Section 2 introduces two characters: an unnamed Orthodox or Hasidic Jew "near burial" and a Catholic, Bunko, who is a certified embalmer. The Jew has twelve sons, eleven of whom are named: They bear the names of eleven of the twelve tribes of ancient Israel. The old man, however, mourns his one lost son, probably Ephraim or Manasseh, and his wives "who bore him sons/ And are past bearing, mourn for the son/ And for the father." Kinnell pairs the Jew and the embalmer Bunko because the "sad-faced" Jew is close to death, but the funeral parlor near him is not for Jews. In the new world, the Jew and the Catholic live side by side, but there is no link between them; in fact, the Jew's final words in the section are: "Bury me not Bunko damned Catholic I pray you in Egypt."

There is one moment of happiness in this second section. The Jew "Confronts the sun" that was introduced in section 1, and he nearly has a religious experience staring at it: "he does not understand/ Fruits and vegetables live by the sun" because he is no mere lover of nature, but "he sees/ A blinding signal in the sky" and smiles. The new world does not prevent the old world values from surviving; his faith in Judaism and God sustains him.

Section 3 begins with a list similar to the epic catalogs in the poems by Homer or

Vergil, but instead of naming families on a journey or warriors preparing for battle, Kinnell lists the signs along the avenue that the "Jews, Negroes, Puerto Ricans" might see as they "Walk in the spring sunlight": everything from "Nathan Kugler Chicken Store Fresh Killed Daily" to an advertisement in Spanish promising death to the most poison-resistant cockroaches. Kinnell then, interestingly, moves to the old women living "in the cockroached rooms" above the stores, and he has them consuming nearly all the products and services the previous lines named; the Avenue is a closed circle. Even when a small boy is introduced watching the pigeons' flight from a rooftop, the pigeons and boy transmogrify into chickens hanging "In Kugler's glass headdown dangling by yellow legs."

The poem moves oddly in section 4 from the first "Sun Day of the year" to the future tense and the nighttime when "The crone who sells the *News* and the *Mirror*" will appear. She has forgotten her dead husband and her children, she has no idea what the papers are reporting, and she is "sure only of the look of a nickel/ And that there is a Lord in the sky overhead." Yahweh lives in the firmament and in the streetlights of the avenue or in the "feeble bulb/ That lights her face"; in her dementia, she is able to see God clearly.

Section 5 returns to the birds whose "pcheek" sounds opened the poem. Now Kinnell wonders if they have matured enough to take up flight, and whether the mother birds are now dead. The mystery of life and death, the cycles of nature, are referred to here. The pushcart market on a Sunday is the focus of section 6. Here Kinnell glories, momentarily, in the beauty of the fruits and vegetables in the sun, but he also realizes they too have been "uprooted,/ Maimed, lopped, shucked, and misaimed," perhaps like the inhabitants of the Lower East Side.

The poet, in section 7, wonders why "Of all places on earth inhabited by men," he finds himself on Avenue C among all the people with "wiped-out lives." The poet is obviously not trapped in the city the way others must be; he has memories of the beauty of nature in New Hampshire and in France. He moves away from these personal memories and returns to the street and an "ancient Negro . . ./ Outside the Happy Days Bar & Grill." The man starts to sing but then is silenced as he "Stares into the polaroid Wilderness" of "Villages,/ . . . on the far side of the river" because the towns are sites of World War II concentration camps: Bergen-Belsen, Treblinka, Buchenwald, Auschwitz.

Section 8 brings to a close the pushcart market as the "merchants infold their stores." More importantly, Kinnell comments on the lives of the people on the avenue. The Jews who survived the Holocaust live in this neighborhood where they survive like "cedars on a cliff, roots/ Hooked in any crevice they can find."

In section 9, Kinnell appears in the first person in perhaps the angriest section of the poem. The biblical story of Abraham and Isaac is transformed: God turns away while Isaac burns in the flames. Walt Whitman appears as a believer in a harmonious cosmos, but Kinnell's friend Isaac, the week before he dies, reads Whitman and can only say, "Oi!/ What shit!"

Gold's junkhouse goes up in flames in section 10, and no one mourns as it burns.

In the evening, however, after the conflagration has gone out, the people appear to witness the destruction: After each person sees the power of the past—the "Carriages we were babies in,/ Springs that used to resist love"—reduced to rubble, "Nobody knows for sure what is left of him."

In section 11, the fish market is described horribly. The varieties of fish for sale are listed, but they are described with such tenderness that the carnage becomes awful. The fish lose their spirit and become flesh only when the store owner "lops off the heads" and "Shakes out the guts as if they did not belong in the first place." The inclusion of a form letter from a concentration camp is incongruously placed in this section. Is the reader somehow to equate the fish deaths with the Holocaust?

Night officially arrives in section 12, and the poet can only imagine what is taking place outside by the sounds he hears from his bedroom; this brings the reader back to the sounds of morning from section 1. In the sentence framing the section, Kinnell hears the "Carols of the Caribbean, plinkings of guitars" outside the Bodega Hispano, but inside the parenthesis there are uncomfortable images: A child cries, "wailing/ As if it could foresee everything"; a hook and ladder truck moves "with an explosion of mufflers"; and a cat caterwauls a "hair-raising shriek." The joy of morning is gone.

The noises of the trash truck arrive in section 13 as it "sucks in garbage in the place/ Where other animals evacuate it." Again, the poet only hears sounds in the darkness. He says, bleakly, "If it is raining outside/ . . . It would be the spring rain." There really is no spring in this poem, however: Death lives too close to life.

The concluding section is as dismal as the previous ones. The street bearing the initial of Christ is a "God-forsaken Avenue," and in the entire neighborhood of the poem, "instants of transcendence/ Drift in oceans of loathing and fear." There is a hint of nostalgia in the last few lines of the poem, as if a paradise has been lost. The people say, "what a kingdom it was!" as if, at some point, life was good. The Yiddish expression of grief is an appropriate place for the poem to end: "oi weih, oi weih."

Forms and Devices

The principal device employed by Kinnell to create meaning through form is the poem's movement from the possibilities of morning to the hopelessness of night. He also transforms traditionally positive stories, such as the biblical tale of Abraham and Isaac, by allowing the innocent Isaac to burn while a useless God turns away and washes his hands like "a common housefly." The avenue that bears the initial of Christ as its name offers a sign to the denizens of the Lower East Side, but the signs are only advertisements for roach killers or a Happy Days Bar. These twists allow the reader to see what has happened to the pure, new world: It has been corrupted.

Humans are not the only ones who are forced to endure in this world. Through metaphor, Kinnell allows the animal and vegetable worlds to also participate in the suffering. Porgies on sale have their "jaws hinged apart/ In a grimace of dejection"; onions sit in the sun "with their shirts ripped"; and cabbages lie about "like sea-green brains/ The skulls have been shucked from." Through personification, the reader is able to sense the suffering of all living things on earth.

In a poem that from the beginning is filled with sounds of birds and brooms and carts, Kinnell accentuates the absence of sound when, in section 12, he lies in bed "Expecting a visitation" of some sort, but hears nothing at all. In addition, the final image of God in section 14 is not one of an immanent deity or a concerned parent figure; instead, "God is a held breath," an absence of sound, a zero in the world.

Themes and Meanings

"The Avenue Bearing the Initial of Christ into the New World" is a large poem that addresses large themes. Kinnell is attempting to do for twentieth century New York what T. S. Eliot did for London in *The Waste Land* (1922), what Guillaume Apollinaire did for Paris in "Zone," and what Walt Whitman accomplished for nineteenth century America in *Leaves of Grass* (1855). By concentrating on a small area of a single city, Kinnell is trying to make a statement about the new world as a whole, and perhaps all of creation.

All of the characters in the poem seem to be suffering from one malady or another. They are all transplants, either from Africa, Puerto Rico, or Jewish ghettos in Europe, and they are not surviving terribly well in this new world. Fathers are removed from sons, and old men and women are headed toward death. The creative power of sex is not felt anywhere in the poem; Whitman's "procreant urge" has been replaced by the sounds of despair, the "oi weih" of the poem's close. Although in the early part of the poem God's presence alleviated some suffering, especially in sections 2 and 4 in which the old Jewish man and woman see God in the sky, by the end of the poem, God is only a "held breath," the Avenue bearing the initial of Christ is "God-forsaken," and a fishmonger who lops off fish heads and nails the fish to wood "stands like Christ" in the new world.

The fault does not lie in America only. The immigrants from Europe, for example, carry the memories of the Holocaust with them. The natural laws that force humans to kill in order to survive operate in Damascus, where twelve goatheads "were lined up for sale," as well as in New York. Kinnell is suggesting that something is wrong with the divine plan; or perhaps, there is no plan or no God. The poem catalogs all the varieties of loss a human can endure, but it offers few possibilities for redemption. The old crone who sells newspapers in section 4 offers some hope. Even though she has forgotten her husband and her children's whereabouts and "She can't tell one newspaper from another," she accepts the mystery of life, and she believes "there is a Lord in the sky overhead." After ten more sections of misery and despair, however, the reader has almost forgotten the old woman's hopeful senility. In the end, the "brain turns and rattles/ In its own black axlegrease" trying to make some sense of the mystery of life.

Kevin Boyle

THE AZURE

Author: Stéphane Mallarmé (1842-1898)
Type of poem: Lyric
First published: 1886, as "L'Azur"; in *Les Poésies de Stéphane Mallarmé,* 1887; collected in *An Anthology of French Poetry from Nerval to Valéry in English Translation with French Originals,* 1958

The Poem

"The Azure," a dramatic lyric poem that consists of nine quatrains and contains thirty-six lines in the original French, utilizes a melodic rhyme scheme that is characteristic of the French Symbolist school of poetry.

The poem reflects on the blue sky, a typically Symbolist aspect of nature, which the poet interfuses with his creative personality; thus art, nature, and the poet merge, and what transpires is a state of poetic meditation of thought, mood, and creativity.

The poem merges the idea of the infinite azure with creativity to develop an artistic and poetic aesthetic. Creativity is blended with the poet's empty soul, the ephemeral fog (an image that appears in the works of Charles Baudelaire, a Symbolist, and T. S. Eliot), and ennui (vexation—a condition of the poetic spirit that also appears in the works of Baudelaire) to represent a poetic state.

The poem presents the nineteenth century in negative terms, in images such as those of "the sad chimneys," chimneys filled with smoke—which reminds one of Charles Dickens' prison of soot. For Stéphane Mallarmé, however, smoke and soot are not related to social or economic oppression; they may represent instead a stifling of poetic creativity. Instead of inspiring the artist, as nature did for the Romantics, the sun in "The Azure" is "dying yellowish on the horizon"—an image that reflects the poet's own mood and soul. There is a sense of stasis in the poem; the poet's stasis is expressed in the stanza that compares his brain to an empty pot of paint: he has no muse to inspire him to create. Sleep and death replace activity and life.

Ambivalence appears in the poem in the images of the azure (infinity) and ennui, and the poem's imagery also expresses the isolation of the poet in society. Essentially, however, the poet's concern is with beauty or perhaps with an unattainable ideal. The poem expresses the desire to achieve perfection and the struggle, apparently unsuccessful, to achieve it. Certainly, the conflict and struggle of the act of creation are apparent in the images of the azure and the ennui. The artist who strives to attain the artistic ideal of the azure must contend with his own fears and inadequacies—the ennui.

The azure triumphs, instilling fear in the poet; instead of the beauty of a peaceful, serene, blue sky, the azure evokes an agony—the poet is "obsessed." The poem ends with a repetition: "The Azure! The Azure! The Azure!" The poem's emphasis is on symbolic meanings, dimensions, and transformations: "The Azure" creates a mood and presents a creative challenge, but it provides no resolution of the conflict it has presented.

Forms and Devices

"The Azure" utilizes the techniques and devices of Symbolism, a nineteenth century poetic movement in France, whose exponents included Charles Baudelaire, Arthur Rimbaud, and Paul Verlaine as well as Mallarmé.

The Symbolist poetic doctrine advocated using language to suggest rather than to explain. The Symbolists used words to evoke moods and feelings, not to name things or describe them in precise terms. Their approach to poetic language was magical and transformational; Rimbaud endorsed what he called "verbal alchemy" (*l'alchimie du verbe*), and Baudelaire described his approach as "an evocative sorcery" (*une sorcellerie évocatoire*). Mallarmé himself believed that a poem was a mystery whose key must be sought by its readers.

The blue of the sky and the ennui that figure so prominently in the poem are symbols that are used frequently in the poetry of the Symbolists. The blue sky, which represents the eternal, the ideal, is particularly important to Mallarmé, who used it as a symbol in his poem "The Windows" (Les Fenêtres) as well as in "The Azure." A mood of ennui, which in "The Azure" represents the fears, indolence, and artistic impotence that the artist must overcome in order to create, is evoked by many poems in the Symbolist tradition.

Among the many stylistic devices that Mallarmé uses in "The Azure" are condensed syntax, difficult grammar, esoteric vocabulary, and enigmatic poetic concepts, which are well suited to Mallarmé's purpose. His intention is to depict the feelings that objects evoke, the effects that they have, rather than the objects themselves. Mallarmé's evocative language, with its use of innovative syntax and complex metaphors, sometimes makes it difficult to determine his meaning.

The opening stanza of "The Azure" is written in the third person, thus setting up an omniscient point of view and casting the poet as the narrator of the poem. The second stanza introduces the pronoun "I," and the first-person point of view is used throughout the rest of the poem.

Themes and Meanings

Mallarmé, a hermetic poet who held poetic gatherings at his home on Tuesday evenings at which poets espoused the cause of art for art's sake, writes a poetry of complex imagery and condensed syntax. His frustration at not finding the right words with which to express an idea is presented in his poetry in the symbol of a white swan whose wings are imprisoned in a frozen lake—the idea of an impasse.

The theme of the impasse that is contained in "The Azure" concerns the difficulty of expressing the artistic ideal in words, not merely the sterility or lack of creativity that hampers the act of creation. The poem's theme is the challenge of writing, the challenge of creativity, the challenge of finding the right words and the right medium in which to express the poetic sensibility. The challenge also lies in finding the right way to connect thoughts, to create a coherent artistic form.

The azure represents the infinite and the eternal, the ideal that the poet can never hope to attain; its very existence mocks the poet, smites him "in serene irony." The poet must struggle to come as close as possible to the artistic ideal; poems and poetic symbols may not be eternal, but they may endure beyond one's own lifetime.

The ennui in the poem represents lamentation or boredom, a recurrent theme in Symbolist works. The death that is referred to is an artistic death; the poet's soul is confined to a state of oblivion, emptiness, and desolation. The bells in which the poet hears the azure singing are poetic bells that awaken him from his torpor, but there is no release for him, and the concluding line of the poem focuses on his obsession with the azure. The blue sky seduces the poet, and he is caught in an inescapable trance.

The poem contains a metaphysical theme that relates to the possibility (or impossibility) of transcending reality and reaching a mysterious world of pure art that exists in the mind and can be expressed in language. Mallarmé focuses on the blue sky not in order to describe it, but in order to relate it to the artist's creative role and to the very essence of creativity itself, thus producing a unique poetic effect. The poem expresses Symbolist critic Arthur Symons' idea that every word is a jewel and every image is a symbol.

Stéphane Mallarmé's "The Azure" embodies the Symbolist idea that to name an object in a poem is to suppress most of the joy of reading poetry, which is derived from divining meaning little by little. The poet who suggests is the poet who creates true poetry.

Clarence McClanahan

BABII YAR

Author: Yevgeny Yevtushenko (1933-   )
Type of poem: Dramatic monologue
First published: 1961, as "Babiy Yar"; collected in *The Poetry of Yevgeny Yevtushenko, 1953 to 1965*, 1965

The Poem

"Babii Yar" is a poem in free verse consisting of ninety-two lines. The title, roughly translated as "Women's Cliff," refers to a ravine near Kiev where thousands of Jews were massacred during the Nazi occupation of the Ukraine in the Soviet Union. The name of the place in itself has no symbolic connotation in the poem, even though Babii Yar has become one of the most recognizable symbols of the Nazi crimes perpetrated against the Jews. The Holocaust is not the main focus of the poem. The very first line, "No monument stands over Babii Yar," reveals the poet's main concern. The original crime was bad enough, he seems to say, but it has been compounded by a lack of visible recognition and respect for its victims. The poet immediately identifies with the Jewish people. He goes back to ancient Egypt and the agony of crucifixion, then leaps across the centuries to Alfred Dreyfus, who was the subject of a celebrated case of prejudice and persecution in nineteenth century France. The poet then turns to a boy in Byelostok, a town in Byelorussia near the Polish border, which has a large Jewish population that has been decimated—first in the pogroms in Tsarist Russia, then during the Holocaust. Finally, the poet identifies with Anne Frank's feelings of fear and needs for love and kindness.

In the final verses, the poet identifies with the victims buried in Babii Yar; this is his most powerful declaration of solidarity. As the trees stand as judges and "all things scream silently," he sees himself transformed into one massive, soundless scream, thus becoming the voice of each old man, each child who was murdered and buried there. He vows never to forget the tragic fate of these innocent victims, which brings him to his last point. He believes that there is no monument at Babii Yar because of the forgetfulness of the non-Jewish survivors and, more ominously, because of the anti-Semitism that existed before the advent of the Nazis and remains latent in the Russian people. This is illustrated by the shout of the pogrom bullies: "Beat the Yids, Save Russia!" By invoking the name of the "Internationale," the battle cry of the Russian revolution, the poet declares that he will fight against the anti-Semites until the last of them is defeated. He is not concerned that the anti-Semites hate him as a Jew even though there is no Jewish blood in his veins. On the contrary, it is because of their hatred that he sees himself as a true Russian, since the Russians are "international to the core."

Forms and Devices

"Babii Yar" is a simple, unambiguous, declarative poem, told in the first person and replete with straightforward rhetorical statements such as "O my Russian people!" "I am behind bars," "I am afraid," "I know the goodness of my land," "And I love." Such direct, terse statements fit a particular style of verse making that was popularized in Russia by Vladimir Mayakovsky and in America by William Carlos Williams. Such verses often consist of only one or two words lined in a cascading fashion. They are used primarily for emphasis, but they also add a dramatic flair, which Yevgeny Yevtushenko, a gifted actor and skillful reader of poetry, inherited from Mayakovsky, who was also a powerful declamator.

The main device used by Yevtushenko in this poem is metaphor. In a series of identification metaphors already mentioned, he not only drives his points home but also makes his references in an interesting way. When he says that he is an old Jew plodding through ancient Egypt, he immediately establishes a link between a history-laden people and himself as a present-day observer of history. When he sees himself crucified, he subtly reminds the reader or listener of the common origin of Christ and the Jewish people. A very brief mention of Alfred Dreyfus (only six words) is sufficient to evoke the terrible injustice done to him and all Jews. The metaphor of a young boy in Byelostok being kicked while lying in the blood that is spilling over the floors brings into stark relief the bestial cruelty of crimes among whose victims are the innocent young.

The poet reserves the most powerful metaphor for Anne Frank, to whom he devotes one-fourth of the poem. During his "conversations" with her, her innocence and tenderness evoke the noblest feelings in him. Even the love he professes for her is ethereal, just as she is "transparent as a branch in April." By emphasizing the innocence of a young girl on a threshold of life, the poet underscores the depth of the injustice perpetrated against her and all young people like her. The images employed here tend to highlight the interplay of innocence and injustice. In addition to the visual image of a branch in April, the poet uses auditory images such as the steps of the police Anne hears and the smashing down of the door; to soothe Anne's fears, he tells her they are the booming sounds of spring and the ice breaking, respectively. The love that his encounter with her brings forth is unreal, desperate, and painfully tender, used to raise hope in a hopeless situation and to confirm the existence of humaneness in an inhumane world. Yevtushenko is at his best in creating metaphors and images that flesh out and animate his references.

Themes and Meanings

It is clear that "Babii Yar" is a poem with a thesis. The thesis is that anti-Semitism exists in the Soviet Union, the official disclaimers notwithstanding. Yevtushenko protests against it by using perhaps the most suitable symbol—Babii Yar. The fact that the atrocities were committed by the hated enemy, the Nazis, amplifies the unforgivability of anti-Semitic attitudes, let alone actions. The fact that this anti-Semitism is camouflaged makes the original crime even more heinous.

Throughout his career, Yevtushenko has been known as a fiery dissident. He has used many of his poems to express his dissatisfaction with, and disapproval of, things that have happened in his country (next to "Babii Yar," "The Heirs of Stalin" is perhaps the best example). His protests have met with varying degrees of success, and his animosity toward the system has had its ebb and flow, but he has never been reluctant to speak his mind. In "Babii Yar," as a member of a post-Holocaust generation of Soviet citizens, Yevtushenko makes a strong statement on behalf of his peers.

"Babii Yar" is, however, more than a political statement about a problem in the Soviet Union. It is a declaration of solidarity with the oppressed, no matter who they may be, no matter where and when the oppression may be practiced. This solidarity with all humankind gives the poem a universal appeal, raising it above local politics and ideology. That is why the poet identifies with ancient figures as well as modern ones such as Dreyfus, Anne Frank, and the boy from Byelostok. It is evident, therefore, that Yevtushenko is warning not only the Soviet authorities and his compatriots but also the entire world against the pernicious effects of anti-Semitism and, in fact, of all injustice. While it is true that he has written other poems to this end, "Babii Yar" can be considered Yevtushenko's main protest against injustice, and a plea for a better world.

The ultimate merits of this poem lie in its aesthetics, however, and in the poet's ability to dress his basically nonliterary aim in a formidable artistic garb that transcends all mundane concerns. The best proof of the effect of the poem is its use by Dmitri Shostakovich in the opening movement of his Thirteenth Symphony.

Vasa D. Mihailovich

BADGER

Author: John Clare (1793-1864)
Type of poem: Lyric
First published: 1920, in *John Clare: Poems Chiefly from Manuscript*

The Poem

"Badger" is written in heroic couplets, its sixty-eight lines divided into five sonnet-length stanzas. Since the copy-text of "Badger" is untitled, some editors have chosen to call it "Badger" and others "[The Badger]"; it has been anthologized in both five- and three-stanza versions. The following description of the poem refers to the five-stanza "Badger."

The first stanza of the poem gives the reader a general sense of the badger's appearance and activities. An awkward and unattractive animal, the badger does not live in harmony with humans and domestic animals: "The shepherds dog will run him to his den/ Followed and hooted by the dogs and men." When the woodman goes hunting for foxes, he does not see the badger's many holes and often tumbles into them.

In the second stanza, the men and their dogs trap the badger and bring him to town to be baited. The noise of the hunt frightens an old fox and a poacher, who misfires, wounding a hare. Although the badger is reputed to be an aggressive animal, much of the violence in the poem seems to come from men, who take a sadistic delight in tormenting the beast.

The badger fights heroically in the third stanza, turning on the crowds and the packs of dogs, beating them all, even the "heavy mastiff savage in the fray" and the bulldog. Despite being relatively diminutive in size, the badger fights for hours against impossible odds, and John Clare describes the beast as grinning throughout the battle. In contrast, the only human mentioned in this stanza is a drunkard who "swears and reels."

The contrast between the valiant badger and the ignoble townspeople is further developed in the fourth stanza, where the badger is finally "kicked and torn and beaten out." His attackers are larger and more numerous; they use sticks and clubs and kick the badger when he is down. The badger plays dead and then, grinning, chases the crowd away, but at last he "leaves his hold and crackles groans and dies." The poem emphasizes the badger's courage and the cowardly bullying of the village mob—although the badger dies, one might say that he wins a moral victory.

Some versions of the poem end with the fourth stanza, which certainly provides the poem with a climax, but Clare wrote a final, concluding stanza, describing a tame badger. This section of the poem presents the badger in another light—rather than a wild animal struggling for survival, the domesticated badger fights dogs when so commanded by his master, but it also "licks the patting hand and trys to play." The last lines of the poem describe the tame badger's essential timidity, as he "runs away from noise in hollow tree[s]/ Burnt by the boys to get a swarm of bees." Given the chance, the badger seems capable of living with people in an affectionate and harmonious manner.

Forms and Devices

Clare's poems are often loose in structure, catalogs of observations about nature that begin and end arbitrarily. Thus some of Clare's editors have felt free to drop the last stanza of "Badger," which seems to take away from the dramatic power of the three middle stanzas. "Badger" is unpunctuated, and this lack of punctuation makes it a fast-paced poem to read, with scarcely a stop (except for the line breaks) for the reader to take a breath. The fact that most lines are end-stopped allows Clare to dispense with punctuation, but he is not able to indicate midline pauses. This lack of punctuation gives the poem a spontaneous quality, as if it were being recited by the poet as he made it up, without much regard to grammar or organization. Unfortunately, many editors have chosen to punctuate Clare's poems for him, and the editorially corrected poems seem less natural and more "literary" than the originals.

"Badger" contains relatively few dialect-words, and thus readers do not need to consult glossaries as much with this poem as they would with many of Clare's other works. Some of the local terms Clare uses in "Badger" are "scrowed" (marked), "clapt the dogs" (set the dogs on), "dimute" (diminished), and "lapt" (wrapped or folded). Although Charles Lamb discouraged Clare from writing in dialect, Clare used Northamptonshire words and phrases in much of his verse. A word such as "scrowed" gives his poetry a regional flavor and distinguishes his verse from the more formally correct writings of his Romantic contemporaries.

In "Badger," Clare piles up verbs in order to show the chaotic violence of the badger's baiting through the streets of the town. In stanzas 3 and 4 the verb "drives" is used six times, as the badger aggressively drives away the sheeplike mob of people and dogs. One gets a sense of the power of the diminutive badger and the mindless cowardice of his tormentors. The violence of the badger-baiting section of the poem reaches a crescendo in stanza 4, with the piling on of the verbs "drives," "beats," "falls," "kicked," "torn," and "dies." The badger, grinning and cackling to the end, is nevertheless the victim of a terrific display of communal violence—the animal is not simply killed, it is beaten to the point of dismemberment. The last stanza, although not without its share of violent verbs, seems almost idyllic in comparison to stanzas 2 through 4, and it ends with the image of a timid, tame badger running away from a noise.

In general, the language of the poem is concrete and unsentimental—some would even say harsh. Clare avoids the literary diction of other poets—he once criticized John Keats for using classical imagery in verse dealing with nature—and renders his descriptions of rural life as realistically as possible. Rather than philosophizing or examining his emotional reactions, Clare describes how the badger is killed in a noncommittal way and allows the reader to come to his or her own conclusions.

Themes and Meanings

The main subject of "Badger" is the relationship of the wild animal to the humans who bait and tame it. What is the reader to make of the townspeople's cruelty to the badger? One response to the poem would be to condemn the badger-baiters as igno-rant sadists, but Clare's avoidance of moral judgment suggest that he would not necessarily agree with this view. Although Clare would not have been aware of Charles Darwin's theory of natural selection, he understood the concept of survival of the fittest from observing animal behavior in the fields near Helpston. For exam-ple, in his natural history notes, Clare carefully describes how green beetles will attack a large moth, devour part of it, and drag the moth's corpse to their hole. There is the same sense of detachment in "Badger"; Clare never expresses pity for the badger nor outrage against the townspeople. In fact, the townspeople and the badger resemble each other in their ferocity—one might even say that in the poem the animal and his tormentors become indistinguishable.

Despite Clare's detachment, the poem does seem to imply that the badger is being cruelly mistreated—certainly the odds, one small badger versus a whole town of dogs and rock-throwing and cudgel-wielding people, do not seem even remotely fair. Thus some readers of the poem consider the baited badger as a victim of the towns-people's capricious exercise of power over a vulnerable creature and, by extension, a reflection of Clare's own feelings about tyranny. As an agricultural laborer, Clare was well aware of abuses of power—his satire *The Parish* is a bitter attack on the tyrants of a country parish—the greedy farmers, constables, overseers, judges, and bailiffs who could make a poor man's life miserable. Clare also considered the acts of enclosure, which destroyed cherished landmarks and drove peasants off the land, as examples of political oppression. Put in the context of Clare's sincere hatred of tyranny and slavery in any form, "Badger" could be seen as a protest against the unfair use of power against a weaker adversary. When the badger runs toward the woods and freedom, the townspeople turn him back with clubs; when the badger is beaten and helpless, he is kicked and torn by the savage mob. Moreover, the last stanza about the tame badger, which must fight at his master's bidding, is yet another example of human tyranny over less fortunate creatures. Examined in this light, "Badger" is more than the description of cruelty against badgers—it is a blanket indictment of the abuses visited upon the powerless by the powerful.

Much of the power of "Badger" comes, however, from its harsh realism: One can tell by reading the poem that this poet-naturalist has carefully studied nature and country life. Clare's main task in "Badger" is to present the reader with a vivid portrait of this misunderstood animal and its sometimes violent relationship with the inhabitants of a rural community, and he succeeds brilliantly.

William D. Brewer

BALAKIREV'S DREAM (1905)

Author: Tomas Tranströmer (1931-   )
Type of poem: Narrative/lyric
First published: 1958, as "Balakirevs dröm (1905)," in *Hemligheter på vägen*;
    collected in *Windows and Stones*, 1972, and in *Tomas*
    Tranströmer: Selected Poems, 1954-1986, 1987

The Poem
    Written almost entirely in the third person, "Balakirev's Dream (1905)" is really
a lyric poem masquerading as a narrative. The poem consists of nineteen unrhymed
couplets, all but three of which are self-contained syntactical units. As the title
indicates, the poem purports to recount the dream of Mily Balakirev (1837-1910), a
famous Russian conductor and composer. Both the date in the title and the reference
to the warship *Sevastopol* carefully situate the poem in time: during or just after the
Sevastopol mutiny, which broke out spontaneously on November 11, 1905, and
which, despite the support of other groups of insurgents, was soon crushed. Like the
much more famous mutiny aboard the battleship *Potemkin*, the *Sevastopol* mutiny
was but a single episode in the ill-fated Russian Revolution of 1905-1907, which was
ruthlessly suppressed by czarist forces.
    The poem begins at a piano recital. Outside the concert hall, the streets are dark-
ened by a strike; inside the hall, a pianist has begun to conjure up a dream world in
which real stones (the brutal outside world?) become as light as dewdrops. The poet
likens the black grand piano to a large spider trembling in its net of music. Listening
to this music, the aging composer dozes off and dreams about a journey he is taking
in the czar's carriage (*droshky*), which is rumbling over cobblestones in a "crow-
cawing" world that is both dark and threatening.
    As frequently occurs in dream situations, the dreamer imagines that he is in two
places at the same time: inside the carriage and running along beside it. Moreover,
his sense of time is distorted: His clock shows that the trip has taken not hours, but
years. He finds himself in a field in which a plow is lying idle; then the plow becomes a fallen bird that is transformed, in turn, into a darkened, icebound ship with
people on its deck. As the carriage approaches the icebound vessel, the grating and
clattering sounds it makes subside, and the wheels spin over the ice with a sound that
is as soft as silk, recalling perhaps the activity of the grand piano-spider, weaving its
delicate net.
    Next, Balakirev finds himself the prisoner of the mutineers on board the
Sevastopol. Handing him a curious "instrument," which is "like a tuba or a phono-
graph/ or part of some unknown engine," the hostile sailors tell him that only by
playing this instrument can he save his life. Paralyzed with fear, Balakirev realizes
that this instrument is the piston that runs the ship. He tries to defend himself by
turning to the nearest sailor and begging him to cross himself. The symbolic gesture
he urges upon the sailor becomes a reality when the man turns his sad eyes on

Balakirev and— "as if nailed in the air"— is crucified. Just as the dreamer is about to witness the execution of the mutineers, the drumrolls that often accompany executions become a round of applause. The pianist has finished weaving his net of music, and Balakirev awakens with the impression that wings of applause are flapping in the hall as the pianist takes a bow. Though the fallen bird from the dream may once again have taken wing, the continued agitation in the street outside suggests that Balakirev's anxiety dream is prophetic.

Forms and Devices

As was mentioned above, the poem consists of nineteen unrhymed, strongly rhythmical couplets. All but three of these couplets are self-contained syntactical units. Tomas Tranströmer uses this structural device, which enables sudden displacements in time and space, to create a realistically presented dream pattern. As each indeterminate dream image recedes, it is replaced by another. The succession of images appears to mobilize the dreamer's repressed fears, finally bringing him to a confrontation with the hostile mutineers aboard the *Sevastopol* who threaten his life at the climax of the dream—that is, in the three couplets that are syntactically connected, from "He turned and faced the nearest sailor" to "as if nailed in the air." This climactic scene—and, indeed, the cinematic presentation of the whole dream sequence—is reminiscent of Sergei Eisenstein's famous film about the revolutionary events of 1905, *Potemkin* (1925). Tranströmer has in fact admitted that memories of this film are associated with the composition of "Balakirev's Dream (1905)."

This poem is partly based on one of Tranströmer's own dreams, which he originally intended to attribute to Anatoly Lyadov, one of Balakirev's colleagues. This leads one to wonder why Tranströmer has chosen to enter the world of political tyranny through a dream that he attributes to Balakirev. As is frequently the case (especially in his earlier poems), he apparently wished both to avoid personal involvement and to gain objectivity by transferring this confrontation between the artist and political reality to a Russian composer who was alive at the time of the Revolution of 1905.

A professional psychologist, Tranströmer has both a deep interest in dreams and a detailed technical knowledge of their function in people's psychic lives. He believes that in dreams— or on the threshold of the dream state— the experiencing self penetrates more deeply into itself and into life's secrets than it can in the waking state. Many of his poems describe dreams, which he sees as mediating between the inner world and the outer world of social life. The vivid dream images in "Balakirev's Dream (1905)" become a series of graphic metaphors that enable the reader to share the emotional reactions of the dreamer, even if the reader is ultimately unable to interpret the dream.

The opening line of the poem transforms the grand piano into a large black spider, trembling in its net of music. The primary aim of this poetic equation is to show that just as the spider makes a net strong enough to support drops of dew, so the music creates an alternative world in which stones (the cares and worries of the outer world) are as light as dewdrops. Yet it is difficult to overlook the fact that the spider's insubstantial net is not only its home, but also a trap for its victims.

Itself a metaphor, the Swedish word for grand piano (*flygel*) means "wing." Thus, besides establishing the setting of the poem, it also subtly introduces the idea of flight and birds that figures so prominently in the dream: for example, the "crow-cawing dark," the "fallen bird," and the "wings of applause" (the "fallen bird" resuscitated?) that flap in the hall when the pianist finishes playing. Near the end of his dream journey, Balakirev sees an abandoned plow (representing the nurturing activities of peace) and then an icebound warship (representing the powerlessness of the insurgents to resist tyranny). These images of disuse, impotence, and death reinforce the dreamer's inability to remedy a desperate situation.

Themes and Meanings

"Balakirev's Dream (1905)" is a poem about the relationship between art and reality. It tests the value of "escapist" art and asks if poetry must inevitably be politically engaged. Written in 1957—one year after the ill-fated revolt of the Hungarian freedom fighters—this appears to be a poem in which Tranströmer asks his readers to consider what is to be gained and what is to be lost if the artist takes a firm stand on political issues and uses his talent primarily as a means of goading others to action. By casting his poem in the form of Balakirev's fictive dream, he not only depersonalizes and objectifies his own strong feelings about the disastrous consequences of the Hungarian revolt of 1956, but also indicates that he believes that this impersonal, quasi-historical approach will be more effective than a first-person lyrical outcry might have been.

The artist he has chosen to play the central role in this poem, Mily Balakirev, is certainly not known to have harbored any deep sympathies for the insurgents—around 1905 he was, in fact, chiefly devoted to preparing a new edition of the works of Mikhail Glinka (1804-1857). Between 1883 and 1895, Balakirev had served as director of the court chapel, which provided music for the imperial family. His divided loyalties seem to be reflected in the fact that in his dream he is both riding in the czar's carriage and running alongside it. Why does he try to defend himself by turning to the nearest sailor and begging him to cross himself? According to Nikolay Rimsky-Korsakov, Balakirev, who had become fanatically religious in the early 1870's, often pressed his friends to cross themselves because he believed that this symbolic gesture might help bring them to religion. His superstitious reaction to the hostile sailor is one of fear, not sympathy, and by urging the rebel to make the sign of the cross—the only thing in the poem that really corresponds to what is known about Balakirev's personal habits—he appears to cause his death. (The leaders of the *Sevastopol* mutiny were shot on March 6, 1906.) In other words, the artist's empty gesture of spiritual aid (or moral support) has only made things worse. Perhaps Tranströmer wants to suggest that highly politicized poetry does more harm than good.

The crisis in Balakirev's dream (that is, the drumrolls betokening execution) coincides with the round of applause that greets the performing artist and wakes the dreamer. Balakirev awakens to applause that is likened to a bird flapping about the hall. The bird (a phoenix?) completes one series of images that bind the poem together. This soaring bird may suggest the idea that art can—at least temporarily— triumph over life. Outside, however, in the streets darkened by the strike, the agitated motion of the droshkies shows that the political situation cannot be ignored. (In the original Swedish, the generally rising meter of the first eighteen couplets changes abruptly and dramatically to a heavily falling meter in the last couplet. This metrical change seems to underscore the fact that Balakirev's dream has alerted him to political reality and to suggest that perhaps the shortest way to political awareness lies within.)

One gains considerable perspective on Tranströmer's position on the question of the proper relation of art to reality by reading "Balakirev's Dream (1905)" in close conjunction with "Allegro," a short poem that appeared in *Den halvfärdiga himlen* (1962, the half-finished heaven), his next verse collection. In "Allegro," the poet sits down at the piano after a bad day and plays a spirited piece by Franz Josef Haydn. The music he makes becomes a house of glass that is assailed by a shower of stones—stones that are by no means as light as dewdrops. Yet though these stones roll right through the glass walls, they cannot shatter them. Tranströmer seems to believe that, far from being a paradise for escapists, the world that artistic experience can provide is a place where freedom exists and persists, despite the brutal assaults of external existence.

Barry Jacobs

THE BALLAD OF READING GAOL

Author: Oscar Wilde (1854-1900)
Type of poem: Ballad
First published: 1898

The Poem

The Ballad of Reading Gaol is not a typical ballad in that commentary ranges beyond the narrative. While Oscar Wilde is focusing on the story of the execution of Royal House Guards trooper Charles Thomas Wooldridge for the brutal murder of his wife, he is also meditating on injustice, betrayal, and the need for prison reform. The poem is divided, rather unevenly, into six "cantos," as Wilde labeled them; each division is further subdivided into groupings usually separated by asterisks.

The first canto (sixteen stanzas: six and ten) concentrates on the condemned man, whom the persona (the voice speaking in the poem) never meets but observes during exercise period, eyeing the sky wistfully. Wilde quickly shifts to presenting the impact on the persona, who reacts to the news that the convict is to be executed. He then meditates on the wider implications of guilt: "each man" is guilty of a crime— killing the thing he loves—but is not held accountable. The persona then resumes his account of the plight of the condemned man, execution (a fate withheld from all the guilty, bonded as they are to the condemned man). The description is remarkable in that Wilde never actually witnessed an execution, but used his creative imagination to help his readers share the agony of the experience.

In the second canto, Wilde reiterates the convicted man's pathos as he enjoys the last delights of the earth: the sun and the morning air. The speaker and his fellow convicts regard the condemned man with awe, and they regret the debt the prisoner must pay. At this point, Wilde unites himself and the condemned man in a strange bond: Both are outcasts caught in a trap of sin and punishment.

Canto 3 is the longest (at thirty-seven stanzas), describing the period of the pre-execution ritual. Cool, unfeeling administrators play their roles: the governor, the doctor, and the chaplain, who seem callously indifferent to the man's plight. The condemned man wishes that the day of execution would come, perhaps to end the unbearable waiting. Guards may wonder about his motives in welcoming death but cannot express any sympathy, or their positions would be intolerable. Wilde empathizes with the warders here, perhaps recalling his own kind treatment by guard Thomas Martin at Reading Gaol. The major emphasis in this section is on the shared feeling of the convicts, who serve almost as a Greek chorus and as fellow victims as the day of execution approaches. The men are shocked to see the open grave readied for the condemned man and spend the night tortured by terror and mad phantoms. Their identification with the condemned man is complete. They dread the dawn, and its arrival is described in a brilliant stanza as the shadows of the window bars move across the persona's cell. Hope for a reprieve dies as the morning progresses. The men do not actually witness the execution, but their imaginations draw a more horrible view than the actual event. When the appointed hour strikes on the prison clock, the execution is signaled by a "wail/ Of impotent despair." The speaker and his fellow convicts share the agony.

Wilde continues to describe the day of execution in canto 4, with the prisoners confined to their cells until noon, when they are released for exercise. Now the impact of the execution is evident as each man avoids the other's eye. They suffer in their shared guilt, stalked by horror and fear. The watchful guards seem insensitive in this section as the speaker remarks on the discrepancy between their fresh uniforms and their quicklime-splattered boots. The executed man has been buried in quicklime to speed the decaying process; unfortunately, the sterile ground over his grave will never yield any growth. The persona wishes for a sign of redemption, roses blooming in the yard or a cross to mark the location. While the executed man may now be at peace, he was allowed no funeral rites; although Christ came to save sinners, the dead man is not allowed any indication of salvation. His only mourners are his fellow outcasts, the convicts. At this point, the poem might have concluded, if Wilde had not chosen to continue with two more cantos, deploring injustice and cruelty. The last four lines of the canto serve as Wilde's epitaph.

Canto 5 is the controversial canto that is often excised by editors to "improve" the poem. Wilde is at his most emotional as he excoriates injustice and the inadequacies of the prison system. Prisons are built with "bricks of shame" (canto 5, line 3), kept from the sight of society. He adds his own indignation at the imprisonment of children (which shocked Wilde in Reading; he offered to pay the children's fine). Food, water, and sanitary facilities are vile and scanty, degrading to the prisoners; the worst torture is isolation. These combine to break men's spirits. Wilde contributes a brief sermon on repentance: "How else but through a broken heart/ May Lord Christ enter in?" (canto 5, line 14). These sorrowing souls have suffered enough punishment to merit salvation.

The shortest of the cantos is the sixth, with only three stanzas. It seems impersonal and objective after the passion of the previous stanzas. It offers a précis of the narrative, reiterating the message of killing the thing beloved, and restating Wilde's theme of universal guilt.

Forms and Devices

The poem represents a break with Wilde's previous poetic style, lush verse heavily indebted to Romantic poets such as Samuel Taylor Coleridge and John Keats, and to Victorian poets Algernon Swinburne and Alfred, Lord Tennyson. Wilde, instead, chooses a more direct, less flamboyant style and often concentrates on detail: "We sewed the sacks, we broke the stones/ We turned the dusty drill" (canto 3, line 9).

Some of the weaker passages depend upon cold abstractions (Death, Dread, Doom), but the strain in poetic technique is eased with vivid personifications: "Sleep walks wild-eyed and cries to Time" (canto 5, line 8); "crooked shapes of Terror crouched" (canto 3, line 19). The grim narrative is brightened by images such as "the little tent of blue" and "clouds with sails of silver." These personifications are often supported by similes: "Like a casque of scorching steel" (canto 1, line 5).

It is not surprising, in a poem about sin and redemption, that Wilde alludes to biblical sources, as in the description of sacrificial victims, "The bitter wine upon a sponge"; in "the holy hands that took/ The thief to Paradise" (canto 5, line 15), suggesting Christ as redeemer; and in the description of the first murder (the story of Cain and Abel). Another powerful allusion is to the legend found in Wagner's *Tannhauser* (canto 4, line 4) when a pilgrim's staff blossoms to signify the redemption of a sinner. These allusions brighten the grim narrative and enhance Wilde's message.

Although the poem is labeled a "ballad," Wilde did not adhere to the traditional, four-line ballad stanza (with the second and fourth lines rhyming) but adopted the six-line stanza used occasionally in Samuel Taylor Coleridge's *The Rime of the Ancient Mariner* (1798) and in Thomas Hood's "The Dream of Eugene Aram" to provide commentary. Wilde also borrowed iambic tetrameter (four repetitions of the iambic pattern of stress on the second syllable) rather than the five repetitions popular in English poetry. Frequently, this pattern has been used in humorous verse (by Lewis Carroll, for example), but Wilde managed it creditably. The metrical form and internal rhyme (a word in midline rhyming with a word at the end), as in "To dance to flutes to dance to lutes," are effective in those passages describing the puppetlike jerking of the phantoms terrifying the convicts, but the general effect can be monotonous.

Indeed, Wilde borrowed more than the stanza form from Coleridge. Like Wilde's phantoms, Coleridge's "death fires" dance "About, about in reel and rout." Early reviewers recognized Wilde's debt to Coleridge and to Hood. They rated Wilde as more realistic in the trenchant narrative of the execution and burial of the convicted murderer, but more mannered and self-conscious in the total presentation.

Themes and Meanings

Writing the poem within months of his release from prison proved cathartic to Wilde and restored his confidence in his creative powers. Wilde had been imprisoned for two years at hard labor after his conviction in May, 1895, for homosexual offenses. The legal proceedings and imprisonment were humiliating; he remarked that he was inspired to write the poem while "in the dock." The poem was originally published with the author's name given simply as "C.3.3," his prison number at Reading, providing the poem with a grim souvenir of his prison life.

He found the opportunity to attack the penal system in the case of trooper Charles Wooldridge, who had slit his wife's throat with a razor and was hanged at Reading. The incident appealed to Wilde on several levels: his pity for the condemned man, his identification with the trooper, and his conviction that humanity shares in guilt. While Wooldridge's crime was vicious, his execution was inhumane. In recognizing that his own punishment exceeded his crime, Wilde accepted a bond with the condemned man, trapped in the same snare (canto 2, line 13).

He extends this identification to the reader; following Charles Baudelaire's taunt "*hypocrite lecteur* [reader]," Wilde embroils the reader in his accusation of guilt: "For each man kills the thing he loves/ Yet each man does not die" (canto 1, line 9). Convicts were punished by the brutal prison system, by insensitive guards, and often by fellow convicts — all unpunished crimes. Furthermore, Wilde boldly convicts humanity of sins of commission and omission, particularly through indifference or betrayal. If his poetic technique changed in this poem, Wilde's themes did not: Betrayal as a theme can be detected in most of his works, including the comedies. Appropriately, his last celebrated work emphasized this same theme.

The betrayed protagonist thus becomes a sacrificial hero, a penitent martyr (illustrated in the poem by the reference to the redeemed Parsifal's staff blooming after his death). Had he been content to restrict himself to this theme, Wilde's poem might have been his masterpiece. Wilde was passionate about the need to expose the brutality of the prison system, however, and wrote to his friend Robert Ross (who had suggested the poem's title) that while he agreed that the poem should end at the lines "outcasts always mourn" (end of canto 5), he insisted that the rest of the poem be included as "propaganda." The reference was to Wilde's exposure of the harsh prison conditions he experienced. He suffered from the poor food, isolation, and inadequate sanitary provision and medical treatment, and used the poem to reveal these deprivations to the public in the hope of initiating reform. He risked ruining the poem, realizing that it suffered from a division in intention, but while he regretted the loss of art, he chose altruism. Ironically, although he consistently used betrayal as a theme, he betrayed his own artistic instincts for propaganda and won a small victory when his poem brought prison conditions to the attention of legislators.

The propagandizing sections, especially canto 5, received the harshest criticism. Most critics agree that exclusion of these sections strengthens the poem; William Butler Yeats printed an abbreviated version in his *Oxford Book of Modern Verse* (1936). In whatever form it is encountered, most readers would agree with Wilde's biographer Richard Ellman: "[O]nce read, it is never forgotten."

Elizabeth Nelson

THE BANQUET

Author: George Herbert (1593-1633)
Type of poem: Meditation
First published: 1633, in *The Temple*

The Poem

"The Banquet" first appeared in a posthumous collection of George Herbert's work published as *The Temple*. Divided into three parts (the church porch, the church, and the church militant), *The Temple* was designed by Herbert to reflect the structure of the Old Testament tabernacle (the outer porch, the Holy Room, and the Holy of Holies). This tripartite division also yields numerical significance as the symbol of the Triune God.

As a religious meditation, "The Banquet" appears in the section labeled "The Church" as a method of preparation for Holy Communion, in which earthly and heavenly elements are combined into a whole that is greater than the sum of its parts. The poem can be roughly divided into two parts. Stanzas 1 through 5 focus on the present, in this case the immediate joys of celebrating the sacrament. In keeping with this pattern, the initial verse contains an allusion to Solomon's *Song of Songs* and welcomes the spiritual cheer provided by the Holy Supper in the way one might welcome a lover. In stanza 2, Herbert goes on to compare the divine sweetness of the wine to a sugared liquor; specifically, he envisions a star melted in the liquid, a combination of heaven and the fruit of earth. This metaphor involves sight as well as taste, perhaps suggesting that in the sacrament an earthly sense (taste) is transformed into a heavenly vision (sight).

Stanzas 3 and 4 shift the emphasis to a sense of smell as the sweetness of the bread is compared to flowers, gums, powders, and perfumes. This smell goes beyond physical sweetness, however, and can "subdue the smell of sin." Verse 4 then assures the reader that by assuming flesh, the Godhead has joined the physical and the spiritual and continues to impart them to believers through a heavenly meal.

Stanza 5 serves as both the climax of the first section and the transition to the second. Herbert argues that just as wood gives off a sweeter scent when the tree is cut than when it is standing whole, so God's love is made sweeter through the sacrifice of His broken body.

The second section (stanzas 6 through 9) provides both a flashback and a projection of the future. Here Herbert explains why the sacrifice of a broken body is necessary and then rejoices in the unity of God and man that is brought about by such a sacrifice. Stanza 6 mirrors verse 5 by dealing with another type of "sweet breaking." Herbert must break with earthly ways and reacquaint himself with his heavenly heritage. This movement from the corporeal to the ethereal can only be accomplished by breaking his willful human spirit, which, by its nature, opposes God. Thus the symbolic "breaking" of worldly desires for Herbert coincides with God's willingness to be "broken" for mankind's sins.

Following the biblical precedent, "whoever humbles himself will be exalted" (Matthew 23:12), stanzas 7 and 8 comprise the movement of sinful man back to his God. The persona gradually moves from the ground to the sky, now viewing God in shared glory rather than in a state of humiliation. The final stanza appropriately returns the reader to earth, where Herbert must continue to serve his Lord. Herbert has learned during his journey, however, and concludes the poem with a paradox resolved. Having experienced Christ's sacrifice as well as His glory, he is unified with the Godhead and can continue "to strive in this" (life) and simultaneously "to love the strife."

Forms and Devices

Perhaps more than other poets of his time, Herbert is known for building the meanings of his poems into the external structure of the work. Although "The Banquet" does not reveal its meaning directly through shape, Herbert has experimented with both rhyme and meter to emphasize religious symbolism. The rhyme pattern is *aabccb*, which suggests the idea of the Trinity (three persons, one God). Moreover, the syllabic structure of the verses is 7-3-7-7-3-7. Once again, the three is Trinitarian, while the seven, another holy number, has often been seen as an archetypal image for the joining of God (three) and man (four for the four corners of the earth). Together they form ten, the number of completeness, while the nine stanzas that compose the poem represent a perfect square of three.

In addition to numeric devices, "The Banquet" relies heavily on metaphor, drawing direct comparisons of two dissimilar things. The metaphysical technique of "conceit" climaxes in verse 5 as Herbert unites several spiritual ideas with the physical concept of sweetness. Earthly taste (sugar) melts into a heavenly vision (star). The metaphors of stanzas 2 and 3 continue this theme of unification as the sweetness of the Host (bread) is compared to the fragrance of "flowers, and gums, and powders." Both star and flower suggest the image of Christ (the star of Bethlehem and the Rose of Sharon) and imply the spiritual and physical oneness created by God putting on human flesh. Thus the God/man (Christ) is the real power and sweetness in communion, in which He gives Himself to redeem sinful man. Like "pomanders and wood," whose scents are better when they are bruised, God's love takes on a sweeter aroma, since he was "bruised for our transgressions" (Isaiah 53).

Thus Christ's sacrifice on the cross is translated into the symbolic breaking of the bread and the blessing of the wine. The body and blood received through the Holy Supper is efficacious in restoring fallen man momentarily to his former glory at the right hand of God. Herbert realizes that the ecstasy provided by the feast is only temporary, yet it is necessary for man's spiritual health, his resurrection to new life on earth. Herbert ends the poem with yet another technique associated with the Metaphysicals: a pun. Utilizing the words "strive" and "strife," he reminds his readers that the Christian life requires struggle, but as Christ overcame the strife of both death and the grave, the believer can "love the strife." For through it, as through Holy Communion, he attains unity with the Savior and both experiences a partial resurrection now and awaits an eternal resurrection after death and the Last Judgment.

Themes and Meanings

Although the first section of "The Banquet" is rich in poetic devices, the second section speaks more personally of the theme of the poem. Section 1 provides a succession of metaphors that build toward a parable of life that emphasizes the unity of flesh and spirit found both in the sacrament and in the God/man, Christ Jesus. This building pattern is also significant because it relates to the title of the collection, *The Temple*. This image suggests not only a physical building but also human beings themselves, who as God's temples constantly desire their bodies to be built up in the Spirit. Thus the abstract combinations of sweetness and wine, fragrance and bread, and the associations of wood and star suddenly become a more personalized parable of the unity of God and man.

This unity is attainable only through bruised wood, an image that recalls not only the cross but also the battered body of Christ, dying for the sins of the world. To emphasize the importance of this event, Herbert flashes back to a time before he was redeemed. Here he pictures himself "drowned" in the delights of the earth. Oddly enough, he is saved from drowning (the punishment for wickedness during the Flood) by another liquid, the blood of Christ. God in His Son comes down to the author and is "spilt with me." Christ joins Himself to human suffering and then adds His victory and resurrection so that man can be restored.

A movement upward, culminating in a heavenly vision, results when man puts on Christ. Literally, Herbert is doing this through the reception of Holy Communion. "Wine becomes a wing," and Herbert beholds a revelation or epiphany as he observes Christ in the fullness of His heavenly glory (the Transfiguration). This vision enables Herbert to make sense even of the insensible. He understands that since he has been lifted up through the sacrament, he must return to earth, and he does so with a greater vision. With "wonder" and awe, he takes up his ditty and returns to his "lines" [poetry] and life. In the last stanza, by joining the senses of touch (hands) and hearing (hearken) to the senses of taste and smell, Herbert seems to suggest that only through receiving the Lord's Supper can one be wholly complete.

Such a completeness overcomes all earthly desires, even those of success and renown. Since it is known that Herbert had aspirations in the court of England, one line from the poem stands out in relationship to his own life. Lines 40 to 42 read as follows: "But still being low and short,/ far from court/ wine becomes wing at last." Whether his hopes were crushed by political disasters in his family or whether he shunned his aspirations for grandeur in favor of the priesthood, Herbert seems to have recognized that the calling of God's kingdom (His court) exceeds the appeals of earthly monarchs and their power. The journey of the soul to its Lord supersedes the finery offered by the world, and "the Banquet" of Holy Communion overshadows and supersedes any physical feast or celebration that might invite individuals to glory in their own abilities and accomplishments rather than in those of their Savior.

Michael J. Meyer

BATTER MY HEART, THREE-PERSON'D GOD

Author: John Donne (1572-1631)
Type of poem: Sonnet
First published: 1633, in *Poems by J.D.: With Elegies on the Authors Death*

The Poem

"Batter my heart, three-person'd God" is a sonnet, a short lyric poem of fourteen lines. In the Renaissance, two kinds of sonnets were popular. The Shakespearean, or English, sonnet has three quatrains, rhyming *abab, cdcd, efef,* and a final couplet, rhyming *gg,* which usually contains a short statement of the theme. The Petrarchan, or Italian, sonnet is divided into an octave rhyming *abbaabba,* and a sestet rhyming *cdecde;* the sestet moves from the questions, causes, or complaints presented in the octave to answers, effects, or resolutions.

John Donne combines both forms in his Holy Sonnet sequence; his octave uses the *abbaabba* rhyme scheme of the Italian sonnet, while his sestet rhymes *cdcdee,* the rhyme scheme of the English sonnet. The couplet usually contains a thematic affirmation of man's sinfulness and God's love for humanity.

The poem uses a first-person narrator. This speaker (not necessarily Donne) is a Christian man trying to come to terms with his own unworthiness in the face of God's never-ending love. In the first four lines, the anguished speaker begs God to make him a new man. He calls God a "three-person'd God" and uses a parallel series of verbs to reflect the three persons of the Trinity. "Knock" and "break" belong to God the Father (representing power); "breathe" and "blow" belong to the Holy Spirit (the Latin root of "spirit" literally means "breathe"; the words also allude to God's spirit breathing over the waters in Genesis); "shine" and "burn" belong to God the Son (incorporating a pun: Christ is both Son and sun). Each subsequent verb used in the verb pairs likewise adds an urgency to the speaker's pleas. It is not enough for God to mend the sinner; the sinner needs the more violent approach of total annihilation and remaking.

The next four lines focus on the depraved state of the speaker, who has been taken over by the Devil (the "another" in line 5). Even reason, the manifestation of God's wisdom in man, is captured by the enemy and unable to lead the sinner back to God.

In lines 9 through 12, the speaker admits his love for God but confesses that he has espoused sin (Satan, God's enemy). Repeating the trinity of supplicating verbs, "Divorce," "untie," and "break," he begs God to divorce him from his relation with sin and to release him from his pact with the Devil.

The couplet brings his petitions to a violent close; the speaker demands that God rape him so that he can be pure.

Forms and Devices

This sonnet employs metaphor and simile, the figurative language of comparison, to illustrate the anguished state of the speaker and his desire to free soul, mind, and body from the captivity of sin. The force of the comparison lies in its power to surprise and instruct by yoking distinctly different ideas or images together.

Donne's power to startle by pairing disparate ideas and images in his metaphors and similes is one of the hallmarks of his strong poetic voice; his figurative language asks from the reader a bold leap in imagination and involves a mental translation that often brings a deeper understanding of the theme of the particular lines. The metaphors and similes in "Batter my heart" are no exception.

In the first four lines, the Trinity is metaphorically compared to a tinker, or metalsmith, who, instead of trying to patch the kettle (the sinner), is asked to create a new kettle by completely destroying the old.

The comparison in lines 5 through 8, this time a simile, focuses on the sinner himself. He is like a town that has been unlawfully taken (usurped) by the Devil. The reasoning power of his mind, likened to God's governor, is also captured and unable to break the bonds of captivity. Although God is outside the gate, the sinner is too weak to hear God's knocking: "Behold I stand at the door, and knock: if any man hear my voice, and open the door, I will come in to him, and will sup with him, and he with me" (Revelation 3:20).

Donne switches back to metaphor in lines 9 through 14, and anchors the relationship of Christ as bridegroom and the Christian as bride in a series of comparisons that are both disturbingly violent and openly sexual. The speaker explains his dilemma: He loves Christ but is engaged to the Devil. He (although a feminine speaker is implied) begs for a release from this relationship. In the last two lines, Donne stretches the tenuous link in the comparison to its breaking point when he asks Christ to rape him so that his soul can be free: "Nor ever chaste, except you ravish me."

In addition to metaphor and simile, Donne employs paradox (a seemingly contradictory statement) to add compression and precision to the poem. Donne cannot express the religious truths imbedded in the poem any other way without distorting them. Christianity itself is built upon the paradox that Christ died in order to restore life to those who believe, and that believers need to emulate this death: "For whosoever will save his life shall lose it: and whosoever will lose his life for my sake shall find it" (Matthew 17:25).

Donne echoes this basic paradox, in his own forcible way, when the speaker claims that only by death to sin can he rise with Christ ("That I may rise, and stand, o'erthrow me"), that only through imprisonment by God can the soul be freed of sin and Satan ("for I/ Except you enthral me, never shall be free"), and that only by using the extreme image of a violent rape by Christ can the sinner obtain a virginal soul.

Themes and Meanings

The best way to understand Donne's religious poetry is to consider each poem as part of a series of progressions of a man depraved by sin but relying on the grace of God for his salvation. Helen Gardner has argued that Donne's Holy Sonnets

(1 through 16, in her numbering) can be divided into three meditative sequences. The first group of six has as a theme the end of time; the theme of the next six sonnets is the love of God for his creation; and the last four deal with sin and repentance. Gardner places "Batter my heart, three-person'd God" as number ten of the series, the central sonnet on the love of God toward His creation, no matter how far man has wandered from the true way. (H. J. C. Grierson, the early compiler of Donne's poetry, assigns number fourteen to this sonnet.)

The metaphors and similes in this sonnet present a Christian man unable to overcome his sinfulness by his own powers, thus underscoring the Christian tenets that "all have sinned and come short of the glory of God" (Romans 3:23) and that only God's unlimiting grace suffices to save the sinner: "For by grace are ye saved through faith; and that not of yourselves: it is the gift of God" (Ephesians 2:8).

The paradoxes incorporated in the sonnet not only give an immediacy to the speaker's dilemma, but also mirror the paradoxical truths of the Christian faith. All the seeming contradictions testify that true spiritual life is only possible through death with Christ so that the Christian's faith may grow to maturity: "Verily, verily, I say unto you, Except a corn of wheat fall into the ground and die, it abideth alone: but if it die, it bringeth forth much fruit" (John 12:24).

The sonnet is centered on the regeneration process, the "making new" of the soul so that God's image may be restored. The passiveness of the sinner, emphasized by his anguished pleas that God begin the renewal process ("Batter my heart," "o'erthrow me," "Divorce me," "imprison me," "ravish me"), reinforces the Christian tenet that God's grace alone can effect this regeneration.

Donne repeats the theme of regeneration through the violent actions of God on the sinful soul at the close of "Good Friday, 1613. Riding Westward." In the same anguished but demanding voice, the speaker asks God to make him a new man: "Burn off my rusts, and my deformity,/ Restore thine image, so much, by thy grace,/ That thou mayst know me, and I'll turn my face."

Although the speakers in Donne's religious poetry express their depravity and their agony over personal salvation, "Batter my heart, three-person'd God" stands as an eloquent and intense witness to the belief that through God's grace the Christian soul can begin its journey of regeneration that will find its ultimate glorification in heaven.

Koos Daley

BAVARIAN GENTIANS

Author: D. H. Lawrence (1885-1930)
Type of poem: Lyric
First published: 1932, in *Last Poems*

The Poem

This short poem in free verse opens with a two-line stanza that implies the speaker has some Bavarian gentians (bright blue flowers) growing in his house in September. The poem then turns into an invocation, or prayer written in the imperative mood, in which the speaker calls to the flowers to act as torches to lead him into the dark underworld of Pluto and Persephone's marriage. "Bavarian Gentians" thus becomes an imaginative journey motivated by the contrast between the somber and unexceptional scene evoked in the opening lines and the vividly described phantasmal underworld of Roman mythology.

The poet's allusions to Pluto, Dis, Demeter, and Persephone invoke a particular Roman myth that explains seasonal change. Pluto, the ruler of the underworld, abducts Persephone, the daughter of the goddess of grain and fertility, Demeter. Though Pluto makes Persephone his underworld queen, Demeter exacts a compromise: Persephone can return each April to her mother for six months, after which (in September) she must return to her husband and the underworld. During the time Persephone is away from her mother, Demeter mourns her absence and the ground becomes barren; with Persephone's return in spring, the earth becomes fertile anew.

Thus, the poem's September setting is significant. The speaker longs to follow Persephone back into Pluto's kingdom at the very time when the earth is dormant and barren: "even where Persephone goes, just now, from the frosted September." The twist D. H. Lawrence gives the myth is his surprising association of vitality with the underworld abode of Pluto. Against the sterility of autumn and winter is posed the dark energy of the mystical underworld.

Into this underworld, the speaker of the poem imaginatively leads us. Images of darkness and blueness abound as we seem to descend deeper. The third and final stanza again cites the gentian flower as a guiding light: "let me guide myself with the blue, forked torch of this flower." The descent continues past a Persephone that exists only as "a voice . . . enfolded in the deeper dark/ of the arms Plutonic." The final image of the poem shows the gentian torch paradoxically "shedding darkness on the lost bride and her groom." The speaker seems to desire to enter this forbidden kingdom, and Lawrence seems to celebrate the Plutonic underworld in the poem. Why this underworld deserves celebration and draws the speaker to it becomes a central interpretive question.

Forms and Devices

Lawrence's mythological allusions structure "Bavarian Gentians," and the reader senses quickly that some knowledge of the myth invoked is necessary for an understanding of the poem. The imagery, however, as reinforced through word repetition, is the poem's most startling technical characteristic. Lawrence repeats references to darkness and blueness throughout the poem. Forms of the word "dark" appear seventeen times in this nineteen-line poem. It seems as if Lawrence is straining the resources of the language to suggest an ultimate darkness, a darkness beyond the power of visual imagery. He refers to "the darker and darker stairs, where blue is darkened on blueness"; the world is a blind one, a "sightless realm where darkness is awake upon the dark." The references to the color blue come, of course, from the gentians' natural color, but the use of blue darkness rather than black allows Lawrence to charge the description with vitality. This underworld is not a realm of lifelessness, nor is its darkness antithetical to light in the sense of knowledge or awareness. Thus the "torch-like" flowers offer a "blaze of darkness." The oxymoron of "torches of darkness, shedding darkness" is crucial to the poem: The darkness attains some of the metaphorical properties of light. The darkness can illuminate, in contrast to "Demeter's pale lamps." All the intense, even hyperbolic imagery of darkness contrasts with the staid quality of the opening lines: "in soft September, at slow, sad Michaelmas."

The use of assonance and alliteration is as blatant and forceful as the use of imagery, as the line above suggests. The *d* and *k* sounds of the oft-repeated "dark" initiate a good deal of alliteration. In one three-line sequence, Lawrence uses "day," "daze," "Dis" (another term for Pluto or his underworld), and "darkness." The *oo* assonance of the "blueness of Pluto's gloom" is similarly prominent, and a link to the words that end the last two lines: "gloom" and "groom" (in this otherwise unrhyming poem). The word repetition, blatant imagery of darkness and light, and prominent assonance and alliteration all create a poem with a potent emotional and poetic charge. Lawrence is not striving for a natural, speechlike level of diction, though his word choice is also not elevated in the sense of traditional poetic diction. The reader enters a world of poetry and myth, but by descent, not ascent, and the language reflects this new poetic territory of a celebrated netherworld.

Themes and Meanings

The poem presents several paradoxes: The darkness is illuminating; the dead underworld possesses vitality; the reluctant journey of Persephone becomes the desired journey of the speaker. These paradoxes are familiar ones for Lawrence, who saw contemporary European society as overly cerebral and stripped of life-giving, primitive physicality. Throughout his poetry and fiction, Lawrence espouses the virtues of blood and earth: The spiritual is rooted in the bodily and the natural, not in the intellectual (at least not in contemporary society, which has corrupted the intellectual). "Bavarian Gentians" is wholly consistent with and expressive of this vision.

The opening lines identify the time of year not only as September but also as Michaelmas, the Christian celebration of the Archangel Michael held on September 29. Significantly, this Christian reference falls in the lines set above ground in the barren world of deserted Demeter. Against this lone Christian allusion, Lawrence places a plethora of pagan images, which he associates with life and sexuality. This contrast identifies the central tension of the poem: between those respectable European and Christian forces of the staid aboveground world and the seething vitality Lawrence locates within the earth and through pagan mythology.

Poet and speaker value the existence of passion in Pluto's kingdom, signified by Pluto's original desire for Persephone and its continued enactment. Enfolded Persephone is "pierced with the passion," and the subterranean world is a place of consummated desire. The sexually charged language of the poem suggests repressed or forbidden pleasures located in the underworld kingdom. Even the "ribbed and torch-like" flowers have phallic connotations (as they clearly do in an earlier version of the poem, in which Lawrence calls them "ribbed hellish flowers erect").

The descent into underground darkness has a psychological quality, as well. The speaker's longing to explore the darkness that lies beneath the somber autumn may well signify a journey into the repressed subconscious. The desires and longings that cannot stand the light of day are here illuminated by the gentians' dark blueness. Lawrence himself resisted Freudian terms, but his project was clearly one of recovery of the repressed. Like Freud, he saw basic human drives and passions distorted by the demands of social propriety. The descent into the underworld as a descent into the subconscious is a distinctively modern theme, and "Bavarian Gentians" is a powerful example of it.

The poem remains ambiguous about what the speaker actually gains from the underworld journey. Indeed, he is a sort of wedding guest at the Plutonic nuptial rites, and he remains an outsider. It is worth remembering that the poem is cast as an invocation: "lead the way," he cries; "let me guide myself." The poem presents the imaginative longing for an entrance into the underworld, rather an account of than the experience itself; however, the very action of the poet's imagination in giving life to the desired experience becomes a kind of experience or journey. That poetry and mythology might point the direction for revivifying humanity is typically Lawrentian. So is the ambiguity, for Lawrence's vision of a world free of the repressions of sterile modernity was never conceived as a wholly literary project. It must, Lawrence believed, be lived.

The poem was written in Lawrence's last year, and, as an imaginative exploration of the afterlife, it could well be read as a study of the poet's own encounter with mortality. Indeed, that theme appears explicitly in other poems written by Lawrence in this period. In "Bavarian Gentians," the celebratory tone and the impassioned vision of underworld vitality suggest an imaginative coming-to-terms with death.

Christopher Ames

THE BEACONS

Author: Charles Baudelaire (1821-1867)
Type of poem: Ode
First published: 1857, as "Les Phares," in *Les Fleurs du mal;* collected in
  Baudelaire: His Prose and Poetry, 1919

The Poem

"The Beacons" uses a catalog of artists to illustrate the relation of the artist to humanity and to God. It is the sixth poem in Charles Baudelaire's principal collection, *Les Fleurs du mal,* set early in "Spleen et idéal" ("Spleen and Ideal"), a section that examines the competing drives of willful degradation and artistic elevation.

In the original French, the poem was written in eleven quatrains using Alexandrines, twelve-syllable lines traditionally chosen for elevated subjects. The rhymes follow a simple, alternating *abab* pattern. The title, which can mean watch fires, as well as beacons, is echoed and explained in the tenth stanza. Each of the eight artists addressed in the first eight stanzas is characterized as a beacon, a warning or guide, in the darkness.

Each of the first eight quatrains addresses and defines the work of a sculptor or painter drawn from periods ranging from the Italian Renaissance through the nineteenth century. The first stanza is dedicated to Flemish artist Peter Paul Rubens, whose work evokes a river of forgetfulness, a garden of indolence, a pillow of flesh, all images of detached opulence. On this pillow of flesh no one can love, although life flows and moves in it.

In the second quatrain, Leonardo da Vinci is a profound, dark mirror where charming, sweetly smiling angels, weighed down with mystery, appear in the shadow of glaciers and pines which enclose their world. Rembrandt is presented as a sad hospital, filled with murmurs, decorated with a great crucifix, where weeping prayer rises from filth, a dark space slashed by a ray of winter light. The fourth quatrain presents the Italian sculptor and painter Michelangelo. His work is a vague place where one sees (pagan) Hercules figures mixed with Christs, where powerful phantoms rise straight up in twilight, tearing their shrouds.

In a break from the general pattern, the fifth stanza names its artist in the last line and addresses him directly. Pierre Puget, French Baroque painter and sculptor, is presented in terms of emotions—boxers' angers and fauns' impudence. A figure of contradictions, he found beauty in the lower classes, had a great heart, yet was swollen with pride, a sickly, yellow man, the melancholy emperor of convicts.

In the sixth quatrain, Antoine Watteau evokes a mad carnival, where hearts wander like butterflies in flames. Fresh and light surroundings are illuminated by lamps that pour madness on spinning dancers. The images are graceful but terrifying, tainted by flame and madness. The seventh stanza, dedicated to Francisco de Goya, presents visions drawn from a witches' Sabbath, a nightmare where fetuses are cooked and old women and naked children tempt demons.

Eugène Delacroix is a lake of blood, haunted by bad angels, shadowed by a wood where strange fanfares pass under a troubled sky. The fanfares are compared to a stifled sigh from the music of Carl Maria von Weber. With these two figures, Baudelaire brings his catalog of immortal artists from the past to his own contemporaries.

The ninth and tenth stanzas join the individual qualities of these artists in their general human character; they are maledictions, blasphemies, complaints, ecstasies, cries, tears, Te Deums. The catalog of terms which takes up the first two lines of the ninth stanza is resumed in the third line as an echo repeated by a thousand labyrinths, multiple, repeated and confined in the most elaborate of traps. The fourth line calls these voices a divine opium, both a deadener of pain and an agent of dreams. The tenth stanza expands their role to a means of escape or rescue from danger, a sentinel cry repeated a thousandfold, an order sent along by a thousand messengers, a beacon lit on a thousand citadels, a cry of hunters lost in great woods.

The eleventh stanza addresses God directly, qualifying the united witness of the great artists as proof of human dignity in suffering and passion, one sob rolling as a wave to die out on the border of eternity.

Forms and Devices

Charles Baudelaire used verse, couched in traditional form, to express personal anguish and aspirations in a way that made him a model for new generations of poets. In "The Beacons," the poet uses the Alexandrine verse and a regular rhyme scheme. The rhetorical pattern of the poem is regular as well. All but one of the eight first stanzas begin with a proper name. Only one is addressed directly (Puget); the others are treated as objective examples through their works. The parallel construction of these seven stanzas emphasizes the deviation of the fifth stanza. In this one stanza, emotion is emphasized. The poet's own emotions and the emotions expressed in his works are described. Here the reader is invited to pause and contemplate the figure of an unhappy invalid who combines qualities from the highest and lowest strata of human societies ("emperor of convicts").

Although the first eight stanzas are treated independently, none is an independent sentence. They do not end until the ninth stanza where they are resumed as "these curses, these blasphemies." Baudelaire uses the mechanism of repetition on several levels. The repeated parallel structure of the first eight stanzas is the most obvious example, but in the first two lines of the ninth stanza he uses the repetitive catalog of verbal complaint forms. In the ninth and tenth stanzas the poet employs repeated parallel grammatical constructions and repeats the word "thousand" four times. The cumulative effect of these multiple repetitions on a formal level reinforces the theme of echo and multiplicity, the swelling wave of voices rolling onward toward God's eternity.

Themes and Meanings

Baudelaire constantly scrutinizes the role of the poet and artist in human society.

"Benediction," the poem that opens "Spleen and Ideal," shows the poet rejected at birth by his mother, reviled by the world, but sustained by the aid of an angel and his own devout aspirations. "The Beacons" presents a number of artists whose works made them spokesmen for humanity. Among them, Puget stars in the role of unhappy artist; he is clearly presented as joining the sublime and sordid aspects of humanity. Not only does the formal structure of the fifth stanza set Puget apart, but he is treated differently thematically, with the themes and emotions of his work brought to the forefront.

The poet Baudelaire was also a music enthusiast and was as well known for his art criticism as for his verse, particularly for his essays on the Paris salons of 1845, 1846, and 1859. His address to the great masters in "The Beacons" comes from a connoisseur of the fine arts as well as literature. In "The Beacons," Baudelaire associates varied sensual images, speaking of the works of visual artists in terms of scent, sound, light and form.

Light and shadow are evoked throughout the poem. In the first stanza, both the river and cool flesh are reflective surfaces for a certain kind of light. The second stanza brings the contrast of light and shadow, with a mirror (essentially a reflective surface) qualified as profound and somber. Rembrandt's dark world is cut through by winter light, cold but powerful in its contrast. The third stanza, however, emphasizes smell and hearing, with a sharp contrast of sublime and sordid elements, into which light intrudes abruptly.

In Michelangelo, the quality of the light is attenuated, vague, and dusky. The atmosphere is ambiguous, threatening with its evocation of physical power and suffering (both Hercules and Christ died in horrible torment), its linking of ancient mythology with Christian themes.

In the sixth stanza, Watteau's light is hectic, the light of flaming butterflies or of lamps which pour madness on the dancers below. Here light implies color with the images of a carnival, of butterflies, of fresh and light settings. Goya's world, dark as a Black Sabbath still has a light-reflective mirror and the naked flesh of children, while Delacroix's lake of blood, with its combination of liquid surface and deep color is shaded by more color, the evergreen fir wood. The common quality of shade from evergreen woods echoes the light effect of the da Vinci stanza.

The ninth and tenth stanzas unite all these evocations of visual images with scent and sound, including Puget's emotions, in a blend of impressions. They are finally transmuted into vocal expressions, both curses and Te Deums. The poet's accomplishment, to transform the visual arts into words, is made explicit in these stanzas.

Only the third line of the tenth stanza, the image of the beacon light, remains visual, and from this line the poet took his title. As the reader is drawn back to the title, he must acknowledge the unity imposed on apparently episodic or particular material. All these voices (with full consciousness of the synesthetic union of visual and vocal) are gathered into one, just as the poem is gathered into one great cry, and this wave is thrown forward as witness toward God and His eternity.

Art lends a measure of immortality to the individual; Baudelaire recognizes this in his choice of a range of artists readily recognized and venerated by the public. "The Beacons" argues that great artists lend a voice to humanity and plead eternally for human dignity.

Anne W. Sienkewicz

BEARDED OAKS

Author: Robert Penn Warren (1905-1989)
Type of poem: Lyric
First published: 1942, in *Eleven Poems on the Same Theme*

The Poem

The title "Bearded Oaks" calls to mind the image of moss-draped stands of trees in the American South. As with many short lyric poems, Robert Penn Warren's poem uses its title to identify the object with which the poet's meditation begins and around which his meaning develops. As objects of immediate perception, the oaks serve as a focal element in the complex of imagery and metaphor that Warren develops. As icons of the idealized past specific to the South, the oaks of the title anticipate the poem's general concern with loss and the claims of history.

The four-line stanzas—quatrains—coupled with a somewhat irregular *abab* rhyme scheme give the poem a visual signature that alerts the reader that the poem is likely to include such traditional formal poetic devices as metaphor and ambiguity. The poetic voice is characteristically lyric: Observations are related in the first person in a manner that implies immediacy of reflection. A second person is present but is not addressed directly until stanza 9: "I do not love you less." Either the reader is overhearing the address or has been implicated in the poem's pronoun "we."

In stanzas 1 to 4, the poet and his companion lie beneath the oaks and hanging moss, through which filter the day's last light. The sensuous surroundings—the "languorous" light and swaying grass—encourage the reader to see the two figures as lovers. A second set of images describes the two lying on the bottom of the darkening sea—"the floor of light and time"—silent and still, similar to coral "atolls" created over "ages" by the work of communities of individual "polyps." Although the lovers are both unmoving and "unmurmuring" and are subjected to a somewhat unflattering comparison with marine invertebrates, there is as yet no reason to see their situation as in any way tragic.

Halfway through the fourth stanza, however, the past ceases to be an orderly unfolding of architectural form. Lines 15 to 24 describe a violent storm at the height of the day, whose effects are still faintly touching the seafloor, where darkness is now spreading. The real objects of the poem's opening scene become secondary, replaced by the metaphoric images of the sea. The sixth stanza further develops the idea that the light above the trees is a storm raging on the ocean surface and provides human terms into which the metaphor can be translated. Intense emotion ("passion") and physical extinction ("slaughter") filter down to the ocean floor, along with their after-effects—"ruth" (regret) and "decay"—where they are somehow responsible for the silent repose of the lovers. The emotional cause and effect described by these images recalls Emily Dickinson's poem "After great pain, a formal feeling comes—." Mere quiet has become "voicelessness."

Stanza 7 has the effect of concluding the previous six stanzas. The literal setting of the poem and its imaginative elaboration in the metaphor of the sea are both replaced by formal logic that struggles against the paradox of "hope is hopeless" and "fearless is fear" and by the somewhat oracular assertion "And history is undone." The inarticulate and inert state of the poet and his companion has now a larger significance: Quiet bliss seems an absence of vitality uncomfortably akin to death.

Abruptly in stanza 8, the poem restarts itself with another image from the poet's memory. The lines might almost begin another poem, for the poet does not reveal why the moment springs to mind. The scene is an empty street where footsteps echo among darkened windows after the couple's car headlights have frightened away a female deer. Both events recall a period prior to the poet's present impasse and seem somehow connected to it, for the deer, so alive and animate in the flash of light, leaves behind only the "hollow street" with its hints of the "shelf of shade" to come.

In stanza 9, the poet claims love is possible in a state that stills the feelings that normally accompany it. The cryptic final stanza explains how this paradox is possible. There also the constellation of silence, stillness, and dark that hints at death is also finally identified explicitly with "eternity." These difficult lines suggest that humans live in mortal time only briefly and that human knowledge of life, including love, is gained with such effort that the duration of an hour can be given over to the easeful anticipation of eternity, even at the expense of human relations. The lines further imply, however, that it is the value of that scarce earthly time that gives meaning to the hour devoted to experiencing eternity.

Forms and Devices

Complex and extended metaphor is typical of Warren's early poetry, as is his use of paradox and fragmented and inverted sentences. These features give his work the flavor of Metaphysical poems such as Andrew Marvell's "To His Coy Mistress" and John Donne's "The Compass." In "Bearded Oaks," the marine metaphor explicitly transforms part of the literal surface of the poem and is then interrupted by the abstract ruminations of the poet on history, love, time, and eternity. These elements work to set up a series of oppositions that describe two states of being.

The literal level of the poem, the physical setting, consists of the poet speaking while gazing toward the light through the oaks and moss above him. The beginning of the translation into metaphor is signaled by "kelp-like" and concludes with the logic and argument of stanza 7. History stops beneath the trees' limbs, where darkness, stillness, voicelessness, and calcified separateness describe the poet and his companion. Above the oaks are light, animation, sound, and emotional vitality. These two states of illumination are tied to the second literal setting of the poem in stanza 8. The remembered images of the startled doe fleeing the car's headlights and of the darkened street reprise the contrast between dark and light.

With the philosophical tone of the last two stanzas, the abstract terms "love" and "eternity" reconceive the problem of what the world of light and the world of dark mean. They are now evaluated according to whether the poet's love is preserved, and the dark, in which light's qualities are revoked, is redeemed by the proposal that immersion in it may be preparation for eternity.

Meaning develops in the poem through the mutual definition of the literal setting and the metaphor of sea and polyps and through their connection to the street and the doe. Although the literal and the metaphoric can be distinguished, that distinction is blurred as the poem evolves, while the emergent realms of light and dark resist being fully explained and interpreted by the abstract passages in the poem. Image, metaphor, and abstraction, then, are not only making meaning in "Bearded Oaks" but also represent meaning itself and the imperfect relations among objects, vision, and intellect.

Themes and Meanings

Warren was concerned in much of his early poetry with the loss of innocence and with the acquisition of self-knowledge in a world of historical contingency where perfect knowledge and an Edenic sense of unity—of oneness between the self and the world—do not exist but are vaguely recalled. He said in "Knowledge and The Image of Man" (1955) that humankind's very process of self-definition is "the discovery of separateness" but that it moves beyond this state: "Man eats of the tree of life and falls. But if he takes another bite, he may get at least a sort of redemption." To "take another bite" is to accept fully humankind's fallen state and to undertake the process of making meaning and knowledge through the perpetual oscillation between the states that Warren calls "doing" and "seeing." Each modifies the other; doing changes what a person is and how he or she sees, thus changing what will be seen, what will be done, and other actions and reactions. To be fixed in the state of seeing or of doing is to suffer the extinction of identity—to become either a chain of acts without the form of identity or an outline of identity lacking acts to give it substance.

In "Bearded Oaks," the poetic self rests in a state of seeing, having withdrawn from the world of light and of making and doing. The suspended state of seeing is not Edenic. The poet, after all, is separate from his love; they are both constructs of history, and neither can ever fully enter the other's heart and mind. For separateness even to be known, however, requires that one have some experience of unity. The fleeting glimpse of the doe—beautiful and unconscious—stands for the momentary inkling of oneness in a world otherwise echoing human beings' own footsteps and isolation back to them. If one pursues a reading of "Bearded Oaks" that acknowledges Warren's views on separateness, identity, and knowledge, then the last stanzas suggest that love is not extinguished in a world that does not allow perfect emotional expression and understanding. Rather than being extinguished, love as human beings know it becomes possible. In "Birches," Robert Frost, too, states that "Earth's the right place for love." Love is identified so strongly with separateness and action in "Bearded Oaks" that the last stanza seems almost an apology for the visionary and reflective state from which the poet writes.

Out of its multiple thematic concerns and its carefully wrought formal tension between objects, metaphor, and intellect, "Bearded Oaks" speaks to the human conviction that the life of the heart and the mind is imperfectly related to the world outside it. The poem urges the reader, nevertheless, to find meaning and redemption in the earthly state.

Peter Lapp

BECAUSE I COULD NOT STOP FOR DEATH

Author: Emily Dickinson (1830-1886)
Type of poem: Lyric
First published: 1890, in *Poems by Emily Dickinson*

The Poem

In "Because I could not stop for Death," one of the most celebrated of any poems Emily Dickinson wrote, the deceased narrator reminisces about the day Death came calling on her. In the first stanza, the speaker remarks that she had been too busy to stop for Death, so in his civility, he stopped for her. In his carriage, she was accompanied by Immortality as well as Death. Many readers have wanted to know why Immortality also rides in the carriage, but when thinking of the courting patterns in Dickinson's day, one recalls the necessity of a chaperon. In any event, Dickinson considers Death and Immortality fellow travelers. This interaction with Death shows the complete trust that the speaker had placed in her wooer. It is not until the end of the poem, from the perspective of Eternity, that one is able to see behind the semblance of Death. Far from being the gentlemanly caller that he appears to be, Death is in reality a ghoulish seducer. Perhaps Dickinson, in her familiarity with the Bible, draws upon Satan's visitation of God in similar pose as a country gentleman. In this way, Dickinson's poem resembles the Gothic novel, a popular Romantic genre given to the sinister and supernatural.

In the second stanza, the reader learns that the journey was leisurely and that the speaker did not mind the interruption from her tasks because Death was courteous. Along the way, they passed the children's school at recess time and fields of ripened grain. They even passed the setting sun—or rather, it passed them, so slow was their pace. With the coming of evening, a coolness had fallen for which the speaker found herself unprepared with regard to clothing. They drew near a cemetery, the place where the speaker has been dwelling for centuries. In the realm of Death, time has elapsed into centuries for the speaker, though it seems shorter than her last day of life when she first "surmised" that her journey was toward Eternity.

Forms and Devices

Tone, or the emotional stance of the speaker in the poem, is a central artifice in "Because I could not stop for Death." Though the subject is death, this is not a somber rendering. On the contrary, Death is made analogous to a wooer in what emerges as essentially an allegory, with abstractions consistently personified. Impressed by Death's thoughtfulness and patience, the speaker reciprocates by putting aside her work and free time. Judging by the last stanza, where the speaker talks of having "first surmised" their destination, it can be determined that Death was more seducer than beau. The tone of congeniality here becomes a vehicle for stating the proximity of death even in the thoroughfares of life, though one does not know it. Consequently, one is often caught unprepared. The journey motif is at the core of the poem's stratagem, a common device (as in poem 615, "Our Journey had Advanced") in Dickinson's poetry for depicting human mortality.

Stanza 3 offers an example of Dickinson's substantial capacity for compression, which on occasion can create a challenge for readers. This stanza epitomizes the circle of life, not so much as to life's continuity despite death, but more in fusion with the journey within the poem—life as procession toward conclusion. Thus, "the School, where Children strove" applies to childhood and youth. Dickinson's dictional acuity carries over to "Recess—in the Ring." Early life, with its sheltering from duress and breakdown and death, its distance in experience from the common fate, is but a deceptive lull—its own kind of seduction and, hence, recess from decline. Yet children are said to be in the "Ring." Time is on the move even for them, though its pace seems slow. Ironically, the dictional elements coalesce in the stanza to create a subrendering of the greater theme of the poem: the seduction of the persona by Death. The children are also without surmise, and like the speaker, they are too busy with themselves (as represented in the verb "strove") to know that time is passing.

Dictional nuance is critical to the meaning of the last two lines of the third stanza. The word "passed" sets up verbal irony (the tension of statement and meaning). The carriage occupants are not merely passing a motley collection of scenes, they are passing out of life—reaching the high afternoon of life, or maturity. Maturation, or adulthood, is also represented in the "Fields of Gazing Grain." This line depicts grain in a state of maturity, its stalk replete with head of seed. There is intimation of harvest and perhaps, in its gaze, nature's indifference to a universal process. Appropriately, the next line speaks of "the Setting Sun," meaning the evening of life, or old age.

Reiteration of the word "passed" occurs in stanza 4, emphasizing the idea of life as a procession toward conclusion. Its recurring use as a past-tense verb suggests the continuation of an action in the past, yet the noncontinuance of those actions in the present in keeping with the norms of the imperfect tense. Human generations will collectively engage in the three life stages, dropping out individually, never to engage in them again.

Dictional elements in stanza 5 hint at unpreparedness for death. The persona's gown was but "Gossamer," a light material highly unsuitable for evening chill. For a scarf ("Tippet"), she wore only silk netting ("Tulle").

The poem is written in alternating iambic tetrameter and trimeter lines, with near rhyme occasionally employed in the second and fourth lines. Regular rhyme occurs sporadically and unexpectedly in its spatial distancing. The use of the dash in the stanza's concluding line compels the reader to pause before entering into the monosyllabic prepositional phrase in which there is a heaviness that suggests the grave's finality. The seemingly disheveled rhyme scheme in actuality intimates one of the poem's central themes: unpreparedness.

Themes and Meanings

Death is a frequent concern of Dickinson's poetry. Often as a means to its exploration, she will seek its objectification through a persona who has already died. In other poems, she is quite sensitive to the fact of death and its impoverishment of those who remain. In some poems, she is resentful toward God, who robs people of those they love and is seemingly indifferent to such loss. One cannot explore the catalyst of life events behind Dickinson's marked sensitivity with any certainty because she lived a remarkably private life. For her, death was only one more form of distancing. As she wrote in poem 749: "All but Death can be Adjusted." Perhaps two of her most famous lines express it best: "Parting is all we know of heaven,/ And all we need of hell" (poem 1732).

Emily Dickinson was very familiar with death. Thirty-three of her acquaintances had died between February, 1851, and November, 1854, including her roommate at Holyoke College. Her mother's family seemed predisposed to early deaths. Then the momentous death of her father occurred in 1874. In 1882, eight years after the death of her father, she wrote that "no verse in the Bible has frightened me so much from a Child as 'from him that hath not, shall be taken even that he hath.' Was it because its dark menace deepened our own Door?"

Some may see this poem as conciliatory, even Christian, given that Immortality rides in the carriage and that the persona speaks of Eternity in the end. Death, by this notion, becomes God's emissary taking one into Eternity. For others, however, there is no resurrection, no specifying of an afterlife. Immortality is employed ironically, not to suggest everlasting life, but everlasting death. As a consort of death, one need not be puzzled by Immortality's presence in the carriage. This is the import of the final stanza, when the speaker exclaims, "Since then— 'tis Centuries— and yet/ Feels shorter than the Day/ I first surmised the Horses Heads/ Were toward Eternity." There is a sense that the journey has never ended and never will. There is much eternity up ahead, for death is a realm without temporal-spatial parameters.

The truth is that life is short and death is long. Perhaps in this sobering truth one may find that Dickinson's poem is as much about life—about how one ought to redeem it from the banal—as it is about death.

Ralph Robert Joly

LA BELLE DAME SANS MERCI

Author: John Keats (1795-1821)
Type of poem: Ballad
First published: 1820; collected in *Life, Letters, and Literary Remains of John Keats,* 1848

The Poem

"La Belle Dame sans Merci" is a remarkably evocative poem attaining subtle effects of mood and music in the short space of forty-eight lines. The twelve stanzas consist of three tetrameter lines followed by a concluding line of only two stresses. The title is taken from a medieval French poem by Alain Chartier in which the speaker is mourning his dead mistress. Other than the title, John Keats' poem has nothing in common with Chartier's.

The poem opens with an unnamed speaker asking a knight at arms what ails him, since he is all alone, pale, and wandering about aimlessly in a barren, desolate landscape. For the first twelve lines the speaker pointedly and persistently questions the knight, describes the landscape, and comments on the knight's physical appearance in a brutally frank and tactless manner. The melancholy tone is created immediately by the speaker's opening words: "O what can ail thee, . . .// The sedge has wither'd from the lake/ And no birds sing."

Beginning with stanza 4 and continuing to the end, the knight tells his strange story, one unlike any other in English poetry. In the flowering fields he met a young woman of supernal beauty, "a fairy's child" who in reality is a femme fatale. The knight came immediately under her spell, perhaps hypnotized by her powerful eyes, losing awareness of all but her. Although he could not understand her strange tongue, the two communicated in other ways. Reminiscent of Christopher Marlowe's passionate shepherd, he made her a garland of flowers, a bracelet, and a belt and set her on his warhorse. She in turn found strange foods for him— sweet roots, wild honey, "manna dew" — and cast a spell upon him which he mistook for words of love: "sure in language strange she said— / I love thee true." She took him to her underground grotto, where, weeping and sighing, she allowed him to comfort her even as she lulled him to sleep.

Once asleep, the knight was shaken by terrible dreams of kings, princes, and warriors all as deathly pale as himself. In vain they were warning him that he was "in thrall" or enslaved by the beautiful lady without pity. Awakening from the nightmare, the knight found himself on the cold hillside alone, the dream figures having vanished. Summer had given way to late autumn, and the beautiful lady had disappeared. The poem ends with the knight's desperate effort to explain to the questioner why he is "Alone and palely loitering." While the final stanza is pregnant with suggestion, it explains nothing. The knight's entire experience is encapsulated in the pronoun "this" (line 45), which has no grammatical antecedent. The initial speaker remains silent, perhaps shocked and befuddled by the knight's account of his experience.

Forms and Devices

This poem draws on a long tradition for much of its power and many of its effects. Ballads are divided into two categories: folk/popular and literary. Folk ballads appear early in a country's literature. They are anonymous and originate as songs. Literary ballads, on the other hand, come only after a literary tradition has been well established, and although they are modeled on a primitive poetic form, they are usually sophisticated compositions in their use of rhetorical devices to create subtle effects. Both categories of ballad share certain characteristics, many of which are evident in Keats's poem. As short narratives rarely exceeding a hundred lines, ballads relate a single event with no background or explanation. The language is simple to the point of starkness, and there is much use of dialogue, refrains, and repetition. Violent and supernatural occurrences are commonplace, and moral commentary is noticeably absent.

Although this poem was only a single evening's work (April 21, 1819), its stanzas, as Walter Jackson Bate has written in *John Keats* (1963), "have haunted readers and poets for a century and a half." Keats had become accustomed to writing iambic pentameter, so the meter here was an experiment. Much of the haunting effect that lingers in the mind long after the poem has been read comes from the stanza form of three four-stressed lines followed by a line of two stresses. The attenuated finality strikes a mournful chord. The effect is clearly seen in the first stanza: "And no birds sing."

Equally important in contributing to the tone is the heavy preponderance of dark vowels in the stressed words of generally a single syllable. Of the 289 words of the poem, all but forty are monosyllabic, and most of these contain long vowels, as in "four," "rose," "cold," "pale," and "wild." The simplicity of the language is as striking an innovation for Keats as is his departure from the comfortable iambic pentameter line. Keats's language is characteristically Spenserian in its rich density of imagery. In the early *Endymion* (1818), the richness tended to excess, blurring the outlines of description. Here, however, the balladlike starkness sets in clearly defined relief the horrid emptiness of the landscape. "The sedge has wither'd from the lake," "the harvest's done," and "cold hill's side" leave indelible marks on the memory. The effect is similar to Thomas Hardy's "Neutral Tones" (1898). The understated matter-of-factness of the narration (there is only a single exclamation) also contributes to the atmosphere of desolation.

Themes and Meanings

"La Belle Dame sans Merci" has been the subject of considerable critical attention. Bate remarks on the wide range of sources that contributed to the poem, to which may be added the strange folk ballad "Thomas Rhymer." The beautiful lady is obviously a femme fatale, an archetypal figure originating in early myth and continuing to the present in the popular image of the vamp. Bate believes the central influence to be Edmund Spenser's Duessa, who in *The Faerie Queene* (1590, 1596) seduces the Red Cross Knight. Other models readily available to Keats of warriors brought low by the wiles of beautiful women are Samson and Antony.

The identification of a specific femme fatale appears less important, however, than relating the knight's experience to the long tradition of a mortal entrammeled by a beautiful female who may possess supernatural powers. One is reminded of the plight of Odysseus' mariners who are bewitched by Circe in Homer's *Odyssey* (c. 800 B.C.). They temporarily lose their human appearance. Keats's knight fares much worse. He may be drained of his blood—he is "death-pale," as are the kings, princes, and warriors of his dream—in which case he would be the zombie victim of a vampire. He is definitely drained of his will. The irony of a knight at arms being reduced to a slave is strong indeed. His "sojourn," or rule, extends merely to the circumscribed area of desolation where "no birds sing," and his activity is reduced from roaming the countryside seeking wrongs to redress to loitering aimlessly about the lake. He is as enervated and purposeless as Alfred, Lord Tennyson's lotus eaters, as out of touch with the world of human concerns as that poet's Mariana. The knight has been victimized through no fault of his own and has suffered the irredeemable loss of his humanness. The pity is that he acquiesces to his fate; he has given up.

To be sure, all critics do not share this view that the lady is a dangerous menace. Bate, for example, sees the poem as premised on the "ultimate impossibility of contact between the human and this elusive, only half-human figure," but he has doubts that the lady is sinister, since the knight "does not actually witness the 'horrid warning' of starvation that this attempted union may bring"; he encounters it only in his dream, which may reflect his own uneasiness. Similarly, Earl R. Wasserman in *The Finer Tone* (1953) exculpates the lady from any evil intent; "she is the ideal whom the lover must pursue but whom he can never possess." The knight "is doomed to suffer her 'unkindness,' which is her nature although not her fault."

This diversity of critical opinion is testimony that the simple language of Keats's poem masks a substantial complexity of meaning. It is highly unlikely that there will ever be a critical consensus as to precisely what the poem "means." There is consensus, however, that "La Belle Dame sans Merci" is a great and unforgettable poem.

Robert G. Blake

BELLS FOR JOHN WHITESIDE'S DAUGHTER

Author: John Crowe Ransom (1888-1974)
Type of poem: Elegy
First published: 1924; collected in *Chills and Fever,* 1924

The Poem

"Bells for John Whiteside's Daughter" is a short funeral poem in five quatrains. Through a series of restrained images, John Crowe Ransom transfixes the grief of the entire community over the inexplicable death of a young girl. He accomplishes this primarily by refusing to admit to the fact of death. The speaker of the poem, representing the community, merely declares perplexity at the little girl's sudden inactivity.

The first stanza uses the past tense to refer to the girl's former busy activity, then leads to contemplation of her current, mystifying "brown study" (an old-fashioned term for rapt daydream). This attitude suggests that her stillness is unnatural, even perverse — as if she were going through one of those childish stages so incomprehensible to the adult world. This fixity contradicts her former habit of action. Yet this is fitting, for the death of children perplexes the standard assumptions of the adult world for the next generation. Faced with that reversal, spectators can only stop and stare, dumbfounded.

The following three stanzas are run together, one leading immediately to the next, to form a unit commemorating the girl's activities. Ransom uses language that elevates the girl's games, giving them public status and the remoteness of romance. In this way, Ransom creates the impression that the townspeople watched this outdoor playing and projected into it their hopes for the future. For example, instead of simply playing war games, she "takes arms against her shadow." Then, those were games of life and death; now, she casts no shadow.

Her major campaigns, however, were waged against the geese that usually inhabited the orchard. These geese occupy the entire third stanza. Ransom paradoxically shows them driven into activity by the girl. Previously the geese possessed the undifferentiated shapelessness of a cloud; now they become a troop of individualists, each reacting in its own way to the driving energy of the girl. She arouses them from their "noon apple-dreams" induced by feeding on windfalls and scatters them in a frenzy of motion.

The engine that drives this activity is the girl's "tireless heart," which ironically has stopped beating. The phrase also suggests the essential innocence of this type of play. It is the kind of thing a good-hearted person does — the kind of play that prepares for and initiates the activities of adulthood.

This leads to the final stanza, which returns to the basic paradox: This girl will never reach adulthood. In language that becomes hard-edged and stark, Ransom returns from reverie about the past to the reality of death. This death stops the breath of the entire community. It seems profoundly wrong. The body lies "primly propped," unnatural in death—forced out of its usual motion, fixed in the brown study it had not known in life. The community is "vexed" at the senseless perversity of this death.

Forms and Devices

The two major techniques used by Ransom in "Bells for John Whiteside's Daughter" are formal diction and understatement, and both work together to reinforce the theme of the poem. Both appear in the title: Instead of "elegy," "lament," or even a more emotive term to announce his subject, Ransom simply uses "bells." This establishes a formal response to an intense emotional situation; it also suggests the futility of any human restitution for this loss. Together, these devices generate the irony that pervades the poem. John Whiteside's daughter is dead, and all one can do is offer the empty gesture of a solemn funeral.

Both devices are used to weave the body of the poem. The first stanza contrasts the former "lightness in her footfall" with her present "brown study," which "astonishes us all." Each of these phrases is either formal or old-fashioned, the language of the older generation left to account for this loss. Again, this generates a fundamental irony: Parents are not supposed to bury their children. The language accentuates this. "Lightness" can suggest emptiness or insubstantiality, reminding readers that those footsteps will never fall again. "Footfall" should refer only to an adult, which this little girl will never become. Further, in life she never would have chosen the rapt, meditative state of brown study. She is in such a state now against her will, and the elders can only stare open-mouthed.

Ransom compounds the ironies in the central section of the poem. The little girl's play activities are described in the terminology of an epic or of a high romance, both old-fashioned conventions. The line "Her wars were bruited in our high window" creates a formal frame about her actions, as if forming a heraldic emblem. The girl's play takes place in an orchard, a region of fertility—no place to memorialize the deeds of the dead before their time. In the orchard, the girl "took arms against her shadow," a phrase that again uses formal terminology inappropriate for one whose combats were innocent, not life-threatening. Nevertheless, these battles seem to have taken her life, and the reader remembers that she now casts no shadow.

The central image within the body of the poem is the girl's driving of the flock of geese, contrasting their pointless somnolence with her directed activity. This interaction is described, as before, in formal, understated terms that generate irony. The geese are an undifferentiated, impersonal mob compared to the girl's intense personality. They are an amorphous "snow cloud," made to cry "in goose" and "scuttle/ Goose-fashion" by the "little body" with the "tireless heart." She is a champion in a war against geese, victor in a trivial mock-epic, made more trivial because that heart has now stopped.

The final stanza announces the bells and ends with a concluding static image of the community "sternly stopped" and "vexed." It is stopped in several ways. The girl's activity—and that of the younger generation—is at a standstill. The routine activities of the town are broken for the funeral. The heart of the community has been taken out. Ransom uses subtle fractures of rhyme and rhythm patterns throughout the poem to underscore this sense of the expected order being frustrated in the death of a child.

Themes and Meanings

In "Bells for John Whiteside's Daughter," Ransom takes an oblique approach to one of the most difficult human experiences: coping with the death of children. He presents no direct resolution for this ethical dilemma. In fact, he treats it as a cosmic irony, properly placed within a context of ironies. It is almost as if he is suggesting that humans need to use intelligence and wit to insulate themselves against the shocks of experience. Life may be inexplicably painful, but one does not have to be broken by it.

The poem may be considered Ransom's notion of the mourning of an intellectual. For this reason, upon first reading it is likely to seem guarded, cold, and impersonal—distant and distancing in its very playfulness. In refusing to grieve, it seems to pretend that human emotions are too elementary to provide satisfying and equivalent responses to loss. It suggests that the heart needs to be shielded against reality.

Subsequent readings disclose that Ransom's lament is deep-rooted, genuine, and sincere, although it certainly does not wear its heart on its sleeve. On any account, it does not evade the question. The death of children is cruel and inhumane; it violates expectations of the normal and the proper. Death provokes immediate emotional reactions: tears and, paradoxically, laughter—reactions that are not very far apart. Death also requires long-term adjustment because the survivors have to go on with the business of living. Overindulgence in emotion can interfere with this recovery, but a tempered response can promote it. Ransom provides this kind of response.

There is deep grief at the core of the poem, although it is masked by irony. Ransom's failure to name the girl or to look directly at the body is not merely a technique of avoidance. By depicting the community as astonished at the girl's inexplicable stillness, "vexed" at her contemplative inactivity, and "sternly stopped" for the funeral, Ransom is using understatement to suggest the inexpressible. Far from minimizing feeling, it is intensified, suggesting that the grief is not expressed directly because it cannot be stated in straightforward language.

In fact, Ransom's use of understatement and ironic distancing here is a technique of transcendence. This technique simultaneously suggests the depth of his grief and the way intelligence can help when coping with grief in order to get beyond it. The ironies abounding in the poem develop out of Ransom's sense that the only suitable response to the irony of early death is multiple irony. Grief is powerful, but it must be overcome. Irony begins by establishing a distance from which healing can begin. In "Bells for John Whiteside's Daughter," Ransom presents a poem in which ironic intelligence suggests a way out of the eternal sadness of the death of children.

James Livingston

BENEDICTION

Author: Charles Baudelaire (1821-1867)
Type of poem: Narrative
First published: 1857, "Bénédiction," in *Les Fleurs du mal*; collected in
Baudelaire: Selected Verse, 1961

The Poem

"Benediction" is composed of nineteen quatrains written in regular Alexandrine, or twelve-syllable, lines with an alternating *abab* rhyme scheme. Charles Baudelaire's choice of this traditional verse form contrasts with his innovative use of imagery that was to inspire a new symbolic form of expression in French poetry.

While the poem uses the third person, the poet it describes clearly represents Baudelaire himself. The autobiographical elements, however, are generalized enough for the poet to represent at the same time the romantic archetype of the poet as an inspired figure misunderstood by society.

The first five quatrains form the most clearly autobiographical section of the poem and emphasize the irony of the title, "Benediction." The idea that a blessing from God is associated with the poet's birth is suggested in the first line, where his appearance is said to be "by a decree of supreme powers." Yet the child is anything but blessed when, immediately after his birth, his mother rejects him.

The mother's rejection echoes Baudelaire's own feeling of abandonment when, after his father died when Baudelaire was only six years old, his mother remarried, choosing a military man with whom the future poet had little in common. As this experience is translated into the poem "Benediction," however, the mother rails against the defects of her child, whom she calls the "damned instrument" of God's persecution of her. This rejection continues in quatrains 8 through 13 as friends and then specific women conspire to torment the poet.

Amid these rejections, quatrains 6 and 7 offer a contrasting hint of the poet's salvation. An angel appears to guide the child amid the perils of the world. These quatrains combine elements of nature and of religion, as the poet "plays with the wind, chats with the cloud/ and becomes drunk while singing the way of the cross." While the angel guides the child in these activities and seems to direct him toward the consoling elements of nature and of religion, the ambiguity of this passage makes it unclear whether the poet will actually achieve a satisfying life.

In the final six quatrains of the poem, the poet experiences a vision of hope. The reader sees him praying and blessing the same God against whom his mother had cried out. These prayers seem to be answered when the poet sees his suffering as a means to salvation: "I know that suffering is the only nobility." The poet then describes a vision of "my mystic crown" that should be the emblem of his redemption. The crown, however, must be described in terms of the objects of the present world. It appears as "pure light" but also as a "diadem" surpassing the brilliance of gems, metals, and pearls. The poet's need to express celestial light in worldly terms prefigures the loss of this vision that will become evident in subsequent poems of *Les Fleurs du mal* (*Flowers of Evil*, 1909).

Forms and Devices

Baudelaire's collection of poems *Flowers of Evil* deals extensively with the elements of good and evil posited in its title. "Benediction" opens the first, and longest, section of the work, "Spleen et idéal" ("Spleen and Ideal"). Baudelaire's concept of "spleen" incorporates the negative elements of fallen nature that contrast with the ideal he envisions at the end of this poem. The poet's tragic fate lies in his consciousness that he is simultaneously drawn to each of these extremes.

Baudelaire created the basis for poetic symbolism by establishing groups of related images that work together to form highly nuanced constructs in his poetry. In "Benediction," both positive and negative references continue the religious theme established in the title. When his friends mock the poet, they sully the "bread and wine" he will consume, thus potentially corrupting a form of Holy Communion. Similarly, the woman, taking advantage of the fact that the poet adores her, assumes the role of "ancient idols," leading him to a pagan form of worship that "usurps" the otherwise Christian devotion of the poem.

The positive vision of the "celestial crown" offers a radiant affirmation of the poet's redemption. That is undercut, however, by certain elements both in this description and in the two quatrains in which the angel seems to protect the poet. Under the angel's care, the child twice "becomes drunk": once from the effects of the sun and once while singing the way of the cross. Drunkenness, as Baudelaire defined it in a prose poem, "Enivrez-vous," was not limited to the action of alcohol, but it does imply a state in which the poet gives up rational control of himself. Thus the angel, even while he permits the child to run this risk, "cries to see him gay as a bird in the wood."

This recognition of the child's vulnerability is based in part on a definition of Baudelaire's language drawn from sources beyond the present poem. This technique exemplifies another source of complexity in Baudelaire's symbolism. The poems of *Flowers of Evil* are clearly meant to be read consecutively, as a whole. When, in the second line of "Benediction," the poet appears in "ce monde ennuyé," this phrase, describing ambiguously a world that is either troubled or bored, draws on the image of Ennui, the monster that Baudelaire described in his preceding poem, "To The Reader."

In the same way, the final lines of "Benediction" undercut the vision of the "celestial crown" with images linked to the poet's moral fall in subsequent poems. The "mortal eyes" seen as "obscure and pitiful mirrors" of celestial light foreshadow the eyes of the woman through whose seduction the poet will be separated from his ideal. Numerous repetitions of the images of both eyes and mirror develop this theme throughout *Les Fleurs du mal*.

The device of linking, through which images are reused from poem to poem, allows Baudelaire to add nuances to his central motifs as they recur in various contexts. The complexity resulting from this multiple redefinition forms the essence of his poetic symbolism.

Themes and Meanings

Baudelaire introduced a number of important themes in "Benediction" that he would develop more fully in subsequent poems. Such themes as the dangerous hostility of women and the painful realities of the poet's life form a part of the negative, and later dominant, dimension of *Flowers of Evil*. The greatest importance of "Benediction" within Baudelaire's work, however, lies in its positive elements. The reader meets the child-poet when he is still naïve enough to believe in the vision of his own salvation. His progressive consciousness of his fall from grace in later poems gains poignancy through its contrast with the vision presented here and never completely regained.

Although Baudelaire's life in the dissipation of nineteenth century Paris could hardly have been further from that of a religious ascetic, he retained a strong sense of traditional Christianity. Religious themes persist even in his most negative descriptions. Thus the poet's mother, turning to God in anger after the poet's birth, says, "Since you chose me from among all women," clearly recalling the similar choice of Mary for the birth of Christ.

The parallelism established between the poet and Christ, both of whom were destined to bring messages of a higher truth to people who would misunderstand them, lends urgency to the poet's desire for salvation. The singing of the way of the cross and the attempt at Communion, when others intercept the bread and wine, prepare the poet for a vision of paradise in which he sees the "splendid throne," implying the presence of God himself.

Interwoven with these images of paradise, however, are suggestions of an earthly paradise. It has already been seen how the celestial crown is related to earthly gems. Similarly, the poet, while accompanied by the angel, finds himself in a seemingly pure natural setting defined by allusions to sun, wind, and cloud. The sun, one source of the poet's drunkenness, takes on more negative connotations later in *Flowers of Evil* until, in "Une Charogne" ("Carrion"), it becomes the source of decay in a corpse.

One need not go beyond "Benediction," however, to find suggestions that paradise cannot be transposed into the context of this world. The angel sees the child as "a bird of the woods," but only six quatrains later, the woman seeks to torment the poet's heart when she finds it as vulnerable as a baby bird. Images such as the sun and the bird, together with the poet's own drunkenness, set the stage for his loss of paradise.

The theme of paradise, both earthly and celestial, persists throughout *Flowers of Evil*, but with increasing indications that the poet is separated from it. His consciousness of this separation gives Baudelaire's protagonist the dimensions of a true tragic hero. Even his most vivid imagining of his own salvation, as he recorded it in "Benediction," contained the seeds of his ultimate failure.

Dorothy M. Betz

BEYOND THE ALPS

Author: Robert Lowell (1917-1977)
Type of poem: Lyric
First published: 1959, in *Life Studies*

The Poem

"Beyond the Alps" is a lyric poem written in iambic pentameter; each of its three stanzas is a sonnet. The rhyming pattern of each sonnet is irregular and typifies, as do other elements in the poem, Robert Lowell's experience with convention.

Lowell's career was marked by several dramatic shifts in style, and this poem does not fit snugly into a formal category. The epigraph suggests that the poem is an occasional piece, written as a consequence of Pope Pius XII's pronouncement that made Mary's bodily Assumption church dogma; however, the structure of the poem is primarily personal narrative. In the first and third stanzas, the speaker, who can only be viewed as Lowell himself, is on a train that has left Rome and is bound for Paris. He notes the "Alpine snow," stewards "banging on their gongs," and the "hush hush of the wheels." The second stanza is a meditation about the pope's decree. The poet's mind moves over the landscape as well as historical, religious, and literary issues. In the third stanza, he refers to his "blear-eyed ego kicking in my berth," which illustrates the depth of his personal religious struggle, which is the emotional center of the poem.

"Beyond the Alps" was the first poem in Lowell's third book, *Life Studies*. It serves as an announcement that he no longer can believe in the dogma of the church. The title is an allusion to the religious debate over papal authority; the transalpiners were a group in the Roman Catholic church who opposed the ultramontanes and their belief in the infallibility of the pope. The poet is literally and figuratively crossing over the Alps, leaving both Rome and traditional Catholic doctrine to arrive in Paris and uncertainty.

Lowell begins the poem very casually by saying that he had read in the newspaper about an expedition of Swiss climbers who had given up trying to scale Mt. Everest. This sets the scene for his own travel and metaphorically suggests that he too has "thrown the sponge/ in once again" — on traditional religion. He says that "Much against my will/ I left the City of God where it belongs." Pius's interpretation of Mary's Assumption, and Lowell's own observations about human nature, have made it impossible for him to reside in his previous convictions. The subsequent lines, "There the skirt-mad Mussolini unfurled/ the eagle of Caesar. He was one of us/ only, pure prose," suggests that the City of God is inhabited by people such as Benito Mussolini. Mussolini was the Fascist dictator of Italy from 1923-1945; he imprisoned, tortured, and murdered people who opposed him. He was also infamous for his mistresses; he and his mistress Clara Petacci were shot and hung by their heels for the public to scorn. Lowell refers to this in the second stanza, when he says, "The Duce's lynched, bare, booted skull still spoke." Lowell implies that all people are potential Mussolinis if they are given enough power; for Lowell, this dramatizes the imperfection of God's creation.

The second stanza illustrates one cost of Lowell's traveling: his vision and moral integrity. His point of view enlarges to that of an omniscient narrator. He therefore can simultaneously observe the crowd yelling "Papa" outside Saint Peter's Basilica and Pope Pius himself. The pope is shocked by the crowd's reaction to the announcement about Mary's Assumption, and he drops the mirror he was holding while shaving. This scene subtly suggests that the pope is merely a man—one who has to shave every day, too. He has an electric razor and a pet canary. This humorous scene is further developed in the next sentence, where Lowell playfully combines two clichés to show how unreasonable and ridiculous he thinks this new interpretation of Mary's Assumption is. The "light" of science is not even a "candle" when compared to Mary rising bodily into heaven "angel-wing'd, and gorgeous as a jungle-bird." He cannot imagine any reasonable person believing this or understanding this belief.

Lowell thinks that people tend to confuse the icon with the saint; the pilgrims to the Vatican still kiss Saint Peter's bronze sandal as if that will bring them good luck. They indulge ostentation and neglect their faith. Lowell suggests that people have not learned much from the example of Mussolini and that God himself, by allowing these traits to flourish, "herded this people to the *coup de grâce.* A *coup de grâce* is a stroke that kills someone who is wounded; it literally means a "stroke of mercy." The "stroke" here can either refer to Mussolini's hanging or to the dogma that ended Lowell's faith. The fact that the Vatican's Swiss guard must guide the pope through the crowd with their pikes to keep the people from crushing him implies that these people have again confused the man with what he represents and that in human nature the light of reason shines rather dimly.

This theme is further developed in the final stanza. The "mountain-climbing train has come to earth," and with it Lowell's aspirations for himself and mankind. Although he had aspired to faith and a more generous view of humanity, his experiences at Saint Peter's and his reading of history have caused disillusionment and despair. Lowell was graduated with a degree in classics from Kenyon College, and in a sense the third stanza can be seen as a yearning for a myth system in which he had once found value. Apollo, the Greek god of the sun, poetry, and music, has had to "plant his heels" on the ground; this questions the value and efficacy of aspiration in general and art in particular. Each disappearing mountain peak becomes a metaphor for some "wasted" and "backward" achievement of the past, such as the Greek Parthenon or Ulysses poking out the eye of the Cyclops. The lack of distinction between historical events, artistic achievements, and mythological feats implies the depth of Lowell's despair. About three thousand years of human history are indicted by this poem— from the "killer" Etruscan kings of the tenth century B.C. to Rome of the 1950's. Lowell is as blind or "blear-eyed" as the Cyclops, because he can find no clear access to "that altitude" to which he once aspired, and his reading of history is no help.

Forms and Devices

The poems that Robert Lowell wrote before *Life Studies* were tightly formal, with a restless urgency, a barely containable energy. "Beyond the Alps" begins this book to announce both an intellectual and stylistic deviation from his previously published poems. Lowell's line relaxes; the syntax is clearer, and there is a confident ease in the language. This casualness is evident in the opening line, where he has just finished reading the paper and looks out the window:

> Reading how even the Swiss had thrown the sponge
> in once again and Everest was still
> unscaled, I watched our Paris pullman lunge
> mooning across the fallow Alpine snow.

He enjambs the lines so that the reader reads past the rhymes; one does not linger on "sponge" because one needs to know the preposition that goes with the verb "thrown." In the second line, one reads past "still" to get to the verb "unscaled." By disguising the rhymes, Lowell puts more weight on the narrative.

There is still a rich medley of sounds in his language. If one considers "mooning across the fallow Alpine snow," one can see how complex it is. The assonance (the *a* and *o* sounds), the consonance (the *l* and *s* sounds), and the meter allow the reader to participate in the beauty Lowell observes.

The only formal deviation from typical sonnets is in the stanzas' rhyme schemes. In fact, the rhyme scheme of each sonnet becomes more and more Shakespearean, which also echoes the intellectual progress of the poem: from chaos to a nostalgic yearning for a classical myth system.

Themes and Meanings

Lowell once remarked that this poem is "about people who go beyond nature, Mussolini or the Pope." Throughout Lowell's work, he was concerned about the way human nature abdicates nature. Although the mountains in the opening stanza are symbolic of man's thwarted ambition and aspiration, they come back in the last stanza to loom over the "mountain-climbing train" that "had come to earth." He is exhausted by his mental traveling and his "blear-eyed ego" that will not allow him any rest. Human ego—whether it is Mussolini's, the pope's, or his own—often causes people to be inhuman. In fact, the occasion for this poem is an example of human ego. Mary must rise bodily into heaven because human vanity does not like to imagine her moldering in the earth like everyone else.

In "Fall 1961" from his subsequent book, *For the Union Dead* (1964), Lowell wrote that "Nature holds up its mirror" to provide a contrast with humans who "have talked our extinction to death." In that poem, his only "point of rest" as he looks out the window of his apartment is an oriole's nest. In both poems, he suggests that humans return to earth, terra firma, and abandon the ego that causes many of humankind's problems.

Joseph Powell

BIRCHES

Author: Robert Frost (1874-1963)
Type of poem: Lyric
First published: 1916, in *Mountain Interval*

The Poem

"Birches" is an enduringly popular lyric by one of the United States' most cele-brated poets. In fifty-nine lines of blank verse, the poem presents a description of birch trees in a New England countryside, scenes of a boy swinging from these trees, and reflections on the meaning that being "a swinger of birches" has in Robert Frost's life. He addresses the reader in an informal, conversational manner, using the first person "I" and addressing the reader casually as "you." Sometimes poets create first-person speakers who are quite different from themselves. In "Birches," however, Frost seems to be speaking in his own voice: as a grown man who has often observed and mused upon the birch trees he is describing, who remembers swinging from birches as a boy, and who has endured the adult tribulations he dis-cusses late in the poem.

Frost reinforces the effect of conversational informality by casting the poem in continuous form. Rather than dividing the poem into stanzas or other formal sec-tions, Frost presents an unbroken sequence of fifty-nine lines. Within this contin-uous form, however, Frost does shift his focus and tone, sometimes abruptly, as if he were digressing in a conversation with the reader. In this way, Frost's major shifts reveal five sections in the poem.

In the brief first section (lines 1-3), Frost muses that when he sees birch trees that are bent over, he "like[s] to think" it is because "some boy's been swinging them." Frost quickly rejects this pleasant thought as whimsical and inaccurate, though. In the second section (lines 4-20), he presents a more dismal and realistic explanation: Winter storms coat the birches with a heavy load of ice that causes them to grow in a bent-over position.

In the third section (lines 21-40), however, Frost playfully reverts to his original theory. In contrast to the ice-storm explanation, he "prefer[s]" to develop the myth of a boy who bends down all the birches on his father's land "by riding them down over and over again." Toward the end of this section, Frost's description vividly dramatizes the skill and exhilaration of the boy's play.

The fourth section (lines 41-49) returns to a tone of burdensome gloom that echoes section 2. Now, however, instead of the birches suffering, it is the poet. Frost reveals that he himself was once "a swinger of birches," and he ruefully admits that he now dreams of returning to this activity as a release from the worry, confusion, and pain of adult life.

In the fifth section (lines 50-59), Frost ends the poem on a note of hopeful recon-ciliation. He realizes that he does not wish for a total escape from the earth and the troubles he experiences there, but only for a temporary respite.

Forms and Devices

The key action described in "Birches" consists of swinging free of the constraints of the earth, up toward heaven and through the air, before landing on the ground again. Through his careful organization of imagery, tropes, and myth, Frost designs the poem as a delightful reflection of its content. That is to say, he takes the reader through a series of swings back and forth between earthbound realities and imaginative possibilities.

The first section of the poem, for example, swings from a real image that Frost has observed (birches bent over) to a myth he would like to believe (that the birches are bent because of a boy's play). In the second section, though, the poem swings back grimly toward reality, as Frost presents dismal images of how ice left by winter storms actually bends the birches: "They are dragged to the withered bracken by the load." Frost also observes ruefully, "once they are bowed/ So low for long, they never right themselves."

The grim power of reality in the second section seems to inspire Frost to assert the countervailing power of his imagination even more strongly. He thus begins the third section by playfully personifying reality as a rude interrupter that he can easily dismiss: "But I was going to say when Truth broke in/ With all her matter-of-fact about the ice-storm." Aware of his own impudence, Frost then imagines a mythical account of how the birches were bent by a boy whose powerful control over reality seems to reflect the power Frost is claiming for his own imagination. The boy "subdued" all his father's birches into bent-over arches until "not one was left/ For him to conquer."

Frost swings back to reality in the fourth section through the surprising revelation that he was once himself "a swinger of birches." The poet has not, however, enjoyed the satisfying mastery over his life that the mythical boy did over his father's birch trees, and Frost "dream[s] of going back to be" a swinger of birches once again as a release from the cares of adult life.

In the first four sections of the poem, then, Frost seems to be largely concerned with dramatizing the conflict between the harsh limitations of earthbound reality, and the more attractive possibilities of play and the imagination. The images of the last ten lines, however, present a surprising and harmonious synthesis of the two extremes. Frost emphasizes that he is no longer so naïve as to wish for complete escape from the earth and its cares. "Earth's the right place for love," he asserts, implying that it need not exist chiefly in heaven or in the imagination. Similarly, he does not take the regressive, whimsical route of imagining that he would swing up and out from a birch tree with the aggressive abandon he had exhibited as a youth. Instead, he imagines the milder pleasures of the gradual climb up the tree "*Toward* heaven" (not the impossible fantasy of soaring into it) and of the gentle descent as the tree would place him down on the ground. In this way, Frost imagines a birch-swinging experience that "would be good both going and coming back," without the conflict between imaginative flight and earthly reality that seemed to prevail earlier in the poem.

Themes and Meanings

"Birches" is a popular poem largely because it so satisfyingly represents the loveable side of Robert Frost. The poem neatly encapsulates much of what is most familiar and endearing about this poet: his vivid description of a New England natural scene, his folksy voice mixing plain talk with whimsy and imagination, and his clear development of simple images and actions into accessible symbolic meanings. Further, the conclusion of the poem is warmly reassuring, making the conflict between realism and romanticism seem reconciled so that earthly realities do not ultimately seem too harsh or discouraging, and playful imaginings do not seem too whimsical or quixotic.

Seen from another perspective, however, "Birches" also reveals a more sophisticated view of the theme of the relation between imagination and reality. Though in general terms the poem presents these two realms as in conflict, Frost also delights in showing that realistic and imaginative language often dissolve into each other, so that the dichotomy between them is not as clear as many people (including the speaker of the poem) seem to think it is. For example, in the second section of the poem (the one mainly concerned with the actual "Truth" about how ice storms bend the birches), the fervor of Frost's observations leads him into some wildly imaginative tropes. Ice shattered by the sun becomes the metaphor "heaps of broken glass to sweep away" that seem to have fallen from the "inner dome of heaven." A simile asserts that the birches with leaves hanging down to the ground are "Like girls on hands and knees that throw their hair/ Before them over their heads to dry in the sun." On the other hand, in the third section, Frost moves almost imperceptibly from imagination to reality—from the myth of the boy who bent down all of his father's birches, to precise images of what could well be an actual launch ("Then he flung outward, feet first, with a swish,/ Kicking his way down through the air to the ground"), to the poet's revelation that "So was I once myself a swinger of birches."

Thus, even in such a seemingly straightforward poem as "Birches," there are moments of subtle strangeness and surprise that show why Frost deserves his current reputation not only as a beloved popular poet in the United States but also as one of the great modern poets of the early twentieth century worldwide. "Birches" shows how the poetry of Robert Frost, perhaps more than that of any other great modern poet, is dedicated to keeping realism and romanticism in close touch with each other. As Frost puts it in the final line of the poem, "One could do worse than be a swinger of birches"—one who knows the pleasures of swinging back and forth between earth and sky and of moving between the realms of reality and imagination.

Terry L. Andrews

THE BISHOP ORDERS HIS TOMB
AT SAINT PRAXED'S CHURCH

Author: Robert Browning (1812-1889)
Type of poem: Dramatic monologue
First published: 1845, in *Dramatic Romances and Lyrics*

The Poem

As the subheading "Rome, 15— " explains, the setting is sixteenth century Rome, Italy. A Catholic bishop lies on his bed, near death. He has summoned his nephews or sons—he is not always sure which—to impart his instructions for his burial in his present church, Saint Praxed's.

The Bishop's primary consideration is that his tomb must outshine the tomb of his old rival, Gandolf, presumably his predecessor as bishop, now dead and buried inside the church, as was customary for high-ranking church leaders. The speaker cherishes the idea that old Gandolf always envied him, especially for his beautiful mistress. The Bishop wants Gandolf to envy his superior tomb as well and plans to enjoy this envy throughout eternity.

The monologue opens with a garbled quote from Ecclesiastes about the vanity of worldly interests. Yet the rest of his long speech reveals him as vain, greedy, and hypocritical, interested only in possessions, pleasures, and besting his rivals. On occasion the Bishop interrupts his instructions about his tomb to utter pious phrases that a bishop would be expected to say, but he himself has not followed these precepts.

Gandolf has already beaten the Bishop to the choice location for his vault, much to the Bishop's annoyance, but he consoles himself that his own spot is satisfactory and that his vault will be much more elaborate. He knows exactly what he wants for every detail. It should be made of the best antique black basalt, with nine peach-blossom-colored marble columns around it, arranged similar to the way the listeners are standing around his bed. When his former church had burned, the Bishop whispers, he had taken from it a huge lapis lazuli gemstone, and now he wants them to dig it up from the vineyard where he had hidden it and use it to adorn the effigy of himself atop his vault. Around the vault he wants a continuous band of bronze sculpture depicting various scenes, including Christ giving the Sermon on the Mount, Moses with the Ten Commandments, and—unsuitable for the Christian theme but totally suitable as a reflection of the Bishop's character—a scene depicting pagan Greek Pans and Nymphs, including one Pan about to "twitch the Nymph's last garment off." Even his epitaph on the vault must be "choice Latin" from Tully (the classical writer Marcus Tullius Cicero); it should clearly outdo Gandolf's epitaph from the less notable Ulpian.

The Bishop hears the young men talking and turns to his son Anselm as though he were the only one he might hope to trust. He worries that they will take his riches for themselves rather than use them for his tomb. He alternately bribes and threatens.

He tells them he can pray to Saint Praxed to send them horses and rare old manuscripts and mistresses. If they disobey his wishes, however, he will disinherit them and leave his villas to the Pope instead.

The Bishop becomes increasingly confused as death approaches. He is unable even to remember which author he wanted quoted for his epitaph. As the nephews/ sons start to leave, he tells them to leave him in his church, where Gandolf still envies him.

Forms and Devices

Robert Browning shows his mastery of the dramatic monologue form in this poem. Browning had an early interest in playwriting, and the poem is a compressed play with one speaking role, that of the Bishop. The minor characters, the nephews/ sons, move together and function almost as a Greek chorus, with only Anselm named. The reader is the audience. Dramatic irony enables the audience to know more than the speaker intends to reveal, and as the Bishop unmasks himself he is inadvertently didactic, instructing the audience in the folly of worldly corruption. Stage directions and props are indicated through the Bishop's remarks about the positioning of the other characters and the lighted candles.

The basic verse pattern of the poem is unrhymed iambic pentameter (blank verse); the central device is irony, created by clusters of images, shifts in tone, and the sense of movement throughout the poem. The poem immediately establishes the scene, with the central character calling reluctant listeners around his deathbed. The other characters (nephew was often a euphemism for a priest's son) seem as preoccupied with selfish interests as does the Bishop. He calls them closer as he whispers his theft of the lapis lazuli from the burned church (possibly he even started the conflagration), and they listen as he tells where the treasure is hidden. Soon he hears them whispering among themselves and exclaims, "Ye mark me not!"

The sense of physical movement throughout the poem is supported by tone shifts. The Bishop gloatingly recalls his worldly triumphs and fondly details his lavish tomb. His description of it, however, increasingly becomes a desperate need to communicate both the instructions and the urgency of carrying out his orders.

As the candles burn down, the Bishop's words show that his mind is drifting into delirium. He seems almost speaking to himself as he says, "strange thoughts/ Grow, with a certain humming in my ears." He mutters a biblical reference about personal evil but immediately stops that thought with a reminder that he wants the lapis. When he has a horrible vision of the body in a coarse, crumbling gritstone box, whose sides "sweat/ As if the corpse they keep were oozing through," he can no longer console himself with thoughts of lapis; the listeners are walking away. The Bishop asks them to arrange the candles in a row so that he can "watch at leisure" if old Gandolf leers at him in envy of his fair mistress.

The central image of the poem is the tomb, the Bishop's obsession, which merges with his revelation of character. Numerous references to stone—marble, travertine, onion-stone, jasper, and pure basalt—rich, rare, hard, and flawless, mingle with images of sensuality, as in the "great smooth marbly limbs" of mistresses or his sacrilegious metaphor that the lapis lazuli is "Blue as a vein o'er the Madonna's breast." Other clusters of images indicate his thorough familiarity with Renaissance art and his thorough immorality. Every word in the poem contributes to the reader's understanding of the total drama.

Themes and Meanings

A major theme of the poem is moral decay. Although this is seen most obviously in the hypocritical and worldly Bishop, similar immorality is also suggested in the greedy and untrustworthy young men, in the envious and conniving Gandolf, in the material wealth of the churches, and in the implication that the Pope himself would welcome new villas to add to his riches. The total effect indicts the dominant Renaissance religious institution as corrupt and spiritually dead.

A bishop should guide his flock and be exemplary in Christian compassion and charity. This bishop, however, devotes himself to personal ambition, wealth, and pleasures. Rather than chastity, poverty, and obedience to God's will, he relishes his memories of his mistress and the thought that Gandolf envied him. His villas and his indulgent luxuries show that he is no follower of Saint Praxed, who gave all she had to the poor. Even now, on his deathbed, rather than repenting his sins and thinking of God's judgment, the Bishop concerns himself only with his earthly remains. Given the example he has set, it is no wonder that he suspects that his nephews/sons will not fulfill his instructions.

The Bishop's closest human tie seems to be his hostile rivalry with Gandolf, which he assumes will continue after death; Gandolf will know the Bishop's tomb is superior to his and will still envy him. The fact that the Bishop is a learned man who has had many privileges makes his attitude and actions especially reprehensible. To him, the Church has meant power, material goods, and sensual stimulation. In a particularly gross perversion of the central Church doctrine of transubstantiation (holy communion), he says that from his tomb he will "hear the blessed mutter of the mass,/ And see God made and eaten all day long."

The poem is one of Browning's finest of many dramatic monologues, and Browning has again created a character whom readers love to hate. The poet has also given readers a means of seeing beyond the surface. The judgment of the Bishop is complicated by one's acquaintance with him. The reader recognizes that it is only because of his dying haziness that he reveals himself, that the nephews/sons will betray his dying wishes, and that the Bishop is only following the example of other ecclesiastics.

This literary example of moral corruption implies the need for change both in institutions and in individuals. Part of the solution is contained in the poem itself— the idea that man's years are short, and the material things of this world are less important than creating a worthy soul.

Lois A. Marchino

THE BLACK ANGEL

Author: Henri Coulette (1927-1988)
Type of poem: Lyric
First published: 1963; collected in *The War of the Secret Agents and Other Poems*, 1966

The Poem

"The Black Angel" is a distilled version of a longer poem by Henri Coulette about a memorial statue of a black angel that stands in the midst of an Iowa City cemetery. A number of Coulette's contemporaries also wrote poems about this statue, though his contemporaries did not publish their poems. Coulette seems to have been uncertain about what he wanted to do with the figure; he wrote at least three versions of the poem, eventually condensing it so far as to make the reference of the title and the line "I will not meet *her* eye" somewhat obscure.

The metrical form of the stanza is the same in all the versions of the poem. It follows a pattern of beats that repeat 5-2-3-4-5-3 in each stanza—a metrical form invented, according to poet Robert Mezey, by Peter Everwine. The first version, of nine stanzas, was not published, but it was printed privately on a double folio that held nine pen-and-ink drawings of the figures invoked by the poem, done by a fellow student. The 1963 version published in *The New Yorker* consisted of the first eight stanzas of the poem, without the original ninth. It was published in *The War of the Secret Agents and Other Poems* (1966) as the four-stanza poem that is discussed here.

The whole poem is in the first person, and while sometimes a poet uses first-person singular even when he or she is writing in the persona of an imaginary speaker, this poem gives no indication that the speaker is anyone but the poet himself. While he is thus speaking of his own thoughts and experiences, the use of the pronoun "I" invites the reader to see through the "eye" of the speaker, to see and experience vicariously what he does.

The stanzas that Coulette excised describe the graveyard statue and muse about those who lie buried about it. He then shifts the focus of his musing from the historical past of prosaic pioneers to ask about others who are gone, or will be gone one day, whose lives were of a different scope. These are the stanzas that make up the poem.

The first stanza begins with a query that, by asking about people of great beauty and longings, draws one's attention to the inevitability and obscurity of their end. The second stanza is more specific, in that it refers to particular friends of Coulette: The "friend too much moved by music" is Donald Justice; "that one too much moved by faces," Robert Mezey; and "that marvelous liar," Philip Levine. All these friends were living, and in fact fairly young men, when this poem was written, so their fates were unknown then.

The third stanza has more to say about these friends: their activity as poets, what it is like to be them, how their lives may end. In the last line of this stanza, the reference to "*her* eye" signals a return to the contemplation of the figure of the black angel.

The fourth stanza describes some very immediate images, things that are found around the speaker as he is standing in the grassy cemetery— "but here's a butter-fly,/ And a white flower." He even describes a bit of himself as one of those immediate things: "the moon rising on my nail" refers to the small, crescent-shaped, white cuticle at the base of the fingernail.

Forms and Devices

Coulette places his poem in a classical context by the use of allusion and conceit. He makes a reference to Thomas Gray, which tells the reader that he understood himself to be writing a poem that on one level was part of the long tradition of graveyard elegies. In those elegies, primarily written in the eighteenth century, the meditation on death stands for a contemplation of the sublime—that which is beyond human comprehension. The use of the Renaissance conceit of *ubi sunt* (Latin for "where are they now?") in the first line ("Where are the people") both reinforces this meditative tone and emphasizes the placement of the poem within a long poetic tradition.

Another connection to poetic tradition is made by the poem's allusion to figures of mythology (if one sees the "idler whom reflection loved" as Narcissus and the "woman with the iridescent brow" as Psyche) and its proposal to "bring them flowers." These references together introduce echoes of John Keats's "Ode to Psyche" (1820). Like Keats's poem, it proposes to do something it never actually begins to do. The speaker who "would" bring flowers, "thinks" of friends, and "will not" but someday "shall" meet the eye of the black angel is very much like the speaker of Keats's poem promising to build a bower to a deity who never arrives.

This poem progresses from very metaphorical to very concrete imagery. The repetition of images of reflection in the first stanza ("mirrors," "oceanic," "reflection," "iridescent") creates a sense of something not plainly visible, but rather something that shimmers and wavers. At the same time, such things as "oceanic longings" and an "iridescent brow" are purely imaginative: While one can have a sense of what is meant, one cannot picture it in the mind's eye.

The image of the "old streetcars buried at sea" is very strong but strange; the intended oddity is plain. Such things are possible, but incongruous. At the same time, to be "buried at sea" is to be beneath the level of shimmer and reflection of the surface of the water. With this image, the poem progresses; it moves from the elusive to the more tangible.

The objects in the fourth stanza are concrete almost to the point of being prosaic but also seem to represent something more than themselves. Their whiteness is an opacity that is the opposite of a reflecting surface. Yet none of these variations— mirroring, murky, or opaque "elements"— imply clear, direct vision, so the impression one gets through the poem is of something not quite comprehended. This sense is made even stronger by the final image, which pairs two seemingly opposite senses of motion.

Themes and Meanings

The figure of the black angel, whether specifically meant or as a general reference, is a signal of death. Combined with the *ubi sunt* theme of the first stanza, one can understand this poem as a contemplation on the passing away of things. The shift from the first stanza to the second stanza, a general query to thoughts of friendship, tells the reader that the poet is contemplating the end of life as he knows it.

In the third stanza, it could be the friendships mentioned in the second stanza that are "the past of what was always future" — that is, friendship is based on what came before but is defined by its lasting forward into time. This line also could place those friends, and thus Coulette himself along with them, among those to be lamented by some future *ubi sunt*. It may be that when others look back upon them, maybe even during their own time, the differences that distinguished them as poets made them as strange as "old streetcars buried at sea"; the experience of being "in the wrong element" may be a kind of death even while they are living.

Further, these lines may also be about poems (which people are "as beautiful as"). It could be that poetry itself, speaking "in tongues,/ Silently, about nothing" is what is so strange, and it is what these friends do that is "what was always future."

In all these possibilities revolve questions about death: Where are those who are gone? Where will my friends be? Where will I be? Will something about me exist in the future? Even the turnings of the friends in the second stanza pose a similar question: Are the turns — from music to games, from faces to the wall ("turned his face to the wall" is in one sense a paraphrase for suicide), from lies to truth — positive change or progress, or are they merely preludes to the final turn to the face of death?

The refusal in the last line of the third stanza puts off that final turn, but the fourth stanza, acknowledging the inevitability of that final meeting ("Although I shall" meet her eye), attempts to put it off by focusing on the "presence of things present" (the butterfly, the flower, the moon). Then death intrudes again, this time as a simile for the hardship of life: "Flying woefully" (life) is like "closing sweetly" (death). Between these two possibilities — living that is as woeful as death and death that may be as sweet as life — which are always all that is present and in everything that is present, "there is nothing else."

"Closing sweetly" also carries a sexual overtone that is not implausible when people's "oceanic longings" and the "woman with the iridescent brow" are considered. This changes the meaning of "I will not meet *her* eye . . ./ Although I shall" somewhat as well. To read the images this way is also not inconsistent with the classical associations of the poem, as the oblivion of the moment of sexual abandonment has been, from the Renaissance on, linked with the "nothing else" of death.

Laurie Glover

BLACK HILLS SURVIVAL GATHERING, 1980

Author: Linda Hogan (1947-   )
Type of poem: Lyric
First published: 1981, in *Daughters, I Love You*

The Poem

The setting for this poem is the Black Hills of South Dakota, specifically at the places where enormous holes drilled into the earth house missile silos. The sites contain nuclear warheads that are capable of traveling thousands of miles and destroying large cities. The occasion is an encampment of people protesting the existence and potential use of these weapons; the poem describes an early morning scene, as the people awaken and begin the day's activities.

In the first stanza, the reader sees Buddhist monks, familiar at peace and antinuclear demonstrations, in their orange-colored togalike robes, outlined against the rising sun. The next two stanzas depict other people beginning to awaken, as bombers fly overhead. While the encampment stirs and comes to life, more people arrive on the dusty roads.

The speaker then turns, in the fourth stanza, from the panoramic view of the whole camp to speak of her family: her husband and two daughters, who are participating in the event with her. She describes her husband bathing their small daughter in a pail of water, then in the next stanza turns to the other daughter combing her hair. The speaker says that she makes coffee, and while doing so tells her daughter that they are camped in the land of the daughter's ancestors. She wonders about her daughter's reaction to this knowledge. The sixth stanza turns again to a slightly more distanced view, as the speaker places her family with respect to the sun and the hills and reflects on the names in her family: Thunder Horse and Dawn Protector for the daughters, and her husband's name, Hogan, which means "home" in Navajo.

In the last two stanzas, the speaker begins to speak first for all of her family, then for all of the people in the encampment. "We" stand, she says, at ground zero, the center of the bombs' target. Enormous power for destruction exists overhead and beneath the earth, in the flying bombers and buried missiles, and this sense is juxtaposed with the description of the people awakening and looking. The increasing light as the sun rises makes the earth almost seem to be on fire, and the speaker sees a mare standing on a distant ridge looking as if she might have been at Hiroshima. The speaker describes the veins within the people carrying life, sees her children's vibrant hair, and begins to hear and feel the monks mentioned at the beginning of the poem as they start to sing to the rhythm of their drums. The poem ends with a single word, "heartbeat."

Forms and Devices

Like almost all Linda Hogan's poems, "Black Hills Survival Gathering, 1980" is written in first-person free verse. The poet alludes directly and deliberately to her family, referring to her husband and daughters by name, and she reinforces the identification between the author of the poem and the voice or speaker within it. The poem proceeds by way of direct description, with very few examples of rhetorical devices such as simile or extended metaphor. One exception is the comparison of the mare seen on a distant hill, which looks like "one burned/ over Hiroshima." This practice of using plain language and straightforward description is in keeping with Hogan's philosophy of writing, which stresses the accessibility of her poetry to ordinary people; as she stated in an interview with Bo Scholer, which was published in *The Journal of Ethnic Studies* (1988), "I don't want my work to be something you can only read if you have gone to a university."

While the description in "Black Hills Survival Gathering, 1980" is unadorned by rhetorical figures, it is highly impressionistic. That is, the reader is constantly drawn to the appearance of things, to the way in which things strike the speaker's eye, and things are often described as if the way they appear is the way they are. In the opening of the poem, for example, the sight of the monks looking as if they are touched by the sun's fire is described in words that state that their bodies actually are "on fire." Later in the poem, the shining of her daughter's hair as it is being combed is portrayed in words that state that the "warm sun" itself is being combed across the hair. The effect of the device, which blurs the distinction between what appears to be and what is, is to suggest metamorphosis and transformation.

Colors play an important part in the description of the process of awakening in the encampment. The monks' orange robes correlate with other images of light and fire in the "fractures of light" (a metaphor for lightning) in the distance, the sulfur-colored grass, and the "burning hills" which appear to be on fire as the sun's light catches them. Close to the light/orange configuration is the red of the horse and the red veins the speaker imagines under the fragile skin of her children. The red of blood and flame contrasts in turn with the sky and the blue of veins. Within this pattern of color is the significant metaphor of the people's veins as "tunnels" — red and blue — carrying the pulsing life within the body, contrasted with the death-dealing tunnels containing warheads and destruction.

Themes and Meanings

"Black Hills Survival Gathering, 1980" is part of a group of poems that resulted from the Black Hills Alliance International Survival Gathering, the event commemorated in the poem. The poems, first printed in *Daughters, I Love You* (1981), are dedicated to Sister Rosalie Bertell, M.D., who inspired the poet with the words quoted in the dedication to the book: "Everywhere I go, women are grieving the death of the species. You can either turn it around or help it to die." The poem, like all the poems in the book, is a plea for life against death. The contrast between life and death, the image of life in the midst of death, permeates the description, imagery and rhetoric of the poem. A secondary theme is the persistent memory, explicit in the description of the monks and the reference to Hiroshima, of the realization of the annihilating power of nuclear destruction. The poem calls for a moral awakening even as the process of awakening is documented in the description.

The life-and-death contrast begins with the description of the B52's leaving "a cross on the ground" over the heads of men awakening on the hilltop. The cross is the cross-shaped shadow of the airplanes passing over the grassy hillside. The figure is also an oblique allusion to the crosshairs on the bombardier's sight, which will locate "ground zero," where the participants of the encampment stand as they assemble in the morning light. Finally, the cross on the ground suggests the association with crucifixion: the sacrificial death of innocent victims.

Throughout the poem, the speaker contrasts the homely, ordinary events of living—bathing children, making coffee, combing hair—with the imminent destruction buried within the earth and flying overhead. The specifically nuclear nature of the threat is woven through the description, from the monks "on fire" against the morning horizon to the dusty roads transforming matter into energy (the energy of the resisters), the electric breeze and, finally, the "radiant" morning. The literal description of people waking up after a night's sleep and beginning their day's activities becomes, in the circumstances, a figure for the moral awakening they undergo with respect to the beauty and fragility of the earth and the necessity for preserving it against the wanton and savage destruction threatened by the missiles and bombers. The poem's reiteration of "waking" constitutes a chorus on this idea: The men wake on the hillside, the speaker's husband wakes, one daughter wakes, then the other, and finally, the entire encampment: "We are waking/ in the expanding light."

Another thread of images links the people and their individual lives with common human life and finally with the life of the earth itself. The speaker reflects that her daughter, as she stands being bathed, contains "wind and fragile fire"—the breath in her lungs and warmth of her body—under her skin; the daughters find their union with the land through their ancestors, "blood and heart." The speaker suggests another potential transformation, speculating that the daughter's hair might become "a mane" in her identification with the plains and its horse culture; this image echoes later in the sight of the red horse, first drooping as if in sickness, but then "surging" toward the sky. Finally, the veins pulsing with life-carrying blood join with the singing and drumming of the monks and all the participants; the poem's final word, "heartbeat," then unites people, land, and inner soul in a single affirmation of life.

Helen Jaskoski

BLACK TAMBOURINE

Author: Hart Crane (1899-1932)
Type of poem: Lyric
First published: 1921; collected in *White Buildings*, 1926

The Poem

"Black Tambourine" is written in three stanzas, each a quatrain with end rhymes on the second and fourth lines. This poem, brief as it is, is like much of Hart Crane's poetry: It carries suggestiveness to an extreme, never openly revealing its hand. The poem, though it appears to take a lyrical pleasure in measure and imagery, is told rather than spoken, allowing the reader to imagine that it may be a meditation rather than a lyric. The words seem to be said for their own sake. There is, in a sense, no definable speaker or audience.

The poem begins with the image of "a black man in a cellar." The second line states, in language reminiscent of a newspaper editorial espousing racial equality, that the black man's downtrodden living conditions "Mark tardy judgment on the world's closed door." The stanza concludes with starkly realistic images of gnats flying in a bottle's shadow and a roach running across the floor.

The second stanza changes the scene so abruptly that the reader struggles to find a connection. The speaker tells about Aesop, the ancient Greek fabler whose moral tales involving animals may have delighted children but clearly pointed at adult behavior. Aesop is generally regarded as a legendary figure, but the most prominent of legends makes him a slave who earned his freedom, or at least a measure of human dignity, through his capacity to tell stories.

There is the hint of a connection here in a double measure: African Americans were brought to the New World as slaves; those who are dehumanized and brutalized by the institution of slavery must, in a sense, "sing for their supper." In a 1921 letter to a friend, Crane offered a further connection between Aesop's fables, with their disarming simplicity, and the sentimental conception of African-American romance, as was popularized by such Caucasian Southern writers as Joel Chandler Harris in his Uncle Remus tales.

The last stanza states that "the black man, forlorn in the cellar,/ Wanders in some mid-kingdom." He is truly no longer of his original world, yet he has not been fully assimilated into the mainstream of the culture in which he and his people were first introduced as slaves. Thus, his tambourine—conforming to a common racist notion that the "childlike" black loves music and dance—is not an active part of his life. Instead, the instrument is "stuck on the wall," while back in his ancestral home, Africa, there is nothing left but a decayed and corrupted—and irrevocable—past symbolized by "a carcass quick with flies."

Forms and Devices

In this poem, Crane works chiefly with two forms of poetic shorthand—

metonymy and synecdoche. Synecdoche, the substituting of the part for the whole, is the easier of the two to define, and it is regarded by some as a special case of metonymy. An example of synecdoche is to use the word "sails" for "ship" or "ships." Metonymy is more complex: offering someone a "mug" when the item being served is actually coffee is one example—the container is substituted for the contained. One might argue that everything in this poem is what it seems to be— and less, and more. "The world's closed door," for example, covers a multitude of socioeconomic injustices, but it is also a door keeping the black man in his cellar (at the bottom of the socioeconomic ladder). Aesop is the fabler, but he also stands for the vision that sees through adversity to higher truths. The tambourine is a real instrument, but it is also the body of African-American culture, that is, the beauty that African Americans managed to salvage from the detritus of the slave culture into which they were forced. The "carcass quick with flies" is a vivid image in concrete terms, but it also stands for what remains of black culture on its native soil as a consequence of the slavers' rapine.

If the carcass is the body of the past, and the tambourine is a token of the slave mentality, which he can put aside but not escape, then Crane wants the reader to see the black man as someone who can neither return to his origin nor advance beyond the figurative cellar of the Europocentric culture into which he has been introduced.

Themes and Meanings

Crane was rather explicit about his intentions for this poem, and although one should generally treat a poet's stated intentions gingerly, in this instance, one may learn from what Crane said he was hoping to achieve.

Referring to the last stanza's "mid-kingdom" analogy (the black man "wanders in some mid-kingdom"), he wrote a letter to his close friend Gorham Munson in the spring of 1921 that the poem was a "bundle of insinuations, suggestions bearing out the Negro's place somewhere between man and beast." He stated that his only personal "declaration" in the poem was that he found "the Negro (in the popular mind) sentimentally or brutally 'placed' in this midkingdom." Crane also noted that a "propagandist for either side of the Negro question could find anything he wanted to in it," insisting that "the value of the poem is only, to me, in what a painter would call its 'tactile' quality—an entirely aesthetic feature."

It is not easy to know what to make of Crane's statements or, therefore, of the poem itself. What may sound, at the one extreme like the most dispassionate of racist attitudes can also sound, at the opposite, like the most dispassionate of aesthetic detachment. Putting those two ends together, however, one can possibly see what Crane means. He is neither depicting the black man as a generic entity nor portraying a particularized African American so much as depicting perceptions of blacks in America—neither from his perspective, nor from theirs, but from the perspective of the dominant white culture of his day.

Although the poem is filled with concrete socioeconomic details and, as noted earlier, a virtual editorial fervor for elucidating the "Negro question," the poem is not "about" the so-called "Negro question." Even that aspect of the poem is a part, not of its theme, but of its texture — its "tactile" quality, as Crane called it.

This is not to say that the poem has no "meaning." Crane is representing something as elusive as attitudes and values, and by evoking them accurately and authentically, he is exposing them to all. As Crane asserts, he does not want to take sides so much as to show the human element at the heart of the matter.

Russell Elliott Murphy

BLACK WOMAN

Author: Léopold Senghor (1906-   )
Type of poem: Lyric
First published: 1945, as "Femme noire," in *Chants d'ombre*; collected in
   Selected Poems, 1964

The Poem
   "Black Woman" is a short poem in free verse, with eighteen lines divided into
three stanzas of five lines each and one stanza of three lines. It is written in the first
person and is addressed directly to the woman of the title, the black woman who
gives the poem its theme.
   This was one of many poems written when Léopold Senghor was living abroad,
away from his own country of Senegal. During this period, he was a student in Paris
and wrote about his childhood, which he viewed as a kind of paradise. These poems
abound in his memories of Africa—an Africa seen in his mind's eye—and are an
imagined return to an idealized Africa.
   Having experienced a feeling of estrangement amid Western society, he set out on
a poetic quest for his homeland. He looked back to the time of his childhood and to
the place where he was reared. The main themes in his first collection of poetry are
a longing for his homeland, a nostalgia for his childhood, and especially an affirmation of his African heritage. "Black Woman" is one of the best-known poems from
this collection. When Senghor writes of Africa, it is frequently in terms of a woman,
a woman who is both wife and mother; she is the "promised land" mentioned in the
poem.
   The first stanza gives the theme of the poem: the natural black woman whose
color is life and whose form is beauty. The poet has grown up in her shadow and has
felt the gentleness of her hands. Now that he is grown, he returns to find her as if he
were coming upon the promised land. He views her through a mountain pass at noon
in the midst of summer, and her beauty strikes him directly to the heart, like the
flash of an eagle.
   In the second stanza, she is seen as a lover, a woman with the flesh of ripe fruit, a
woman who can transport the poet with somber ecstasies of black wine, a woman
with a mouth that makes his own mouth lyric. The poet elaborates, finding her a
woman who is like a limitless savanna that shudders beneath the caresses of the east
wind; a woman who is like a tight, well-sculpted drum that resounds under the
fingers of the conqueror; a woman whose solemn contralto voice becomes the spiritual song of the loved one.
   In the third stanza, she is almost a goddess, so perfect that even her skin is
smooth as the oiled skin of an athlete or a prince. She is like a graceful gazelle with
celestial adornments. Pearls become stars on the darkness of her skin. The reflections of the setting sun on her glistening skin are delights on which the mind can
exercise itself. The poet's anguish is lightened by the sunlike glance from her eyes,

when he is in the shadow of her hair.

In the fourth and last stanza, the poet—more philosophical—informs the black woman that he is celebrating in verse her beauty, which is passing, and her form, which he establishes eternally in his poetry, before fate can turn her to ashes in order to nourish the roots of life.

Forms and Devices

The poem is a hymn of praise to the black woman—not only as an individual, but also as a symbol of African women and as a representative of her race. The first two lines serve as a statement of the poem's theme: the beauty of the natural black woman, who though naked, is "clothed" in her color, which is life. There is also the poet's response to this beauty, as the black woman is perceived in both a sensory and in an emotional way. The poet has experienced the touch of her hand, and he is struck to the heart by her beauty.

Even though the musical language and the rhythm of the original poem may lose something in translation—and many of Senghor's poems were written to be accompanied by African musical instruments—one nevertheless perceives the impact of this poem through the imagery, metaphor, and personification that the poet employs.

In an enumerative style, similar to that of a litany, Senghor presents a series of images that are, in effect, the attributes of the black woman. He thus seems to summarize her qualities, beginning with a description of the natural woman, then—elaborating metaphorically—he describes her as the promised land, a plain that rustles, and the nocturnal sky. The poet thereby sees her not only in terms of a person, but in terms of the earth itself, and even the universe.

There are other metaphors: In the second stanza—more erotic than the first—the black woman is seen in terms of ripe fruit, black wine, a savanna that shudders beneath the "caresses" of the east wind, and an object—a sculpted drum—that responds to the touch. Even her voice is the song of the loved one. In the third stanza, the oil on her skin is seen by the poet as the oil on the limbs of an athlete or on those of the princes of Mali. She is now more of a goddess, a graceful but celestial gazelle, perhaps a totem for her people.

Associating her with eternity, the poet uses terms dealing with things eternal: earth, wind, summer, noon, stars, night, suns. The poet thus sees the woman not only in terms of a person, not only in terms of the earth, but also in a more cosmic sense. The poet also employs words dealing with color, many of which are synonymous with black—shadow, dark, and somber. These words that are images of darkness are contrasted with words that are images of light: brighten, gold, stars, and suns.

The poet also uses the device of inversion. The first line of the first stanza—"naked woman, black woman"—becomes "naked woman, dark woman" in the second stanza, and these words are inverted in the first lines of the last two stanzas. Inversion is again used, as the repetition of the theme in the final stanza uses the words of the first stanza—life, form, and beauty—but in inverted order.

Use of punctuation is sparse, the end of the lines serving as the end of the word group. A change of tense occurs only in the third line of the first stanza, where the poet uses the past tense in order to recall the comfort that black womankind has given him. He immediately resumes the present tense for the rest of the poem. This effect helps to connect the past with the present. He had grown up under the black woman's shadow; now he seeks solace again in the shadow of her hair.

Personification is another device, as the poet writes in the fourth stanza of Fate, which is jealous and capable of reducing one to ashes. It is in this stanza that he reveals his vocation of poet, as he informs the black woman that he is celebrating her beauty and her form in poetry, before she returns to ashes in order to nourish the roots of life. Thus the poet has moved, by means of description, metaphor, and personification, from praise of the black woman herself to an affirmation of the continuation of life. He has saved the best for last as he ends on a note of optimism.

Themes and Meanings

The meaning of this poem revolves around Senghor's contemplation, description, and glorification of the natural black woman. Woman holds a place of importance in Senghor's life and in his poetry. When he writes of Africa in his poetry, it is frequently in terms of a woman. His glorification of the black woman is quite different from that of Western poetry, which had so often glorified women of Western society. The black woman of this poem is more than an individual person; she is also the progenitor of his race, and thus symbolic of Africa itself and an embodiment of Senghor's African heritage. Senghor takes pride in his race, and here especially, he shows his love and respect for the black woman. He uses her very color as part of his praise and seems to abstract her characteristics into an idea of a black woman in order to praise her.

This deservedly famous and often-quoted poem was written when he was away from his homeland. The nostalgia that one finds in the other poems of his collection *Chants d'ombre* are reflected in this poetic return to an Africa that was almost unspoiled by the ways of the Western world and that was, for him, a sort of paradise where all seemed to be in harmony and at peace, where he felt secure in his place in the world. In this Africa of his childhood, there was a sense of a life spent in common with his family, his village, his clan, his tribe, and even his ancestors.

In this poem, he sees, in his imagination, an idealized African woman in several roles: in the first stanza, as mother, and thus comforting; in the second stanza, as lover, and thus erotic; and in the last line of the last stanza, as nourisher of life. There is a certain sweetness in this poem, a contemplative quality, a quiet appreciation of the African woman, and the emotions the poet experiences at her sight and at her touch. He details his pleasure on contemplating her and the comfort he experiences in her presence.

He realizes that life is transitory, that even though beauty seems permanent, time works on the individual woman. He is a poet, however, and he informs this woman that he is celebrating her beauty and her form in poetry, before she returns to ashes.

The final stanza affirms the gift and the mission of the poet as someone who can relate the temporal to the eternal; as Pierre de Ronsard wrote to immortalize the passing beauty of his Helen, or Cassandra, or Marie, so can Senghor immortalize the beauty of the black woman. Thus the last stanza, even though potentially tragic as to the fate of the individual black woman, ends on a note of hope. These very ashes will be used to nourish life anew.

George Craddock

BLACKBERRY EATING

Author: Galway Kinnell (1927-   )
Type of poem: Lyric
First published: 1980, in *Mortal Acts, Mortal Words*

The Poem

"Blackberry Eating" is a short poem in free verse, its fourteen lines (in one stanza) all parts of one compound-complex sentence. One-sentence poems are not uncommon for Galway Kinnell. The title plunges into the immediacy of the context of the poem by focusing on an action as subject. The poem is written in the first person. There is no indication that the speaker's persona is someone other than the poet, so the poem fits into the classic tradition of lyric poetry wherein the poet directly informs the reader about a personal experience.

A subject that is clearly in the realm of the ordinary is the starting point of "Blackberry Eating." Kinnell introduces the activity of picking blackberries by grounding the experience in a particular mood, love, and a particular season, autumn. Autumn suggests the time of harvest, when the prospect of impending death weighs heavily on the mind. No drape of melancholy is allowed here, though; the enthusiasm of love keeps it pushed aside.

A descriptive series of words, a vibrant picture of blackberries begging to be picked, helps the reader see, smell, and feel the clusters of fruit. A blending of wilderness and civilization follows when the speaker links his exploration of nature with humankind's regularity and demands: The blackberries are for breakfast.

When Kinnell draws attention to the prickly stalks, he focuses on the significance of small details and comments on the mystical process of creation. He suggests that the stalks earn their prickles as a penalty for "knowing the black art of blackberry-making," a parallel with the myth of Adam and Eve's loss of Eden for "knowing" too much. The "knowing" here has mysterious and sexual connotations, as well as moral ones, since what is referred to as a "black art" is the knowledge of reproduction, which requires a penalty that serves as a flag of warning or an obstacle to be overcome for the speaker. Standing among the prickly stalks, the speaker raises clusters of blackberries to his face. The berries are framed in a close-up now, so ready to enter his mouth that they almost drop in, but the inclusion of "almost" qualifies the relationship of berry and tongue so that the necessity for deliberate involvement on the part of the eater remains.

The poem shifts away from the actual wilderness setting when blackberries are compared to a certain class of "words" in the latter portion of the long sentence. Kinnell limits these words to those with many letters and one syllable, and then, keeping blackberries within sight, he calls the words "lumps." The poet suggests "strengths" and "squinched" as examples of words that invoke a sensory experience like that of the provocative berries when such words, like the berries, engage the tongue. The interaction between the words and the poet, described in a series of actions of increasing intensity, emphasizes the sensory experience. In the last two lines, Kinnell returns the reader to a vantage point distant enough to glimpse the relationship between his satisfaction in encountering nature's empowering impetus in the creative wild and his satisfaction in realizing the same empowering impetus in his own creative impulse. The familiar blackberry-eating terminology in the description is not what it seems, however, since it now describes an inner place in which the black art of language making resides.

Forms and Devices

Its fourteen-line length demonstrates that "Blackberry Eating" is an unrhymed, free-verse sonnet in the style of Robert Lowell. The strict sonnet forms specify definite patterns of meter and rhyme but can also be interpreted on the basis of spirit and passion. The poem's first eight lines, or octave, consistent with the Italian sonnet form, serve as an introduction of the theme, developing the theme in the direction of the sensory experience of blackberry eating. Also true to form, the poem's last six lines, or sestet, introduce a new development or application of the proposition, wherein words are substituted for berries as sensory objects. This flow and ebb are sonnetlike, even though none of the other aspects demanded by the sonnet form is present.

The controlling image of the poem is a simile: the comparison of blackberries and words. Each element of the simile, however, has a specific definition. The blackberries are "fat, overripe, icy," and the words are "many-lettered and one-syllabled." In the first instance, Kinnell uses a series of somewhat hyperbolic adjectives to enhance the reader's appreciation of the sensate function of the blackberries. The "words" of the simile, restricted by Kinnell's imposition of rules, are heightened in meaning as well, since they directly relate to "strengths" and "squinched" by being the kind of words that sound "strong" because they "squinch" their few vowels among an abundance of consonants.

Kinnell's simile is framed by an analogy between the mysterious "art of blackberry-making" and the mysterious power of words. By use of a mirroring syntax including the repetition of the phrase "in late September" in the first and last lines of the poem, and the repetition of the adjectives "icy, black" in the second and next-to-last lines at the end of a series of adjectives modifying blackberries and language, respectively, the poem conveys the message that, in the same way that the blackberry bush produces blackberries, language produces succulent words that, when boldly embraced by the tongue, introduce sensations akin to the pleasure derived from devouring luscious blackberries.

The very sounds of "Blackberry Eating" underline its sense-oriented theme. The alliteration of *b*'s and long *e*'s, and the repetition of *p* in the first four lines, together with the *s*'s sprinkled generously throughout, work the lips and tongue. Especially involving are the *l*'s and *s*'s of line 9 followed by "squeeze, squinch . . . splurge" and then "silent, startled, icy" — words that infuse both energy and surprise into the images they evoke.

Themes and Meanings

With a Whitmanesque receptivity to experience, Kinnell transmits his wonder and delight in nature's creative power, and his own, in "Blackberry Eating." The speaker, frank about his love of nature, provides an idealized picture of rural life by describing a fall morning's experience that he implies he has repeated many times. The experience is not an end in itself, however, but acts as a sounding board for a more personal phenomenon: the eruption of words into his consciousness to be manipulated into their most effective mode.

"Blackberry Eating" concerns the origin of creative power, a playful presentation of the creative process as evidence of what Andrew Taylor has called the positive aspect of darkness that appears throughout Kinnell's work. This positive aspect, writes Taylor, "is the nonself, the unconscious, the preconscious, the unpredictable source of vitality, the Mystery."

Kinnell's mysterious "source of vitality" here touches the speaker in the form of inspiration, in compact words that bring with them a fullness of experience that awakens the speaker's senses to a mysterious void that lies just beyond the knowable. The void, however, does not loom in its "silent, startled, icy" blackness as a pit of destruction, but becomes, through its dramatic association with the extreme sensory pleasures of blackberry eating in the wild, a communicator of a life-affirming bias in the inexplicable design of the universe.

From its opening clause, "Blackberry Eating" reveals its Romantic underpinnings. Its form, that of a nature lyric replete with intimate observations of the beauty and bounty of the wild, displays Romanticism in the exaltation of detail and in the relationship imposed by its comparison of the speaker's sensory interaction with the physical world to his spiritual interaction with his own inner world. The influence of Austrian poet Rainer Maria Rilke on Kinnell's poetic vision shines through in this poem's organic vehicle. Although Rilke's emphasis is on transformation and Kinnell's is on empathetic participation, both poets use contact with the earth to penetrate the surface of things in order to achieve an understanding of the life/death cycle.

When Kinnell writes of the blackberry stalks "knowing the black art of blackberry-making" and later describes "the silent, startled, icy, black language of blackberry-eating," he is hinting at a metaphysical philosophy of a kind of Jungian collective unconscious that employs sensory, or even sensual, experience as its messengers. In *Walking Down the Stairs* (1978), Kinnell comments that "language itself comes from the deepest place, from sex." "Blackberry Eating" introduces this "deepest place" in a wider, yet still sensory and sensual context, and invites one to realize such ecstasy for oneself.

Virginia Starrett

BLACKCURRANT RIVER

Author: Arthur Rimbaud (1854-1891)
Type of poem: Lyric
First published: 1886, as "La rivière de Cassis," in *Les Illuminations*; collected
  in *Rimbaud: Complete Works, Selected Letters*, 1966

The Poem

"Blackcurrant River" is a short poem, composed in May, 1872, that was not published by the author. It remained a manuscript until 1886, when it was published together with a number of other pieces, entirely without the poet's knowledge. By the time "Blackcurrant River" appeared, Arthur Rimbaud had abandoned poetry and left Europe to live as a trader in Ethiopia.

The poem is composed of three rhyming six-line stanzas. In the French original, the lines are of unequal lengths, alternating eleven-syllable lines with lines of five to seven syllables. The rhyme scheme is also slightly irregular. While the rhymes of the first and third stanzas alternate in a simple *ababab* pattern, the second-stanza rhyme repeats a single nasalized vowel (*revoltants, temps, importants, entend, errants, vent*). Formal deviations such as these are difficult to render in a translation; their effect in the original French is considerable.

"Cassis" is a fruit, a popular flavor of sweetened syrup, and a liqueur. Thus the French title suggests a stream of sweet liquid, an inviting counterpart to the Big Rock Candy Mountain. When translated into English, the title contains a pun (currant-current) that is absent in French. Rimbaud spoke English, however, and may have been conscious of the possibility. In any case, the title helps establish a deceptively mild tone for the poem, although "black currents" run throughout.

The opening stanza evokes a pastoral landscape of a stream that rolls unknown through strange valleys. The stream is accompanied by the voices of a hundred ravens (or crows), and these are true, good "angel voices." Another element of this scene is the great movements of fir thickets in plunging winds. An undercurrent of tension troubles the ideal countryside: Why is the river unknown? Why are the valleys strange? How can the cawing of crows be hailed as angel voices? Even the winds, in the verb "plunge," are characterized with unusual violence.

The second stanza adds picturesque references in a guidebook tone. Everything rolls (as the river rolls), with mysteries of campaigns of ancient times, visited dungeons, important parks. All the elements of a country ramble in château country are here, yet the poet compromises his pastoral by terming his mysteries "revolting." Within these boundaries are heard the passions of knights errant, but the passions are dead. Again, the stanza ends with the wind, here set in opposition to the rest of the scene: "But how salubrious is the wind!"

The final stanza brings human figures to the landscape, a foot-traveler and a crafty peasant. An impersonal voice directs the hiker to look at latticework fences; if he does so, he will feel braver. Ravens are called soldiers of the forests, sent by the

Lord. They are "dear, delicious ravens," directed to chase away the peasant. The peasant figure, crafty and guzzling (the verb used can also mean offering a toast), has the old stump of an amputated limb. In its final image, the poem offers a degraded figure, deformed by some old injury, a blot upon the fairy-tale pastoral landscape. Disturbing undercurrents in the description of that landscape suggest, however, that the sympathies of the poet lie with this "crafty peasant."

Forms and Devices

"Blackcurrant River" was written during the young Rimbaud's close early association with fellow poet Paul Verlaine. This was a very productive period, and several poems from roughly the same time, such as "Larme" ("Teardrop"), "Bonne Pensée de Matin" ("Good Morning Thought"), and the four "Fêtes de la Patience" ("Feast Days of Patience"), show the poet's formal experiments.

One element of experimentation is the length of the lines. Rimbaud's earliest poems are often written in formal Alexandrine (twelve-syllable) lines — even sonnet form. The poems of May, 1872, use shorter lines, although they rhyme and use regular verse form, sometimes inconsistently. In the "Fêtes de la Patience," for example, three of the four poems are written in lines of five syllables, the fourth in lines of eight.

The uneven rhythm of "Blackcurrant River" is one of its most distinctive features; it halts briefly after each shorter line, suggesting a limping step or the irregular flow of water over stones. This effect may not be rendered in all translations. The longer lines could be read separately and produce a legible text. The shorter lines throw the poem into its essential imbalance, and their content is emphasized. These lines often carry the more unsettling thoughts and images of the poem. In the briefer lines, crows' croaks are qualified as "angel voices," winds plunge and are praised, crows are called "dear" and "delicious," and an amputated limb serves to lift a toast or guzzle. These lines are longer by two syllables in the last two stanzas, adding to the irregularity of the poem.

Rhythm is not the only element that unifies "Blackcurrant River." The two first stanzas of "Blackcurrant River" are bound by an internal echo; both have the same main verb, "roll," and both evoke the wind. The first and third share the image of crows and their qualification as angels or soldiers of the Lord. Within the overall rhyme structure, which tends toward "rich" rhymes (that is, rhymes in which two or more elements of the word ending are the same), the rhyme scheme of the second stanza, which is built around the same nasalized vowel for all six lines and has a full syllable rhyme for the first four, produces a closed atmosphere. It emphasizes the suggestion of confinement that is thematic within this stanza, with its dungeon keep, river banks, and formal park.

Themes and Meanings

If the image of a "blackcurrant river" evokes a vagabond's paradise, the development of the poem expands that image by coupling it with medieval, fairy-tale commonplaces and a little faintly ironic advice to the timid hiker. This pastoral thematic is, however, accompanied by hints of violence. The wind, for example, is not always a tame breeze, but sometimes a violent one. In the first stanza, the movement of the fir thickets is produced by several winds "plunging." In the second stanza, the wind is set in contrast to the enclosed atmosphere of revolting mysteries, ancient campaigns, dungeon keeps, important parks, and dead passions. It is "salubrious," healthy and unconfined.

Also important in "blackcurrant river" are the ravens or crows, harsh-voiced birds of ill omen, which frequently devour dead heroes in traditional ballads. Within a poem that stresses the theme of medieval romance, this link cannot be denied, yet the birds are addressed positively as the forest's soldiers, sent by the Lord, "dear . . . delicious." Rimbaud's poem "Les Corbeaux" ("The Ravens"), published in September of 1872, deals directly with crows as scavengers of the battlefields of the Franco-Prussian war. He uses the same positive language, calling the birds "dear . . . delicious" and addressing them as "saints of the sky." In both poems, the use of quasi-religious vocabulary is ironic. Nature's imperative of decay and destruction is carried out by scavengers, and the carrion birds fill this role. They are addressed positively in opposition to traditional values, as the violent unconfined wind is valued above the romantic figures of the second stanza in "Blackcurrant River."

The third stanza presents the reader with two more figures in opposition: the hiker and the peasant. The first is only hinted at, in a manner suggesting that he is both threatened and in need of reassurance. What danger he fears is not explicitly mentioned, but wicker-work fences seem scant protection. He may be the eye that observes the picturesque features of the earlier stanzas, the tourist in these strange valleys.

The peasant figure completes the disintegration of the picturesque scene. While the knights errant of medieval romance are noble figures, and their ruined castles, formal gardens, and ancient wars and passions are popular clichés for elevated sentiment and beauty, the peasant is common, crafty, and deformed. The ravens are ordered to make him flee, but their role is an ironic one, and the peasant still holds the emphasized position at the end of the poem. It is he, after all, who actually drinks from the blackcurrant river and does so with gusto.

As for the stream from which he guzzles, if it is made of cassis syrup, it is thick and dark red, suggesting blood, another stream that flows unseen in dark valleys. Ravens and crows, as eaters of flesh and blood, reinforce this equivalence. One could go further and see, in the references to ancient romantic and military themes, a source of the river of blood from which the deformed peasant drinks, as well as an attempt to discredit the romantic glorification of war.

Any deliberate step-by-step logical interpretation, however, would directly oppose the declared intentions of the poet. In May of 1871, Rimbaud had formulated a poetic theory that envisioned a direct assault on the senses and sensibilities of his reader through manipulation of poetic form. The reader is, in some sense, placed in the position of the timid foot-traveler, seeking reassurance behind a wicket gate but faced with the uneasy knowledge that the sympathies of the poet lie with the powers of disintegration: the crows, the wind, the crafty peasant with his old stump of a limb. All the forces of the poem, from the unsettling rhythm and uneven rhyme to the seditious and troubling images, combine to provide a vivid landscape that is undercut by an unpredictable black current.

Anne W. Sienkewicz

THE BLESSED DAMOZEL

Author: Dante Gabriel Rossetti (1828-1882)
Type of poem: Ballad
First published: 1850; revised and collected in *Poems*, 1870; revised again for
Poems, 1881

The Poem

There are four versions of "The Blessed Damozel," which was written in 1847, when Dante Gabriel Rossetti was eighteen years old. The first version was published in *The Germ* in 1850, the second in *The Oxford and Cambridge Magazine* in 1856, the third in 1870 in Rossetti's collection *Poems*, the fourth in *Poems*, 1881. The changes appearing in the second and third versions are generally regarded as improvements.

Many years after the poem was written, Rossetti is said to have attributed it to his admiration of Edgar Allan Poe's "The Raven" (1845). Rossetti is reported to have said that Poe had done the most that was possible to do with the grief of a lover on earth longing for a lover in heaven and that he (Rossetti) was determined to reverse the conditions in "The Blessed Damozel."

Both a poet and a painter, in 1848 Rossetti, along with Holman Hunt and John Everett Millais, established the Pre-Raphaelite Brotherhood. The term "Pre-Raphaelite" was first used to describe a group of German artists who early in the nineteenth century formed a brotherhood in Rome to restore Christian art to the medieval purity of the great Italian masters preceding Raphael. The German group was short-lived, and the term was later used to designate the English school founded by Rossetti and his followers. In general, the English Pre-Raphaelites reacted against the neoclassic tendencies and low standards of the art of their day. Both their painting and their literature are characterized by an interest in the medieval and the supernatural, simplicity of style, love of sensuous beauty, exactness of detail, and much symbolism.

"The Blessed Damozel" not only is Rossetti's best-known work, but it also epitomizes the Pre-Raphaelite school. He used the medieval form of damsel, "damozel" — a young, unmarried woman of noble birth — in the title to emphasize the medieval setting and visionary aspects of the poem. He was commissioned in 1871 to do a painting of the poem and by 1879 had given it a *predella* showing an earthly lover (wearing a cloak and a sword) lying under a tree in the forest looking up at his beloved. The poem is presented as his reverie. He dreams that she leans out from the golden bar of heaven. Although she has been in heaven ten years, to her it scarcely seems a day. In the forest, the lover imagines that the autumn leaves are her hair falling on his face. Around her, lovers, met again in heaven, speak among themselves, and souls ascending to God go by "like thin flames."

Her gaze pierces the abyss between heaven and earth, and she speaks. (Her lover imagines that he hears her voice in the birds' song.) She wishes that he would come to her, for when he does they will lie together in paradise and she herself will teach him the songs of heaven. She will ask Jesus that they be allowed to live and love as they once did on earth — but for eternity. She sees a flight of angels pass by and lays her head on the golden barrier of heaven and weeps. The lover asserts that he has heard the tears.

Forms and Devices

Originally, the ballad was a narrative lyric poem preserved by oral tradition. The ballad meter of England derived from the *septenarius*, a rhymed Latin hymn meter of seven feet or accents. These long lines, technically known as "fourteeners," as they often numbered fourteen syllables, were afterward broken up into four shorter lines of iambic tetrameter alternated with iambic trimeter, which accounts for the alternating unrhymed lines.

In the case of "The Blessed Damozel," Rossetti has broken three long septenarian lines into six shorter lines of alternating tetrameters and trimeters. Thus, the second, fourth, and sixth lines in each stanza rhyme, as in stanza 2: "adorn," "worn," and "corn." The ballad was predominantly a medieval poetic form, and Rossetti's use of it exemplifies the Pre-Raphaelite preoccupation with medievalism.

Another important aspect of Rossetti's poetry is his "painterly" style. It is often said that reading one of his poems is almost like looking at a painting. Rossetti himself said that the supreme perfection in art is achieved when the picture and the poem are identical — that is, when they produce the same effect. Rossetti achieves this effect by paying meticulous attention to detail and by using concrete images. The damozel's eyes are as deep as waters "stilled at even" (at twilight); she wears seven stars in her hair, which is yellow like corn; holds three lilies in her hand (seven and three are mystical numbers); and wears a white rose on her robe. The earth spins in the void "like a fretful midge"; the "curled moon" is a "little feather" in the gulf — all of these are concrete images that present a portrait of the damozel, the earth, and the moon.

Finally, the poem abounds with Christian imagery and symbolism. Arising from the tradition of courtly love, one of the great medieval themes was an idealized, platonic, spiritual love. Although this tradition had its carnal aspects, the spiritu-alized love and adoration are best exemplified by Dante Alighieri's mystical devotion to Beatrice and his portrayal of her in paradise. True to his intention, Rossetti has reversed the roles in this poem. By setting the poem in heaven, within a medieval Christian framework, he has tried to suggest the spiritual nature of the damozel's love for her earthly lover. The heavenly lover wears the white rose — a symbol of virginity — and is therefore fitted to be in the service of Mary, who is the ultimate symbol of pure, chaste love. It is Mary herself who will approve their love and bring the lovers before Christ (lines 115 to 126).

Themes and Meanings

The reader can see in "The Blessed Damozel" the expression of an ancient and well-known theme: the desire of an isolated, separated lover to achieve unity with the beloved. Rossetti has framed this vision as a reverie, a daydream, a wish-fulfilling dream in the mind of a lover. The heart of the poem is the ironic conflict between the earthly bodily desire and the tradition that heaven is a place of disembodied souls, comforted and joyful in the presence of God. This irony is emphasized by the poem's religious framework.

The earthly, fleshly dimension of the lover in heaven is unconsciously revealed in several places in the poem: Her bosom "warms" the bar of heaven (line 46); she imagines taking her lover's hand (line 75), lying together in the shadow of the mystic tree (lines 85 to 86), laying her cheek against his (line 116), and, finally, living in heaven "as once on earth" (line 129).

These are all images of touching in the earthly sense. Yet, by the standards of medieval theology—which the whole framework of the poem implies—she ought to be contemplating the joy of God and exhorting her lover to lay aside grief and remember that she now enjoys the real reward of life: eternal life with God.

The Christian imagery, which is largely derived from Dante and other medieval Italian poets, is used decoratively and in this context does not support the sensuous desires of the lover. As much as Rossetti tried to emulate the austere spiritual idealization of Dante, his own sensuousness prevented him from achieving it.

The heavenly lover yearns passionately, intensely, for her earthly companion. In her yearning, she moves from a vision of their reunion, to hope of everlasting unity, and finally to doubt and despair. The void between heaven and earth is immense. What is emphasized is the separateness of the lovers: The wish is not the thing itself; the traditional Christian sops about being in heaven hold no comfort for the bereaved lover, for without the beloved, the heaven becomes a hell.

Dean Davies

BOBO'S METAMORPHOSIS

Author: Czesław Miłosz (1911-   )
Type of poem: Lyric
First published: 1965, as "Gucio zaczarowany," in *Gucio zaczarowany*; collected
in *The Collected Poems, 1931-1987,* 1988

The Poem

"Bobo's Metamorphosis" is a 102-line poem—or cycle of poems—in eight sections, each having its own style, subject, and structure. Despite the differences, the poem develops cohesiveness on the basis of recurrent imagery and consistent thematic focus.

Drawn from an eighteenth century Polish text entitled *Zabawy przyjemne i pożyteczne* (1776; entertainments pleasant and useful), the poem's epigraph, "The distance between being and nothingness is infinite," serves as an excellent introduction to both the poem and the six typographically distant lines that make up its opening section. In this section, which resembles Wallace Stevens' "Thirteen Ways of Looking at a Blackbird," the first three lines are lyrically intense but only barely sketched word-pictures. The fourth and longest line introduces a narrative "I." The fifth is the most abstract, as an annunciation of the reader's dilemma and the poem's theme: "Life was given but unattainable." The sixth line, a reprise of the preceding five, transforms seeing into feeling and telescopes time and space into a single, fragmentary transtemporal moment: "From childhood till old age ecstasy at sunrise."

Dawn and dusk serve as ways of establishing a painterly and almost mythic frame of reference and of creating an odd continuity between the poem's otherwise discontinuous parts. Section 2, for example, begins with a fragment which almost seems an afterthought to section 1, an attempt to complete what was left unfinished: "As life goes, many of these mornings." Section 2 also reintroduces the "I" who only fleetingly appeared in section 1. Again there is a telescoping of time ("I was grown up and small"), but now this telescoping is contextualized as the seemingly random recollections of a narrator who may be Miłosz, as suggested by the geographical references in line 9, but who may also be an insect, as suggested by the fourth line of section 1, the fifth line of section 2, and the seventh section of the poem.

Section 3 presents, in a highly naturalistic yet semifantastic manner, a solitary "consciousness" hiking somewhere in California. The relative continuity gives way to the complexity of the poem's fourth and longest section, which begins with a mention of the story of Philemon and Baucis from Ovid's *Metamorphoses* (c. A.D. 8). The mention of the "wandering god" and the "advancing weevil" recalls the hiking consciousness earlier and prepares the way for the return of the wandering, advancing "I," who will recall his own version of Baucis in a jumbled sequence of images ending with her sudden aging and departure. In the final two stanzas of section 4, the narrator's cinematic memory jump-cuts from autobiographical recollection back to literary fantasy: to Prospero's island from William Shakespeare's *The*

Tempest (1611) and more specifically to Miranda, the sorcerer's daughter. Miranda is seen briefly against a backdrop which includes spirits looking strangely like skin divers, another of the poem's many temporal and spatial discontinuities.

The narrative "I" abandons the role of Prospero and returns to autobiographical recollection in the next two sections, the only time in the poem that a single narrative is carried over from one section to the next. The subject is the unnamed artist whom "I liked . . . as he did not look for an ideal object"—he commits himself to the impossible art of painting things as they are.

Section 7 clarifies the poem's title even if it does not identify its source: Zofia Urbanowska's children's book of the same name in which, as the poem points out, "Bobo, a nasty boy, was changed into a fly." In the novel, Bobo is restored to human form and given the opportunity to reform. The poem's version of Bobo's metamorphosis is equally humorous and fantastic but less moralistic. It is far more lyrical and is also, in its hint of death, a bit somber.

"Bobo's Metamorphosis" is a poem of dust and death but also of excess and ecstasy. Nowhere are the two combined so effectively as in the final stanza, which serves as a reprise and distillation. The table introduced in section 2 takes on a more overtly important role, separating the narrative "I" from the woman who sits across from him. The efforts of the "I" to know this minutely observed person recalls the realist artist's desire to draw both object and essence in sections 5 and 6. The distance between "I" and "other" is imaged in terms of Zeno's arrow moving across an infinitely divisible space of time. The image creates a paradoxical sense of both the despairingly impossible and the joyously inexhaustible. Looking across that endless expanse, the narrator believes that the woman knows what he knows. From this mutual knowledge of endless separation comes what the poem affirms, that "humanness, tenderness" which may not be two distinct qualities at all.

Forms and Devices

Although it refers specifically to a single children's story, the title "Bobo's Metamorphosis" implies a profusion of endlessly metamorphosing autobiographical materials (people, places, events, as well as literary texts), which in turn implies Miłosz's belief that poetry comes from personal experience, not from other poetry. For Miłosz, however, poetry must never be merely personal, or merely historical. A poem is not a confession but a distillation and transformation of life into art through form. By form, Miłosz means something quite different than meter, rhyme, and the other trappings of conventional verse. He means the "search" for "direct forms," a search which may, as in the case of "Bobo's Metamorphosis," involve the bringing together of many different forms, including (as in the first section) ones that may be mere notes or jottings.

The language of these notelike lines, and indeed of the entire poem, is simple and direct—surprisingly so given the range and depth of Miłosz's religious and philosophical interests. This simple speech is well suited to what Miłosz has called his "struggle to seize hold of fragments of reality." His need to capture in words "something that actually happened" becomes most clearly articulated in section 5. There, Miłosz takes exception to Poland's other great contemporary poet, Zbigniew Herbert, for claiming in one of his own poems that "The most beautiful object/ is the one that doesn't exist." The artist who appears in the fifth section of "Bobo's Metamorphosis," like Miłosz, rejects the privileging of abstraction and metaphor over reality. Miłosz and his artist (anonymous but, by virtue of "his tobacco-stained beard," not abstract) choose a more realistic approach in their efforts "to name, paint, draw" existing objects. This naming implies something more than mere photographic depiction. It implies that contemplative state toward which Miłosz's "realistic" yet highly meditative poetry is invariably drawn and against which he feels as invariably compelled to offer the counterweight of events in all their immediacy and time in all its fluidity.

The immediacy and fluidity of "Bobo's Metamorphosis" is most artfully apparent in the repeated metamorphoses of subjects, scenes, styles, and time, such as the frequent shifts from present to past tense and the change of mood in section 4 from indicative to subjunctive. Objects, people, places and certain key words appear, disappear, and suddenly, almost randomly, reappear in a text which strikes the reader as specific in detail yet strangely elusive in meaning. The poem is realistic in approach yet fantastic, even magical in effect, like the original *Bobo's Metamorphosis.* Overall, the poem operates within the opposing claims established by the two forms of what, after "metamorphosis," is its most important word: the kinetic physicality of the verb "to attain" and the static spirituality of the noun "the attainable."

Themes and Meanings

The ideal task of the poet, Miłosz pointed out in his Nobel Prize lecture, "is to contemplate the word 'is.' " In Miłosz's case, this "is" encompasses ontology (over the more fashionable contemporary preoccupation with epistemology), on the one hand, and a preoccupation with "the complexity and richness of the visible world," on the other. Conceiving the world as indissolubly double—as objective existence and ontological essence—and drawing on Urbanowska's children's story about a boy turned into a fly, Miłosz embodies in his poem that "basic curiosity about the world" which he, both as "witness to poetry" (the title of his Harvard lectures) and as witness to history (the German occupation of Poland and the rise of the Stalinist state), warns is fast disappearing. About "flying into the center of things" and exploring "reality from various angles, in various guises," according to the poet, "Bobo's Metamorphosis" conforms to Miłosz's definition of poetry as "the passionate pursuit of the Real," but a Real which remains stubbornly, magically unattainable.

Against history's generalizations and its annihilation of the individual, Miłosz posits the sensuous apprehension of the world in all its immediacy as it is experienced, remembered, or contemplated. Although experience and memory act as checks on each other and so would appear to have more or less equal status, memory in fact occupies a special place in Miłosz's philosophical scheme, mediating between the experiential and the eternal. Marked by two temporal worlds, memory exhibits the duality of humanity's at once timebound and timeless existence.

The linkage of the sensual and the spiritual in "Bobo's Metamorphosis" derives at least in part from the Catholicism in which Miłosz was trained and to which he continued to subscribe. The essential paradox at the very heart of the poem, however, summed up in the line "Life was given but unattainable" and even more succinctly in the phrase "the eternal moment" from "Notebook: Bon by Lake Leman," written a decade earlier, derives in large measure from a quite different source: the writings of Simone Weil, and her thoughts on contradiction in particular. One must not become "at home" with contradiction too easily, Weil has warned; rather, one must struggle against it with all one's intelligence and only then admit to its inevitability. In "Bobo's Metamorphosis," the contradictory forces do not merely oppose one another: They meet and merge (or metamorphose) one into the other. The "eternal moment" that is the poem "Bobo's Metamorphosis" develops from the fluid movement of various styles, forms, subjects and the "passionate pursuit of a Real" which is at once ephemeral and eternal, fragmentary and whole, "given" and "unattainable."

Robert A. Morace

BODY OF SUMMER

Author: Odysseus Elýtis (Odysseus Alepoudhélis, 1911-   )
Type of poem: Lyric
First published: 1943, as "Soma tou kaloukariou," in *Ílios o prótos*; collected in
The Sovereign Sun, 1974

The Poem

"Body of Summer" is a free-verse poem of four stanzas. The poem can be divided in half: The first two stanzas describe a landscape in the voice of a third-person narrator; the last two stanzas address the personified landscape directly in the song of the "little siren."

A deceptively simple description of midsummer opens the poem: "A long time has passed since the last rainfall was heard." The landscape is dry, parched from long drought. "Now the sky burns endlessly." Populated by ants and lizards, the landscape seems inhuman, yet the fruit trees "paint their mouths" with the colors of overripe fruit splitting in the sun, and the earth is slowly opening its thirsty pores. Instead of the elemental sound of rain from above, the "syllabic" drip of water is heard from a hidden spring below that trickles the rudiments of language, as though the earth itself is beginning to speak.

Beside the spring, a "huge plant" gazes into the eye of the sun. Like the fruit trees and the water, which are nonspecific (neither pears nor pomegranates, neither fountain nor stream), the plant is generic and anonymous. Perhaps it is a sunflower, which, like the soul of man (especially Greek man), follows the sun.

The second stanza compares this landscape to a personage, not really a person, that is reclining sensuously on the shore, huge and naked, smoking olive leaves, like Gulliver stranded on the beach. Like Lilliputians, cicadas are in his ears, ants are on his chest, and lizards are in his armpits. He swarms with life. The question is asked: "Who is this who sprawls on the far beaches?"

This is the body of summer. The reader discovers this in the second half of the poem, an apostrophe sung by the "little siren," who addresses the personified season directly: "O naked body of summer." Unlike the aloof narrator of the first two stanzas, the singing siren is celebratory, admiring, perhaps even seductive, and certainly erotic. Her catalog of physical traits gives the abstract season substance, weight, and texture. His skin is eaten by oil and salt, his body is rock, his heart throbs. His hair is the willow, and his breath is as fragrant as "basil on the curly groin." Like a sailing ship, his body is a "vessel of day!"

This lazy eroticism gives way to a violent sexual coupling in the final stanza, as winter returns to descend on this vessel-rock, whose "hills plunge into thick udders of clouds." Winter is depicted as a "savage" beast with claws and udders, the female equivalent of the masculine body of summer. When this period of strife is over, however, the body of summer reemerges, smiling "unconcernedly" in its "deathless hour" and reasserting its "naked health" and vigor under both sun and sky.

Forms and Devices

In an interview with Ivar Ivask (March, 1975), Odysseus Elýtis cites "Body of Summer" as an example of the way in which he has kept "the mechanism of myth-making but not the figures of mythology." In this poem, he says, it is "the idea of summer which is personified by the body of a young man." Such transformations are typical of his first period of poetry, which was influenced by Surrealism and written before and during World War II. "In my first period nature and metamorphoses predominate (stimulated by surrealism, which always believed in the meta-morphosis of things)."

Elýtis is a visual artist as well as a poet, and his collages are reminiscent of his poetry in the way they transpose various photographic images. In "Body of Sum-mer," for example, there are visually surprising images that could occur only in the literal medium of collage—cicadas in the ear, lizards in the grass of armpits—images that employ synesthesia, using one sense to evoke another, the visual evoking the tactile: one hears, sees, and also feels the cicadas' warmth and the lizards' glide.

The figure of the little siren animates the physical world of the first two stanzas, in which the transformations are merely metaphorical, with the mythical world of the last two stanzas. By addressing the body of summer directly, the little siren turns the poet's metaphorical language into living myth. She is the poem's animating soul (its anima, in Jungian terms).

This is what connects Elýtis' poetry with the Surrealism of Paul Éluard (1895-1952), for whom the poem exists as a vehicle by which to discover the erotic link between landscape and the human psyche. Elýtis felt such a sensuous and loving connection between the language and the landscape of his native Greece.

Elýtis insists on the untranslatable significance of objects named in their own language. "If I say in Greek, for example, 'olive tree' or 'sea,' these words have completely different connotations for us than, say, for an American." The poet's pri-vate associations are similarly untranslatable. Lizards are, for example, creatures who thrive in a parched landscape; they are, for Elýtis, personal symbols. In the Ivask interview, he tells how "once, at high noon, I saw a lizard climb upon a stone . . . and then, in broad daylight, commence a veritable dance, with a multitude of tiny movements, in honor of light. There and then I deeply sensed the mystery of light."

Themes and Meanings

"Body of Summer" aims, as does all Elýtis' poetry, to reveal what he calls the mystery of light: limpidity, clarity, transparency. This is why the sun (*hylios*) and sky (*ouranos*) figure so prominently in his poems. Some translators have exchanged the two terms, as in line 3: "Now the *sun* burns endlessly," although Elýtis has written *ouranos* (sky or heavens) and not *hylios* (sun).

This is a key difference in this poem because it points out the distinction between the pagan Greek sun worship and the Byzantine Greek yearning for heavenly tran-scendence. Elýtis would hope to unite the two, the Christian and the pagan, in his modern poem.

The final lines of the poem illustrate this theme of the poem, which can best be seen by comparing two translations. The Keeley-Sherrard translation reads: "As the sun finds you again on the sandy shores/ As the sky finds you again in your naked health." The pagan sun beats down, earthward, while the Byzantine sky lifts up, heavenward. The final emphasis is on the sky's approval of "naked health."

The poem ends with the word *ouranos*, however, which in Greek (like the French *ciel*) means both sky and heaven. This detail is captured in Kimon Friar's translation: "As once more you are found on the beaches by the sun/ And amid your naked vigor by the sky." Here, the final position of the subject of the verb (which is active in Greek syntax) makes the sky's discovery more forceful and memorable. The naked vigor and health of the body is approved by both the sun *and* the sky (*hylios* and *ouranos*), the final word turning the emphasis away from the pagan "naked health" of the Keeley-Sherrard translation toward the Christian "sky" of Friar's. It is important to end the poem on this high note, because it turns a poem of hedonistic sun worship into a poem of spiritual transcendence.

Elýtis calls this movement upward in his poems "meteorism" or "a tendency to mount up to the sky, to rise toward the heights." This is why he denies being a pagan or Dionysian poet, insisting always on the "clarity" of his poems—not *la belle clarté* of French rationalism, but rather what he calls "limpidity." "What I mean by limpidity," he notes in the Ivask interview, "is that behind a given thing something different can be seen and behind that still something else, and so on and so on. This kind of transparency is what I have attempted to achieve. It seems to me something essentially Greek."

This double-exposure or montage effect is what attracted Elýtis to Surrealism. The Surrealist juxtaposition of images allows the emanative essence of a thing to break through, to rise above the surface of things. This is particularly evident in the poet's collages, in which certain images, a Greek *kouros* statue or a naked girl, seem to be emerging through a rip in the surface of the colorful Greek postcard landscape.

Yet it is not only the classical world that emanates through Elýtis's poetry, as it is for example in that of his contemporary George Seferis, but also the Christian heritage of Byzantine Greece. The collage that serves as frontispiece to *Odysseus Elýtis: Analogies of Light* (1981) is a good example. "Votive Offering" shows a Byzantine angel rising above a cluster of whitewashed island rooftops as though bestowing a blessing on the village; from the village blossoms a cluster of shells. Clearly, the elements of water, earth, and sky are connected in these figures that represent the animal, human, and divine worlds.

This benediction of the Byzantine that is bestowed on what is sensuous and "pagan" is at the heart of Elýtis' erotic poetry, which is always striving to change the world "through continual metamorphoses more in harmony with my dreams," and to create "a contemporary kind of magic whose mechanism leads to the discovery of our true reality."

Richard Collins

THE BOOK OF THEL

Author: William Blake (1757-1827)
Type of poem: Narrative
First published: 1789

The Poem

The *Book of Thel* is one of William Blake's early "Prophetic Books," illustrated and printed by Blake himself on eight plates, in a process he invented. The poem itself consists of a motto followed by four sections of blank-verse paragraphs of varying lengths.

After the motto has posed some cryptic questions about how knowledge and wisdom might be acquired, the reader is introduced to Thel, a young girl wandering in a mythological pastoral setting, the vales of Har. The unhappy Thel is asking many questions about the purpose of her life. She is particularly distressed about the transience of existence. Why must everything in creation, including Thel herself, fade and die?

Various nonhuman aspects of nature, appearing to her in human form, try to answer her questions. First, a "Lilly of the valley" explains that although it is small and weak, it receives continual blessings from heaven during its brief span of life. When it fades away it flourishes again in "eternal vales." The Lilly tells Thel that she has no reason to complain. Thel replies that although she can see how the Lilly plays a useful part in nature — providing nourishment for the lamb and, with its perfume, reviving the cows after milking — she cannot see that her own life has any useful function. The Lilly tells her to ask the Cloud.

Thel asks the descending Cloud why it does not complain, even though it fades away so quickly. The Cloud replies that when it vanishes, it is to a far richer life, "to love, to peace, and raptures holy." It gives up its separate existence and merges into the morning dew which then provides food for all the flowers. Thel is still not comforted. She fears that she is not like a cloud. She does not provide food for the flowers, even though she can enjoy the sweetness of their smell. She will die and become the food of worms, and there will have been no purpose to her life.

The Cloud replies that this is not so, because "every thing that lives,/ Lives not alone, nor for itself," and calls to a worm to confirm this. Thel sees a worm on the Lilly leaf, and thinks it is weeping like a newborn baby. A Clod of Clay emerges and repeats that nothing lives merely for itself. The Clod may appear to be the least significant thing, but God pours blessings on her as mother of all the children of the earth. The Clod does not understand how this can happen, but she lives and loves without questioning. Thel, still weeping, replies that although she knew that God might cherish a worm, she did not not realize the full extent of the divine love. The Clod of Clay invites Thel to enter her domain and play her full part in earthly existence. Thel has nothing to fear and will be able to return to her vales.

Thel enters the domain of earth, but she discovers it to be "A land of sorrows & of tears where never smile was seen." She wanders around in a distressed condition until she sees her own grave. She hears a voice coming from the grave, asking a series of questions about why the five senses are permitted to register such intense and horrifying experiences in life. Thel is terrified and rushes back to the peaceful vales of Har.

Forms and Devices

The Book of Thel is the gentlest of Blake's illuminated books, a complete contrast to the harshness of *Tiriel*, which was written at about the same time. The poem is written in iambic heptameters, usually with a caesura after the third or fourth foot of each line. Blake adapted the ballad form, in which lines of three feet and four feet alternate, consolidating this pattern into one line. The meter is fairly regular, although there is enough variation to avoid monotony. The repetition of soft consonants, such as *l* and *f*, in the opening sections create the dominant tone of the poem's language. The overall effect is one of sweetness and femininity; the word "gentle," for example, is repeated four times in lines 12-13.

The only major change in the musical, flowing language and meter comes in the last few verse paragraphs, when Thel contemplates the harshness of earthly existence. The line length becomes irregular, varying between five feet and eight feet. There is an increased use of trochees rather than iambs. In addition, the insistent and cumulative repetitions in the questions Thel hears about the roles of the senses (a technique Blake used frequently in his later prophetic books) impart a feeling of intensity and urgency that has not been felt in the languid and passive atmosphere of the poem up to that point.

Unusual names and settings, such as the river of Adona, Luvah's horses, and the vales of Har, create a mythological atmosphere. Thel herself is described as a daughter of Mne Seraphim, a name Blake may have found in the work of the Renaissance magician and alchemist Cornelius Agrippa. The mythological elements provides an appropriate background for the poem's major device, the pathetic fallacy, which allows the elements of nature, both animate and inanimate, to find a voice.

All Blake's illuminated books involve both text and designs. The illustrations do not merely illustrate the text; sometimes they provide a counterpoint, a new angle on the matter of the poem, or put the text in a wider context. *The Book of Thel* has six illustrations, the most interesting of which is the final one. It shows a young girl, possibly but not necessarily Thel, and two smaller children, riding on a serpent. Thel holds the reins in her hands and appears to be in control of the beast, and the children look as if they are enjoying themselves.

The serpent is an ancient symbol with many meanings. In alchemy, the serpent is often shown with its tail in its mouth and symbolizes nature in its unregenerate or untamed form. Seeing the young figure riding the serpent of nature with such ease gives the reader another perspective on the ending of the poem. Perhaps Thel is needlessly afraid of the powers of nature, which may be more benevolent than she realizes.

Themes and Meanings

The Book of Thel has been variously interpreted. Some commentators believe it is a Neoplatonic allegory. According to this view, Thel is an unborn soul contemplating its descent from the eternal, spiritual world into the realm of matter. For the Neoplatonists the material world was only a shadow, a reflection, of the eternal world, and life on earth was a kind of death, or imprisonment, of the soul. Blake was familiar with Neoplatonic theory, which he would have found explained in Thomas Taylor's translation of Porphyry's *Cave of the Nymphs*, which was published in 1788. Much of the imagery of the poem is of water in its various forms, and water is a Neoplatonic symbol of the material world.

According to the Neoplatonic view, Thel would be showing some wisdom in rejecting her incarnation; however, the philosophies espoused by Lilly, Cloud, and Clod of Clay are very different. They are closer to the worldview Blake would have found in alchemy, with which he was also familiar through the writings of Paracelsus and Jakob Böhme. In the alchemical philosophy, the divine spirit interpenetrated the natural world, and every particle of creation served a spiritual purpose. Blake expressed this idea many times in *The Marriage of Heaven and Hell* (c. 1790-1793), especially in the phrase, "Every thing that lives is holy." Thel's rejection of earthly life shows that she has failed to grasp this principle.

A more naturalistic interpretation of the poem views Thel as a young girl in a state of innocence, who is reluctant to enter the state of Experience. In his *Songs of Innocence and of Experience* (1794), Blake called these the "Two Contrary States of the Human Soul"; the unreflective joy and naïveté of innocence had to give way to the more somber realities of maturity before innocence could be recaptured at a higher level. Thel's intellectual questioning and her unhappiness shows that she has already outgrown innocence, but her refusal to move on to the next stage in life shows her lack of maturity. She is refusing to grow up; her egotism and selfishness block her progress. The name Thel was probably taken from a Greek word meaning "will," and this may imply that Thel is also showing a deficiency of will.

Thel would cease her lamentation if she could learn to go beyond seeing life solely in terms of the individual ego and absorb the philosophy taught by the Lilly, Cloud, and Clod of Clay. They all take delight in what Blake was later to call "self-annihilation"; they willingly give up their individual identities so as to serve the larger purposes of creation. In doing so, they feel constantly blessed and fulfilled. This is the central paradox of all religious faith: He who loses his life shall save it. Blake's achievement in *The Book of Thel* is to have expressed this view with such charm and delicacy, giving a voice to the humblest and apparently most insignificant aspects of creation.

Bryan Aubrey

BRAHMA

Author: Ralph Waldo Emerson (1803-1882)
Type of poem: Lyric
First published: 1857; collected in *May-Day and Other Pieces*, 1867

The Poem

"Brahma" is an excellent reflection and representation of Ralph Waldo Emerson's work as a whole. Though he is more widely known as a writer of essays, several of his poems may be seen as keys to his use of style and theme in all of his work, and this is one of those poems. Stylistically, he uses the same spiral or circular method that he does in his prose, rather than the more straightforward linear development used by most poets of his time. Thematically, he insists on the same spiritual and physical unity and harmony in the universe, expressed in a similarly intensive and dense language, as he does in his essays. These qualities demand much from the reader.

"Brahma" is a poem of sixteen lines, divided into four quatrains. In order to understand and appreciate this poem fully, one must know something about Eastern religion, especially Hinduism. In Hindu theology, Brahma (or, more commonly, Brahman) is the supreme spirit or divine reality in the universe, the eternal spirit from which all has come and to which all shall return (similar to what Emerson more commonly called the Over-Soul). The "strong gods" (line 13) are secondary gods who, like all mortals, seek ultimate union with the supreme god, Brahma: They include Indra, the god of the sky; Agni, the god of fire; and Yama, "the red slayer" (line 1), or god of death. The "sacred Seven" (line 14) are the highest holy persons or saints in Hinduism, who also seek union (or reunion) with Brahma.

In stanza 1, Emerson insists that in the creative spirit of the universe, nothing dies; if death thinks that in fact it kills, or if those who are killed think that they are really dead, they are wrong, for death is maya, or illusion. Brahma is subtle; the patterns of life and death, of eternal return, are not always obvious to the human eye or mind. Through the intuition, however, a person can see and understand his or her role in these patterns and can accept and learn from them.

In the second stanza the reader discovers the essential unity of opposites—what Emerson called polarity. The physical and spiritual are intimately intertwined, with the physical being the concrete representation in the material world of the spiritual, which alone is real. In Emerson's terms, "both shadow and sunlight are the same" (line 6); in other words, light and dark, good and evil, life and death, happiness and sadness, and "shame and fame" (line 8) are all the same. They are illusions which mortals believe to be real, but which are not. In the same way, all human experience is one, and is eternally present; what is "far or forgot" (line 5) is in fact near, and both past and future are encapsulated in the present moment.

Stanza 3 suggests that one can never escape this creative energy, since it is present everywhere in the universe. Humans ignore it at their own peril, since it alone is real, and it encompasses both "the doubter and the doubt" (line 11). It is the song of creative joy sung by the Brahmin, the highest caste in Hinduism. Fortunately, however, even if one does ignore the creative spirit, it remains present in one's life, and eventually one's spiritual eyes will open and one will recognize it. Both the person who doubts and the doubts themselves are essential parts of the universal plan.

Stanza 4 states that all seek union with this eternal spirit—whether lesser gods, saints, or those persons who are considerably farther down on the spiral of spiritual enlightenment. If one loves the good, regardless of one's faults, one shall find it. Even if one is insecure or "meek" in one's beliefs, one should turn away from the illusion of the Calvinist Christian heaven, where entrance is limited to the very few elect, and all others are rejected and damned. One should seek the Brahma, or Over-Soul, the eternal spirit of creativity and life in the universe, from which all have come and to which all will return.

Forms and Devices

"Brahma" reflects Emerson's periodic use of the standard poetic meter and rhyme of his time: The four quatrains are in iambic tetrameter, and his use of coupled rhymes (*abab*) is a reflection of his thematic sense of the inescapable polarity in the universe.

The central figure in the poem is the speaker, who is Brahma, or the Over-Soul, the creative spirit in the universe. Having the Brahma as the speaker allows Emerson to posit the unity within the world's polaric structure; though contradictions seem to exist, he suggests, they are in fact meaningful paradoxes and not meaningless contradictions. Emerson makes extensive use of irony in his poetic strategy; he indicates that death is not really death, that shadow and sunlight are the same, and that both the doubter and doubt are contained within the Brahma, to which all persons aspire to return. There are other ironies as well: It is clearly implied that it is the abode of Brahma (line 13) which is to be sought rather than a Christian heaven, and that those who adopt the Darwinian perspective of the survival of the fittest miss the realization that, in reality, all survive.

Emerson has, in "Brahma," used a series of images borrowed from Hindu scriptures (many of which he translated in the issues of the Transcendentalist magazine *The Dial*, which he co-edited with Margaret Fuller for two years and then edited himself) to reflect the coordinated pattern and unity in the physical universe, which is itself a reflected pattern of the same unity in the spiritual universe.

Themes and Meanings

Emerson insists in his writings that it is only the spiritual world which is "real"; the material world is simply an illusion, created by human senses, that must eventually be transcended. He frequently used one segment of the world (as did Henry David Thoreau, who learned the method from him) as a microcosm of the universe as a whole, believing that if one could but understand all of one aspect of the reality, one would have a clear entry into understanding the whole.

Another central Emersonian theme is implied in this poem, one that has to do with the relationship between people and nature: Physical nature can be a mirror to reflect back to humankind the spiritual facts which lie behind and inform all physical facts. Shadow and sunlight, for example, can reveal that they are inescapable parts of one phenomenon, and thus one spiritual reality. Just as a person may come to realize that shadow is only the absence of light, so may one come to realize that evil is only the absence of good.

Other central themes in Emerson's work are reflected in this poem: the idea of compensation, for example, which shows that there is a principle of balance in the universe, since for everything that is given, something is taken away, and vice versa. In the whole (or spiritual) sense, nothing is ever lost. There is also a commentary on the nature of experience, which Emerson saw — in a metaphor which he used in several works — as being like beads strung on the string of one's temperament. In other words, what one sees and finds in the world is directly connected to one's perspective, or point of view, since how one looks at things determines what one sees. It is much like holding up a string of colored beads to the light and looking through them with all their varied colors — except, as Emerson states in his essay "Experience," that these beads are named desire, reality, temperament, succession, and subjectiveness. It is also the case, as he argued in his essay "Fate," that the universe is structured as much or more by one's internal fate or destiny as it is by any external fate. Since everyone desires to return to the Brahma or Over-Soul, from which they have come (whether they realize it or not), and since the Brahma, Over-Soul, or creative principle in the universe is waiting to accept or re-accept them when they are ready, the purpose of free will is to lead people to choose what has already been chosen (another paradox, and another polarity), to return to the ultimate unity and harmony from which everyone originally came.

Clark Mayo

BREAD AND WINE

Author: Friedrich Hölderlin (1770-1843)
Type of poem: Elegy
First published: 1894, as "Brod und Wein," in *Friedrich Hölderlin: Sein Leben und sein Dichten*; collected in *Poems and Fragments*, 1967

The Poem

"Bread and Wine" is a nine-stanza poem written in an elegiac form based on Greek and Roman elegies—a form used to express a sense of tragedy. Written by Friedrich Hölderlin in 1800, it is often cited by critics as a poem that marks the culmination of his younger period. That is, it is the work of a poet who is reaching the peak of his powers.

The nine stanzas that constitute the poem divide easily into three sections of three stanzas apiece. The first section begins in contemporary times (that is, Hölderlin's times) by looking at a town at night. As people head home from their work, night is presented as a time of rest, a time of quiet reflection when one can think of love and of distant friends. When the moon and the stars come out, however, night becomes "Night, the fantastical," "Night, the astonishing, . . . the stranger to all that is human."

The second stanza develops the view of night as "astonishing." "No one," the poet says, "Knows what it is," and not even the wisest understand what the purpose of night is; the reason of day is better suited to humankind. Nevertheless, people find the darkness of night attractive. To the mad and the dead, night is sacred, but even to other people night offers a hint of "holy drunkenness" and "frenzied oblivion," of "a life more intense and more daring" than the life of day. It should be noted that the original dedication of this poem was to the "Wine god"—traditionally, Dionysus. Associating night with the idea of holy drunkenness is thus also a way of associating it with Dionysus, who will become an important figure as the poem progresses.

In the third stanza, the narrator associates the attraction of night with a divine fire that, day and night, urges people to be gone. "Let us go then!" he says, and later adds, "Off to the Isthmus," referring to the Isthmus of Corinth where the ancient Olympic games were held, and "Off to Olympian regions." He will guide the reader to ancient Greece, because "back there points the god who's to come."

The middle section, stanzas 4 through 6, describe an imaginary journey to ancient Greece, a journey that begins when the narrator laments the loss of ancient Greece, with its festival halls and its temples dedicated to singing to the gods. He then goes on to imagine the beginning of Greek culture, which begins with a visitation of gods, especially "Father Aether," conceived of by Hölderlin as the father of the gods.

It is this visitation of the gods that the fifth stanza, which is structurally and thematically the center of the poem, details. When the gods first appear, they are not immediately recognized, except by children. Nevertheless, the gods offer gifts to humankind, which humankind is pleased to receive but immediately begins to waste. At that point, the gods appear "in truth," meaning in their corporeal persons, and people grow accustomed to joy and to "the sight of godhead revealed." For the first and only time, humankind is completely happy, with every desire satisfied by the presence of the gods. Humankind remains blind to the value of this enormous gift, but does find words "like flowers" to name these gods.

The sixth stanza records the heyday of Greek civilization, which Hölderlin conceives of as a civilization whose art and achievements were dedicated to praising the gods. Again the poet asks: Where are the heavenly temples and cities of the Greeks? What happened to the sacred theaters that celebrated joy, and why do the gods no longer appear at the feast with humankind?

The seventh stanza opens the section of the poem that returns to contemporary times. The gods are still living, Hölderlin says, although not in this world, because humanity can no longer stand a direct encounter with godhood. Humanity must be hardened through its encounters with night and frenzy before it will be able to face the gods again. In the meantime, Hölderlin wonders, "who wants poets at all in lean years?" — that is, the job of poets is to praise present gods, but there are no gods present. Poets, an imaginary listener responds, are today like the priests of Dionysus who once roamed the night. That is, poets (as Martin Heidegger comments in an essay inspired by these lines, "What Are Poets For?") are the ones today who stay on the trail of the absent gods, trying to find the traces of their movements.

In stanza 8, Hölderlin explores this comparison. When the gods disappeared, they left behind a few gifts that would remind humanity of the time of spiritual joy. Bread and wine, which were used in sacraments to Dionysus in much the same way that they have been used in Christian Communion ceremonies, are two such gifts, and when people taste them in religious ceremonies, they can experience a taste of divine joy. Similarly, poets in another way provide a small taste of this divine bliss.

In the final stanza, Hölderlin prophesies the ultimate return of the gods. In the meantime, however, even though humankind lives today as a mere shadow of its past and future self, the wise can find the "Son of the Highest" — which is a reference to Dionysus but is presented as a Christlike figure — whose torch can bring light to wise men and who will eventually lead the way to a second golden age.

Forms and Devices

The form of the elegy came to Hölderlin ultimately from Classical literature, but was in fact being invigorated in German literature at the time Hölderlin was writing by Johann Wolfgang von Goethe and Friedrich Schiller. Traditionally, an elegy entails a poet looking at the tragic aspects of life but finding consolation in some principle. As the critic Richard Unger notes in his remarks on "Bread and Wine" in *Friedrich Hölderlin* (1984), Hölderlin also follows Schiller's lead in using the form to express a longing for an absent ideal — in this case, to lament the absence of divine presence.

In Hölderlin's hands, however, the elegy also becomes a prophecy. In this regard,

Michael Hamburger, a critic and translator of Hölderlin, notes that a fruitful comparison can be drawn to Hölderlin's English contemporary, William Blake. Like Blake in such prophecies as "America," Hölderlin in "Bread and Wine" foresees a time when humankind will be able to see the divine world directly. Unlike Blake, though, who created an enormous system of his own in his poetry, Hölderlin worked closely with existing religious systems in "Bread and Wine"—primarily the ancient worship of Dionysus, but also the modern worship of Christ, which he presents as similar.

Images of light and darkness play a key role in the prophetic aims of this poem. The description in the opening stanza of night falling in a contemporary village plays a crucial role, drawing the reader into Hölderlin's prophecy with its very homeliness. Night is a time of rest, a time for reflection, and a time for drunken celebration. As the poem develops in the second stanza, however, the problem being presented is that there is something about the night that is foreign to human reason. To an extent, Hölderlin seems to be accepting the common opposition by which day is associated with reason and darkness is associated with madness and lack of reason.

Darkness, however, is also associated with the "holy drunkenness" granted by the wine god (Dionysus). Thus night offers a lack of reason that, rather than being disabling, is in fact enabling. The night not only allows the poet to travel imaginatively to ancient Greece, but also provides the divine inspiration, in the form of holy drunkenness and madness, that will prepare humanity for its ultimate encounter with the gods.

At the end of the poem, Hölderlin is clearly trying to resolve this opposition. The "Son of the Highest" is already among human beings, who live as shadows; he is holding his torch to lighten the "gloom." Although the night allowed Hölderlin to travel back to ancient Greece in spirit, what the night revealed was the light of this torch, which is the light of inspiration, not of reason. This light will not eliminate the shadows—humankind—but allow humankind to become fully real.

Themes and Meanings

Much of this poem's meaning can be found in the title. The bread and wine mentioned are important not only to the Hellenistic feasts of Dionysus, but also to the Christian ceremony of Communion. This is merely one of several hints throughout the poem of a subtle but crucial aim of this poem—to reconcile the ancient worship of Dionysus with the modern worship of Christ.

Toward this end, the view of Dionysus that this poem presents is not the view that Friedrich Nietzsche (who was nevertheless much influenced by Hölderlin) was to present later in the nineteenth century in *Die Geburt der Tragödie aus dem Geiste der Musik* (1872; *The Birth of Tragedy Out of the Spirit of Music*, 1909), a work that in the twentieth century did much to shape views of Dionysus. As Richard Unger points out, Nietzsche's Dionysus is a god of orgiastic violence; Hölderlin's is a god of drunken inspiration. Both writers present gods who are associated with the uncanny, but (as is shown in Hölderlin's description of the night, in which he associates the "inhuman night" not only with madness, death, and inspiration, but also with rest and reflection) Hölderlin's view of an encounter with this god—while not devoid of the fearsome—is gentler, reconcilable with views of Christ as a bringer of comfort.

The eighth and ninth stanzas of the poem especially call attention to this comparison. The identity of the "Genius" who in stanza 8 dispenses divine comfort and then leaves is left deliberately vague; it could be either Christ or Dionysus. The bread and wine, which are all that remain to contemporary humanity of divine grace, also promise that the "Heavenly who once were/ Here . . . shall come again," another reference that seems to have been deliberately constructed to invoke Christian promises of a divine return.

Similarly, in the final stanza, the poet promises that the "Son of the Highest" is already among humanity, bringing his torch to dispel the gloom of people living in an age devoid of the gods. The "Son of the Highest" could be Dionysus, a son of "Father Aether," or Christ.

It is important to recognize, however, that while Hölderlin takes pains to present a Christlike view of Dionysus, the fundamental sensibility underlying the poem is not particularly Christian, and Hölderlin was not, when he wrote this poem, a conventional Christian. As Richard Unger points out, what the taste of bread and wine remind one of today is that all the gods—Hellenistic as well as Christian—were once here, and all shall return. Furthermore, the time of this return, as Hölderlin conceives it, will be marked by a society based on the ancient Greek model, a society that—when humankind is once again able to endure the direct presence of the divine—will live among and for the gods.

Finally, a related theme in "Bread and Wine" (which remains important in Hölderlin's later poetry) concerns the relationship between man and language. While the visitation of the gods to the Greeks is not presented as the origin of language, that time is presented as a time when language lived most fully, "like flowers leaping alive" to name the gods. For Hölderlin, the most vital task for language—and poetry especially—is to name the gods; however, as he acknowledges when he asks "who wants poets?" in a time when the gods are absent, all a poet can do is trace the potential presence of these gods. By performing this role, this poem can serve the same purpose as the bread and wine of its title. It cannot bring the gods back, but it can provide a taste of the divine presence that is absent from the world.

Thomas Cassidy

THE BRIDGE

Author: Hart Crane (1899-1932)
Type of poem: Poetic sequence
First published: 1930

The Poem

   The Bridge belongs to the tradition of the long poem in America—they are works that ask philosophical and religious questions about life and the fate of nations. Walt Whitman was the originator of this mode of lyrical epic *Leaves of Grass*, first published in 1855. Others who followed Whitman's techniques in the long poem include Ezra Pound and T. S. Eliot; William Carlos Williams, Louis Zukofsky, and Charles Olson wrote long poems in the post-World War II era. Hart Crane's effort to write his own sequential work found a rich context from which to draw for ideas, allusions, echoes, and conscious reference.

   Other classics of the modernist era had their influence on Crane's poem. In particular, Crane was influenced by James Joyce's *Ulysses*, published in 1922, a novel of modern Dublin life in which two characters are followed closely by the narrator as they go about their affairs over a single twenty-four-hour period. This absorption with a city and the emotional lives of its citizens gave Crane the basis for the organization of his poem about modern New York City. Joyce's protagonist, Stephen Dedalus, is based on himself, as is Crane's speaker in *The Bridge*, a sensitive young man who yearns for visionary enlightenment.

   The Bridge is the last great poem of the modernist era, a period crowded with experiments in which Western culture and ideology underwent close scrutiny and sweeping revision. In essence, modernism was the rediscovery of the primitive world, where nature dominated human affairs, and myth, magic, and ritual were the principal forms of expression. Modernist writers rejected the artificiality of urban industrialism and celebrated the natural bonds between humans and wild nature as the more healthful and spiritually satisfying way. Most of these works responded to the religious crises of the early twentieth century by seeking alternative forms of vision and belief in non-Western traditions.

   Crane's poem begins with a paean, or hymn of praise, to the Brooklyn Bridge, John Augustus Roebling's engineering wonder that spans the East River between Long Island and Manhattan. While composing this poem, Crane rented the apartment at 110 Columbia Heights from which Roebling had overseen the completion of his project. The section entitled "Proem" takes the angle of vision of that apartment window, which looked down at the bridge, and follows a sea gull as it rises up over the top of the bridge and disappears—a metaphor for imaginative flight. The reader contemplates the bridge at early dawn, at noon (when a suicide leaps from its parapets), then in the evening, when the poet admires its looming shadow against the snow falling on a cold December night, the end of the "iron year."

   What follows are eight sections of varying lengths and poetic forms, each with a thematic title. The longest section, part II, entitled "Powhatan's Daughter," contains five poems (the section runs to sixteen pages in most editions). Part IV, "Cape Hatteras," has the longest poem of the group, an eight-page ode on the airplane as the new wonder of the industrial era. "The Tunnel," which forms part VII, is a lyrical account of a subway ride back to Brooklyn. Other sections depict Columbus' voyage back to Europe after his discovery of the New World ("Ave Maria"), the history of navigation on the Mississippi ("The River"), canoeing on the small rivers of Indian America ("The Dance"), the land migrations of the pioneers and gold-rushers ("Indiana"), and the adventures of merchant mariners and whalers ("Cutty Sark"). Large and diverse as the work may be, one of its unifying themes is transportation — what the bridge itself monumentalizes in its great span.

"Ave Maria" opens the sequence in stately eight-line stanzas that dramatize Columbus' returning voyage to Spain after discovering what he thinks is China. He is disappointed, however, to return without a "delirium of jewels." The discovery of America began in error and from motives of greed, but it ends with Columbus's vision of the mysterious gods that rule time and space and of the human longing to discover "still one shore beyond desire!"

From this "dawn," the reader begins the journey through the day and night to follow. "Powhatan's Daughter" opens with a sinuous lyric on early waking. This is followed by the poem "Van Winkle"; Rip Van Winkle slept for twenty years in Washington Irving's tale and woke to find himself at the crossroads of American history, somewhere between its colonial origins and the sprawling macadam highways racing off into the future. His memories of the time before he slept, the childhood of the nation, preface the historical themes of the next three poems. "The River" recounts the migrations to the western territories by train and by Mississippi riverboat. Pioneering destroyed the wilderness and primal nature, however, and the human effort to conquer the land ends in a spent dream, as the river ends "turbid,/ Tortured with history" in the Gulf of Mexico.

"The Dance" that follows goes upriver by canoe to rediscover Amerindian culture. The presiding spirit over these poems is Pocahontas, the sensuous Indian princess who fell in love with John Smith and spared his life. The speaker imagines falling in love with Pocahontas, of mating with her and joining Indian life in the wilds. "Indiana" concludes the section with a dramatic monologue spoken by a tired, resigned pioneer wife whose husband joined the Colorado gold rush but, like others, lost the American dream. Columbus' search for gold in "Ave Maria" began a futile search for El Dorado in the New World.

In "Cutty Sark," an old mariner recounts his adventures at sea, sometimes as a whaler, and the reader looks down from the bridge to the ships in the harbor as the speaker returns home. "Cape Hatteras" is an ambitious ode composed in long paragraphs of iambic pentameter. This section pays homage to Whitman's "Passage to India" (his hymn to the opening of the Suez Canal) before taking up its own subject, the Wright brothers' inaugural airplane flight at Kitty Hawk (on Cape Hatteras, North Carolina) and the grim future of aircraft as war machines.

"Cape Hatteras" concludes Crane's survey of the history of America to the early twentieth century. "Three Songs," in part V, begins a commentary on the troubled present of America, depicting a culture that possesses wealth and power but lacks spiritual vision. As Henry Adams remarked in his autobiography, *The Education of Henry Adams* (1907), America lacks a female muse. Crane considers three types of muse—Eve, or motherhood; Magdalene, the seductress; and Mary, the goddess of imagination and wisdom—and finds only the last suitable as a spiritual guide. In "Quaker Hill," the old religions have perished; they are viewed from an old Quaker graveyard, where a modern golf course and clubhouse now preside.

In "The Tunnel," the reader plunges below the East River and enters the unconscious realm of American life. Here the roots of ghostly ideals are found, the old vision dating back to sunken Atlantis, as well as those subway riders who struggle in a living death of dispirited modern reality. T. S. Eliot accepted this poem for publication in his journal *Criterion*; it bears a close resemblance to Eliot's *The Waste Land* (1922) in its treatment of the modern city.

"Atlantis" brings the sequence to a close with its hymn to the bridge as both "harp," or artistic instrument, and "altar," or place of vision. The bridge spans many things at once, land and sea, earth and sky, self and soul, underworld and heaven. Its form articulates the link between realities and is the necessary symbol for a culture lacking in unity or faith.

Forms and Devices

The poem employs a welter of poetic forms, stanzaic patterns, and figures of speech. Its chief forms are the dramatic monologue, as used by Eliot, and the ode, an irregular, open form, as developed by John Keats and Percy Bysshe Shelley and raised to ecstatic meditation in Whitman. Monologues occur in "Ave Maria," where Columbus speaks, and in "Indiana," where a pioneer woman remembers her hard life; a dialogue poem occurs in "Cutty Sark," interwoven with lyrics of various songs. "The Tunnel" uses several voices to enrich the meditation. The principal odes occur in "Cape Hatteras" and "Atlantis." Though much of the language is based on iambic pentameter, the poems are essentially irregular and use a variety of rhythms to control shifting tones and moods in the work, as in an orchestral suite. The "Proem" uses "heroic couplets," an epic convention that rhymes two lines of iambic pentameter; Crane's rhymes are "slant," or partial rhymes. Crane also favors the stately eight-line stanza for sombre subjects, as in "Ave Maria," "Quaker Hill," and "Atlantis," and quatrains for lighter subjects, such as "The Harbor Dawn" and "The Dance." Irregular stanzas of greater length indicate complex thinking and dense meditative structures, as in "Cape Hatteras" and "The Tunnel."

Crane's diction is notable for its lush, compacted phrases and for its range—from mannered eloquence and fragile images to jazzy lyrics and harsh, realistic descriptions. Metaphors abound on all the important objects of the poem: bridge, water, highways, the landmass, the underground. Everything is transformed from literal and earthbound description to visionary and spiritual abstraction. The towers of the bridge are musical "staves," the cables the "orphic strings" of the harp; the women of "Three Songs" present myriad possibilities for their ultimate meaning. Eve, for example, is the constellation of the Southern Cross as well as mother, Venus, the source of "lithic trillions of your spawn," the stars.

Elsewhere one finds a continuous thread of puns and wordplay on key images, as language reflects upon itself and transforms its literality into figuration and back again. A notable pun occurs in "Van Winkle," in which Rip is asked upon waking, "Have you got your *Times*" — *The New York Times*, but also the new day to which he has rudely awakened. Typical of metaphoric brilliance is the description of a trout in a pond at night as a "moon whisper." The bridge itself, in "Atlantis," is a "flight of strings," a "telepathy of wires," and its traffic is a "crystal-flooded aisle."

Themes and Meanings

The Bridge is a celebration of technique, the human agency by which things are related and unified. The Brooklyn Bridge is a piece of sublime artistry by which two islands are joined by work of dazzling precision and majestic boldness. The bridge stands for the work of art itself—for the power of art to link together great dissimilarities of experience, and to do so in an act of daring and invention that celebrates its own process as it joins the ends of life together. That is why Crane dissects the elements composing the bridge and finds in each of them an emblem of artistic energy: in particular, the bridge as a musical figure, with its columns rising as staves in a musical score, its cables representing strings, and the birds flying over it as the notes struck on them. In music, a bridge refers both to a brief connecting passage between two longer passages and to a support for strings on an instrument. Crane once described "The Harbor Dawn" as "legato" — a smooth and connected style of musical performance; its Latin root means "to bind." There are songs and lyrical interludes throughout the work.

In undertaking this poem, Crane believed that he had discovered the essential symbol for a country and New World culture that lacked a vision of its spiritual aspirations. America was young, materialistic, and brash, and its formation was violent from the start. Whitman had already sung the song of its inner life in "Song of Myself," but the country lacked unity, a collective selfhood in which action and revery, dreams and reason came together. The bridge thus stood as an industrial achievement that Crane strove to interpret as a symbol linking modern man with the primal depths of the New World.

In "Ave Maria," Columbus is himself the divided man, at once looking for gold and jewels—plunder from the innocent native world of America—and pleading with the gods of his vision as he returns to Europe. The poems that follow explore this separation, running like a seam through all the actions of modern humans as they exploit the resources of the continent and show little or no respect for the suffering nature on which they wreak their havoc. Even the pioneer wife who returns to the Midwest in "Indiana," after the gold rush, notes the pathetic figure of an Indian squaw along the road—Pocahontas grown weary with the years. Pocahontas is the dream betrayed, a figure of nature who began in friendship and ended in tragic suffering.

In "Cape Hatteras," the reader learns that the Wright brothers' invention of the airplane is an unfulfilled promise; the plane soon becomes a machine of death and destruction as the rapacious will of commerce turns its violence from nature to the world at large. The history of America, Crane asserts, is the failure of numerous visions and dreams that stemmed from greed and self-indulgence. The bridge remains the constant symbol of the need to join the two ends of America itself, its wilderness and primal life with the heights of its reason and sophistication. Only when the speaker enters the subway and descends to the depths below the East River does he communicate with that hidden world of America, its great unconscious realm of myth and ritual; he returns to understand the full meaning of the bridge in "Atlantis." The sunken island of Atlantis lies somewhere in the depths of the ocean and represents all that America has ignored in nature and Indian life in its urge to plunder the wilderness of the New World. The Brooklyn Bridge is for Crane a more imposing symbol of America than is the Statue of Liberty, the other monument of the New York harbor. The bridge links the commercial towers of Manhattan with Whitman's island—the island he celebrates by its Indian name, Paumanok.

The Bridge is also about the writing of poetry, the act of confronting a datum of reality and of transforming it into a burning image of spiritual truth. Crane knows that the other subjects of his poem are serious and compelling, and are the essential purpose of his poem, but the poetry must come first. The construction of the poem is foremost an act of language, of finding the musical phraseology and the imaginative solutions to turning this powerful figure of the bridge into a central symbol of America. Everything in the poem must be measured by the density and music of the speech; the poems must be as well crafted as the bridge itself before it can be said to comment upon its symbolic function.

Reading the poem over many times reveals hidden depths and lush textures of speech that one reading alone cannot fully exhaust. Like its subject, the poem's craftsmanship is its most notable achievement. The artful construction of the poem is a reminder to its readers that accomplishment must first of all be a form of love of the materials and of the principles by which it is shaped, joined, and executed. Even this attitude of making and enjoying has its thematic place in the poem: The work must first of all pay homage to the materials and not exploit them for gain. Everywhere in the poem, the evidence of rewriting and rethinking are present. The individual phrase has luster, originality, and daring departure from convention. The plot has the bold simplicity of the bridge as well, its units inexorably formed to construct a vision of linked worlds.

Paul Christensen

THE BRIEF JOURNEY WEST

Author: Howard Nemerov (1920-   )
Type of poem: Meditation
First published: 1950, in *Guide to the Ruins*

The Poem
"The Brief Journey West" is a meditative poem of twenty-eight lines divided into seven stanzas. The title suggests not only a particular journey, but a frontier push, and most important, the brevity of human life. The iambic pentameter of the poem gives it a formal, almost elegiac quality, which suits the subject of aging and death.

Written in the third person, the poem features an omniscient speaker with the stately quality of a court storyteller, an Anglo-Saxon "scop," or bard. The "fathers" of the poem represent the fathers of any nation, movement, or race; the decline refers both to the pioneers and to their visions.

The poem opens with a description of the fathers coughing and spitting in a room by a "dry road." Both the illness of the fathers and the arid land outside their "room" convey impotence and sterility. The reader is reminded that these ineffectual men once so conquered and crushed their environment that they "hung/ That bloody sun upon the southern wall." Now, however, as the second stanza reveals, they are so old that the wrinkles of their skin duplicate the maps they made when, forging new territory, they drained wild swamps. They wanted to make a place for themselves in history, but now youth and discovery have vanished—they are only history's "cracked precipitate."

The poem's third verse describes the decay of youth and vision through images of shattered glass and a sun that "burn[s] the prosperous flesh away/ Of the filthy world, so vilely fathered on/ The fathers." These lines suggest that decay results in part from corruption of the fathers' ideals. These fathers are now so old that they are only "black cinders, sitting there."

In the fourth stanza, the poem's speaker then addresses the fathers, asking them what vitality, specifically "lecheries," remain. He comments mournfully that nothing flows in the blood of the old fathers except, "When schoolgirls pass," the "custom of desire." Instead of being disturbed by passion, the fathers now enjoy "the sarcastic triumph of the mind . . . letting their lust alone," because age has robbed them of passion.

"The Brief Journey West" becomes increasingly somber in the final two stanzas. The sixth stanza states that the aged fathers, no longer naïve or passionate, wish neither for "reformation of the past," nor for inevitable disease. Instead, in the silence of the wise, they recognize a world that is "A shrivelled apple in the hand of God." The last verse shows these once impassioned trailblazers routinely hanging their "somber flags" and pursuing "their theme/ Of common images," through the night in sleep. Completely spent, these old men hope for nothing more than sleep. They want to be through with all crises, but "the one," the inevitable disaster of death.

Forms and Devices

References to destruction and a somber tone give "The Brief Journey West" its power. Words that convey aridity and heat express both the shriveling of the fathers and of the world as "apple in the hand of God." The first three stanzas contain varied images of sterility resulting from lack of moisture. There is the "dry road," and the fathers' skin, which is "seamed and dry" as a drained swamp, presumably now so dry that all that is left is "cracked precipitate"—like the fathers themselves, who are now so scorched with age that they are "black cinders." The "cracked precipitate" image refers to both swamp and man. As a drained swamp leaves deposits, so the "black cinders" of the fathers are the aged residue of history. Not only are the fathers scorched into black cinders, but their triumphs are also withered for the "bloody sun" has burned "the prosperous flesh away/ Of the filthy world."

These references to withering heat are followed by equally harrowing images of cold, hardness, and brokenness. Metaphors of hardness and cold imply death through the deadening of desire. The "black cinders" of the fathers are so lifeless that they are no longer moved by much of anything. When women pass, their flesh are "Cold gleams" that provoke only the "custom of desire" in the fathers' eyes, which have hardened into the likeness of cold gems. The triumph of the mind over lust is "sarcastic," for the fathers have no choice but to twist the cooling of desire into a triumph. These images of cold stones coupled with those of brokenness, crushed beetles, "the cracked precipitate," and shattered glass, add to the poem's desolation.

The most powerful metaphor of the poem, however, is of the world as a "shrivelled apple in the hand of God," a comparison that functions on several levels. The world is round like an apple, and it has become old and corrupt as a withered apple. This line is also a biblical allusion to the Garden of Eden apple, the consumption of which led to the Fall.

The poem's concluding images refer to sleep and the oblivion it brings. In the last stanza, the fathers desire only sleep. Sleep, as a symbol for oblivion, emphasizes not only the old men's disintegration, but their resignation. They want only to sleep, not to fight or blaze new trails. The words "somber," "dark," and "sleep" suggest the old men's slide into death. They are unwilling to deal with any other challenges, but "the one"—death.

The images in "The Brief Journey West" progress from active to passive images of decay, an advance that imitates the sequence of aging. The poem starts with coughing and spitting, a road, a room, and trophies in the room. Glass shatters, sun burns. Thereafter, the images slowly become more passive: cooling desire, silence, sleep, death.

Themes and Meanings

"The Brief Journey West" is about, in the poet's own words, man's transitory life span. Many poets have addressed mutability in their work, specifically the transience of man, and Howard Nemerov is no exception. There are at least two ways, however, in which the poem differs from many on the same theme. The first is in the darkness of its vision; the second is the poet's outrage.

"The Brief Journey West," written when Nemerov was twenty-six, indicates what was to be a hallmark of the poet's work, his pessimism. In this poem focusing on aging and death, man's lot is portrayed as the anguished Macbeth termed it, "Full of sound and fury, signifying nothing." The poem's tone is one of bitterness and rage; all comes to nothing—all heroics, all heroes. There is no implication of either personal or collective immortality.

What sets this meditative poem apart from other poems on the same subject is the darkness of Nemerov's vision. The only surcease offered from the relentless process of decay is the oblivion of indifference through sleep, and the bitterness of the poet's tone suggests that, to the speaker, such a solution is unacceptable. The anger of the speaker suggests that there should be more than aging, death, and oblivion to follow all of man's efforts. Implicit in the bitter tone is an angry spiritual question: Why?

The unacceptability of death as a fitting end to man's strivings is emphasized through the painful, often violent images of burning and brokenness ("shattered," "cracked"). That life is not as it should be, that it is metaphysically flawed, is further suggested by the biblical allusion to the apple, which led Creation to groan and to Fall.

Although Nemerov's later work on the same subject expresses some serenity, there is none in "The Brief Journey West." It has not only an outraged, but a hopeless quality. Despite the biblical allusion, there is no redemption, either by God or man. Man is alone; he strives, conquers, only to be conquered by the same sun that he hung (or thought he hung) on the southern wall. The poem's elegiac quality, resulting from the sonorous tone of its stately rhythms, recalls the Anglo-Saxon bard's sad ballads, but it has none of the Old English sense of man's collective solidarity in the midst of a bad fate. There is no sense of brotherhood present among the "black cinders, sitting there," nor does the poet suggest hope in a kind of collective consolation. There is not even God to rage against; life has a useless, mechanistic quality to which the speaker cannot adjust.

The poem is saved from complete misery by the grandeur of its rhythms and language. No matter how absurd man's fate, "The Brief Journey West" implies, by its sweeping pictures of man's triumphs before his inexorable demise, that man has dignity. "The Brief Journey West," written in Nemerov's youth, is both an example and a presage of later work in which the speaker questions, but receives no answers.

Mary Barnes Bruce

BRIEF PAUSE IN THE ORGAN RECITAL

Author: Tomas Tranströmer (1931-   )
Type of poem: Lyric
First published: 1983, as "Kort paus i orgelkonserten," in *Det vilda torget*;
collected in *Tomas Tranströmer: Selected Poems, 1954-1986*, 1987

The Poem

"Brief Pause in the Organ Recital" is a lyric poem that contains twelve carefully balanced, four-line stanzas of free verse. The immediacy of the experience recounted in the poem is emphasized by the fact that almost all the verbs in the poem are in the present tense.

The poet/speaker is attending an organ recital in a medieval cathedral. The sudden silence during a brief pause in the program breaks into his elevated mood and makes him aware of the traffic noises—"that greater organ"—outside the cathedral. He perceives that though it lacks the rigidly formal structure of the organ music to which he has been listening, the traffic noise has a freer rhythm of its own. Next, he becomes aware, as if it were part of the street noise, of the pulsing of his own blood, what he calls "the cascade that hides inside me." The passing of a trailer-truck heavy enough to shake the six-hundred-year-old walls of the cathedral brings to mind an experience he had as a child of four: Seated on his mother's lap, he listened to the distant voices of contending adults ("the winners and the losers"). Though he initially appears to reject the idea, he senses a similarity between the mother's lap and the sheltering church. In effect, he is reinventing a metaphor that became a cliché in an earlier age of firm religious faith: the Church as the believer's mother.

Gazing at the pillars that support the roof of the cathedral, he appears to rediscover a common Romantic symbol, that of nature (the forest) as a vital, protective force. The mental image that likens the interior of the cathedral to a forest serves as a transition to a remembered dream with an outdoor setting. The poet vividly relives this dream: He is standing alone in a churchyard that is surrounded by blooming heather; he is waiting for someone, a mysterious friend who is never identified, even though the dreamer soon notices that this friend has already arrived. The setting (a graveyard) and the heather (a familiar portent of death in Swedish folk tradition) suggest that the awaited friend might be Death; indeed, in the following lines, when the dream reaches its climax, the reader learns that "death turns up the lights from underneath, from the ground." If what the dreamer is experiencing is a vision of his own death, however, it seems to hold no terrors for him. When death intensifies the purplish (heather-colored) light, that light is transformed into a color that is beyond human experience. Finally, this hue converges with the rosy light of dawn that "whines" in through the eyelids of the dreamer and awakens him. This example of synesthesia (in this case, color becoming sound) finally gains semantic content and is articulated as a word: "PERHAPS." Tentative though it may seem, this message from beyond the grave (or from the depths of his own self) gives the poet enough hope to sustain him in this unstable world and to persuade him that he must not expect to be able to reduce it to an abstract picture—anymore than he could hope to find the blueprint of a storm.

This acceptance of uncertainty and earthly mutability leads to the poet's final reinvention of a traditional symbol: the world as a book. He remembers that he learned to read by scanning the pages of the family encyclopedia, a book that intends to reduce the world to an abstract picture, to certainties. As a result of his dream experience, he now realizes that each individual produces a personal encyclopedia, a book of contradictions that is constantly being updated and revised by each new wave of experience. Returning to the positive image of the forest that he likened to the interior of the cathedral, the poet now uses the same image to characterize the vitality of this internal encyclopedia that is growing inside each person, as near to one as one's blood, as dynamic as the sea. In Swedish, the poem ends with an incomplete line, as wave succeeds wave, and an ellipsis, indicating the continuation of the process.

Forms and Devices

One of the most striking features of this poem is its extremely regular formal structure. As he frequently does in his poems, Tomas Tranströmer carefully establishes a distinct rhythmic pattern in the first stanza that he repeats with little variation throughout the remainder of the poem. The first two sentences of this poem fall into a stanzaic pattern in which two long lines (the first and the third) alternate with much shorter lines (the second and the fourth). These expanding and contracting lines may be thought of as imitating the diastolic and systolic actions of the heart, a bodily rhythm that figures importantly in this poem. (Robin Fulton's English translation of this piece achieves a similar effect by sharpening the rhythmic contrast between the long and the short lines.) One can only guess whether the rigid metrical order of this poem is meant to suggest that the universe too has a meaningful structure.

The speaker of this poem clearly longs for some proof that life has meaning and purpose, that there is some basis for religious belief. Though Tranströmer makes little mention of overt religious observances in his poetry, many conventional religious values seem to correspond not only to his own deepest personal needs, but also to his poetic intuitions. In an interview with Richard Jones in 1979, Tranströmer speaks of his "religious longing" and of the direction in his poetry toward "some sort of cosmic feeling" (*Poetry East* 16, 1980). In this poem, he expresses the "cosmic feeling" by adducing a series of analogies that tend to show that nature is a nest of boxes: During a pause in the music, the speaker hears first the pulse of society, then his own pulse; finally—in the dream he so vividly relives—he thinks he hears the pulse of the universe. The traffic circulating around the cathedral is a "larger organ" that produces a music of its own, a music that is echoed in the circulation of the blood through the poet's vascular system. The rhythmic pumping of his heart also corresponds to the regular surge of the seas, the ebb and flow of the tides that metaphorically wash through the text of the reader's inner encyclopedia at the end of the poem. The correspondences he perceives between the rhythm of his own body and the rhythms of the outer world—evidence, in other words, that man is a harmonious part of nature—might have led Tranströmer to the facile conclusion that "God's in his heaven—/ All's right with the world" (Robert Browning, *Pippa Passes*, 1841). What prevents him from doing so is his awareness that the order he perceives is constantly at risk: Potentially disruptive or destructive energies (the cascade that hides inside him, the storm that cannot be mapped) may at any moment be unleashed.

The moment of insight comes, therefore, not from the poet's perception of outer correspondences between man and nature, but from within his own psyche—at the end of the dream that is the spiritual climax of this poem. Tranströmer, a trained psychologist, has more than a clinical interest in dreams. He believes, as one can tell from many of his poems, that dreams not only link one's inner with one's outer self but also enable one to penetrate more deeply into one's essential self than is possible in the waking state. The manifest content of this dream (the churchyard, the heather, the friend he is awaiting, the way in which death "turns up the lights from underneath, from the ground") might lead one to conclude that the dreamer has an overwhelming awareness—if not fear—of death. Tranströmer is, however, more interested in conveying the emotional impact of the dream than in interpreting it.

Themes and Meanings

"Brief Pause in the Organ Recital" is a poem about religious experience. Though the words "mystic" and "mysticism" are often applied to Tranströmer and his work, it is important to notice that no revelation, no vision bringing certainty, is vouchsafed to the speaker of this poem. The dream that leads him to affirm the world with "an unshakable PERHAPS" can best be characterized as a secular epiphany or a moment of extraordinary insight.

The cessation of the music enables the poet to hear the traffic outside the cathedral. In Tranströmer's poetic vocabulary, "traffic" usually symbolizes human intercourse at all levels—the social order and its contextual situation in time and space. The vaguely disturbing murmur of the traffic outside becomes more threatening when the rumble of a heavy trailer-truck causes the cathedral walls to tremble, and the poet immediately associates this with a similarly jarring experience that he had when he was four: Then, safely seated on his mother's lap, he was protected from social discord. These two images (the sheltering cathedral walls and the mother's lap) help the poet define the barrier between the safe inner world and the menacing world outside, a characteristic concern of Tranströmer's. In the interview mentioned above, he said, "I like border regions. I am interested in borders and I am always writing on the borderline—the borderline between the inner world and the outer world. I call this borderline 'the truth barrier'... because that's the point where you can see the truth."

The sudden silence also enables him to cross another border. Listening to the beating of his pulse, he becomes aware that, like the music, it too will someday stop. Will it be only a short pause? Placed on the borderline between life and death, the poet finds new meaning in a dream he once had: Alone in a churchyard, surrounded by heather, he is waiting for a friend who, he soon realizes, is already there; death begins turning up the purple light until, becoming a hitherto unknown hue, it merges with the light of dawn and becomes articulate. Is the mysterious friend death or—as one Swedish critic suggests—Christ? Does the purple heather portend death, or does the liturgical association of the color purple with Christ's passion suggest the idea of resurrection? There is not enough evidence to enable one to answer "yes" or "no" to any of the questions that the poem raises. The most positive answer Tranströmer can give is PERHAPS, which is unshakable.

In crossing the border between dreaming and the waking state, Tranströmer appears to have glimpsed the divine, timeless world that has always been at the heart of religious belief. He senses—but cannot verify—a meaningful order in the universe. This is the point at which humankind usually takes refuge in belief, but Tranströmer seems to feel that it is as limiting to believe in the existence of meaning where none may exist as it is to deny its existence on the grounds of insufficient evidence. Seen in this light, PERHAPS (which is understood to include contradictions and uncertainties) is neither a defeat nor a compromise, but a proclamation that the poet chooses to remain open to all possible blueprints of reality.

In the last three stanzas of the poem, Transtömer uses the image of the book to justify his endorsement of uncertainty. He thinks of the family encyclopedia, with which he taught himself to read as a child. He now realizes, however, that because it attempts to give an abstract picture of the world, to reduce it to a closed and static system, this kind of encyclopedia—ironically described as "all-knowing"—is an inadequate guidebook to the world. His dream experience has convinced him of the supreme value of uncertainty, and he sees that each person contains his or her own individual encyclopedia, one that is written from birth onward on the tabula rasa (or formatted disk) of the mind. No book of certainties, this is one that encompasses contradictions; its pages, as vital as the quivering leaves in a forest, are—like a database—always being updated and restructured by each new wave of information. Although this "open system" is subject to constant revision, however, its basic structure is never destroyed. Would one be justified in seeing the permanence of this inner encyclopedia's essential structure as somehow analogous to the medieval notion that nature is a book written by God to show humankind how He works in the world? Undoubtedly, Transtömer's answer would be "PERHAPS."

Barry Jacobs

BROKEN BOAT

Author: Tu Fu (Du Fu, 712-770)
Type of poem: Lyric/meditation
First published: wr. c. 764, as *"P'o ch'uan"*; in *Ch'üan T'ang shih*, early
  eighteenth century; collected in *Travels of a Chinese Poet*, 1934

The Poem

In 757, Tu Fu angered Emperor Su-tsung and was demoted to a minor position away from the capital. Widespread unrest and famine soon forced him to give up the post and travel in search of a livelihood. In 760, he managed to settle down in a "straw cottage" on the western suburbs of Ch'eng-tu (in Sichuan). The Straw Cottage became the focal point of interest in his poetry thereafter. Unfortunately, in 762, the uprising of Ch'eng-tu's Vice Prefect Hsü Chih-tao caused him to flee again. In 764, after turning down an offer of a minor position in the capital, Tu Fu returned to the Straw Cottage. A year had scarcely passed when Yen Wu, a military friend, recommended him to serve under the Council of Military Advisors. He accepted and took office in the city of Ch'eng-tu. Soon, however, he gave up the post and returned to the Straw Cottage, where he stayed until 766. "Broken Boat" was probably written in 764 upon his first return. As the poem begins, the poet states that all his life he has had "a heart for rivers and lakes" and that he was early equipped with a tiny boat, which was not meant merely for cruising along the stream and traveling in the vicinity of his modest abode. The implication here is that the poet has had lofty aspirations but has always been frustrated. For example, he had to flee in haste from the horrendous revolt only recently. Even at a distance, however, he has longed for a return to the sanctuary that he cherishes as home. Written in the form of a couplet, lines 5 and 6 highlight the chaotic nature of Tu Fu's times by accentuating his attachment to the Straw Cottage.

Upon his return, the poet discovers that his neighbors are gone and the place has been overgrown with wild bamboos. The boat itself, with "No one to rap its rim [while singing a song]," has sunk. The images of desolation in lines 7 and 8 carry the poignant hint that, in an age of turmoil and suffering, peace can be only a matter of nostalgia. The contrast between the past and present conditions of the homestead is so devastating that, in the couplet that follows, the nostalgia grows into an existential crisis:

> [I am] looking at the west-flying wings above;
> [I am] ashamed of the east-fleeting flow below.

The migration of the birds and the flow of the water seem to be the only constants in a world of tumultuous change. The spatio-temporal images here hint at a cosmic order that is not perturbed by human destiny. Such indifference renders one inconsequential and vulnerable. Feeling helpless and futile, the poet remarks that he is not saddened by the submerged boat— "The old one can perhaps be dug up;/ A new one is easy to be had" (lines 13 and 14)— but rather by the fact that, obliged to flee again and again, he cannot stay even in a humble house for long.

Forms and Devices

In the T'ang dynasty, poetry was written mainly in either the "recent" or the "ancient" style. All the lines in a recent-style poem follow a set pattern of tonal contrasts and harmonies. An ancient-style poem, however, does not have a predetermined length, and there is no rigid tonal arrangement. Because its format can be tailored to the needs of the poem itself, since it is free from prosodic constraints, the ancient style is an appropriate vehicle for narration and cursive expression.

T'ang poetry is also categorized according to whether each line has five or seven characters. The seven-character format is suitable for weighty and complex subjects because of its larger capacity and greater flexibility. The succinct five-character format, which has a longer tradition behind it, is ideal for essentialistic expression because the minimal language enhances a sense of immediacy through unadulterated concentration on thoughts and feelings.

"Broken Boat" is an ancient-style poem with sixteen five-character lines. Two important couplets are present in the poem.

The first couplet, which juxtaposes the hasty escape from the uprising (line 5) with the passionate yearning that materializes into the return visit (line 6), is characterized by a tension between the fragile order the poet once established and the disastrous disorder he has had to endure. This tension points up other tensions in the human condition: that between war and peace, and that between the transience of tranquillity and the permanence of irremediable disruption.

The second couplet (lines 11 and 12), though deceptively simple, is meticulously constructed according to the principles of antithesis and incremental reinforcement. "Above" and "west" (line 11) are contrasted with "below" and "east" (line 12), but the directional antithesis also serves to underscore the insentient nature of the cosmic order exemplified by the migrating birds and the flowing water. The two lines are also incremental in emotional intensity — while line 11 describes an action (looking up at the birds), line 12 highlights a mental condition (feeling ashamed). In sum, this couplet dramatizes the poet's tragic sense of life by juxtaposing human nature in all its frailty with insensate Nature itself.

From a broader perspective, because its subject matter is a person returning home, "Broken Boat" also reminds one of "Returning to the Farm and the Fields to Stay," a poetic sequence by the recluse T'ao Ch'ien (365-427). One may even regard "Broken Boat" as a dialogue with *t'ien-yuan shih* (pastoral poetry). According to this genre, a rustic existence, which has pleasures of its own to offer, is definitely preferable to the anxieties and taboos of civil service. "Broken Boat" is both an outgrowth and an offshoot of this pastoral tradition. While Tu Fu also tried to lead a private life, eulogizing it in the earlier, relatively complacent days of the Straw Cottage, this poem raises important questions about the validity and even possibility of security and serenity in rural life. Special circumstances in his times, it seems, have led him to write a poem that questions the validity of the pastoral genre itself.

Themes and Meanings

The poem begins with an allusion, in the phrase "a heart for rivers and lakes." The meaning of Tu Fu's poem hinges on this phrase, which originally appears in the Taoist anthology *Chuang-tzu*. In a dialogue quoted in the essay *"Jang wang"* ("On Relinquishing the Throne"), a prince raises an existential question: "When a person's *body* is loitering about the rivers and lakes, and yet his *heart* is settled under the lofty portals [of the court], how does one handle this problem [of discrepancy]?" In other words, how can one reconcile the conflict between one's aspiration to be free (at the cost of deprivation) and one's desire to be a member of the court (at the cost of being free)? To this the interlocutor replies that one should regard life as more valuable than material gains. This dialogue sheds important light on the poem.

The allusion suggests primarily that Tu Fu, like T'ao Ch'ien before him, may have eventually endorsed the Taoist position, feeling that the integrity of self is more precious than public life. The allusion does not, however, preclude the possibility that in Tu Fu's case the Taoist position can still be accompanied by a desire to contribute to the well-being of the state. Does Tu Fu, a diehard patriot, not wish to be doing something better? Has he, practically a refugee and vagrant, not had enough wandering? Because both conditions are sadly true, it would seem that in cataclysmic times the aspiration to be free and the desire to have a part to play are not meant to exclude each other, but rather to be interwoven into an irresolvable conflict.

In the final analysis, the predicament of irreconciliation arises because a choice between aspiration and desire does not exist. Indeed, the absence of choice is the major theme of "Broken Boat," and it begins to develop after the opening allusion. The poet has chosen a home, but numerous social upheavals have rendered that choice null and void. A similar destiny also affects his neighbors (line 7). A boat would have kept him free at least in principle, but not even this option is left open. The realization that he is living through a social tragedy makes the poet conclude that his grief is not over a broken boat, but rather the perpetual condition of homelessness.

The boat can indeed be regarded as a thematic symbol of this homelessness. The east-flowing river may have put the poet to shame because of the factual vagabondage rather than the metaphysical liberation it symbolizes. Indeed, "Broken Boat" is emblematic of the last decade or so of Tu Fu's life and career. Spending a large part of this period traveling by boat not in order to feel free but to take refuge, he wrote the last line of his poetry on the deck of a boat, which is also the place where he breathed the last breath of his life.

Balance Chow

THE BROKEN HOME

Author: James Merrill (1926-   )
Type of poem: Poetic sequence
First published: 1965; collected in *Nights and Days*, 1966

The Poem

"The Broken Home" is a sequence of seven sonnets that are connected by imagery and themes, yet each is formally and narratively self-contained. The title refers to the poem's autobiographical subjects — the divorce of James Merrill's parents and his concern for the brokenness or incompleteness of his own childlessness.

The first sonnet begins with the poet outside, watching parents and a child framed by a window — a tableau he contrasts with his own "Sunless, cooler" room below. Thoughts of his childless ("Sunless") existence as a poet for whom "The flame quickens" and "The word stirs" prompt him to ask his "tongue of fire" (either his muse or his homosexual lover) whether "you and I are as real/ At least as the people upstairs."

The second sonnet focuses on the adult life of his father, Charles Merrill, founder of the brokerage firm Merrill Lynch, Pierce, Fenner and Smith. In the first two quatrains, Merrill discovers in his father the soul of a visionary "eclipsed" by a desire for business and sex that drove him to warm "up for a green bride" every thirteen years. "Too late now" the poet realizes that, like himself, his father could have "invested" in "cloud banks well above Wall Street and wife."

The third sonnet provides a historical backdrop for the particular breakdown of the marriage of the poet's parents. Merrill describes a set scene from the 1920's in which a veiled suffragette in "hobble skirt" attacks a famous man in a public place with insults: *"War mongerer! Pig! Give us the vote!"*

In the fourth and fifth sonnets, Merrill moves from outside, where at the poem's beginning he watched the idealized family "gleaming like fruit/ With evening's mild gold leaf," to inside the window to probe the harsh realities of two particular memories from his own childhood. The fourth sonnet presents an oedipal scene in which the young boy is led by his Irish setter to enter the bedroom of a sleeping woman — apparently his mother, "clad in taboos" — who awakens from a deathlike sleep to terrify dog and boy. Thinly veiled sexual images allow Merrill to explore troubling aspects of his own sexuality. In describing the bedroom that "throbbed like a bruise," Merrill creates an oedipal pun about "Blinds that beat sun from the bed." The phallic Irish setter Michael, "satyr-thighed" with "head/ Passionately lowered," penetrates the closed door but "slumps" "to the floor" at the possibility of a heterosexual encounter.

In the fifth sonnet of "The Broken Home," Merrill remembers overhearing his parents (who "love each other still") discussing their frenzied life-style outside his window after a party. The lead soldier guarding the boy's windowsill in the octave introduces a cluster of images the poet uses in the sestet to describe the gradual cooling of his parents' feelings, which were once intense "Like metal poured at the close of a proletarian novel,/ Refined and glowing from the crucible."

The sixth sonnet again focuses on the present status of Merrill as childless poet with which "The Broken Home" begins. In addition to defending his childlessness, this section of the poem introduces Merrill's justification for breaking with the examples of his parents by refusing to be political and rejecting a traditional family for himself. This sonnet also provides Merrill's rationale for his particular poetics by asserting the validity of the artifice of his apolitical poems—those rare avocados "gemmed with air" with "small gilt leaves."

The octave of the final sonnet presents Merrill's memories as a house in which "A child, a red dog roam the corridors,/ Still." The sestet describes the "real house" that Merrill's family occupied, which is now converted into a boarding school from which another child can watch a setting sun without the "stiflement" of the nightmares "The Broken Home" describes.

Forms and Devices

Throughout "The Broken Home," Merrill "confesses" through the "unstiflement" of his poetry his anxiety about his childlessness, his sadness over the rift in his family, and his discomfort over his strained relationships with his mother and father. Yet in the seventh sonnet, Merrill makes it clear that he is no "confessional" poet by carefully setting himself apart from those poets who, like Edgar in William Shakespeare's *King Lear* (c. 1605), expose their nakedness and madness to the elements, "Who on the heath impersonate Poor Tom/ Or on the barricades risk life and limb."

In "Broken Home," Merrill masks the painful issues he probes through his favorite device of wordplay. For example, in the second sonnet, he develops witty puns associated with his father—"had flown in World War I," "cloud banks," and "chilled wives/ In sable orbit—rings, cars, permanent waves"—to distract himself and the reader from the painful subject at hand (the philandering father's abandonment of Merrill's mother).

Merrill also uses puns and homophones to create multiple levels of meaning that operate simultaneously with the more obvious literal meaning often disguising more sensitive and volatile subjects. For example, he disguises his concerns for his own childlessness within his puns on his "Sunless, cooler" room in the first sonnet and "small gilt leaves" in the sixth sonnet (suggesting "guilt" over childlessness and homosexuality as well as "gold leaf" artifice). In the fourth sonnet, Merrill uses the homophones "satyr" and "setter" and the pun on "sun" in "Blinds beat sun from the bed" to mask his fairly explicit attempt to come to terms with his oedipal relationship with his mother.

The most significant pun in "The Broken Home," however, occurs in the final lines of the poem as the house is exorcised and Merrill himself gains relief from his confessions. Merrill develops puns on "cool," "story," and "setter" as he concludes that in the converted boarding school, "Someone at last" may "cool/ With the unstiflement of the entire story,/ Watch a red setter stretch and sink in cloud." On one level, the poet suggests that the house's new inhabitant may be able to watch a sunset cooled by the open window and the departure of Merrill's haunted family. At the same time, Merrill seems to be "Someone" who, having purged himself of "the entire story" of "broken home," can now with cool detachment watch the memories of the Irish setter (and its sexual baggage) disappear into his imagination.

Themes and Meanings

A central theme of "The Broken Home," as the title suggests, is the disintegration of a marriage. As he observes the "gold leaf" tableau of the ideal unbroken family in the first lines of the poem, Merrill is led to attempt to discover reasons for the breakup of his parents' marriage. In each of the next four sonnets, he explores potential explanations for his broken home: his father's being too absorbed in "sex/ And business," the conflict between the roles of men and women, the ghastliness of a mother-turned-corpse, his parents' indulgence in the aristocratic frenzy of the 1920's. By the end of the fifth sonnet, however, Merrill has no explanation, no certainties, and is forced to bury without judgment both mother and father and their once-glowing hearts "Cool here in the graveyard of good and evil."

A perhaps less obvious although no less important theme in "Broken Home" is childlessness. Just as the opening family tableau reminds Merrill of his parents' divorce, so it also contrasts with his childless life of art and homosexuality in the "room on the floor below." As he did with his parents' failed marriage, Merrill attempts to find explanations for his own choices in the sonnets that follow: a lack of connection with his father; his oedipal relationship with his mother; something in him growing "heavy, silver, pliable" as he observes his parents' deteriorating relationship; his reaction against his parents' world.

Once again left with no clear explanations for the phenomenon that troubles him, Merrill turns in the sestet of the sixth sonnet to look tenderly at the "offspring" he does produce—his poems. While in his poem "Childlessness" Merrill refers to his life as a garden in which "Nothing's been seeded," in "The Broken Home" he announces that he does not "try to keep a garden." Instead, he presents his poetry writing as another, more artificial form of gardening: the "rooting" in water of an exotic avocado "gemmed with air." He recognizes that his "offspring" poems—his "small gilt leaves"—are only provisional artifacts that grow "Fleshy and green." He knows he must again and again probe his past in an attempt to transform his painful memories into jeweled poems: "I let them die, yes, yes,/ And start another." When Merrill sadly concludes, "I am earth's no less," he means that he is no less a part of earth's fertility cycle than "the people upstairs" and also that producing his gilded "children" will neither assure his immortality nor prevent his death.

Janice Moore Fuller

THE BROKEN TOWER

Author: Hart Crane (1899-1932)
Type of poem: Lyric
First published: 1932; collected in *Collected Poems*, 1933

The Poem

"The Broken Tower" was the last poem that Hart Crane composed before committing suicide in 1932, and the poem does indeed have the eerie quality of a poetic last will and testament. Crane suffered from a chronic bent toward self-destructiveness, however, and much of his poetry explored the processes, purpose, and frustrations of the poetic sensibility confronting raw experience head-on in highly charged verbal arenas.

"The Broken Tower," whose title connotes a shattered or fractured vision, is composed in ten stanzas, each a perfect quatrain. In the very opening verse, the reader is asked to envision a bell tower and to hear the bells ringing at dawn; the speaker, however, is not in tune with these uplifting images. Rather, he has "dropped down the knell/ Of a spent day," his feet "chill on steps from hell."

The poem's central idea centers on this initial contrast between the power to make sounds that bespeak the godhead and the earthbound, or worse, condition of the maker of such sounds, who feels miserable in his inadequacy to write a poetry equal to his vision (the bells) and yet equally compelled to continue: "And I, their sexton slave!" The speaker engages the reader in his travail by the use of direct address: "Have you not heard, have you not seen. . . ?" While he has toiled and has in fact heard, it has been only from this worldly and imperfect end. The bells sound, but their source eludes him; the resulting poetry has become "my long-scattered score/ Of broken intervals."

After an intervening stanza rhapsodizing the power of that godly music that he has only imperfectly approximated in verse, the poet abandons the self-critical, confessional tone with which the poem opened in favor of an apologia. For if he entered the "broken world," it was only in an effort to "trace the visionary company of love." His aim was not wrong; the problem was, and is, that this sort of insubstantial vision does not linger long enough for anyone to limn its features. "Its voice/ An instant in the wind," there is not time enough "to hold each desperate choice." The poet questions whether the words which he "poured . . . [were] cognate, scored" of the Word Itself or were, instead, though "pledged to hope—cleft to despair." Was it, in other words, nothing more than self-deception?

The speaker admits that there is no answer, unless it is "she/ Whose sweet mortality stirs latent power." The surprise introduction of a beloved this late in the poem (the seventh stanza) may seem odd unless one realizes that the speaker has taken a necessary third step in his growth away from despair and toward acceptance. He abandons the solitude of the visionary quest and of self-critical evaluation in favor of a sharing of himself through physical union with a fellow, flawed creature like himself.

The new commitment made, the two lovers'—or at least sexual partners'—fleshly mortality evokes, through their heartbeats, an "angelus of wars" in his chest. It is from a different source, but it is no less music. He no longer needs to hear the sound of the mystical bells; he accepts himself and others as a part of the sound that the godhead makes. As his sights have been lowered to a wholly earthly level, so, too, the tower is itself internalized and, realized in his flesh, healed as it transforms finally into the male erection that, in the act of coitus, "Unseals her earth"; in the rhythms of the orgasmic climax, it "lifts love in its shower." What the speaker could not invoke, he evokes; what he could not bring down, he raises; what he could not repair, he reconstructs.

Forms and Devices

Though it is very much a twentieth century poem composed in the spirit of literary modernism, "The Broken Tower" utilizes a complex metaphorical technique that harks back to the so-called English Metaphysical poetry of the seventeenth century composed by poets such as John Donne and Andrew Marvell.

The conceit or extended metaphor is the foundation of such poetry. As the eighteenth century English critic Samuel Johnson once put it in rather disparaging terms, it is yoking two disparate things violently together; it is a farfetched comparison that, on balance and further consideration, actually does have the ring of truth. The twentieth century poet and critic T. S. Eliot was among the first to observe that Metaphysical poetry was actually a sort of precursor of the modern imagination, with its quest for up-to-date, startlingly fresh imagery within traditional themes and forms.

"The Broken Tower" is ostensibly relating a quasi-religious experience, but while biographical data suggests that the poem was inspired by Crane's attending a religious festival in Mexico while on a Guggenheim Fellowship in that country, one does both Crane and the poem an injustice if one fails to see that, in any real terms, religion has very little to do with it. The poem is structured around an extended metaphor for the visionary quest and the perils and frustrations that generally attend such a tenuous exercise. That metaphor is so layered and textured that it becomes the visionary quest itself, the striving to give voice to the inarticulate, and the effort to find entry into the spiritual through contact with another's flesh.

Without diminishing the validity of any of those readings, the poem ultimately comments on the creative process as an individual endeavor. The speaker/poet is first a sexton ringing bells he cannot see and can barely hear; then he is an acolyte hoping that his offerings might be found worthy by his God; and finally he is a lover who approaches the object of his passion as if she were herself a religious icon. That extended metaphor in each instance works best when its final reading is rendered wholly in terms of a poet trying to master the very substance, and duality, of his material: the word as it evokes the world.

Crane wishes to foster those other readings as well, however, so he subtly blends musical and religious terminology and references—"cathedral," "crucifix," "antiphonal carillons," "sexton," "encyclicals," "score," "intervals," and "angelus"—

thus making the experience of the poem a richer one than if he had spoken only in terms of poems and verses, similes and metaphors, words and images. He is also able to glide from the ideal to the real by slipping through a virtually explicit description of male sexual arousal and penetration of the female without diminishing the spiritual tone of the verse or suggesting any less profound an intention.

Themes and Meanings

The image of the tower is the most outstanding signal of the poem's central theme. True, one can argue that it is indeed a bell tower. The Tower of Babel comes to mind as well; but when a poet talks about a tower, he invites his reader to think of the fabled ivory tower wherein he finds his necessary isolation and elevated point of view from which to contemplate and comment on the human condition.

Yet this is a "broken" tower. One cannot avoid the further implication that this poet believes that he has somehow lost his vision, perhaps even his talent. It is known, for example, that Crane did spend much of his Guggenheim grant in Mexico involved in alcoholic binges and other debaucheries, and he was much depressed by the relatively poor reception that his major poem, *The Bridge* (1930), had received.

The speaker/poet first carries on an argument with his readers. Life is hell, he tells them, and all humans are imperfect, limited creations. It is impossible to bring back from the edges of hope and despair words and images that will ring true. Then he finds the courage to admit that he nevertheless has tried to serve a cause larger than self, the cause of human love and enlightenment.

Finally, as if it were himself that he was arguing with and trying to assuage, he remembers that life after all is for the living, as is love. Where he had felt defeated, he now sees that transcendence unmindful of the human element is an empty triumph. Thus it is in another's embrace that he finds the proper expression of all the joy and all the meaning he has been seeking. The poem ends on the powerfully liberating insight that one has within oneself a creative force quite capable, if need be, of creating love where there had been nothing before.

Russell Elliot Murphy

BUCKDANCER'S CHOICE

Author: James Dickey (1923-   )
Type of poem: Lyric
First published: 1965, in *Buckdancer's Choice*

The Poem

"Buckdancer's Choice" is a short poem written in an anapestic meter. The poem's narrator recalls that during his childhood, he would listen to his invalid mother whistle a song, which he now realizes represented the last assertions of her will and life force as she faced death. To highlight the human refusal to give in to death, the narrator develops an analogy between his mother's whistling and the dance of the buck-and-wing men who performed in minstrel shows.

The poem begins with the narrator remembering how his mother, who was confined to bed with angina—an inflammatory affliction of the throat and lungs— would "split" the air into "nine levels," as she continually whistled endless variations of the same song, "Buckdancer's Choice." The song originates from traveling minstrel shows, which were once popular but have almost died out since. Like the old minstrel shows, the narrator's mother is nearing the point when she will no longer exist. Though the disease from which she suffers affects her breathing by stripping the air from her lungs, the dying woman continues to whistle. Her whistling makes a profound impression on her son, who recalls creeping up to the closed door of her bedroom and intently listening to the countless versions of "Buckdancer's Choice" she could create. The narrator realizes that through her whistling, his mother was "Proclaiming what choices there are/ For the last dancers of their kind." In other words, he comes to see that she was doing the only thing she could in order to show that she was still alive and not ready to give in to death. Though his mother was not conscious of his listening to her whistling, the song makes the narrator aware of the power of the human will to survive. This realization culminates in the narrator imagining that such efforts in the face of death possess an almost magical or transcendental dimension.

Forms and Devices

James Dickey uses anapestic meter in "Buckdancer's Choice," giving the poem a strong rhythmic quality. Anapestic meter consists of three syllables, with two unaccented syllables followed by an accented one. The anapest's strong melodic quality is especially appropriate for a poem that involves music.

Dickey uses point of view both to relate how the child is drawn to his mother's whistling and to make a sophisticated assessment of the whistling's significance. The poem is narrated by an individual who recalls that as a child he would listen to his mother whistle. This perspective lets the narrator reflect and comment on the importance of this occurrence, and allows him to suggest how as a child he was almost magically attracted to the song, which related a message whose significance would not be clear until years later.

The use of an older and more experienced narrator also allows Dickey to develop convincingly the poem's central metaphor, which likens the mother's whistling to former slaves' performances in minstrel shows. The mother continues to whistle to herself, just as the minstrel show performers continue their acts despite the fact that their audience has practically disappeared. As the poem progresses, the narrator develops this metaphor, imagining the minstrel-show performers dancing to his mother's whistling; finally, he draws an analogy between his mother, the performers, and all of humanity. The music his mother makes and the performances of the ex-slaves become reflective of the human need to express emotion and live, even if no one else fully appreciates the value of that effort. Dickey's mature narrator is able to look back through time and develop the full implications of the analogy in a manner that he could not articulate or completely comprehend as a child.

Themes and Meanings

Like many of Dickey's poems, "Buckdancer's Choice" addresses the theme of the human will to exist when confronted with the inevitability of death. By comparing the narrator's mother to ex-slaves who continued to express themselves through their songs even as the minstrel-show tradition was nearing extinction, Dickey affirms the human will to celebrate life and shows how displays of the will to live provide people with a vital message.

In the first stanza, the narrator describes his mother's ability to whistle as a "gift of tongues." This description suggests the profound communication the mother's song holds for the listening child. A person who possesses the ability to speak in tongues is often regarded as a conduit who relays some essential message that emanates from a supernatural source. Similarly, the mother's message is not conveyed directly to the child but through a medium, the ex-slaves' song. Moreover, the mother whistles to herself and is not conscious of the child's presence, but the whistling enables the boy to gain greater insight into his mother's plight and, more generally, into the process of life and death.

The mother's whistling is also characterized as "The thousand variations of one song," with each variation symbolizing another continuing effort to ward off death by asserting her existence. Since her illness confines her to bed, her whistling becomes a way to declare that she is still in this world and not ready to give it up. Indeed, her whistling becomes a heroic act, something she continues to do despite the fact that she must battle "breathless angina."

Listening to the song conjures an image in the child's mind of a freed black who, "with cymbals at heel," forms a "one-man band" that dances to his mother's song. The narrator imagines that the buck-and-wing men's dance, in which the dancers flap their elbows, is an attempt to fly, to transcend the human and escape death. Like his mother's whistling, the dance becomes symbolic of the desire to live. This image is central to the poem because through it, the narrator expresses that seemingly trivial acts such as whistling or dancing can become deeply significant: Through them, people may be "Proclaiming what choices there are/ For the last dancers of their kind." A key word here, one that is echoed in the poem's title, is "choice." Having choice suggests that individuals retain some power of volition, some means to express themselves; it is a declaration that though their existence and autonomy may be slipping away, they can continue to fight for whatever life they still possess.

In the final three stanzas, the narrator widens the poem's frame of reference. Instead of referring to his dying mother, he speaks of "women"; instead of referring to his childhood, he speaks of "children." This broadening generalizes the significance of the exchange between the particular mother and child described in the poem to include all of humanity, for, as the poem declares, all are "slaves of death." The poem concludes with an image of "children enchanted at walls," listening to the song and imagining the dance. The children are "not dancing but nearly risen." The words "enchanting" and "risen" imply that the connection the song creates between people is magical, a revelation of the human spirit's insatiable appetite for life and significance. Though the word "nearly" modifies this optimistic vision, suggesting the impossibility of such a dream, what remains of uttermost importance is the human will to resist death, even if such an endeavor is inevitably futile.

Ernest Suarez

BUDDHA IN GLORY

Author: Rainer Maria Rilke (1875-1926)
Type of poem: Lyric
First published: 1908, "Buddha in der Glorie," in *Der neuen Gedichte anderer Teil*; collected in *Rainer Maria Rilke: Fifty Selected Poems*, 1940

The Poem
"Buddha in Glory" (or as one translator titles it, "The Buddha in the Glory") is a short poem of twelve lines divided into three stanzas of four lines each. The original poem is predominantly in trochaic meter (with alternating stressed and unstressed final syllables in each line); it begins in trochaic pentameter and ends in trochaic tetrameter. The original German rhymes *abab, cdcd, efef.*

The poem's title calls up visions of Eastern religion, mysticism, and meditation on the right path to Nirvana or salvation. Buddhism is a religion of eastern and central Asia that developed from the teachings of Gautama Buddha. The name Buddha is Sanskrit for "the enlightened"; the goal of the Buddhist is to arrive at a state of perfect spiritual fulfillment. This mental and moral self-purification is said to free one from the suffering that is inherent in life.

While Rilke undoubtedly had this religious history in mind as he wrote the poem in Paris in the summer of 1908, he was also probably working from a particular statue of Buddha that was located in the garden of the French sculptor Auguste Rodin, to whom Rilke was personal secretary for several years. Rilke described this sculpture in a letter to his wife Clara on September 20, 1905:

> Then the huge blossoming starry night is before me, and below, in front of the window, the gravel path goes up a little hill on which, in fanatic silence, a statue of Buddha rests, dispensing, with quiet discretion, the unutterable self-containedness of his gesture under all the skies of day and night. C'est le centre du monde [It is the center of the world], I said to Rodin.

Buddha is clearly a subject that fascinated Rilke, who wrote two earlier Buddha poems in the first part of the *Neue Gedichte* (1907; *New Poems*, 1964); "Buddha in Glory" is the closing poem of *New Poems, Part II*.

While the poem seems mystical in tone, speaking of the "center of all centers" and the "kernel of all kernels," one can follow the general movement of its imagery. In the first stanza, the persona of the poem acknowledges Buddha as the center of all being and compares this central position to an almond centered within its shell. Buddha is like a vital and dynamic almond, the fruit of which encompasses everything, including the heavens themselves. The persona clearly admires this spiritual accomplishment and salutes Buddha. The poem is addressed directly to the Buddha.

In stanza 2, Buddha's consciousness and the almond which serves as a metaphor for it continue to expand and to grow beyond time into infinity. The sap that fills the almond's fruit and Buddha's veins presses on infinity itself. The image of Buddha finally subsumes even the heavens, which are filled with Buddha's own suns that send their rays to assist the sap that drives through the almond's flesh. Having enveloped time and space, in stanza 3, Buddha participates in the heavenly realm itself as the rays of his own suns now burn and glow. Yet these external symbols are nothing compared to the intensity of consciousness that burns within the Buddha and that will long outlast the external glory of the sun: "But in you is already begun/ that which will outlive the sun." The spiritual growth of consciousness within Buddha is thus more crucial than any image of physical expansion.

Forms and Devices

Perhaps the most striking device Rilke uses in this poem is that of the doubled metaphor. Buddha himself is an image of spiritual perfection and expanded consciousness, but Rilke adds a second level of metaphor by comparing the statue of Buddha to the living system of the almond. The technique of embodying spiritual meaning in a specific physical object (often an artwork of some kind) is typical of many of the poems in *New Poems*. In this case, Rilke complicates matters further by using a metaphor from the natural world (the almond) to explicate the vital spiritual significance of the sculpture, which in turn symbolizes the perfected consciousness of Buddha himself. Sitting silently and self-contained at the center of time and space, Buddha resembles the seed or kernel at the center of the almond. This usually limited germ or nucleus expands along with Buddha's consciousness to encompass all of space, including the starry skies, as well as all of time as the almond's (and Buddha's) physical shell swells into infinity. The almond's casing (or Buddha's body) no longer serves to limit the consciousness it contains. The metaphors allow the spiritual world to subsume the physical world and thus to eliminate all physical boundaries. The idea of perfected spirituality is embodied in the perfectly taciturn statue but then linked to a natural image that can grow to include all of time and space. By describing the unfolding of his image, Rilke is able to symbolize a very complex and mystical spiritual development.

A second technique Rilke employs in this poem is that of constant expansion of his poetic vision. Rilke begins the poem at a single point of extreme concentration: "Center of centers, seed of seeds." From this single point, his image of the almond and of Buddha's spiritual perfection constantly expands until it envelops the heavens themselves. The image of Buddha thus unites many levels of existence. The Buddha statue is made of stone and embodies the inanimate world; the metaphor of the almond represents the natural world; Buddha as a historical figure brings in the human world; and finally, Buddha's spiritual perfection encompasses the transcendent realm of the heavens or the divine. Rilke thus accomplishes in his imagery his own unification of realms and of levels of consciousness. The poem itself becomes an act of spiritual unification and perfection.

To emphasize this unity, Rilke employs a rhyme scheme in German that links *Kerne* (seeds, kernels) and *Sterne* (stars) in lines 1 and 3 of stanza 1. His rhyme connects the concentrated point of the nucleus or seed to the stars, the infinitesimal to the infinite, just as his description does. In lines 2 and 4 of stanza 2, Rilke rhymes *Schale* (shell, husk) and *Gestrahle* (rays) to produce the same effect of breaking open the image so that it becomes boundless.

Themes and Meanings

"Buddha in Glory" is a poem about the triumph of the spiritual world over the physical world. Buddha himself symbolizes this triumph. Buddha's perfected and all-encompassing consciousness allows him to merge with all of existence. The suns are now his suns; the rays of the heavens are his. Rilke thus succeeds in embodying in his poem a very complex mystical experience of spiritual perfection, of the attainment of Buddhahood. While it would be extremely difficult for a poet to explain such an experience to a reader in discursive language, Rilke manages to capture this mystical fulfillment in a striking image (the almond) drawn from the natural realm more familiar to the reader.

The tone of the poem is one of admiration. The persona of the poem greets and celebrates Buddha and his spiritual accomplishments. The persona recognizes that Buddha has achieved the purification of consciousness that allows him to merge with all of existence, to burn with a spiritual intensity that will outlast the sun itself. The sculptor has captured this spirituality in his sculpture just as nature captures it in the perfection of its fruits. Rilke now attempts to do the same in his poem. In a gesture of unification reminiscent of German Romanticism, Rilke manages to merge the aesthetic world (the sculpture), the world of spirit (Buddha's consciousness), and the natural world (the almond) in a single image of metaphysical wholeness. Rilke creates in his poem something of the same experience that Buddha achieves in his unification with all of existence. Thus the poem, like Buddha, provides an example of perfected consciousness and reunified existence.

Although Rilke begins with a single point of concentration (perhaps akin to T. S. Eliot's "still point of the turning world" in the *Four Quartets*, 1943), his poem is about expansion of that center of centers into infinity — that is, about the elimination of all boundaries. Here Buddha (and the almond that symbolizes him) surpasses all dependencies, all limits of space and time, in order to become his own universe, his own suns. The apparent limitations of the shell or husk are overcome as the image encompasses all existence. The sap that flows in the almond's veins (and in Buddha's) is part of the system of the stars' rays. Yet the real growth and expansion is an inward one. Returning to that point of concentration within Buddha himself, the poem comes to rest on the internal rather than the expansive external universe it has opened up. Within, in the realm of the spiritual, is the source and beginning of an intensity that will outlive even the sun that symbolizes the life force of our ordinary universe. Consciousness, internal life, outstrips all external existence. Finally, Rilke suggests that the enlightenment signified by Buddha's name is to be found within.

Kathleen L. Komar

THE BUILDING

Author: Philip Larkin (1922-1985)
Type of poem: Lyric
First published: 1974, in *High Windows*

The Poem

"The Building" is a poem of nine seven-line stanzas plus a single final line. It is written in Philip Larkin's characteristic rough iambic pentameter, with an equally characteristic subtle rhyme scheme. All the lines are not exactly ten syllables each; nevertheless, the pattern of stress is that of the iamb: a two-part (disyllabic), stressed-unstressed foot.

The poem is a description of a place that is never definitively named, although it is clearly a hospital or other health-care facility. The first stanza describes the building in contrast to what is around and outside it. The last lines of the first stanza, along with the entire second and third stanzas, describe the building's interior, including the inhabitants. The fourth and fifth stanzas describe what the building is like from the inside, from the point of view of the people waiting there: how being there is an interruption of their daily lives, and what they are afraid will happen to them.

Stanza 6 returns to the exterior of the building, this time looking out from the inside. The outside world seems very far off; it goes on and on, out of sight. Further, in stanza 7, the world is addressed as a separate thing and is even said to be "beyond the stretch/ Of any hand from here." For a brief three-line sentence, the speaker of the poem is present and includes himself in the condition of the people in the building: The "loves" and "chances" of the world are only a "touching dream to which we are all lulled." Then he separates himself again in a way that he says is inevitable, because everyone will "wake from" that dream "separately." Awakening from that illusion of "self-protecting ignorance" is brought about by a more real confrontation with death in a building such as this.

Stanza 8 shifts back from speculation to more particulars about the experience of the people in the building. The sense of uncertainty remains, however, because the particulars of death are unknown on any level. So, continuing on to stanza 9, what is being said about the people in the building— "Each gets up and goes at last" and "All know they are going to die" — is being said about all humanity. The poem explains this when it says in the final lines, "That is what it means,/ this clean-sliced cliff; a struggle to transcend/ The thought of dying." The confrontation with death forced upon the people who arrive at this building is no different from that which faces those who have not arrived there yet, and what is done in the building of the poem is in a certain way no different from what is done in "cathedrals," because neither "contravenes . . ./ The coming dark" of death. The desire of all people to do so, to contravene both their own and others' coming dark, is poignantly represented by their offerings of "wasteful, weak propitiatory flowers."

Forms and Devices

Larkin's subtle rhyme scheme contributes significantly to the overall impact of the poem. While the stanzas run seven lines, the poem uses an eight-rhyme pattern: *abcbdcad*. This has two effects. First, because the rhyme carries over from one stanza to the next, the reader, too, is carried forward through the description by an imperceptible force; it is an experience akin to that which is being described. Second, through the middle stanzas of the poem this has the effect of disturbing the unity of each stanza. For example, the rhyme scheme begins at the second line of the third stanza, the third line of the fourth stanza, and so on, so that the reader is made to feel an unease and a lack of resolution, until the final stanza and the single final line.

This effect is further accomplished by a technique called enjambment, in which the sense of one line is carried over into the next. This occurs frequently within stanzas; more important, it occurs from one stanza to the next in every stanza except the first. The midsentence pause creates a momentary sense of meaninglessness. When that pause carries over across stanzas the sense of disorientation generated by the poem is more intense.

With the last eight lines of the poem, the beginning of the rhyme pattern and the beginning of the stanza coincide, as they did in the first stanza, and the pattern is allowed to complete itself with the final single line. This coincidence, the completion of the pattern and the end of the unrelenting enjambment, provide a sense of resolution for the reader, but one which is itself uneasy as the final line, standing alone, also breaks completely with the stanzaic form of the poem.

The absence of a first person, a narrative "I," in this poem contributes to its troubling sense of depersonalization. Not only is the first person absent, the only second-person reference is not to a singular "you" but to the whole "world" (stanza 7), after which there is a single reference to "we" (all of "us" in this world). All the other references to people are by category— "porters," "nurse," "kids," "girls"— or only as "humans" or "faces," lumped together in indefinite or plural third-person pronouns— "someone," "those who tamely sit," "some" who are young or old, "they" and "them," and even "all." The only exception occurs when the indistinct "they" see a singular "him" "wheeled past," in stanzas 5 and 6; that is, when someone is separated from the waiting mass and goes to face his fate alone.

The anonymity of the building, emphasized by all the indefinite pronouns as well as the poem's title, is reinforced by Larkin's repeated use of similes using the comparative word "like." The streets are "like a great sigh"; the waiting room is "[l]ike an airport lounge." Finally, in the ninth stanza, all that the waiting people know is that they will die in a place "somewhere like this."

Themes and Meanings

Larkin combines three themes that contribute to one another: questions of health and sickness are hinted at in terms of bodily health, but also in terms of mental and spiritual health. Outside the building is a living, normal world of "close-ribbed streets" that "rise and fall" in an image of breathing, "like a sigh," where people are "free" and go about their business. This everyday normalcy is belied by the later reappearance of images of the body in stanza 7. The dream of life occurs only when "conceits" (vanities) and "ignorance congeal" like blood within a vein, a vein which itself "collapses," taking that dream of life with it as death is confronted.

The confrontation with death is also sometimes cast in terms of crime and imprisonment. In stanzas 3 and 4, the presence of those "humans" in the waiting room is associated with something that "has gone wrong," with "error of a serious sort." In stanza 5, when someone is wheeled away, the "rooms, and rooms past those" into which they disappear and which are "hard to return from," carry a sinister implication of torture. At the same time, the references to confession and to a building of many rooms also has Christian connotations of the confessional and Christ's words about there being a place for everyone in heaven. This association is strengthened in later stanzas, with references such as the communionlike "Each gets up and goes," and "congregations" in "white rows." At the same time, however, that image of "white rows" could be prison cells and/or slabs of a morgue.

By mixing these three images, Larkin communicates the mixed attitudes society takes toward disease and death. The onslaught of fatal illness can be regarded as the result of moral failure, of "not living right," or, alternatively, as an opportunity to come to terms with things that are not of this world or as the beginning step toward eternal life. The cultural reluctance to name certain forms of terminal disease renders them even more mysterious and terrifying. Larkin reduplicates this effect by leaving the building and the plight of its inhabitants unnamed.

Finally, this poem has strong associations with Matthew Arnold's poem "Dover Beach" (1867). The image of the cliff appears in both, as does the lament that the world is a land of dreams. Most important, the "crowds" in "the coming dark" are the same as those clashing on Arnold's darkling plain. By this connection, Larkin's poem can be understood to be functioning at a level far beyond the immediate portrayal; it becomes a lament for the very nature of the human struggle.

Laurie Glover

THE BURIED LIFE

Author: Matthew Arnold (1822-1888)
Type of poem: Lyric
First published: 1852, in *Empedocles on Etna, and Other Poems*

The Poem

"The Buried Life" is a ninety-eight-line poem divided into seven stanzas of varying length with an irregular rhyme scheme. A monologue in which a lover addresses his beloved, the poem yearns for the possibility of truthful communication with the self and with others.

The first line evokes the banter of a loving couple, but it is immediately checked by the deeply sad feelings of the speaker. Troubled by a sense of inner restlessness, he longs for complete intimacy and hopes to find it in his beloved's clear eyes, the window to her "inmost soul."

As the second stanza suggests, not even lovers can sustain an absolutely open relationship or break through the inhibitions and the masks that people assume in order to hide what they really feel. Yet the speaker senses the possibility of greater truth, since all human beings share basically the same feelings and ought to be able to share their most profound thoughts.

In a burst of emotion, expressed in two intense lines, the speaker wonders whether the same forces that prevent people from truly engaging each other must also divide him and his beloved.

The fourth stanza suggests that direct contact is only possible in fugitive moments, when human beings suddenly are aware of penetrating the distractions and struggles of life and realize that their apparently random actions are the result of the "buried stream," of those unconscious drives that motivate human behavior.

In the long meditative fifth stanza, the speaker advances the idea that there are occasions in the midst of busy lives when people are suddenly overwhelmed with the desire to understand their "buried life," the wellspring of all that they do. Yet no one ever seems to penetrate the origins of things and articulate what remains a mystery, what the speaker calls "nameless feelings." There is a "hidden" aspect of life, an underground sense that haunts people, that beckons to them, just as, in the sixth stanza, the lover beckons to his beloved, taking her hand and expressing—if only for a moment—a sense of complete communion between themselves and their emotions. It is at these times that people become aware of the deeper currents of their beings.

The final stanza expresses the utter peacefulness of this communion between lovers, when they feel at rest, when they are no longer bothered by the elusiveness of their beings' purpose and they comprehend the sources of their lives.

Forms and Devices

The poem is built around a central metaphor: the evocation of an individual's life and of life itself as a stream or river, ever flowing, ungraspable, and possessed of great depths. In the first line, for example, the lovers' conversation "flows" — a delightful and yet troubling metaphor because their words, like water, resist definition and do not reach the core of identity or meaning.

The poet uses the metaphor explicitly in the fourth stanza in referring to the "unregarded river of our life . . . eddying at large in blind uncertainty," for human beings usually ignore the true roots of their selves.

The fifth stanza is even more explicit, as the speaker uses the phrase "our buried life" to parallel his use of "buried stream" in the fourth stanza. To track the "mystery of this heart," to observe the "nameless feelings that course through our breast," again continues the metaphor of the stream, the watercourse that contains within it unanalyzed elements. When the speaker evokes the moment of communion in the sixth stanza, it is also in the terms of water, as "a man becomes aware of his life's flow." Knowing his life's basis is, as the last line of the poem suggests, similar to following the "sea where it goes."

Comparing human lives to a stream, to the flowing of water, is a traditional metaphorical conception of human life, which Matthew Arnold uses to capture both the enigma and the energy of life. Even the speaker's tears in the first stanza are an expression of this life flow — at once so soothing and troubling, so appealing and frustrating to human beings who wish to plumb the depths of their existence.

The poet also uses the device of a dramatic monologue, of a lover addressing his beloved, to generalize about human experience, to suggest that the lovers' feelings are a microcosm of the feelings that all human beings share. Beginning with a dramatic scene — the speaker moved to tears and wishing that he could see in his beloved her "inmost soul" — the poem gradually, stanza by stanza, develops the universal import of the speaker's feelings, showing how all human beings partake of this quest for self-knowledge and communion with one another.

Arnold also achieves an impressive unity in the poem by repeating certain key words — particularly those with which he evokes a "benumbed" and "jaded" world. This world is blind to the depths of things and distracted and deafened by its own surface affairs — by all the sounds and sights that obscure the quieter, softer, cooler forces at play in human nature, which are observed only at those rare moments of self-awareness. By implication, nature itself, its buried streams and its rising hills, evoke in the poem's last lines a sense of life's peaks and valleys, its origins and outcomes, that become apparent only in the lovers' momentary transcendence of daily cares and expressions.

In the poem's shift from first to third person, Arnold effectively transforms a personal, individual experience into a universal experience as well. For example, in the fifth and sixth stanzas, he moves from the speaker's address to his beloved to a hypothetical situation in which "a beloved hand is laid in ours," thus making his appeal to the human heart which, earlier in the poem (line 23), is described as beating "in every human breast." When the tones of a lover's voice suddenly open the beloved's heart, "a bolt is shot back somewhere in our breast" (line 84) — a line of shocking visual force that describes a moment of unlocking the heart that the speaker had yearned for earlier in the poem (line 13).

Themes and Meanings

A poem of great frustration and sadness, "The Buried Life" yearns for an openness which the poet fears that he will never achieve. Saddened by his own inability to express his deepest, truest self, he turns to his beloved, thinking that in her "limpid" eyes he can find true communion with another soul. He knows that people fear to reveal themselves, suspecting that they will be ignored or, worse, criticized for what they expose of themselves. Yet, his counterargument is that all human beings contain essentially the same feelings and thus should be able to bare their souls more freely than they do.

It has been pointed out that there may be a slight confusion in the poem, perhaps explained by the poet's shifting use of metaphor. On the one hand, lines 38-40 and 55-56 suggest that the river of life is subterranean and only rarely accessible. On the other hand, the river of life in lines 43-44 is treated as a surface flow interrupted or broken by eddies, emanations of a "genuine self" referred to in line 36. Evidently, Arnold is identifying the discrepancy between the self who thinks that he is determining his fate, who thinks he can "well-nigh change his own identity" (line 34), and the self who seems to pursue life with "blind uncertainty" (line 43) while actually "driving on with it [the buried life] eternally."

Thus, the poem raises but does not resolve disturbing questions about fate and free will. Human beings clearly deceive themselves—that much is clear from the fourth stanza—yet the poet just as clearly entertains the possibility that the lovers, and indeed all human beings, at least have the capacity to see truly and to understand the ultimate reasons for their actions.

Although the poem does not settle the "fate versus free will" conundrum, its use of metaphor does suppose that, as in nature where all rivers have their source, so in human nature all lives have their origin, which a man can glimpse, who "thinks he knows/ The hills where his life rose,/ And the sea where it goes." The ending is tentative because it refers to what the man "thinks he knows," yet it is positively rendered in the simple declarative rhymes of the last words, mimicking the "unwonted calm," of the knowledge that the speaker has acquired.

Carl Rollyson

BURNING A BOOK

Author: William Stafford (1914-   )
Type of poem: Lyric
First published: 1987, in *An Oregon Message*

The Poem

"Burning a Book" is in free verse, its nineteen lines divided into three verse paragraphs, units of thought of eight, nine, and two lines, respectively. Book burning is often seen as a symbol of censorship and ignorance, but this poem looks at book burning from a unique viewpoint. It is unwise to assume automatically that the poet and the speaker of a poem are speaking with the same voice, but very often such is the case. "Burning a Book" so closely identifies with William Stafford's own views on writing that one can conclude there is no distinction between the two.

The poem begins with a detailed, even graphic description of the burning of a book; it recognizes the destructive nature of book burning and apparently supports the conventional symbolism associated with it. Yet there is a hint of the direction the poem will take when the reader is told that lies are burning as well as truth. Apparently, book burning may not be all bad. The last sentence of the first paragraph sets a conversational tone and includes the reader in the process: "You can usually find a few charred words in the ashes." Within the first few words of the second verse paragraph, the poet's viewpoint is stated directly: "some books ought to burn." Stafford's poems often state opposing attitudes. It is almost as if he wants to speak both for and against.

The latter part of the second verse paragraph speaks metaphorically of the perceived danger: Worse than the act of burning books (or, by symbolic association, rejecting written ideas) deemed failures is the fact that some books that should have been written were never written at all; some subjects—good or bad, weighty or insignificant—were never explored. There are "whole libraries" of undiscovered subjects, worthy and unworthy, in towns, cities, and countrysides. The ironic crux of the poem's message is in the last sentence of the paragraph: "ignorance can dance in the absence of fire." The implied viewpoint is that fire is needed for knowledge, even the fire of burning books; for even a burned book has had something to say, whether truthful, controversial, proved wrong or dangerous, or simply poorly stated. How could its worth be determined if it had never been written?

The final paragraph, which opens with a challenging, defiant tone, unites the reader and the speaker. The poet has burned books and perhaps, like the reader, has found "a few charred words in the ashes." More important to him are the books he has not written, that "nobody has," whole libraries of potential fuel for knowledge, testing, even controversy.

Forms and Devices

An openness to the possibilities in language characterizes Stafford's poetic method. He is eager to explore unique modes of perception in language in order to express meanings in objects and ideas. Figures of speech allow the poet to say things in new ways. Stafford uses figures of speech—personification and metaphor—to great effect in "Burning a Book."

Nearly every object and idea in the poem seems alive. The pages protect each other, truth and lies both burn, the flame's attitude is one of indifference, some books are "trying for character but just faking it," and ignorance dances. Personifying these things, attributing human characteristics to the nonhuman, causes the poem to bristle with energy. The effect supports the concept in the poem that what the words say in a book is not as important as the creative energy, the impulse, that takes the writer through the process. If the process leads to a failure, so be it, implies the poet, but one never knows unless the process is brought to life and new ideas and methods are explored. Only ignorance has energy in the absence of creative exploration, and it dances gleefully.

Pages that contain both truth and lies try to protect themselves from the fire. They appear victimized, and the reader is pulled, by the personification, into empathy for the writings being destroyed. One can easily visualize a repressive society burning books that threaten conventional and acceptable standards.

Some of these personified books, however, are fakes whose ideas have no validity. Put simply, books are, like people, all different. Like people, all deserve at least the chance to have their say. As well as infusing energy into the poem, then, the personification also highlights the poem's pragmatic outlook, which explores the abstract, conventional symbolism of book burning in terms with which the reader can identify—and even participate in—by realistically examining it from all sides.

The extended library metaphor in the second paragraph of the poem indicates the vastness of the material that could be written about. Books represent ideas, and libraries are the places where those ideas are found—in towns and cities and countrysides, anywhere there is life. If writers do not explore these places, even the evils—"wild dogs" who terrorize the countryside and who "own anything that moves"—will not be identified. The comparatively small fire a few books make (shown by the description of the burning of one book) cannot compare to the enormous waste and potential danger of not writing at all.

Themes and Meanings

"Burning a Book" is a poem about taking risks—specifically, taking risks in writing. Stafford has always admired, and practiced in his own writing, the quixotic approach of plunging into the unknown. He maintains that no subject, as long as it involves the heart and intuition of the writer, is too small to write about. As Stafford himself says, "[L]ike Don Quixote you must expect some disasters. You must write your bad poems." (Perhaps one must write some poems worthy of nothing better than "burning.") Not to write intuitively, on impulse, is "to guarantee that you will not find the unknown, the risky."

Following a creative impulse may lead to something worthwhile or it may lead to windmills in the sky, but one thing is certain in the poem: Neither truth nor lies will be found without the attempt. Stafford's sense of irony admits that "Truth, brittle and faint, burns easily,/ its fire as hot as the fire lies make," and his wisdom says that if neither is accessible, there is no way to distinguish between truth and lies.

Although book burning is conventionally associated with ignorance, in his usual attitude of openness to both sides of an issue, Stafford observes that, ironically, ignorance dances equally well in the absence of fire. He takes a wry look at the whole concept. Where there are books being burned, there is something with which to disagree; there is knowledge, however faulty. To be judged unworthy, a book must be read and must be written in the first place. How could book burning itself be deemed repressive without the words that can expose its dangers?

The reader is invited to risk being fallible. The imaginative space of the poem includes writer and reader alike. "You" and "I" are almost equated, for the participation of the reader is required if one is to find the words in the ashes. When the poet admits figuratively to burning books that no doubt meet the criterion "trying for character/ but just faking it," he is quite possibly talking about some of his own writing. The tone is finally optimistic as he casually shrugs at his own failures (and perhaps at his critics) and looks forward to the endless possibilities of discovery.

Stafford is one of the most prolific of American poets. In his view, even the most ordinary ideas are worth examining and exploring. "Burning a Book" exemplifies his deep-rooted beliefs about writing; his words are designed to rekindle vigor and excitement in exploring the boundaries of thought.

Marilyn Schultz

THE BURNING BABE

Author: Robert Southwell (1561-1595)
Type of poem: Lyric/narrative
First published: 1595, in *Maoeniae*

The Poem

"The Burning Babe," by Robert Southwell, is one of the most famous and powerful Christmas poems in the English language. Written in carefully crafted rhyming couplets of iambic heptameter, the poem is sixteen lines long, and each of its long lines is skillfully broken by a caesura (pause), which occurs after the first four feet and before the last three. Yet, despite its structural complication, "The Burning Babe" relates its astonishing, mystical occurrences in a smoothly flowing narrative.

In the first four lines of the poem, a cold and isolated narrator stands "shivering" in the snow at night when he suddenly senses a comforting "heat" which lifts his spirits and causes his "heart to glow." Nevertheless, he casts a "fearful" glance at the source of the heat and, astonishingly, he sees, suspended in the air, "A pretty babe all burning bright." This "burning babe" is the infant Jesus Christ.

In lines 5 through 8 of the poem, the Christ child's peculiar condition is carefully described: the babe is "scorchèd with excessive heat" and shedding "floods of tears." Finally, this amazing and sorrowful image speaks, not with the joy usually associated with Christmas, but with the complaint that "none approach to warm their hearts." Clearly, the babe is reminding the stunned narrator that the extraordinary miracle of the Incarnation (Christ's human birth) is too often taken for granted and that men too often refuse to undertake a true and necessary commitment to Christ's warming love.

Then, in lines 9 through 12, the love of God is portrayed not only as warming, but also as purifying: "My faultless breast the furnace is" and the "metal in this furnace wrought are men's defilèd souls." Through this extraordinary metaphor (Jesus as a purifying furnace), the Christ child reminds the narrator that the great news of the Incarnation is not only that God is among us, which is extraordinary enough, but also that this Incarnation also initiates a redemption through which all men can purify themselves before God.

In the poem's final four lines, the Christ child reinforces the furnace imagery with a related metaphor of purification and cleansing: the promise to all men to "melt into a bath to wash them in my blood." With these words, the burning babe suddenly vanishes from sight and the amazed narrator immediately recalls "that it was Christmas day." Thus the poem, through the Christ child, reminds the narrator (and the reader) that Christmas and the Redemption cannot be separated, and that the best awakening that one could possibly have each Christmas is to remember that the purpose of the Incarnation is one's personal salvation.

Forms and Devices

The great Elizabethan poet Ben Jonson once said that if he could have written "The Burning Babe," he would have been glad to destroy many of his own best poems. There are many reasons this poem is so affecting, but the strangeness of the narrative and the unusual central metaphor are two of the poem's most memorable aspects.

The very incident itself—the encounter with an enflamed Christ child suspended in the air—is both a stunning and miraculous apparition. The babe's strong admonition and unusual language increase the peculiar and marvelous aspects of the narrative. Finally, when the narrator's conscience has been awakened, the babe simply vanishes. Thus Southwell, by combining the traditional "strangeness" of early folk ballads with the miraculous events recorded in hagiographies (lives of the saints), creates a scene that is both mystical and unforgettable.

Even more amazing, however, than the action of the poem is its central metaphor of the infant Jesus as a furnace, explained when the burning babe first appears: " 'Alas!' quoth he, 'but newly born in fiery heats I fry.' " As critic Linda Ching Sledge points out, in her book *Shivering Babe, Victorious Lord: The Nativity in Poetry and Art* (1981), this powerful image of the newly born Christ child literally enflamed in a nonconsuming fire clearly recalls the primary two symbolisms of fire imagery in the Bible: the presence of God (as in the burning bush of Exodus 3:2, the pillar of fire in Exodus 13:21, and the tongues of fire in Acts 2:3-4) and the nature of sacrifice (as in the story of Abraham and Isaac in Genesis and in the many Old Testament burnt offerings to God).

In the poem, the child explains that he burns with a purifying love that burns away men's sins: "My faultless breast the furnace is, the fuel wounding thorns." Thus, through the Passion of Jesus (which included the crowning with thorns), this furnace will consume man's sins. Although divine justice demands retribution for human sin, God's mercy "blows the coals," and the resultant fire is Christ's love. As a result of this extraordinary love, "men's defilèd souls" can now be transformed "to their good."

The poem "The Burning Babe" is a marvelous blend of many striking poetic elements: haunting rhythm and rhyme, powerful language, sharp images, intellectual complexity, and fervid spirituality. It is its very strange narrative and its memorable central metaphor, however, that make the poem more powerfully effective than the many other interesting, but less memorable, nativity poems which have been written by a wide range of English poets, including John Donne, Ben Jonson, John Milton, and William Blake.

Themes and Meanings

"The Burning Babe" is a poem about Christian redemption. It was written by Robert Southwell, a young Jesuit priest, who violated an English decree that no Catholic Masses could be celebrated in England. As a result, Southwell was hunted, captured, and viciously tortured by Richard Topcliffe, one of Queen Elizabeth's most brutal "pursuivants" (priest-hunters). At the time he wrote the poem, Southwell was awaiting trial and certain execution in the Tower of London. In his poem, Southwell clearly reflects on his own coming death and his hopes of personal redemption.

Unlike most Christmas poems that focus on the nativity scene and emphasize the joy of the Incarnation, Southwell's poem is a strange, deep, and often somber meditation which clearly reflects his own situation as a tortured prisoner awaiting death in solitary confinement. At the beginning of the poem, the narrator, as indicated by his isolation and deep "shivering" cold, appears as a lost or misguided soul clearly in need of spiritual direction. Thus the very purpose of the entire poem is to indicate the sudden and astonishing impact which the strange apparition of the burning Christ child has upon the narrator. The lost soul's shock upon first seeing the suspended child is similar to that of the Bethlehem shepherds on Christmas night when the angel suddenly appears to them: "And lo, the angel of the Lord came upon them, and the glory of the Lord shone about them; and they were sore afraid" (Luke 2:9).

Then, when the burning babe has admonished all men (including the narrator) for not apprehending the love and sacrifice of God, he further explains his ability to burn away (and wash away) all human sin. This great and divine power had been foretold by the angel Gabriel when he spoke to Mary of her coming child: "For He shall save His people from their sins" (Matthew 1:21). Finally, at the end of the poem, when the babe vanishes, the awestruck narrator "callèd unto mind that it was Christmas day." Thus, the lost and lonely soul has clearly been awakened by his miraculous experience as he recalls the great significance of the day. Like Dante in *The Divine Comedy* (c. 1320), the narrator has now been directed back to the right and true path.

Robert Southwell sincerely believed that poetry could be used for higher, more spiritual ends, and he was determined to show "how well verse and virtue suit together" (*The Life of Robert Southwell, Poet and Martyr,* Christopher Devlin, 1956). While awaiting his execution (he was hanged at Tyburn on February 21, 1595), Southwell proved his convictions by writing his small masterpiece, "The Burning Babe." In this most unusual and powerful of all Christmas poems, Robert Southwell, who was canonized in 1970, explains that the miracle of Christmas should inspire all men to recall the ultimate miracle of redemption and salvation.

William Baer

BURNING THE TOMATO WORMS

Author: Carolyn Forché (1950-   )
Type of poem: Meditation
First published: 1975; collected in *Gathering the Tribes*, 1976

The Poem

"Burning the Tomato Worms" is a long poem of thirteen stanzas in free verse, the key poem among seven others in the section of Carolyn Forché's *Gathering the Tribes* that bears the same name. At first, the poem seems not to be about the event named in its title. Stanza 5 finally mentions burning the tomato worms, an act that is transformed in stanza 10, when the tomatoes and their worms are brought in for shelter from an early frost. The symbolic significance of the round, red tomatoes and the cylindrical worms that destroy them becomes clear by the end of the poem.

The epigraph for the poem offers a suggestion for interpreting it. The epigraph speaks of the cycles of creation and destruction, a cycle that is readily apparent in tending crops and, in the poem, is applied to human life. Moreover, the epigraph gives the injunction that poetry must be an attempt to "know" and name and order these important patterns of life, that it must strive to capture the roots of birth and death and to tell people what to do in the interim between them.

In the first stanza, the narrator is stimulated by the sights and feelings of autumn into remembering her grandmother. Although the stanza is brief, only seven lines, it introduces the reader to several important aspects of the poem. The dark spines of the pine trees seem to be phallic, an image of masculinity. In contrast, the clouds (perhaps billowy and rounded), the fertility of the plowed ground, and the bulging beaks of the pelicans as they bring food to their young suggest femininity. The narrator is careful to place this scene in the United States. The memory comes during a transitional time, an interim, "Between apples and the first snow." All of this suggests that the poem will reenact a rite of passage for the narrator: from naïve and innocent childhood to the age-old knowledge of womanhood and a kinship with her female ancestor. She will attain the knowledge of creation but also of pain, suffering, and loss.

As the memory of her grandmother becomes more focused, the narrator projects into the circumstances of her own conception and birth by imagining a time prior to her own existence. She divides the society before her birth into communities of men and communities of women, each with their own work to do and images that represent them. Most notable are the climatic contrasts: the frozen blood that thaws at her conception, for example.

She pictures her grandmother in her native Uzbek and imagines her daily occupations. Most of the images surrounding her grandmother evoke sustenance and nurturance; yet, the implication is that the tasks of farm life and motherhood took her away from a life of creativity. At the end of stanza 3, the grandmother beckons to the narrator to join her in a cyclic ritual, and the narrator feels connected, linked to both womanhood and her personal history, despite the differences in the two women's ages and experience.

It is unclear as to where her grandmother leads her; blood reappears here in the footprints pointing away from the house—away from domestic chores and responsibilities. That blood could be creative or destructive; the grandmother seems ready for an escape, a quick getaway. Perhaps she is the victim of a pogrom, or perhaps she is merely running away from the drudgery of being a farm wife.

Stanzas 5 through 10 offer a different cycle, beginning and ending with the tomato worms. Now, more realistically, the narrator paints pictures in the life of her grandmother: her appearance, her knowledge, her life-style. Interspersed are comments spoken by the grandmother herself, phrases etched in a young girl's memory but now recalled only in fragments. In all these memories is a sense of loss, of an opportunity that passes all too quickly, leaving one's life already determined and perhaps wasted. All the images used to describe the grandmother are closely allied with the natural world and with religion. The child can re-create the image of the grandmother and walk in her footsteps but with a difference of removal through space and time.

In stanza 5, the narrator burns tomato worms and strings useless gourds. Symbolically, she destroys the male principle and finds her own fertility, or productivity, equally destitute. In stanza 10, the tomatoes, complete with their worms, are brought into the home and retained and accepted rather than destroyed—salvaged at the last minute from the destruction of the frost. Even though the narrator can imaginatively experience the pain of achieving sexual maturity through the life of her grandmother and its expansion to archetypal dimensions, she cannot avoid the experience herself, and her time has arrived. The scene is set, but there is a confusion as to its nature: It can be both destructive and creative. Nature seems to encourage her boldness, offering her examples at every turn. She enacts her rite of sexual passage in stanza 12.

Stanza 13 gives a glimpse of the narrator after becoming a woman. Ironically, the passage has not brought her clarity of vision but rather reveals that the answers are simply in the living. Her grandmother had her own truth and keeps it to herself; the narrator must also find her own answers and cope with the pain of existence on her own.

Forms and Devices

The thirteen sections of the poem intermix memorial reconstruction of the grandmother's life, the actual voice of the grandmother, and the narrator's personal history revolving around the hardships and rhythms of a life linked to the land.

The poem attains unity through alliteration and assonance. Although it does not rhyme, the repetition of consonant and vowel sounds lends the poem an air of mystery and remoteness, as if it were an incantation.

This remoteness takes the poem away from the specific details of the narrator's life and memory of her grandmother and renders it archetypal, that is, an enduring and endlessly recurring pattern of human behavior. All the images and symbols of the poem align themselves along poles of masculinity and femininity. For the male principle, there are the tomato worms, logs, bonfires, cucumbers, gladioli, daggers, and knives; for the female, there are the gourds, tomatoes, apples, beads, candles and the worship of the Virgin Mary, hearts, and the moon.

The recurring image of blood points to the ambivalence that the poem retains from beginning to end. In ancient cultures, the wedding sheets were hung on the clothesline the day after the marriage to show the entire community by means of the bloodstains that the bride was a virgin and that the union had been consummated. Nature teaches the necessity of fertility and renewal, yet blood also appears at destruction, as when animals dying in traps bleed on the snow. Humankind seems to be the agent of destruction indicated by the blood, yet humans are also necessary partners in the renewal of life.

The central section of the poem employs the trope called metonymy, which is the use of a crucial part of something to represent the whole. The hands of the grandmother—both their potential and the actual work that they do—tell her entire story. Other female images reinforce the feeling of magic and transformation traditionally associated with women: worship of the moon, tending to growth and sustenance, the mysteries of birth. Yet, if procreation is a natural and necessary process, it is hard to account for pain in the world. Interestingly, the female initiate feels like an animal of prey, as suggested by the analogy to the rabbit in stanza 11.

Themes and Meanings

"Burning the Tomato Worms" is more of an experience than a statement of specific and definitive meaning. It dramatizes a rite of passage into womanhood, the sexual awakening of a girl who, through that passage, finds the dark bond that links her to all other women. It depicts the necessity of succumbing to the processes of being human, which entails both joy and pain. The poem affirms the importance of relations, especially familial relations, in establishing a personal identity. It enjoins the reader to live according to her own inner promptings and personal history at the same time as it reveals the inexorable and universal processes that unite all women, all humanity.

Returning to the epigraph with which the poem began, the reader may consider the poem an attempt to tell a truth, to capture both the personal and universal inherent in a single experience. "Burning the Tomato Worms" explores the ways in which an individual acquires knowledge and constructs truths, a process that logic and reason cannot necessarily capture. The end of the poem implies, too, that truth is neither simple nor clear. Like many poems, "Burning the Tomato Worms" requires the reader to accept the ambiguous and the paradoxical in life.

Sandra K. Fischer

BUT SO AS BY FIRE

Author: George Oppen (1908-1984)
Type of poem: Lyric
First published: 1972; collected in *Seascape: Needle's Eye*, 1972

The Poem

George Oppen's "But so as by Fire" is a poem in free verse, its twenty-six short lines divided into thirteen verse paragraphs resembling brief phrases. The paragraphs, or phrases, vary in length from one to four lines. The title suggests an alternative to the effects of fire—effects achieved by something else as though "by fire." Fire often triggers new growth, as seen, for example, in the forest after a fire. Another fitting example within the poem's context is the rebirth of the mythological phoenix from the ashes of its own fiery death. The word "fire" is not in the poem; the regenerative connotation is unspoken.

There is immediacy of place in the first sixteen lines of the poem as the reader observes "this" life that is guarded by the trees' dark shade. Describing and extolling the virtues of nature are frequent themes of lyric poetry. In this poem, the "magic" of the natural world is protected by darkness, a significant departure from most poems about nature, wherein darkness is associated with fear or even death. The darkness here is not forbidding but nurturing.

The first two paragraphs present the larger picture, from a viewpoint of some distance—a general image of thick-foliaged woods covering the rocky ground. Then, suddenly, the author focuses in on his subject, and the images become more specific. The next four paragraphs—lines 7 through 14—detail the world under the trees. Broken boughs on the ground foster the decomposition cycle, as new life sprouts from the rotting matter on the ground. Small animals thrive in protective shadows, and pools, not stagnant but clean with the "trickle of freshwater," nourish the healthy life cycle.

The shift in perspective from the small, detailed world of the woods to the world of humanity begins in paragraph 7. The only punctuation in the poem occurs in line 15 as all that has gone before is identified, emphasized, and set apart by the comma and the white space after the phrase "New life." Oppen's poetry often involves clean-cut silences framing words; the usage here is consistent with the "beauty of silence" of the shadowed world.

The rich compost generates its own gentle heat on the forest floor and engenders new life. Unrealized potential is intimated in the "hidden starry life" that is "not yet/ A mirror like our lives." In paragraphs 8 through 10, the speaker intensifies his focus on struggling humanity and speaks with inclusive spokesmanship, likening "our lives" to a mirror: hiding nothing in light and reflecting mere copy images. Nothing new is produced in a mirror, in sharp contrast to the new life created by decay in the shaded forest.

In the generalizing manner of the sage, the poet muses in the last four lines (three concise phrases) that, paradoxically, light is to be feared more than shadows. He implies that in the silent dark places, literally and figuratively, are found possibilities, creativity, and strength to "Summon one's powers."

Forms and Devices

Precision of language is characteristic of Oppen's poetry. It is evident in the compressed language and spare method used in the poem as well as in Oppen's use of imagery. Oppen's poetry is most approachable through its imagery. As John Taggart states in an essay entitled "Deep Jewels: George Oppen's *Seascape*," in the journal *Ironwood* (1985), "Oppen has chosen to stand fast to the conception of image as center, foundation, and base for composition."

Oppen's imagery renders the abstract in concrete terms throughout the poem. For example, the new life generated by "the dark green moss/ In the sweet smell of rot" conveys the poem's concept of darkness as nurturer. Plain and original dispensing of ordinary words mark the precise and concrete imagery.

As with the objectivist method of poetry that he helped to originate in the 1930's, Oppen strove for a new refinement of imagery toward a poetry of simplicity and most important, thought. Imagery involves only the eye, but objectivism engages both the eyes and the mind equally. Oppen once said that in his poetry he was trying to describe how "the test of images can be a test of whether one's thought is valid." Consistent with that statement, in this poem the imagery is arresting, but its thrust is toward thought.

This thrust toward thought is accomplished in three ways. The first is characteristic of Oppen's bare, terse style. The language may be spare, but with a single word it can establish an attitude or a mood. The "thin ground/ That covers the rock ledge" is rendered beautiful because it is "magic." The darkness is not fearsome for it "guards" life. The rot is "sweet" smelling. Clearly, the organic structures are generated to lead toward thought.

Key patterns of sound accompany the word pictures in the second method of supporting the poem's meaning. The alliteration is subtle, but in this poetry of such reticence that it almost moves toward silence, compression and precision of language give each letter greater significance. Gentle, explosive *b* sounds link and grant "beauty" to "broken boughs." One can sense the forest's subtle regenerative heat in the quiet hiss of the phrase "moss/ In the sweet smell of rot." In contrast, the assonance in "lives reflect light/ like mirrors" is loudly bright and penetrating.

Finally, it is the combination of imagery and didacticism that leads the reader to meditative conclusions. The shadow imagery suggests protection and creativity. When, however, attention is turned to the situation in which humanity finds itself—exposed in light and "gone/ As far as possible"—the tone becomes didactic. The positive connotations of darkness—the images of safety in shadows—are replaced by the shock of rhetoric that defines the stated paradox that the danger to humanity exists in the light, not in the darkness. For example, the poet asks who knew "To be afraid/ Not of shadow but of light." Thus is traditional thought undermined by the restrained but powerful amalgam of statement with imagery. The "test of images" successfully guides the reader to final, thoughtful conclusions.

Themes and Meanings

"But so as by Fire" is a poem about regeneration. A frequent theme in poetry, with roots in ancient mythology, regeneration is typically perceived as a fount of possibility, creativity, and strength. That perception applies literally to organic life, as seen in the womblike environment of the forest in the poem, and figuratively to the mind and to the works of humanity.

In reality, fire often triggers rebirth in the forest, but the poem offers the organic life in the shaded forest as its representation of the beauty of the regenerative cycle. It then explores the subject further and declares that not only has humanity turned away from nurturing its own dark pockets of vision and apparently lost figurative regenerative capabilities but also there appears to be a tragic inevitability about the process.

The poem represents the loss by likening "our lives" (although the pronoun is ambiguous, the poet's inclusivity indicates the modern society all humans share) to mirrors. What is reflected in a mirror is not substantive and is not creatively new — it is a copy. Compared to the activity of rebirth in the darkened, symbiotic forest, humankind can be said to have lost all forward momentum. The poem implies that humans are stalled, creativity blocked, and that they stand exposed and vulnerable in the light that they themselves sought, having rejected the internal quiet, shadowed places out of fear of the dark. The poem does not explain further as to what light it means or in what way humans have "Gone/ As far as is possible." The effort is simply to lay out the human facts more clearly, to describe what it means to investigate the human condition.

The suggested inevitability of the move from the occurrence of regeneration to the figurative loss of it in humanity renders the poem nearly tragic. The perception of the tragic in the poem can be defined as the ceaseless conflict (the terms of which are never quite clear) that cannot be won.

The evidence that the process is inevitable is most clear in two places in the poem. The first is in the finality of the past tense used in the phrase "We have gone/ As far as is possible." The second is in the prophetic outlook that the new life, the "Hidden starry life," is not "yet" attained. The inference is clear: It is merely a matter of time.

"Hidden starry life" is a marvelous transitional image to demonstrate what it means to lose the strength of unrealized potential. A star is "hidden" while it gathers energy in the cool hydrogen gases of dark space, but after it ignites into fiery visibility, it begins consuming its own gases until its eventual death.

The poem ponders whether humanity will regenerate somehow, "as by fire," as life in the forest does, and find new possibilities. There are no answers given in the poem, although the tone remains upbeat. The exhortation is, after all, to "Summon one's powers," even if for no other reason than for courage to face the inevitable.

Marilyn Schultz

BUTTERFLY

Author: Nelly Sachs (1891-1970)
Type of poem: Lyric
First published: 1949, as "Schmetterling," in *Sternverdunkelung*; collected in *O the Chimneys*, 1967

The Poem

"Butterfly," written in free verse, consists of sixteen lines arranged in three groups of six, six, and four lines. At the core of the poem is a typical nature reverie, except that here the processes of observation and abstraction are reversed. In conventional nature poetry, observation of a concrete object inspires the poet to achieve a deeper insight, but in this poem the actual butterfly is embedded in interpretive associations. As the poet contemplates the butterfly, two different images are summoned. The first image, a visionary flight from the center of the earth, can be regarded as an association inspired by the second image, a butterfly lighting on a rose.

The poem begins with the poet directly addressing the butterfly and admiring its beautiful colors. Paradoxically, its colorfulness is tied to the image of dust and the concept of "aftermath." The presence of dust is easily explained in terms of a natural phenomenon—when one lightly brushes a butterfly's wings, a powdery residue remains. Yet dust connotes death as well: "For dust you are and to dust you shall return" (Genesis 3:19). In view of this second interpretation of dust, the connection to "aftermath" and the implied destruction is clearer.

The poet's subsequent observation is equally contradictory on the surface. The reader is told that the butterfly has made the journey from the earth's flaming core, passing through the stony outer layer. These cataclysmic images of fire and stone conflict with the butterfly's fragility. If one remains on the level of visual association, one can picture how the butterfly has caught some of the fire's luminosity in the vibrant coloring of its wings. One might also appreciate the lapidary quality of its markings, like brilliant enamels fired in a kiln. The final line of this section, however, "Webs of farewell in the transient measure," invites one to consider the butterfly's journey in metaphoric terms. One is confronted with the concepts of death and transition.

Next the poet hails the butterfly as a creature of night, not in a demoniac sense, but a blessed one. This is a highly unusual label for the butterfly, which depends on sunlight for its survival. It has been suggested by Matthias Krieg that the butterfly's positive connection to the night lies in its being an image of dreams. If one considers the dream state as one of transition between consciousness and unconsciousness, then the projection of life's and death's burden onto the butterfly's delicate wings follows logically. Finally one arrives at the concrete image of the butterfly coming to rest on a rose. For a moment the butterfly is only a butterfly, not an abstract fusion of life and death, stasis and transition.

These ideas, however, permeate the poem's atmosphere and are transposed onto the wilting rose and fading sun in the last line of the second section.

Lines 13 and 14 repeat the opening pair of lines. Here the butterfly's colorful designs become abstract as they are transposed into the realm of metaphor and are transformed into a system of signs. The grammatical ambiguity of the final lines deliberately leaves the reader alternating between viewing the butterfly as a royal sign or as bearing a royal sign. The question is unresolved, but the reverential implication of "royal" bespeaks an optimistic faith in the order of the world. The butterfly becomes the ultimate symbol of signs and their meanings, carrying on its wings a mysterious, yet kingly, system of ciphers.

Forms and Devices

"Butterfly" contains no traditional metrical patterns, but the poem achieves a lyrical quality through its evocative associations and descriptions. It opens with a direct address to the butterfly and continues as an extended apostrophe. The poet's one-sided discourse consists of admiring epithets and descriptions.

The principal poetic device used by Nelly Sachs is the metaphor. This poem provides an excellent example of how she expands and adapts a metaphor, creating an all-inclusive symbol. The multiple possibilities of her metaphor's meaning exist somewhere between conventional references and a highly personal system of associations inspired by biographical experiences and a study of mysticism—both Jewish and Christian.

The butterfly traditionally evokes spring, renewal, and hope. Deeply bound to the sun for survival, it is connected to the symbolism of light, representing optimism and enlightenment. Its vibrant coloring is another aspect of this connection to the positive symbolism of light; hence, the butterfly is ascribed yet another abstract dimension. In many Western cultures it also serves as an icon for the soul, capturing visually the moment of the soul's separation from the body in death. So, too, does Sachs's butterfly carry a message that speaks to the human condition.

For the most powerful implications of this metaphoric butterfly, one must turn to the biological fact that the butterfly is a creature of metamorphosis. Its beautiful, evocative form is but a phase; indeed, it already has one "death" behind it—the death of the pupa. The butterfly carries a dual association: It symbolizes at once death (or the transient quality of life) and a hopeful cycle of renewal. The English version of this poem inclines one to favor the more pessimistic interpretation of the butterfly, for it translates the word *Jenseits* as "aftermath," which has decidedly negative connotations. *Jenseits* literally means "beyond" and indicates the afterlife or immortality. In one other instance the English translation opts for a darker view: The rose "withers," when in the original language it "wilts" in the fading sun. A wilting rose is part of a cycle of regeneration, as is the setting sun, while withering implies a more permanent state of decay. In the German text, then, the concepts of death and renewal do not form a duality of opposition; rather, they coexist as aspects of natural life and allow for a transcendence beyond its limitations.

Themes and Meanings

In Nelly Sachs's mature poetry, one finds echoes of her childhood passion for the fossils and insects that she studied as keys to nature's secrets. Later, as she tried to understand a distorted world which had engendered the Holocaust, she returned to this realm and found a rich source of symbols and metaphors. Her poem focuses on natural phenomena that emphasize constant flux and the potential for transformation, making it an especially poignant statement in the light of the historical background against which she wrote.

Sachs, who received the Nobel Prize for Literature in 1966, was known as the "poet of the Holocaust." This particular poem appeared in a volume of poetry dedicated to commemorating its victims and understanding their suffering. The butterfly is a recurring image in this collection, where it serves most often as an icon for the souls of the innocent. In this poem, however, the individual's metamorphosis through death is placed in the context of the earth's life cycles: The butterfly symbolically embraces a phase of transformation lasting eons (the planet's core is constantly creating) and one lasting a single day. Each end leads to a new beginning. The pain of leavetaking, of death, is not erased, but is mitigated by the promise of renewal. Thus did Sachs attempt to come to terms with the senseless deaths of her people during the Holocaust.

The metaphor is the poem's formative poetic device as well as its thematic content. In writing poetry, Sachs faced an unusual dilemma: The language she used, German, was also the language of the oppressor. Moreover, the experiences of her time seemed overwhelming and inexpressible. Her solution was her system of metaphors. At a time when many poets were experimenting with meaninglessness and with the arbitrariness of language, her metaphoric approach allowed her, in a sense, to reinvent her language. The metaphoric butterfly expresses the paradoxical relationship between death and transformation. It is the "royal sign" which encodes the patterns of this mystery and serves as an example of Sachs's transformed language in which words seem to include concepts and their opposites. When confronted with such paradoxes, one is indeed challenged to reconsider assumptions about how narrowly one perceives the world and one's position in it.

Elisabeth Strenger

BYPASSING RUE DESCARTES

Author: Czesław Miłosz (1911-   )
Type of poem: Lyric
First published: 1982, as "Rue Descartes," in *Hymn o perle*; collected in *The Separate Notebooks*, 1984

The Poem

"Bypassing Rue Descartes" is a poem thirty-five lines long and arranged in ten irregular stanzas. The poem is written in the first person, as is traditional in lyric poetry. The poet remembers a walk taken in Paris, which occasions a meditation on history, exile, and guilt. The poem has the qualities of nostalgia and intimacy that insist the poem is autobiographical rather than a portrayal of a persona.

"Bypassing Rue Descartes" (which was tellingly retitled in translation from simply "Rue Descartes") describes a walk the poet, "A young barbarian just come to the capital of the world," took that initiated his life as an exile from Lithuania and Poland. The title establishes a place and a locus for meditation. The poet, however, bypasses this street and figuratively bypasses what this street signifies: Cartesian certainty, with its insistence on analysis and division. Bypassing Rue Descartes, the poet descends toward the Seine, hence proposing a traditional departure from abstraction and a movement toward nature.

The poem's first stanza establishes the poet's place and identity. In the second stanza, the poet considers himself one among many exiled nationalities, including Poles, North Africans, and Vietnamese. Implicit in his catalog is the history of empires and colonialism. The poem continues, describing the difference between the immigrant's customs, "About which nobody here should ever be told," and the cosmopolitan world. While the poet is speaking from his own experience, he also is describing the condition of the exile. The poet contrasts his homeland's "cloudy provinces" with the "universal" city he enters "dazzled and desiring."

In the fourth and fifth stanzas, both of which are unrhymed couplets, the poet shifts to a conditional future that describes certain specific political conditions. In these lines, the tone is clipped, aphoristic, and ironic. Readers should recall that when Czesław Miłosz permanently left Poland for France in late 1951, France was the colonial power in Algeria and Vietnam. Nationalists of both these countries were active in Paris, hence many of these exiles "Would be killed because they wanted to abolish the customs of their homes." Many of their peers were "seizing power/ In order to kill in the name of the universal, beautiful ideas."

The poem returns to the specifics of the walk in the sixth stanza with the sensuous catalog of a street market: rustling laughter in the dark, baked breads, lemons and garlic, and wine poured from clay pitchers. These sights and sounds return the poet to the immediate and commonplace world, yet his meditations on empire and power are not mitigated, for the poet finds he is surrounded by monuments attesting periods of glory. What these monuments represent, however, is forgotten.

The final four stanzas consist of a movement toward a vision of time where empires always rise and fall. This traditional vision of fortune is then displaced by a more earthly, almost pagan, vision that "the time of human generations is not like the time of the earth." The large vision narrows to focus on the poet, and the poem concludes with the poet's confession of his own guilt.

Forms and Devices

Although "Bypassing Rue Descartes" is essentially a lyric, Miłosz is a poet who never rests easily in a single recognizable form. Like many of his other poems, this one is allegorical and ironic. It also shares with Miłosz's prose writing a philosophical interest in the nature of power. Because the poem continually verges on the allegorical and philosophical, and departs from the personal or lyrical, it contains elements of generalization.

The city of Paris is named through its epithet, "the capital of the world." The city then becomes "the universal," suggesting not only its cosmopolitan atmosphere but also its metaphysical absoluteness. It is a manifestation of *idea*. The poet quickly undercuts this portrayal with the personification of the city behaving in accordance with its nature ("Rustling" with laughter, "baking" breads, "pouring wine," "buying" garlic and fish), all the while shamelessly indifferent. Though this lists the commonplace, Miłosz uses its vitality and the sense of being engrossed with the transactions of life to contrast with the attraction of the exiled to the "universal."

The poem employs the classical allegorical structure of the journey to convey meaning. Like the pilgrim Dante, the young exile Miłosz makes a descending journey toward revelation. The journey from postwar Poland into exile also is implied as part of this allegorical journey. When the poet reaches the Seine and leans on the "rough granite of the embankment," he senses he has "returned from travels through the underworlds." Like Dante, he has witnessed the cataclysms of history. At the river's edge, symbolically another threshold, he "suddenly saw in the light the reeling wheel of the seasons/ Where empires have fallen and those once living are now dead." Not simply a traditional view of the vicissitudes of Fortuna, the poet assumes the role of prophet. Much in the tradition of Ecclesiastes, the poet sees the emptiness of human existence and the need for dispensations other than those offered by politics and philosophy.

If the first part of the poem can be considered ironic (the poet self-deprecatingly calls himself a "young barbarian," which echoes Constantine Cavafy's poem "Waiting for the Barbarians"; the decidedly ironic repetition of "Soon enough" marks the fate of exiles involved in politics) and the second part an allegorical vision, then the third part, the last two stanzas, returns to the personal but without the opening stanzas' ironic detachment. The poem turns to an earlier memory of a walk through a forest, where the poet encountered a water snake coiled in the grass and killed it. The poem concludes with a deeply personal memory and a profoundly symbolic image. While one may wish to assign a biblical meaning to the snake, one must note that it is a water snake and that in Lithuanian folklore these creatures are sacred;

hence, it is taboo to harm them, as Miłosz states in a footnote to the poem. The poem describes the poet's exile from nature in that he has committed a transgression against life.

Themes and Meanings

"Bypassing Rue Descartes" is a deceptively complex poem. Among its considerations are exile, the mutability of power through time, and guilt. The poem's journey is in many ways a searching back to reach a personal moment of guilt, an original but personal sin that has resulted in what amounts to a life of punishment and purgation through the condition of exile. That everyone has committed transgressions against life, that everyone is guilty of destruction, is the human condition and not one borne of a strictly religious sensibility. Insofar as everyone is guilty of transgression, everyone lives in a condition of exile.

"Bypassing Rue Descartes" implicitly asks: For what do we live? It does not ask the question of dogma—how do we live?—but the question of choices, responses, and responsibilities. The poem offers many dichotomies: civilized-barbarian, abstraction-sensuousness, metaphysical-tangible, empire-local, universal-specific, and death-life. It traces the poet's movement from desiring the universal to understanding it as part of the complex of empire, dogmatic politics, abstraction, and finally the force of death—the same force that has driven him into exile.

The poem insists on life: the sensuous particularity of life as illustrated by the catalogs of the provincial customs and the details of the street market as well as the symbolic value of the water snake as a sign of generative forces. The emphasis on the fully lived moment is found throughout Miłosz's poetry, as exemplified by "Rivers," "It Was Winter," "A Poetic State," "Reading the Japanese Poet Issa (1762-1826)," or the movement of the entire collection of poems *Nieobjęta ziemia* (1984), translated as *Unattainable Earth* (1986).

Miłosz's poetry exemplifies what has become known as the poetry of witness. His work has revolved consistently around the question of history and the individual's position within history. Poetry, for Miłosz, is the witnessing of history. Poetry thus serves as memory; however, poetry is also moral, in that daily it stands before what is real and it must name that reality. "Bypassing Rue Descartes" is not a rejection of history, but an understanding of mutability. To be a witness, one must also be willing to bear responsibility of one's guilt, which comes at the very moment of the exercise of power. No one can escape the judgment of history, for "just punishment/ . . . reaches, sooner or later, the breaker of a taboo."

James McCorkle

BYZANTIUM

Author: William Butler Yeats (1865-1939)
Type of poem: Lyric
First published: 1932, in *Words for Music Perhaps*

The Poem

"Byzantium" is written in five eight-line stanzas that are, in their metrical precision and complex rhyme scheme, reminiscent of the unique stanzaic patterns of the early nineteenth century odes composed by such English Romantic poets as William Wordsworth, Percy Bysshe Shelley, and John Keats. The twentieth century Anglo-Irish poet William Butler Yeats certainly shares many traits with those, and other, nineteenth century precursors. Nevertheless, despite all the intensity of its emotion and the rich intricacies of its imagery, "Byzantium" is hardly the sort of effusive outburst one has come to associate with the ode; the speaker seems to be more engulfed in his vision than in any attempt to share its emotional quadrants with the reader.

"Byzantium" takes its name from an ancient city upon whose site the Roman Emperor Constantine constructed his eastern, Christian capital about A.D. 330. Called Nova Roma, that city eventually became known as Constantinopolis and is the modern-day Turkish city Istanbul. For more than a thousand years the capital of the Byzantine Empire, it was regarded as the premier city of the Western world. While Yeats prefers the city's older name, there is no doubt that his Byzantium is medieval Constantinople.

As the poem begins, night is falling. The day's sights and even the night's sounds draw back, leaving the reader's undistracted senses free to explore other realms of reality and ranges of experience. Soon it is after midnight. The soldiers' nightly revelries have ended, although a "night walker," who may simply be someone out very late or a streetwalker plying her trade, is singing, and in the "great cathedral," the Hagia Sophia, the gong that calls the faithful to prayer has already rung.

In this dreamy atmosphere, pregnant with mystery and anticipation, "A starlit or a moonlit dome disdains" all that human beings are—human complexities and the "fury and the mire" of human veins. That dome may be the night sky or it may be the dome of the Hagia Sophia. Earthbound in this most worldly of cities, an imperial capital, the speaker reminds the reader of that extreme emblem of power and glory, the boundless heavens that dwarf the scope of the human imagination, let alone human accomplishments, let alone one mere mortal.

As if he, too, has been called to prayer and is inspired by this setting to free his spirit of its sensory limitations, the speaker now has a vision. He cannot be certain if the image he sees is a man or a shade—that is, a ghost—although it is an image apparently so awesome in its reality that it overwhelms him to such an extent that he does not know if he is alive or dead—or what life or death is. Yielding to the strength of his vision, he "hail[s] the superhuman;/ I call it death-in-life and life-in-death."

The vision increases in its intensity as the darkened physical world all about him is transfigured. He is "seeing" with the mind's eye—although it would be more proper, given the quasi-religious tone of much of the imagery thus far, to imagine the so-called third eye of the mystic. The reader now sees a golden bird that may be a miracle, a real bird, or a man-made, mechanical bird. The speaker decides that it is a miraculous bird; it is "Planted on the starlit golden bough" and "by the moon embittered." The imagery recalls the disdainful dome of the opening stanza, for the bird also "scorn[s] aloud" the day's commonplaces and "all complexities of mire or blood."

In the fourth stanza, the visionary frenzy increases as the reader is swept up with the speaker "into a dance,/ An agony of trance." Flames are flitting on the pavement. These are not the result of the fires of our physical world, however, but are manifestations of the fire of the spirit. Although they are begotten of blood, those spirits who have finally transcended their physical being—that "fury and mire"—are escaping the purgatorial fires that have cleansed them of their worldliness.

In the last stanza, the vision is fulfilled, and the reader is allowed to see the liberated souls of the dead. "Astraddle on the dolphin's mire and blood," these souls have breached all those earthly and sensory barriers that in life normally confine one to the prosaic plane of this world. As if on a floodtide that bursts like a fountain up from the midnight streets of ancient Byzantium, the spirits make their journey to the Isle of the Blessed across "That dolphin-torn, that gong-tormented sea" that divides the living both from their peace and from the ultimate source of the speaker's vision.

Forms and Devices

Yeats never abandoned the Symbolist tradition that shaped him as a poet in his youth. Though "Byzantium" is a product of his later years, written well after he had transformed himself into a modernist poet, surely the chief device that gives the poem its other-worldly ambiance is the symbol.

Indeed, in Yeats's view, only the symbolic can express the highest truths, for symbols are "hints too subtle for the intellect"—that is, they can speak to the deeper and more enduring faculties that are generally categorized as the soul. Furthermore, the symbol can do so with an incredible economy, whereby a series of symbols in the right combination can encompass the sorts of truths that would require reams of philosophical discourse to approximate.

By the same token, Yeats was himself too serious a student and seeker of human enlightenment to trust to the unregenerate dream imagery that often beguiles the visionary poet. Thus all his life he steeped himself in traditional symbologies—ancient Celtic lore; occult symbolism and ritual, including astrology; and, finally, the rich Christian iconography of Byzantine Europe.

Yeats's studies had taught him that the ancient Romans used dolphins to depict the spirit's voyage from this world to the next; that the starry dome was symbolic of the soul's astral destiny in the ancient mystery cults associated with Mithra and

Orpheus; that a crowing cock carved on a tombstone was intended to ward off evil spirits and influences; that the Byzantine emperors had mechanical birds that sang to the delight of visitors; that the golden bough signifies that point at which the temporal and eternal mingle their mysteries. Precisely how these and other symbols that Yeats half appropriated and half created combine to form new or larger meanings in his poetry is left, as it should be, to the creative energies of each reader.

Themes and Meanings

While the symbol may leave the analytical mind that eschews speculative reasoning high and dry, Yeats's poetry is not incapable of yielding precise meanings, even if they remain debatable. If one can balance the symbolic coordinates, "Byzantium" yields a rich harvest.

It is generally accepted, for example, that Byzantium is for Yeats a city of art to which the soul might escape whenever the pressures or sheer corruption of the world in particular and the physical universe in general become too much to bear. Much of this sort of reading of "Byzantium" is based on pairing that poem with comments Yeats made in a long prose work entitled *A Vision* (1925, 1937), as well as with another, earlier Yeats poem, "Sailing to Byzantium," which does seem to express a desire to escape from the decay and tedium of cyclical nature and which also mentions a golden bird.

On a wholly spiritual level, "Byzantium" clearly does contrast the mere mundane level of daylight vision with the infinitely richer possibilities that contemplations of the eternal and the miraculous offer. If the poem seems to trivialize day-to-day despairs and travails, it does so by asserting that enduring glories that are as yet unimagined, albeit hinted at in the symbols and icons of artistic and religious traditions, will eventually reward the patient soul.

The less one categorizes the nature of these glories—whether they are religious or aesthetic—of the eternal and spiritual or of the temporal and perceptual, the more one can appreciate Yeats's main point that they are in fact transcendent and beyond corruption, and are therefore unchanging.

Thus the "superhuman" that the speaker hails can be Yeats's way of suggesting that humanity has yet to achieve its full potential in the capacity to imagine a transcendent reality. The poem also comments on that element of the divine that seems to commingle irresistibly with humanity's mortal nature, creating the complexities and confusions and conflicts on which the poem comments. This divine element could be the Christ, who, in the Byzantine image called the Pantokrator, represented in Yeats's view the apogee of all Western thought and development to that moment in history and so seemed, as an image, to embody the perfection the race is perpetually seeking in its visionary quests.

Russell Elliott Murphy

CALIFORNIA SWIMMING POOL

Author: Sharon Olds (1942-   )
Type of poem: Lyric
First published: 1987, in *The Gold Cell*

The Poem

"California Swimming Pool" is a short poem in free verse. It is made up of five long, descriptive sentences, which form one stanza. In it, the poet evokes the mood—the sounds, the sights, the atmosphere, and the intrigue—of summer afternoons at a public swimming pool.

The scene is described from a young girl's perspective, most likely a girl approaching puberty. She speaks informally in the first person, remembering the scene, using the conversational "you" to describe the place and what she did and saw there. Sharon Olds often describes personal experiences in her poems; in fact, many of her poems are clearly autobiographical. Thus, the speaker, who is actually an adult looking back on herself as a girl, is probably indistinguishable from the poet herself.

The first two sentences set the scene. Around the pool, the poet recalls, the dead leaves "lay like dried-out turtle shells," and the air was filled with summer insects: "sated" mosquitoes and yellow jackets. The bright sun and intense heat of a California summer are easily evoked. The leaves were "scorched and crisp," and mosquitoes hung in the air. As the poet describes it, not only does the weather seem oppressive but also the mood, which borders on the sinister: The dead leaves have "points sharp as wasps' stingers," and the mosquitoes are compared to sharks. Even the yellow jackets, usually harmless if annoying, "moved when you moved," in a threatening manner implying the futility of escape.

In fact, for the poet, there was no escape. A ritual, common and irresistible, unfolded daily, and the boys and girls of summer were participants in the ceremony. The site for the ritual, the "great pool" around which "everything circled," is described as if it were in an ancient temple, its water "blue and/ glittering as the sacred waters at Crocodilopolis." Furthermore, there was even the ritual of mock sacrifice when "the boys came from underwater . . ./ to pull you down." The swimming pool in which the children played becomes in the poet's memory a sacred place where the youngsters performed their own rites of passage, marking their entrances into adulthood.

That transformation naturally included the girl's first knowledge of sex—an awareness of her own sexual feelings and a curiosity about the sexuality of others. That is why "the true center was the/ dressing rooms," because behind the splintered pine wall "were boys, actually/ naked there in air clouded as the/ shadows at the bottom of the pool. . . ." As part of her initiation into adulthood, the girl seeks sexual knowledge. The reader is reminded, however, that she suspected the quest was dangerous: The bottom of the pool was "where the crocodiles/ glistened in their slick skins." Boys—and the power of sexuality—are like crocodiles, fascinating yet threatening, even deadly.

Nevertheless, the urge to sacrifice herself for sexual knowledge was hard to resist—temptation (in the form of a knothole in the pine wall), says the poet, "hissed at me" all summer. Thus, the poem ends with an allusion to Eve's temptation by the serpent, and the girl (not yet a woman) considering the invitation to partake of the forbidden fruit: "*come see, come see, come eat and be eaten.*"

Forms and Devices

In "California Swimming Pool," the poet's vantage point in time and maturity lends an irony to this description of the summertime experience of a girl on the threshold of sexual awakening. The poet speaks in the past tense; she has had time to reflect on her experiences. In other words, the speaker (and perhaps the reader) fondly recalls as well as painfully relives what will happen—what did happen—in the weeks or months after the summer scene this poem describes. The girl in the poem, however, is still an innocent, no matter how attuned she has become to the forbidden pleasures and hidden dangers of sex and boys.

"California Swimming Pool" is packed so full of concrete language that it has the richness and density of a copiously arranged still life. Olds does not rely on rhyme or strict meter to give her poem unity and form; she uses related images to "hinge" the four sentences together. The dead leaves "like dried-out turtle shells," with "points sharp as wasps' stingers" and the "sated" mosquitoes "like sharks" are similes that suggest not only the summer climate but also the peril later clearly associated with the boys. These images create an aura of danger and prepare the reader for the later comparisons, which are bolder.

The central metaphor describes the boys as crocodiles, coming from underwater "to pull you down" and lying in shadows at the bottom of the pool "in their slick skins." The references to predators—mosquitoes, wasps, sharks, and finally crocodiles—unify the poem and reinforce the sense of unknown danger the poet then felt about her attraction to the opposite sex.

The combined effect of these images is to transform the swimming pool into a magical, almost mythical place of sacred waters and fabulous beasts. The place at the center of the fable, however, is described in literal terms: The dressing rooms are familiar, with their "smell of chlorine" and their "cold concrete." It is almost as if the fantasy of the pool fades to stark reality in the dressing rooms, where "boys, actually naked" were for the girl a temptation all too real.

Themes and Meanings

Danger is probably not all that the girl sensed that summer, but her inexperience hindered a mature appreciation of her sexuality. Sex, a frequent theme in Olds's poetry, is often explored, always celebrated. She reveres and respects its power in human lives and rejoices in its power to express absolute love. For Olds, sex is a fundamental and needed language. So for the girl, the message of the hissing knothole was undeniable. The mysterious attraction of sex, for Olds, is similarly not to be denied.

The "clouded" air of the dressing rooms and the "shadows" in the pool are also accurate metaphors. The clouds and shadows hid and distorted the objects of the girl's curiosity; they represent the obstacles that the girl, in her quest for sexual knowledge, would have to confront and overcome. They also could represent her own naïve beliefs, possibly misconceptions, which might have impeded her quest.

The reference to "sacred waters" reinforces the idea of the girls and boys as initiates in an ancient ceremony. "Crocodilopolis" is an allusion to the Acropolis of Athens, Greece, site of some of the best-known ancient Greek temples and a sacred place of worship. This allusion suggests again that what encircled the "great pool" was worship of the sacred power of sexuality and the raw vitality of youth. The summer-long ceremony was a dance for the coming-of-age the youths were experiencing. At this temple of the crocodiles, the youths paid homage to themselves and to the waters of life.

In the popular imagination, crocodiles — direct descendants of prehistoric reptiles — are particularly fierce and terrifying. Their actions are propelled by millions of years of honed instinct. When a crocodile attacks, it is efficient and, to humans, remorseless. Yet these cold-blooded creatures fascinate human beings. They are savage yet awe-inspiring; they are beautiful.

In "California Swimming Pool," the crocodile becomes a symbol for sex, for its impenetrable mystery and powerful jaws, for its primitive attraction, and for its unspeakable beauty. This symbol vitalizes Olds's description of a young girl's first reckonings with her own sexual energy and power. The poem conveys the poet's awe for the beauty and mysterious power of sex and her deep reverence for the life force in everyone.

JoAnn Balingit

THE CANONIZATION

Author: John Donne (1572-1631)
Type of poem: Lyric
First published: 1633, in *Poems by J. D.: With Elegies on the Authors Death*

The Poem

The forty-five lines of John Donne's "The Canonization" are divided into five nine-line stanzas, a form that suggests a five-act play. The title reflects the speaker's conviction that in opposing the claims of the world (business, courtly ambitions), he and his beloved have become love's martyrs, and therefore saints.

The first-person speaker appears to be addressing an outsider who is unsympathetic to his romantic involvement and who has said as much prior to the first line. The poem, then, is a type of dramatic monologue, in which the speaker defends and later celebrates his love against the outsider's objection. In the first stanza, he commands the outsider to hold his tongue and tells him to scold him about being too old for love if he wishes, but not about being in love. He suggests that the outsider pursue his own ambitions or do whatever he likes, so long as he leaves him alone to love.

In the second stanza, the speaker adopts a defensive tone, arguing that no one is "injured" by his love, as the outsider may have charged. Donne employs several conventional Petrarchan metaphors (poetic clichés by that time), insisting that his lover's sighs have not sunk any merchant ships, nor has his heated passion caused an early spring to be delayed. He concludes that argumentative soldiers and lawyers can still bicker even though he finds contentment in love.

In the third stanza, the speaker reacts to apparent name-calling on the part of the outsider, insisting that he and his beloved are "flies" (in the diction of his age, moths or butterflies) or "tapers" (candles), which gain fullness of life even as they consume themselves. (Renaissance English poets commonly employed the word "die" as a sexual pun, based on the folk belief that each orgasm shortened one's life by a day.) Likening the physically and spiritually united lovers to the phoenix, a mythical bird that was thought to erupt into flame and then be resurrected from its own ashes, the speaker claims that they are proven "mysterious" (in the spiritual sense) by this ideal love. This constitutes the climax or turning point of this small drama.

Perhaps the outsider has now argued that the paradox is too much for him, for in the fourth stanza the speaker explains that if they do literally die from their love, it will be a martyrdom, and their saints' legend will be an appropriate subject for poetry (as this poem itself proves), so they will also live because of their love. He expands his point metaphorically by suggesting that if their love is not suitable for chronicles, it will do for sonnets, and that a carefully made funeral urn is as suitable for famous personages as "half-acre tombs" like the pyramids.

The last stanza amounts to an imagined prayer of intercession. In short, the busy world will request a "pattern" or model of ideal love from these martyrs, who have found in each other a peaceful "hermitage."

Forms and Devices

This poem is a triumph in the "complex stanza" form, which derives from the classical ode and which requires that the poet contrive a fresh rhyme scheme (*abbaccca* in the present case) and use a variable line length as well. The Donne employs a free iambic foot and a meter that varies from pentameter (ten syllables per line) in the first, third, fourth, and seventh lines to trimeter (six syllables) in the last line of each stanza. The remaining lines are in tetrameter (eight syllables). Donne frames each stanza by closing off the first and ninth lines with the word "love," which accordingly echoes throughout the poem.

Within the formal structure, Donne uses frequent balance and antithesis (as in line 2, in which "my palsy" is balanced with "my gout"). Occasionally this binary pattern, which operates throughout the poem, leads to paradox, for the speaker argues that the apparent dangers of passionate love actually sustain life in the best sense. The paradoxical pairing of the lover's "colds" (chills) and "heats" (fevers) in the second stanza are conventional and even somewhat playful, but the pairing of dying and rising later in the poem is more profound. Antitheses abound in the poem: chronicles/sonnets, well-wrought urn/half-acre tombs, peace/rage. These tend to counter the more obviously balanced pairs in the first stanza: "With wealth your state"/"your mind with arts," a course/a place (in court, presumably), His Honor/His Grace, "the King's real"/"or his stamped face" (on a coin).

The metaphorical play in this poem can be confusing to those who are unaware of the traditions and conventions of Renaissance poetry. The typical Petrarchan lover, for example, who is teased in the second stanza, was pictured as an unfortunate man who was spurned by his mistress and who consequently sighed up a storm, wept floods, and alternately suffered chills and fevers. Donne's lover is beloved in turn, so he does not suffer such maladies.

Donne draws on the emblem tradition for conventional metaphors in the second stanza. Emblem books in that era provided woodcuts or engravings that had moralizing mottoes and poems. The moth drawn to a deadly candle was one such emblem, as was the image of the eagle (representing physical power, often that of the male) and the dove (representing peace or spirituality). The phoenix was also a popular emblem.

Donne concludes his poem with a metaphor in which the lovers, staring into each other's eyes, reflect themselves and indeed the whole world, as represented by "Countries, towns, courts." They become, then, the epitome or summation of the universe.

Themes and Meanings

"The Canonization" argues for the superiority of love's unifying and reconciling potential over the divisive and antagonistic impulses of the ordinary world. In pursuing personal ambitions in business or at court, people like the imagined outsider and courtiers, soldiers, and lawyers trade serenity for strife. The speaker argues that an ideal love, which is both physical and spiritual, can provide a paradigm for the confused world, and he asserts that this poem proves his point.

The reference to the king in the first stanza causes some scholars to associate the poem with the accession of James I in 1604. Only three years earlier, Donne had put a disastrous halt to his own courtly ambitions when he eloped with Ann More, the ward of his employer, Sir Thomas Egerton, Lord Keeper of the Seal. Ann More's father had Donne blackballed, in effect, and the couple experienced severe financial strain for several years. This poem might be seen, then, as an explanation or even a justification of his apparently impulsive behavior.

If his intended audience for the poem was King James himself, Donne's appeal must have fallen on deaf ears, since another ten years were to pass before his fortunes improved. The marriage was apparently a happy one, however, and Ann Donne was to bear nine children before her death in 1617. John Donne did not remarry.

Ronald E. McFarland

CANTO 1

Author: Ezra Pound (1885-1972)
Type of poem: Poetic sequence
First published: 1925, in *A Draft of XVI Cantos*

The Poem

Canto 1 is the first poem in a long sequence of 120 cantos making up what the poet, Ezra Pound, conceived of as a twentieth century epic. Pound worked on the *Cantos* for nearly fifty years, weaving scores of subjects and themes into the longest important poetic work of the modern era. When he set out on his poetic odyssey, Pound conceived of his poem as a modern version of Dante's *The Divine Comedy* (c.1320); his intention was to mirror Dante's epic organization into "inferno," "purgatory," and "heaven." Pound, following Dante, called the individual units of the epic cantos.

When Pound finished Canto 1, in 1921, he had no idea what the final shape of his modern epic would be, but he was aware that this first canto would have to act as an overture to whatever followed. So in many ways, Canto 1 is a capsule form of many of the themes and poetic devices that would come in the succeeding cantos. At the same time, this poem reflects many of Pound's interests in subject and form that appear in his earlier works.

Canto 1 can be divided into two sections: The first, longer section (ending with "Lie quiet Divus") is drawn from the *Odyssey* (c.800 B.C.), Book XI, and certain other Homeric works; the second half is a pastiche, which, although it still refers directly to Odysseus, also echoes other classic poems, chiefly a Homeric hymn to Aphrodite.

Although the speaker in the earlier part of Canto 1 is clearly Odysseus, the personae in the poem's later parts are more difficult to identify. Odysseus speaks first, and is followed by a quotation from the blind sage Tiresias, whom Odysseus meets in his journey to the underworld. Then, at the line beginning "Lie quiet Divus," Pound himself intervenes as both epic storyteller and classical scholar.

The first half of the poem retells the story of Odysseus' journey to Hades: Odysseus describes setting out to find the entrance to Hades, which had been described to him by the sorceress Circe. His crew loads the ship, and they push off, sailing until they reach the "place aforesaid by Circe." There they perform sacred rites — pouring wine on the ground, saying prayers, sacrificing a sheep — to summon up the dead.

A number of souls appear, including one of Odysseus' crew, Elpenor, who had been killed accidentally when Odysseus and his men had been delayed by Circe. One night, having drunk too much, Elpenor fell off a ladder, breaking his neck ("shattered the nape-nerve"). He asks Odysseus to build a tomb for him, including his epitaph, "A man of no fortune, with a name to come." Then Anticlea, Odysseus' mother, appears, followed by Tiresias, from whom Odysseus wants a prophesy. Tiresias does foretell Odysseus' future, telling the hero that he will eventually return to his homeland but will lose all his shipmates in the process.

At this point in the poem, it is as though Pound the narrator looks up from the old book in which he has been reading Odysseus' story—the Latin translation by Andreas Divus, produced in 1538. Pound also finds in the back of this book some hymns said to be composed by Homer. One of these is a poem in praise of Aphrodite, and Pound ends Canto 1 by quoting the hymn's description of the goddess of love.

Forms and Devices

Although scholars argue about the exact verse structure of the *Cantos*, it is fair to say that generally Canto 1 is written in free verse—poetic lines that have no set rhythm or consistent number of feet and do not rhyme. This is not to say that Canto 1 is without structure: The first section of the poem echoes the rhythms of Anglo-Saxon poetry, while the final lines loosely mimic certain classic verse patterns.

The language that Pound uses in the first part of Canto 1 is that of the Old English "seafarer poet." The result is a story drawn from Greek literature told in the mock-language of early medieval England. Throughout the Cantos, Pound uses this kind of juxtaposition of subject matter drawn from one literary or historical period and poetic language drawn from another. In making such junctions, Pound's intention was to show the reader certain important similarities—in thought and feeling—between eras that might seem at first glance very different.

In this case, Pound believed that Odysseus and the anonymous seafarer from the European Dark Ages were spiritual brothers. Both were animated by the desire to sail unknown seas in small, perilous ships, simply for the sake of discovery. Both find that the discoveries they make have more to do with their own inner landscape than with the geography of new lands.

Devices echoing Anglo-Saxon poetry include reversal ("Circe's this craft," "unpierced ever,"), alliteration ("swart ship," "sun to his slumber"), and archaic language ("swart," "ell-square pitkin," "ingle," "bever," "fosse"). Overall, the rhythm of this section suggests the rolling of the small ship over the sea's breakers.

"Kennings," compound terms that describe metaphorically some common object, are another Anglo-Saxon poetic device used in Canto 1 ("nape-nerve" for "neck").

Pound wants his readers to pay close attention to his poem's sources, its allusions. Generally, allusion takes place in poetry through mention of a name, place, or idea associated with some other work of literature or with some historical event. More rarely, a poet may quote or mimic another writer. In the *Cantos*, however, Pound goes even further: In the section describing Odysseus' journey to the underworld, for example, Pound is freely translating a Latin translation (that of Divus) of Homer's original Greek. In the last lines ("Cypri munimenta sortita est," or "Cyprus is allotted to her"), Pound even reproduces Divus' exact words. Pound's abundant use of foreign languages throughout the Cantos—sometimes with English translations following, sometimes not—forces the reader to pay attention to the literary and cultural sources of his allusions. Untranslated words and phrases in Canto 1 include "in officina Wecheli" (a reference to the place of publication of Divus' translation);

"Venerandam," "worthy of veneration"; "Argicida," "killer of Argus" (a reference to the Greek god Hermes); and "orichalchi," "coppery." In this canto, all foreign-language phrases are in either Greek or Latin.

There are also abundant allusions to classical myth and Homeric epic. Perimedes, Eurylochus, and Elpenor are all members of Odysseus' crew. Erebus and Avernus are different names for the underworld. Finally, Canto 1 displays a formal device that, although it runs throughout the *Cantos*, is generally nontraditional: Many lines are fragmented, having no clear grammatical subject or object. The final phrase— "So that:"—is characteristic of this device. Moreover, Pound shifts abruptly from speaker to speaker in Canto 1, as in the jump from "And then Anticlea came" (spoken by Odysseus) to "Lie quiet Divus" (ostensibly Pound himself). As a result, fragmentation and abrupt shifts in persona create much disorientation in most readers, but Pound's intention here is to spur the reader to greater efforts, to motivate him or her to participate more fully than usual in generating meaning from the poem.

Themes and Meanings

As difficult as Canto 1 may be in form, its theme is a traditional, straightforward one: descent into the underworld. In fact, Homer's account of Odysseus' search for knowledge among the dead spirits of Hades is the earliest version in Western literature of this motif.

In speaking to the dead, Odysseus acquires knowledge that is normally forbidden to mortals: He learns the cause of Elpenor's death, for example, and, more tellingly, discovers his own fate. This kind of supernatural knowledge can be won only through sacrifice, and Odysseus' journey over unknown seas and the deaths of his crewmen prepare him for this knowledge. The holy, sacrificial rites with which he calls up the spirits of the dead are part of this mystery, whereby mortal human intelligence exceeds the usual limits of reality.

Pound uses this theme for two reasons: so he can create variations on it at the end of Canto 1, and to introduce what he projected to be the grand theme of the *Cantos* as a whole.

Just as Odysseus summons the dead to acquire knowledge, so Pound, the narrator and the scholar, calls up the dead Renaissance translator Divus to step from his own historical and literary period into world culture as a whole. By studying Divus' Renaissance Latin version of the *Odyssey*, Pound animates a dead era and two dead languages. In fact, Pound's admonition to "lie quiet Divus" suggests that the experience has been too enlivening, too overwhelming. Moreover, in another historical layer, Pound discovers that Odysseus and the anonymous Anglo-Saxon seafarer are spiritual brothers.

This swirl of characters and eras may account for the confusion at the end of the poem, at which point the various currents of history and literature threaten to dislocate the narrator's consciousness.

John Steven Childs

CANTO 49

Author: Ezra Pound (1885-1972)
Type of poem: Poetic sequence
First published: 1937, in *The Fifth Decad of Cantos*

The Poem

Canto 49—often called the "Seven Lakes" canto—is one of a set of ten cantos appearing in the third book of Ezra Pound's twentieth century epic, the *Cantos*. This long poetic sequence, including 120 cantos, weaves scores of subjects and themes into the longest important poetic work of the modern era. By the time the "Fifth Decad" of cantos was published, Pound had already been at work on his epic for nearly twenty years; he would continue to write new cantos for thirty more.

The time is late autumn, and the persona is evidently someone journeying down a canal, noting the passing landscape. In the poem's first line, however, Pound tells us that "these verses" are "by no man"; his intention here is possibly to suggest that the poem itself is a natural object, swelling up from the landscape like the mist or the flocks of birds who live by the banks of the canal.

The persona is evidently standing in the riverboat's small cabin, lit by a single lamp; later, in stanza 4, he describes the "hole of the window" from which he views the landscape he describes. The canto's second line sets the scene: The persona travels late in the year, when the normally busy canal is empty. The weather is turning cold; during the course of the poem, the rain noted in the second line becomes a snow flurry. Meanwhile, under the heavy rain, plants growing on the banks, the reeds and bamboos, bend and creak. The cold rain and the persona's loneliness evoke an aura of sadness, and he feels that the natural world empathizes with him.

Finally, in the second stanza, the weather clears. The sun sets and the moon rises over the surrounding hills. Although Pound gives the reader too little information to be certain about the exact landscape through which the persona passes, the canal on which he travels may link the "seven lakes" of the poem's first line. As the persona sails over one of these lakes, he hears a distant bell from a monastery. The boat voyages on downstream, floating on the silver river lit by the dying sun.

In the short third stanza, the persona now sees the banner of a canalside wine shop and a small settlement adjacent to the shop. Snow begins to fall. There are signs of other people moving about on the lake; a fisherman's boat hung with a small lamp looks from a distance like one of the floating paper lanterns used during Chinese festivals. The village of San Yin, on which the persona comments in the stanza's fourth and fifth lines, may be either the wine-shop settlement the persona is now viewing or another village the persona simply remembers. Throughout the poem, the persona's current perceptions and past memories are often mixed, reflecting time's unimportance to him. Migrating geese alight on a sandbar for a moment and then take off. Other birds, rooks, circle the fishermen's boats, looking for fish. On the distant shore, small boys with lamps turn over rocks, looking for shrimp.

In stanza 5, there is a definite change of tone, probably caused by a shift in persona, from the anonymous Chinese traveler to Pound himself, who comments on the building of the canal. The canal, built by a civic-minded Chinese ruler, represents to Pound the right use of state wealth. Instead of using the state's riches to accumulate debt, the "old king" has used his resources to improve his country. Pound contrasts this with the lending and borrowing of state money for profit. "Geryon," in the stanza's second line, is a mythical beast used in Dante's *Inferno* (c. 1320) to signify usury, the immoral accumulation of wealth through lending at interest—in other words, using money to make money, rather than using money to create the physical means to generate wealth, such as a canal that facilitates commerce.

The next stanza is a Japanese transliteration of a Chinese poem. The lines mean "Bright colorful auspicious cloud/ Hang gracefully/ Let sun and moon shine/ Morning after morning."

Stanza 8 describes in shorthand the natural cycle of ordinary human life and work, which is contrasted with the life of the state. The poem ends with a cryptic reference to classical mythology—probably relating to Bacchus' enchantment of wild beasts.

Forms and Devices

The Seven Lakes canto is generally considered one of the most beautiful portions of the *Cantos*. In theme and language, it reflects Pound's lifelong love of Chinese and Japanese poetry. Although it is impossible to render oriental verse forms into English, Pound here tries to capture the flavor of a classic Chinese poem, using short free-verse lines and syntax that often dispenses with the subject-verb-object structure of English sentences. Largely, then, the canto is made up of traditional natural images drawn from Chinese poetry.

Canto 49 is an imitation of the classical Chinese *shih*, or song, first collected in the ancient *Shih Ching* (Classic of Songs). The main structural characteristic of the shih, which Pound adopts here, is the use of short one- or two-syllable words, grouped in four-word lines. Stanza 6 exactly reproduces one such shih. As a result, the rhythm of the poem is terse and far more clipped than most Western poetic styles.

Even though the language of the Seven Lakes canto is direct, the imagery attempts to suggest emotion rather than state it openly. Thus the persona never tells the reader what he himself is feeling; instead, he allows the imagery of the natural world to do that for him. The heavy rain falling in the twilight of the first stanza, the bent reeds, and the "weeping" bamboos all strongly indicate the persona's sadness and loneliness, and the fire and ice of the cloud in the third line suggest a deep unstated conflict within the persona's psyche.

Contrasted to this imagery of cold, rain, and emptiness, however, is another set of images suggesting delicacy, light, and calm. The poem's second stanza introduces both the light of the bright autumn moon and the silvery blaze of sunset on the canal.

The persona is also calmed by what he hears: The thin tune carrying through the canalside reeds seems to echo the chill of the air, and the gong of the monk's bell picks up the echo.

The flag waving in the sunset and the chimney smoke from the village reinforce the imagery evoked by this delicate, transitory landscape, which is as constantly changing as the persona's viewpoint as he moves downstream.

The imagery of the poem's fourth stanza is perhaps the jewel of the canto. The flurried snow, the jade-colored landscape, the pinpoint lights of the fishing boats, and the small boys strongly suggest a classical Chinese painting. In such a painting, elements of line and color are subtly implied, giving viewers the impression of a vivid dreamworld.

Themes and Meanings

In many ways, the Seven Lakes canto is simply a masterly imitation of classical Chinese verse. Thus many of its themes may be treated as the traditional ones associated with Oriental poetry. On the other hand, Pound introduces an important sub-theme toward the end of the canto, which throws the earlier, more conventional meanings into contrast.

As in much of the *Cantos* (and as in much poetry throughout history), the theme here centers on a journey. In this case, the poem deals with the voyage of a solitary traveler on a nearly deserted waterway late in the year. Because of the mixture of past and present in the voyager's perceptions and because of his loneliness, his journey readily suggests the voyage this person makes through life. One of the great themes of Chinese and Japanese poetry — perhaps in part because of the strong Buddhist influence in those cultures — is the transience of life, its evanescent and even illusory quality.

Much of what the persona sees as he travels downstream seems insubstantial: The changing weather of autumn, the changing of day into night, the moon, the migrating birds, the chimney smoke — all these images combine to create a picture of a universe that Buddhism views as only partly real. Although the reader is never told exactly what troubles the persona, the speaker's emotions are clearly the most solid element in his world.

A key line in stanza 2 — "Sail passed here in April; may return in October" — may reflect the poem's central meaning, the coming and going of human relationships. Here Pound relies upon a conventional theme in Chinese poetry: the departure of a beloved person on a long journey. In poems that employ this theme, the persona, the person being left behind, is often uncertain that the traveler will return.

Thus the smaller incident of saying goodbye to one person — perhaps forever — mirrors the larger course of any individual's life, from which friends, lovers, and family are eventually taken by death or distance.

This theme in the poem might be termed the "personal" one, but the canto concludes with another theme, the "social" one. Here Pound turns his emphasis from the emotions of one lonely person to passions having to do with statecraft. The image that links the private and the public is the canal: For the lonely traveler, the canal symbolizes life's solitary journey through an achingly beautiful natural landscape; but for the social observer, the canal symbolizes the just use of a state's wealth—to promote commerce, to enhance the lives of all the people who live by the thoroughfare. These are the people who live simple, direct lives, untroubled by the more sophisticated worries of the traveler. When the sun comes up, they work; when it sets, they rest. Their efforts are concentrated on not merely observing nature, but making it productive—they dig wells and work the fields.

Pound possibly suggests at the end of the poem that there is another dimension that transcends both the public and the private. In this, he is simply following the Chinese sage Confucius (who was much admired by Pound). Confucius argued that there was no separation between the good of the individual and the good of the people as a whole—that, like the flow of the canal through the lakes, individual health moved naturally into the public realm.

John Steven Childs

CANTO 74

Author: Ezra Pound (1885-1972)
Type of poem: Poetic sequence
First published: 1948, in *The Pisan Cantos*

The Poem

Canto 74 is the first poem in an eleven-poem set called *The Pisan Cantos*, which occurs about midway in the long poetic sequence the *Cantos*. Most Ezra Pound scholars agree that *The Pisan Cantos* contains some of the most powerful and beautiful passages in the entire sequence of 120 cantos. Like the remainder of the poem, *The Pisan Cantos* interweaves scores of themes and motifs into a tapestry containing elements drawn from world history, the literature of many countries and periods, and from Pound's own life. In fact, Pound often described the *Cantos* as "a poem containing history," including his own life history, and Canto 74 is a particularly good example of the ways in which Pound used personal and universal history as the foundation of the *Cantos'* poetic structure.

The sequence was written during Pound's internment in the Detention Training Camp, a U. S. Army prison outside Pisa, Italy, during 1945 and 1946. During World War II, Pound had sided with Benito Mussolini's Fascists and had spent much of the war making pro-Fascist propaganda broadcasts for Rome Radio. When the Allies captured northern Italy, Pound was arrested as a traitor and held in Italy to await trial in the United States. Pound's incarceration in the camp forms the autobiographical basis for these cantos, and much of their subject matter has to do with Pound's day-to-day life in the open-air prison.

There are two difficulties with presenting a straightforward summary of Canto 74's content. The first is that by the time the reader reaches *The Pisan Cantos* (at page 425 of the American edition of the *Cantos*), he or she is expected to have assimilated dozens of references and allusions developed more fully in earlier cantos. The second is that this is one of the lengthiest of the cantos, running to nearly fifty pages in the standard edition.

In the opening seventy-four lines, for example (ending with "thereby making clutter"), nearly each line contains a different allusion, either to an earlier section of the *Cantos* themselves or to literature or history. The first eight lines allude to the death of Mussolini ("Ben"), who, having been captured by Italian Resistance fighters was killed along with his mistress ("Clara") and hung by his feet in a public square in Milan. Yet this reference immediately flows into one having to do with the "resurrected-god" motif of Mediterranean folklore and religion (in Greek, *Digonos* means "twice born"), and that in turn spurs the persona, Pound himself, to recall his friend T. S. Eliot's famous line about humankind ending with a "whimper" not a "bang" — Pound reverses this idea and thus introduces a note of defiance and even hope in the middle of his own defeat.

Next, a series of references to the writings of Confucius and to classic Chinese poetry intervene ("rain is also of the process"). These lines are followed by allusions to the journeys of Odysseus and of the Argonauts. One line in this sequence, "when Lucifer fell in N. Carolina," remains a mystery to Pound scholars, who are baffled by its meaning. In fact, the "Lucifer" line is typical of many others in this canto, making a coherent summary difficult.

The poem opens with Pound's lament for the death of Mussolini, who, Pound felt, was to lead Italy into a new Renaissance. Pound then contrasts political upheaval with the steady processes of nature praised in the Chinese classics. The reference to Confucius leads to remarks on the financial probity of the Chinese emperors and the contrasting usury practiced against Indian peasants during the last years of the British raj. Pound believed that the economic structure of the modern world was the source of its evils, including war and the loss of freedom, to which he refers in "the Constitution in jeopardy."

Returning to Odysseus, Pound compares one meaning of the Greek hero's name, "no man," with that accorded to an Australian god, Wanjina, who, like the God of the Old Testament, brought the created world into being through naming. The poem now shifts (at "from the death cells") to Pound's own impressions of the landscape in and around the detention camp. That landscape includes gallows for hanging criminals, and the gallows remind him of various executed criminals, including the medieval French poet François Villon and Barabbas. In the lines following, Pound introduces some of his fellow prisoners, "Thos. Wilson" and "Mr. K."; at "there was a smell of mint under the tent flaps," Pound inserts a lyrical passage having to do with the beauties of nature, visible even in the camp.

The Chinese character that then appears ("shien") means "to manifest, shining," and this ideogram is meant to stand for the light of the natural world, which illuminates everything, even the prison, with the clarity of truth. From light, Pound then returns to the darkness of economic falsehood (at "Never inside the country . . .") and to the hidden machinations of usurers (those who lend money at exorbitant interest—Pound's chief villains).

At "Pisa, in the 23rd year . . . ," Pound describes the execution of a fellow prisoner, Till, and the natural wisdom of another prisoner, called "Snag." The Chinese character here means "mo," or evening; Pound expands the character's meaning to "a man on whom the sun has gone down," such as the executed Till. That is followed by a series of lines contrasting the illumination of mystical light with the darkness of history. The verse paragraphs beginning "Lordly men are to earth o'ergiven" relate Pound's memories of his fellow writers, some of whom are now dead: Ford Madox Ford, William Carlos Williams, James Joyce, and others. These memories are followed by others having to do with various twentieth century events, which had been related to Pound through anecdotes told by witnesses of them.

These main subjects—Pound's life in the camp, his memories, the evils of a corrupt economic system, the beauty and light of the natural world, the fleeting events of history—recur throughout the remainder of Canto 74 and on into the rest of *The Pisan Cantos*. As the poem picks up its pace, however, the subjects are interwoven at smaller and smaller intervals. For example, in the passage beginning "autumnal heavens under sha-o," Pound moves in rapid succession through Chinese poetry (three lines), Old Testament dictates on money (three lines), the fees charged on an ancient toll road (three lines), Confucius (four lines), a description of a fellow prisoner (five lines), usury (two lines), state funding of the Athenian navy (two lines), and the infamy of Sir Winston Churchill (two lines). Often, the change of subject occurs in the middle of a line, complicating matters greatly for the reader intent on detecting a consistent narrative thread.

Forms and Devices

As are the other cantos in general, Canto 74 is written in free verse—poetic lines that have no set rhythm or consistent number of feet and that do not rhyme. The poem is broadly segmented into verse paragraphs; there are stanzas, which, similar to free verse, follow no regular structure and run anywhere from one line to several pages.

One immediately recognizable structural feature of this canto—again as with nearly all the other cantos—is fragmentation: Normal syntactic patterns are often absent, so that individual lines may lack subjects, objects, or verbs. Moreover, such lines may begin abruptly, in midsentence, and may often be written in a foreign language. A good example occurs at the beginning of Canto 74, where "sorella la luna" ("sister the moon") on one separate line is followed by an imperative sentence ("Fear god . . ."), followed by a noun phrase begun by a conjunction ("but a precise definition").

Another unfamiliar structural device, which Pound used increasingly toward the end of the *Cantos*, is the Chinese character, often inserted to the side of the text as a kind of commentary on the Western-language lines. Pound believed that such ideograms were "picture writing," able to be read as visual images without knowledge of Chinese. Thus, ideograms provided direct, unmediated messages embodying the themes of certain portions of the poem.

Largely, however, it is the striking imagery of Canto 74 that most readers admire. Although a simple paraphrase of the many subjects Pound addresses in this canto makes the poem appear incomprehensible, the poet's imagery helps these divergent motifs to cohere.

The main imagery comprises three elements: light, natural processes, and the Celestial City. Much of Pound's imagery in Canto 74 is in direct contrast to the drab realities of prison life. In fact, Pound uses the simple details of his life in the detention camp as symbols of natural forces that flow on, oblivious to human beings and their history. In the passage beginning "and there was a smell of mint under the tent flaps," for example, the many small, piquant details seem to shine like the universal light that is one of the canto's main themes. The odor of rain-drenched wild mint, the brilliant white of oxen on the road outside the prison, the dark sheep standing out against the rainy mountainside take on the quality of eternal emblems of the natural world. Because this world has nothing to do with Pound, it "upholds" him—keeps him going—precisely as watching the lizards crawling around the camp keeps his mind off his coming trial.

In the lines that follow the "mint" passage, Pound uses the imagery of universal light "to manifest" (as the Chinese character here says) the underlying reality reflected in individual elements of the natural world. Such light also appears in imagery concerning the Celestial City, where the "light of light . . . virtu" illumines human works as well. The "four giants at the four corners," who appear following the above images, were the colossal ancient statues that marked the boundaries of an ideal city-state; however, the statues also symbolize the "giant" that lies dormant in human potential.

Themes and Meanings

The imagery in Canto 74 suggests that human beings will only fulfill their real potential when they bring themselves into harmony with the light of the gods— when, along with the animals and plants, they move in natural sympathy with the universe.

Standing in the way of such potential are a number of obstacles; not the least of these is economic corruption. For Pound, usury symbolized that corruption, because, he believed, usurers make money with money; that is, they contribute nothing to the actual physical well-being of humankind. Earning money through interest on loans occurs only on paper: Lenders are not manufacturers or farmers or artisans, and thus they are out of tune with the natural world.

Canto 74 frames this generalized theme in Pound's own individual perspective. He places the dry world of economics and the abstractions of history in a human context, his own. An aging poet awaiting trial for treason, Pound sees himself as a victim of the modern world's corruption. He also views himself, with all human beings, as a victim of time itself: Throughout the poem, he is flooded with memories of his own past. Yet, as a citizen of the world, as a well-known poet and thinker, Pound's personal life intersected with some of the greatest events of the twentieth century, and so in the lyrical intensity of *The Pisan Cantos*, he welds together these major themes: the disharmony of the modern world and his own personal tragedy.

John Steven Childs

CASUALTY

Author: Seamus Heaney (1939-   )
Type of poem: Elegy
First published: 1979, in *Field Work*

The Poem

"Casualty" is a lament for the unknown citizen, an anonymous victim not merely of the social violence of the poet's native province but also of those tribal attachments that make the violence so aggravated, interminable, and difficult to understand—those elements that are referred to toward the second section of the poem as "our tribe's complicity." Since the poet himself was born and reared in Northern Ireland, he speaks with particular, if understated, eloquence and with an intimacy that is typical of his work as a whole on the complex of human inevitability and historical happenstance of which his subject has fallen foul.

The poem is one of a number of elegies in *Field Work*, a collection that also includes, among other poems of this type, one on a murdered cousin as well as an elegy on the American poet, Robert Lowell. In addition, *Field Work*—the author's first book after leaving his native province and coming to live in the Republic of Ireland—contains numerous poems on the possibility of renewal. The collection's overall concern with death and rebirth and the impact of that historical, social, and natural cycle on an individual consciousness is conveniently, if not necessarily definitively, condensed in the three parts of "Casualty," making it one of the emblematic statements in a pivotal work in the poet's development.

Although the poet has, in a biographical sense, left his native place, in other senses, he is, as "Casualty" shows, very much attached to it. The acts of public respect and private mourning bridge the gap between the poem's sections and provide evidence of that attachment. The event in question is the killing of thirteen unarmed civil rights protesters—not all of them from the Bogside area of Derry, which has become a facile synonym for die-hard Provisional Irish Republican Army (IRA) sympathizers ("the Provisionals" mentioned in the poem)—by British Forces on January 30, 1972, commonly remembered as Bloody Sunday. (Derry is the capital city of the county in which Seamus Heaney was reared.) As the poet is assimilated to, and detached from, that notorious event, so is his subject, and the poem effectively addresses itself to the awkward existence of both distance and intimacy between the poet and his material.

The very anonymity of the casualty becomes a challenge to the poet, like a question he feels he must answer or a ghost ("Dawn-sniffing revenant") he has no desire to exorcise. The three-part division of the poem facilitates a slow, tentative, oblique approach ("my tentative art") to the violent absence that the poet feels obliged to confront. Opening with a fondly detailed evocation of the subject—his habits, gestures, and bearing, which recount the natural facts of his actual presence—the poem moves to the different kind of attentiveness in its treatment of the funeral of the Bloody

Sunday Thirteen. On that occasion, communal feeling held sway. The mourners formed the facsimile of a community ("braced and bound/ Like brothers in a ring").

This communal mode of observance has been denied by the casualty, who met his death indifferently breaking the law, expressing a loyalty to his own nature rather than to reflexes conditioned by larger forces. The poet who "missed his funeral" problematically preserves him in a poem, ensuring that this unassimilated citizen is assimilated in an other-than-communal order of witnessing.

Forms and Devices

Heaney's poetry is widely admired—even by readers without direct access to the poems' contexts or allusions—for its fidelity to the actual and its ability to render the world of things with a direct, sensory appeal. The opening stanza of "Casualty" is a good example of the poet's economical conjuring up of his subject's physical presence. The oxymoronic "observant back" vividly connotes the man's ready presence and complements the sense of his being "a natural for work." This economy of means is underlined by the poem's almost laconic three-foot line—a line that seems to replicate the casualty's "deadpan sidling tact." Immediacy of language and simplicity of metrical structure also make acceptable the disarming candor and the poet's attitude: "I loved his whole manner."

The poem's patent disavowal of rhetoric, the means whereby it is able to "manage by some trick/ To switch the talk" from the loftiness often considered endemic to elegies, makes its larger project of reclamation and commemoration seem feasible. Nothing in the poem seems beyond the bounds of nature, except the various violences that it addresses. The same plain and rather plaintive tone is maintained even in the act of imagining the victim's moment of death ("I see him as he turned"). Sustaining a steady tone to guide the supple range of his associative mode of writing has always been one of Heaney's principal characteristics. The effects of doing so can be readily experienced in "Casualty," where such issues as historical contingency and social solidarity are installed as tributaries to the main theme of individual fate and choice so that the theme is seen more revealingly as a result.

The continuity of the poet's witnessing voice throughout the poem, weaving its chronologically random way through various levels of a recent personal past, also adds greatly to the poem's overall effect. The events recounted in "Casualty" happened with an abruptness that is unanswerable. This fact is preserved in the poem's discontinuous narrative, in which what is the irenic equal and opposite to the subject's death ("that morning/ When he took me in his boat") is kept till last. The poem's relaxed, yet steadfast, tone ensures that a means of both admitting and accommodating those discontinuities can be found, shocking "puzzle" though they may be. The discontinuities are reflected in the poem's form, both in its three-part organization and in the variable lengths of its stanzas. Within those forms, however, the same meter remains constant, and subtle rhymes and half-rhymes supply an understated but persistent sense of order. In other words, the very aspects that are the poet's fundamental attributes articulate a degree of coherence and containment that are lamentably and destructively unavailable to the world outside the poem. With the casualty presented in this manner, the reader as well as the recollecting author should be in a position to admit the tragic awareness that "I tasted freedom with him."

Themes and Meanings

Students of Irish poetry will find many intriguing echoes between "Casualty" and William Butler Yeats's "The Fisherman." Published in a pivotal collection in Yeats's development — *The Wild Swans at Coole* (1919) — this poem conjures up a remote, anonymous, isolated figure and holds him up as an ideal whereby the aspirations of the day might be revealed in all their tawdry (though not necessarily violent) opportunism. In particular, Yeats makes a strong case for the fisherman as the embodiment of cultural integrity based on personal distinctiveness.

Heaney's "Casualty" is less politically ambitious than Yeats's "The Fisherman," and it is much more quiescent in tone, as befits the personal tenor of this elegy. With its emphasis on questioning and on thought as an experience of difficulty rather than of release ("you're supposed to be/ An educated man"), "Casualty" is also less didactic than its Yeatsian predecessor. Nevertheless, Heaney's poem may be instructively read as a critical companion piece to Yeats's, particularly in its Yeatsian tendency to seek redemption in nature for what society manifestly disdains to supply. Since Heaney's fisherman is "A dole-kept breadwinner" (that is, a recipient of unemployment benefits), it is tempting to see him in the poem's concluding section as a poacher, a fisher of waters not his own. Such a view would be consistent with the sense of his going his own way that the poet both admires and is disturbed by, since it is the occasion of his untimely death.

It seems, however, that the poem needs a sense of the sea ("fathoms," "haul/ Steadily off the bottom," "well out, beyond") in order to give a sense of scope to the freedom being "tasted." Such scope is necessary in order for the full measure of risk and self-sufficiency to emerge. The sense of self-sufficiency is present in the reader's introduction to the character, while the understanding of risk emerges in the victim's paying with his life for a forbidden drink. The fact that "he would not be held/ At home by his own crowd" (those to whom by reason of culture, social standing, and background he might be presumed to owe allegiance) is both the unnerving cause of his death and the reason he is the poem's subject.

In the obscure fate of an anonymous citizen, Heaney trawls the emptiness for an image of adequacy. What he comes up with is a potent recognition of independence as something that is not only provided for by militant activity and tribal prescriptions: It may also be something innate. By means of a typical verbal maneuver, Heaney uses the colloquial Irish expression, "he drank like a fish," to invoke a sense of the casualty's larger-than-social existence. It is by virtue of his nonaligned, nonconforming aspects, and the poet's insistence on their relevance, that "Casualty" becomes an elegy for the "cornered outfaced stare" of humanity in Heaney's homeland.

George O'Brien

CATS

Author: Charles Baudelaire (1821-1867)
Type of poem: Sonnet
First published: 1847, as "Les Chats"; in *Les Fleurs du mal*, 1857; collected in
  The Flowers of Evil, 1955

The Poem

"Cats" is a sonnet, a poem of fourteen lines, in which the octave is divided into two quatrains and the sestet is made up of two tercets. The poem was first published in the journal *Le Corsaire* in 1847 and was ultimately included in Charles Baudelaire's collection of 1857 known in English as *The Flowers of Evil*. The poem is both elegant and magical in its descriptions of cats. The first line (in the translation by Anthony Hecht) introduces "Feverish lovers, scholars in their lofts," and the second line states that both lovers and scholars will eventually "love the cat." In the first two lines, the poet has given the reader a glimpse of the hold cats have even on people from diverse walks of life. The third line of the first quatrain describes the cat as being both "gentle" and "powerful" and states that this creature is "king of the parlor mat." In the last line of the quatrain, Baudelaire notes that the cat is "Lazy," like the lovers and scholars, and "sensitive to draughts." One can assume that cats, by their nature, exert a hold over those who let them into their homes.

The second quatrain—the second half of the sonnet's octave—presents unsettling attributes of the "Gentle but powerful" creature. The first line speaks of the cat as being "linked to learning and to love." The cat "Exhibits a taste for silences and gloom"; it is more complex than first imagined. It has a dark side, which has been heightened through long silences. The conclusion put forth in the closing lines of the second quatrain speaks of the cat becoming a "splendid messenger of doom/ If his fierce pride would condescend to serve." There is an ominous cloud hanging over the poem now, which could lead to frightening prospects if the cat were so inclined. It is perhaps a small consolation that the cat will not be the "messenger of doom" because of its "fierce pride."

The sestet of "Cats" moves away from the "gloom" of the octave and introduces mystery and magic. The cat is "Lost in his day-dream" as the first tercet begins and resembles "sphinxes in the desert." It has become timeless and almost godlike. The first tercet ends with the image of this royal creature being "Fixed in a reverie that has no end." The cat has transcended the conscious world and has become something that is more myth than reality. The poem closes with a tercet that revels even more in the magical qualities of the cat. The first line points to the cat's loins being "lit with the fires of alchemy"; it has become more than the sum of its parts. From whatever angle the cat is observed, there is some new quality to be discovered. The poem closes with "And bits of gold, small as the finest sand,/ Fleck, here and there, the mystery of his eyes." The cat ultimately remains a mystery, and the deepest mystery is in its eyes.

Forms and Devices

Baudelaire's collection *The Flowers of Evil* was not assembled in a random fashion. The collection is divided into sections, and the poems included in each section help to build a thematic pattern for that section. The American author Edgar Allan Poe had a major influence on Baudelaire. Structure, rhythm, and rhyme, according to both Poe and Baudelaire, should be employed by the poet to give each poem its own independent identity; each poem should create a unique atmosphere. Baudelaire constructed every poem as a unit, and the unit then fit into the larger thematic patterns to create the whole of *The Flowers of Evil*. The most successful poems in the collection have a strong rhetorical structure. Baudelaire's greatest poems are relatively short. The shortness was by design, since Baudelaire (and Poe) believed that the power of one poem to stimulate its reader could not be sustained over an extended length.

"Cats" can be found in the first section of *The Flowers of Evil*. This section, "Spleen et Idéal" ("Bile and the Ideal"), is the largest of the collection; there are eighty-eight poems included, and "Cats" is the sixty-ninth. A number of sonnets are included in "Bile and the Ideal," and "Cats" is certainly one of the best. The sonnet form was ideally suited to Baudelaire's expressed need to create emotional impact in a brief number of lines. A sonnet is only fourteen lines long and traditionally has been employed to express emotional power through a lyrical mood. Each line of "Cats" is an Alexandrine, which means that the line has twelve syllables consisting of six iambics. There must also be a caesura (or interruption) after the third iambic.

In the original French, "Cats" draws much of its power from metrical stresses. Baudelaire also makes use of the compound doublet, which consists of the repetition of two, or possibly more, sounds in the same sequence. Baudelaire's skillful handling of rhythm, marvelous manipulation of rhyme, and strong sense of metaphor all enhance the power of "Cats." The evolution of the cat from a creature of the house to be loved in the first quatrain to a magnificent creature of mystery in the last tercet is beautifully unified. The sonnet form is a precise style of expression, and "Cats" is a concise poem. A subtly magical work is built upon a realistic base; the balance of the poem exemplifies Baudelaire's belief that the emotional content of a poem could be mastered through its formal structure.

Themes and Meanings

The publication of *The Flowers of Evil* in 1857 caused a great scandal. It was ruled by a French court to be an obscene collection, and some of the poems had to be excised in subsequent editions. The preface of *The Flowers of Evil* stated Baudelaire's belief that sin overwhelmed the world, and in each section of the collection, the poet confronted different ways of personal escape. "Cats" was included in the opening section, in which Baudelaire escaped into a quest for beauty in art and love. Within this section there is charm, music, and sensuality; Romanticism is strong in these poems. It is clearly evident in a poem such as "Cats." The spell that is created within this sonnet has close ties to English Romanticism and especially to the work of Samuel Taylor Coleridge.

Baudelaire can also be considered a bridge to modern poetic art. He used the bold repudiation of bourgeois normality found in Romanticism and added his own sharp images, framed within a rigid poetic structure, to legitimize a wide range of topics otherwise thought to be indelicate. "Cats" does not approach some of the more scandalous subjects; it does speak powerfully about a creature that is exotic, however, and the exotiç also runs counter to bourgeois normality. The cat of the first quatrain receives love by being different but not existing outside normal boundaries. Baudelaire refuses to leave it at that. In the second quatrain, the cat takes on qualities that are dark, or at least potentially dark (the cat's pride will not allow it to "condescend to serve").

The sestet introduces a magical world. The common house cat is no longer—if it ever really was—common. It assumes a pose comparable to the "sphinxes in the desert"; it is beyond complete human comprehension. When the last tercet begins with an image of the cat's loins being "lit with the fires of alchemy," it is evident that cats are magical creatures with special powers. The last line mentions "the mystery of his eyes," which is a fitting summation of what cats symbolize. The cat represents (as do tigresses or women in other of Baudelaire's poems) a fantastic creature that will consume any human who tries to understand or love it. *The Flowers of Evil* attempted to pierce bourgeois society from every possible angle. In "Cats," Baudelaire created a sonnet that struck at society's respectability through the exotic and mysterious world of cats.

Michael Jeffrys

THE CEMETERY BY THE SEA

Author: Paul Valéry (1871-1945)
Type of poem: Meditation
First published: 1922, as "Le Cimetière marin," in *Charmes, ou poèmes*;
    collected in *An Anthology of French Poetry from Nerval to Valéry in English
    Translation with French Originals*, 1958

The Poem

"The Cemetery by the Sea," written in 1920, is Paul Valéry's best-known poem. It consists of twenty-four stanzas of six lines each. The poet returns in imagination to the cemetery of Sète, a city on a cliff above the Mediterranean, where he was born and where he dreamed as a youth among the tombs of his ancestors. He imagines himself sitting on a tombstone at noon and contemplating the white sails on the calm sea, which he describes as doves pecking on a roof, while he wrestles with the problems of life and death, of being and nonbeing, and thinks about the future course of his life.

In his monologue, Valéry thinks of the sea as the roof of the temple of time sparkling with diamonds, and he enjoys the idea of mingling with the sky and the sea. As his shadow passes over the tombs, he realizes that he himself is subject to change; he recalls his nineteen years of what he calls indolence. (Actually, since 1894 he had been working first in the Ministry of War and later in the news agency Havas. He was a married man and the father of two children, devoting his free time to research on the nature of thought.) He accuses himself of idleness because he has not made full use of his poetic talent.

In stanza 11, the poet imagines himself a shepherd among the quiet white sheep, the tombs. He refuses the Christian consolation symbolized by the marble doves and angels and contemplates eternal nothingness, reflecting in stanza 13 that the dead buried in the cemetery are quite comfortable.

In the next two stanzas the noonday sun, symbol of unchanging perfection, is contrasted with ephemeral man—with the poet himself, who is filled with fear, repentance, and doubt. Man, he decides, is the flaw, the changing element in the perfection of the universe. The dead lose their individuality and return to the great Whole; their bodies feed the flowers.

In the seventeenth stanza, Valéry chides himself for dreaming of a more perfect world and asks himself if he expects to write poetry when he is dead. Immortality is only an illusion; those who compare death to a maternal breast are guilty of a beautiful lie and a pious trick. The empty head of a skeleton laughs forever. Stanza 19 states that the true worm is not that which has destroyed the bodies, but is thought that feeds on life and never leaves man. Even in his sleep, the worm of thought pursues him. Valéry is referring to the dictum of René Descartes, *Cogito ergo sum*: "I think, therefore I am."

In stanza 21, Valéry asks Zeno, a Greek philosopher who denied the reality of movement by asserting that a flying arrow is immobile at each instant, if he has pierced him with the arrow that is killing him. He rejects the idea that time does not pass; movement exists, therefore life and time exist and action is possible.

In the last three stanzas, the poet reacts: The weather has changed, and a breeze has sprung up. Its salty freshness returns his soul to him. Like a man who has plunged into the refreshing sea, he emerges from his reverie filled with a taste for life. He will plunge into action.

Forms and Devices

All six lines in each stanza end with a rhyme in the pattern *aabccb*. This rigidity called for great expertise on the part of Valéry and his translators. If a translator is truly faithful to the thought of a poem, it is the music that suffers most in passing from one language to another. If he must limit each line to ten syllables and adhere to a difficult rhyme scheme, he can hardly hope to imitate the music of the original.

This difficult poem requires the reader to penetrate a host of metaphors. The reader must equate the calm sea with a roof and the sails with doves pecking on the shining roof of the temple of time under a blazing noontime sky while the poet meditates on great philosophical problems and on his own existence. Stanza 5 contains a simile: The poet inhales his future as a hungry mouth obscures the contour of a piece of fruit. This is perhaps the only reasonably simple comparison in a forest of unexpected (and unexplained) images used as symbols.

The theme of the poem rests on these original, complicated, and obscure symbols. One eminent critic insists that the whole poem is a metaphor, to which each image refers. Another famous scholar declares that the noonday sun is the symbol of eternity and the sea is the symbol of human consciousness. Less difficult to conceive is the idea that the sea seen through the trees is a prisoner of the leaves. It devours the cemetery grills because the sea, sparkling in the sun, causes them to seem to disappear.

Comprehensible also is the metaphor of the poet as a shepherd among his sheep, the white marble tombs, and the sea as watchdog. The angels and doves (unfortunately translated sometimes as "pigeons") obviously represent the consolation of the Christian religion. He urges the watchdog to frighten them as a sign that he rejects this idea of life after death.

In the second-to-last stanza, Valéry describes in startling images the sea as it reacts to the rising wind: It is delirious; it resembles a panther's skin and a torn Greek cloak; it is a hydra, the serpent with nine heads which, according to Greek mythology, replaced each lost head with two others; it is a serpent biting its tail.

Valéry employed figures of speech and symbols to express philosophic ideas. The metaphor which unifies the structure of the poem, according to one critic, establishes a parallelism among the three separate elements: the sea, the cemetery, and the poet. Each of these elements has two aspects, one on the surface, the other interior. Other poetic devices, such as alliteration, embellish the original but cannot be preserved in translation. For example, stanza 4 of the French has nine pronounced *t* sounds and eight pronounced *s* sounds; the effect is striking.

Themes and Meanings

Scores of books have been written about Paul Valéry and "Le Cimetière marin," as well as hundreds of articles by critics, teachers, poets. In 1928, Gustave Cohen, a professor at the Sorbonne, gave a series of lectures entitled *Essai d'interprétation du "Cimetière marin"* (attempt to interpret "The Cemetery by the Sea") to a large audience that included Paul Valéry himself. The poet expressed his pleasure at having the intentions and the wording of the poem, reputedly obscure, so well understood. Valéry explained in a preface to the publication of the lectures that he had decided to write a monologue that would be at the same time personal and universal, one that would contain the simplest and most constant themes of his emotional and intellectual life. His poem is a meditation on life and death, on mobility and immobility, on being and nonbeing. Since, in the fashion of his friends the Symbolists, he does not explain his metaphors, the reader must puzzle out the meanings. This is harder to do from a translation than from the original, because the translator has had to incorporate English rhymes and meter as well as preserve the meanings.

The personal problem at issue in the poem is how the poet should spend the rest of his life. For the past nineteen years, his chief intellectual efforts have been directed to mathematics, art, music, and linguistics at the expense of his great poetic talent. He is trying to discover his true self. He meditates on life and eternity. The surface of the sea is calm, but underneath there is turbulence; the poet thinks of the activities of life with philosophic disdain, but behind the disdain there is a living organism. The cemetery offers the immobility of the tombs, but underneath them are the remains of the poet's ancestors. As he looks at the sea he is filled with the idea of changelessness, but his own shadow rejects the light. He needs some assurance of the fact of change to prove his own existence. He cannot accept the idea of immortality. The true irrefutable worm is not in the grave but in life.

The story of Zeno's stationary arrow and the tale of Achilles and the tortoise were meant to illustrate the fact that change is illusion. He must reject this idea, however; he cannot escape from change and action. At the end of the poem, the calm sea becomes turbulent, and with a triumphant cry the poet accepts the prospect of an active life.

Dorothy B. Aspinwall

THE CHANGING LIGHT AT SANDOVER

Author: James Merrill (1926-   )
Type of poem: Poetic Sequence
First published: "The Book of Ephraim," 1976, in *Divine Comedies*; *Mirabell: Books of Number*, 1978; *Scripts for the Pageant*, 1980; *The Changing Light at Sandover* (complete poem), 1982

The Poem

The Changing Light at Sandover is an epic poem in three books along with a supplemental coda. The title refers to the house owned by the poet in Stonington, Connecticut, where much of the action (both internal and external) of the poem takes place. More generally, the title expresses the central preoccupation of the poem: its interest in the possibilities available in the occult and the spirit world. The fact that the light changes rather than remains constant hints that this world sometimes appears genuine yet seems sometimes a contrivance of the human imagination.

The first book of the poem "The Book of Ephraim," begins with the poet, James Merrill, in his dining room at Sandover. He, along with his friend David Jackson, is at the Ouija board, looking for otherworldly communication. They manage to make contact with a spirit named Ephraim, who in his earthly existence was a Greek Jew of the first century A.D., murdered by the Roman emperor Tiberius about the time of Jesus. Ephraim gives them information about the organization of the afterlife, pictured as a complicated set of layers of consciousness. Ephraim also liberally dispenses scandal and gossip about various historical personages. Ephraim's messages are written down by Jackson and then are used as the base for the excerpts that are presented in the poem. Further sessions with Ephraim are interspersed frequently with an account of the daily lives of Merrill and Jackson. The reader is made familiar with a circle of friends of the two men, dead friends as well as living ones. Several of these friends will appear as characters in the poem's messages from the spirit world, including the experimental film director Maya Deren, the voice and presence of the distinguished poet W. H. Auden (a major influence on Merrill), and friends—Maria Mitsotaki, Hans Lodeizen, and Robert Morse—whose main renown is through this poem itself. This overlap between Merrill's mundane life and the world of his Ouija-channeled visions is characteristic of this portion of the poem. In "The Book of Ephraim," messages from the spirit world do not make up the majority of the book. Those messages that do occur are interwoven subtly with sensitive and amusing observations about the life and art of this world. The presence of the Ouija messages lends an aura of the uncanny and the mysterious to even the daily elements of Merrill's narrative. One has a sense that something is about to happen, that there are mysterious forces lurking in the present that make one uneasy about whether what one has known about the world will suffice. This mystery will become more explicit in the remainder of the trilogy.

Merrill and Jackson journey to New Mexico, Greece, and Venice as the years pass, and their contacts with Ephraim continue. The poet begins to write a novel about his experiences with Ephraim but finds himself blocked by what Merrill believes are the overly broad evocations required by the novel form. Merrill begins to envision revealing Ephraim and his spirit world in a work much like the poem now being read. A momentary intrusion during one of the sessions of a terrifying, powerful force, a spirit far mightier than Ephraim, disrupts contact with the spirit world. "The Book of Ephraim" ends with the poet in his home, waiting for the repair of his broken furnace. The poem seems to have returned to the material world. Yet a glimpse of an enigmatic "ancient, ageless woman of the stars," who refuses to surrender her uncanny otherness to the inquiring eye of the poet, shows that there is still a lingering mystery that will be explored in future volumes.

The second part of the poem, *Mirabell: Books of Number*, begins where the first book left off, in Merrill's house in Stonington. After some characteristically wry and rich reflections on having acquired "the wrong wallpaper" for his parlor, Merrill reestablishes contact with Ephraim. That leads to contact with another spirit who reveals far more of the content of the afterlife. This spirit, called by the number 741 but eventually named Mirabell by its human contacts, is described as being one of the winged "men before mankind" whose appearance is similar to that of the bats that are represented on the parlor wallpaper, but who is later shown to be a beautiful peacock. Mirabell is not the chatty confidant that Ephraim was; he is far more elemental, far less domesticated. Mirabell shows his more cosmic reach by demanding that Merrill write "poems of science." Much of the rest of this part of the poem is taken up, indeed, with scientific analogies and speculations.

Mirabell describes a universe fashioned by a "God Biology," or, as his title is abbreviated, "God B." This god is within the shaping processes of life rather than outside and above them as in traditional religions. Mirabell's account mixes established scientific facts with wildly imaginative visions as he lays out the nature and history of the cosmos. Mirabell lays stress on the leading role of certain extraordinary individuals whose gifted minds constitute God B's primary resource in ordering the universe against his adversary: chaos. According to Mirabell, there are five of these souls, who have through the ages been reincarnated continually. Because there are five of them, their cultivation and succoring of God B's realm is known as "V work," after the symbol for the number five in the Roman numeral system. Mirabell's revelations give a sense of the beauty of God B's works, as well as their potential destructiveness.

The third section, *Scripts for the Pageant*, is taken up almost totally with the spirit world. There are many occasions for rendezvous with those of Merrill's friends who have passed into the other realm. As Merrill and Jackson journey once again to Greece, the tempo picks up and the action becomes crowded with a panoply of figures and messages about life and death. Several of the world's major religious figures, such as Buddha and Muhammad, appear, along with the angels of traditional Christian cosmology, who remain even though their God is not present. Much of this part is told in dramatic dialogue (suitable for a "pageant"), in which "JM" and "DJ" (as the names of Merrill and Jackson are often abbreviated) engage in prolonged questioning of their otherworldly interlocutors. The reader learns that Maria Mitsotaki will soon be reborn as a scientist in Bombay, to take up the mission of "V work." The angel Michael, who may all along have been the ultimate presence behind the seemingly minor Ephraim, presents a series of revelations about the future of humankind and its world. Michael and his angelic counterparts seem to paint a picture of humankind's ultimate redemption from its own vast potential for self-destruction. The heavenly instruction ends as Auden and other of Merrill's friends prepare to leave the spirit world for their eventual reincarnation upon Earth, where they will continue to propagate the healing and cultivating virtue of "V work."

The three parts originally appeared as separate volumes; upon publishing the overall work, Merrill added a short coda. The coda brings the provisional affirmation of the cosmic grandeur of *Scripts for the Pageant* once again to more intimate terms. Merrill moves from wondering whether the cosmos will be saved to determining what within it is worth saving. In answer, he pictures the ballroom at Sandover inhabited by all the great artists of the past, along with some of his own personal friends. As this scene exists in the spirit world, in the "real" Sandover, Merrill begins himself to write the poem; the last line of the poem is also its first: "Admittedly."

Forms and Devices

The Changing Light at Sandover is an epic not because it follows the formal techniques of works such as Homer's *Iliad* (c.800 B.C.), but because, in the manner of earlier long poems in English such as William Wordsworth's *The Prelude* (1850) or Walt Whitman's "Song of Myself," its ambition and its imaginative reach are of epic dimensions. Its vast range of characters, its Dantesque revelation of the afterlife and the heavens, and the sheer degree of personal, historical, and artistic information it includes give it a prodigious dimension that is equaled strikingly by its poetic achievement.

Unusually for a poem of its epic nature, though, the greatest asset of *The Changing Light at Sandover* is its mastery of linguistic rhythm and nuance. Merrill, in the many excellent lyric poems he wrote prior to the composition of this epic, had exhibited a tendency to write almost exclusively in traditional forms, employing rhyme and meter. That made him unpopular in the 1960's, when free verse was seen as a sign of authenticity and personal liberation. On the other hand, it made him quite popular in the 1980's, when young poets once again began enthusiastically to practice formal verse. What is captivating about Merrill, though, is the flexibility of his forms. One never feels that his use of them is merely an academic exercise; they flow so seamlessly into the story he is telling that their intricate architecture is often noticed only on a second reading. For example, the section of "The Book of Ephraim" describing his visit to Venice is in terza rima, the rhyme scheme used by

Dante; the witty suggestion is that it is appropriate to the Italian setting. Yet Merrill's imagery and his subject matter are so engrossing that the form does not obtrude. The form becomes an auxiliary comment on the poem it helps structure, rather than simply a confirmation of its authority.

Merrill's finest formal achievement in the poem is the "Samos" section of *Scripts for the Pageant*. Using another Italian form, the canzone, Merrill ends every line with one of these five words: "sense, water, fire, land, light." The five words (note the recurrence of the number five from "V work") clang together with an almost deafening and exhilarating intensity as they describe the lyrical tumult of Merrill's visit to the Greek isle of Samos, as well as its sober aftermath, in which shadows of death and loss intrude.

Merrill's wordplay is also a pivotal element of his formal apparatus. Through punning, alliteration, and a shrewd grasp of the verbal possibilities inherent in the different senses of words, Merrill creates combinations of language that assist him in reconciling the many different chords present in the poem. For example, in the "Samos" section, Merrill describes "the upward-rippling rungs of fire/ the outward-rippling rings (enough!) of water." Yet after this visionary torrent, Merrill uses "water" in a much more comic sense, as he asks in a parenthesis, "Now some details — how will this hold water?" The same word that before denoted a primal element now is used as an almost banal figure of speech.

What is first noticed about the poem is how the messages from the Ouija board are printed exclusively in capital letters. This device permits them to stand out on the page and conveys a sense of how strange they are, how unable to be accommodated within one's usual ways of looking at things. The capitalization deliberately gives them a tone of power and drama, as in this line from *Mirabell: Books of Number*: "A BASIC PRECEPT U WILL NEED TO TAKE ON FAITH; THERE IS/ NO ACCIDENT."

The poem's organization as a whole is also very deliberate. The first part is divided into sections by means of the letters of the alphabet, whereas the second goes through the first ten numbers, zero to nine. The third section is divided into three parts, "YES," "&," and "NO." All these signs appear on the Ouija board. Thus the board underlies the poem's formal principles and provides access to its spiritual revelations.

Themes and Meanings

One expects great truths from an epic poem. The reader expects to be told about the meaning of the world and to be instructed on how to live within it. *The Changing Light at Sandover* is a very contemporary poem in its refusal to provide fully these sorts of truths. The world conveyed through the Ouija board is a work of fantasy and imagination, not one that is intended to be an imitation of what reality is or an admonition as to what it should be. Merrill is adamant in his claim that the Ouija sessions occurred as in the poem. He insists that the spirit world, not himself, was responsible for the portions of the poem in capital letters, and that he only served as an editor who molded them into a suitable poetic shape. Even so, the reader is not compelled to accept the veracity of the poem's narrative but to enjoy it as a work of art.

The way the poem combines spirituality and imagination can be seen in miniature in the character of Ephraim. In the nineteenth century, Matthew Arnold made a famous distinction between the "Hellenic" and the "Hebraic": The Hellenic sensibility is filled with the beauty and grace found in Greek sculpture; the Hebraic sensibility possesses the zeal and faith found in the Bible. Ephraim, a Greek Jew, combines these sensibilities; the values he represents are both transcendent and sensuous. The fact that Ephraim is murdered at about the time of the death of Jesus hints that Merrill is proffering his vision as a comic and ironic version of the long-held truths of Judeo-Christian belief.

Merrill does not offer an easy substitute for the God of this faith. Merrill's cosmology values both art and nature, without worshiping either of them. The heart of Merrill's implicit creed may be found in *Mirabell: Books of Number*, when the voice of Auden advises, "THINK WHAT A MINOR/ PART THE SELF PLAYS IN A WORK OF ART/ COMPARED TO THE GREAT GIVENS/ THE ROSEBRICK MANOR/ ALL TOPIARY FORMS & METRICAL/ MOAT ARIPPLE!" "THE GREAT GIVENS" of art or nature are shaped by individual hands, whether those of humans or of God B, but their beauty, their display of the wonders of being a created entity, redeems the self by integrating it into a larger whole. This whole is overtly the cosmos portrayed by the voices speaking through the Ouija board, but Merrill clearly also has in mind the legacy of art and imagination passed from the past to the present. "Sandover" is thus not only Merrill's own house but also the entire edifice of art, the rosebrick manor that persists while being laid over by the sands of time.

Thus *The Changing Light at Sandover* can affirm either a lavishly described afterlife or the artistic power and heritage that have enabled the creation of such a vision. The glory of Merrill's poem is that he leaves the options open. The reader has the capacity to choose between revelation and imagination, and perhaps to accept both.

Nicholas Birns

CHANNEL FIRING

Author: Thomas Hardy (1840-1928)
Type of poem: Narrative
First published: 1914, in *Satires of Circumstance*

The Poem

The title refers to the firing of naval guns on the English Channel, guns apparently engaging in a military exercise. The poem registers a complex response to this event, using nine stanzas, each a quatrain set in an *abab* rhyme scheme, one of the most common forms of English poetry.

In "Channel Firing," Thomas Hardy uses the first-person plural, though the "We" might be thought of as a single individual speaking for his companions as well as for himself. The "We" are all dead and buried in a graveyard situated beside a church. This location is indicated not only by the reference to an "altar-crumb" but also by the word "chancel," which means the space around the altar of a church for the clergy and the choir, as well as by the term "glebe cow," which means a cow pastured on church grounds for the pastor's use.

The first two stanzas describe the arousal of the dead by the sound of the guns, a sound that is interpreted by them as signaling the arrival of Judgment Day. That occasion, according to Christian belief, will see the destruction of the world as humans know it, the resurrection of the dead, and their assignment by God, along with those still living, to eternal bliss or eternal torment.

God does in fact enter but not to proceed to judgment. Rather, He assures the dead that the sounds they have heard are simply those of guns at sea practicing to make war even bloodier ("redder") than it has been in ages past. God accuses the nations preparing for war of being insane. The living, he says, are doing no more for promulgating Christian principles than are the dead, who are helpless to affect the course of human events. God further states that it is a good thing He has not arrived to deliver judgment, because if He had, some of the living would be consigned to hell for engaging in military threats. God's statement, which dominates the middle section of the poem, concludes by His saying that "It will be warmer" if He ever does blow the trumpet signaling Judgment Day. By that, he apparently means the flames of hell will engulf the world.

Assured that Judgment Day has not arrived, the dead, who had sat up in response to the sounds they heard, resume their horizontal position. One of them wonders aloud whether humanity will ever prove to be saner than it was when he and his companions were sent to their death by God. Another, who had been a clergyman, wishes that he had spent his life enjoying himself (smoking and drinking) rather than preaching.

As the poem concludes, the sounds of the guns are heard once again, creating an impression of their readiness to carry out acts of revenge. The guns' reverberations extend inland to Stourton Tower, a structure built to commemorate the victory of

Alfred the Great over Danish invaders. The sounds also reach Camelot, the site of the legendary King Arthur's court, and, finally, Stonehenge, a ring of monoliths that may have been used by a sun-worshiping cult or for astronomical observation.

Forms and Devices

Hardy has made a daring choice of speakers for the telling of this curious anecdote, employing not only the dead, whose actions and speech are reported to the reader directly, but also God Himself, who speaks condemningly of humankind. The presence of these beings, along with the graveyard setting, would seem to make for an unrelievedly solemn and moralistic piece, but in fact "Channel Firing" works to subvert such an effect through the use of irony.

Irony comes in various forms, but it always involves a gap or discrepancy of some sort. One such gap occurs between the thrust of the first six lines and that of the next three. The initial somberness and spookiness created by guns shaking coffins, the disturbing of the dead, and the awakening of dogs who then proceed to howl in a "drearisome" manner is undercut by the distinctly unthreatening details of the mouse, the withdrawing worms, and, most of all, the drooling cow. Hardy heightens the incongruous presence of the cow by having it enter the poem in the same line that sees the entrance of God. The setup of that line— "The glebe cow drooled. Till God called, 'No' " —creates the momentary impression that God is enjoining the cow not to drool, a patently ridiculous effect.

Even when the reader continues and realizes that the "No" refers to the fact that God is informing the dead that it is not Judgment Day, irony persists. It now involves the discrepancy between the way one would commonly expect God to talk and the way Hardy's creation speaks. While God's statement is given a touch of the elevated and archaic by His employment of the medieval "Christés" (instead of "Christ's"), His speech is notable for its use of the all-too-human taunting remark, "Ha, ha," as well as for the cliché "Mad as hatters" (which alludes to the occupational hazard once faced by people who made hats because of a chemical used in their production). Even "for Christés sake" carries with it the echo of the common human and secularized expression "for Christ's sake."

Related to God's use of "Ha ha" is the irony involving His attitude. Functioning neither as the figure of mercy nor the solemn deliverer of justice that common belief would expect, God taunts and teases the dead on the matter of Judgment Day. Instead of having the coming of that momentous occasion continue to be regarded as a certainty, He leaves the matter open. He says, when referring to His blowing of the trumpet signifying judgment, "if indeed/ I ever do," bringing into question a fundamental Christian belief under the cover of His solicitousness for the dead ("for you are men,/ And rest eternal sorely need"). It is no wonder that in response to the appearance of this sort of divinity, one of the dead should regret having given his life to being a Christian preacher.

Themes and Meanings

Unless the comic undercutting of the original atmosphere of the poem is recognized, along with the irony attached to the figure of God, "Channel Firing" might be read as a fairly straightforward and unrelentingly serious condemnation of humankind for continuing to make war, a judgment coming from within a Christian perspective. The moralizing figure of the poem, God, cannot be taken seriously, however, or at least not entirely so. Ultimately, He is an unattractive figure.

The poem is registering the fact of war and its cost in human life. Indeed, the piece might be regarded as prescient, for Hardy wrote it in April of 1914, only months before the outbreak of World War I. Yet Hardy is pointing to the costly use of force less to shake a judgmental finger at humankind than to register such use as apparently inescapable. The poem might be said to replace judgments with facts, and Christian theology, which it finds absurd, with history.

It is interesting to note Hardy's handling of place names in the last stanza. They are arranged so as to have the sounds of the guns carry not merely inland through space but also backward through time. The reader moves from Hardy's century to the eighteenth century, the period when Stourton Tower was constructed. The reference to that edifice moves the reader back even further, for it commemorates an event of the ninth century. The mention of Camelot carries the reader still further back, to the sixth century, and the reference to Stonehenge goes back furthest of all, for that prodigious structure is prehistoric.

It is as if Hardy is saying that the use of force, the making of war, has been with humankind for as long as there have been human beings. That, along with the gunnery practice that opens the poem, would suggest that violence will continue to be a fact of human life. A solemnity returns to "Channel Firing" as Hardy offers the reader this bleak but in a way grand perspective on human existence, setting that existence in the framework of the cosmos with the notable phrase that closes the poem, a phrase marked by alliteration and four strong beats — "starlit Stonehenge." Bloody as it has been, the human enterprise acquires a certain substance and dignity here. Unlike the poem's handling of God and fundamental presuppositions of Christianity, it does not undercut that dignity by subjecting it to irony.

Alan Holder

CHICAGO

Author: Carl Sandburg (1878-1967)
Type of poem: Lyric
First published: 1916, in *Chicago Poems*

The Poem

"Chicago" is a poem in free verse, one without a set meter or rhyme scheme, running twenty-three lines. The title gives the name of the city that the poet is praising, which does not appear elsewhere in the poem. Without the title, this poem could refer to any industrial city, suggesting a universal love of place.

The poem, written in the first person so that the poet addresses the reader directly, celebrates both the virtues and vices of the city. It begins with a staccato list of occupations found in Chicago (hog butcher, tool maker, stacker of wheat), followed by three adjectives that attach an emotion to those occupations. Carl Sandburg calls them "Stormy, husky, brawling," creating an aura of vitality. This first section of the poem is abrupt and rapid, like the city being portrayed.

The second section departs from the brief phrasing and turns to long, flowing, melodic sentences. Each of the first three sentences acknowledges a vice of the city in the first half of the sentence. It is wicked, corrupt, and brutal. The poet agrees to each accusation, supplying a specific detail that supports the charge in the second half of the sentence. There are "painted women," "gunmen," and "wanton hunger." The city does, in fact, have its failings.

The poet more than accepts the failings of his city, however; he answers in the remaining lines with a list of positive attributes. His city is singing and loud, "proud to be alive and coarse and strong and cunning." Sandburg celebrates this strength, and it is clear that the vices are a small enough price to pay for the overwhelming vitality and life the city contains.

In the last four lines, an important shift of perspective occurs. The poet personifies the city, saying it laughs as a young man does, laughs "as an ignorant fighter who has never lost a battle." This suggests a sense of innocence despite the previously mentioned corruption. Only youth laughs and feels confident regardless of circumstances. Only youth swaggers with the assurance of victory. Hence, a sense of immaturity mingles with the confidence and vitality.

The last line repeats the major attributes the poet grants the city. It is laughing, stormy, and proud. This line concludes with the repetition of the poem's beginning, but as fragments of a single line rather than separate lines. This gives the poem a circular effect, ending right where it began, and creates a sense of closure.

Forms and Devices

Sandburg wrote in free verse, but this does not mean that the poem lacks any structure. The structure supports the subject matter. A poem about a loud, brawling city would hardly be appropriately conveyed in a tightly constructed sonnet. Sandburg sought to capture the mood of the city in the arrangement of the poem's language.

The short phrases in the first section are simply a list of occupations. This suggests that the city is primarily a place of industry, all efficiency and business. When the second section begins, the lines are long compound sentences that capture the depth of emotion the poet feels. The poet is in awe of the city even as he admits its weaknesses.

Sandburg was greatly influenced by the poetry of Walt Whitman. Both poets wrote of the common man, democratic society, and celebrations of the ordinary rather than the sublime. Sandburg utilizes the free-verse form that Whitman had made so popular in the nineteenth century, but Sandburg owes other debts as well — particularly to the Bible. The repetition of "and" in the first several lines, for example, is distinctly biblical. By using "and" rather than writing sentences with dependent clauses, Sandburg creates the effect that each independent clause is equally important. The poet's emotions are equally significant regarding the city's vices and its virtues.

This parallelism is one of the chief poetic devices employed. In addition to the repeated "and," the use of the "-ing" form of the verbs after line 13 implies that the action is occurring presently. These are the things the city is doing; it is not resting on its laurels and traditions like other "little soft cities," but moving rapidly.

The poem is written in the present tense, which lends it immediacy. The poet is currently experiencing the city and its emotion, which is a radical departure from what the nineteenth century English poet William Wordsworth said poetry ideally was: emotion recalled in tranquility. There is nothing tranquil about "Chicago," and the use of the present tense helps convey this.

Sandburg's use of metaphor further supports his themes. He compares the city to a dog to show its fierceness. He compares it to a young man, endowing the city with youth and enthusiasm and energy. These comparisons are commonplace; there is no elaborate use of mythology or classical allusions, so the reader has immediate access to the meanings. Sandburg does not employ traditional poetic devices such as alliteration or assonance, preferring the rhythms of natural speech. This is a conscious appeal to the common man, as Sandburg believed that poetry should address the common man.

Perhaps one of the most outstanding devices the poet uses is the personification of the city. Personification, giving human characteristics to inanimate objects, is clear in the attribution of physical traits to Chicago, such as saying the city has a mouth and head. The city behaves in a human fashion, laughing and brawling and singing. In this way, Sandburg furthers the concept of the city's vitality and life.

Additionally, Sandburg addresses the city directly — the poetic voice is speaking to the city. "They tell me you are wicked," he says, as if the city will answer him. This conveys the idea that the city will continue, in the same fashion, regardless of the occupants. Indeed, if people move away, the city's character will not change, and Sandburg acknowledges this self-perpetuating ability in the direct address.

Themes and Meanings

"Chicago" is a celebration of America's vitality. It is about boundless energy, about love of life, about the zest and laughter that Sandburg found. Granted, the city has its dark side, but Sandburg's city laughs in the face of terrible destiny. This attitude is a prominent theme in American literature, especially in the latter half of the twentieth century.

The destiny to which the poet refers is death. Many of Sandburg's poems address this theme directly, but in "Chicago" it is implied rather than directly stated. The terrible destiny is inevitable; no matter how much life is packed into the sprawling city, its inhabitants will perish. The spirit of the city will eventually soften and become like other cities. This impression of death is reaffirmed in the metaphor of the ignorant fighter. Fighters do lose eventually, even if it has not happened yet. Despite the certainty of destiny, however, the important thing is to live. The affirmation of life lies in the attempts to live life fully, to work, and most of all, to laugh.

Unlike many of his contemporaries, notably T. S. Eliot, Sandburg was a poet of the people. He was widely read in his own time, and his poetry reflects his preoccupation with the common person. The people of his city may be underfed, criminal, or immoral, but they are real people. He writes of workers and farmers. He writes of those people who strain and sweat and swear and laugh and cry in order to celebrate the very existence of humanity. His concern for common people is more than intellectual; throughout his life, he kept in close contact with the laboring classes and was motivated by his experiences with the Populist movement. It is no coincidence that in addition to his many volumes of poetry Sandburg wrote a massive biography of Abraham Lincoln. He viewed Lincoln much the same way that he viewed his city, Chicago — as a folkloric figure of the people, standing for the average worker.

Sandburg contributed an important dimension to the poetry of his time. His use of blunt language helped liberate poetry from the nineteenth century's formal prettiness. His subject matter appealed to working people rather than to strict intellectuals. The form was loose and free, like the dreams of the people. This poem, perhaps his greatest, provides a glimpse of the talent and power of one of America's early twentieth century poets.

Christine F. Sally

"CHILDE ROLAND TO THE DARK TOWER CAME"

Author: Robert Browning (1812-1889)
Type of poem: Narrative
First published: 1855, in *Men and Women*

The Poem

The title is a direct quotation from a song of Edgar in William Shakespeare's *King Lear* (c. 1605-1606). It has traditionally been assumed that the persona is Roland, although such an assumption is unwarranted. This poem is an interior monologue, a hybrid of the soliloquy and the dramatic monologue, and the "narrator" is simply thinking aloud. The thinker-narrator is a quester of many years, something that the mythical Roland was not. Moreover, the persona does not appear to be a very young man preparing for knighthood, as the word "childe" would suggest.

"Childe Roland to the Dark Tower Came" begins *in medias res*. Since no background or explanation is given for what is happening, the reader is initially confounded. Gradually, it becomes clear that the persona is searching for the "Dark Tower" and has just asked an aged cripple for directions. Suspicious that the cripple has maliciously misdirected him even to his death, he nevertheless proceeds on the appointed path. He is exhausted by his search, "drawn out through years," and would be glad to reach an end of any kind, even if the end should mean failure or death.

At line 43, the persona turns away from the ominous cripple-guide to continue his search. Immediately on entering the gray plain, the safe road vanishes. The protagonist finds himself amid gathering darkness, entrapped in a grotesque, alien environment. Much of the remainder of the poem describes changing scenes from this landscape of nightmare, which in many ways parallels the diseased garden of *The Sensitive Plant* (1820) by Percy Bysshe Shelley, one of Robert Browning's favorite poets. From the tenth stanza intermittently to the thirty-first, the poem is, in large measure, a series of vivid verbal pictures that put one in mind of the surreal paintings of Hieronymus Bosch, Pieter Bruegel, and Salvador Dalí.

As he continues his search for the Dark Tower, the persona confronts not only the physical horrors of a stunted, deformed nature but also the memory of earlier comrades who, in their quest for the Dark Tower, came to miserable ends. His memory of "Cuthbert's reddening face" and Giles, "the soul of honor," is more harrowing to him than the "starved ignoble nature" by which he is surrounded. At last, the plain gives way to mountains, and in a final ray of sunset between two hills the Tower is revealed to the persona. His mind filled with the names of "all the lost adventurers" who had gone before him and feeling like a helpless prey for the gigantic hills, which are "Crouched like two bulls locked horn in horn in fight," the persona is dauntless and sounds his horn in defiance and triumph: *"Childe Roland to the Dark Tower Came."* On this note the poem ends — as abruptly as it began.

Forms and Devices

The poem consists of 204 lines divided into thirty-four stanzas. As is the case with many of Browning's dramatic poems, the meter keeps to a conversational (in this case thoughtful) rhythm while remaining predominantly iambic pentameter. "In the dock's harsh swarth leaves, bruised as to balk" is a telling exception. The rhyme scheme of the six-line stanzas is fixed at *abbaab*. A powerful effect of emphasis and finality is often achieved by means of the rhyme of the final line of the stanza echoing that of the third line. Stanzas 2, 9, and 16 are good examples of this sound effect.

In the hands of a lesser poet, the use of a fixed stanza form could inhibit the free flow of thought and reduce credibility by making the reader question the appropriateness of the form for the substance. Such is not the case, however, with this poem. Through the frequent use of enjambment and internal stops, Browning is able to approximate the fluidity of consciousness. In this freeing of the restraints of form, this poem is a tour de force in the manner of Browning's "My Last Duchess," in which naturalness of speech is achieved within the confines of rhymed couplets.

In *"Childe Roland to the Dark Tower Came,"* Browning makes extensive use of cacophony, simile, and metaphor. The harsh ugliness of the landscape is conveyed by means of such shrill words and phrases as "cockle," "spurge," "blotches," "chopped," "bespate," "ugh," "ragged thistle stalk," "dank/ Soil to a plash," and "ugly heights and heaps." Browning was especially comfortable using unpleasant sounds to create desired effects, as one may see in "Soliloquy of the Spanish Cloister" and "How They Brought the Good News from Ghent to Aix."

Similes in this poem are what might be called "organic." They are vital embodiments of the persona's perceptions. The persona's comparison of the "sudden little river" to a serpent indicates his sense of danger; the phrase "quiet as despair" in stanza 8 suggests his exhaustion. That he has "supp'd full with horrors" is seen in his perception of the cleft in the oak tree as "a distorted mouth that splits its rim/ Gaping at death" in stanza 26.

The various states of the persona's consciousness are similarly delineated by metaphors. As he leaves the public path in stanza 8, he sees himself as a lost farm animal: The sun "shot one grim/ Red leer to see the plan catch its estray." The doomed ship in stanza 31 and the exposed, vulnerable prey of gigantic hunters in stanza 32 are additional indications of the persona's acute fear and sense of danger.

Themes and Meanings

According to Browning, *"Childe Roland to the Dark Tower Came"* descended upon him as a sort of dream and was written in a single day, January 2, 1852. Browning denied any allegorical intentions in writing it and was characteristically reluctant to offer any help in interpreting it. Many years later, Browning said that the poem had demanded to be written and that he was aware of no particular meaning when he composed it. When a friend asked if the poem's meaning could be described as "He that endureth to the end shall be saved," Browning replied affirmatively.

"Childe Roland to the Dark Tower Came" has been the subject of numerous studies. William Clyde DeVane has found in Gerard de Lairesse's *The Art of Painting* (translated into English in 1778), a book that had a profound and permanent influence on Browning, the origin of many of the poem's images, including the cripple, the pathless field, the diseased vegetation, the river, the water rat, the claustrophobic mountains, and the malevolent sunset. The image of the tower was suggested by one he had seen several times in Italy, and he told Mrs. Orr, his early biographer, that the horse came to him from a figure in a tapestry he owned.

Because of its suggestion of allegory, this poem has been a favorite subject of interpretation of Browning societies. Some see in the poem a dark pessimism reflecting unresolved conflicts in the poet's psyche. Others see it as a study of courage. Clearly, the poem draws heavily on the conventions of quest literature, and it has many affinities with *Sir Gawain and the Green Knight* (fourteenth century). Both Browning's persona and Gawain traverse dangerous and frightening terrains in their search; they are beset with self-doubt and fear; they are forced to look deep within themselves and summon up their last vestiges of courage and will. Finally, the objects of their quests are disappointing. The Green Chapel is merely an earthen mound, and the Dark Tower is no more than a "round squat turret" made of brown stone. The tower has no intrinsic beauty or value. What is important is the quest itself. Considered in this way, *"Childe Roland to the Dark Tower Came"* is a clear statement of "success in failure," a theme Browning explored often. Making the effort to overcome obstacles to Browning is far more spiritually fulfilling than anything the world regards as success. Browning's heroes embrace life and death fully and fiercely. The "ungirt loin and the unlit lamp" are sins that loom large in Browning's writing. Timidity and a turning away from challenges have no place in Browning's strong optimism.

The persona of *"Childe Roland to the Dark Tower Came"* is a hero. His life is fulfilled in a splendid expenditure of energy; he has far more in common with Alfred, Lord Tennyson's Ulysses than with T. S. Eliot's J. Alfred Prufrock. Taken in the broad context of Browning's poetry, *"Childe Roland to the Dark Tower Came,"* despite its general ambience of gloom, affirms the ultimate value of human effort. It is a poem of unbridled optimism.

Robert G. Blake

THE CHIMNEY SWEEPER

Author: William Blake (1757-1827)
Type of poem: Lyric
First published: 1789, in *Songs of Innocence*

The Poem

"The Chimney Sweeper," a poem of six quatrains, accompanied by William Blake's illustration, appeared in *Songs of Innocence* in 1789, the year of the outbreak of the French Revolution, and expresses Blake's revolutionary fervor. It exposes the appalling conditions of the boys known as climbing boys, whose lot had been brought to public attention but had been only marginally improved by the 1788 Chimney Sweepers' Act. Blake published a companion poem in *Songs of Innocence and of Experience* in 1794.

The speaker is a young chimney sweeper, presumably six or seven years old, and the style is appropriately simple. Much of the imaginative power of the poem comes from the tension between the child's naïveté and the subtlety of Blake's own vision.

In the first stanza, the sweeper recounts how he came to this way of life. His mother—always in Blake's work the warm, nurturing parent—having died, he was sold as an apprentice by his father, the stern figure of authority. His present life revolves around working, calling through the streets for more work, and at the end of the day sleeping in soot, a realistic detail since the boys did indeed make their beds on bags of the soot they had swept from chimneys.

The second stanza introduces Tom Dacre, who comes to join the workers and is initiated into his new life by a haircut. As Tom cries when his head is shaved, the speaker comforts him with the thought that if his hair is cut it cannot be spoiled by the soot. The consolation is, from any adult point of view, totally inadequate, but for Tom it is effective. He falls asleep and dreams happily.

The next three stanzas give the substance of the dream. Tom dreams that thousands of sweepers locked in coffins are released by an angel. Suddenly, they find themselves in a pastoral landscape, where, freed from their burdens, they bathe in a river and then rise up to the clouds. There, the angel tells Tom, "if he'd be a good boy,/ He'd have God for his father & never want joy." The dream is an obvious instance of wish fulfillment, and its pathos rests on the fact that while it reveals the child's longing to escape, the opening and closing of the poem make it clear that his only ways of escape are dreams and death.

The last quatrain opens with a brutal contrast. Having dreamed of playing in the sun, Tom awakes, and the sweepers begin their day's work, a day to be spent in the total darkness of the cramped chimneys. Yet, restored by his dream, Tom is happy, and the poem ends with the pious moral, akin to the angel's speech, "So if all do their duty, they need not fear harm."

Forms and Devices

The poem is built around a series of powerful, closely related contrasts. The first, introduced in the second line, is that of bondage and freedom, for the child is literally sold into a state of both servitude and imprisonment within the chimneys. This contrast is reinforced by the parallel contrast between black and white. Covered in soot, the sweepers are habitually black; Tom's white hair is cut off, and the whiteness of his skin is only regained in the dream, when he, along with the other boys, is able to wash in the river. The color contrast suggests the condition of the African slave, whose plight Blake, an ardent supporter of abolition, describes in "The Little Black Boy." Like that little boy, the blackened chimney sweeper suffers the injustice of a white society that puts commercial values before moral ones and treats him as an outcast from the human condition.

A second group of contrasts juxtaposes work and play, sorrow and joy, tears and laughter. In the streets, the sweeper can only call, "weep weep," and Tom cries when his head is shaved, but in the dream, the scene that is the subject of Blake's illustration, the boys leap, laugh, and play.

The final antithesis is that between death and life, coldness and warmth, darkness and light. The sweepers endure a death-in-life, the literal cold and dark of their days matched by their deprivation and the cold indifference of society. In Tom's dream, however, the washing in the river assumes the significance of a baptism into a better life and counters the ritual head shaving of the entry into prison. The child glimpses a new heaven and a new Earth before he returns to the fallen world.

From these contrasts, certain images acquire symbolic significance. The bags, abandoned in the dream and picked up again with the brushes the next morning, suggest the terrible burden of the child's life; the soot indicates the corruption of a society that uses and abuses him; and the coffins represent both the chimneys in which he works and the actual death to which he will soon come. In contrast, the sun, river, and plain express the joys that should be natural to childhood. Yet, even symbols associated with happiness intensify the harsh facts of existence. The bright key recalls imprisonment; the harmony of the leaping boys emphasizes their isolation in the chimneys; and the lamb, whose curling fleece Tom's hair resembles, is often, as is the sweeper, a helpless victim.

These emotionally charged contrasts and images underscore the ironic understatement. The speaker describes his life plainly, indulging in neither denunciation nor sentimentality. The facts speak for themselves, however, forcefully opposing the three pieces of comfort in the poem, the first provided by the speaker for Tom, the second provided by the angel, and the third offered by the speaker as a final moral. When God the Father, like the father on Earth, seems to have turned His face from the child, injunctions for Tom to be good and to do his duty betoken a bitter irony.

Themes and Meanings

While presenting the nonjudgmental viewpoint of the child, Blake makes a passionate indictment of a society that exploits the weak and at the same time hypocritically uses moral platitudes about duty and goodness to further its selfish interests. Moreover, the reader is made aware of his own complicity in social evil when the sweeper addresses him directly with the words "your chimneys I sweep."

Yet, the poem is more than social criticism. In *Songs of Innocence and of Experience*, Blake contrasts the two states of being. Usually the condition of childhood, innocence is that state in which evil is not known; it is characterized by joy and love, is normally associated with the peaceful harmony of a pastoral background, and is often guarded by the presence of the good mother. Experience, on the other hand, brings awareness of evil; it is accompanied by feelings of outrage and hatred; and it finds its appropriate setting in the city. In Blake's philosophy, passage through experience is necessary before entrance into a final state of vision, a higher innocence in which joy is regained but transformed by deeper spiritual awareness.

Although most poems in *Songs of Innocence* directly reflect the happiness of innocence, a few — notably, "The Chimney Sweeper," "Holy Thursday," and "The Little Black Boy" — place innocent children in a world of experience. Surrounded by evil, these children still retain their innocence, an innocence marked not so much by their own freedom from guilt as by their unawareness of the guilt of others.

The chimney sweeper is robbed of everything that should be the accompaniment of innocence. Yet, he bears no ill will, accepting without question both his lot and the moral clichés of a corrupt adult world. He transcends circumstances and in a sense re-creates his world. Deprived of his own mother, he becomes Tom's protector as he soothes the sobbing child. Thus comforted, Tom enjoys, in a dream, the light, laughter, and freedom denied him in real life. Significantly, the joy does not dissipate with the start of the day's work, and Tom, secure in his innocence, remains "happy & warm."

The last line, "So if all do their duty, they need not fear harm," is then a paradox. On the level of social protest, the moral is deliberately inadequate and ironic. Yet, it also asserts a fundamental truth, since duty implies not the obligation to climb the chimneys or to acquiesce in the social pattern but the need to retain as long as possible an innocence that allows its possessor to triumph over the restrictions of the material world.

"The Chimney Sweeper" juxtaposes two points of view: that of the poet, who attacks society by indirections, and that of the sweeper, who presents directly the mode of perception characteristic of innocence. The interplay of the two gives the poem its unique depth and complexity.

Muriel Mellown

CHRISTABEL

Author: Samuel Taylor Coleridge (1772-1834)
Type of poem: Narrative
First published: 1816, in *Christabel; Kubla Khan: A Vision; The Pains of Sleep*

The Poem

Christabel is a long narrative poem, most of which is written in tetrameter couplets. As Samuel Taylor Coleridge himself pointed out in the original preface to the work, although the meter is standard, the number of syllables is somewhat irregular, varying from seven to twelve. The simple title emphasizes the fact that the story told by the poet is indeed Christabel's story, the story of her struggle against possession by a demonic force.

From the scenic description in part 2 of *Christabel*, critics have deduced that the geographical setting Coleridge chose for his poem was the Lake District of England, where he had lived for some time near his friend and fellow poet William Wordsworth. The historical setting is the Middle Ages and, appropriately, the physical milieu is the castle of a baron, Sir Leoline.

Christabel begins in the forest outside the castle. Although it is a chilly night in early spring, the protagonist, Christabel, has sought the solitude of the woods to pray for her absent lover. Suddenly a mysterious lady emerges from the darkness. After introducing herself as "Geraldine," she says that she was abducted from her own home by five knights, who deposited her in the woods but will return for her. Taking pity upon Geraldine, Christabel helps her into the castle, ignoring such warnings of evil as the lady's seeming inability to walk across the threshold, which had been blessed against evil spirits, and the growls of the usually good-natured old mastiff as the guest passes.

When they reach her room, Christabel speaks of her dead mother, who she believes still guards her from evil. The statement calls forth a strange, defiant exclamation from Geraldine, but Christabel attributes it to her guest's frightening experience, and the two settle down to sleep. While she holds the sleeping Christabel in her arms, Geraldine puts a spell on her, so that although she will be able to recognize evil, Christabel will not be able to speak about it.

When Christabel awakens the next morning, she has a confused sense of having sinned, perhaps in a dream. It is difficult for her to believe that Geraldine is evil, however, especially after Sir Leoline discovers that their guest is the daughter of his former friend, Lord Roland de Vaux of Tryermaine, from whom he has long been estranged. Resolving to heal the breach between them, Lord Roland commands the bard Bracy to take word to Lord Roland that his daughter is safe.

Bracy asks for a day's grace, so that he can expel from the woods the evil which he senses is lurking there. He tells the Baron of a troubling dream, in which he saw a snake devour a dove. Unfortunately, Sir Leoline assumes that the dove is not Christabel but Geraldine. When Christabel begs him to expel the guest, he accuses her of jealousy and, in a fury, sends Bracy on his mission. The poem ends with a few lines about the relationship between a father and a child.

Although Coleridge published the poem unfinished, he left an account of his intentions for two or three more parts, which would bring it to a conclusion. Geraldine would vanish, to reappear in the guise of Christabel's lover, and Sir Leoline would insist on proceeding with a wedding. The real lover would appear just in time and prove his identity. The evil spirit would disappear forever and all would end happily.

Forms and Devices

In the late eighteenth century, the Middle Ages had once again become fashionable. Readers were fascinated with the Gothic: knights in armor, ladies in distress, exotic religious trappings—such as rosaries, matins, bells, guardian spirits, and prayers to the Virgin—and, above all, supernatural suspense. It was this side of Romanticism that Coleridge had claimed when he and Wordsworth divided up the subject matter to be included in *Lyrical Ballads* (1798), and even though it appeared in a later collection, *Christabel* also clearly illustrates this kind of work.

The images in *Christabel* are those conventionally associated with mystery and the supernatural; for example, the sounds mentioned in the first lines: the chiming of the midnight hour, the hoots of owls, and the howling of the mastiff. The poet stresses the fact that the cock is crowing at the wrong time; clearly, this is a hint of disorder in the natural environment. The full moon is significant, too; although it brightens the dark woods, it is partially covered by a gray cloud, symbolizing the struggle between light and dark.

As the poem proceeds, this conflict becomes more explicit, and the images suggest the theme. Conventionally, light represents good, and dark, evil. It is also light that reveals the truth. Thus, when Geraldine enters the castle, the cold brands flare up so that Christabel can see Geraldine's snakelike eyes. Later, it is Christabel who lights the lamp, Geraldine who seems to shrink from the light. The fact that Geraldine is garbed in white, denoting goodness and purity, indicates that she is involved in a carefully planned deception.

The snake or serpent is the major symbol of evil in part 2 of the poem. Sir Leoline applies this symbol to Geraldine's supposed attackers, who he says must have "reptile souls." Later, he misinterprets Bracy's warning about the dove and the snake by assuming that the innocent-looking Geraldine is the dove. It is Christabel who now begins to see her as a snake or a serpent. It is clear that the images in the poem do more than create a mood; they are integrally related to the central conflict of the poem.

Themes and Meanings

Christabel is a poem about the conflict between good and evil. Christabel is good; Geraldine is evil. Geraldine has appeared at the castle with the obvious intention of drawing Christabel into evil, perhaps, it is implied, through a sexual seduction.

Early in the poem, the forces on both sides of the conflict are clearly lined up.

Christabel has her faith, as expressed in her prayers to God and to the Virgin Mary. Moreover, she has a spiritual guardian in her dead mother as well as an earthly guardian in her beloved father.

Although Geraldine does not actually call upon satanic powers, it is clear that she has their skills. Like the biblical serpent, she is a deceiver. She can invent plausible lies; she can feign goodness; and, as Coleridge's projected continuation suggests, she can appear in any guise, even that of another living person.

The reason that Geraldine is so successful in deceiving Christabel and Sir Leoline is that she appeals to the very vulnerability of virtue. Because she has been taught to be compassionate toward others, Christabel pities Geraldine. The fact that Geraldine seems to be another girl of high rank, almost a second self, makes Christabel's action even more predictable.

Sir Leoline, too, is made vulnerable by the seeming helplessness of a daughter so much like his own; however, his greatest weakness is his devotion to the code of chivalry. A knight is bound by hospitality; he cannot honorably cast out a guest and certainly not if she is a helpless damsel who has put herself under his protection.

Even in the fragment of *Christabel* which was published there are hints that while recognizing the power of evil, Coleridge did not intend for it to win. Despite the spell placed upon her, Christabel feels an increasing revulsion toward Geraldine; Bracy believes his dream, warning of evil; and certainly Sir Leoline will eventually once more be governed by his love for Christabel. In the conclusion, just as in Coleridge's *The Rime of the Ancient Mariner* (1798), nature will be justified; the woods, as well as the castle, will be rescued from evil by the power of good.

Rosemary M. Canfield Reisman

CHURCH GOING

Author: Philip Larkin (1922-1985)
Type of poem: Meditation
First published: 1955, in *The Less Deceived*

The Poem

"Church Going," a poem of seven nine-line stanzas, is a first-person description of a visit to an empty English country church. The narrator is apparently on a cycling tour (he stops to remove his bicycle clips), a popular activity for British workers on their summer holiday. He has come upon a church and stopped to look inside. Not wishing to participate in a worship service, the visitor checks first to make "sure there's nothing going on." He will eventually reveal that he is an agnostic and that his interest in churches is not derived from religious faith.

This church is empty, so he walks in, observing all of the usual accoutrements: "matting, seats, and stone,/ And little books." His irreverence is captured in his tone as he observes "some brass and stuff/ Up at the holy end." Yet he is not totally irreverent. He knows that he should take off his hat, but he is not wearing one. Instead, he removes his bicycle clips.

As he moves around the building, he touches the baptismal font, observes the roof, and climbs into the lectern to look at the large-print lectionary. He even plays church for a moment, speaking the words ("Here endeth the lesson") that are usually announced at the end of each scripture reading. Clearly, he has some familiarity with religious practices. He also knows enough to leave an offering in the alms box at the door of the church. All he leaves, however, is an Irish sixpence, a coin worth less than its English equivalent.

After the narrative/descriptive beginning, the poem changes direction. The narrator wonders why he stopped at the church, why he often stops at churches. What is he looking for? Before answering that question, however, he asks another. What will happen to church buildings when we stop using them as churches? This is not an entirely irrelevant question for a man who has lost his faith and who assumes that others will do likewise.

He imagines that some churches will become museums, while others will fall to ruin. They might be avoided as places of bad luck, or approached as places for magical cures. Certainly, there will be superstition associated with these places for a time, the narrator observes, but even superstition will eventually fade.

Who will be the last to remember what church buildings were used for, he wonders: an archaeologist perhaps, who would know the name for the rood-loft, the high beam between the choir and the nave that held a cross or crucifix, or someone looking for an antique or a decorative artifact. It might be a "Christmas-addict," assuming with comic irony that the celebration of Christmas will go on long after Christianity has been forgotten. Or it might be someone like the narrator, someone who comes to "this cross of ground" (traditional English churches are shaped like crosses) looking for *something*.

This last thought returns the narrator to his original question: What is it that he is looking for? And now he is ready to venture a tentative answer. This place has held "what since is found/ Only in separation—marriage, and birth,/ And death, and thoughts of these." The importance of these moments was recognized here. Furthermore, church buildings have been places for serious thoughts, and even when they are no longer used for worship, they will still be sought by people who need to be serious. It is a place that is "proper to grow wise in,/ If only that so many dead lie round."

Forms and Devices

"Church Going" looks and sounds almost casual in its structure, but that appearance is deceptive. The poem is, in fact, an expertly constructed work. The rhyme scheme of each stanza is complexly intertwined: *ababcadcd*. The middle lines (lines 5 and 6) reverse the expected alternating rhymes.

Furthermore, the rhyme is so subtle as to be almost unnoticed in the reading. Only a few of the rhyming words are exact rhymes, and these are often very ordinary words (for example, "door" and "for" in stanza 2, and "do" and "too" in stanza 3) that do not call attention to themselves. Other rhyming words are half-rhymes (also known as imperfect rhymes, near rhymes, or slant rhymes). These words have similar vowel sounds, or similar consonant sounds, but not both. Some of the many half-rhymes in "Church Going" are "on," "stone," and "organ," and "silence" and "reverence."

The other dominant structural device in the poem is rhetorical. "Church Going" carefully follows the structure of the meditation, beginning with a detailed description of a place, leading to an internal debate, and finally reaching a tentative conclusion. Larkin's place, a church, is evoked in sufficient detail to let readers re-create it in their minds and imagine themselves there with the narrator. The internal debate begins in stanza 3 and continues through the beginning of stanza 6. Here the narrator raises many questions, answering none of them. The questions explore the possible significance and uses of church buildings once people no longer use them for religious worship. What will happen when their purpose has been forgotten? The questions lead inevitably to considering why the narrator himself is drawn to these places.

His conclusion, which begins halfway through stanza 6, remains tentative. The narrator discovers some important purposes for church buildings, at least for himself, and he offers them for his readers to consider. True to the meditation format, the poem does not seek to prove a point logically or solve a problem absolutely. Instead, it allows the mind to take direction from the external environment and consider various aspects of an issue, letting the discussion lead to a new discovery. That discovery may be a momentary resolution, not the final answer.

Themes and Meanings

"Church Going" records the spiritual longings of a man who has lost religious faith. It may be seen as representing the spiritual longings of a generation of British citizens for whom the church has ceased to be important.

That religion has lost its central position is assumed. After all, the narrator would have observed the serious decline in church attendance in England since the nineteenth century. He would also, perhaps, think of Stonehenge, a religious site whose purpose has been forgotten. The narrator does not wonder *if* churches will fall out of use. Instead, he wonders what will happen *when* they do. Understanding the rest of the poem requires the recognition of that assumption.

The discussion about what will become of the unused church buildings is, in fact, an exploration of what has caused religion to be so important to so many for so long. Uncovering those reasons also reveals the needs that must still be met in the secular world.

The church, the narrator discovers, "held unspilt/ So long and equably what since is found/ Only in separation—marriage, and birth,/ And death, and thoughts of these." People have always turned to the church for these major life events. Weddings, baptisms, and funerals are conducted in churches (or at least by ministers), and even in an age that lacks religious faith, people need to affirm the special significance of these events. They want God to take notice of them, even if, paradoxically, they don't believe in God. Love, birth, and death all transcend the ordinary and must be "recognised/ And robed as destinies."

Finally, the church is a place that is "proper to grow wise in." The secular world, the world of work, bicycling holidays, suburbs, and sheep, can do very well without the influence of the church, but "someone will forever be surprising/ A hunger in himself to be more serious." That hunger, a spiritual longing, can be met only by going to a place where it is valued, where it has been valued for centuries.

Bruce H. Leland

THE CIRCUS ANIMALS' DESERTION

Author: William Butler Yeats (1865-1939)
Type of poem: Lyric
First published: 1939, in *Last Poems and Two Plays*

The Poem

"The Circus Animals' Desertion" is a five-stanza poem in three parts. Part 1 introduces the poet's problem: a lack of inspiration. Part 2 explores three earlier writing experiences, and part 3 offers a solution to the problem.

The circus animals of the title are William Butler Yeats's earlier symbols and themes, which until now "were all on show," but now have deserted the elderly poet. In the first stanza, the speaker bemoans that desertion: "I sought a theme and sought for it in vain,/ I sought it daily for six weeks or so." When inspiration does not come, he blames old age.

The list of circus performers that concludes part 1 begins the references to Yeats's earlier works which fill the poem. The "stilted boys" are probably young men suffering from unrequited love. They were like acrobats performing on stilts, and they were "stilted," artificially formal, in their love (such as the "lovers who thought love should be/ So much compounded of high courtesy" in Yeats's 1902 poem "Adam's Curse"). The burnished chariot may belong to Helen of Troy or to Cuchulain, frequent subjects of Yeats's earlier work. The lion and woman is a direct reference to the sphinxlike "rough beast" of "The Second Coming."

Part 2 of the poem discusses three of Yeats's major early works in specific detail. Since his inspiration is blocked, he can do nothing but "enumerate old themes." The first of these is the narrative poem *The Wanderings of Oisin* (1889). In that poem, the hero Oisin tells Saint Patrick of his adventures with his fairy bride visiting three islands (which may be seen as youth, middle age, and old age).

The second early work to be recalled is the play *The Countess Cathleen* (1892), in which the title character offers to sell her soul to the devil in order to save the souls of the peasants on her land. Yeats explains that Maud Gonne ("my dear") had inspired the play. Like Cathleen, Maud risked her own well-being for others in her fanatical opposition to British occupation of Ireland. Once that theme was developed into a story, however, the thought that inspired it diminished. The "dream itself had all my thought and love."

The final work considered is the play *On Baile's Strand* (1904). Just as the Fool in the play is tricked by the Blind Man, Cuchulain is tricked by Conchubar into fighting a young hero who has arrived on the shore. Cuchulain kills the young man, only to learn that the stranger was his son. In remorse, "Cuchulain fought the ungovernable sea," attempting to chop the heads from the waves until he drowned. Here again, the art itself finally took control. "Players and painted stage took all my love/ And not those things that they were emblems of."

All three of Yeats's specific examples reveal the pattern of thought of the artist.

Specific people, events, or stories may inspire him, but the act of creation, the details of the particular poem or play, quickly become the center of the artist's attention.

Thus removed from life, the creations become complete and perfect in a way that life can never be. Part 3 of "The Circus Animals' Desertion" asks where they began. The answer comes quickly: They began in the messiness of life. In a stunning list of images of corruption and chaos, Yeats exemplifies that origin:

> A mound of refuse or the sweepings of a street,
> Old kettles, old bottles, and a broken can,
> Old iron, old bones, old rags, that raving slut
> Who keeps the till.

This "foul rag and bone shop of the heart" is the only source available to the poet for the creation of new poems.

Forms and Devices

The six stanzas of "The Circus Animals' Desertion" are written in iambic pentameter with a regular rhyme scheme: *ababbcc*. Though Yeats wrote occasionally in blank verse (most often in his plays), his poetry usually works with traditional rhyme and meter. Within the tradition, however, Yeats felt free to experiment. He uses half-rhyme from time to time in the poem ("vain" and "man," "enough" and "love"); the occasional use of imperfect rhymes keeps the rhyme scheme from becoming insistent.

There are also variations from the iambic meter. For example, line 8, "Lion and woman and the Lord knows what," ends with three accented syllables following three unaccented syllables. The phrase "the Lord knows what" is thus emphasized, underlining the speaker's frustration. Further, the emphasis of this colloquial phrase helps to create a less formal tone for the poem.

Yeats's division of the poem into three parts provides a clear rhetorical structure. Part 1 presents the problem, part 2 examines it via specific examples, and part 3 reaches a conclusion. The conclusion—that poetic inspiration begins in the sordid chaos of the heart—is predicted from the beginning: In part 1, he suspects that "I must be satisfied with my heart." References to the heart continue through the second part, and the poem concludes with a resounding final image of the "foul rag and bone shop of the heart."

The image of the heart is such a conventional poetic symbol that readers may be tempted to ignore its significance here. In "The Circus Animals' Desertion," Yeats does not use the heart to symbolize romantic love. Rather, "heart" here refers to the wide and confusing range of human emotions. It is clearly distinguished from thought, themes, and art. That distinction between the feelings and the art is central to the theme of the poem.

An unusual device that Yeats uses in the poem is the reference to his own earlier works. While poets regularly use allusions to other famous works of literature, they do not as often allude to their own works. There may even seem to be arrogance in the assumption that readers will have read *The Wanderings of Oisin* or recognize the sphinx image from "The Second Coming." On the other hand, it seems not only appropriate but also right for an introspective poem which reflects on a lifetime of poetic work to include details of that work.

Themes and Meanings

That poets find inspiration in chaotic life is not a new theme for Yeats. In fact, the whole poem can be seen as a new occasion to "enumerate old themes." As early as "Adam's Curse," Yeats was noting the distinction between art (and artifice) and life. In that poem he speaks of lovers who worked hard at love, turning it into a work of art, but "now it seems an idle trade enough." The work of love is too exhausting to sustain; the lovers weary of it.

Much later, in "Sailing to Byzantium," an old man seeks to leave the messy world which celebrates "Whatever is begotten, born, and dies." In contrast to that all-too-human life is the city of Byzantium, symbol of eternal and unchanging art. That symbol is developed further in "Byzantium," where the world of art "disdains/ All that man is,/ All mere complexities,/ The fury and the mire of human veins." In these poems the world of art, because organized, unchanging, and eternal, seems superior to mere humanity and mutable human feeling. Yet there is ambiguity throughout. Lovers become tired with the art of love. The golden bird in "Sailing to Byzantium" sings only of events from the world of nature that was left behind. Images of death pervade "Byzantium."

"The Circus Animals' Desertion" addresses this ambiguity directly and seeks to reconcile it in a balance between messy human feeling and idealized, unchanging art. Yeats explains what happened to him in the process of creating three works. In each instance, he began with real human feelings. For example, when he began *The Countess Cathleen*, he was genuinely concerned that Maud Gonne was destroying herself in her political work on behalf of the Irish peasants. He hoped to warn her of the dangers of such self-sacrifice. From that source in human feeling, however, the play emerged as something quite different.

The works of art are thus removed from life and human feeling. The very process of creation forces this removal: "Players and painted stage took all my love/ And not those things that they were emblems of." The contradiction is resolved in the final stanza, when Yeats recognizes the creation of art requires a continually repeated process of returning to chaotic human feelings. The heart, the symbol for those feelings, must finally be recognized as the source for art. Art is not generated by the intellect; one cannot merely seek a theme. The feelings of the heart, no matter how sordid, chaotic, messy, and unartistic, are the only source for poetry.

Bruce H. Leland

THE CISTERN

Author: George Seferis (Giorgos Stylianou Seferiades, 1900-1971)
Type of poem: Lyric
First published: 1932, as "E sterna," in *E sterna*; collected in *George Seferis: Collected Poems, 1924-1955*, 1967

The Poem

"The Cistern" is a lyric poem of twenty-five stanzas (if one counts the blank twenty-third stanza); each stanza contains five lines. The variable rhyme scheme utilizes off-rhyme in a resourceful and modern way.

"The Cistern" is prefaced with a quotation from the Cretan painter Doménikos Theotokópoulos, called El Greco, who worked in Toledo, Spain. The quotation is from the artist's inscription to his *View and Plan of Toledo* (c. 1609). The significance of the quotation has to do with the artist's poetic license to change reality to fit his aesthetic purposes. El Greco thought it "preferable" to shift the hospital's position and aspect to fit the painting's composition. "As for its actual position in the town," he says, "that appears on the map."

The poem's cistern is no ordinary reservoir to catch rainwater. The reader knows immediately that this cistern exists only in the mind; its symbolism is resonant in the opening line: "Here, in the earth, a cistern has taken root." Though it is an organic part of the landscape, the cistern gathers only "secret water" for one's interior life.

Above it the world goes on, time passes, and human cares and joys resound on its dome like "pitiless night." The cistern is as unconcerned about the world as the heavens are about mortals: "The stars/ don't blend with its heart." In pursuing their "destined suffering," human faces light up for a moment and die out. Caught up in "the pulse of nature," man bends toward earth like roses, thirsty with love, but "turns to marble at time's touch," returning to the earth and "sweetened" in his grave.

Though the world does not touch it, the cistern gathers human suffering, replenished by "pain, drop by drop." It hoards tears, "the groan of each body in the air," hopes that fail "at the edge of the sea." It "casts its nets far into a world" and feeds on the "bitter undulation" of human passion, taking away the embraces it once gave. In sleep one comes close to the cistern's hidden "garden where silver drops," but only in "the cave of death" is one able to talk to "the black roots."

The cistern is closer to "the root of our life/ than our thoughts and our anxiety." The regard of others or one's own pain does not affect this inner resource of one's being, for the cistern is "nearer than the spear still in our side." That one is unable to express this inner resource is a "crime," because if one could, perhaps he or she "might escape" both the painful knowledge and the hunger with which life leaves one.

Suffering is what intimates to men and women that they have this inner resource. The "body's bitterness" nourishes "our souls" so that beauty may "bloom in the blood of our wound." In this rebirth, which is a kind of death, everything may "become as it was at first," like a snake shedding its skin. Then one may find "Great and immaculate love, serenity."

Even though the cistern is known, "the blind earth/ that sweats from the effort of spring" drags human beings from the cool of the cistern back into the "Flames of the world." They know that " 'We are dying! Our gods are dying,' " but are as powerless as the statues who watch "the crowds of death pass by." (Here, a stanza consisting entirely of ellipses represents the silent procession of the dead.) When the dead have passed, the "magic spells" have been broken, but one's vision of the thirst-quenching cistern has already taught him or her the value of "silence," even in the midst of "the flaming city."

Forms and Devices

"The Cistern" is considered the culmination of George Seferis' early period, before the influence of T. S. Eliot's free verse and dramatic method have taken hold, as in *Mythistorema* (1935). The cinquains experiment with off-rhyme and a line resembling English pentameter, showing Seferis to be turning away from the traditional Greek pendecasyllabics and other formal restrictions, toward a rhythm more suitable to the modern Greek idiom.

Nevertheless, the language of "The Cistern" is abstract in a way that Seferis never repeats. The narrator speaks from a spiritual height, aloof from any specific scene or direct human experience. As Zissimos Lorenzatos says, in *The Lost Center and Other Essays in Greek Poetry* (1980): "the language is hardly audible. It has surrendered. In the end, you find you have received the poem's message without anyone having given it to you." There is power in the poem, but it is the power of seduction rather than persuasion; the reader must surrender to the poem as Seferis has surrendered to the language.

"The Cistern" is full of phrases that attribute human feelings to inanimate things. The characters, if they can be called that, are all abstractions. The cistern is an organism with a life of its own; it has "taken root" and has a heart. The day "grows, opens and shuts," like a flower. In such metaphors, the symbol is asserted rather than achieved.

Abstractions are personified. Night is "pitiless," cares "tread," joys "move by," fate has a "quick rattle," the fates "have woken gently," hope "may follow," expectation is "open-eyed," shadows are "mournful," the earth is "blind" and "sweats," warmth is "tame" or "calmly avoided fear" or "knocked on sleep to ask" directions. One also hears of "the wind's breath," "the skin of silence," "the root of our life," "the thirst of love," "the pulse of nature," and "the effort of spring."

What human presences do arrive on the scene are ghostly: "faces light up, shine a moment/ and die out." Otherwise, they appear only as bodies, living or dead: "Man's body bends to earth," "the groan of each body," "the body's bitterness," "a body hidden" in "the cave of death." Bodies may appear only in parts: "fingers eyes and lips," eyes that "roll in a gutter," the victim "full of eyelids," "palm on the temple,"

"Faces that go!" When the narrator addresses an unspecified "you," who "bent humbly, naked curve,/ white wing over the flock," the erotic possibility of a human presence dissolves in the apostrophe to the abstraction of "Great and immaculate love, serenity."

Themes and Meanings

"The Cistern" is a poem that locates the source of the poet's inspiration in what Philip Sherrard calls "a still centre of contemplative understanding." The poem leads away from the world of action to the poet's inner resources; for the cistern, where all human experience is gathered in secret, "teaches silence/ in the flaming city."

This view of poetic inspiration owes something to ancient Greek and Christian ethics as well as to modern psychology. The heroic ethic of Homer held that suffering leads to wisdom not only personally but also for the race in general. The ancient dead of the statues, for example, "our stern brother/ who looks at us with eyelids closed" communicates, however obliquely, what he has learned. Similarly, Christ in his martyrdom suffered for humanity's sins, and through him is felt "the spear still in our side." Yet the cistern, which gathers all this mythic and historical pain "drop by drop," is "nearer the root of our life" than these, just as it is nearer than the "destined suffering" of personal fate.

In modern psychology, the cistern replenished by individual experience has an analog in C. G. Jung's idea of the "universal unconscious." In sleep and dreams, as well as in meditative states such as artistic creation, one taps this storehouse of archetypal images, which have a power and significance of their own, derived from but no longer dependent on the things of the world. The "secret water" of the cistern is gathered from human experience but is not subject to the world, which "doesn't touch it."

It is toward the cistern that "Man's body bends" when it is "thirsty" for love or art, to nourish the root of his life. Then is when "our souls," like roses, put forth shoots of beauty, "so that we may escape the body's bitterness/ so that roses may bloom in the blood of our wound." There in the cistern of tears the poet finds his inspiration. Like the night that "does not believe in the dawn," or like love that "lives to weave death," the poet is a paradox, aloof from the world, yet distilling his unique vision of the world, observing a contemplative "silence/ in the flaming city." It is in this way that he becomes a "free soul."

Richard Collins

THE CITY IN THE SEA

Author: Edgar Allan Poe (1809-1849)
Type of poem: Lyric
First published: 1832, as "The Doomed City," in *Poems*; collected in *The Raven and Other Poems*, 1845

The Poem

"The City in the Sea" is a poem of four uneven stanzas, the divisions between which Edgar Allan Poe reworked in the several editions of this lyric. The title of the poem and the revisions Poe made in that title suggest connections with the biblical Sodom and Gomorrah, ancient cities condemned for their wickedness and licentiousness. The city that Poe depicts here is certainly a doomed, dreary, and lonely place, one characterized by death rather than life, by stillness rather than human activity.

The poem is primarily descriptive, and by beginning as he does with the exclamation "Lo!" — meaning "Look closely!" — Poe emphasizes that he wants the reader to pay careful attention to the surprising and important picture he is about to paint.

Poe begins by introducing the sole inhabitant of this city in the sea — death — for death has erected his throne here and rules the unusual and alien landscape. The city is located in the "West," the land of the setting sun and endings rather than the land of beginnings and hope, and eventually everyone — both the good and the bad — arrives in this region for "eternal rest." The city seems, however, deserted, and a sense of hopelessness, resignation, and melancholy prevails. Poe infuses the poem with the quality of a nightmare — something familiar but terrifyingly abnormal — by asserting that the city resembles nothing that anyone would recognize while at the same time describing the city with conventional words and concepts ("towers," "shrines," and "palaces"). A vast stillness dominates the scene, and even the wind has forgotten to blow here.

Poe turns his attention to the distance between this city and heaven when he comments on the light. This light is not a holy or natural light (as light from heaven would be) but rather one that gleams from the "lurid" sea onto walls that remind the poet of Babylon, another condemned and sinful city of the ancient world. Despite the fact that the domes, spires, and halls are highly decorated in this city, they remain deserted and forgotten. Poe focuses again on the surreal quality of this landscape when he tells the reader that the turrets and shadows seem to blend and to hang suspended in air. With this assertion, Poe implies that there is no distinction here between what is real (the turrets) and what is unreal (the shadows). Substance and shadow become one, and death rules majestically over all.

The feeling that everything is reduced to immobile similarity is intensified in the third stanza, where Poe shows that both churches (fanes) and graves, symbols of life and death, are "level" with the waves. The scene is so threateningly still that it causes one to think that there may not even be normal, "happier" seas elsewhere in the world. The stillness of both sea and air enhances the unnaturalness of this city, and both make the apparent serenity of the scene hideous rather than comforting. Poe concludes his description, however, with a final appeal to the reader to look carefully, for he again says, "lo," and calls attention to the fact that movement finally occurs: The city seems to sink and settle, and as it does so, hell rises to meet and honor the city.

Forms and Devices

One characteristic of the lyric poem is its focus on pictorial and melodic aspects of experience. "The City in the Sea" is no exception to this rule, for in this work a detailed picture of a city is offered, and the language in which the picture is rendered is intensely melodic and beautiful. The pictorial aspects of "The City in the Sea" are conveyed primarily through imagery, that is, language that appeals to the senses. The sense to which this poem makes its greatest appeal is the visual. Poe wants the reader to see this city; he wants him or her to visualize this beautiful and yet doomed human edifice. His choice of language reveals his preoccupation with sight; words such as "gleam," "shadow," "sculptured," "resemble," "streams," "open," "ripples," "glass," and "diamond" remind the reader that he or she is looking at something, that Poe wants his readers to see what he places before them.

The visual beauty of this city is further emphasized by the melodic beauty of Poe's skillful versification, his use of rhyme and meter. While the poem does not conform to a fixed form (such as a sonnet or a rondel), it does employ various patterns of sound that enhance its appeal. All the lines are arranged in rhymed couplets (two lines), tercets (three lines), or quatrains (four lines), and some lines and words are repeated for emphasis and effect ("Resignedly beneath the sky/ The melancholy waters lie"). Poe makes frequent use of rhymes other than these end rhymes (rhyming words at the end of the line). He uses initial rhyme, or rhyme that comes at the beginning of a line ("Streams up the turrets silently—/ Gleams up the pinnacles far and free"), as well as internal repetition of sounds ("The viol, the violet, and the vine") to intensify his description. In general, each line has four metrical beats, but because the number of syllables in each line varies, the rhythm of the poem is sometimes surprising and emphatic (as in the longest line of the poem—"Where the good and the bad and the worst and the best"—in which the stress falls heavily on the significant words of the passage: "good," "bad," "worst," and "best").

The poem also contains allusions to several real places, although it clearly presents a fantasy of these places rather than a realistic depiction of them. Babylon is mentioned in line 18, a reference to the ancient city devoted to material and sensual pleasures, and the entire poem reminds the reader of the story of Sodom and Gomorrah, which—as is this city—were utterly destroyed for their wickedness. That the city Poe has created is, indeed, evil becomes even more obvious when one considers how unnatural it seems—the wind does not blow, nothing moves, the light is strange—and how far from heaven it is: The light does not come from heaven, the waters are sad rather than joyful, and the gods there are death and "idols."

Themes and Meanings

Essentially, Poe's "The City in the Sea" is not obviously metaphoric; that is, it does not talk about one thing as though it were something else. (It does not, for example, discuss a beloved woman as if she were a rose.) Rather, this poem presents what Poe wants to discuss—a city—in nightmarish and frightening terms. When Poe asks his readers to consider this city, however, he is also asking them to think about all that cities have come to represent for civilized humans—activity, work, pleasure, art, music, and society ("The viol, the violet, and the vine"). This city is filled with the accomplishments of human beings, with "shrines and palaces and towers," but the city is ruled over by death, and the city exists in a land where resignation, melancholy, and stillness prevail. While no one is present in the city save death, everyone comes here eventually, and the poem seems to hint that all human efforts are vain and hopeless and—according to the final lines of the poem—honored only by hell and death.

Poe would probably resist this reading of the poem since he did not believe that poetry existed to teach; he believed rather that poetry existed for its own sake, for the beauty of its lines, mood, atmosphere, and feeling. For Poe, the importance of this poem would lie in how eloquently and elegantly he had represented this doomed city, how poignantly he had sketched the city's fall, how fully he had developed the atmosphere of resignation and sadness. Yet, it is exactly for this reason that many readers find Poe objectionable. No one would argue that Poe has depicted here a healthy and moral environment. The city is clearly corrupt; however, Poe has made something beautiful of this corruption. The reader must decide for himself or herself whether such an effort is laudable, whether a poem should be more uplifting and hopeful.

Given all the stillness in the poem and in the city, a rising or hopeful movement would finish the poem with some triumph, with some sense of morality, but the movement at the end of "The City in the Sea" is instead a sinking that ends with hell "rising from a thousand thrones." Only hell seems ascendant at the end of the poem. In this sense, the poem very much embodies the nightmarish state of mind that so fascinated Poe. He seemed to look at the world of familiar objects the way one looks at the elements of a very bad dream: Things look familiar, but they are really evil and terrifying. It is as if Poe takes a slightly different focus, an altered perspective, on the city, and in so doing he reveals it to be a place of death not life, stillness not activity, melancholy not hope, resignation not determination.

Kathleen Margaret Lant

CLAREL

Author: Herman Melville (1819-1891)
Type of poem: Narrative
First published: 1876

The Poem

Herman Melville wrote *Clarel: A Poem and Pilgrimage in the Holy Land* during the twenty years that followed his journey to Europe and the Middle East in 1856-1857. Although he had earlier achieved fame through his novels of adventure, he was weakened physically and mentally, a condition exacerbated by his now unsuccessful efforts to provide for his family through his writing. Melville accepted the trip as a gift from his father-in-law, Judge Lemuel Shaw. Judge Shaw and Melville's wife, Elizabeth, hoped the extended tour would ease the author's debilitating depression. The trip, which covered fifteen thousand miles and touched on three continents and nine countries, began with a visit to his old friend Nathaniel Hawthorne in Liverpool. From Liverpool, Melville sailed through the Straits of Gibraltar into the Mediterranean Sea, visiting Constantinople and the pyramids before coming to port in Jaffa. From Jaffa he traveled inland to Jerusalem. Like many tourists of the time, Melville arranged to make a three-day trip eastward from Jerusalem to the Dead Sea, passing through Jericho, down the Jordan River to the Dead Sea, and returning to Jerusalem through the ancient monastery of Mar Saba and the village of Bethlehem. This experience provided the basis for the two-volume narrative poem about the spiritual pilgrimage of a young divinity student named Clarel that Melville published in 1876 with a bequest from his uncle Peter Gansevoort.

Melville struggled through the late 1850's and early 1860's. Having abandoned fiction, he tried his hand unsuccessfully at the lecture circuit, wrote poetry about the Civil War that was published as *Battle-Pieces and Aspects of the War* (1866), failed in attempts to procure a consulship, and was troubled by bouts of rheumatism and sciatica. Financially drained, he sold his country home in Pittsfield, Massachusetts, in 1863. In 1866, he was appointed to a four-dollar-a-day job as a customs inspector in New York City. This position placed Melville in the center of one of the most corrupt bureaucracies of postwar America, but it provided him with a steady income and the freedom to write without the pressure of pleasing a public that had long forgotten him. *Clarel*, the narrative of a young theologian's attempt to regain the faith he lost during his years of study, is Melville's personal effort to come to terms with the philosophical uncertainties that troubled him throughout his life.

The poem is divided into four parts, each part culminating in death. Beginning in Jerusalem, the four parts take Clarel and a changing band of companions and guides on a symbolic, circular journey in an ambiguous search for meaning across a debilitated and infertile wasteland.

In part 1, Clarel is repulsed by the barrenness of Jerusalem and overwhelmed by feelings of loneliness. Instead of the traditional vision of a sacred and glorious city,

Clarel is confronted by "Dismantled, torn,/ Disastrous houses, ripe for fall," dwellings that look like "plundered tombs." A bleak and confusing maze of walls and enclosures, Jerusalem seems a city forsaken by God and hostile toward man. Disillusioned by the decay and disorder of the city, Clarel is overwhelmed by the diversity of people and beliefs he encounters in Jerusalem. He feels surrounded by men "in each degree/ Of craze, whereto some creed is key," men who, in the privacy of their personal visions, "Walk like somnambulists abroad."

In an effort to clarify the confusion he feels in Jerusalem, Clarel seeks spiritual guides. While wandering in the dry, stony lands outside the city's walls, and while visiting the faded monuments and shrines of the ancient city, he meets Nehemiah, a millenarian dispenser of tracts, who has traveled from America to be witness to the Second Coming; Celio, a hunchbacked renegade Catholic, whose sudden, unexplained death seems the terrible price of religious rebellion; Vine, a sensitive, meditative, middle-aged American, who is reminiscent of Nathaniel Hawthorne; and Rolfe, an assertive, argumentative American, who is a partial self-portrait of Melville. During the course of the poem's narrative, Clarel turns to these and other possible guides whom he meets along the way for help, but none of these diverse characters is able to provide him with the guidance he desires.

Clarel's desperate yearning for some hope in existence is answered when he meets a beautiful young Jewish woman named Ruth with whom he immediately falls in love. Impulsively he asks for her hand in marriage, but their courtship is interrupted by the death of Ruth's father, and Clarel decides to pass the required time of mourning by joining his newfound guides in a pilgrimage toward the Dead Sea.

In part 2, Clarel and the other pilgrims are joined by Derwent, a melioristic Anglican priest, and together they journey down from Mount Olivet toward Jericho. Their physical descent is paralleled by a building sense of doom. When they reach Mount Quarantania, the traditional site of Christ's temptation, Mortmain, a cynic whose belief in human progress has been destroyed by the failure of the French Revolution of 1848, leaves the group to spend the night alone under the mountain. As Mortmain leaves, the group is joined by the geologist Margoth, who argues coldly for the primacy of science. Set amid the formidable and barren landscape of the Siddom Plain, part 2 moves through ominous banks of fog toward the encampment on the shores of the Dead Sea. There Mortmain, visibly aged by his nightlong vigil, recklessly drinks the bitter water of the Dead Sea, "Hades water shed . . . the Sodom waters dead" and has a vision of his own coming demise. That night, Nehemiah, hallucinating a vision of the New Jerusalem, walks somnambulistically into the waters. The grim pilgrims find his corpse the next morning floating near the shore.

In part 3, the pilgrims ascend the rugged Judah ridge toward Mar Saba, the ancient Coptic monastery and oasis. At Mar Saba, the starkness of the pilgrims' journey is relieved by the conviviality of the monks, the comfortable quarters, and the plentiful food and drink. The humanism of this center of Christian belief stands in contrast to the closed doors and dust-covered shrines of Jerusalem. A lone, majestic palm, which grows from the side of the mountain, becomes a problematic symbol of the hope for immortality, but the reader is reminded that the intricate passages of Mar Saba lead down as well as up. In this place of reassessment the pilgrims once again encounter death when they discover the corpse of Mortmain, its open eyes transfixed upon the sacred palm and an eagle feather at its lips. Mortmain's ambiguous demise, which hints at both beatitude and annihilation, leaves the poem's young protagonist feeling "Suspended 'twixt the heaven and hell."

In part 4, the pilgrims stop in Bethlehem on their return journey to Jerusalem. In this portion of their journey they are joined by two others: Agath, an illiterate Greek seaman who has survived the brutality of a hostile world through the tenacity of his will, and Ungar, an embittered Confederate who has fled America and the defeat of his cause to become a soldier of fortune. Clarel, who has had second thoughts and dark premonitions regarding his betrothal to Ruth while on his journey, discovers that she has died while he was traveling. Confused and alone, Clarel is last seen joining another band of pilgrims.

The poem concludes with a brief epilogue that asks "If Luther's day expand to Darwin's year,/ Shall that exclude the hope—foreclose the fear?" Critics have argued over the interpretation of the poem's conclusion. Some see in it a Melville who, near the end of his life, had made peace with the conflict between disbelief and belief. Others, however, see in it a reaffirmation of Melville's lifelong inability to resolve this conflict and his conviction that it could not be resolved.

Forms and Devices

Clarel is a massive work, comprising more than eighteen thousand lines of iambic tetrameter in which lines rhyme at irregular intervals. Melville's decision to use short octosyllabic lines and his decision to create a rhyme at the end of each short line, a particularly difficult task in English, decrease the readability of the poem and help to explain why many critics have dismissed *Clarel* as bad poetry; however, others have argued that the limitations of the form Melville selected are the result of a conscious effort on the author's part to force his reader to experience an uneasiness similar to the spiritual disorientation that confronts the protagonist. In a sense, the reader feels as trapped between the narrow walls of the iambic tetrameter lines as Clarel feels between the conflicting pressures of faith and cynicism.

The poem is divided into four parts of roughly equivalent length. The poem's 150 cantos average about 120 lines each. The cantos are thematically or narratively gathered in groups of two to five and are irregularly divided into sections that indicate a minor change in subject or merely relieve visual monotony. Within each of the four parts, the groups of cantos form a pattern of nine to ten movements. Some slight relief from the confines of the poem's rigid structure is provided by more than forty short lyric pieces—hymns, songs, invocations, and chants—that are interspersed throughout the narrative.

Although limited in its prosody, the poem is rich in symbolic imagery. The topography of the Holy Land provides Melville with his most powerful images. The pilgrims' physical journey down toward the Dead Sea, 1,300 feet below sea level, mirrors their increasing gloom, just as their ascent to Mar Saba's towers offers a brief hope of beatitude. Throughout their journey the sterile images of the desert remind the reader of the sterility that plagues their spirits. The walls and winding alleyways of Jerusalem echo the confusion of the young protagonist; the brackish waters of the Dead Sea serve as a frightening image of annihilation. Most of the poem's landscape is a wilderness, separated from the civilization the pilgrims have voluntarily abandoned. It is at once a place of potential revelation and a place of possible spiritual death. The bleakness of the desert landscape is frequently juxtaposed with the pilgrims' fond memories of lusher landscapes at home, the green fields, orchards, and of families that they have left in their pasts. Of course, the poem's setting also offers numerous biblically significant sites that provide Melville with opportunities to elaborate on his theological themes. Most often, however, these holy places are portrayed as ruined or defiled, becoming additional symbols of disillusionment and loss of faith. Finally, it is not surprising that the author of *Moby Dick* (1851) uses sea images throughout his desert poem, for in his earlier work Melville frequently described the vast loneliness of the oceans as a kind of wasteland.

Freed from the pressure to make his writing pay, Melville clearly did not overly concern himself with the commercial potential of *Clarel*; however, his narrative does relate to some important literary and social interests of his time: the popularity of letters from abroad, which related travelers' reactions to famous places; nineteenth century Protestant America's fascination with the Holy Land; and the still popular English genre of the Oriental romance.

Themes and Meanings

Despite its length and intellectual complexity, Melville's *Clarel* has one overriding theme. The poem focuses on the major philosophical crisis of the later nineteenth century, the apparent destruction of the credibility of revealed religion in the wake of Darwin's discoveries. Although the poem is filled with disillusionment and death and permeated with a sense of gloom, it draws no final conclusion regarding the conflict between reason and faith.

The question of faith was always central to Melville's thought. In Liverpool before departing for the Holy Land in 1856, Melville visited Hawthorne, and his friend wrote a remarkable description of their afternoon: "Melville . . . began to reason of Providence and futurity . . . and informed me that he had 'pretty much made up his mind to be annihilated'; but still he does not seem to rest in that anticipation; and, I think will never rest until he gets hold of a definite belief. It is strange how he persists . . . in wandering to and fro over these deserts, as dismal and monotonous as the sand hills amid which we were sitting. He can neither believe, nor be comfortable in his unbelief." The multiple characters with whom Clarel travels represent a broad range of beliefs, from the self-satisfied, comfortable faith of Derwent to the cold, scientific analysis of Margoth, but none of his fellow pilgrims can serve as a model for Clarel, and in the end he leaves to continue his spiritual pilgrimage alone. In the epilogue to *Clarel*, Melville's narrator calls this conflict the "running battle of the star and clod" that will "run forever—If there be no God" to settle the matter by divine intervention. The poem shows Clarel's failure to find belief, concluding with his murmured complaint that " 'They wire the world—far under the sea/ They talk; but never comes to me/ A message from beneath the stone.' " Yet the poem's epilogue advises the protagonist to "keep thy heart," for "Even death may prove unreal at the last,/ And stoics be astounded into heaven."

As a corollary to the examination of faith, *Clarel* confronts the prevalent optimism of American civilization in the late nineteenth century, questioning the inevitable triumph of Protestant democracy. The poem shows that man's technological and commercial advances have not dented the age-old questions at the heart of existence. In fact, the poem implies that modern man is turning away from even the consideration of such questions.

Finally, the poem explores the limitations of human relationships, their inability to stem the overwhelming tide of spiritual destruction that washes away man's hopes and dreams. The love theme that is brought forth with such promise in part 1 of the poem, quickly fades during the long dry pilgrimage and the endless theological discussions of the pilgrims. Long before he returns to Jerusalem, Clarel senses that his love for Ruth will not be consummated. When he discovers her funeral upon his return to Jerusalem, the sight merely confirms the tragic intuition he has already felt. During his journey, Clarel turns from one companion to another, seeking companionship as well as revelation. In part 2, as he and Vine rest in a secluded bower, Clarel feels strongly attracted to his countryman: "O, how but for communion true/ And close; let go each alien theme;/ Give me thyself!" But Vine rejects the young man's advances by asking, "Why bring oblations of thy pain/ To one who hath his share?" and asserts that "Lives none can help ye; . . . Go live it out." Vine's gentle rebuke underscores the poem's assertion that companionship cannot assuage the pain of spiritual unrest. Most of the characters in the poem are Ishmaels, renegades who have turned away from the comforts of home in the hope of embracing some higher comfort, but like the ceaseless wanderers of Melville's fiction, they seem destined to find no rest.

Carl Brucker

CLEAR NIGHT

Author: Octavio Paz (1914-   )
Type of poem: Lyric
First published: 1962, as "Noche en claro," in *Salamandra*; revised in *Poemas*,
    1979; collected in *Collected Poems of Octavio Paz, 1957-1987*, 1987

The Poem
    "Clear Night" is a long poem of 141 lines in free verse. It is divided into seven
stanzas of varying length. The poem is dedicated to André Breton and Benjamin
Péret, two influential Surrealist poets with whom Octavio Paz became associated in
the 1940's while he lived in Paris. From the opening two stanzas, one is led to believe
that the three characters in the poem correspond directly to Paz, Breton, and Péret,
and the rest of the lyric confirms this belief. The poet uses the first person with no
suggestion of artifice; that is, one can safely assume that the speaker of the poem is
Paz himself and not a fictional persona. The poem is cast as a recollection of an
experience, so much of the time the past tense is used. At moments of special importance the poet shifts to the present tense, as if he were reliving those moments.
    Contrary to the suggestion of the title, the poem begins with the three poets sitting
in a café at ten o'clock on a misty autumn evening. They are the only ones lingering
there. They feel the ominous approach of autumn, which is compared to a "blind
giant" (line 5) and "faceless man" (line 8) advancing toward the city. Suspending
such dark thoughts, the poet shifts the reader's attention to scenes of the city, and the
reader views these scenes as if through the same window as the three friends in the
café. It is this experience of carefully attending to the city—not only to its main
streams but also to its underlife—that informs the poet's observations throughout
the rest of the poem. In particular, he focuses on a teenage couple. The boy is
streetwise and tough. The girl is more innocent, small and pale but also resilient and
surprisingly durable, like a "pale branch in a patio in winter" (line 54). She is wearing a red jacket on which one sees the boy's hand. The word "love" is spelled on his
fingers. One imagines the boy grasping the back of the girl's neck as they pass by the
poets' window. Although they seem an unlikely match in some ways, their interaction is characterized by an entwining passion and sexual energy.
    The poet's attitude toward the boy's gesture is ambivalent. In the apostrophe to
the hand, he seems at first to deplore the predatory relation between the boy and the
girl implied in the grasping. The hand as "collar" (line 64) seems to choke the
"eager neck of life." In the next lines, however, the poet admires the sign of love
painted on the hand. The hand becomes a symbol of redemption rather than a fetter.
    In the fourth stanza, there is a shift back to the three friends who now are walking
through the city. The language here is highly symbolic—they see at least two distin-
guishable rivers, the river of centuries and the river of stars. The poet re-creates the
excitement of the moment by adopting the present tense and by recalling the urgent
voices that direct and manipulate his gaze. It is at this point that the night "opens"

(line 79). This marks the first epiphany, or revelation, of the poem.

The fifth stanza returns to a more narrative mode. It begins by describing the friends' separation and a brief observation about the wind and the river which remind the reader of the literal setting of the poem. This literalness is, however, short-lived, for the poet quickly moves to pondering the violence of time. He seems to conclude that man inevitably loses the battle with time. Poetry is the only means of defeating time. Paz is not invoking the classical idea that poetry is a means to immortality through fame; rather, he is defining poetry as a particular way of experiencing reality that does not view time as linear and death as an end.

The last long division of the poem describes a second epiphany, one which the poet experiences apart from his friends. It is here that Paz explores in erotic imagery the relation between poetry and the point of silence from which poetry begins and toward which it leads. This silence is not negative; rather, it is the necessary condition for the observer who would penetrate the surface of reality with "the light push of a thought" (line 17).

Forms and Devices

The reader of "Clear Night" is rewarded when she or he perceives the network of images that Paz has woven into the poem, for the interconnectedness of these images offers an interpretative key to the poem. In the central image of the night as it "opens" (line 79) its hand, for instance, one recalls the earlier description of time, not progressing as one normally understands it, but as opening up — the "minute opened into two" (line 20). Shortly after, the poet perceives the city as revealing itself in a similar way: "The city opens like a heart" (line 28). Finally, in the last long section of the poem, the city "unfolds" (line 106) itself to the sensitive poet. Thus, Paz invites the reader to link thematically the images of the hand, time, the city, and the clear night.

Such attention to imagery helps interpret the most enigmatic parts of the poem. In section 3, one is given a sense of a great disaster in a London subway, but the poet speaks in a highly symbolic code and depends on imagery rather than literal description to convey the significance of the event. It is no accident that the poets sit in "Café d'Angleterre" (line 1) as this event is recalled. Although their café is situated in Paris, its name (café of England) reinforces the sense that the poets are connected to the tragedy. The mutilation of the victims is described in a way that evokes the earlier image of autumn. Just as autumn is a "faceless man," so these victims become "faceless" and lose their identities through the mutilation. The poet uses the first person plural to speak for the victims as if all humanity, past and present, share in that disaster. Paz is exploring the relation between human identity and a reality that seems intent on erasing it.

Much of the difficulty and much of the beauty of "Clear Night" derives from Paz's reliance on imagery and the narrative discontinuity that results from this emphasis. Once the poet sets the scene in the first section, he quickly moves to a meditation cast in opaque symbolic language. Although he does mark a break in thought by capitalizing the first letter of a line, the absence of punctuation throughout the whole poem gives the sense of fertility, abundance, and overflow of energy. This energy is precisely what the poet hopes to capture of the city's activity. Lines such as "walking flying ripening bursting" (line 23), "a vagabond grey sparrow streetsmart a bully" (line 51), "embracing splitting joining again" (line 75), "centuries generations epochs" (line 83), "echoes calls signs labyrinths" (line 87), and "towers plazas columns bridges streets (line 109) not only describe the variety of ways one can experience reality at the same time, but more important, such lines also convey the energy with which the poet is manipulating language in order that it correspond to the richness of his experience.

Manipulating language is one way to convey the wealth of experience. Another way is to go outside language. The most noticeable device in the poem is Paz's simple illustration of the hand of the boy, which is set within his verbal description of it. In a very basic way this drawing challenges the reader's preconceived notions about poetry; poetry is more than words organized in a certain way. The simplicity of the drawing is in marked contrast to the network of images in the poem, and although this hand is linked thematically to the more complex corpus of the poem (the hand is not completely devoid of language, for the hand contains the word "love" on its fingers), it remains apart, as if to hint that this image remains the seed of the poem.

Themes and Meanings

"Clear Night" is about the poet's revelation of the interconnectedness or coexistence of things that are usually seen as opposing and separate, such as life and death, past and present, and the heavenly and the mundane. "Everything is a door" (line 16 and line 69), one reads, and "everything a bridge" (line 70). If one waits and observes closely, one will see beneath the superficial divisions in the world and understand that everything is comparable to everything else. The "light push of a thought" (line 17) is all that is needed for such a revelation.

The vision that is celebrated is one that depends on the viewer's arrival at a point that is neither a door nor a bridge, but a point prior to time and space, pure essence. Quite simply, in order to perceive that everything is connected, one must be outside the network of connections. At this point outside time and space, the poet is most aware of, and sensitive to, chance occurrences which would challenge the appearance of reality and reveal something more fundamental than convention or unearth something below consciousness. This is the point of expectation—the expectation that is returned to several times in the poem with the refrain, "Something's about to happen" (lines 18, 32, and 113).

One could also say that this isolated point is the point of pure desire, for desire that is sullied with appetite and acquisitiveness must be suspended in this state. This pure desire could be called poetic desire, the desire to challenge the common view of reality through daring comparisons, through the linking together of things that seem very different. This desire is what allows Paz, in the final long section of the poem, to see woman and city as connected. The effect of this extended comparison is double. Woman becomes objectified and fragmented. This objectification of woman has been a source of criticism of Surrealist art by recent scholarship; Paz's poem certainly bears the marks of Surrealism's influence on him, and this treatment of woman is one of them. More positive, the second effect of the comparison is that the city is transformed from a mere construct to a living organism. Both effects, however different, show the transforming power of poetry.

In stanza 5, Paz makes an explicit claim about the power of poetry. Lamenting the human failure to defeat strife, cruelty, and misfortune, the poet finds hope in the transformative power of poetry. Even though time, which is connoted by the advance of autumn, brings death, the poet takes consolation in the fact that poetry allows one to suspend time — to get outside it. It is poetry that allows Paz to view time in a new way, as opening up. It is poetry that inspires him to link boldly life and death in the present: "the living are alive/ walking flying ripening bursting/ the dead are alive/ oh bones still hot" (lines 22-25).

Poetry is a way of experiencing reality, of reading the signs in the world. It is not a fanciful or delusory indulgence in language. It is the perception of the elusive and mysterious love painted on the hand of the world that redeems and renews the world.

"Clear Night" is a difficult poem that presents the reader with a series of paradoxical images that are finally resolved when one gets outside the poem and views it as a structure of interlinking images rather than a linear process with a beginning, middle, and end. In this way, the experience of the poem demands as much from the reader as the experience of life demands from the poet.

Thomas Mussio

THE COLLAR

Author: George Herbert (1593-1633)
Type of poem: Dramatic monologue
First published: 1633, in *The Temple*

The Poem

"The Collar" is George Herbert's most extensive and detailed poem of rebellion. Thirty-two of its thirty-six lines describe what the poem itself calls the ravings of a person growing "more fierce and wild" as he strains to release himself from the restrictive pressures that surround him. Much like John Donne's energetic complaints to God in several of his Holy Sonnets, "The Collar" gives full expression to the speaker's resentment of the pain and rigor of leading a life that is moral and holy. Only after these complaints are freely, almost hysterically voiced is the speaker taught how quickly they can be banished by a patient God who ultimately gives more than he asks.

The poem begins with a dramatic statement of refusal — "I struck the board, and cried, No more" — and the following lines give examples of the kind of life that the speaker wants to leave behind. He is a person of ambition and desire, yet everything in life seems to conspire to frustrate or torment him. His life is one of "sighs" and "tears," a situation he finds particularly distressing because he can readily imagine the joys and glories, the wine, fruit, and flowers, that are withheld from him.

The process of describing his past failure to seize the available pleasures of life makes him more determined to change his ways immediately and exchange his tears for the pursuit of "double pleasures." Like a libertine, he suggests that inhibitions and moral laws are only a "rope of sands" once a person decides not to be bound by them. Instead of being blind to the forbidden pleasures of life, he will now serve only his needs and desires. Enraptured by his own enthusiasm, even the death's-head, the traditional reminder of mortality and the nearness of judgment, is no longer intimidating and will certainly not be part of his luggage as he prepares to go abroad. He is confident that all of his fears can be neatly bundled up and left behind, and he attempts to wind up his argument with what sounds like a proverb celebrating his new creed of practical selfishness: "He that forbears/ To suit and serve his need,/ Deserves his load."

This is not, however, the true finale of his argument, which is provided by the intervention of a holy voice, a device used in several other key poems by Herbert. All the ravings of the speaker are answered by one gentle word, *"Child,"* an almost miraculous reminder that not only is the speaker always overheard by God, but, more important, he is always protected, instructed, and accepted. This is the way the world of rebellion ends, not with a bang but with a whisper, and when the speaker replies *"My Lord,"* he acknowledges not only that his rebelliousness is at an end but that devotion to such a Lord is not painful servitude but joyful freedom. In a curious way, the story of this poem is thus foretold by the multiple meanings hinted at by the title: "The Collar" suggests a restrictive collar that the speaker wants to slip and the angry "choler" to which he gives voice throughout most of the lines; yet even in the depths of his anger and rebelliousness, the speaker is a "caller," and God is always ready to answer.

Forms and Devices

One of the most interesting aspects of "The Collar" is the way the form of the poem helps to convey not only the dramatic rebelliousness of the speaker but also the concluding resolution. The speaker's anger and nervousness are underscored in several ways. His speech pattern is halting and constantly interrupted. Many of the statements are short, and the frequent punctuation in the lines gives them a clipped, staccato sound, adding to the impression of uneasiness. Any sense that this is the speech of a confident and determined man is also undermined by the fact that much of it takes the form of questions. These are meant to be rhetorical questions, but still they suggest that the speaker is plagued with doubts.

At first glance, the overall structure of "The Collar" seems to mirror the state of mind of the speaker. The line lengths alternate in an apparently irregular pattern, and the rhyme scheme is difficult to assess. As a result, the structure of the poem may be taken as an embodiment of the rebelliousness of the man who is in the process of swearing off all laws and restrictions. "My lines and life are free," he says, and the irregular lines of the poem signify his first step toward a life of pleasurable transgression. From another perspective, the form of the poem seems not so much free as chaotic, thus subtly indicating that a person who repudiates the legal and moral restrictions of life abandons the basic principles of order and thereby begins a descent into incoherence, the necessary by-product of rebelliousness.

The structure of "The Collar," however, is neither completely free nor chaotic, but extremely subtle, discernible only after careful and patient analysis. Beneath the superficial disorder, or developing progressively through it, is an orderly pattern that climaxes in the last four lines of the poem. This is best seen in the rhyme scheme. As Joseph H. Summers points out in *George Herbert: His Religion and Art* (1954), every line in "The Collar" finds a rhyme somewhere, but through most of the poem there are many off-rhymes, and because rhymes do not occur at predictable, regular intervals, they sometimes undermine rather than create a sense of closure. Near the end, the rhyming lines begin to occur closer and closer, but the speaker's last assertion that he is tying up his fears is still belied by the irregular off-rhymes (abroad/load, fears/forbears). Only in the last four lines do the rhymes become regular (alternating *abab*) and purposeful: The designation of the speaker as "wild" is replaced by the new name given to him, "Child," and his every "word" of rebelliousness gives way to "Lord," the divine word capable of redeeming human anger, weakness, and folly.

Themes and Meanings

The recurrent topic of Herbert's poems is not perfection but correction. Perfection is unreachable, but constant correction is one of the rules of religious life (and religious poetry) for Herbert. The speaker of "The Collar" is by no means wicked or reprehensible. He is, in fact, all too human, and his protest against the inevitable disappointments, restrictions, and pains of life is one with which most of the readers of this poem can sympathize and identify. Much to his credit, Herbert never denies the validity of the experiences described in "The Collar" or suggests that such feelings, however confused or disordered or angry, are unworthy of expression. Herbert knew that the Bible, especially the book of Psalms, one of his great spiritual and poetic models, dwells repeatedly on laments and complaints as radical as those in "The Collar."

Alongside the Bible, perhaps there is also something of a different kind of social and religious ritualism here—the carnivalesque spirit. Carnival is a festival time of at least temporary release from the obligations and restraints of daily life, and one is not only freed but even encouraged to abuse, parody, or otherwise flout the figures of authority and "cold dispute[s]/ Of what is fit, and not" and grab for the physical pleasures at hand. Carnival functions not only as an individual and societal relief valve, letting off pressure that might otherwise build to intolerable levels, but also an important acknowledgment of the claims of the body and a person's legitimate right to cry out against the strains of religion, law, and morality.

In works by William Shakespeare, according to C. L. Barber in *Shakespeare's Festive Comedy* (1959), carnivalesque release leads to clarification, and this is precisely the pattern of "The Collar," where Herbert allows the speaker full expression of his freedom as part of a rhythm of spiritual life that returns him to a deepened understanding of his obligations and his relationship to God. One of the ironies of the speaker's protests throughout "The Collar" is that everything valuable that he seeks by rebellion is available through religious obedience. God surfaces dramatically at the end of the poem, and this is a surprising, wondrous moment. Yet there are signs of God subtly in evidence long before the last two lines: in the "board" of line 1 that the speaker strikes, which calls to mind the Communion table, and in the thorn, tears, blood, wine, and corn (by which Herbert meant grain or wheat), which the speaker mistakenly thinks are absent from the holy, moral life or are signs only of his pain and disappointment. Properly understood, the true desires of the speaker reinforce not his momentary rebellion from but his ineradicably close connection to God. As in so many of Herbert's other poems, in "The Collar" one comes to God in a surprising way, in this case after exhausting oneself in an impatient struggle against a God who is overwhelmingly patient, kind, and understanding.

Sidney Gottlieb

THE COLOSSUS

Author: Sylvia Plath (1932-1963)
Type of poem: Lyric
First published: 1960, in *The Colossus*

The Poem

"The Colossus" is a fairly short poem in free verse, with six stanzas of five lines each. The title of the poem, which also serves at the title of Sylvia Plath's first collection of poetry, suggests both the classical world in which huge statues or monuments were constructed (for example, the Colossus of Rhodes, an ancient wonder of the world) and the enormity of the subject for the writer.

The poem is written in the first person, but the speaker of the poem does not place herself in a recognizably contemporary world; instead, she chooses a strange environment that seems to be partially a reconstruction of classical Greece and Rome and partially a bizarre world of exaggerated, nightmarish metaphors. As with many first-person lyrics, this poem is addressed to a specific "you"; however, the identity of the person addressed is withheld from the reader through the first three stanzas.

Plath begins with an image that suggests Humpty-Dumpty rather than the classical world. She can never get her colossus "pieced, glued, and properly jointed" together, no matter how hard she tries. Despite her attempts to "dredge the silt" from the throat of this thing (is it monster, statue, human, or animal?), all she hears are the untranslatable brays, grunts, and cackles proceeding from its lips. Because the oracles of Greece and Rome communicated by nearly incomprehensible messages, Plath thinks that perhaps these sounds are coming from a "mouthpiece of the dead, or of some god or other." Although she has worked for thirty years on her dredging project, she is "none the wiser"; no god's message has been heard.

The third and fourth stanzas remain focused on the image of the incomprehensible head, but they move from the lips to the brow, the eyes, and the hair. In addition, the fourth stanza finally removes some ambiguity by stating specifically that the "you" she is trying to recompose and listen to is, in fact, the speaker's father. The images become increasingly bizarre and macabre as the speaker crawls all over the "skull plates" of her father, trying still to clean and mend him. She then proceeds to eat her lunch in this huge burial ground. The father's enormity is clear not only because of the physical size of his ruined corpse/statue, but also because of the exaggerated comparisons he elicits from the speaker: Her father, all by himself, is "pithy and historical as the Roman Forum." The reader is convinced that the father is immensely important to the speaker by the sheer size and outrageousness of the comparisons.

The final stanzas end one workday for the tireless speaker and begin another. During the night, she protects herself from the elements by squatting "in the cornucopia/ Of [his] left ear," but she still hears nothing from him. The morning sun rises "from under the pillar of [his] tongue," but it rises silently: No message comes from the land of the dead. The speaker is "married to shadow," not substance, because she is still enamored of her deceased father. The poem ends with a striking image, taken once again from the classical world, of a boat's keel scraping the shore as it lands; she no longer listens for this sound of rescue or deliverance — either because she does not expect a husband-type figure to win her or because she has resolved herself to the fact that her father will never return.

Forms and Devices

The chief literary technique employed by Plath is the conceit, or extended (and often exaggerated) metaphor. A reader can easily accept a quick metaphor which compares a person with a statue, but Plath allows this metaphor to surprise the reader when she insists on focusing her attention on the comparison for the entire poem.

Because of its subject matter, the poem could have easily become a macabre or sentimental piece, but because of the exaggerated and therefore humorous nature of the conceit, the poem is saved from the problems inherent in a poem about mourning a parent. The poem's seriousness is undercut by the oddity of her comparisons.

The scattered remains of a dead parent are horrific, but Plath's conceit allows her to challenge the horror by placing the absurd alongside it. The speaker imagines herself "crawl[ing] like an ant in mourning/ Over the weedy acres of [his] brow," but she complicates the picture by having the metaphorical ant scale "little ladders with gluepots and pails of Lysol." The poem becomes cartoon-like in its images: the ant carries glue to fix the "immense skull plates" and Lysol to clear his eyes. When the poem regains its seriousness with an allusion to Aeschylus' *Oresteia* (458 B.C.), the Greek tragedy, Plath again disrupts the sober scene by explaining, "I open my lunch on a hill of black cypress." She eats surrounded by her father's bones and hair "littered . . . to the horizon line." She has followed the metaphor for so long that the normal biological demands, the ingredients usually of comedy, interrupt the poem, and she picnics amid the littered scene. Finally, at night, when she protects herself from the elements near the poem's close, she squats in "the cornucopia" of her father's severed left ear. This hyperbolic, or exaggerated, comparison between a cornucopia and an ear, as with the other metaphors in the poem, becomes oddly humorous because the conceit, or the analogy between the father and the ruined statue, has become strained: He is her father, a Greek or Roman ruin, litter, and a cornucopia.

Plath's successes come from her ability to risk the excesses of her metaphors, and her work is important at least partly because of the extremes — in both subject matter and style — she was able to reach in her writing.

Themes and Meanings

Many American poets writing after World War II concentrated on their own personal histories or family trees for poetic subject matter. Sylvia Plath is often linked with Anne Sexton, Robert Lowell, and John Berryman, all poets writing in postwar

America, because of the self-analysis and self-reflection present in the poems. Often these writers are called "confessional poets" because they reveal their own personal obsessions, psychological quirks, or tawdry misdeeds in the poems. Plath's "The Colossus" fits into this school of poetry because of its self-absorption and the ambivalent feelings the speaker has toward her father.

Sylvia Plath's relationship with her father, who died when she was eight, is the subject of much of her poetry. In later poems, especially "Daddy," she reveals astonishingly strong and disturbing feelings toward her father. She imagines herself as a Jew and her father as a Nazi and confesses that she, in some way, relishes the role: "Every woman adores a Fascist,/ The boot in the face, the brute/ Brute heart of a brute like you." The poet seems to enjoy the need for punishment, perhaps to erase feelings of guilt about her father's death.

"The Colossus," an early poem, does not go quite so far in examining the psychologically disturbing relationship of father and daughter as "Daddy" does, but it does examine archetypal patterns of behavior. It is no accident that the poem's one direct allusion to a classical text comes with the "blue sky out of the Oresteia." That trilogy by the Greek tragic playwright Aeschylus deals in part with Electra's attempt to come to terms with the death of her father, Agamemnon. Sigmund Freud, working with this Greek myth, thought the Electra complex paralleled in many ways the male Oedipus complex, and he suggested that daughters often want to displace their mothers in order to capture totally their father's affections.

Plath's obsessive quest to reestablish contact with her father in "The Colossus" participates in some ways in this Freudian theory. The mother is invisible in the poem (and in most Plath poems); she is removed from the scene by the author's inattention to the relationship. The speaker confesses that her "hours are married to shadow" because of her devotion to her father's memory. In the poem, she labors to piece together her father in order to establish some type of relationship with him again; she wants to hear him speak, to listen to his words of advice.

The fact that the father lies scattered across the poem, littering the horizon, perhaps suggests the ambivalence the poet feels for her father. On one hand she wants to become reunited with him, but on the other the image she creates of a dismembered ruin perhaps suggests her anger at her father for leaving her when she was a young girl.

When a poem deals with a psychologically complex relationship, its meaning is often difficult to pin down. The seriousness of the poem's subject combines with the comic exaggerations of the conceit, and the desire of the speaker for reunion with her father is linked with Plath's own capacity to "create such a ruin" in the first place. To say that the poem's meaning is difficult to express is to say that Plath's relationship with her father was extremely ambivalent. Like most good poems, "The Colossus" creates its power from the tensions and ambiguities it contains.

Kevin Boyle

THE COMPANY

Author: Robert Creeley (1926-   )
Type of poem: Lyric
First published: 1988, in *The Company*

The Poem

In the poetry Robert Creeley wrote during the 1980's, he began to turn back to the early stages of his life, placing his present thoughts in a larger perspective through reflection on decisive moments of the past. The recollective sense of "The Company" is immediately established by the first word, "Backward," which is instantly qualified by the phrase "as if retentive," suggesting how experience accumulates. Creeley's placement of the well-known line from William Wordsworth's "My Heart Leaps Up," "The child is father of [Creeley says "to"] the man," then gives the poem specific direction; a dual track from childhood is drawn in terms of "use" (or personal choice) and "circumstance" (the outside world). The first quatrain, written in open verse in a flowing line dense with information, is followed by three similarly shaped stanzas that examine the implications of this formulation. The poet draws conclusions from his experience, summarized in terse, almost aphoristic form. The randomness of existence and the difficulty in determining the presence of any form or meaning in most human actions are posed as a central theme, as the "great expectations" of the "next town" repeatedly turn into an "empty plate" in actuality.

The fifth stanza epitomizes this situation. The poet looks back at the young men such as himself who were reaching maturity in the historical moment of World War II. The war pulled them out of a comparatively privileged cultural position and set them between "all the garbage/ of either so-called side." The poet remembers clinging to "an existential/ *raison d'être* like a pea/ some faded princess tried to sleep on," but this turns out to be merely a trendy philosophical scheme with no real value for the poet.

In the last three stanzas, the poet shifts to the present and reaches beyond it toward the future. Proposing a philosophical position that would permit an understanding of his generation's (or company's) life and times, the poet envisions a "recorder" (another version of the writer) who must attend not only to the official version of events of historians ("in books") or archaeologists ("under rocks") but, more crucially, to what is central to human survival— "some common places of feeling."

Although there is clearly a positive aspect to "the good times" that people must "take heart in remembering," there is also a constant consciousness of an almost nameless dread, referred to as "whatever it was,/ comes here again," a chilling indicator of the tenuousness of existence. The terrifying abruptness with which life can end engenders a feeling of unease, yet an adult's awareness of this threat might enliven each moment in an oblique fashion through the energy generated by the fear of extinction. The repeated use of the word "last" in the final stanza suggests both closure and a continuance into the unknown.

Forms and Devices

Creeley has said that he is "very at home" with colloquial language, and "The Company" is written with "a sense of source in common speech" characteristic of Creeley's voice. The vernacular is qualified by interposition of quotations from familiar poetry and brief catch-phrases with origins in foreign languages, which have become a part of American culture. These provide a contrasting context, establishing a tension between an official version of history and what Creeley feels are the genuinely significant elements of most people's lives. The Wordsworth quote recalls not only "My Heart Leaps Up" but also the much more famous "Ode: Intimations of Immortality." The Wordsworth reference seems to set a direction for the poem, but the data from one's early years are called into question by a barrage of words such as "banality," "vacant," "disjunct," and "ambivalent," which question the data's validity. Similarly, the line "Out of all this emptiness/ something must come . . ." is countered by the diminution of "great expectations" into "empty plates." In both cases, the somewhat portentous, lofty prospects promised by official culture have been turned into hollow shells. Even the adventure and excitement of foreign travel combined with the epoch-making danger of a global war, turn into a groping for meaning through reliance on historical slogans.

Creeley describes himself as "one who has been long in city pent," quoting from a sonnet by John Keats that also echoes John Milton's *Paradise Lost* (1667, 1674) and Samuel Taylor Coleridge's "Frost at Midnight" and "This Lime-Tree Bower My Prison." The references again set up a mood of expectation, but while "trying to make sense of it," Creeley's generation was "blasted" out of what he calls "humanistic" obligations. The use of the word "humanistic" is a reduction of the much more positive "human" of the last three stanzas, while the "*oblige*" of "*noblesse oblige*" carries again the pressure of externally imposed responsibility. The culmination of all these attempts to control "the company" Creeley speaks for is the failure of the more hip academic mind to offer some kind of explanation, its "existential *raison d'être*" — replete with sophisticated European connotations — collapsing into the simile of a "faded princess" (an exhausted Old-World image) who "was expectably soon gone."

The clash between the dominant political and cultural ideas and a growing awareness of their inadequacy is ingeniously developed through the close control of words and their location, an important element of Creeley's style in all of his work. There is a sense of qualification, even resistance, when the scientifically precise "scale" of the second stanza becomes the poetically suggestive "implication"; in the third stanza, the removal of the article before "small, still" compresses and intensifies the image of emptiness. The implication, without actual statement, of "we were" before "moving along" in the fourth stanza contributes to a growing sense of urgency expressed in rhythmic momentum. The first four stanzas are written in short word bursts, hesitant and incomplete, which mark the poet's confusion and distrust. An expository section that follows (stanzas 5 through 7) is composed of longer lines, a flowing narrative that encapsulates the deceptive and unsatisfactory "solutions" presented in polished rhetoric by the spokesman for a settled society. The last three stanzas occur as a single long, deliberative line. In a final rejection of what is expected, the repetition of the word "last" produces a pattern of continuance, so that even the feared end of life is qualified by the resonant reverberation of the words themselves.

Themes and Meanings

Robert Creeley has spoken of his friends and fellow artists as "a *company*, a kind of leaderless Robin Hood's band, which I dearly love. . . . There is no company dearer, more phenomenal, closer to my heart." He further describes this loose community as writers for whom poetry is "not a purpose, not discretion, not even craft — but *revelation*, initial and eternal." "The Company" is an attempt to express the sensibility that informs this conviction and to describe some of the conditions that contributed to its occurrence.

Creeley begins with negative assumptions because so much of his education and cultural conditioning seemed to interfere with the goal of his writing, "an actual possibility of revelation." While he respects the literary achievements of various canonical writers, the weight of their reputations and the force of their mastery of form tended to narrow his own possibilities. Even while accepting many of the traditional aspects of a New England upbringing, his inclusion of the phrase "ages hence," from Robert Frost's "The Road Not Taken," suggests that for him, neither road was appropriate, that he and his "company" had to blaze their own trail.

The tentativeness, the hesitancy, that characterizes much of Creeley's poetry is not evident here in the commanding, declarative tone the poet uses to dismiss the false assumptions that he and his contemporaries had to overcome. The last section attempts, as Creeley did in much of his work during the middle and late 1980's, to mingle (as Charles Molesworth says) "quiet acceptance" with "ineradicable doubt" in search of some enduring human qualities. The "common places of feeling" recall the Ezra Pound dictum "Only emotion endures," which Creeley often uses as a guiding precept. The tension between the "good times" one wants to remember and "whatever it was" (the nameless dread) one "can't forget" is part of the ultimate burden of human existence. This final juxtaposition of hope and fear defines the poet's existence, while the poem is itself an instrument in the maintenance of an optimistic attitude. It is typical of Creeley that by using language to confront and frame his fear in the repetition of an occasion ("the last, the last") that haunts his thoughts, he is doing all he can to overcome it.

Leon Lewis

COMPOSED UPON WESTMINSTER BRIDGE, SEPTEMBER 3, 1802

Author: William Wordsworth (1770-1850)
Type of poem: Sonnet
First published: 1807, in *Poems in Two Volumes*

The Poem

This poem's title, "Composed upon Westminster Bridge, September 3, 1802," tells the reader its setting: William Wordsworth is in London on the bridge that crosses the Thames River by the houses of Parliament, close to where Big Ben's Tower stands today. When he tells the poem's place and date of composition, however, the poet may not be strictly accurate. He probably began composing the poem on July 31 as he crossed the bridge at the beginning of a journey to France; he may have then finished it by his return on September 3. His sister, Dorothy Wordsworth, records that on July 31 as they drove over Westminster Bridge they saw St. Paul's Cathedral in the distance and noticed that the Thames was filled with many small boats. "The houses were not overhung," she reports, "by their cloud of smoke, and they were spread out endlessly, yet the sun shone so brightly, with such a pure light" that it seemed like "one of nature's own grand spectacles." Dorothy Wordsworth's description can help one to read the poem.

The reader may first think that the poet is musing to himself, but his somewhat public tone suggests a general audience. One may first be puzzled; if it were not for its title, the general subject of the poem would not be immediately apparent. Lines 1 through 3 make a forceful assertion, but it is a negative one: Whatever the "sight" turns out to be, nothing on earth is more beautiful, and only a very insensitive person could ignore it. All one knows of this "sight" so far is that it is impressive ("majestic") and moving ("touching").

In line 4, the reader discovers that the subject of the poem is the beauty of the city. One should probably take "City" to mean all the parts of greater London that could have been seen from Westminster Bridge in 1802, and perhaps in particular the sections called the City of Westminster (located by the bridge) and the City of London, with its towers and spires visible downriver on the north bank of the Thames. The poet, echoing his sister's description, describes the panorama of this vast city in the silence and clear air of an early morning in summer. He sees the tops of many different manmade structures; he sees ships on the river, but most of all such urban landmarks as theaters and churches. The dome must be that of St. Paul's itself. His eyes move easily from these buildings to the sky and to the open hills and fields that in those days lay close to central London to the southwest and were visible on hills to the north.

At line 9, the poet stops his description of London and begins to compare it to those wonderful sights he has seen in nature. He has never seen anything in nature more beautiful than this view of the city. He has never seen a sight any more calm than this, nor presumably has any sight ever caused him to feel more calm himself. In the poem's final three lines, the poet returns to give vivid, even extravagant pictures of the beautiful city and the river. He exclaims to God that London's "mighty heart" is alive and motionless in houses that themselves "seem asleep."

Forms and Devices

This poem is a sonnet—a fourteen-line lyric poem with a moderately rigid rhyme scheme. In his sonnets, Wordsworth rhymes in the manner of the Italian Petrarch and the Englishman John Milton, not in that of William Shakespeare (the most famous sonneteer in English). Here Wordsworth rhymes *abba, abba, cdcdcd*. Two groups of four lines (or quatrains) form the octave (or opening eight-line grouping). This sonnet does not break down into units as markedly as do more traditional examples of the form. Although like most sonnets it changes direction after the octave, the change is less sharp than usual. The sestet's meaning shifts between lines 10 and 11, but the shift is not abrupt.

In spite of its rather strict form, the poem seems unconstrained. In most ways, its sentences proceed in a normal conversational English way, with a list here or a parenthetical remark there. One exception to this generalization is that the poet often inverts normal word order to achieve emphasis: "Dull would he be," "Never did sun," "Ne'er saw I." As a result, the poem reads somewhat like dramatic prose, even though the reader does feel a regular musical pulse. Wordsworth said elsewhere that he tried to write poetry in a language close to real speech, and here he appears to succeed. As in ordinary conversation, this poem's language has few extravagant figures of speech. A simile compares the city's morning beauty to "a garment" that it wears; valleys "steep" in sunlight. In the last three lines, the poet employs obvious personifications: The river has its own will, houses sleep, and London has a dormant mighty heart.

The force of the poem's language lies in its vigorous emphasis and its descriptions (and perhaps one allusion). As noted above, inversions of words often create strong emphases. Many lines, particularly in the octet, are enjambed; that is, many lines run into the next, propelling the poem's rhythm forward. The last six lines provide successive short, forceful, and somewhat unconnected exclamations and statements. Most readers can respond to the sights of the city that this poem provides. The image of the London skyline is vivid even to those who have never seen a picture of London, as are the separate pictures (the river, the houses) evoked by the personifications in the last three lines of the poem. (Note that Wordsworth has simplified what he must have seen; the boats that Dorothy mentioned do not appear in William's account.)

The poem reads easily. It presents its ideas forcefully by means of comparatively simple devices and vivid images. Nevertheless, many readers come away with a sense that there is more to the poem than an uncomplicated, vigorous description of what Wordsworth saw from Westminster Bridge.

Themes and Meanings

Between July 31 and September 3, 1802, William and Dorothy Wordsworth traveled to France to visit William's former lover, Annette Vallon, and William and Annette's illegitimate daughter, Caroline. Even though at this time Wordsworth was preparing to marry someone else, one should not assume that the visit was at all traumatic. The reader gets quite the opposite impression from the poet's account of a walk with his daughter that he describes in another sonnet, "It Is a Beauteous Evening." War had separated Wordsworth and Annette for ten years, and any idea that they might marry had been put aside. Undoubtedly, Wordsworth was living intensely at this time, but the reader should resist trying to find any specific autobiographical meaning in this poem.

To a reader of Wordsworth's other poetry, the most unusual thing about "Composed upon Westminster Bridge, September 3, 1802," is its subject matter. In most of his poetry, Wordsworth describes natural scenes: streams, hills, mountains, woods, and meadows—natural sights located in Switzerland, Wales, and most of all in the Lake District in northwestern England. He not only describes those scenes but also explains how experiencing them refreshes and ennobles the human spirit. In contrast, he usually pictures cities in general, and London in particular, as the opposite of the country, as places where those ennobling experiences do not happen, places where human nature is degraded. He celebrates his own escape from a city in the opening lines of *The Prelude* (1850), and later in that poem he describes the depravity of London at great length. He often sympathizes with his friend Samuel Taylor Coleridge because he was unlucky enough to have spent much of his boyhood in London.

So it is unusual that in this poem Wordsworth finds the city fully as beautiful as natural scenery. He celebrates London's beauty in many of the ways he talks about natural sights. As in "Lines Composed a Few Miles Above Tintern Abbey," what one sees on the earth's surface in London blends into the sky and harmonizes with it. The London scene is suffused in glorious light. As in other poems, this scene and its observer are "calm"—a word that to Wordsworth never means simply "without motion," but rather describes a profound and life-giving peace.

Wordsworth knows that he is not seeing the city in all of its aspects. He sees London at its best, early in the morning of a beautiful summer day. He knows that, later, the city will awake and that the streets will fill up with their normal noise and bustle. In colder seasons, smoke from fireplaces will darken the sky. Wordsworth's simile in lines 4 and 5 makes this point clearly: The beauty of the morning is like a garment which makes its wearer beautiful, but which can be taken off— presumably to reveal a different, less lovely city underneath. If line 6 contains an allusion to the insubstantial, soon-to-disappear "cloud-capp'd towers" of William Shakespeare's *The Tempest* (1611; act 4, scene 1), one sees even more vividly how ephemeral is Wordsworth's vision.

Nevertheless, the vision is real. Its effect is powerful, and it lasts in the memory. It is a vision of calm beauty—and something more. In other passages in his poetry, most notably in Book 1 of *The Prelude*, one senses a force outside the poet, pressing upon him. This force can be terrifying (as when great hills stride after him) or simply exciting or invigorating. In this poem, many readers sense that the poet has seen and evoked such a force in the autonomous river gliding "at his own sweet will," in the soon-to-awaken houses, and in the energy and potential activity of the sleeping collective heart of the inhabitants of London.

George Soule

CONCERNING EXAGGERATION,
OR HOW, PROPERLY, TO HEAP UP

Author: Charles Olson (1910-1970)
Type of poem: Lyric
First published: 1953, in *In Cold Hell, in Thicket*

The Poem

"Concerning Exaggeration, or How, Properly, to Heap Up" is a long poem of one hundred lines describing the ideal poet and the fully realized human being, both of whom reject conventional limitations for identification with the totality of reality through exaggeration (literally, from the Latin root, "to heap up"), requiring a movement of the self into a reimagined world of fulfilling possibilities.

Written in 1951, the poem first appeared in *In Cold Hell, in Thicket*, edited by a poetic disciple, Robert Creeley, in 1953. The volume was the only book of short poems to be completed when Charles Olson was rector of Black Mountain College, an experimental alternative to conventional colleges, located in North Carolina. Both Black Mountain College and this collection of poems were intended as antidotes to the status quo in modern Western literature and culture, and the poems established Olson as a new force in American poetry.

In part 1, the speaker advises circumspection (meaning both "caution" and "a fully rounded perspective") regarding conventional notions of "blood" (restricted social perceptions of one's inherited identity). The advice is that people must all take a revolutionary look at all their "economies" and conventional systems and assumptions. The speaker then makes a major affirmation; namely, that he is more than the restricted, detached, or conventional self conditioned by society; he is everything, feels and affects everything, and expresses (or poetically sings) everything, be it wild or indifferent (lines 1 through 9).

Part 2 focuses on "How, Properly, to Heap Up"—in other words, how the speaker and the reader can best create such oneness with the totality of reality through conjuring up epic exaggeration in Greco-Roman, Hebraic, and other cultural myths of birth and engendering, as in the cases of Venus ("She/ came out of a wave"), Agamemnon ("who came back from the war to find his double," Aegisthus), and other legendary personages. The mythological figures in this section all suggest a reaching out (their "heaping up") beyond the individual self into a plethora of complex, even if grotesque, familial relationships. As such, they are mythic role models for human identification with a whole universe of becoming, yet they are no more fantastic ("No wonders") than the setting sun that in its descent touches everything, from tree branch to earth root (lines 10 through 37).

Part 3 changes the focus from blood and birth to the head and celebrates a mythic hero of the mind, a leader rendered all the more powerful from his union (his "heaping up") with a hawk whose wings encircle "the sides of his head." This role model had appeared in a dream that had generated exaggerations or fancies in the mind of the speaker, who thereby moved out of the self (his "heaping up") into a universe of possibility, becoming a "horse on both sides of a river" fondled by others, "each on each side." There is more self-aggrandizement in a charade converting a single individual into "two of us" in the united form of a "centaur." Such is the process of reorienting the self and reimagining the world ("And I twist,/ in the early morning, asking/ where/ does it stop") in order to enter the totality of reality (lines 38-57).

Part 4 begins with a statement of Olson's literary and philosophical creed. The totality of reality and its infinity of possibilities transcend the bounds of conventional realism that pigeonholes one's identity and perception of things. To apprehend infinity within the moment requires a receptivity within one that is as all-inclusive as reality is. One must exaggerate and "heap up" beyond the self. People must become living metaphors, creating vital bridges between their selves and the otherness of existence. Such living metaphors are the liberating movement of selves into a universe of multiple possibilities ("than as fabulous as to move") and express human achievement of an integration with total reality worthy of the Hindu goddess Shiva, who unites the opposites of destruction and creation ("he who is presented with her answer is/ that answer"). The poem closes as it began, with a call for circumspection (an all-encompassing perspective on things) and with a warning against restricted notions of "blood" that delimit one's identity, whose very symbol of imprisonment appears in the typography of the last three lines:

> (was what he said,
> at that point of
> his time).

Forms and Devices

"Concerning Exaggeration, or How, Properly, to Heap Up" is an experimental lyric poem divided into four parts and written in free verse. Its form was directly influenced by the poetic techniques of Ezra Pound. Pound helped to spearhead a modernist revolution in early twentieth century poetry of the Western world, and Olson was perhaps the most prominent, if not uncritical, follower of the methods practiced in Pound's *Cantos* (1917-1970). Both men shared an abhorrence of vague abstractions, with Olson going so far as to consider the generalizing tendency of the modern mind to be the major obstacle preventing the achievement of fulfilling totality of being.

Both poets strove for the exact word (*le mot juste*) and the precise image and discarded discursive poetic statement. Both favored intense compression and ellipsis—the deletion of all unnecessary words ("All, is of the matter")—to achieve a complex suggestiveness of meaning and a mythic resonance with an absolute economy of language.

They both indulged in maximum allusiveness by references to both Eastern and Western literary and historical figures and events to lend mythic richness and universality of significance to their poems. Olson, for example, piled on cryptic references to legendary figures serving as role models for a human totality of being in this poem, especially in parts 2 (lines 10 to 17 and 22 to 37), 3 (lines 38 to 45), and 4 (lines 72 to 87).

Finally, Olson imitated Pound's penchant for exploiting the literal and pictorial character of words that reached its zenith with the use of ideograms (word signs capturing a physical actuality in place of detested abstractions). Olson's poem literalizes words such as "exaggeration" and "circumspection" for a dramatic communication of his philosophy of experiencing the totality of reality. The poem does not merely represent but at times also presents meaning, as in the series of metaphors and similes (lines 72 through 87) expressing self-realization in the living act of metaphor (lines 68 through 71). Similarly, the concluding three lines constitute an ideogram picturing the circumscribed identity trapped in delimiting notions of conventional thought.

Themes and Meanings

"Concerning Exaggeration, or How, Properly, to Heap Up" is about the full flowering of the ideal poet and human being through movement beyond delimiting social conditioning (literally, the exaggeration of the self in the form of a "heaping up") into a whole universe of being and becoming.

Olson's influential essay "Projective Verse" (1950) rejected the partitioning of reality separating the human from the natural world as well as the subjective from the objective realm of being. Poetry is to assist readers in breaking down conventional boundaries and in experiencing the totality of things by avoiding abstraction and logical deduction and by striving for a cumulative inductive barrage of disordered feelings and thoughts to humble the intellect into a reoriented perception of a whole universe of being and becoming. Poetry is, therefore, inherently an exaggeration because it reimagines the world, enabling readers to transcend socially conditioned boundaries and grasp at new possibilities of seeing and self-realization.

As Sherman Paul wrote in *Olson's Push: "Origin," Black Mountain, and Recent American Poetry* (1978), such self-actualization through projective verse is the ultimate end of the poet's art and thought: "Felicity comes of obeying what [Ralph Waldo] Emerson called the soul's emphasis." In another of Olson's experimental essays, published in *Origin*, there is an attack on Socrates for fathering the delimiting Western system of education: "his methodology still the RULE: 'I'll stick my logic up, and classify, boy, classify you right out of existence.' "

Olson's "Concerning Exaggeration, or How, Properly, to Heap Up" is one of many experimental poems designed to dispel the conventional rule-mongering of his contemporaries and to extend the reach of the human psyche into the totality of reality. To achieve this end, the poem must not simply represent reality; it must also present and project a total reality to its readership through elaborate exaggeration.

Thomas M. Curley

CONCERNING NECESSITY

Author: Hayden Carruth (1921-   )
Type of poem: Narrative
First published: 1973, in *From Snow and Rock, from Chaos: Poems 1965-1972*

The Poem

"Concerning Necessity" is a narrative poem of forty-two lines, which are divided into seven six-line stanzas. Each stanza has inexact, or slant, rhymes in an *ababcc* scheme. The poem is written in the first person. Although authors often create a persona that is distinct from themselves, the persona of this poem is commonly seen in Hayden Carruth's poetry: The speaker is a man (a husband and father) who is living in a difficult environment filled with physical labor. To anyone who is aware that Carruth spent more than twenty years of his life as a laborer and handyman in a rural area of Vermont, it is clear that this poem arises from Carruth's personal experiences.

The poem begins in the first-person plural ("we"), indicating that there are many people who live in the rural hardship described. Stanzas 1, 2, and 3 depict a work-filled, arduous existence, in which he and others live in a "kind of rural twilight." These stanzas contain precise details of this existence, beginning with stanza 1 and its references to "hard dirt" and "difficult woods." The emphasis on work is continued in stanza 2, with a catalog of the types of work performed. The use of cataloging, which often occurs in poetry as a list of supportive examples or statements in parallel order, works well here because it intensifies the sense of the relentless labor of these people. The work involved is very physical—for example, driving a wedge, and making a chain saw "snarl once more." Stanza 3 shows dramatically that everything is "falling to pieces" and creates a near-despairing tone. The mood of the first three stanzas is dark and foreboding.

In stanza 4, however, the poem turns from physical description to meditation. The speaker now ruminates upon his situation, realizing that he had been deluded in thinking, like "that idiot Thoreau," as he says, that "necessity could be saved" by the natural facts of his rural existence. He now sees his delusion in believing that the "necessity" of his life, including hard work, suffering, and, eventually, death, could be compensated for solely by the objects of nature.

The poet again uses a catalog of natural objects in stanza 5 with references to trees, bird, mountain, and stars. Carruth, a noted observer and lover of nature, often turns in his poems to such natural phenomena for solace. Yet the stanza ends with the realization that "these things do serve/ a little though not enough," and the reader is left wondering what would be "enough." Carruth gives the answer in stanzas 6 and 7, in which the speaker states directly what "saves the undoubted collapse/ of the driven day and the year": He sees a woman "asleep in the field" or "telling a song to a child." These observations of tenderness and love in stanza 7 enable the speaker to "fall in love/ all over with human beauty."

Forms and Devices

"Concerning Necessity" has a formal structure of seven six-line stanzas which employ an *ababcc* slant-rhyme scheme and a line that varies between six and ten syllables. Within this structure, the poet uses strong images and direct, colloquial statement to convey his concerns. Although this combination may seem contradictory, it is often seen in Carruth's poetry, with the formal structure helping to "contain" the message of the content.

The slant rhymes are not exact, but each set of rhymes contains an echoing vowel or consonant. For example, the last word of line 1 "live," echoes the last word of line 3, "giving." This use of inexact rhyme gives the poem a structure which, at the same time, does not force it into a rigid pattern (as a full rhyme might). In the same way, the six-to-ten-syllable lines give the poem a sense of regularity without a strict syllable count. Most of the lines are six or seven syllables, and this repetition of length creates a strong rhythmic expectation, as may be seen clearly in the last four lines of stanza 2: "dig the potato patch/ dig ashes dig gravel/ tickle the dyspeptic chain saw/ make him snarl once more."

Appropriately for a poem about the difficult lives of people living in rural areas, Carruth often uses simple declarative statements that contain colloquial words and direct, easily understood images. Since this is a poem about people working in a natural environment, the actions are fundamental ones: cleaning a hen house, cutting corn, and watching a woman "telling a song" to a child.

Images are also basic: "dirt," "weeds," "potato patch," "white birch." The strength of these images dramatically re-creates the scenes and also anchors the speaker's meditations in the physical world. For example, the major meditation, "that necessity could be saved/ by the facts we actually have," is followed by a catalog of natural images such as the "white birch," "hemlock," "baybreasted nuthatch." This pattern does not allow the speaker to drift off into abstraction; rather, it brings his thoughts back into the world.

Also appropriately for the simple, rural context of the poem, Carruth does not use figures of speech or thought, such as similes or metaphors. Since the poem is about the bare, unadorned lives of rural people, the poet creates a poetic language that is also bare and unadorned. Digging a potato patch, or watching a woman who is "done in or footsore," is not like anything else, Carruth implies; the reality portrayed must be taken for what it is, and this imbues that reality with importance and solidity. He does, however, present this reality in catalogs. For example, stanza 3 contains a catalog of the deteriorating situations in which the speaker finds himself: "the house is falling to pieces/ the car coming apart/ the boy sitting and complaining." These catalogs intensify the individual images and, through accumulation, give them a power they would not have separately.

Themes and Meanings

The essential question of the poem is hinted at in the title, "Concerning Necessity." What, the poet asks, can sustain the speaker in the face of his difficult, rural existence? How can "necessity," or the determinants of one's life, be compensated for? This question is often raised in Carruth poems, which usually have a speaker who is alone in nature and is meditating on the meaning of his usually difficult life. In his poem, as in other Carruth poems, the speaker does not turn to metaphysics, to intuitive responses, or to nature for his answers: He looks for and finds them in his loved one—or, as the speaker says at the end of the poem, "right here where I live."

After depicting the hard work and deteriorating situations of his existence, the speaker says, "this was the world foreknown," meaning that he had sensed his life would come to this end. He admits to his "delusion" that nature could provide him with the answers he seeks. Like "that idiot Thoreau," he had held romantic notions that nature can provide the meaning for man's existence, if he would only search for such meaning. This notion, that man can find the answers to the basic questions of his existence in nature, was one of the dominant ideas of the great Romantic period of American literature, during the nineteenth century. Authors such as Ralph Waldo Emerson, Henry David Thoreau, and Walt Whitman were the more optimistic representatives of this period, and it is their belief in nature's ability to give complete meaning to man's existence that the speaker of the poem no longer accepts. Nature, he says, does "serve/ a little though not enough."

Instead, the speaker realizes, it is "human beauty" that "saves" him and, by implication, also saves "necessity" by compensating for all the hard work and suffering the man and his loved ones undergo. This human beauty is seen in the woman portrayed in stanzas 6 and 7, the one who is "down asleep in the field/ or telling a song to a child," the one who moves "in some particular way" and makes the speaker "fall in love all over with human beauty" again. Thus, the poem, which begins on a somber, laborious note and turns, in stanza 4, to a meditation on the speaker's condition, ends with a confirmation: It is the beauty of human beings in his everyday world that provides the speaker with meaning.

This poem, as are so many of Carruth's poems, is similar in an essential way to the poems of Robert Frost. Using nature as a backdrop, the poets place their personae in extremely difficult, almost overwhelming situations. These personae do not find easy answers in God and nature; rather, they must rely upon their own dogged perseverance and constant searching in order to find meaning in their lives. Carruth, though, goes one step beyond Frost, for he has his speaker find meaning in another human being, in love.

Len Roberts

CONNOISSEUR OF CHAOS

Author: Wallace Stevens (1879-1955)
Type of poem: Meditation
First published: 1938; collected in *Parts of a World*, 1942

The Poem

"Connoisseur of Chaos" is a short poem divided into five boldly numbered stanzas of very loose blank verse—unrhymed lines, each with five stresses. While II, III, and IV are full stanzas of ten to twelve lines, the opening and closing units (I and V) do not work as stanzas so much as brief propositions of only two and three lines.

Stanza I, in fact, is an opening gambit consisting of two ruthlessly opposing propositions, as if this connoisseur (an expert in chaos) is beginning a logical proof: *A*, any violent order is finally merely disorder; and *B*, any great disorder is really a kind of order. The mind-tease of *A* and *B* can be illustrated endlessly, and the rest of the poem seems, at first, to be an attempt to illustrate the point.

Stanza II contains more propositions, but now readers have several "if x, then y" proposals cast in material of a rather whimsical nature—if flowers are bright in both Connecticut and in South Africa, which obviously they are, the speaker states, then there is an essential unity in the world. Disorder is really orderly if the big picture is considered.

Yet in stanzas III and IV the speaker damns this sense of order as being perhaps too easy, even sentimental. Things fall apart when readers remember how "squamous" (encrusted) humans minds become when confronted with all the squirming facts in a world that can never be ordered. Finding illustration or lovely order in the world is not enough to endure a realization of vastly limited human perception. There are things in this part of the poem which indicate that humans in the twentieth century are at an impasse. The speaker uses a collective voice which states the impossibility of returning to a simpler world order—to the "old order," say, of the church. Because that order seems violent—forced and even destructive—it is strongly implied that the way orthodoxy or institutions attempt to impose order leads to repression and war. The knowledge that old orders end badly almost forces an acceptance that all new orders will have a similar fate. Despair is the result. Each human attempt at making sense of life falls into "the immense disorder of truths," as if dropping into an abyss. By implication, the contemporary world will end there as well.

One last time the speaker makes a proposal: What if the disorder of truths itself should ever become so largely perceived, by minds with unvested interests, that another great order is suddenly perceived? The result is "the pensive man"—a person who can live with ideas and not fall hopelessly into despair when order is again elusive.

The connoisseur abandons his argument in stanza V and gives one last teasing set of lines. He gives up his propositions for a quick image of the one-in-the-many paradox.

Forms and Devices

An important device, almost a trick, in this poem is in the extralogical jump from the cold, unpromising propositions of "*A*" and "*B*" to the lovely matched brevity of the eagle image at the end. Readers have to make a violent connection between those cold, opening propositions and that lovely closing image.

Wallace Stevens helps by putting rather proselike, longer stanzas in the middle of his poem. There are many repetitions of Stevens' "if [x is true] . . . and it is" in these longer stanzas. He perhaps does this in order to provide a strongly implied "therefore." This is the language of logical argument; it is also the impasse out of which the poem must find its way. If readers hear how prosaic and logical Stevens sounds in his sentence structures, they may also hear this "if/then/therefore" language suddenly given up with a kind of shrug— "Well . . ." (IV, line 1).

Up to this point, the connoisseur has not been the kind of speaker who uses conversational shrugs. In adopting more relaxed phrases from this point, he also abandons the collective "we" in favor of the personal "I." He locates himself in an intimate way by declaring, almost out of nowhere, that it is April as he writes and that the wind is blowing after days of constant rain. This relaxing of the language and mood is part of the poem's formal strategy. A mock-pedantic tone has been set up and then discarded so that readers might be given something linguistically fresh, if still puzzling, at the end. Section V is yet another proposition, but it comes from an entirely different realm from that of the propositions given at the beginning.

Themes and Meanings

The thematic thrust of this poem is in its demonstration of using poetry to make a leap from one realm of thinking to another. Stevens had a very long career as a poet, and he never tired of composing poems which get at the nature of what it means to think poetically. Thinking poetically is not whimsical for Stevens; it is separate, but no less real than other ways of thinking. "Connoisseur of Chaos" is a poem about Poetry with a capital *P* — the aesthetics of human experience and what Stevens called the "Supreme Fiction." The persona in this particular poem (the cold-eyed pedant) speaks convincingly of a possible impasse leading to despair in Western twentieth century thinking if people did not have access to poetry's truths. Stevens thought it might be a despair which cuts deeper than anything previously experienced in the history of humankind. During the poet's life, emerging areas of scientific discovery — of non-Euclidean mathematics, to offer only one example — made uncertainty the only certainty in the universe. Science prevented a return to the confidence of Sir Isaac Newton's so-called laws of nature, which once explained much about the physical world while enabling people to imagine a god having set those laws into motion. That order had been deposed. The poem suggests that many experience the bliss and then the horror in the vastly limited powers of everyday perception. The speaker himself is skilled at illustrating how language encourages him to make gorgeous order (nonsense?) of the world. He states, in effect, "I can make all the lovely correspondences in life and nature seem 'as pleasant as port.' " Stevens is making fun of his own task as a poet quite possibly immersed in mere pleasantries. Even ordinary use of language forces those who speak it into analogies they do not wish to make. Some of the despair over reaching impasses in everyday thinking is related to Stevens' sense of his times. Not stated here, but lying behind the dilemma of the poem, is the following address to the collective "we" at the center of this poem: Living in an age of advanced linguistic and psycholinguistic studies, findings have made people aware of what has been called an imprisonment in language.

The connoisseur/speaker strives for a way out of the impasse. One way is for the connoisseur to play with the independent domains of art and science and turn those domains on their heads. Late in the poem he likens his "*A*" and "*B*" propositional thinking, which initially got him started, to that which is rigid, "statuary, posed/ For a vista in the Louvre." Science can lead straight to the prisonhouse if discoverers begin to worship their own discoveries. The discoveries themselves become museum pieces.

To find the domain of truth which is only possible in art, Stevens eschews museums for something more fleeting—for "things chalked on the sidewalk." The chalk, associated with a scientist doing complex mathematical proofs, is placed in the hands of the poet ("the pensive man"), whose blackboard is the exposed, vulnerable sidewalk slate where proofs are temporary.

The pensive man is the other side of the pedantic-sounding speaker, the connoisseur of chaos. Both modes of being—pensive and pedantic—can exist in the same mind. Most people have "*A*" and "*B*" ways of thinking. Such thinking must be integrated; it must become consonant with all other ways of thinking. Only the pensive man, the person perhaps ready to give up every proposition he ever chalks, has the ability to see an eagle float in the sky and to perceive that one bird as part of a huge scheme. Implied is the idea that the eagle's nest is only briefly available as an order, and a vision of God is presented here in Stevens' near-religious wording. The meaning in this Imagist ending is all created by implication: The mind presumably returns to doubt, in the same way the mind goes back and forth between a certainty of huge orders and disorders. From this sense of all that is out there, all poetry springs. Hence the mind is not defeated by chaos, whose vastness the mind cannot begin to fathom. Poets and their readers have in them the courage and the vision to be the connoisseurs of chaos. The vast spheres of chaos will never be tapped, but neither will the sheer human verve to think on chaos and make it one of life's richest experiences.

Beverly Coyle